Data Structures and Program Design

SECOND EDITION

Data Structures and Program Design

Robert L. Kruse

St. Mary's University
Halifax, Nova Scotia

Prentice-Hall, Inc.
Englewood Cliffs, New Jersey 07632

Library of Congress Cataloging-in-Publication Data

KRUSE, ROBERT LEROY (date)
    Data structures and program design.

    Bibliography: p.
    Includes index.
    1. Electronic digital computers—Programming.
2. Data structures (Computer science)   3. PASCAL
(Computer program language)   I. Title.
QA76.6.K77 1987   005.1   86-17081
ISBN 0-13-195884-4

Prentice-Hall Software Series
Brian W. Kernighan, adviser

Editorial/production supervision: Joan L. Stone
Interior design and page layout: Kenny Beck
Manufacturing buyer: Ed O'Dougherty

Printed in the United States of America

10 9 8 7 6 5

ISBN 0-13-195884-4 025

Prentice-Hall International, Inc., *London*
Prentice-Hall of Australia Pty. Limited, *Sydney*
Prentice-Hall Canada, Inc., *Toronto*
Prentice-Hall Hispanoamericana, S.A., *Mexico*
Prentice Hall of India Private Limited, *New Delhi*
Prentice Hall of Japan, Inc., *Tokyo*
Prentice Hall of Southeast Asia Pte. Ltd., *Singapore*
Editora Prentice-Hall do Brasil, Ltda., *Rio de Janeiro*

for my mother
Esther Kruse

C O N T E N T S

P R E F A C E _____

An apprentice carpenter may want only a hammer and a saw, but a master craftsman employs many precision tools. Computer programming likewise requires sophisticated tools to cope with the complexity of real applications, and only practice with these tools will build skill in their use. This book treats structured problem solving, the process of data abstraction and structuring, and the comparative study of algorithms as fundamental tools of program design. Several case studies of substantial size are worked out in detail to show how all the tools are used together to build complete programs.

Many of the algorithms and data structures studied here possess an intrinsic elegance, a simplicity that cloaks the range and power of their applicability. Before long the student discovers that vast improvements can be made over the naive methods usually used in introductory courses. And yet this elegance of method is tempered with uncertainty. The student soon finds that it can be far from obvious which of several approaches will prove best in particular applications. Hence comes an early opportunity to introduce truly difficult problems of both intrinsic interest and practical importance and to exhibit the applicability of mathematical methods to algorithm verification and analysis.

The goal of programming is the construction of programs that are clear, complete, and functional. Many students, however, find difficulty in translating abstract ideas into practice. This book, therefore, takes special care in the formulation of ideas into algorithms and in the refinement of algorithms into concrete programs that can be applied to practical problems. The process of data specification and abstraction, similarly, comes before the selection of data structures and their implementations.

I believe in progressing from the concrete to the abstract, in the careful development of motivating examples, followed by the presentation of ideas in a more general form. At an early stage of their careers most students need reinforcement from seeing the immediate application of the ideas that they study, and they require the practice of writing and running programs to illustrate each important concept that they learn. This book therefore contains many sample programs, both short procedures and complete programs of substantial length. The exercises and programming projects, moreover, constitute an indispensable part of this book. Many of these are immediate applications of the topic under study, often requesting that programs be written and run, so that algorithms may be tested and compared. Some are larger projects, and a few are suitable for use by a group of several students working together.

SYNOPSIS

Programming Principles

By working through the first large project (CONWAY's game of Life), Chapter 1 expounds principles of top-down refinement, program design, review, and testing, principles that the student will see demonstrated and is expected to follow throughout the sequel. At the same time, this project provides an opportunity for the student to review the syntax of Pascal, the programming language used throughout the book.

Chapter 2 introduces a few of the basic concerns of software engineering, including problem specification and analysis, prototyping, algorithm design, refinement, verification, and analysis. These topics are illustrated by the development of a second program for the Life game, one based on an algorithm that is sufficiently subtle as to show the need for precise specifications and verification, and one that shows why care must be taken in the choice of data structures.

The study of data structures begins in Chapter 3 with stacks, queues, and lists in contiguous implementation, always emphasizing the separation between the use of data structures and their implementation. Chapter 4 continues by studying the same data structures in linked implementations and culminates with a discussion of abstract data types. Compatible packages of Pascal procedures are developed for each implementation and are used in both large and small sample programs. The major goal of these chapters is to bring the student to appreciate data abstraction and to apply methods of top-down design to data as well as to algorithms.

Chapters 5, 6, and 7 present algorithms for searching, table access (including hashing), and sorting. These chapters illustrate the interplay between algorithms and the associated abstract data types, data structures, and implementations. The text introduces the "big Oh" notation for elementary algorithm analysis and highlights the crucial choices to be made regarding best use of space, time, and programming effort.

These choices require that we find analytical methods to assess algorithms, and producing such analyses is a battle for which combinatorial mathematics must provide the arsenal. At an elementary level we can expect students neither to be well armed nor to possess the mathematical maturity needed to hone their skills to perfection. My goal, therefore, is only to help students recognize the importance of such skills and be glad for later chances to study mathematics. Appendix A presents some necessary mathematics. Most of the topics in the appendix will be familiar to the well-prepared student, but are included to help with common deficiencies. The final two sections of Appendix A, on Fibonacci and Catalan numbers, are more advanced and are not needed for any vital purpose in the text, but are included to encourage combinatorial interest in the more mathematically inclined.

Recursion is a powerful tool, but one that is often misunderstood and sometimes used improperly. Some textbooks treat it as an afterthought, applying it only to trivial examples and apologizing for its alleged expense. Others give little regard to its pitfalls. I have therefore essayed to provide as balanced a treatment as possible. Whenever recursion is the natural approach it is used without hesitation. Its first use in this text is the second half of Chapter 7, where mergesort and quicksort are introduced. Chapter 8 (which may be read any time after stacks are defined) continues to study recursion in depth. It includes examples illustrating a broad range of applications, an exposition of the implementation of recursion, and guidelines for deciding whether recursion is or is not an appropriate method to employ.

Binary trees are surely among the most elegant and useful of data structures. Their study, which occupies Chapter 9, ties together concepts from lists, searching, and sorting. At the same time, binary trees provide a natural example of recursively defined data structures and therewith afford an excellent opportunity for the student to become more comfortable with recursion applied to both data structures and algorithms.

Trees and Graphs   Chapter 10 completes the study of data structures by collecting several important uses of multiway trees as data structures, including tries and B-trees, after which the chapter introduces graphs as more general structures useful for problem solving. The presentations in each major section of Chapter 10 are independent from each other.

Case Study: An   Chapters 11 and 12 are large case studies, worked out in detail. Chapter 11
Index Writer develops a program to produce a word list or index of a text, thereby illustrating the top-down design and refinement of data structures together with algorithms, and demonstrating nontrivial applications of hash tables and of binary search trees. The resulting program (nearly 1000 lines in Pascal) also illustrates techniques for processing of textual information and files.

Case Study: The   The case study in Chapter 12 examines the Polish notation in considerable detail,
Polish Notation exploring the interplay of recursion, trees, and stacks as vehicles for problem solving and algorithm development. Some of the questions addressed can serve as an informal introduction to compiler design. Again, the algorithms are fully developed within a functioning Pascal program. This program accepts as input an expression in ordinary (infix) form, translates the expression into postfix form, and evaluates the expression for specified values of the variable(s).

Removal of recursion is a topic that, I hope, most programmers may soon no longer need to study. But at present much important work must be done in contexts (like FORTRAN or COBOL) disallowing recursion. Methods for manual recursion re-
Removal of moval are therefore required, and are collected for reference as Appendix B. Some
Recursion instructors will wish to include the study of threaded binary trees with Chapter 9; this section is therefore written so that it can be read independently of the remainder of Appendix B.

Pascal Notes   Appendix C, finally, includes the standard diagrams and tables describing Pascal syntax, as well as further information to help with programming problems.

CHANGES IN THE SECOND EDITION

In this edition, the first half of the book has been extensively rewritten, and many changes have been made in the remainder as well. The principal changes are summarized as follows.

▶ The process of data abstraction and information hiding, often practiced silently in the first edition, has now been brought to the forefront. The definition and choice of abstract data types are emphasized and carefully separated from implementation decisions.

▶ Major aspects of software engineering receive more emphasis, aspects such as specifications for problems, data, and algorithms, verification, testing, and maintenance. These topics are treated in conjunction with both small sample programs and large case studies.

▶ New sections have been added on graphs and graph algorithms and on simulation as a use of queues. Several sections have been expanded, including those on records and on applying linked lists to manipulating polynomials.

▶ Each of the first ten chapters now concludes with "Pointers and Pitfalls" giving helpful hints for problems of algorithm design and with "Review Questions" to help the student collect the principal concepts of the chapter.

▶ Notes in the left margin pick out key words and help the reader locate specific topics.

▶ The two-color printing and improved diagrams are intended to increase the pedagogical effectiveness of the book by distinguishing appropriate elements of the text, diagrams, and programs.

▶ Supplementary materials are now available to instructors teaching from this book. These materials include a manual of solutions to exercises and programming projects, an instructor's guide with transparency masters, and a software tape with all the sample programs from the text and the programming projects.

COURSE STRUCTURE

prerequisite

The prerequisite for this book is a first course in programming, with experience using the elementary features of Pascal. Chapter 2 includes a discussion of records and Chapter 4 a study of pointer types, in case students have not previously met these topics. A good knowledge of high school mathematics will suffice for almost all the algorithm analyses, but further (perhaps concurrent) preparation in discrete mathematics will prove valuable.

content

This book includes all the topics of the ACM Course CS2, August 1985 version (*Program Design and Implementation*), with additional emphasis on data abstraction, data structures, algorithm analysis, and large case studies, so that it is also suitable for a version of Course CS7 (*Data Structures and Algorithm Analysis*) that emphasizes program design along with implementations and applications of data structures. The book contains significantly more material than can usually be studied in a single term, and hence it allows flexibility in designing courses with different content and objectives.

CS2

The core topics specified for ACM Course CS2 occupy Chapters 1–8 and the first third of Chapter 9. A one-term course based closely on CS2 will normally include almost all the content of these chapters, except for the more detailed algorithm analyses, verifications, and some of the sample programs. The later chapters include all the advanced optional topics suggested for possible inclusion in CS2.

data structures

An elementary course on data structures and algorithms should consider Chapters 1 and 2 briefly (to look at the questions of data specification and time-space tradeoffs), emphasize Chapters 3–10, and select other topics if time permits.

CS7

A more advanced course in Data Structures and Algorithm Analysis (ACM course CS7) should begin with a brief review of the topics early in the book, placing special emphasis on data abstraction, algorithm analysis, and criteria for choosing data structures and algorithms under various conditions. The remaining chapters will then provide a solid core of material on data structures, algorithm design, and applications.

two-term course

A two-term course can cover the entire book, thereby attaining a satisfying integration of many of the topics from both of ACM courses CS2 and CS7. Students need time and practice to understand general methods. By combining the study of data abstraction, data structures, and algorithms with their implementation in projects of realistic size, an integrated course can build a solid foundation on which later, more theoretical courses can be built.

Even if it is not covered in its entirety, this book will provide enough depth to enable interested students to continue using it as a reference in later work. It is important in any case to assign major programming projects and to allow adequate time for their completion.

ACKNOWLEDGMENTS TO THE SECOND EDITION

Since the first publication of this book, various readers have made comments and suggestions that have been incorporated in this edition, and for which I am grateful. My thanks go especially to the following people.

My colleague PAUL MUIR has shared many good ideas with me and has carefully read the revised manuscript, thereby contributing valuable suggestions that are reflected in many places in the book. My students STEVEN A. MATHESON and J. DAVID BROWN have worked with me long and faithfully in producing solutions to all the exercises and programming projects, in preparing the solutions manual and the software tape, in testing all the programs from the book, in bringing the text files up to date, and in improving the consistency and clarity of exposition. Further solutions and suggestions have come from T. CHIASSON, S. MACKEIL, S. DOYLE, L. FRASER, and S. MANSFIELD.

The field staff and the editorial staff of Prentice-Hall have contributed much to the success of this book. The production editor, JOAN STONE, and the staff whose names appear on the copyright page have worked to improve the quality of this edition and to make up for bureaucratic delays. But it is JAMES F. FEGEN, JR., Executive Editor for Computer Science and Engineering, who has contributed most through his keen enthusiasm, through his constant support for my work from the preliminary plans for the first edition of the book to the present day, and through his true Christian friendship.

ACKNOWLEDGMENTS TO THE FIRST EDITION

The writing, rewriting, and production of this book have been an arduous task, but one that has been made easier by the help of other people. My mother, first of all, gave me the patient understanding and love without which the work could not have been completed. Family and friends have spoken words of encouragement; colleagues have given valuable suggestions and advice; and students have shown the enthusiasm and joy of discovery that make the effort worthwhile.

Several reviewers have helped, by questions and comments, to clarify the aims and exposition of the book. BRIAN W. KERNIGHAN was particularly helpful in reading several versions of the manuscript and providing many careful, detailed comments.

Preliminary versions of the manuscript have been used by several classes, with different levels of preparation, at Saint Mary's University, the University of Alberta, and (by T. B. McLean and his students) at Georgia Southern College. Student reaction has led to many improvements in the exposition. H. O'Connell and B. Lee were especially helpful in pointing out misprints and obscurities.

Computer facilities for the production of this book have been provided by Saint Mary's University, the University of Alberta, and Dalhousie University. The Computing Science Department at Alberta extended generous hospitality to me during a sabbatical leave in 1982.

Robert L. Kruse

Data Structures and Program Design

C H A P T E R   1

Programming Principles

▶ *This chapter summarizes important principles of good programming, especially as applied to large projects, and illustrates methods for discovering effective algorithms. In the process we raise questions in program design that we shall address in later chapters and review many of the special features of the language Pascal by using them to write programs.*

1.1 INTRODUCTION

The greatest difficulties of writing large computer programs are not in deciding what the goals of the program should be, or even in finding methods that can be used to reach these goals. The president of a business might say, "Let's get a computer to keep track of all our inventory information, accounting records, and personnel files, and let it tell us when inventories need to be reordered and budget lines are over-spent, and let it handle the payroll." With enough time and effort, a staff of systems analysts and programmers might be able to determine how various staff members are now doing these tasks and write programs to do the work in the same way.

problems of large programs

This approach, however, is almost certain to be a disastrous failure. While inter-viewing employees, the systems analysts will find some tasks that can be put on the computer easily and will proceed to do so. Then, as they move other work to the computer, they will find that it depends on the first tasks. The output from these, unfortunately, will not be quite in the proper form. Hence they need more programming to convert the data from the form given for one task to the form needed for another. The programming project begins to resemble a patchwork quilt. Some of the pieces are stronger, some weaker. Some of the pieces are carefully sewn onto the adjacent ones, some are barely tacked together. If the programmers are lucky, their creation may hold together well enough to do most of the routine work most of the time. But if any change must be made, it will have unpredictable consequences throughout the system. Later, a new request will come along, or an unexpected problem, perhaps even an emergency, and the programmers' efforts will prove as effective as using a patchwork quilt as a safety net for people jumping from a tall building.

purpose of book

The main purpose of this book is to describe programming methods and tools that will prove effective for projects of realistic size, programs much larger than those ordinarily used to illustrate features of elementary programming. Since a piece-meal approach to large problems is doomed to fail, we must first of all adopt a consistent, unified, and logical approach, and we must also be careful to observe important principles of program design, principles that are sometimes ignored in writing small programs, but whose neglect will prove disastrous for large projects.

problem specification

The first major hurdle in attacking a large problem is deciding exactly what the problem is. It is necessary to translate vague goals, contradictory requests, and perhaps unstated desires into a precisely formulated project that can be programmed. And the methods or divisions of work that people have previously used are not necessarily the best for use in a machine. Hence our approach must be to determine overall goals, but precise ones, and then slowly divide the work into smaller problems until they become of manageable size.

program design

The maxim that many programmers observe, "First make your program work, then make it pretty," may be effective for small programs, but not for large ones. Each part of a large program must be well organized, clearly written, and thoroughly understood, or else its structure will have been forgotten, and it can no longer be tied to the other parts of the project at some much later time, perhaps by another programmer. Hence we do not separate style from other parts of program design, but from the beginning we must be careful to form good habits.

Even with very large projects, difficulties usually arise not from the inability

data structures

to find a solution but, rather, from the fact that there can be so many different methods and algorithms that might work that it can be hard to decide which is best, which may lead to programming difficulties, or which may be hopelessly inefficient. The greatest room for variability in algorithm design is generally in the way in which the data of the program are stored:

▶ How they are arranged in relation to each other.

▶ Which data are kept in memory.

▶ Which are calculated when needed.

▶ Which are kept in files, and how the files are arranged.

A second goal of this book, therefore, is to present several elegant, yet fundamentally simple ideas for the organization of data and several powerful algorithms for important tasks within data processing, such as sorting and searching.

analysis

When there are several different ways to organize data and devise algorithms, it becomes important to develop criteria to recommend a choice. Hence we devote attention to analyzing the behavior of algorithms under various conditions.

testing and verification

The difficulty of debugging a program increases much faster than its size. That is, if one program is twice the size of another, then it will likely not take twice as long to debug, but perhaps four times as long. Many very large programs (such as operating systems) are put into use still containing bugs that the programmers have despaired of finding, because the difficulties seem insurmountable. Sometimes projects that have consumed years of effort must be discarded because it is impossible to discover why they will not work. If we do not wish such a fate for our own projects, then we must use methods that will

program correctness

▶ Reduce the number of bugs, making it easier to spot those that remain.

▶ Enable us to verify in advance that our algorithms are correct.

▶ Provide us with ways to test our programs so that we can be reasonably confident that they will not misbehave.

Development of such methods is another of our goals, but one that cannot yet be fully within our grasp.

maintenance

Informal surveys show that, once a large and important program is fully debugged and in use, then less than half of the programming effort that will be invested altogether in the project will have been completed. *Maintenance* of programs, that is, modifications needed to meet new requests and new operating environments, takes, on average, more than half of the programming investment. For this reason, it is essential that a large project be written to make it as easy to understand and modify as possible.

Pascal

The programming language Pascal has several features that make it the most appropriate choice to express the algorithms we shall develop. Pascal has been carefully designed to facilitate the discipline of writing carefully structured programs, with requirements implementing principles of program design. It contains relatively few features, in comparison with most high-level languages, so that it can be mastered quickly, and yet it contains powerful features for handling data that ease the translation from general algorithms to specific programs.

Several sections of this and later chapters mention features of Pascal informally as they appear while we write programs. For the precise details of Pascal syntax (grammar), consult Appendix C.

1.2 THE GAME OF LIFE

If I may take the liberty to abuse an old proverb:

One concrete problem is worth a thousand unapplied abstractions.

case study

Throughout this chapter we shall concentrate on one case study that, while not large by realistic standards, illustrates both the methods of program design and the pitfalls that we should learn to avoid. Sometimes the example motivates general principles; sometimes the general discussion comes first; always it is with the view of discovering general methods that will prove their value in a range of practical applications. In later chapters we shall employ similar methods for much larger projects.

The example we shall use is the game called *Life*, which was introduced by the British mathematician J. H. CONWAY in 1970.

1.2.1 Rules for the Game of Life

definitions

Life is really a simulation, not a game with players. It takes place on an unbounded rectangular grid in which each cell can either be occupied by an organism or not. Occupied cells are called *alive;* unoccupied cells are called *dead.* Which cells are alive changes from generation to generation according to the number of neighboring cells that are alive, as follows:

transition rules

1. The neighbors of a given cell are the eight cells that touch it vertically, horizontally, or diagonally.
2. If a cell is alive but either has no neighboring cells alive or only one alive, then in the next generation the cell dies of loneliness.
3. If a cell is alive and has four or more neighboring cells also alive, then in the next generation the cell dies of overcrowding.
4. A living cell with either two or three living neighbors remains alive in the next generation.
5. If a cell is dead, then in the next generation it will become alive if it has exactly three neighboring cells, no more or fewer, that are already alive. All other dead cells remain dead in the next generation.
6. All births and deaths take place at exactly the same time, so that dying cells can help to give birth to another, but cannot prevent the death of others by reducing overcrowding, nor can cells being born either preserve or kill cells living in the previous generation.

1.2.2 Examples

As a first example, consider the community

The counts of living neighbors for the cells are as follows:

moribund example

By rule 2 both the living cells will die in the coming generation, and rule 5 shows that no cells will become alive, so the community dies out.

On the other hand, the community

stability

has the neighbor counts as shown. Each of the living cells has a neighbor count of three, and hence remains alive, but the dead cells all have neighbor counts of two or less, and hence none of them becomes alive.

The two communities

alternation

and

continue to alternate from generation to generation, as indicated by the neighbor counts shown.

variety

It is a surprising fact that, from very simple initial configurations, quite complicated progressions of Life communities can develop, lasting many generations, and it is usually not obvious what changes will happen as generations progress. Some very small initial configurations will grow into large communities; others will slowly die out; many will reach a state where they do not change, or where they go through a repeating pattern every few generations.

popularity

Not long after its invention, MARTIN GARDNER discussed the Life game in his column in *Scientific American,* and, from that time on, it has fascinated many people, so that for several years there was even a quarterly newsletter devoted to related topics. It makes an ideal display for home microcomputers.

Our first goal, of course, is to write a program that will show how an initial community will change from generation to generation.

1.2.3 The Solution

method

At most a few minutes' thought will show that the solution to the Life problem is so simple that it would be a good exercise for members of a beginning programming class who had just learned about arrays. All we need to do is to set up a large rectangular array whose entries correspond to the Life cells and will be marked with the status of the cell, either alive or dead. To determine what happens from one generation to the next, we then need only count the number of living neighbors of each cell and apply the rules. Since, however, we shall be using loops to go through the array, we must be careful not to violate rule 6 by allowing changes made earlier to affect the count of neighbors for cells studied later. The easiest way to avoid this pitfall is to set up a second array that will represent the community at the next generation and, after it has been completely calculated, then make the generation change by copying it to the original array.

Next let us rewrite this method as the steps of an informal algorithm.

algorithm

Initialize an array called map to contain the initial configuration of living cells.

Repeat the following steps for as long as desired:
  For each cell in the array do the following:
    Count the number of living neighbors of the cell. If the count is 0, 1, 4, 5, 6, 7, or 8, then set the corresponding cell in another array called newmap to be dead; if the count is 3, then set the corresponding cell to be alive; and if the count is 2, then set the corresponding cell to be the same as the cell in array map (since the status of a cell with count 2 does not change).
  Copy the array newmap into the array map.
  Print the array map for the user.

1.2.4 Life: The Main Program

The preceding outline of an algorithm for the game of Life translates into the following Pascal program.

main program

```
program Life(input, output);
{Simulation of Conway's game of Life on a bounded grid.}
{Version 1}
const
   maxrow = 50;                            {maximum number of rows allowed}
   maxcol = 80;                            {maximum number of columns allowed}
type
   row    = 1 .. maxrow;
   col    = 1 .. maxcol;
   status = (dead, alive);
   grid   = array[row, col] of status;
var
   map,                                    {description of current generation}
   newmap: grid;                           {description of the next generation}
   i:      row;
   j:      col;
   again:  Boolean;                        {continue for another generation?}
{The declarations of the procedures and functions will go here.}
begin                                      {main program Life}
```

initialization

```
   Initialize(map);
   WriteMap(map);
   repeat
```

calculate changes

```
      for i :=1 to maxrow do for j :=1 to maxcol do
         case NeighborCount(i, j) of
            0, 1:       newmap[i, j] := dead;
            2:          newmap[i, j] := map[i, j];
            3:          newmap[i, j] := alive;
            4, 5, 6, 7, 8: newmap[i, j] := dead
         end;
```

advance generation

```
      map := newmap;
      WriteMap(map);
      Enquire(again)
   until not again
end.                                       {main program Life}
```

subprograms

action of program

In this program we still must write the procedures Initialize and WriteMap that will do the input and output, the procedure Enquire that will determine whether or not to go on to the next generation, and the function NeighborCount(i, j) that will count the number of cells neighboring the one in i, j that are occupied in the array map. The action of the program Life is entirely straightforward. First, we read in the initial situation to establish the first configuration of occupied cells. Then we commence a loop that makes one pass for each generation. Within this loop we first have a nested pair of loops on i and j that will run over all entries in the array map. The body of these nested loops consists of the one special statement **case . . . end,** which is a multiway selection statement. In the present application the function NeighborCount(i, j) will return one of the values 0, 1, . . ., 8, and for each of these cases we can take a separate action, or, as in our program, some of the cases may lead to the same action. You should check that the action prescribed in each case corresponds correctly to the rules 2, 3, 4, and 5 of Section 1.2.1. Finally, after using the nested loops and **case** statement to set up the array newmap, the assignment statement map := newmap copies it into array map, and the procedure WriteMap writes out the result.

Exercises
1.2 Determine by hand calculation what will happen to each of the communities shown in Figure 1.1 over the course of five generations. [*Suggestion:* Set up the Life configuration on a checkerboard. Use one color of checkers for living cells in the current generation and a second color to mark those that will be born or die in the next generation.]

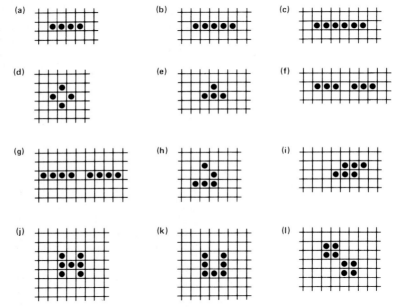

Figure 1.1.   Life configurations

1.3 PROGRAMMING STYLE

Before we turn to writing the subprograms for the Life game, let us pause to consider several principles that we should be careful to employ in programming.

1.3.1 Names

In the story of creation (Genesis 2 : 19), God brought all the animals to Adam to see what names he would give them. According to an old Jewish tradition, it was only when Adam had named an animal that it sprang to life. This story brings an important moral to computer programming: Even if data and algorithms exist before, it is only when they are given meaningful names that their places in the program can be properly recognized and appreciated, that they first acquire a life of their own.

purpose of careful naming

For a program to work properly, it is of the utmost importance to know exactly what each variable represents, and to know exactly what each subprogram does. Documentation explaining the variables and subprograms should therefore always be included. The names of variables and subprograms should be chosen with care so as to identify their meanings clearly and succinctly. Finding good names is not always an easy task, but is important enough to be singled out as our first programming precept:

> ### Programming Precept
> *Always name your variables and subprograms*
> *with the greatest care, and explain them thoroughly.*

Pascal goes some distance toward enforcing this precept by requiring a section to declare variables and allows a more extensive use of names than most languages. Constants used in different places should be given names, and so should different data types, so that the compiler can catch errors that might otherwise be difficult to spot.

The careful choice of names can go a long way in clarifying a program and in helping to avoid misprints and common errors. Some guidelines are

guidelines

1. Give special care to the choice of names for procedures, functions, constants, and all global variables and types used in different parts of the program. These names should be meaningful and should suggest clearly the purpose of the subprogram, variable, and the like.

2. Keep the names simple for variables used only briefly and locally. A single letter is often a good choice for the variable controlling a **for** loop, but would be a poor choice for a procedure or for a variable used three or four times in widely separated parts of the program.

3. Use common prefixes or suffixes to associate names of the same general category. The files used in a program, for example, might be called

   InputFile TransactionFile TotalFile OutFile RejectFile

4. Avoid deliberate misspellings and meaningless suffixes to obtain different names. Of all the names

   index   indx   ndex   indexx   index2   index3

   only one (the first) should normally be used. When you are tempted to introduce multiple names of this sort, take it as a sign that you should think harder and devise names that better describe the intended use.

5. Avoid choosing cute names whose meaning has little or nothing to do with the problem. The statements

   while TV **in** hock **do** study;
   if not sleepy **then** play **else** nap;

   may be funny but they are bad programming!

6. Avoid choosing names that are close to each other in spelling or otherwise easy to confuse.
7. Be careful in the use of the letter "l" (small ell), "O" (capital oh), and "0" (zero). Within words or numbers these usually can be recognized from the context and cause no problem, but "l" and "O" should never be used alone as names. Consider the examples

$$l := 1; \quad x := l; \quad x := 1; \quad x := O; \quad O := 0$$

1.3.2 Documentation and Format

purpose for documentation

Most students initially regard documentation as a chore that must be endured, after a program is finished, to ensure that the marker and instructor can read it, so that no credit will be lost for obscurity. The author of a small program indeed can keep all the details in his head, and so needs documentation only to explain the program to someone else. With large programs (and with small ones after some months have elapsed), it becomes impossible to remember how every detail relates to every other, and therefore to write large programs, it is essential that appropriate documentation be prepared along with each small part of the program. A good habit is to prepare documentation as the program is being written, and an even better one, as we shall see later, is to prepare part of the documentation before starting to write the program.

Not all documentation is appropriate. Almost as common as programs with little documentation or only cryptic comments are programs with verbose documentation that adds little to understanding the program. Hence our second programming precept:

> ### Programming Precept
> *Keep your documentation concise but descriptive.*

The style of documentation, as with all writing styles, is highly personal, and many different styles can prove effective. There are, nonetheless, some commonly accepted guidelines that should be respected:

guidelines

1. Place a prologue at the beginning of each subprogram including

   (a) Identification (programmer's name, date, version number).
   (b) Statement of the purpose of the subprogram and method used.
   (c) The changes the subprogram makes and the data it uses.
   (d) Reference to further documentation external to the program.

2. When each variable, constant, or type is declared, explain what it is and how it is used. Better still, make this information evident from the name.

3. Introduce each significant section (paragraph or subprogram) of the program with a comment stating briefly its purpose or action.

4. Indicate the end of each significant section if it is not otherwise obvious.

5. Avoid comments that parrot what the code does, such as

count := count + 1;   {Increase counter by 1}

or that are meaningless jargon, such as

{horse string length into correctitude}

(This example was taken directly from a systems program.)

6. Explain any statement that employs a trick or whose meaning is unclear. Better still, avoid such statements.

7. The code itself should explain *how* the program works. The documentation should explain *why* it works and *what* it does.

8. Whenever a program is modified, be sure that the documentation is correspondingly modified.

format

Spaces, blank lines, and indentation in a program are an important form of documentation. They made the program easy to read, allow you to tell at a glance which parts of the program relate to each other, where the major breaks occur, and precisely which statements are contained in each loop or each alternative of a conditional statement. There are many systems (some automated) for indentation and spacing, all with the goal of making it easier to determine the structure of the program.

prettyprinting

A *prettyprinter* is a system utility that reads a Pascal program, moving the text between lines and adjusting the indentation so as to improve the appearance of the program and make its structure more obvious. If a prettyprinter is available on your system, you might experiment with it to see if it helps the appearance of your programs.

consistency

Because of the importance of good format for programs, you should settle on some reasonable rules for spacing and indentation and use your rules consistently in all the programs you write. Consistency is essential if the system is to be useful in reading programs. Many professional programming groups decide on a uniform system and insist that all the programs they write conform. Some classes or student programming teams do likewise. In this way, it becomes much easier for one programmer to read and understand the work of another.

> ***Programming Precept***
> *The reading time for programs is much more than the writing time.*
> *Make reading easy to do.*

1.3.3 Refinement and Modularity

problem solving

Computers do not solve problems; people do. Usually the most important part of the process is dividing the problem into smaller problems that can be understood in more detail. If these are still too difficult, then they are subdivided again, and so on. In any large organization the top management cannot worry about every detail

subdivision

of every activity; the top managers must concentrate on general goals and problems and delegate specific responsibilities to their subordinates. Again, the middle-level managers cannot do everything: They must subdivide the work and send it to other people. So it is with computer programming. Even when a project is small enough that one person can take it from start to finish, it is most important to divide the work, starting with an overall understanding of the problem, dividing it into subproblems, and attacking each of these in turn without worrying about the others.

Let us restate this principle with a classic proverb:

> ### Programming Precept
> *Don't lose sight of the forest for its trees.*

top-down refinement

This principle, called **top-down refinement,** is the real key to writing large programs that work. The principle implies the postponement of detailed consideration, but not the postponement of precision and rigor. It does not mean that the main program becomes some vague entity whose task can hardly be described. On the contrary, the main program will send almost all the work out to various subprograms (procedures and functions), and as we write the main program (which we should do first), we decide *exactly* how the work will be divided among them. Then, as we later work on a particular subprogram, we shall know before starting exactly what it is expected to do.

specifications

It is often not easy to decide exactly how to divide the work into subprograms, and sometimes a decision once made must later be modified. Even so, two guidelines can help in deciding how to divide the work:

> ### Programming Precept
> *Each subprogram should do only one task, but do it well.*

That is, we should be able to describe the purpose of a subprogram succinctly. If you find yourself writing a long paragraph to specify the task of a subprogram, then either you are giving too much detail (that is, you are writing the subprogram before it is time to do so) or you should rethink the division of work. The subprogram itself will undoubtedly contain many details, but they should not appear until the next stage of refinement.

> ### Programming Precept
> *Each subprogram should hide something.*

A middle-level manager in a large company does not pass on everything he receives from his departments to his superior; he summarizes, collates, and weeds out the information, handles many requests himself, and sends on only what is needed at the upper levels. Similarly, he does not transmit everything he learns from higher management to his subordinates. He transmits to each person only what he needs to do his job. The subprograms we write should do likewise.

One of the most important parts of the refinement process is deciding exactly what the task of each subprogram is, specifying precisely what its input will be and what result it will produce. Errors in these specifications are among the most frequent program bugs and are among the hardest to find. First, the data used in the subprogram must be precisely specified. These data are of five kinds:

parameters

▶ *Input parameters* are used by the subprogram but are not changed by the subprogram. In Pascal, input parameters are usually value parameters. (Exceptions: Files must always be **var** parameters, even if used for input only; often large arrays are passed as **var** parameters to avoid the time and space needed to make a local copy.)

▶ *Output parameters* contain the results of the calculations from the subprogram. In Pascal, output parameters must be **var** parameters.

▶ *Inout parameters* are used for both input and output; the initial value of the parameter is used and then modified by the subprogram. In Pascal, inout parameters must be **var** parameters.

variables

▶ *Local variables* are declared in the subprogram and exist only while the subprogram is being executed. They are not initialized before the subprogram begins and are discarded when the subprogram ends.

▶ *Global variables* are used in the subprogram but not declared in the subprogram. It can be quite dangerous to use global variables in a subprogram, since after the subprogram is written its author may forget exactly what global variables were used and how. If the main program is later changed, then the subprogram may mysteriously begin to misbehave. If a subprogram

side effects

alters the value of a global variable, it is said to cause a *side effect.* Side effects are even more dangerous than using global variables as input to the subprogram because side effects may alter the performance of other subprograms, thereby misdirecting the programmer's debugging efforts to a part of the program that is already correct.

> ### Programming Precept
> *Keep your connections simple. Avoid global variables whenever possible.*

> ### Programming Precept
> *Never cause side effects.*
> *If you must use global variables as input, document them thoroughly.*

For functions, the definition of *side effect* is expanded to include changes made to parameters as well as global variables. A function should calculate just one result, returned as the value of the function. If a subprogram needs to produce more than one result, it should be written as a procedure, not as a function.

before and after conditions

The second way in which the specifications of a subprogram should be made precise is in describing the action of the subprogram. The documentation should include a statement of exactly what conditions the subprogram expects to find when it is started. These are called the *preconditions* for the subprogram. The documentation should also indicate what changes the subprogram will make, and therefore what conditions will hold after the subprogram finishes. These are called the *postconditions* for the subprogram.

While all these principles of top-down design may seem almost self-evident, the only way to learn them thoroughly is by practice. Hence throughout this book we shall be careful to apply them to the large programs that we write, and in a moment it will be appropriate to return to our first example project.

Exercises
1.3

E1. Given the declarations

```
var A:   array[1 .. n, 1 .. n] of integer;
    i, j:  integer;
```

where n is a constant, determine what the following statement does, and rewrite the statement to accomplish the same effect in a less tricky way.

```
for i := 1 to n do
  for j := 1 to n do
    A[i, j] := (i div j) * (j div i);
```

E2. Rewrite the following procedure so that it accomplishes the same result in a less tricky way.

```
procedure DoesSomething(var first, second: integer);
begin
  first := second − first;
  second := second − first;
  first := second + first
end;
```

E3. Determine what each of the following procedures does. Rewrite each procedure with meaningful variable names, with better format, and without unnecessary variables and statements.

(a)
```
function Calculate(apple, orange: integer): integer;
var peach, lemon: integer;
begin peach := 0; lemon := 0; if apple < orange then begin
peach := orange end else if orange <= apple then begin
peach := apple end else begin peach := maxint; lemon := maxint
end; if lemon <> maxint then begin Calculate := peach end end;
```

(b) For this part assume the declaration **type** vector = **array**[1 .. max] **of** real.
```
function Figure(var vector1: vector): real;
var loop1: integer; loop2: real; loop3: real; loop4: integer;
begin loop1 := 1; loop2 := vector1[loop1]; loop3 := 0.0;
loop4:= loop1; for loop4 := 1 to max do begin loop1 := loop1 + 1;
loop2 := vector1[loop1 − 1];
loop3 := loop 2 + loop3 end; loop1 := loop1 − 1; loop2 := loop1;
loop2 := loop3/loop2; Figure := loop2 end;
```

(c)   **procedure** question(**var** a17: integer; **var** stuff: integer);
     var another, yetanother, stillonemore: integer;
     begin another := yetanother; stillonemore := a17;
     yetanother := stuff; another := stillonemore; a17 := yetanother;
     stillonemore := yetanother;
     stuff := another; another := yetanother; yetanother := stuff; **end;**

(d)   **function** mystery(apple, orange, peach: integer): integer;
     begin if apple > orange **then if** apple > peach **then if**
     peach > orange **then** mystery := peach **else if** apple < orange **then**
     mystery := apple **else** mystery := orange **else** mystery := apple **else**
     if peach > apple **then if** peach > orange **then** mystery := orange **else**
     mystery := peach **else** mystery := apple **end;**

E4. The following statement is designed to check the relative sizes of three integers, which you may assume to be different from each other:

     if x < z **then if** x < y **then if** y < z **then** c := 1 **else** c := 2 **else**
     if y < z **then** c := 3 **else** c := 4 **else if** x < y **then**
     if x < z **then** c := 5 **else** c := 6 **else if** y < z **then** c := 7 **else**
     if z < x **then if** z < y **then** c := 8 **else** c := 9 **else** c := 10;

(a) Rewrite this statement in a form that is easier to read.

(b) Since there are only six possible orderings for the three integers, only six of the ten cases can actually occur. Find those that can never occur, and eliminate the redundant checks.

(c) Write a simpler, shorter statement that accomplishes the same result.

cube roots

E5. The following Pascal function calculates the cube root of a real number (by the NEWTON approximation), using the fact that, if y is one approximation to the cube root of x, then

$$z = \frac{2y + (x/y^2)}{3}$$

is a closer approximation.

     function Fcn(stuff: real): real;
     var April, Tim, Tiny, Shadow, Tom, Tam, Square: real; flag: Boolean;
     begin Tim := stuff; Tam := stuff; Tiny := 0.00001;
     if stuff <> 0 **then repeat** Shadow := Tim + Tim;
     Square := Tim ∗ Tim;
     Tom := (Shadow + stuff/Square);
     April := Tom / 3;
     if April ∗ April ∗ April − Tam > −Tiny **then if** April ∗ April ∗ April − Tam
        < Tiny **then** flag := true **else** flag := false **else** flag := false;
     if flag = false **then** Tim := April **else** Tim := Tam **until** flag = true;
     if stuff = 0 **then** Fcn := stuff **else** Fcn := April **end;**

(a) Rewrite this function with meaningful variable names, without the extra variables that contribute nothing to the understanding, with a better layout, and without the redundant and useless statements.

(b) Write a function for calculating the cube root of x directly from the mathematical formula, by starting with the assignment $y := x$ and then repeating

$$y := (2 * y + (x/\text{sqr}(y)))/3$$

until $\text{abs}(y * y * y - x) < 0.00001$.

(c) Which of these tasks is easier?

statistics

E6. The *mean* of a sequence of real numbers is their sum divided by the count of numbers in the sequence. The (population) *variance* of the sequence is the mean of the squares of all numbers in the sequence, minus the square of the mean of the numbers in the sequence. The *standard deviation* is the square root of the variance. Write a well-structured Pascal function to calculate the standard deviation of a sequence of n numbers, where n is a constant and the numbers are in an array indexed from 1 to n, which is a parameter to the function. Use, then write, subsidiary functions to calculate the mean and variance.

plotting

E7. Design a program that will plot a given set of points on a graph. The input to the program will be a text file, each line of which contains two numbers that are the x and y coordinates of a point to be plotted. The program will use a procedure to plot one such pair of coordinates. The details of the procedure involve the specific method of plotting and cannot be written since they depend on the requirements of the plotting equipment, which we do not know. Before plotting the points, the program needs to know the maximum and minimum values of x and y that appear in its input file. The program should therefore use another procedure Bounds that will read the whole file and determine these four maxima and minima. Afterward, another procedure is used to draw and label the axes; then the file can be reset and the individual points plotted.

(a) Write the main program, not including the procedures.

(b) Write the procedure Bounds.

(c) Write the header lines for the remaining procedures together with appropriate documentation showing their purposes and their requirements.

1.4 CODING, TESTING, AND FURTHER REFINEMENT

The three processes in the title above go hand-in-hand and must be done together. Yet it is important to keep them separate in our thinking, since each requires its own approach and method. *Coding*, of course, is the process of writing an algorithm in the correct syntax (grammar) of a computer language like Pascal, and *testing* is the process of running the program on sample data chosen to find errors if they are present. For further refinement, we turn to the subprograms not yet written and repeat these steps.

1.4.1 Stubs

early debugging and testing

After coding the main program, most programmers will wish to complete the writing and coding of the subprograms as soon as possible, to see if the whole project will work. For a project as small as the Life game, this approach may work, but for larger projects, writing and coding all the subprograms will be such a large job that, by the time it is complete, many of the details of the main program and subprograms that were written early will have been forgotten. In fact, different people may be writing different subprograms, and some of those who started the project may have left it before all subprograms are written. It is much easier to understand and debug a program when it is fresh in your mind. Hence, for larger projects, it is much more efficient to debug and test each subprogram as soon as it is written than it is to wait until the project has been completely coded.

Even for smaller projects, there are good reasons for debugging subprograms one at a time. We might, for example, be unsure of some point of Pascal syntax that will appear in several places through the program. If we can compile each subprogram separately, then we shall quickly learn to avoid errors in syntax in later subprograms. As a second example, suppose that we have decided that the major steps of the program should be done in a certain order. If we test the main program as soon as it is written, then we may find that sometimes the major steps are done in the wrong order, and we can quickly correct the problem, doing so more easily than if we waited until the major steps were perhaps obscured by the many details contained in each of them.

stubs

To compile the program correctly, there must be something in the place of each subprogram that is used, and hence we must put in short, dummy subprograms, called *stubs*. The simplest stubs are those that do nothing at all:

```
procedure Initialize(var map: grid);    begin  end;
procedure WriteMap(map: grid);    begin  end;
function NeighborCount(i: row; j: col): integer;    begin  end;
```

Even with these stubs we can at least compile the program and make sure that the declarations of types and variables are syntactically correct. Normally, however, each stub should print a message stating that the subprogram was invoked. When we execute the program, we find that some variables are used without initialization, and hence, to avoid these errors, we can add code to procedure Initialize. Hence the stub can slowly grow and be refined into the final form of the subprogram.

For a small project like the Life game, we can simply write each subprogram in turn, substitute it for its stub, and observe the effect on program execution.

1.4.2 Counting Neighbors

Let us now refine our program further. The function that counts neighbors of the cell in i, j requires that we look in the eight adjoining positions. We shall use a pair of **for** loops to do this, one running usually from i − 1 to i + 1 and the other usually from j − 1 to j + 1. We need only be careful, when i, j is on a boundary of the grid, that we look only at legitimate positions in the grid. To do so we introduce four variables for the lower and upper limits of the loops, and make sure that they remain within range. Since the loops will incorrectly consider that the cell in position i, j is a neighbor of itself, we must make a correction after completing the loops.

```
function NeighborCount(i: row; j: col): integer;
var
  x,                                          {loop index for row}
  xlow, xhigh: row;                           {limits for row loop}
  y,                                          {loop index for column}
  ylow, yhigh: col;                           {limits for column loop}
  count:  integer;                            {counter of occupied neighbors}
begin                                         {function NeighborCount}
  if i = 1 then                               {First determine the boundaries.}
    xlow  := 1
  else
    xlow  := i − 1;
  if i = maxrow then
    xhigh := i
  else
    xhigh := i + 1;
  if j = 1 then
    ylow  := 1
  else
    ylow  := j − 1;
  if j = maxcol then
    yhigh := j
  else
    yhigh := j + 1;
  count := 0;                                 {Use nested loops to count neighbors.}
  for x := xlow to xhigh do
    for y := ylow to yhigh do
      if map[x, y] = alive then
        count := count + 1;
  if map[i, j] = alive then
    count := count − 1;
  NeighborCount := count
end;                                          {function NeighborCount}
```

1.4.3 Input and Output

careful input and output

It now remains only to write the procedures Initialize, WriteMap, and Enquire that do the input and output. In computer programs designed to be used by many people, the procedures performing input and output are often the longest. Input to the program must be fully checked to be certain that it is valid and consistent, and errors in input must be processed in ways to avoid catastrophic failure or production of ridiculous results. The output must be carefully organized and formatted, with considerable thought to what should or should not be printed, and with provision of various alternatives to suit differing circumstances. The programming tools needed to design comprehensive input and output procedures, unfortunately, still differ considerably from one computer system to another, and in any case are more concerned with the details of the language and the problem at hand than with general ideas. It is therefore impossible to include as much error checking as we would wish, working only within the provisions of standard Pascal. When the programs are implemented in a particular system, additional error checking can usually be included.

> ***Programming Precept***
> *Keep your input and output as separate modules,*
> *so they can be changed easily*
> *and can be custom-tailored to your computing system.*

1. Pascal Conventions

Both input and output files in Pascal are abstractions of magnetic tapes, with operations done strictly sequentially. Pascal also sets up buffers that sometimes interact peculiarly with input or output on the terminal. When the Pascal language was first devised, it was required that the system would immediately (before executing any statements in the program) obtain the first datum from the input file and place the datum in the "file window." This meant that it was impossible in the original Pascal language to write a prompting message to an interactive terminal before the program requested the first input from the terminal. Since this situation is clearly unacceptable, various solutions to this problem have been implemented in different systems, and there is, unfortunately, no universal method to accomplish interactive input and output in Pascal.

lazy input

In this book we shall use the conventions that are now standard and that work properly on many, but not all, systems. This convention is called *lazy input.* The reference manuals for your Pascal system should discuss input-output conventions, and from these manuals you can determine what changes, if any, will be required to run the Life program on your computer. We shall use the standard procedures read to obtain input data and readln to complete reading one line of input. We also use the standard procedure eof that takes on Boolean values, being true if and only if an end-of-file mark has been encountered. With lazy input, the system does not try to fill its file window until it is necessary. Hence there is no difficulty in writing a prompt (or doing other instructions) before the first read from the terminal. When we check for end of file, however, using the function eof forces the system to fill its file window. Hence we must write a prompt *before* checking eof. Reading input will therefore take the following general form.

sample input
procedure

```
write('First prompt');
while not eof do
begin
   read(data);
   Process(data);
   write('Continuing prompt')
end;
```

2. Initialization

The task that procedure Initialize must accomplish is to set the map to its initial configuration. To initialize the map, we could consider each possible coordinate pair separately and request the user to indicate whether the cell is to be occupied or not. This method would require the user to type in

$$\text{maxrow} * \text{maxcol} = 50 * 80 = 4000$$

input method

entries, which is prohibitive. Hence, instead, we input only those coordinate pairs corresponding to initially occupied cells.

initialization

```
procedure Initialize (var map: grid);
var
   x, y: integer;                                      {coordinates of cell}
begin                                                  {procedure Initialize}
   writeln('This program is a simulation of the game of Life.');
   for x := 1 to maxrow do
     for y := 1 to maxcol do
       map[x, y] := dead;
   writeln('On each line give a pair of coordinates for a living cell.');
   writeln('Terminate the list with the special pair   0 0');
   readln(x, y);
   while (x <> 0) or (y <> 0) do                       {Check termination condition.}
   begin                                               {Check input for legality.}
     if (x >= 1) and (x <= maxrow) and (y >= 1) and (y <= maxcol) then
       map[x, y] := alive
     else
       writeln('Values are not within range.');
     readln(x, y);
   end                                                 {loop processing pair x, y}
end;                                                   {procedure Initialize}
```

output

For the output procedure WriteMap we adopt the simple method of writing out the entire array at each generation, with occupied cells denoted by * and empty cells by blanks.

```
procedure WriteMap(map: grid);
const
  full = '*';
  empty = ' ';
var
  x: row;
  y: col;
begin
  page(output);
  writeln('The map is below:');
  for x := 1 to maxrow do
  begin
    for y := 1 to maxcol do
      if map[x, y] = alive then
        write(full)
      else
        write(empty);
    writeln
  end
end;
```
{procedure WriteMap}
{Commence a new page of output.}

{processing row x}
{procedure WriteMap}

response from user
Finally comes the procedure Enquire that determines whether the user wishes to go on to calculate the next generation. The task of Enquire is to ask the user to respond yes or no; to make the program more tolerant of mistakes in input, this request is placed in a loop, and a blank or carriage return is considered equivalent to an affirmative answer. Pascal sets provide a convenient way to check several possibilities at once.

```
procedure Enquire(var again: Boolean);
var
  response: char;
begin
  repeat
    write('Continue (y, n)? ');
    readln(response)
  until response in ['n', 'y', 'N', 'Y', ' '];
  again := response in ['y', 'Y', ' ']
end;
```
{procedure Enquire}

{procedure Enquire}

At this point, we have all subprograms for the Life simulation. It is time to pause and check that it works.

1.4.4 Drivers

separate debugging
For small projects, each subprogram is usually inserted in its proper place as soon as it is written, and the resulting program can then be debugged and tested as far as possible. For large projects, however, compilation of the entire project can over-

whelm that of a new subprogram being debugged, and it can be difficult to tell, looking only at the way the whole program runs, whether a particular subprogram is working correctly or not. Even in small projects the output of one subprogram may be used by another in ways that do not immediately reveal whether the information transmitted is correct.

driver program

One way to debug and test a single subprogram is to write a short auxiliary program whose purpose is to provide the necessary input for the subprogram, call it, and evaluate the result. Such an auxiliary program is called a ***driver*** for the subprogram. By using drivers, each subprogram can be isolated and studied by itself, and thereby bugs can often be spotted quickly.

As an example, let us write drivers for the subprograms of the Life project. First, we consider the function NeighborCount. In the main program its output is used, but has not been directly displayed for our inspection, so we should have little confidence that it is correct. To test NeighborCount we shall supply it with the array map, call it for each entry of the array, and write out the results. The resulting driver hence uses procedure Initialize to set up the array and bears some resemblance to the original main program.

```
program DriveNeighborCount(input, output);
{Declarations of constants, types, and variables may be taken from the main
    program.}
begin
  Initialize(map);
  for i := 1 to maxrow do
  begin
    for j := 1 to maxcol do
      write(NeighborCount(i, j): 3);
    writeln
  end
end.
```

Sometimes two subprograms can be used to check each other. The easiest way, for example, to check procedures Initialize and WriteMap is to use a driver whose declarations are those of the main program, and whose action part is

```
                begin    Initialize(map);  WriteMap(map)    end.
```

Both procedures can be tested by running this driver and making sure that the configuration printed is the same as that given as input.

1.4.5 Program Tracing

group discussion

After the subprograms have been assembled into a complete program, it is time to check out the completed whole. One of the most effective ways to uncover hidden defects is called a ***structured walkthrough.*** In this the programmer shows the completed program to another programmer or a small group of programmers and explains exactly what happens, beginning with an explanation of the main program followed by the subprograms, one by one. Structured walkthroughs are helpful for three reasons. First, programmers who are not familiar with the actual code can often spot bugs or conceptual errors that the original programmer overlooked. Second, the questions that other people ask can help you to clarify your own thinking and discover your own mistakes. Third, the structured walkthrough often suggests tests that prove useful in later stages of software production.

It is unusual for a large program to run correctly the first time it is executed as a whole, and if it does not, it may not be easy to determine exactly where the errors are. On many systems sophisticated *trace tools* are available to keep track of subprogram calls, changes of variables, and so on. A simple and effective debugging tool, however, is to take *snapshots* of program execution by inserting write statements at key points in the main program. A message can be printed each time a subprogram is called, and the values of important variables can be printed before and after each subprogram is called. Such snapshots can help the programmer converge quickly on the particular location where an error is occurring. *Scaffolding* is another term frequently used to describe code inserted into a program to help with debugging. Never hesitate to put scaffolding into your programs as you write them; it will be easy to delete once it is no longer needed, and it may save you much grief during debugging. Some Pascal compilers, in fact, treat the two comment constructions { . . . } and (* . . . *) as different, allowing one to be nested inside the other. If your compiler does this, then it is often helpful to leave the scaffolding permanently in the program by using one kind of brackets for ordinary comments and the other kind for scaffolding that is no longer needed.

write statements for debugging

For very large programs yet another tool is sometimes used. This is a *static analyzer,* a program that examines the source program (as written in Pascal, for example) looking for uninitialized or unused variables, sections of the code that can never be reached, and other occurrences that are probably incorrect.

1.4.6 Principles of Program Testing

So far we have said nothing about the choice of data to be used to test programs and subprograms. This choice, of course, depends intimately on the project under development, so we can make only some general remarks. First, we should note

choosing test data

> ### Programming Precept
> *The quality of test data is more important than its quantity.*

Many sample runs that do the same calculations in the same cases provide no more effective a test than one run.

> ### Programming Precept
> *Program testing can be used to show the presence of bugs,*
> *but never their absence.*

It is possible that other cases remain that have never been tested even after many sample runs. For any program of substantial complexity, it is impossible to perform exhaustive tests, yet the careful choice of test data can provide substantial confidence in the program. Everyone, for example, has great confidence that the typical computer can add two floating-point numbers correctly, but this confidence is certainly not based on testing the computer by having it add all possible floating-point numbers and checking the results. If a double-precision floating-point number takes 64 bits, then there are 2^{128} distinct pairs of numbers that could be added. This number is astronomically large: All computers manufactured to date have performed altogether but a tiny fraction of this number of additions. Our confidence that computers add correctly is based on tests of each component separately, that is, by checking that each of the 64 digits is added correctly, and that carrying from one place to another is done correctly.

testing methods

There are at least three general philosophies that are used in the choice of test data.

1. The Black-Box Method

Most users of a large program are not interested in the details of its functioning; they only wish to obtain answers. That is, they wish to treat the program as a black box; hence the name of this method. Similarly, test data should be chosen according to the specifications of the problem, without regard to the internal details of the program, to check that the program operates correctly. At a minimum the test data should be selected in the following ways:

data selection

1. *Easy values.* The program should be debugged with data that are easy to check. More than one student who tried a program only for complicated data, and thought it worked properly, has been embarrassed when the instructor tried a trivial example.

2. *Typical, realistic values.* Always try a program on data chosen to represent how the program will be used. These data should be sufficiently simple so that the results can be checked by hand.

3. *Extreme values.* Many programs err at the limits of their range of applications. It is very easy for counters or array bounds to be off by one.

4. *Illegal values.* "Garbage in, garbage out" is an old saying in computer circles that should not be respected. When a good program has garbage coming in, then its output should at least be a sensible error message. It is preferable that the program should provide some indication of the likely errors in input and perform any calculations that remain possible after disregarding the erroneous input.

2. The Glass-Box Method

The second approach to choosing test data begins with the observation that a program can hardly be regarded as thoroughly tested if there are some parts of its code that,

path testing

in fact, have never been executed. In the *glass-box* method of testing, the logical structure of the program is examined, and for each alternative that may occur, test data are devised that will lead to that alternative. Thus care is taken to choose data to check each possibility in every **case** statement, each clause of every **if** statement, and the termination condition of each loop. If the program has several selection or iteration statements, then it will require different combinations of test data to check all the paths that are possible. Figure 1.2 shows a short program segment with its possible execution paths.

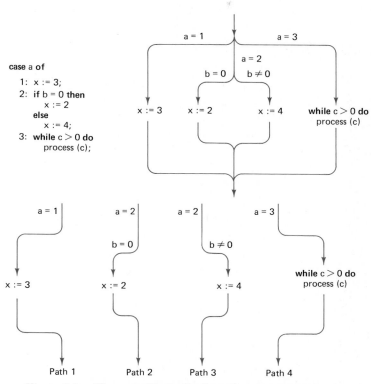

Figure 1.2. The execution paths through a program segment

For a large program the glass-box approach is clearly not practicable, but for a single small module, it is an excellent debugging and testing method. In a well-designed program, each module will involve few loops and alternatives. Hence only a few well-chosen test cases will suffice to test each module on its own.

modular testing

In glass-box testing, the advantages of modular program design become evident. Let us consider a typical example of a project involving 50 subprograms, each of which can involve 5 different cases or alternatives. If we were to test the whole program as one, we would need 5^{50} test cases to be sure that each alternative was tested. Each module separately requires only 5 test cases, each of which is easier, for a total of $5 \times 50 = 250$. Hence a problem of impossible size has been reduced to one that, for a large program, is of quite modest size.

comparison

interface errors

Before you conclude that glass-box testing is always the preferable method, we should comment that, in practice, black-box testing is usually more effective in uncovering errors. Perhaps one reason is that the most subtle programming errors often occur not within a subprogram but in the interface between subprograms, in misunderstanding of the exact conditions and standards of information interchange between subprograms. It would therefore appear that a reasonable testing philosophy for a large project would be to apply glass-box methods to each small module as it is written and use black-box test data to test larger sections of the program when they are complete.

3. The Ticking-Box Method

To conclude this section, let us mention one further philosophy of program testing, the philosophy that is, unfortunately, quite widely used. This might be called the *ticking-box* method. It consists of doing no testing at all after the project is fairly well debugged, but instead turning it over to the customer for trial and acceptance. The result, of course, is a time bomb.

Exercises 1.4

E1. Find suitable black-box test data for each of the following:

  (a) A function that returns the largest of its three parameters, which are real numbers.

  (b) A function that returns the square root of a real number.

  (c) A function that returns the least common multiple of its two parameters, which must be positive integers. (The *least common multiple* is the smallest integer that is a multiple of both parameters. Examples: The least common multiple of 4 and 6 is 12, of 3 and 9 is 9, and of 5 and 7 is 35.)

  (d) A procedure that sorts three integers, given as its parameters, into ascending order.

  (e) A procedure that sorts an array A of integers indexed from 1 to a variable n into ascending order, where A and n are both parameters.

E2. Find suitable glass-box test data for each of the following:

  (a) The statement

    if a < b **then if** c > d **then** x := 1 **else if** c = d **then** x := 2
    else x :=3 **else if** a = b **then** x := 4 **else if** c = d **then** x := 5
    else x := 6;

  (b) The function NeighborCount(i, j).

Programming Projects 1.4

P1. Enter the Life program of this section on your computer and make sure that it works correctly.

P2. Test the Life program with the examples shown in Figure 1.1.

P3. Run the Life program with the initial configurations shown in Figure 1.3.

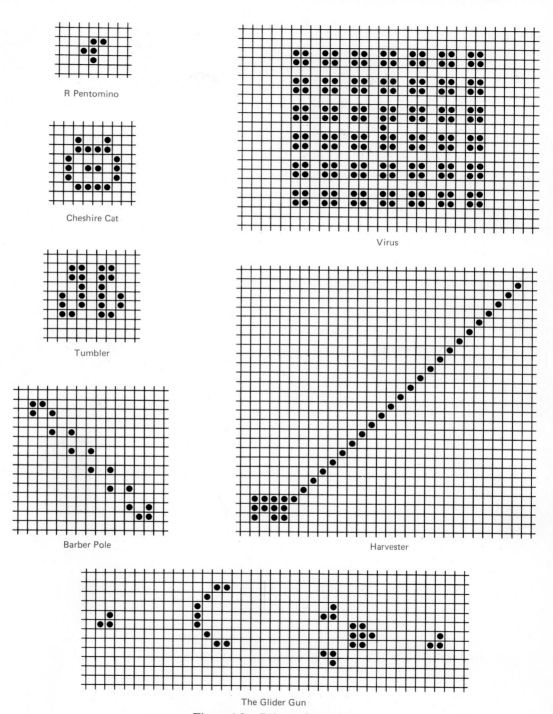

Figure 1.3. Life configurations

POINTERS AND PITFALLS

1. Be sure you understand your problem before you decide how to solve it.
2. Be sure you understand the algorithmic method before you start to program.
3. In case of difficulty, divide the problem into pieces and think of each part separately.
4. Keep your subprograms short and simple; rarely should a single subprogram be more than a page long.
5. Use stubs and drivers, black-box and glass-box testing to simplify debugging.
6. Use plenty of scaffolding to help localize errors.
7. In programming with arrays, be wary of index values that are off by 1. Always use extreme-value testing to check programs that use arrays.
8. Keep your programs well-formatted as you write them—it will make debugging much easier.
9. Keep your documentation consistent with your code, and when reading a program make sure that you debug the code and not just the comments.
10. Explain your program to somebody else: Doing so will help you understand it better yourself.
11. Remember the Programming Precepts!

REVIEW QUESTIONS

Most chapters of this book conclude with a set of questions designed to help you review the main ideas of the chapter. These questions can all be answered directly from the discussion in the book; if you are unsure of any answer, refer to the appropriate section.

1.3
1. When is it appropriate to use one-letter variable names?
2. Name four kinds of information that should be included in program documentation.
3. Why should side effects of subprograms be avoided?

1.4
4. What is a program stub?
5. What is the difference between stubs and drivers, and when should each be used?
6. What is a structured walkthrough?
7. Name two methods for testing a program, and discuss when each should be used.
8. If you cannot immediately picture all details needed for solving a problem, what should you do with the problem?

REFERENCES FOR FURTHER STUDY

Pascal

The programming language Pascal was devised by NIKLAUS WIRTH, who first published its description in 1971. For older versions of the language, the standard reference manual was

K. JENSEN and N. WIRTH, *PASCAL User Manual and Report,* second edition, Springer-Verlag, Berlin, Heidelberg, New York, 1974, 167 pages.

More recently, the International Standards Organization (ISO) has specified a standard version of Pascal to which most newer compilers adhere. This standard Pascal is succinctly but clearly described in the following book, to which you may refer with subtle problems in Pascal behavior:

DOUG COOPER, *Standard Pascal User Reference Manual,* W. W. Norton, New York, 1983, 176 pages.

Many good textbooks provide a more leisurely description of Pascal, too many books to list here. These textbooks also provide many examples and applications. Some books designed for introductory courses, however, omit important "advanced" features of Pascal that will be used often in this book. Be sure that any textbook you select covers the full syntax of standard Pascal.

Programming Principles

Three books that contain many helpful hints on programming style and correctness, as well as examples of good and bad practices, are

BRIAN KERNIGHAN and P. J. PLAUGER, *The Elements of Programming Style,* second edition, McGraw-Hill, New York, 1978, 168 pages.

HENRY F. LEDGARD, PAUL A. NAGIN, and JOHN F. HUERAS, *Pascal with Style: Programming Proverbs,* Hayden Book Company, Hasbrouck Heights, N.J., 1979, 210 pages.

DENNIE VAN TASSEL, *Program Style, Design, Efficiency, Debugging, and Testing,* second edition, Prentice-Hall, Englewood Cliffs, N.J., 1978, 323 pages.

EDSGER W. DIJKSTRA pioneered the movement known as structured programming, which insists on taking a carefully organized top-down approach to the design and writing of programs, when in March 1968 he caused some consternation by publishing a letter entitled "Go To Statement Considered Harmful" in the *Communications of the ACM* (vol. 11, pages 147–148). DIJKSTRA has since published several papers and books that are most instructive in programming method. One book of special interest is

E. W. DIJKSTRA, *A Discipline of Programming,* Prentice-Hall, Englewood Cliffs, N.J., 1976, 217 pages.

The Game of Life

The prominent British mathematician J. H. CONWAY has made many original contributions to subjects as diverse as the theory of finite simple groups, logic, and combinatorics. He devised the game of Life by starting with previous, technical studies of cellular automata and devising reproduction rules that would make it difficult for a configuration to grow without bound, but for which many configurations would go through interesting progressions. CONWAY, however, did not publish his observations, but communicated them to MARTIN GARDNER. The popularity of the game skyrocketed when it was discussed in

MARTIN GARDNER, "Mathematical Games" (regular column), *Scientific American* 223, no. 4 (October 1970), 120–123; 224, no. 2 (February 1971), 112–117.

The examples at the end of Sections 1.2 and 1.4 are taken from these columns. These columns have been reprinted with further results in

MARTIN GARDNER, *Wheels, Life and Other Mathematical Amusements,* W. H. Freeman, New York, 1983, pp. 214–257.

This book also contains a bibliography of articles on Life. A quarterly newsletter, entitled *Lifeline,* was even published for some years to keep the real devotees up to date on current developments in Life and related topics.

C H A P T E R   2

Introduction to Software Engineering

▶ *This chapter continues to expound the principles of good program design, with special emphasis on techniques required for the production of large software systems. These techniques include problem specification, algorithm development, verification, and analysis, as well as program testing and maintenance. These general principles are introduced in the context of developing a second program for the Life game, one based on more sophisticated methods than those of the last chapter.*

Software engineering is the discipline within computer science concerned with techniques needed for the production and maintenance of large software systems. Our goal in introducing some of these techniques is to demonstrate their importance in problems of practical size. Although much of the discussion in this chapter is motivated by the Life game and applied specifically to its program, the discussion is always intended to illustrate more general methods that can be applied to a much broader range of problems of practical importance.

2.1 PROGRAM MAINTENANCE

Small programs written as exercises or demonstrations are usually run a few times and then discarded, but the disposition of large practical programs is quite different. A program of practical value will be run many times, usually by many different people, and its writing and debugging mark only the beginning of its use. They also mark only the beginning of the work required to make and keep the program useful. It is necessary to *review* and *analyze* the program to ensure that it meets the requirements specified for it, *adapt* it to changing environments, and *modify* it to make it better meet the needs of its users.

Let us illustrate these activities by reconsidering the program for the Life game written and tested in Chapter 1.

1. Review of the Life Program

problems

If you have run the Life program on a small computer or on a busy time-sharing system, then you will likely have found two major problems. First, the method for input of the initial configuration is poor. It is unnatural for a person to calculate and type in the numerical coordinates of each living cell. The form of input should instead reflect the same visual imagery as the way the map is printed. Second, you may have found the program's speed somewhat disappointing. There can be a noticeable pause between printing one generation and starting to print the next.

Our goal is to improve the program so that it will run really efficiently on a microcomputer. The problem of improving the form of input is addressed as an exercise; the text discusses the problem of improving the speed.

2. Analysis of the Life Program

We must first find out where the program is spending most of its computation time. If we examine the program, we can first note that the trouble cannot be in the procedure Initialize, since this is done only once, before the main loop is started. Within the loop that counts generations, we have a pair of nested loops that, together, will iterate

operation counts

$$\text{maxrow} \times \text{maxcol} = 50 \times 80 = 4000$$

times. Hence program lines within these loops will contribute substantially to the time used.

nested loops

The first thing done within the loops is to invoke the function NeighborCount(i, j). The function itself includes a pair of nested loops (note that we are now nested to a total depth of 5), which usually do their inner statement 9 times. The function also does 7 statements outside the loops, for a total (usually) of 16.

Within the nested loops of the main program there are, along with the call to the function, only the comparison to find which case to do and the appropriate assignment statement; that is, there are only 2 statements additional to the 16 in the function. Outside of the nested loops there is the assignment of arrays map := newmap, which, in copying 4000 entries, is about equivalent to 1 more statement within the loops. There is also a call to the procedure WriteMap, some variation of which is needed in any case so that the user can see what the program is doing. Our primary concern is with the computation, however, so let us not worry about the time that WriteMap may need. We thus see that for each generation, the computation involves about

$$4000 \times 19 = 76,000$$

statements, of which about $4000 \times 16 = 64,000$ are done in the function. On a small microcomputer or a tiny share of a busy time-sharing system, each statement can easily require 100 to 500 microseconds for execution, so the time to calculate a generation may easily range as high as 40 seconds, a delay that most users will find unacceptable.

Since by far the greatest amount of time is used in the function calculating the number of occupied neighbors of a cell, we should concentrate our attention on doing this job more efficiently. Before starting to develop some ideas, however, let us pause momentarily to pontificate:

> ### Programming Precept
> *Most programs spend 90 percent of their time doing 10 percent of their instructions.*
> *Find this 10 percent, and concentrate your efforts for efficiency there.*

It takes much practice and experience to decide what is important and what may be neglected in analyzing algorithms for efficiency, but it is a skill that you should carefully develop to enable you to choose alternative methods or to concentrate your programming efforts where they will do the most good.

3. Problem-Solving Alternatives

use of array

Once we know where a program is doing most of its work, we can begin to consider alternative methods in the hope of improving its efficiency. In the case of the Life game, let us ask ourselves how we can reduce the amount of work needed to keep track of the number of occupied neighbors of each Life cell. Is it necessary for us to calculate the number of neighbors of every cell at every generation? Clearly not, if we use some way (such as an array) to remember the number of neighbors, and if this number does not change from one generation to the next. If you have spent some time experimenting with the Life program, then you will certainly have noticed that in many interesting configurations, the number of occupied cells at any time is far below the total number of positions available. Out of 4000 positions, typically fewer than 100 are occupied. Our program is spending much of its time laboriously calculating the obvious facts that cells isolated from the living cells indeed have no occupied neighbors and will not become occupied. If we can prevent or substantially reduce such useless calculation, we shall obtain a much better program.

As a first approach, let us consider trying to limit the calculations to cells in a limited area around those that are occupied. If this occupied area (which we would have to define precisely) is roughly rectangular, then we can implement this scheme easily by replacing the limits in the loops by other variables that would bound the occupied area. But this scheme would be very inefficient if the occupied area were shaped like a large ring, or, indeed, if there were only two small occupied areas in opposite corners of a very large rectangle. To try to carry out this plan for occupied areas not at all rectangular in shape would probably require us to do so many comparisons, as well as the loops, as to obviate any saving of time.

4. A Fresh Start and a New Method

Let us back up for a moment. If we can now decide to keep an array to remember the number of occupied neighbors of each cell, then the only counts in the array that will change from generation to generation will be those that correspond to immediate neighbors of cells that die or are born. We can substantially improve the running

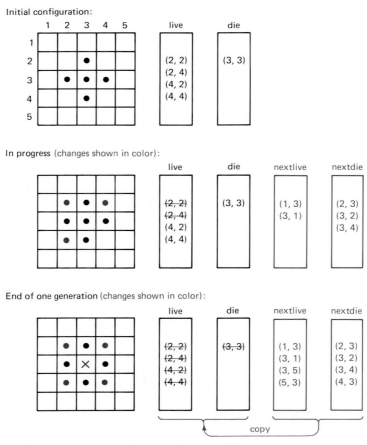

Figure 2.1. Life using lists

arrays and functions

time of our program if we convert the function NeighborCount into an array and add appropriate statements to update the array while we are doing the changes from one generation to the next embodied in the **case** statement, or, if we prefer (what is perhaps conceptually easier), while we are copying newmap into map we can note where the births and deaths have occurred and at that time update the array.

To emphasize that we are now using an array instead of the function Neighbor-Count, we shall change the name and write numbernbrs for the array.

*algorithm
development*

The method we have now developed still involves scanning at least once through the full array map at every generation, which likely means much useless work. By being slightly more careful, we can avoid the need ever to look at unoccupied areas. As a cell is born or dies it changes the value of numbernbrs for each of its immediate neighbors. While making these changes we can note when we find a cell whose count becomes such that it will be born or die in the next generation. Thus we should set up two lists that will contain the cells that, so to speak, are moribund or are expecting in the coming generation. In this way, once we have finished making the changes of the current generation and printing the map, we will have waiting for us complete lists of all the births and deaths to occur in the coming generation. It should now be clear that we really need two lists for births and two for deaths, one each for the changes being made now (which lists are depleted as we proceed) and one list each (which are being added to) containing the changes for the next generation. When the changes on the current lists are complete, we print the map, copy the coming lists to the current ones, and go on to the next generation.

5. Algorithm Outline

Let us now summarize our decisions by writing down an informal outline of the program we shall develop.

initialization

Get the initial configuration of living cells and use it to calculate an array holding
 the neighbor counts of all cells. Construct lists of the cells that will become
 alive and that will become dead in the first generation;
Repeat the following steps as long as desired:

main loop

For each cell on the list of cells to become alive do

 Make the cell alive;
 Update the neighbor counts for each neighbor of the cell;
 If a neighbor count reaches the appropriate value, then add the cell to
  the list of cells to be made alive or dead in the next generation;

For each cell on the list of cells to become dead do

 Make the cell dead;
 Update the neighbor counts for each neighbor of the cell;
 If a neighbor count reaches the appropriate value, then add the cell to
  the list of cells to be made alive or dead in the next generation;

*prepare for next
generation*

Write out the map for the user;
Copy the lists of cells to be changed in the next generation to the lists for
 the current generation.

Clearly a great many details remain to be specified in this outline, but before we consider these details, we need to develop some new tools.

Exercises 2.1

E1. Sometimes the user might wish to run the Life game on a grid smaller than 50×80. Determine how it is possible to make maxrow and maxcol into variables that the user can set when the program is run. Try to make as few changes in the program as possible.

E2. One idea for changing the program to save some of the **if** statements in the function NeighborCount is to add two extra rows and columns to the arrays map and newmap, by changing their dimensions to

$$[0 .. \text{maxrow}+1, \ 0 .. \text{maxcol}+1].$$

Entries in the extra rows and columns would always be dead, so that the loops in NeighborCount could always run their full range from $i-1$ to $i+1$ and $j-1$ to $j+1$. How would this change affect the count of statements executed in NeighborCount?

Programming Projects 2.1

P1. Rewrite the procedure Initialize so that it accepts the occupied positions in some symbolic form, such as a sequence of blanks and X's in appropriate rows, rather than requiring the occupied positions to be entered as numerical coordinate pairs.

P2. On a slow-speed terminal writing out the entire map at every generation will be quite slow. If you have access to a video terminal for which the cursor can be controlled by the program, rewrite the procedure WriteMap so that it updates the map instead of completely rewriting it at each generation.

2.2 PASCAL RECORDS

As we develop the revised Life program that follows the scheme we have devised in the last section, we must make some decisions about what variables we shall need and the ways in which we shall implement the lists we have decided to use. In doing so we shall use an important feature of Pascal that aids greatly in displaying the logical connections between different pieces of data, the Pascal category of types called *records*.

1. The Logical Structure of Lists

A list really has two distinct parts associated with it. First is a variable that gives the number of items in the list. Second is an array that contains the items on the list. In most languages the programmer must carry the counter variable and the array separately (and doing so is a frequent source of trouble for beginners). Sometimes tricks are used, such as establishing the array to have indices commencing at 0, and using entry 0 as the counter.

2. Definition and Examples

The type declaration

record   . . .   end

in Pascal establishes a type consisting of several *fields* (also called *components*), each of which is itself of some (arbitrarily defined) type. In our case, we may define a type called list with declarations such as the following:

declaration of list

```
const    maxlist = 200;                          {maximum size of lists}
type     list = record
           count:  0 .. maxlist;
           entry:  array[1 .. maxlist] of entrytype        {defined elsewhere}
         end;
```

The four lists that we wish to have are now variables of type list, declared as usual:

var   die, live, nextdie, nextlive: list;

3. Accessing Records

Individual parts of a Pascal record variable are referenced by giving first the name of the variable, then a period (.), then the name of the part as declared in the type statement for the record. Thus the counters of entries in our four lists are denoted

field access

```
die.count     nextdie.count
live.count    nextlive.count
```

The kth entry in list live is denoted live.entry[k].

4. Hierarchical Records: Data Abstraction

The entries in our lists will be coordinate pairs [x, y], and there is no reason why we should not think of these pairs as a single record, by defining

declaration of coordinate

```
type coord = record
               x: row;
               y: col
             end;
```

If we then define entrytype = coord, we shall have put these coordinates into our lists, as we wish to do.

hierarchy of records

Note that we now have an example of a record (coord) contained as entries in arrays that are fields of another record (list). Such records are called **hierarchical.** By putting records within records, records in arrays, and arrays in records, we can build up complicated data structures that precisely describe the relationships in the data processed by a program.

top-down design of data structures

When we work with records, however, we should never think of them as having such a complicated structure. Instead, we should use top-down design for data structures as well as for algorithms. When we process the large, outer records, we need not be concerned about the exact structure of each component within the record. When we write algorithms to manipulate the innermost components, we should treat them only in terms of their simple structure and not be concerned as to whether they may later be embedded in larger records or arrays. We can thus use records to accomplish **information hiding,** whereby we can design the upper levels both of algorithms and data structures without worrying about the details that will be specified later on lower levels of refinement.

5. The **with** Statement

To access the individual fields within a hierarchical record, we must work our way from the top level down, using a period (.) each time we take a field within a record and brackets ([ ]) each time we take an entry of an array. To obtain, for example, the x coordinate of entry k of the list nextdie, we must write

nextdie.entry[k].x

Although, as you can see, this notation is entirely logical, it can become a bit cumbersome when there are several records and arrays, one within the next, so Pascal allows the special statement

field access
with recordvariable **do** . . . .

In the block under control of the **with** statement the specified record variable has a special status, so that its various fields can be accessed by giving only their names, without having to repeat the name of the record variable each time.

Continuing with our example of lists, we note that the list nextdie can be processed with statements such as

```
with nextdie do
  for k := 1 to count do
    with entry[k] do
      {Calculations with coordinates need specify only x or y to denote
       nextdie.entry[k].x or nextdie.entry[k].y};
```

As one further example of processing hierarchical records, we can write a short procedure that will add an entry x to the end of a list L.

adding to a list
```
procedure Add(var L: list;   c: coord);
begin                                                {procedure Add}
  with L do
    if count = maxlist then
      Overflow          {A separate procedure is needed to handle overflow.}
    else begin
      count := count + 1;
      entry[count] := c
    end
end;                                                 {procedure Add}
```

6. Variant Records

With the preceding discussion, we have all the information concerning records that we need for the Life program, but for completeness we mention some further aspects of records that will be useful in future applications. For more details and examples, consult a textbook on Pascal programming.

Depending on the particular information stored in a record, some of the fields may sometimes not be used. If the data are of one kind, then one field may be required, but if they are of another kind, a second field will be needed. Suppose,
example

for example, that records represent geometrical figures. If the figure is a circle, then we wish a field giving the *radius* of the circle. If it is a rectangle, then we wish the *height* and the *width* of the rectangle and whether or not it is a *square*. If it is a triangle, we wish the three *sides* and whether it is *equilateral, isosceles, or scalene*. For any of the figures we wish to have the *area* and the *circumference*. One way to set up the record type for all these geometrical figures would be to have separate fields for each of the desired attributes, but then, if the figure is a rectangle, the fields giving the radius, sides of a square, and kind of triangle would all be meaningless. Similarly, if the figure is a circle or a triangle, several of the fields would be undefined.

fixed and variant parts

To avoid this difficulty, Pascal provides *variant records* in which certain fields are defined only when the information in the record is of a particular kind. Variant records have two parts: In the *fixed* part, all the fields remain the same no matter what kind of information is in the record, but in the *variant* part, the fields differ according to the kind of information. What kind of information is in the record (and therefore which variant is used) depends on the value of a special field called

tag field

the *tag field*. The type of the tag field can be any ordinal type, and the variant part, introduced by the word **case**, is superficially similar to a **case** statement with the tag field in place of the case selector. The different variants are selected by constants of the ordinal type, and the fields in each variant are enclosed in parentheses (. . .).

All this will be clarified by returning to our geometrical example. The ordinal type specifying the kind of information in the record is the enumerated type

> **type**   figuretype = (circle, rectangle, triangle);

and the record can then be declared as follows:

geometry example

```
type
  figure = record
             area,                                  {This is the fixed part of the record.}
             circumference: real;
           case shape: figuretype of               {This is the tag field.}
             circle:                                {first variant}
               (radius: real);
             rectangle:                             {second variant}
               (height,
               width:   real;
               square: Boolean);
             triangle:                              {third variant}
               (side1,
               side2,
               side3:   real;
               kind:   (equilateral, isosceles, scalene))
           end;                                     {end of record declaration}
```

advantages of variant records

The first advantage of variant records is that they clarify the logic of the program by showing exactly what information is required in each case. A second advantage is that they allow the system to save space when the program is compiled. Since the fields in only one of the variants are usable for a particular record, the fields in different variants can be assigned to the same space by the compiler, and hence the total amount of space that needs to be set aside for the record is just the amount needed if the largest variant is the one that occurs. This situation is illustrated in Figure 2.2 for the example of records describing geometrical shapes.

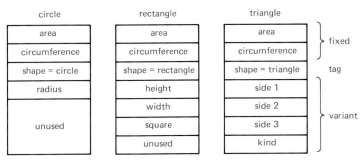

Figure 2.2   Storage of variant records

Here are some rules and guidelines concerning the use of variant records in Pascal:

rules and guidelines
for records

1. The fixed part of the record must come first, then the tag field and the variant part, if any.

2. A record may contain only one variant part, although any fields within a record may be other records with their own variant parts.

3. All the field identifiers used in a record must be different, even when they appear in different variants.

4. The tag field identifier may be omitted, but it is not recommended to omit it, and the tag *type* must be included if there is a variant part.

5. The variants are selected by constants from the tag type. Several constants, separated by commas, can specify the same variant.

6. The list of fields in a variant is enclosed in parentheses (. . .). A field list for a variant can be empty; this is denoted by ( ).

7. The variant to be used in a particular record is determined at run time by assigning a value to the tag field and the fields of the corresponding variant. The variant can be changed at any time by changing the tag field and the variant fields. If the variant is changed, the variant fields belonging to the previous variant are lost.

Exercises   **E1.** Define record types (no variant records needed) for each of the following applica-
2.2   tions:

(a) A *complex number* consisting of a *real* part and an *imaginary* part, both of which are real numbers.

(b) A *string* of characters consisting of an integer *counter* together with an array of characters.

(c) An *address* consisting of a *street,* a *city,* and a *state* or country, each of which is a string (defined in part **(b)**).

(d) The type personaldata consisting of a *name,* which is a string (defined in **(b)**), an *address* (defined in **(c)**), a *sex* (one of *male* or *female*), a *marital status* (one of *single, married, widowed,* or *divorced*), and a number of *dependents* between 0 and 20.

E2. Write a procedure that will delete the last coordinate from a list (as defined in the text) or will invoke a procedure Error if the list was empty.

E3. Write procedures that will copy one list to another list (as the record type defined in the text). Use the following methods: **(a)** copy the entire records; **(b)** use a loop to copy only the entries. Which version is easier to write? Which version will usually run faster, and why?

E4. Define a record type using variant records for the following simplified kind of bank account. The record includes a *name,* which is a string (as defined in Exercise **E1(b)**), an *address* (as defined in **E1(c)**), an integer account *number,* the date the account was *opened* (a string), and an account *balance* (real number). There are three kinds of accounts, *savings, checking,* and *term.* For a savings account there is a *deposit* list, a *withdrawal* list, and a current interest *credit* (a real number). For a checking account there is a *transaction* list (including deposits, credits, cheques, and debits as positive or negative numbers) and a current *service charge* (a real number). All these lists are set up similarly to the lists in the text, but their entries are real numbers. For a term account there is an *initial* balance (real number), an interest *rate* (real number), an *accumulated* interest amount (real number), and a *maturity* date (string).

2.3 ALGORITHM DEVELOPMENT: A SECOND VERSION OF LIFE

After deciding on the basic method and the overall outline of the data structures needed for solving a problem, it is time to commence the process of algorithm development, beginning with an overall outline and slowly introducing refinements until all the details are specified and a program is formulated in a computer language.

2.3.1 The Main Program

In the case of the Life game, we can now combine our use of records as the data structures for lists with the outline of the method given in part 5 of Section 2.1, thereby translating the outline into a main program written in Pascal. With few exceptions, the declarations of constants, types, and variables follow the discussion in Sections 2.1 and 2.2 along with the corresponding declarations for the first version of the Life game.

Life2
main program

```
program Life2(input, output);
   {Simulation of Conway's game of Life on a bounded grid}
   {Version 2}
```

{maximum size of grid}

```
   const
      maxrow = 50;
      maxcol = 80;
      maxlist = 400;
```

declarations

{maximum size of lists}

```
   type
      row       = 1 .. maxrow;
      col       = 1 .. maxcol;
      status    = (alive, dead);
      grid      = array[row, col] of status;
      gridcount = array[row, col] of integer;
      coord     = record
                     x: row;
                     y: col
                  end;
      list      = record
                     count: 0 .. maxlist;
                     entry: array[1 .. maxlist] of coord
                  end;
   var
      map:        grid;
      numbernbrs: gridcount;
      live,
      die,
      nextlive,
      nextdie:    list;
      again:      Boolean;
   {Declarations of procedures will be inserted here.}
```

```
   begin                                                    {main program Life2}
```

initialization

```
      Initialize(live, die, nextlive, nextdie, map, numbernbrs);
      WriteMap(map);
      repeat
```

main loop

```
         Vivify(live, map, numbernbrs);
         Kill(die, map, numbernbrs);
         WriteMap(map);
         AddNeighbors(live, nextlive, nextdie, numbernbrs);
         SubtractNeighbors(die, nextlive, nextdie, numbernbrs);
         Copy(nextlive, live);
         Copy(nextdie, die);
         Enquire(again)
      until not again
   end.                                                     {main program Life2}
```

description

Most of the action of the program is postponed to various procedures. After initializing all the lists and arrays, the program begins its main loop. At each generation we first go through the cells waiting in lists live and die in order to update the array map, which, as in the first version of Life, keeps track of which cells are alive. This work is done in the procedures Vivify (which means *make alive*) and Kill. After writing the revised configuration, we update the count of neighbors for each cell that has been born or has died, using the procedures AddNeighbors and SubtractNeighbors and the array numbernbrs. As part of the same procedures, when the neighbor count reaches an appropriate value, a cell is added to the list nextlive or nextdie to indicate that it will be born or die in the coming generation. Finally, we must copy the lists for the coming generation into the current ones.

2.3.2 Refinement: Development of the Subprograms

specifications and problem solving

After the solution to a problem has been outlined, it is time to turn to the various parts of the outline, to include more details and thereby specify the solution exactly. While making these refinements, however, the programmer often discovers that the task of each subprogram was not specified as carefully as necessary, that the interface between different subprograms must be reworked and spelled out in more detail, so that the different subprograms accomplish all necessary tasks, and so that they do so without duplication or contradictory requirements. In a real sense, therefore, the process of refinement requires going back to the problem-solving phase to find the best way to split the required tasks among the various subprograms. Ideally, this process of refinement and specification should be completed before any coding is done.

Let us illustrate this activity by working through the requirements for the various subprograms for the Life game.

1. The Task for AddNeighbors

Much of the work of our program will be done in the procedures AddNeighbors and SubtractNeighbors. We shall develop the first of these, leaving the second as an exercise. The procedure AddNeighbors will go through the list live, and for each entry will find its immediate neighbors (as done in the original function NeighborCount), will increase the count in numbernbrs for each of these, and must put some of these on the lists nextlive and nextdie. To determine which, let us denote by n the updated count for one of the neighbors and consider cases.

cases for AddNeighbors

1. It is impossible that $n = 0$, since we have just increased n by 1.
2. If $n = 1$ or $n = 2$, then the cell is already dead and it should remain dead in the next generation. We need do nothing.
3. If $n = 3$, then a previously live cell still lives; a previously dead cell must be added to the list nextlive.
4. If $n = 4$, then a previously live cell dies; add it to nextdie. If the cell is dead, it remains so.
5. If $n > 4$, then the cell is already dead (or is already on list nextdie) and stays there.

2. Problems

One subtle problem arises with this procedure. When the neighbor count for a dead cell reaches 3, we add it to the list nextlive, but it may well be that later in procedure

spurious entries

AddNeighbors, its neighbor count will again be increased (beyond 3) so that it should not be vivified in the next generation after all. Similarly, when the neighbor count for a live cell reaches 4, we add it to nextdie, but the procedure SubtractNeighbors may well reduce its neighbor count below 4, so that it should be removed from nextdie. Thus the final determination of lists nextlive and nextdie cannot be made until the array numbernbrs has been fully updated, but yet, as we proceed, we must tentatively add entries to the lists.

postpone difficulty

It turns out that, if we postpone solution of this problem, it becomes much easier. In the procedures AddNeighbors and SubtractNeighbors, let us add cells to nextlive and nextdie without worrying whether they will later be removed. Then when we copy nextlive and nextdie to lists live and die, we can check that the neighbor counts are correct (in live, for example, only dead cells with a neighbor count of exactly 3 should appear) and delete the erroneous entries with no difficulty.

duplicate entries

After doing this, however, an even more subtle error remains. It is possible that the same cell may appear in list nextlive (or nextdie) more than once. A dead cell, for example, may initially have a count of 2, which, when increased, adds the cell to nextlive. Its count may then be increased further, and in SubtractNeighbors decreased one or more times, perhaps ending at 3, so that SubtractNeighbors again adds it to nextlive. Then, when neighbor counts are updated in the next generation, this birth will incorrectly contribute 2 rather than 1 to the neighbor counts. We could solve this problem by searching the lists for duplicates before copying them, but to do so would be slow, and we can again solve the problem more easily by postponing it. When, in the next generation, we wish to vivify a cell, we shall first check whether it is already alive. If so, then we know that its entry is a duplicate of one earlier on list live. While we are postponing work, we might as well also postpone checking the neighbor counts, so that the copying procedure will now do nothing but copy lists, and all the checking is done in Vivify and Kill. Figure 2.3 shows the trace of Life2 for one small configuration and exhibits the appearance and deletion of spurious and duplicate entries in the various lists.

> ***Programming Precept***
> *Sometimes postponing problems simplifies their solution.*

2.3.3 Coding the Procedures

Now that we have spelled out completely and precisely the requirements for each procedure, it is time to code them into our programming language. In a large software project it is necessary to do the coding at the right time, not too soon and not too late. Most programmers err by starting to code too soon. If coding is begun

specifications complete

before the requirements are made precise, then unwarranted assumptions about the specifications will inevitably be made while coding, and these assumptions may render different subprograms incompatible with each other or make the programming task much more difficult than it need be.

> ***Programming Precept***
> *Never code until the specifications are precise and complete.*

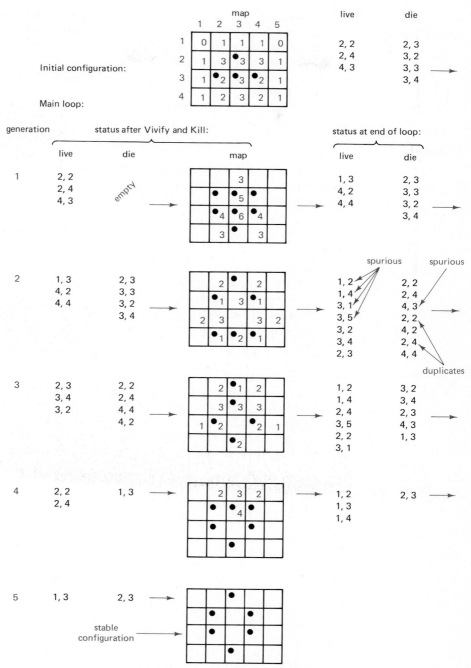

Figure 2.3.   A trace of program Life2

top-down coding

It is possible, on the other hand, to delay coding too long. Just as we design from the top down, we should code from the top down. Once the specifications at the top levels are complete and precise, we should code the subprograms at these levels and test them by including appropriate stubs. If we then find that our design is flawed, we can modify it without paying an exorbitant price in low-level procedures that have been rendered useless.

Now that the specifications for several of the Life subprograms are complete, let us embody our decisions into procedures coded in Pascal.

1. Procedure Copy

Since we decided to postpone all the checking for spurious entries in the lists, the final version of the copying procedure is trivial. It need only copy one list to another and leave the first empty:

copy one list

```
procedure Copy(var A, B: list);
{Copies list A into list B and leaves list A empty}
   var   k:   1 .. maxlist;                          {used to traverse lists}
   begin                                             {procedure Copy}
      for k := 1 to A.count do                       {Copy the entries}
         B.entry[k] := A.entry[k];
      B.count := A.count;                             {and the count.}
      A.count := 0                                    {Set list A to be empty.}
   end;                                               {procedure Copy}
```

2. Procedure Vivify

The procedure Vivify goes through the list live and vivifies each cell, provided that it was previously dead and had a neighbor count of exactly 3. Otherwise, the cell is one of the spurious entries, and Vivify deletes it from the list. Hence at the conclusion of the procedure, list live contains exactly those cells that were vivified and whose neighbor counts must therefore be updated by AddNeighbors.

make cells alive

```
procedure Vivify(var live: list; var map: grid; var numbernbrs: gridcount);
   var
      k: 1 .. maxlist;                                {used to traverse list live}
   begin                                              {procedure Vivify}
      k := 1;
      with live do                                    {Work on the list live.}
         while k <= count do with entry[k] do
         if (map[x, y] = dead) and (numbernbrs[x, y] = 3) then
         begin                                        {Make the cell alive.}
            map[x, y] := alive;
            k := k + 1
         end
         else begin                                   {Delete entry k from the list.}
            entry [k] := entry[count];
            count := count − 1
         end
   end;                                               {procedure Vivify}
```

3. Procedure AddNeighbors

At the conclusion of procedure Vivify, the duplicate and spurious entries have all been removed from list live, and what remains are the cells that were actually vivified. Hence the procedure AddNeighbors can update all the related neighbor counts without problem. This procedure has the following form.

update neighbor counts

```
procedure AddNeighbors(var live, nextlive, nextdie: list;
                           var numbernbrs: gridcount);
var
  i,                                        {loop index for row of neighbor loops}
  ilow, ihigh: row;                                          {row loop limits}
  j,                                                       {column loop index}
  jlow, jhigh: col;                                        {column loop limits}
  k:           0 .. maxlist;                               {used to traverse list}
  nbr:         coord;                                  {record form of a neighbor}
begin                                                   {procedure AddNeighbors}
  with live do
    for k := 1 to count do
      with entry[k] do                        {Loop through the vivified cells.}
      begin                              {Prepare to loop through the neighbors.}
```

bounds for loop

```
        if x = 1       then ilow  := 1       else ilow  := x − 1;
        if x = maxrow  then ihigh := maxrow  else ihigh := x + 1;
        if y = 1       then jlow  := 1       else jlow  := y − 1;
        if y = maxcol  then jhigh := maxcol  else jhigh := y + 1;
        for i := ilow to ihigh do for j := jlow to jhigh do
```

find a neighbor

```
          if (i <> x) or (j <> y) then                      {Skip the cell c itself.}
          begin
            nbr.x := i;    nbr.y := j;                  {Set up a coordinate record.}
            numbernbrs[i, j] := numbernbrs[i, j] + 1;
```

put cells onto lists

```
            case numbernbrs[i, j] of
              0:          writeln('Impossible case in AddNeighbors.');
              1,2:;                                          {No action is needed.}
              3:          if map[i, j] = dead then Add(nextlive, nbr);
              4:          if map[i, j] = alive then Add(nextdie, nbr);
              5,6,7,8:;                                              {no change}
            end                                                 {case statement}
          end                                                {processing one neighbor}
      end                                             {processing one entry from live}
end;                                                    {procedure AddNeighbors}
```

4. Remaining Procedures

The procedures Kill and SubtractNeighbors are similar in form to Vivify and AddNeighbors; they will be left as exercises. The procedure WriteMap can be used without change from the first version, but a much more efficient version is possible that makes use of the lists live and die to update the screen rather than rewriting it at each generation. The procedure Add appears in Section 2.2. We shall postpone writing procedure Initialize to the end of the next section.

Programming Projects 2.3	**P1.** Write the missing procedures for the second version of Life: **(a)** Kill and **(b)** SubtractNeighbors.
	P2. Write driver programs for the procedures **(a)** Kill and **(b)** SubtractNeighbors, and devise appropriate test data to check the performance of these procedures.

2.4 VERIFICATION OF ALGORITHMS

purpose

Another important aspect of the design of large programs is algorithm verification, that is, a *proof* that the algorithm accomplishes its task. This kind of proof is usually formulated by looking at the specifications for the subprograms and then arguing that these specifications combine properly to accomplish the task of the whole algorithm. While constructing such a proof we may find that the specifications must be changed to enable us to infer the correctness of the algorithm, and, in doing so, the proof itself helps us formulate the specifications for each subprogram with greater precision. Hence algorithm verification and algorithm design can go hand-in-hand, and sometimes the verification can even lead the way. In any case, algorithm verification should precede coding.

2.4.1 Proving the Program

Let us again illustrate these concepts by turning to the Life program, first, to be sure that its algorithm is correct and, second, to assist us in designing the remaining procedure, Initialize.

caution

Indeed, the fact that there were subtle errors in our initial attempts to organize the work done in procedures Vivify, Kill, AddNeighbors, SubtractNeighbors, and Copy should alert us to the possible presence of further errors, or at least to the necessity of exercising considerably more care to be sure that our algorithms are correct.

1. Possible Problems

By postponing the checking of neighbor counts, we were able to avoid difficulties both with the problems of duplicate and of erroneous entries. But, for example, how can we be sure that it is not still possible that the same cell might erroneously be included in both lists nextlive and nextdie? If so, then it might first be vivified and then killed immediately in the following generation (clearly an illegal happening). The answer to this particular question is *no,* since the main program calls both procedures Vivify and Kill before either procedure AddNeighbors or SubtractNeighbors. Thus the cell keeps the same status (alive or dead) from the end of procedure Kill until the next generation, and the procedures AddNeighbors and SubtractNeighbors check that only dead cells are added to nextlive and only living cells to nextdie.

How can we be sure that there are not more subtle questions of this sort, some of which might not be so easy to answer? The only way we can really be confident is to *prove* that our program does the right action in each case.

2. The Main Loop

The difficulty with our program is that what happens in one generation might affect the next generation in some unexpected way. Therefore we focus our attention on the large loop in the main program. At the beginning of the loop, it is the contents of lists live and die that determine everything that happens later. Let us therefore summarize what we know about these lists from our previous study.

loop invariant

> *At the beginning of the main loop, list* live *contains only dead cells, and list* die *contains only living cells, but the lists may contain duplicate entries, or spurious entries whose neighbor counts are wrong. The lists* nextlive *and* nextdie *are empty.*

At the very start of the program, it is one task of procedure Initialize to ensure that the lists live and die are set up properly, so that the preceding statements are correct at the start of the first generation. What we must prove, then, is that if the statements are true at the start of any one generation, then after the eight procedure calls within the loop, they will again be true for the next generation.

3. Proof by Mathematical Induction

At this point, you should note that what we are really doing is using the method of **mathematical induction** to establish that the program is correct. In this method of proof, we begin by establishing the result for an initial case. Next we prove the result for a later case, say, case n, by using the result for earlier cases (those between the initial case and case $n - 1$). See Appendix A.1 for further discussion and examples of proof by mathematical induction.

initial case

induction step

For our program, verification of the initial case amounts to a verification that Initialize works properly. For the second part of the proof, let us examine the actions in the main loop, assuming that the statements are correct at its beginning. Procedure Vivify uses only list live and carefully checks each entry before it vivifies a cell, removing erroneous and duplicate entries from list live as it goes. Hence at the conclusion of Vivify, list live contains only those cells that were properly vivified, and no duplicates. Procedure Kill similarly cleans up list die. Since the two lists originally had no cells in common, and none has been added to either list, no cells have been improperly both vivified and killed. Next, procedure WriteMap is called, but does not change the lists. Procedure AddNeighbors works only from list live and puts only dead cells on list nextlive, and only living ones on list nextdie. Similarly, procedure SubtractNeighbors keeps the dead and living cells properly separated. Together these two procedures add all the cells whose status should change in the next generation to the lists, but may add duplicate or spurious entries. Finally, the copying procedure sets up lists live and die and empties lists nextlive and nextdie, as required to show that all conditions in our statements are again true at the beginning of the next generation. The logic of our program is therefore correct.

end of proof

2.4.2 Invariants and Assertions

Statements such as the one we established in the preceding proof are called *loop invariants.* In general, a loop invariant is a statement that is true at the beginning of every iteration of the loop. The statements we made about the status of various lists at different points of the loop are called *assertions,* and assertions that hold at the beginning and end of each procedure (or, more generally, before and after any statement) are called *preconditions* and *postconditions.*

As an example, let us write down preconditions and postconditions for some of our procedures:

Vivify:

> *precondition:*   List live contains only dead cells and contains all cells ready to be vivified.
>
> *postcondition:*   Array map has been updated with vivified cells, and list live contains only those cells that were vivified, with no duplicates or spurious entries.

AddNeighbors:

> *precondition:*   List live contains all vivified cells whose neighbor counts have not yet been updated.
>
> *postcondition:*   Array numbernbrs has increased counts for all cells neighboring cells in list live. If the increased neighbor count makes the cell a candidate to be vivified [*resp.* killed], then the cell has been added to list nextlive [*resp.* nextdie].

Initialize:

> *precondition:*   None.
>
> *postcondition:*   Array map contains the initial configuration of living and dead cells. Array numbernbrs contains counts of living neighbors corresponding to the configuration in array map. List live contains only dead cells and includes all candidates that may be vivified in the next generation. List die contains only living cells and contains all candidates that may die in the next generation.

simplification

The purpose of loop invariants and assertions is to capture the essence of the dynamic process. It is not always easy to find loop invariants and assertions that will lead to a proof that a program is correct, but it is a very useful exercise. Attempting to find invariants and assertions sometimes leads to simplifications in design of the algorithm, which make its correctness more obvious. Our goal should always be to make our algorithms so straightforward and clear that their logic is obviously correct, and the use of loop invariants can help in this process.

> ### Programming Precept
> *Know your problem.*
> *Give precise preconditions and postconditions for each procedure.*

Algorithm verification is a subject under active research, in which many important questions remain to be answered. Correctness proofs have not yet been supplied for a large number of important algorithms that are in constant use. Sometimes exceptional cases appear that cause an algorithm to misbehave; correctness proofs would provide a consistent means to delineate these exceptions and provide for their processing.

2.4.3 Initialization

design of Initialize

As we turn, finally, to the procedure Initialize, let us use the postconditions for the procedure to help in its composition. The first postcondition states that the array map is to be initialized with the starting configuration of living and dead cells. This task is similar to the initialization of the first version of the program, and we leave the resulting procedure ReadMap as an exercise. We shall, however, need the list of initially living cells for calculating the neighbor counts, so we shall also require Read-Map to put this list into list live. As one of its postconditions, ReadMap will be required to make sure that there are no duplicates in this list. (This can be achieved easily if the reading is done properly.)

The second task is to initialize the neighbor counts in array numbernbrs. But we have required ReadMap to set up list live so that it contains exactly the information needed for procedure AddNeighbors to set the neighbor counts properly for all neighbors of living cells, provided that before calling AddNeighbors we first set all entries in numbernbrs to 0. As well as initializing numbernbrs, procedure AddNeighbors will locate all dead cells that will become alive in the following generation and add them to list nextlive. Hence by setting nextlive to be empty before calling AddNeighbors and copying nextlive to live afterward, we accomplish another of the postconditions of Initialize.

The final postcondition is that list die contain all living cells that should die in the next generation. Some, but perhaps not all, of these may be found by AddNeighbors (in the main loop, the remainder would be found by SubtractNeighbors, which we have no way to use in Initialize). We can accomplish the postcondition more easily, however, by simply putting *all* the living cells into list die: Recall that procedure Kill allows spurious entries on its input list.

In this way the postconditions lead to the following procedure:

initialization

```
procedure Initialize(var live, die, nextlive, nextdie: list;
                     var map: grid; var numbernbrs: gridcount);
var
  x, y: integer;                        {used to set all entries in numbernbrs to 0}
begin                                                     {procedure Initialize}
  ReadMap(live, map);                                          {initializes map}
  for x := 1 to maxrow do                     {Set all the entries in numbernbrs to 0.}
    for y := 1 to maxcol do
      numbernbrs[x, y] := 0;
  nextlive.count := 0;                       {Initialize the lists used by AddNeighbors.}
  nextdie.count := 0;
  AddNeighbors(live, nextlive, nextdie, numbernbrs);
  Copy(live, die);                    {Some of the cells just read in should die in the first
                                                       generation. Kill will catch them.}
  Copy(nextlive, live);               {Put output from AddNeighbors where needed.}
  nextdie.count := 0
end;                                                      {procedure Initialize}
```

Exercises **E1.** Write down preconditions and postconditions for each of the following proce-
2.4   dures:

   (a) **procedure** SquareRoot(x: real; **var** y: real) sets y to the square root of x.
   (b) **function** Meanx(**var** A: list): real calculates the mean (average) x value in a
        list of coordinates (x, y) as declared in Section 2.2.
   (c) **procedure** Copy(**var** A, B: list).
   (d) **procedure** Kill.
   (e) **procedure** SubtractNeighbors.
   (f) **procedure** WriteMap.

E2. (a) Write down the precondition and postcondition for the procedure ReadMap.
   (b) Code the procedure ReadMap.
   (c) Write a driver for ReadMap and test it.

2.5 PROGRAM ANALYSIS AND COMPARISON

In designing algorithms we need methods to separate bad algorithms from good
ones, to help us decide, when we have several possible ways in which to proceed,
which way will prove the most effective for our problem. For this reason the analysis
of algorithms and the comparison of alternative methods constitute an important
part of software engineering.

1. Statement Counts

Let us now see about how much more quickly the program Life2 should run than
the previous version. As we did for the first version, let us ignore the time needed
for input and output in the main program, and look only at the statements inside
the principal loop counting generations. Since all the work of Life2 is done within
procedures, we must analyze each in turn. Each of the procedures does most of its
work within a loop that runs through the entries of one of the lists live, die, nextlive,
or nextdie. Thus the key improvement of Life2 over the original program is that the
amount of computation is no longer proportional to the size of the grid but to the
number of changes being made. For a typical configuration, there might be about
100 occupied cells, with likely no more than 50 dying or being born in a single
generation. With these assumptions, we see that each statement within the inner
loops will be executed about 50 times. In Vivify there are 3 statements within the
loop, in Copy only 1. Within the loop of AddNeighbors there are first 4 **if** statements,
then 2 statements each done 9 times, and the **case** statement done 8 times, for a
total count of 30. The counts for Kill and SubtractNeighbors are similar; thus we
obtain for each generation about

count for Life2
$$50 \times (3 + 1 + 30 + 3 + 1 + 30) = 3400$$

statements. The number of statements executed outside the loops is insignificant (it
is less than 10), so 3400 is a reasonable estimate of the statement count for each
generation.

count for Life1
Our first version of the Life program had a count of 76,000 statements per
generation. Thus our revised program should run as much as 20 times faster. This

constitutes a substantial improvement, particularly in view of the fact that when program Life2 slows down, it is because many changes are being made, not because it is repeating the same predictable calculations.

2. Comparisons

programming effort

From other points of view, however, our second program is not as good as the first. The first of these is the point of view of programming effort. The first program was short and easy to write, simple to understand, and easy to debug. The second program is longer, entailed subtle problems, and required sophisticated reasoning to establish its correctness. Whether this additional work is worthwhile depends on the application and the number of times the program will be used. If a simple method works well enough, then we should not go out of our way to find a more sophisticated approach. Only when simple methods fail do we need to try further devices.

> ### Programming Precept
> *Keep your algorithms as simple as you can.*
> *When in doubt, choose the simple way.*

space requirements

The second point of view is that of storage requirements. Our first program used very little memory (apart from that for the instructions) except for the two arrays map and newmap. These arrays have entries that, in assuming only the two values alive and dead, can be packed so that each entry takes only a single bit. In a typical computer with word size of 32 or 16 bits, the two arrays need then occupy no more than 250 or 500 words, respectively. On the other hand, program Life2 requires, along with the space for its instructions, space for one such array, plus 4000 words for the array numbernbrs and 401 words for each of its four lists, giving a total of more than 5700 words.

3. Time and Space Trade-offs

We have just seen the first of many examples illustrating the substantial trade-offs that can occur between time and space in computer algorithms. Which to choose depends on available equipment. If the storage space is available and otherwise unused, it is obviously preferable to use the algorithm requiring more space and less time. If not, then time may have to be sacrificed. Finally, for an important problem, by far the best approach may be to sit back and rethink the whole problem: You will have learned much from your first efforts and may very well be able to find another approach that will save both time and space.

> ### Programming Precept
> *Consider time and space trade-offs in deciding on your algorithm.*

> ### Programming Precept
> *Never be afraid to start over.*
> *Next time it may be both shorter and easier.*

Exercises
2.5

E1. We could save the time needed to copy lists if we did two generations instead of one inside the main loop. We would pass the names of which of the lists to use to all the procedures, and in writing the instructions for the second generation, we would simply swap the pairs of lists. How many statements, approximately, would be saved per generation? Do you think this change is worth implementing? If so, do it.

E2. We could save the space needed for the array map by making a slight modification in how we keep information in the array numbernbrs. We could use positive entries in numbernbrs to denote living cells and negative entries to denote dead cells. However, we could then not tell whether an entry of 0 meant a dead cell or a living cell with no living neighbors. We could easily overcome that problem by changing the definition of neighbor so that a cell is considered its own neighbor (so the neighbor count for a dead cell would range from 0 to 8, stored in numbernbrs as 0 to −8, and that for a living cell from 1 to 9).

    (a) With this change of definition, write down the revised rules (from Section 1.2.1) for the game of Life.

    (b) Do you think that implementing the changes to eliminate array map is worth the effort? Why or why not?

    (c) If you answered the last question positively, describe exactly what changes are needed in the program.

E3. Note that there is some inefficiency in the program Life2 in having procedures AddNeighbors and SubtractNeighbors called once from the main program, since these procedures must loop through the lists live and die just as Vivify and Kill already do. It would be faster if these procedures were written to update the neighbors of only one cell and were called from Vivify and Kill whenever a cell was vivified or killed.

    (a) Will the program work correctly if these changes are made?

    (b) If not, what further changes will make it work?

    (c) With your revised program, find the proper loop invariants and verify that your algorithm is correct.

Programming
Projects
2.5

P1. If you use a video terminal with direct cursor addressing, write a version of the procedure WriteMap that takes advantage of the lists live and die to update the map rather than completely rewriting it at each generation.

P2. Run the complete program Life2 and compare timings with those of Life1.

2.6 CONCLUSIONS AND PREVIEW

This chapter has surveyed a great deal of ground, but mainly from a bird's-eye view. Some themes we shall treat in much greater depth in later chapters; others must be postponed to more advanced courses; still others are best learned by practice.

2.6.1 The Game of Life

1. Future Directions

We are not yet finished with the game of Life, although we next shall turn to other topics. When we return to the Life game (at the end of Chapter 6), we shall find an algorithm that does not require us to keep a large rectangular grid in memory.

2. Problem Specification

For the moment, however, let me make only one observation, one that you may well have already made and, if so, one that has likely been bothering you. What we have done throughout this chapter and the previous one has been, in fact, incorrect, in that we have not been solving the Life game as it was originally described in Section 1.2. The rules make no mention of the boundaries of the grid containing the cells. In our programs, when a moving colony gets sufficiently close to a boundary, then room for neighbors disappears, and the colony will be distorted by the very presence of the boundary. That is not supposed to be.

It is of course true that in any computer simulation there are absolute bounds on the values that may appear, but certainly our use of a 50 by 80 grid is highly restrictive and arbitrary. Writing a more realistic program must be one of our goals when we return to this problem. But on a first try, restrictions are often reasonable. Nevertheless,

> **Programming Precept**
>
> *Be sure you understand your problem completely.*
> *If you must change its terms, explain exactly what you have done.*

When we started in Section 1.4, we did nothing of the sort, but plunged right in with an approach leaving much to be desired. Almost every programmer learns this experience the hard way and can sympathize with the following:

> **Programming Precept**
>
> *Act in haste and repent at leisure.*
> *Program in haste and debug forever.*

The same thought can be expressed somewhat more positively:

> **Programming Precept**
>
> *Starting afresh is usually easier than patching an old program.*

A good rule of thumb is that, if more than ten percent of a program must be modified, then it is time to rewrite the program completely. With repeated patches to a large program, the number of bugs tends to remain constant. That is, the patches become so complicated that each new patch tends to introduce as many new errors as it corrects.

3. Prototyping

An excellent way to avoid having to rewrite a large project from scratch is to plan from the beginning to write two versions. Before a program is running, it is often impossible to know what parts of the design will cause difficulty or what features need to be changed to meet the needs of the users. Engineers have known for many years that it is not possible to build a large project directly from the drawing board. For large projects engineers always build *prototypes*, that is, scaled-down models that can be studied, tested, and sometimes even used for limited purposes. Models of bridges are built and tested in wind tunnels; pilot plants are constructed before attempting to use new technology on the assembly line.

software prototypes   Prototyping is especially helpful for computer software, since it eases communication between users and designers early in the project, thereby reducing misunderstandings and helping to settle the design to everyone's satisfaction. In building a software prototype, the designer can use programs that are already written for input-output, for sorting, or for other common requirements. The building blocks can be assembled with as little new programming as possible to make a working model that can do some of the intended tasks. Even though the prototype may not function efficiently or do everything that the final system will, it provides an excellent laboratory for the user and designer to experiment with alternative ideas for the final design.

> ### Programming Precept
> *Always plan to build a prototype and throw it away.*
> *You'll do so whether you plan to or not.*

2.6.2 Program Design

1. Criteria for Programs

A major goal of this book is to evaluate algorithms and data structures that purport to solve a problem. Amongst the many criteria by which we can judge a program, the following are some of the most important:

1. Does it solve the problem that is requested, according to the given specifications?
2. Does it work correctly under all conditions?
3. Does it include clear and sufficient information for its user, in the form of instructions and documentation?
4. Is it logically and clearly written, with short modules and subprograms as appropriate to do logical tasks?
5. Does it make efficient use of time and of space?

Some of these criteria will be closely studied for the programs we write. Others will not be mentioned explicitly, but not because of any lack of importance. These criteria, rather, can be met automatically if sufficient thought and effort are invested in every stage of program design. I hope that the examples we study will reveal such care.

2. Software Engineering

Software engineering is the study and practice of methods helpful for the construction and maintenance of large software systems. Although small by realistic standards, the program we have studied in this chapter illustrates many aspects of software engineering.

Software engineering begins with the realization that it is a very long process to obtain good software. It begins before any programs are coded and continues maintenance for years after the programs are put into use. This continuing process is known as the *life cycle* of software. This life cycle can be divided into phases as follows:

phases of life cycle

1. *Analyze* the problem precisely and completely. Be sure to *specify* all necessary user interface with care.

2. *Build* a prototype and *experiment* with it until all specifications can be finalized.

3. *Design* the algorithm, using the tools of data structures and of other algorithms whose function is already known.

4. *Verify* that the algorithm is correct, or make it so simple that its correctness is self-evident.

5. *Analyze* the algorithm to determine its requirements and make sure that it meets the specifications.

6. *Code* the algorithm into the appropriate programming language.

7. *Test* and *evaluate* the program on carefully chosen test data.

8. *Refine* and *repeat* the foregoing steps as needed for additional subprograms until the software is complete and fully functional.

9. *Optimize* the code to improve performance, but only if necessary.

10. *Maintain* the program so that it will meet the changing needs of its users.

Most of these topics have been discussed and illustrated in various sections of this and the preceding chapter, but a few further remarks on the first phase, problem analysis and specification, are in order.

3. Problem Analysis

Analysis of the problem is often the most difficult phase of the software life cycle. This is not because practical problems are conceptually more difficult than are computing science exercises—the reverse is often the case—but because users and programmers tend to speak different languages. Here are some questions on which the analyst and user must reach an understanding:

specifications

1. What form will the input and output data take? How much data will there be?

2. Are there any special requirements for the processing? What special occurrences will require separate treatment?

3. Will these requirements change? How? How fast will the demands on the system grow?

4. What parts of the system are the most important? Which must run most efficiently?

5. How should erroneous data be treated? What other error processing is needed?

6. What kinds of people will use the software? What kind of training will they have? What kind of user interface will be best?

7. How portable must the software be, to move to new kinds of equipment? With what other software and hardware systems must the project be compatible?

8. What extensions or other maintenance are anticipated? What is the history of previous changes to software and hardware?

4. Requirements Specification

The problem analysis and experimentation for a large project finally lead to a formal statement of the requirements for the project. This statement becomes the primary way in which the user and the software engineer attempt to understand each other and establishes the standard by which the final project will be judged. Among the contents of this specification will be the following:

1. *Functional requirements* for the system: what it will do and what commands will be available to the user.

2. *Assumptions* and *limitations* on the system: what hardware will be used for the system, what form the input must take, the maximum size of input, the largest number of users, and so on.

3. *Maintenance requirements:* anticipated extensions or growth of the system, changes in hardware, changes in user interface.

4. *Documentation requirements:* what kind of explanatory material is required for what kinds of users.

The requirements specifications state *what* the software will do, not *how* it will be done. These specifications should be understandable both to the user and to the programmer. If carefully prepared, they will form the basis for the subsequent phases of design, coding, testing, and maintenance.

2.6.3 Pascal

In this chapter and the previous one, we have had a whirlwind tour of many features of Pascal. No attempt has been made to present an orderly or complete description of Pascal features. A concise summary of Pascal appears in Appendix C, to which you should refer with questions of Pascal syntax. For further examples and discussion, consult a Pascal textbook.

By far the most powerful feature of Pascal is the flexibility and strength of its

data types

data types. We have hardly scratched the surface in uncovering these resources. As occasions arise, we shall use the other Pascal tools in making data types: files, sets, and the pointer types that we shall introduce in Chapter 4 and use frequently thereafter. The ability to combine the type definitions in flexible ways (files of records, records containing arrays, arrays of records, etc.) gives almost endless ways to organize our data structures.

Programming Projects 2.6

P1. A *magic square* is a square array of integers such that the sum of every row, the sum of every column, and sum of each of the two diagonals are all equal. Two magic squares are shown in Figure 2.4.*

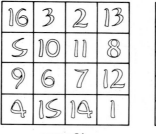

sum = 34   sum = 65

Figure 2.4.   Two magic squares

magic squares

(a) Write a program that reads a square array of integers and determines whether or not it is a magic square.

(b) Write a program that generates a magic square by the following method. This method works only when the size of the square is an odd number. Start by placing 1 in the middle of the top row. Write down successive integers 2, 3, . . . along a diagonal going upward and to the right. When you reach the top row (as you do immediately since 1 is in the top row), continue to the bottom row as though the bottom row were immediately above the top row. When you reach the rightmost column, continue to the leftmost column as though it were immediately to the right of the rightmost one. When you reach a position that is already occupied, instead drop straight down one position from the previous number to insert the new one. The 5×5 magic square constructed by this method is shown in Figure 2.4.

one-dimensional Life

P2. *One-dimensional Life* takes place on a straight line instead of a rectangular grid. Each cell has four neighboring positions: those at distance one or two from it on each side. The rules are similar to those of two-dimensional Life except (1) a dead cell with either two or three living neighbors will become alive in the next generation, and (2) a living cell dies if it has zero, one, or three living neighbors. (Hence a dead cell with zero, one, or four living neighbors

---

* The magic square on the left appears exactly as shown here in the etching *Melancolia* by Albrecht Dürer. Note the inclusion of the date of the etching, 1514.

stays dead; a living cell with two or four living neighbors stays alive.) The progress of sample communities is shown in Figure 2.5. Design, write, and test a program for one-dimensional Life.

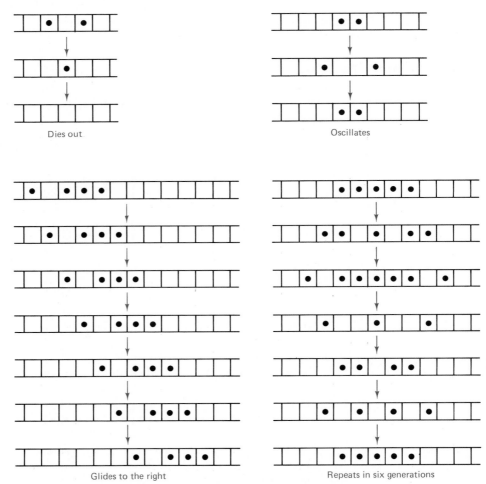

Figure 2.5.   One-dimensional Life configurations

P3. (a) Write a program that will print the calendar of the current year.

(b) Modify the program so that it will read a year number and print the calendar for that year. A year is a leap year (that is, February has 29 instead of 28 days) if it is a multiple of 4, except that century years (multiple of 100) are leap years only when the year is divisible by 400. Hence the year 1900 is not a leap year, but the year 2000 is a leap year.

(c) Modify the program so that it will accept any date (day, month, year) and print the day of the week for that date.

(d) Modify the program so that it will read two dates and print the number of days from one to the other.

(e) Using the rules on leap years, show that the sequence of calendars repeats exactly every 400 years.

(f) What is the probability (over a 400-year period) that the 13th of a month is a Friday? Why is the 13th of the month more likely to be a Friday than any other day of the week? Write a program to calculate how many Friday the 13ths occur in this century.

POINTERS AND PITFALLS

1. To improve your program, review the logic. Don't optimize code based on a poor algorithm.

2. Never optimize a program until it is correct and working.

3. Don't optimize code unless it is absolutely necessary.

4. Use records to clarify the logic of your programs.

5. Nest your **with** statements as you nest your procedures: Use one level of **with** statement for each procedure.

6. Keep your procedures short; rarely should any procedure be more than a page long.

7. Be sure your algorithm is correct before starting to code.

8. Verify the intricate parts of your algorithm.

9. Keep your logic simple.

10. Review the Programming Precepts!

REVIEW QUESTIONS

2.1   **1.** What is program maintenance?

2.2   **2.** What is the main reason for using records rather than separate variables in Pascal?

3. What are hierarchical records, and how should they be processed?

4. Give two reasons why variant records are useful.

2.3   **5.** When should allocation of tasks among procedures be made?

6. How long should coding be delayed?

2.4   **7.** What is mathematical induction?

8. What is a loop invariant?

9. What are preconditions and postconditions of a subprogram?

2.5   **10.** What is a time-space trade-off?

2.6   **11.** What is a prototype?

12. Name at least six phases of the software life cycle and state what each is.

13. Define software engineering.

14. What are requirements specifications for a program?

REFERENCES FOR FURTHER STUDY

software engineering

A thorough discussion of many aspects of structured programming is

> EDWARD YOURDON, *Techniques of Program Structure and Design,* Prentice-Hall, Englewood Cliffs, N.J., 1975, 364 pages.

A perceptive discussion (in a book that is also enjoyable reading) of the many problems that arise in the construction of large software systems is

> FREDERICK P. BROOKS, JR., *The Mythical Man-Month: Essays on Software Engineering,* Addison-Wesley, Reading, Mass., 1975, 195 pages.

A good textbook on software engineering is

> IAN SOMMERVILLE, *Software Engineering,* second edition, Addison-Wesley, Wokingham, England, 1985, 334 pages.

Program testing has been developed to the point where its methods can fill a large book:

> WILLIAM E. PERRY, *A Structured Approach to Systems Testing,* Prentice-Hall, Englewood Cliffs, N.J., 1983, 451 pages.

algorithm verification

Two books concerned with proving programs and using assertions and invariants to develop algorithms are

> DAVID GRIES, *The Science of Programming,* Springer-Verlag, New York, 1981, 366 pages.

> SUAD ALAGIĆ and MICHAEL A. ARBIB, *The Design of Well-Structured and Correct Programs,* Springer-Verlag, New York, 1978, 292 pages.

Keeping programs so simple in design that they can be proved to be correct is not easy, but is very important. C. A. R. HOARE (who invented the quicksort algorithm that we shall study in Chapter 7) writes, "There are two ways of constructing a software design: One way is to make it so simple that there are obviously no deficiencies, and the other way is to make it so complicated that there are no obvious deficiencies. The first method is far more difficult." This quotation is from the 1980 Turing Award Lecture, "The emperor's old clothes," *Communications of the ACM* 24 (1981), 75–83.

problem solving

Two books concerned with methods of problem solving are

> GEORGE PÓLYA, *How to Solve It,* second edition, Doubleday, Garden City, N.Y., 1957, 253 pages.

> WAYNE A. WICKELGREN, *How to Solve Problems,* W. H. Freeman, San Francisco, 1974, 262 pages.

The programming project on one-dimensional Life is taken from

> JONATHAN K. MILLER, "One-Dimensional Life," *Byte* 3 (December 1978), 68–74.

C H A P T E R   3

Lists

▶ *This chapter introduces the study of data structures by studying various kinds of lists, including stacks and queues, together with their implementations in computer storage and Pascal procedures. The separation between the use of data structures and their implementation is emphasized. Several examples are developed, including a simulation problem.*

3.1 STATIC AND DYNAMIC STRUCTURES

Soon after the introduction of loops and arrays, every elementary programming class attempts some programming exercise like the following:

> *Read an integer n, which will be at most* 25, *then read a list of n numbers, and print the list in reverse order.*

This little exercise will probably cause difficulty for some students. Most will realize that they need to use an array, but some will attempt to set up the array to have *n* entries and will be confused by the error message resulting from attempting to use a variable rather than a constant to declare the size of the array. Other students will say, "I could solve the problem if I knew that there were 25 numbers, but I don't see how to handle fewer." Or "Tell me before I write the program how large *n* is, and then I can do it."

lists and arrays

The difficulties of these students come not from stupidity, but from thinking logically. In a beginning course, there is sometimes not enough distinction drawn between two quite different concepts. First is the concept of a *list* of n numbers, a list whose size is variable, that is, a list for which numbers can be inserted or deleted, so that, if *n* = 3, then the list contains only 3 numbers, and if *n* = 19, then it contains 19 numbers. Second is the programming feature called an *array* or a vector, which contains a constant number of positions, that is, whose size is fixed when the program is compiled. The two concepts are, of course, related in that a list of variable size can be implemented in a computer as occupying part of an array of fixed size, with some of the entries in the array remaining unused.

implementation

In this chapter we shall see that sometimes there are several different ways to implement a list within computer memory, and therefore the careful programmer needs to make a conscious decision about which of these to choose. The need for careful decision making about how to store data, in fact, extends back even further in the process of program design. We shall soon see that there is more than one kind of list (*stacks* and *queues* are the first two kinds we study), and therefore the programmer must first decide what kind of list (or what other conceptual structure) is needed for the data and then must decide how the conceptual structure will be implemented in computer memory. By keeping these decisions separate, we shall be able both to simplify the programming process and to avoid some of the pitfalls that attend premature decisions.

choice of data structures

choice of implementation

Already in Section 2.2 we have discussed the implementation of lists inside Pascal arrays. We set up a record type, so that we could keep track both of the array and of the variable that counts entries in the list, tied together as one logical structure. In this chapter we shall continue with similar methods.

3.2 STACKS

3.2.1 Definition and Operations

The easiest kind of list to use is called a *stack* and is defined formally as a list in which all insertions and deletions are made at one end, called the *top* of the stack.

stacks

A helpful analogy (see Figure 3.1) is to think of a stack of trays or of plates sitting on the counter in a busy cafeteria. Throughout the lunch hour, customers take trays off the top of the stack, and employees place returned trays back on top of the stack. The tray most recently put on the stack is the first one taken off. The bottom tray is the first one put on, and the last one to be used.

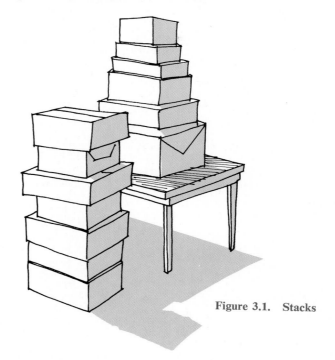

Figure 3.1.   Stacks

Sometimes this picture is described with plates or trays on a spring-loaded device so that the top of the stack stays near the same height. This imagery is poor and should be avoided. If we were to implement a computer stack in this way, it would mean moving every item in the stack whenever one item was inserted or deleted. This would be costly. It is far better to think of the stack as resting on a firm counter or floor, so that only the top item is moved when it is added or deleted. The spring-loaded imagery, however, has contributed a pair of colorful words that are firmly embedded in computer jargon, and which we shall use. When we add an item to a stack, we say that we *push* it onto the stack, and when we remove an item, we say that we *pop* it from the stack. From the same analogy, the term ***push-down list*** is used synonymously with stack, but we shall not employ this term. See Figure 3.2.

push and pop

3.2.2 Examples

1. Stack Frames for Subprograms

As one important application of stacks, consider what happens within the computer system when subprograms are called. The system (or the program) must remember the place where the call was made, so that it can return there after the subprogram is complete. It must also remember all the local variables, CPU registers, and the

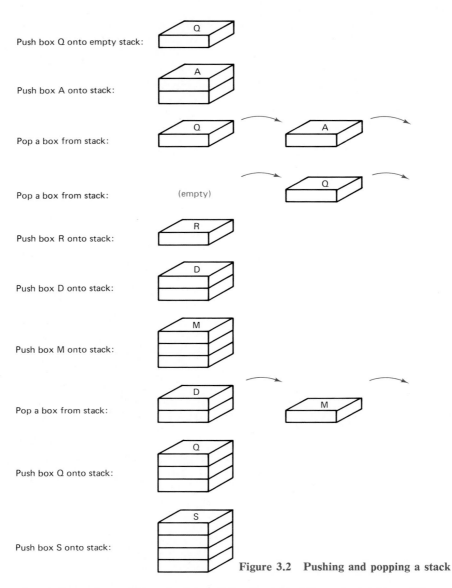

Push box Q onto empty stack:

Push box A onto stack:

Pop a box from stack:

Pop a box from stack: (empty)

Push box R onto stack:

Push box D onto stack:

Push box M onto stack:

Pop a box from stack:

Push box Q onto stack:

Push box S onto stack:

Figure 3.2   Pushing and popping a stack

like, so that information will not be lost while the subprogram is working. We can think of all this information as one large record, a temporary storage area for each subprogram.

subprogram data storage

Suppose now that we have three subprograms called A, B, and C, and suppose that A invokes B and B invokes C. Then B will not have finished its work until C has finished and returned. Similarly, A is the first to start work, but it is the last to be finished, not until sometime after B has finished and returned. Thus the sequence by which subprogram activity proceeds is summed up as the property *last in, first out*. If we consider the machine's task of assigning temporary storage areas for use by subprograms, then these areas would be allocated in a list with this same property,

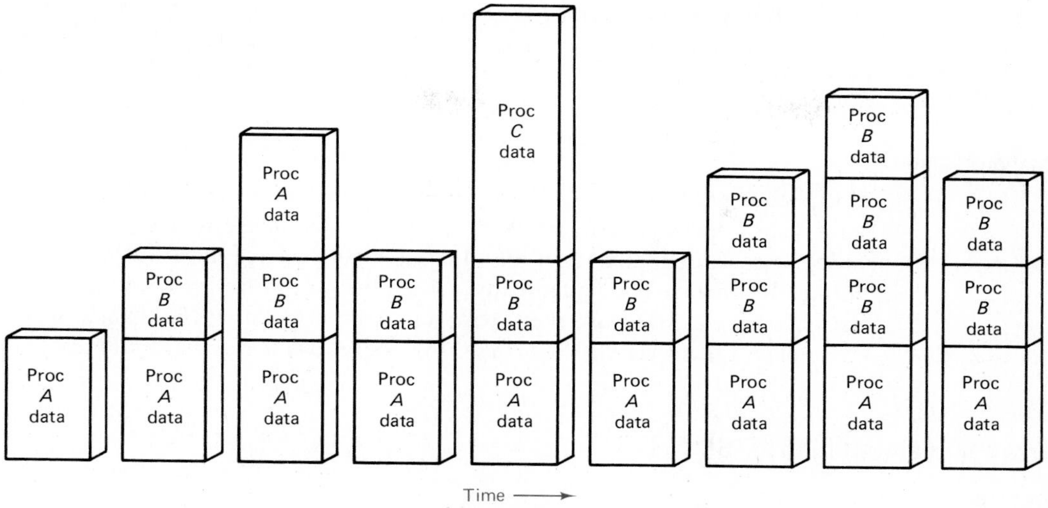

Figure 3.3   Stack frames for subprogram calls

that is, in a stack (see Figure 3.3). Hence yet one more name sometimes used for stacks is *LIFO lists,* based on the acronym for this property.

2. Reversing a Line

As a simple example of using stacks, let us suppose that we wish to make a procedure that will read a line of input and will then write it out backward. We can accomplish this task by pushing each character onto a stack as it is read. When the line is finished, we then pop characters off the stack, and they will come off in the reverse order. Hence our procedure takes the following form:

```
procedure ReverseRead;
{Read one line of input and write it out backward.}
var
  S: stack;
  ch: char;
begin                                              {procedure ReverseRead}
  Initialize(S);
  while (not eoln) and (not Full(S)) do
  begin                        {Push each character on the line onto the stack.}
    read(ch);
    Push(ch, S)
  end;
  readln;
  while not Empty(S) do
  begin                        {Pop each character from the stack and write it.}
    Pop(ch, S);
    write(ch)
  end;
  writeln
end;                                               {procedure ReverseRead}
```

In this procedure we have used not only Push and Pop but also a procedure Initialize that initializes the stack to be empty and Boolean-valued functions Empty that checks whether the stack is empty or not and Full that checks if it is completely full.

3. Information Hiding

use of procedures

Notice that we have been able to write our procedure before we consider how the stack will actually be implemented in storage and before we write the details of the various procedures and functions. In this way we have an example of ***information hiding:*** If someone else had already written the procedures and functions for handling stacks, then we could use them without needing to know the details of how stacks are kept in memory or of how the stack operations are actually done.

3.2.3 Array Implementation of Stacks

1. Declarations

To implement a stack in a computer we shall set up an array that will hold the items in the stack and a counter to indicate how many items there are. In Pascal we can make declarations such as the following, where maxstack is a constant giving the maximum size allowed for stacks and item is the type describing the data that will be put into the stack. Type item depends on the application and can range from a single number or character to a large record with many fields.

stack type

```
type    stack = record
             top:      0 .. maxstack;
             entry:    array[1 .. maxstack] of item
        end;
```

2. Pushing and Popping

Pushing and popping the stack are then implemented as follows. We must be careful of the extreme cases: We might attempt to pop an item from an empty stack or to push an item onto a full stack. We shall regard such attempts as errors fatal to execution of the program, and therefore we must also write Boolean-valued functions so that by checking emptiness or fullness the program can guard against these errors ever occurring.

push

```
procedure Push(x: item; var S: stack);
begin                                          {procedure Push}
  with S do
    if top = maxstack then
      Error            {The external procedure Error will terminate the program.}
    else begin
      top := top + 1;
      entry[top] := x
    end
end;                                           {procedure Push}
```

pop

```
procedure Pop(var x: item; var S: stack);
begin                                                    {procedure Pop}
  with S do
    if top = 0 then
      Error              {The external procedure Error will terminate the program.}
    else begin
      x := entry[top];
      top := top − 1
    end
  end;                                                   {procedure Pop}
```

3. Other Operations

empty

```
function Empty (var S: stack): Boolean;
begin
  Empty := (S.top = 0)
end;
```

full

```
function Full(var S: stack): Boolean;
begin
  Full := (S.top = maxstack)
end;
```

One more procedure is needed to initialize a stack to be empty before it is first used in a program:

initialize

```
procedure Initialize (var S: stack);
begin
  S.top := 0
end;
```

4. Advantages of the Operational Approach

If you think that we are belaboring the obvious by introducing all these procedures and functions, then in one sense you are right, since their substance is so simple that they could easily be written out wherever they are needed in a program, rather than keeping them as separate procedures. For large programs there is one important advantage, however, to using a record type to implement stacks and separate proce-

flexibility of implementation

dures and functions to process them. It may well happen that, after we start work on a large project, we realize that another way of implementing our stacks in storage would prove better than the method we had used. If the instructions have been written out every time a stack is pushed or popped, then every occurrence will need to be changed. If we have used records and procedures, then only the definition of the record type and the declarations of the procedures must be altered. A second

clarity of program

advantage, of course, is that the very appearance of the words *Push* and *Pop* will immediately alert a person reading the program to what is being done, whereas the instructions themselves might be more obscure. A third advantage we shall find is

top-down design

that separating the use of data structures from their implementation will help us improve the top-down design of both our data structures and our programs.

**Exercises
3.2**

E1. Draw a sequence of stack frames showing the progress of each of the following segments of code. (S is a stack of characters and x, y, z are character variables.)

(a)

```
Initialize(S);
Push('a', S);
Push('b', S);
Push('c', S);
Pop(x, S);
Pop(y, S);
Pop(z, S);
```

(b)

```
Initialize(S);
Push('a', S);
Push('b', S);
Initialize(S);
Push('c', S);
Pop(x, S);
Push('a', S);
Pop(y, S);
Push('b', S);
Pop(z, S);
```

(c)

```
Initialize(S);
Push('a', S);
Push('b', S);
Push('c', S);
Pop(x, S);
Pop(y, S);
Push(x, S);
Push(y, S);
Pop(z, S);
```

(d)

```
Initialize(S);
Push('a', S);
Push('b', S);
Push('c', S);
while not Empty(S) do
    Pop(x, S);
```

E2. Let S be a stack of integers and x be an integer variable. Use the procedures Push, Pop, Initialize and the functions Empty, Full to write procedures doing each of the following tasks. [You may declare additional variables in your procedures if needed.]

(a) Set x to the top element of the stack S and leave the top element of S unchanged. If S is empty, set x to maxint.

(b) Set x to the third element from the top in S, provided that S contains at least three integers. If not, set x to maxint. Leave S unchanged.

(c) Set x to the bottom element of S (or to maxint if S is empty), and leave S unchanged. [*Hint:* Use a second stack.]

(d) Delete all occurrences of x from S, leaving the other elements of S in the same order.

two coexisting stacks

E3. Sometimes a program requires two stacks containing the same type of items. If the two stacks are stored in separate arrays, then one stack might overflow while there was considerable unused space in the other. A neat way to avoid this problem is to put all the space in one array and let one stack grow from one end of the array and the other stack start at the other end and grow in the opposite direction, toward the first stack. In this way, if one stack turns out to be large and the other small, then they will still both fit, and there will be no overflow until all the space is actually used. Declare a new record type doublestack that includes the array and two indices topA and topB, and write procedures PushA, PushB, PopA, and PopB to handle the two stacks within one doublestack.

E4. Write a program that uses a stack to read an integer and print all its prime divisors in descending order. For example, with the integer 2100 the output should be

prime divisors

7   5   5   3   2   2.

[*Hint:* The smallest divisor greater than 1 of any integer is guaranteed to be a prime.]

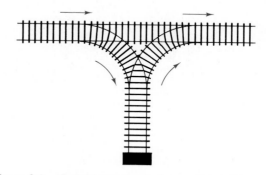

Figure 3.4.   Switching network for stack permutations

stack permutations

E5. A stack may be regarded as a railway switching network like the one in Figure 3.4. Cars numbered 1, 2, . . ., *n* are on the line at the left, and it is desired to rearrange (permute) the cars as they leave on the right-hand track. A car that is on the spur (stack) can be left there or sent on its way down the right track, but it can never be sent back to the incoming track. For example, if *n* = 3, and we have the cars 1, 2, 3 on the left track, then 3 first goes to the spur. We could then send 2 to the spur, then on its way to the right, then send 3 on the way, then 1, obtaining the new order 1, 3, 2.

(a) For *n* = 3, find all possible permutations that can be obtained.

(b) Same, for *n* = 4.

(c) [Challenging]   For general *n*, find how many permutations can be obtained by using this stack.

3.3 QUEUES

3.3.1 Definitions

In ordinary English a queue is defined as a waiting line, like a line of people waiting to purchase tickets, where the first person in line is the first person served. For computer applications we similarly define a *queue* to be a list in which all additions to the list are made at one end, and all deletions from the list are made at the other end. Queues are also called *first-in, first-out lists*, or *FIFO* for short. See Figure 3.5.

Figure 3.5.   A queue

applications

Applications of queues are, if anything, even more common than are applications of stacks, since in performing tasks by computer, as in all parts of life, it is so often necessary to wait one's turn before having access to something. Within a computer system there may be queues of tasks waiting for the line printer, for access to disk storage, or even, in a time-sharing system, for use of the CPU. Within a single program, there may be multiple requests to be kept in a queue, or one task may create other tasks, which must be done in turn by keeping them in a queue.

front and rear

The item in a queue ready to be served, that is, the first item that will be removed from the queue, we call the ***front*** of the queue (or, sometimes, the ***head*** of the queue). Similarly, the last item in the queue, that is, the one most recently added, we call the ***rear*** (or the ***tail***) of the queue.

3.3.2 Implementations of Queues

1. The Physical Model

As we did for stacks, we can create a queue in computer storage easily by setting up an ordinary array to hold the items. Now, however, we must keep track of both the front and the rear of the queue. One method would be to keep the front of the queue always in the first location of the array. Then an item could be added to the queue simply by increasing the counter showing the rear, in exactly the same way as we added an item to a stack. To delete an item from the queue, however, would be very expensive indeed, since after the first item was removed, all the remaining items would need to be moved one position up the queue to fill in the vacancy. With a long queue, this process would be prohibitively slow. Although this method of storage closely models a queue of people waiting to be served, it is a poor choice for use in computers.

2. Linear Implementation

defect

For efficient processing of queues, we shall therefore need two indices so that we can keep track of both the front and the rear of the queue without moving any items. To add an item to the queue, we simply increase the rear by one and put the item in that position. To remove an item, we take it from the position at the front and then increase the front by one. This method, however, still has a major defect. Both the front and rear indices are increased but never decreased. Even if there are never more than two items in the queue, an unbounded amount of storage will be needed for the queue if the sequence of operation is

Add, Add, Delete, Add, Delete, Add, Delete, ...

The problem, of course, is that, as the queue moves down the array, the storage space at the beginning of the array is discarded and never used again. Perhaps the queue can be likened to a snake crawling through storage. Sometimes the snake is longer, sometimes shorter, but if it always keeps crawling in a straight line, then it will soon reach the end of the storage space.

advantage

Note, however, that for applications where the queue is regularly emptied (such as when a series of requests is allowed to build up to a certain point, and then a task is initiated that clears all the requests before returning), at a time when the queue is empty, the front and rear can both be reset to the beginning of the array, and the simple scheme of using two indices and straight-line storage becomes a very efficient storage method.

3. Circular Arrays

In concept we can overcome the inefficient use of space simply by thinking of the array as a circle rather than a straight line. See Figure 3.6. In this way as items are added and removed from the queue, the head will continually chase the tail around the array, so that the snake can keep crawling indefinitely but stay in a confined circuit. At different times the queue will occupy different parts of the array, but we never need worry about running out of space unless the array is fully occupied, in which case we truly have overflow.

4. Implementation of Circular Arrays

modular arithmetic

Our next problem is to implement a circular array as an ordinary linear (that is, straight-line) array. To do so, we think of the positions around the circle as numbered from 1 to max, where max is the total number of entries in the circular array, and to implement the circular array, we use the same-numbered entries of a linear array. Then moving the indices is just the same as doing modular arithmetic: When we increase an index past max we start over again at 1. This is like doing arithmetic on a circular clock face; the hours are numbered from 1 to 12, and if we add four hours to ten o'clock, we obtain two o'clock.

Perhaps a good human analogy of this linear representation is that of a priest serving communion to people kneeling at the front of a church. The communicants do not move until the priest comes by and serves them. When the priest reaches the end of the row, he returns to the beginning and starts again, since by this time a new row of people have come forward.

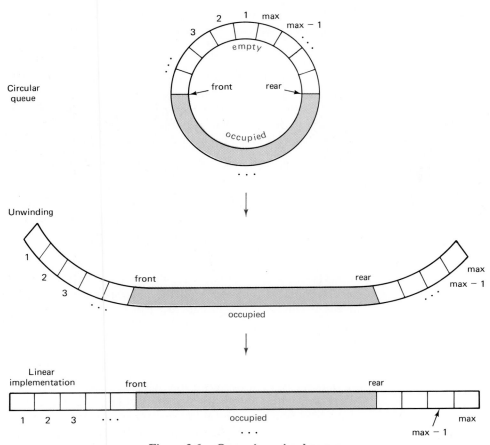

Circular
queue

Unwinding

Linear
implementation

Figure 3.6.   Queue in a circular array

5. Circular Arrays in Pascal

In Pascal we can increase an index i by 1 in a circular array by writing

if i = max **then** i := 1 **else** i := i + 1;

or even more easily (but perhaps less efficiently at run time) by using the **mod** operator:

i := (i **mod** max) + 1.

A more natural way to express this latter form is to index the array from 0 to max − 1, so that the addition comes before the mod:

i := (i + 1) **mod** max.

(You should check to verify that the result of the latter expression is always between 0 and max − 1, whereas the previous expression is always between 1 and max.) Starting the indices at 0 proves even more natural when it is necessary to increase the index i by an arbitrary amount k > 0. If we index the array from 0 to max − 1, we need only write

$$i := (i + k) \textbf{ mod } max$$

whereas if we index the array from 1 to max, we must write

$$i := (i + k - 1) \textbf{ mod } max + 1.$$

In Pascal, unfortunately, starting the indices at 0 means that we must declare two constants, both max and another equal to max − 1, and doing so sometimes causes confusion. For simplicity we therefore retain the traditional indexing starting at 1 whenever we implement a queue in a circular array.

6. Boundary Conditions

Before writing formal algorithms to add to and delete from a queue, let us consider the boundary conditions, that is, the indicators that a queue is empty or full. If there is exactly one entry in the queue, then the front index will equal the rear index. When this one entry is removed, then the front will be increased by 1, so that an empty queue is indicated when the rear is one position before the front. Now suppose that the queue is nearly full. Then the rear will have moved well away from the front, all the way around the circle, and when the array is full the rear will be exactly one position behind the front. Thus we have another difficulty: The front and rear indices are in exactly the same relative positions for an empty queue and for a full queue! There is no way, by looking at the indices alone, to tell a full queue from an empty one. This situation is illustrated in Figure 3.7.

empty or full?

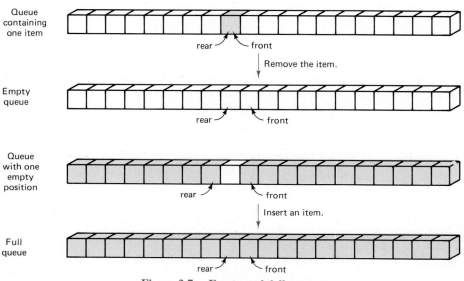

Figure 3.7.   Empty and full queues

7. Possible Solutions

1. empty position

2. flag

3. special values

There are at least three essentially different ways to resolve this problem. One is to insist on leaving one empty position in the array so that the queue is considered full when the rear index has moved within two positions of the front. A second method is to introduce a new variable. This can be a Boolean variable that will be used when the rear comes just before the front to indicate whether the queue is full or not (a Boolean variable to check emptiness would be just as good) or an integer variable that counts the number of items in the queue. The third method is to set one or both of the indices to some value(s) that would otherwise never occur in order to indicate an empty (or full) queue. If, for example, the array entries are indexed from 1 to max, then an empty queue could be indicated by setting the rear index to 0.

8. Summary of Implementations

To summarize the discussion of queues, let us list all the methods we have discussed for implementing queues.

1. The physical model: a linear array with the front always in the first position and all entries moved up the array whenever the front is deleted (this is generally a poor method for use in computers).

2. A linear array with two indices always increasing (this is a good method if the queue can be emptied all at once).

3. A circular array with front and rear indices and one position left vacant.

4. A circular array with front and rear indices and a Boolean variable to indicate fullness (or emptiness).

5. A circular array with front and rear indices and an integer variable counting entries.

6. A circular array with front and rear indices taking special values to indicate emptiness.

postpone implementation decisions

In the next chapter we shall find still other ways to implement queues. The most important thing to remember from this list is that, with so many variations in implementation, we should always keep questions concerning the use of data structures like queues separate from questions concerning their implementation, and in programming we should always consider only one of these categories of questions at a time. After we have considered how queues will be used in our application, and after we have written the procedures employing queues, we will have more information to help us choose the best implementation of queues suited to our application.

3.3.3 Circular Queues in Pascal

Next let us write formal Pascal procedures for some of the possible implementations of a queue. We shall choose the last two implementations and leave the others as exercises. In all cases, however, we take the queue as stored in an array indexed with the range

$$1..\text{maxqueue}$$

and containing entries of a type called item. The variables front and rear will point to appropriate positions in the array.

1. Implementation with a Counter

First, we take the method in which a variable count is used to keep track of the number of items in the queue. The record declaration for a queue takes the form

type queue

```
queue = record
           count,
           front,
           rear:      0..maxqueue;
           entry:     array[1..maxqueue] of item;
        end;
```

The first procedure we need will initialize the queue to be empty.

initialize

```
procedure Initialize(var Q: queue);
begin                                          {procedure Initialize}
   with Q do begin
      count := 0;
      front := 1;
      rear := 0
   end
end;                                           {procedure Initialize}
```

The key procedures for adding to and deleting from a queue follow our preceding discussion closely. We use a procedure Error (assumed to be written elsewhere) to keep track of error conditions.

insertion

```
procedure AddQueue(x: item; var Q: queue);
begin                                          {procedure AddQueue}
   with Q do
      if count = maxqueue then
         Error                                 {external procedure}
      else begin
         count := count + 1;
         rear := (rear mod maxqueue) + 1;
         entry[rear] := x
      end
end;                                           {procedure AddQueue}
```

deletion

```
procedure DeleteQueue(var x: item; var Q: queue);
begin                                            {procedure DeleteQueue}
with Q do
  if count = 0 then
    Error
  else begin
    count := count − 1;
    x := entry[front];
    front := (front mod maxqueue) + 1
  end
end;                                             {procedure DeleteQueue}
```

We shall also find use for three functions concerning the size of the queue, all of which are easy to write with this implementation.

size

```
function Size(var Q: queue): integer;
begin
  Size := Q.count
end;
```

empty?

```
function Empty(var Q: queue): Boolean;
begin
  Empty := (Q.count = 0)
end;
```

full?

```
function Full(var Q: queue): Boolean;
begin
  Full := (Q.count = maxqueue)
end;
```

2. Implementation with Special Index Values

Next let us turn to the method that relies on special values for the indices. Most of the necessary changes in declarations are clear. We have

type queue

```
queue = record
          front,
          rear:    0 .. maxqueue;
          entry:   array[1 .. maxqueue] of item;
        end;
```

We shall use the condition

$$rear = 0 \quad \text{and} \quad front = 1$$

to indicate an empty queue. The initialization procedure is

initialize

```
procedure Initialize(var Q: queue);
begin
  Q.front := 1;
  Q.rear  := 0
end;
```

To write the procedure for adding to the queue, we must first (for error checking) find a condition indicating whether the queue is full or not. Fullness is typically indicated by rear = front − 1 together with rear > 0, but it is also possible that front = 1 and rear = maxqueue. Building these conditions into the procedure, we obtain

insertion

```
procedure AddQueue(x: item; var Q: queue);
begin                                                  {procedure AddQueue}
  with Q do
    if ((rear = front − 1)  and (rear > 0)) or
       ((rear = maxqueue) and (front = 1)) then
      Error                                            {external procedure}
    else begin
      rear := (rear mod maxqueue) + 1;
      entry[rear] := x;
    end
end;                                                   {procedure AddQueue}
```

Since emptiness is indicated by rear = 0, the deletion procedure closely resembles the previous version.

deletion

```
procedure DeleteQueue(var x: item; var Q: queue);
begin                                                  {procedure DeleteQueue}
  with Q do
    if rear = 0 then
      Error                                            {external procedure}
    else begin
      x := entry[front];
      if front = rear then                             {The queue is now empty.}
      begin
        front := 1;
        rear := 0
      end
      else
        front := (front mod maxqueue) + 1
    end
end;                                                   {procedure DeleteQueue}
```

The three functions Size, Empty, and Full will be left as exercises.

Exercises 3.3

E1. Suppose that Q is a queue that holds characters and that x, y, z are character variables. Show the contents of the queue Q at each step of the following code segments.

(a)

```
Initialize(Q);
AddQueue('a', Q);
AddQueue('b', Q);
DeleteQueue(x, Q);
AddQueue(x, Q);
DeleteQueue(y, Q);
DeleteQueue(z, Q);
```

(b)

```
Initialize(Q);
AddQueue('a', Q);
x := 'b';
AddQueue('x', Q);
DeleteQueue(y, Q);
AddQueue(x, Q);
DeleteQueue(z, Q);
AddQueue(y, Q);
```

E2. Suppose that you are a financier and purchase 100 shares of stock in Company X in each of January, April, and September and sell 100 shares in each of June and November. The prices per share in these months were

accounting

Jan	Apr	Jun	Sep	Nov
$10	$30	$20	$50	$30

Determine the total amount of your capital gain or loss using **(a)** FIFO (first-in, first-out) accounting and **(b)** LIFO (last-in, first-out) accounting (that is, assuming that you keep your stock certificates in (a) a queue or (b) a stack). The 100 shares you still own at the end of the year do not enter the calculation.

E3. Use the procedures developed in the text to write other procedures that will
   (a) Empty one stack onto the top of another stack.
   (b) Move all the items from a queue onto a stack.
   (c) Start with a queue and an empty stack, and use the stack to reverse the order of all the items in the queue.

E4. Implement the simple representation of queues in a linear array when it can be assumed that the queue can be emptied when necessary. Write a procedure AddQueue that will add an item if there is room and, if not, will call another procedure that will empty the queue. While writing this second procedure, you may assume the existence of an auxiliary procedure Service(x: item) that will process a single item that you have just removed from the queue.

E5. Write Pascal procedures and functions to implement queues by the simple but slow method of keeping the head of the queue always in the first position of a linear array.

E6. Write Pascal procedures and functions to implement queues in a linear array with two indices head and rear, such that when rear reaches the end of the array, all the items are moved to the front of the array.

E7. Write the three functions Size, Empty, and Full for the implementation of a queue in a circular array with special index values to indicate emptiness.

E8. Rewrite the first set of Pascal procedures for queue processing from the text, using a Boolean variable full instead of a counter of items in the queue.

E9. Write Pascal procedures and functions to implement queues in a circular array with one unused entry in the array. That is, we consider that the array is full when the rear is two positions before the front; when the rear is one position before, it will always indicate an empty queue.

Programming Project 3.3

P1. Write a procedure that will read one line of input from the terminal. The input is supposed to consist of two parts separated by a colon ':'. As its result, your procedure should produce a single character as follows:

N No colon on the line.
L The left part (before the colon) is longer than the right.
R The right part (after the colon) is longer than the left.
D The left and right parts have the same length but are different.
S The left and right parts are exactly the same.

Examples:

Input	Output
Sample Sample	N
Short:Long	L
Sample:Sample	S

Use a queue to keep track of the left part of the line while reading the right part.

3.4 APPLICATION OF QUEUES: SIMULATION

3.4.1 Introduction

Simulation is the use of one system to imitate the behavior of another system. Simulations are often used when it would be too expensive or dangerous to experiment with the real system. There are physical simulations, such as wind tunnels used to experiment with designs for car bodies and flight simulators used to train airline pilots. Mathematical simulations are systems of equations used to describe some system, and computer simulations use the steps of a program to imitate the behavior of the system under study.

computer models   In a computer simulation, the objects being studied are usually represented as data, often as data structures like records or arrays whose entries describe the properties of the objects. Actions in the system being studied are represented as operations on the data, and the rules describing these actions are translated into computer algorithms. By changing the values of the data or by modifying these algorithms, we can observe the changes in the computer simulation, and then, we hope, we can draw worthwhile inferences concerning the behavior of the actual system in which we are interested.

While one object in a system is involved in some action, other objects and actions will often need to be kept waiting. Hence queues are important data structures for use in computer simulations. We shall study one of the most common and useful kinds of computer simulations, one that concentrates on queues as its basic data structure. These simulations imitate the behavior of systems (often, in fact, called *queueing systems*) in which there are queues of objects waiting to be served by various processes.

3.4.2 Simulation of an Airport

As a specific example, let us consider a small but busy airport with only one runway (see Figure 3.8). In each unit of time one plane can land or one plane can take off, but not both. Planes arrive ready to land or to take off at random times, so at any given unit of time, the runway may be idle or a plane may be landing or taking off, and there may be several planes waiting either to land or take off. We therefore *rules* need two queues, called landing and takeoff, to hold these planes. It is better to keep a plane waiting on the ground than in the air, so a small airport allows a plane to take off only if there are no planes waiting to land. Hence, after receiving requests from new planes to land or take off, our simulation will first service the head of the queue of planes waiting to land, and only if the landing queue is empty will it allow a plane to take off. We shall wish to run the simulation through many units of time, and therefore we embed the main action of the program in a loop that

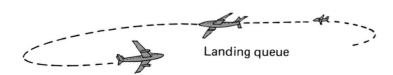

Landing queue

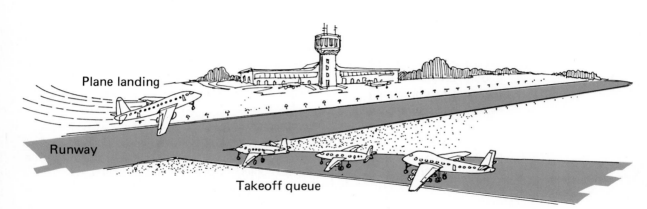

Plane landing

Runway

Takeoff queue

Figure 3.8. An airport

runs for curtime (denoting *current time*) from 1 to a variable endtime. With this notation we can write an outline of the main program.

first outline

```
program Airport(input, output);
var
    p:          plane;                    {plane currently being processed}
    landing,
    takeoff:    queue;                    {lines of planes waiting}
    curtime,                              {current time unit}
    endtime,                              {time when simulation ends}
    i:          integer;                  {loop control variable}
begin
    Initialize(landing);                  {Set the queues to be empty at the start.}
    Initialize(takeoff);
    for curtime := 1 to endtime do  {Commence the main loop on units of time.}
    begin
```

new plane ready to land

```
        for i := 1 to RandomNumber do     {Add new planes to the landing queue.}
        begin
            NewPlane(p);                  {Get information on the new plane.}
            if Full(landing) then         {Include error processing if the queue is full.}
                Refuse(p)
            else
                AddQueue(p, landing)      {Put each new plane into the queue.}
        end;
```

new plane ready to take off

```
        for i := 1 to RandomNumber do     {Add new planes to the takeoff queue.}
        begin
            NewPlane(p);
            if Full(takeoff) then
                Refuse(p)
            else
                AddQueue(p, takeoff)
        end;
```

plane landing

```
        if not Empty(landing) then        {If a plane is waiting to land, let it.}
        begin
            DeleteQueue(p, landing);
            Land(p)                       {Process a landing plane.}
        end
```

plane taking off

```
        else if not Empty(takeoff) then   {Only if none landing can one take off.}
        begin
            DeleteQueue(p, takeoff);
            Fly(p)                        {Process a departing plane.}
        end
```

idle runway

```
        else
            Idle                          {Runway is idle; there is nothing to do.}
    end;
    Conclude                              {Finish up the simulation.}
end.
```

3.4.3 The Main Program

Although this outline clearly shows the use of queues in this simulation, more detail is needed to keep track of all the interesting statistics concerning the problem, such as the number of planes processed, the average time spent waiting, and the number of planes (if any) refused service. These details are reflected in the declarations of constants, types, and variables to be inserted into the main program. We shall then need to write the subprograms to specify how this information is processed. The declaration of type queue is deliberately omitted from the following list, in order that we can postpone until later the decision concerning which method will be used to implement the queues. Most of the remaining declarations are self-explanatory, except for the last three variables, which are concerned with generating random numbers, and will be explained when we consider the use of random numbers.

declarations

```
const
   maxqueue = 5;                          {Use a small value for testing.}
type
   action = (arrive, depart);             {What is the plane wishing to do?}
   plane = record
               id,                        {identification number of plane}
               tm: integer;               {time of arrival in queue}
           end;
   item = plane;
{Insert declaration of type queue here.}
var
   landing,
   takeoff:      queue;
   p:            plane;
   curtime,          {current time; one unit = time needed for takeoff or landing}
   nplanes,                             {number of planes processed so far}
   endtime,                             {total number of time units to run}
   idletime,                            {number of units when runway is idle}
   nland,                               {number of planes landed}
   ntakeoff,                            {number of planes taken off}
   nrefuse,                             {number of planes refused use of airport}
   landwait,                            {total waiting time for planes landed}
   takeoffwait,                         {total waiting time for planes taking off}
   i:            integer;               {loop control variable}
   expectarrive, {expected number of planes arriving to land in one unit of time}
   expectdepart: real;      {expected number of planes newly ready to take off}
   seed:         integer;               {used for generating random numbers}
```

simulation statistics

The version of the main program in runnable Pascal differs little from the preceding outline except for the inclusion of the many parameters used to update all the variables just declared.

initialize

```
program Airport(input, output);
{Declarations of constants, types, and variables are to be inserted here.}
begin                                              {main program Airport}
   Initialize(landing);
   Initialize(takeoff);
   Start(endtime, nplanes, nland, ntakeoff, nrefuse, landwait, takeoffwait,
         idletime, expectarrive, expectdepart);
   for curtime := 1 to endtime do
```

new plane(s) ready to land

```
   begin
      for i := 1 to RandomNumber(expectarrive) do
      begin                               {Add a new plane to the landing queue.}
         NewPlane(p, nplanes, curtime, arrive);
         if Full(landing) then
            Refuse(p, arrive, nrefuse)
         else
            AddQueue(p, landing)
      end;
```

new plane(s) ready to take off

```
      for i := 1 to RandomNumber(expectdepart) do
      begin                               {Add a new plane to the takeoff queue.}
         NewPlane(p, nplanes, curtime, depart);
         if Full(takeoff) then
            Refuse(p, depart, nrefuse)
         else
            AddQueue(p, takeoff)
      end;
      if not Empty(landing) then
```

plane landing

```
      begin                                              {Bring a plane in to land.}
         DeleteQueue(p, landing);
         Land(p, curtime, nland, landwait)
      end
      else if not Empty(takeoff) then
```

plane taking off

```
      begin                                              {Allow a plane to take off.}
         DeleteQueue(p, takeoff);
         Fly(p, curtime, ntakeoff, takeoffwait)
      end
```

runway idle

```
      else
         Idle(curtime, idletime);
   end;
```

finish simulation

```
   Conclude(nplanes, nland, ntakeoff, nrefuse, landwait, takeoffwait, idletime,
                                              takeoff,  landing)
end.                                               {main program Airport}
```

3.4.4 Steps of the Simulation

The actions of the procedures for doing the steps of the simulation are generally straightforward, so we proceed to write each in turn, with comments only as needed for clarity.

1. Initialization

```
procedure Start(var endtime, nplanes, nland, ntakeoff, nrefuse, landwait,
                takeoffwait, idletime: integer; var expectarrive, expectdepart: real);
```
{provides first message and initializes all variables specified as parameters}

```
var
  OK: Boolean;                                  {Are the input numbers acceptable?}
  response: char;                                            {answer from user}

begin                                                          {procedure Start}
```
initialize counters
```
  nplanes := 0;
  nland := 0;
  ntakeoff := 0;
  nrefuse := 0;
  landwait := 0;
  takeoffwait := 0;
  idletime := 0;
```
instruct user
```
  writeln('This program simulates an airport with only one runway.');
  writeln('One plane can land or depart in each unit of time.');
  writeln('Up to ', maxqueue:3, ' planes can');
  writeln('be waiting to land or take off at any time.');
```
input parameters
```
  write('How many units of time will the simulation run? ');
  readln(endtime);
  Randomize(seed);                      {required for random number generation}

  repeat
    write('Expected number of arrivals per unit time (real number)?');
    readln(expectarrive);
    write('Expected number of departures per unit time?');
    readln(expectdepart);
```
error checking
```
    if (expectarrive < 0.0) or (expectdepart < 0.0) then
    begin
      writeln('These numbers must be nonnegative.');
      OK := false
    end
    else if expectarrive + expectdepart > 1.0 then
    begin
      write('The airport will become saturated. Read new numbers?');
      readln(response);
      OK := response in ['N', 'n']
    end
    else
      OK := true
  until OK
end;                                                           {procedure Start}
```

2. Accepting a New Plane

```
procedure NewPlane(var p: plane; var nplanes: integer;
                        curtime: integer; kind: action);
{makes a new record for a plane and updates nplanes}
begin                                              {procedure NewPlane}
  nplanes := nplanes + 1;
  p.id := nplanes;
  p.tm := curtime;
  case kind of
    depart:   writeln('  Plane ', nplanes:3, ' ready to take off.');
    arrive:   writeln('  Plane ', nplanes:3, ' ready to land.')
  end
end;                                               {procedure NewPlane}
```

3. Handling a Full Queue

```
procedure Refuse(p: plane; kind: action; var nrefuse: integer);
{processes a plane wanting to use runway, but the queue is full}
begin
  case kind of
    depart:   writeln('  Plane ', p.id: 3, ' told to try later.');
    arrive:   writeln('  Plane ', p.id: 3, ' directed to another airport.')
  end;
  nrefuse := nrefuse + 1
end;
```

4. Processing an Arriving Plane

```
procedure Land(p: plane; curtime: integer; var nland, landwait: integer);
{processes a plane p that is actually landing}
var
  wait: integer;
begin
  wait := curtime - p.tm;
  writeln(curtime: 4,': Plane ', p.id: 3, ' landed; in queue ', wait: 2, ' units.');
  nland := nland + 1;
  landwait := landwait + wait
end;
```

5. Processing a Departing Plane

```
procedure Fly(p: plane; curtime: integer; var ntakeoff, takeoffwait: integer);
{processes a plane p that is actually taking off}
var
   wait: integer;
begin
   wait := curtime − p.tm;
   writeln(curtime:4,': Plane ', p.id:3, ' took off; in queue ', wait:2, ' units.');
   ntakeoff := ntakeoff + 1;
   takeoffwait := takeoffwait + wait
end;
```

6. Marking an Idle Time Unit

```
procedure Idle(curtime: integer; var idletime: integer);
{updates variables for a time unit when the runway is idle}
begin
   writeln(curtime:4, ': Runway is idle.');
   idletime := idletime + 1
end;
```

7. Finishing the Simulation

```
procedure Conclude(nplanes, nland, ntakeoff, nrefuse, landwait, takeoffwait,
                         idletime: integer; var takeoff, landing: queue);
{writes out all the statistics and concludes the simulation}
begin
   writeln('Simulation has concluded after ', endtime:4, ' units.');
   writeln('Total number of planes processed:    ', nplanes:4);
   writeln('     Number of planes landed:         ', nland:4);
   writeln('     Number of planes taken off:      ', ntakeoff:4);
   writeln('     Number of planes refused use:    ', nrefuse:4);
   writeln('     Number left ready to land:       ', Size(landing):4);
   writeln('     Number left ready to take off:   ', Size(takeoff):4);
   if endtime > 0 then
      writeln(' Percentage of time runway idle:   ', (idletime/endtime)*100.0:7:2);
   if nland > 0 then
      writeln(' Average wait time to land:        ', (landwait/nland):7:2);
   if ntakeoff > 0 then
      writeln(' Average wait time to take off:    ', (takeoffwait/ntakeoff):7:2)
end;
```

3.4.5 Random Numbers

A key step in our simulation is to decide, at each time unit, how many new planes become ready to land or take off. Although there are many ways in which these decisions can be made, one of the most interesting and useful is to make a random decision. When the program is run repeatedly with random decisions, the results will differ from run to run, and with sufficient experimentation, the simulation may display a range of behavior not unlike that of the actual system being studied.

system random number generator

Many computer systems include random number generators, and if one is available on your system, it can be used in place of the one developed here. Since standard Pascal, however, does not include random number generation, we discuss it briefly here.

The idea is to start with one number and apply a series of arithmetic operations that will produce another number with no obvious connection to the first. Hence the numbers we produce are not truly random at all, as each one depends in a definite way on its predecessor, and we should more properly speak of *pseudorandom* numbers. The number we use (and simultaneously change) is called the *seed*.

seed for pseudorandom numbers

If the seed begins with the same value each time the program is run, then the whole sequence of pseudorandom numbers will be exactly the same, so we normally begin by setting the seed to some random value, for example, the time of day:

```
procedure Randomize(var seed: integer);
begin
    seed := clock;            {System dependent: function clock is not part of
                               standard Pascal, but many systems provide some such facility.}
end;
```

A sample function for producing one pseudorandom number from its predecessor is

sample generator

```
function Random(var seed: integer): real;
const
    m = maxint;
    a = 2743;
    c = 5923;
begin
    seed := (seed * a + c) mod m;
    if seed < 0 then seed := seed + m;
    Random := seed/m
end;
```

The constants m, a, and c in this function should not be chosen at random, but should be carefully chosen to make sure that the results pass various tests for randomness. The given constants seem to work fairly well on 16-bit computers, but other choices should be made for other machines.

uniform distribution

The function Random, like most pseudorandom generators, produces as its result a real number between 0.00 and 1.00. We must take numbers produced this way and convert them to the form we need. For our simulation we wish to obtain an integer giving the number of planes arriving ready to land (or take off) in a given time unit. We can assume that the time when one plane enters the system is independent of that of any other plane. The number of planes arriving in one unit of time then follows what is called a *Poisson distribution* in statistics. To calculate the numbers,

Poisson distribution

we need to know the *expected value,* that is, the average number of planes arriving in one unit of time. If, for example, on average one plane arrives in each of four time units, then the expected value is 0.25. Sometimes several planes may arrive in the same time unit, but often no planes arrive, so that taking the average over many units gives 0.25.

The following function determines the number of planes by generating pseudo-random integers according to a Poisson distribution:

Poisson generator

```
function RandomNumber(expectedvalue: real): integer;
{generates a random nonnegative integer according to a Poisson distribution
    with the expected value given as parameter}
var
    em: real;                               {e^{-v} where v is the expected value}
    n: integer;                                          {count of iterations}
    x: real;                               {pseudorandom number, 0 < x < 1}
begin                                                     {function RandomNumber}
    em := exp(− expectedvalue);
    x := Random(seed);
    n := 0;
    while x > em do
    begin
      n := n + 1;
      x := x * Random(seed)
    end;
    RandomNumber := n
end;                                                      {function RandomNumber}
```

3.4.6 Sample Results

We conclude this section with the output from a sample run of the airport simulation. You should note that there are periods when the runway is idle and others when the queues are completely full, so that some planes must be turned away.

This program simulates an airport with only one runway. One plane can land
    or depart in each unit of time. Up to 5 planes can be waiting to land or take
    off at any time.
How many units of time in simulation? 30
Expected number of arrivals per unit time (real number)? 0.47
Expected number of departures per unit time? 0.47

idle

        Plane 1 ready to land.
    1: Plane 1 landed; in queue 0 units.
    2: Runway is idle.
        Plane 2 ready to land.
        Plane 3 ready to land.
    3: Plane 2 landed; in queue 0 units.

  4: Plane 3 landed; in queue 1 units.
     Plane 4 ready to land.
     Plane 5 ready to land.
     Plane 6 ready to take off.
     Plane 7 ready to take off.
  5: Plane 4 landed; in queue 0 units.
     Plane 8 ready to take off.
  6: Plane 5 landed; in queue 1 units.
     Plane 9 ready to take off.
     Plane 10 ready to take off.
  7: Plane 6 took off; in queue 2 units.
  8: Plane 7 took off; in queue 3 units.
  9: Plane 8 took off; in queue 3 units.
     Plane 11 ready to land.
 10: Plane 11 landed; in queue 0 units.
     Plane 12 ready to take off.
 11: Plane 9 took off; in queue 4 units.
     Plane 13 ready to land.
     Plane 14 ready to land.
 12: Plane 13 landed; in queue 0 units.
 13: Plane 14 landed; in queue 1 units.
 14: Plane 10 took off; in queue 7 units.
     Plane 15 ready to land.
     Plane 16 ready to take off.
     Plane 17 ready to take off.
 15: Plane 15 landed; in queue 0 units.
     Plane 18 ready to land.
     Plane 19 ready to land.
     Plane 20 ready to take off.
     Plane 21 ready to take off.
 16: Plane 18 landed; in queue 0 units.
     Plane 22 ready to land.
 17: Plane 19 landed; in queue 1 units.
     Plane 23 ready to take off.
takeoff queue full   Plane 23 told to try later.
 18: Plane 22 landed; in queue 1 units.
     Plane 24 ready to land.
     Plane 25 ready to land.
     Plane 26 ready to land.
     Plane 27 ready to take off.
     Plane 27 told to try later.
 19: Plane 24 landed; in queue 0 units.
     Plane 28 ready to land.
     Plane 29 ready to land.
     Plane 30 ready to land.
     Plane 31 ready to land.
landing queue full   Plane 31 directed to another airport.

20: Plane 25 landed; in queue 1 units.
    Plane 32 ready to land.
    Plane 33 ready to take off.
    Plane 33 told to try later.
21: Plane 26 landed; in queue 2 units.
22: Plane 28 landed; in queue 2 units.
23: Plane 29 landed; in queue 3 units.
    Plane 34 ready to take off.
    Plane 34 told to try later.
24: Plane 30 landed; in queue 4 units.
    Plane 35 ready to take off.
    Plane 35 told to try later.
    Plane 36 ready to take off.
    Plane 36 told to try later.
25: Plane 32 landed; in queue 4 units.
    Plane 37 ready to take off.
    Plane 37 told to try later.
26: Plane 12 took off; in queue 15 units.
27: Plane 16 took off; in queue 12 units.
28: Plane 17 took off; in queue 13 units.
29: Plane 20 took off; in queue 13 units.
    Plane 38 ready to take off.
30: Plane 21 took off; in queue 14 units.

summary

Simulation has concluded after 30 units.
Total number of planes processed: 38
  Number of planes landed: 19
  Number of planes taken off: 10
  Number of planes refused use: 8
  Number left ready to land: 0
  Number left ready to take off: 1
  Percentage of time runway idle: 3.33
  Average wait time to land: 1.11
  Average wait time to take off: 8.60

Exercises 3.4

E1. In the airport simulation we did not specify which implementation of queues to use. Which of the implementations would be best to use, and why? If the choice of implementation does not make much difference, explain why.

E2. The function Random has the side effect of changing the value of its parameter seed. Side effects in functions are normally very dangerous. By considering the use of the variable seed, explain why this side effect is not as dangerous as most, and may actually help to indicate what the function does.

Programming Projects 3.4

P1. Experiment with several sample runs of the airport simulation, adjusting the values for the expected numbers of planes ready to land and take off. Find approximate values for these expected numbers that are as large as possible subject to the condition that it is very unlikely that a plane must be refused service. What happens to these values if the maximum size of the queues is increased or decreased?

P2. Modify the simulation to give the airport two runways, one always used for landings and one always used for takeoffs. Compare the total number of planes that can be served with the number for the one-runway airport. Does it more than double?

P3. Modify the simulation to give the airport two runways, one usually used for landings and one usually used for takeoffs. If one of the queues is empty, then both runways can be used for the other queue. Also, if the landing queue is full and another plane arrives to land, then takeoffs will be stopped and both runways used to clear the backlog of landing planes.

P4. Modify the simulation to have three runways, one always reserved for each of landing and takeoff and the third used for landings unless the landing queue is empty, in which case it can be used for takeoffs.

P5. Modify the original (one-runway) simulation so that when each plane arrives to land, it will (as part of its record) have a (randomly generated) fuel level, measured in units of time remaining. If the plane does not have enough fuel to wait in the queue, it is allowed to land immediately. Hence the planes in the landing queue may be kept waiting additional units, and so may run out of fuel themselves. Check this out as part of the landing procedure, and find about how busy the airport can get before planes start to crash from running out of fuel.

P6. Write a stub to take the place of the random number function. The stub can be used both to debug the program and to allow the user to control exactly the number of planes arriving for each queue at each time unit.

P7. Write a driver program for function RandomNumber; use it to check that the function produces random integers whose average over the number of iterations performed is the specified expected value.

scissors-paper-stone

P8. In a certain children's game, each of two players simultaneously puts out a hand held in a fashion to denote one of scissors, paper, or rock. The rules are that scissors beats paper (since scissors cut paper), paper beats rock (since paper covers rock), and rock beats scissors (since rock breaks scissors). Write a program to simulate playing this game with a person who types in S, P, or R at each turn.

random walk

P9. After leaving a pub a drunk tries to walk home as shown in Figure 3.9. The streets between the pub and the home form a rectangular grid. Each time the drunk reaches a corner he decides at random what direction to walk next. He never, however, wanders outside the grid.

(a) Write a program to simulate this random walk. The number of rows and columns in the grid should be variable. Your program should calculate, over

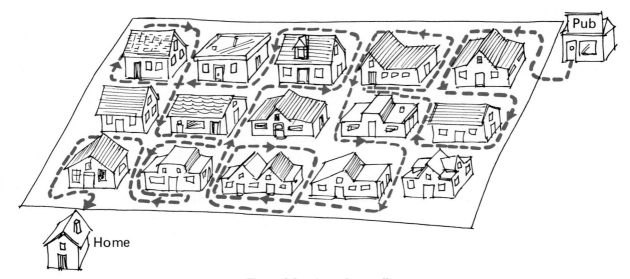

Figure 3.9.   A random walk

many random walks on the same grid, how long it takes the drunk to get home on average. Investigate how this number depends on the shape and size of the grid.

(b) To improve his chances, the drunk moves closer to the pub—to a room on the upper left corner of the grid. Modify the simulation to see how much faster he can now get home.

(c) Modify the original simulation so that, if the drunk happens to arrive back at the pub, then he goes in and the walk ends. Find out (depending on the size and shape of the grid) what percentage of the time the drunk makes it home successfully.

(d) Modify the original simulation so as to give the drunk some memory to help him, as follows. Each time he arrives at a corner, if he has been there before on the current walk, he remembers what streets he has already taken and tries a new one. If he has already tried all the streets from the corner, he decides at random which to take now. How much more quickly does he get home?

3.5 OTHER LISTS AND THEIR IMPLEMENTATION

1. General Lists

Stacks are the easiest kind of list to use because all additions and deletions are made at one end of the list. In queues changes are made at both ends, but only at the ends, so queues are still relatively easy to use. For many applications, however, it is necessary to access all the elements of the list and to be able to make insertions or deletions at any point in the list. It might be necessary, for example, to insert a new name into the middle of a list that is kept in alphabetical order.

2. Two Implementations

1. counter

The usual way of implementing a list, the one we would probably first think of, is to keep the entries of the list in an array and to use an index that counts the number of entries in the list and allows us to locate its end. Variations of this implementation are often useful, however. Instead of using a counter of elements, for example, we can sometimes mark entries of the array that do not contain list elements with some special symbol denoting emptiness. In a list of words, we might mark all unused positions by setting them to blanks. In a list of numbers, we might use some number guaranteed never to appear in the list.

2. special value

relative advantages

If it is frequently necessary to make insertions and deletions in the middle of the list, then this second implementation will prove advantageous. If we wish to delete an element from the middle of a list where the elements are kept next to each other, then we must move many of the remaining elements to fill in the vacant position, while with the second implementation, we need only mark the deleted position as empty by putting the special symbol there. See Figure 3.10. If, later, we wish to insert a new element into a list in the first implementation, we must again move many elements. With the second implementation, we need only move elements until we encounter a position marked empty. With the first implementation, on the other hand, other operations are easier. We can tell immediately the number of elements in the list, but with the second implementation, we may need to step through the entire array counting entries not marked empty. With the first implementation, we can move to the next entry of the list simply by increasing an index by one; with the second, we must search for an entry not marked empty.

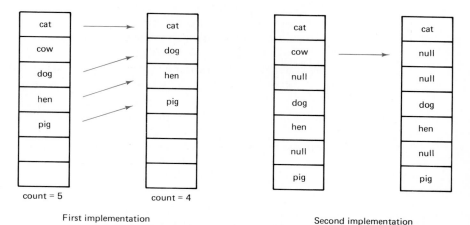

First implementation   Second implementation

Figure 3.10   Deletion from a list

3. Operations on Lists

Because variations in implementation are possible, it is wise in designing programs to separate decisions concerning the use of data structures from decisions concerning their implementation. To help in delineating these decisions, let us enumerate some of the operations we would like to do with lists.

First, there are three functions whose purposes are clear from their names:

status operations

function Empty(**var** L: list): Boolean;
function Full(L: list): Boolean;
function Size(L: list): integer;

For most other operations we must specify the place in the list to use. At any instant we are only looking at one entry of the list, and we shall refer to this entry as the ***window*** into the list. Hence, for a stack, the window is always at the same end of the list; for a queue, it is at the front for deletions and at the rear for additions. For an arbitrary list we can move the window through the list one entry at a time, or position it to any desired entry. The following are some of the operations we wish to be able to do with windows and lists:

window into a list

window positioning

procedure Initialize(**var** L: list);   {initializes L to be empty}
function IsFirst(w: window; **var** L: list): Boolean;   {Is w the first entry of L?}
function IsLast(w: window; **var** L: list): Boolean;   {Is w the last entry of L?}
procedure Start(**var** w: window; **var** L: list);
                                    {positions the window to the first entry of L}
procedure Finish(**var** w: window; **var** L: list);
                                    {positions the window to the last entry of L}
procedure Next(**var** w: window; **var** L: list);
                                    {positions the window to the next entry of L}
procedure Preceding(**var** w: window; **var** L: list);
                                    {positions the window to the preceding entry of L}

list changes

procedure Delete(**var** w: window; **var** L: list);
        {deletes the entry in the window of L and moves the window to the next entry}
procedure InsertAfter(**var** w: window; x: item; **var** L: list);
        {inserts item x into L in a new position after the window; does not change w}
procedure InsertBefore(**var** w: window; x: item; **var** L: list);
                {inserts item x into L in a new position before the window; w still points to
                                                                the same item}
procedure Replace(w: window; x: item; **var** L: list);
                                    {replaces the item in the window position with x}
procedure Retrieve(w: window; **var** x: item; **var** L: list);
                                    {sets x to the item in the current window position}

4. List Traversal

One more action is commonly done with lists—*traversal* of the list—which means to start at the beginning of the list and do some action for each item in the list in turn, finishing with the last item in the list. What action is done for each item depends on the application, for generality we say that we ***visit*** each item in the list. Hence we have the final procedure for list processing:

traverse and visit

procedure Traverse(**var** L: list; **procedure** Visit(**var** x: item));

procedural parameters (Yes, this declaration is standard Pascal; procedures are allowed as formal parameters for other procedures, although this feature is not often used in elementary programming and is not implemented in all compilers.) When procedure Traverse finishes, the window has not been changed. To be sure of proper functioning, it is necessary to assume that procedure Visit makes no insertions or deletions in the list L.

5. Pascal Programs

Let us now finally turn to the Pascal details of the two implementations of lists introduced earlier. Both methods will require the declaration of a constant maxlist giving the maximum number of items allowed in a list and types

declarations

```
index = 1 .. maxlist;
window = index;
```

The first method then requires a record declaration for a list:

type list

```
type list = record
              entry: array[index] of item;
              count: 0 .. maxlist
            end;
```

In the second method we require a variable of type item named null that will contain the special value denoting an empty position. The type declaration then becomes

```
type list = array[index] of item;
```

To show the relative advantages of the two implementations, let us write the function Size and the procedure Delete for each implementation.

Size, *version 1*

```
function Size(var L: list): integer;                    {first implementation}
begin
   Size := L.count
end;
```

Size, *version 2*

```
function Size(var L: list): integer;                    {second implementation}
var
   i:      index;
   count: integer;
begin
   count := 0;
   for i := 1 to maxlist do
      if L[i] <> null then
         count := count + 1;
   Size := count
end;
```

As you can see, the first version is somewhat simpler. On the other hand, for the Delete procedure, the second version is simpler.

deletion, version 1

```
procedure Delete(var w: window; var L: list);          {first implementation}
    {deletes the entry in the window of L and moves the window to the next entry}
var
    i: index;
begin
    for i := w + 1 to L.count do              {Move each item one position earlier.}
        L.entry[i − 1] := L.entry[i];
    L.count := L.count − 1;
    if Empty(L) then                          {Ensure that w is in the range of the list.}
        Start(w, L)
    else
        if w > Size(L) then
            Finish(w, L)
end;
```

deletion, version 2

```
procedure Delete(var w: window; var L: list);          {second implementation}
    {deletes the entry in the window of L and moves the window to the next entry}
var
    flag: Boolean;
begin
    flag := IsLast(w, L);
    L[w] := null;
    if flag then                              {Ensure that w is in the range of the list.}
        Start(w, L)
    else
        Next(w, L)
end;
```

Although there remain a good many functions and procedures to write in order to implement these list structures fully in Pascal, most of the details are simple and can safely be left as exercises. It is, of course, permissible to use procedures and functions already written as part of later procedures or functions. To illustrate this, let us conclude this section with a version of procedure Traverse that will work with either implementation.

traversal

```
procedure Traverse(var L: list; procedure Visit(var x: item));
var
  w: window;
begin                                            {procedure Traverse}
  if not Empty(L) then              {There is nothing to do for an empty list.}
  begin
    Start(w, L);
    while not IsLast(w, L) do       {Loop through all positions except the last.}
    begin
      Retrieve(w, x, L);
      Visit(x);
      Next(w, L)
    end;
    Retrieve(w, x, L);              {Consider the last position separately.}
    Visit(x)
  end
end;                                             {procedure Traverse}
```

Exercises 3.5

E1. Write Pascal functions and procedures to implement the following operations on a list implemented with **(1)** a record type including an array of items and a counter of items in the list and **(2)** an array and special item null denoting an empty position.

(a) **function** Empty(L: list): Boolean;

(b) **function** Full(L: list): Boolean;

(c) **function** IsFirst(w: window; **var** L: list): Boolean;

(d) **function** IsLast(w: window; **var** L: list): Boolean;

(e) **procedure** Initialize(**var** L: list);

(f) **procedure** Start(**var** w: window; **var** L: list);

(g) **procedure** Finish(**var** w: window; **var** L: list);

(h) **procedure** Next(**var** w: window; **var** L: list);

(i) **procedure** Preceding(**var** w: window; **var** L: list);

(j) **procedure** InsertAfter(**var** w: window; x: item; **var** L: list);

(k) **procedure** InsertBefore(**var** w: window; x: item; **var** L: list);

(l) **procedure** Replace(w: window; x: item; **var** L: list);

(m) **procedure** Retrieve(w: window; **var** x: item; **var** L: list);

E2. Given the functions and procedures for operating with lists developed in this section, do the following tasks.

(a) Write a procedure that deletes the last entry of a list.

(b) Write a procedure that deletes the first entry of a list.

(c) Write a procedure that reverses the order of the entries in a list.

(d) Write a procedure that splits a list into two other lists, so that the entries that were in odd-numbered positions are now in one list (in the same relative order as before) and those from even-numbered positions are in the other new list.

deque

The word *deque* (pronounced either "deck" or "DQ") is a shortened form of *double-ended queue* and denotes a list in which items can be added or deleted from either the first or the last position of the list, but no changes can be made elsewhere in the list. Thus a deque is a generalization of both a stack and a queue.

E3. Is it more appropriate to think of a deque as implemented in a linear array or in a circular array? Why?

E4. Write the four algorithms needed to add an item to each end of a deque and to delete an item from each end of the deque.

E5. Note from Figure 3.4 that a stack can be represented pictorially as a spur track on a straight railway line. A queue can, of course, be represented simply as a straight track. Devise and draw a railway switching network that will represent a deque. The network should have only one entrance and one exit.

E6. Suppose that data items numbered 1, 2, 3, 4, 5, 6 come in the input stream in this order. By using **(1)** a queue and **(2)** a deque, which of the following rearrangements can be obtained in the output order?

(a) 1 2 3 4 5 6	**(c)** 1 5 2 4 3 6	**(e)** 1 2 6 4 5 3
(b) 2 4 3 6 5 1	**(d)** 4 2 1 3 5 6	**(f)** 5 2 6 3 4 1

scroll

E7. A *scroll* is a data structure intermediate to a deque and a queue. In a scroll all additions to the list are at its end, but deletions can be made either at the end or at the beginning. Answer the preceding questions in the case of a scroll rather than a deque.

E8. Suppose that we think of dividing a deque in half by fixing some position in the middle of it. Then the left and right halves of the deque are each a stack. Thus a deque can be implemented with two stacks. Write algorithms that will add to and delete from each end of the deque considered in this way. When one of the two stacks is empty and the other one not, and an attempt is made to pop the empty stack, you will need to move items (equivalent to changing the place where the deque was broken in half) before the request can be satisfied. Compare your algorithms with those of Exercise 4 in regard to

(a) clarity;

(b) ease of composition;

(c) storage use;

(d) time used for typical accesses;

(e) time used when items must be moved.

unordered list

E9. In this section we have implicitly assumed that all operations on a list were required to preserve the order of the items in the list. In some applications, however, the order of the items is of no importance. In the lists live and die that we set up for the Life game in Chapter 2, for example, it made no difference in what order the entries were in the lists, and so when we needed to delete an item from the list, we could fill its hole simply by moving the last item from the list into the vacant position and reducing the count of items on the list by 1. Procedure Vivify thus had the form

```
        procedure Vivify;                          {algorithm outline}
        begin
          i := 1;
          while i <= count do
          begin
            if entry[i] is OK then                 {Process a good entry.}
            begin
              process entry[i];
              i := i + 1
            end
            else begin                             {Delete a bad entry.}
              entry[i] := entry[count];
              count := count − 1
            end
          end
        end;
```

Determine which of the operations on lists from this section will be simplified if the order of entries in the lists can be changed as desired. Rewrite the associated procedures for these operations.

file   **E10.** A file declared as **file of** item in Pascal is a list whose elements are items of type item. If F is a file, then the file window F↑ is analogous to the list window discussed in this section. The operations that can be done conveniently with a file, however, are more restricted than are those given in the text. Determine which list operations correspond to each of the following standard file operations (where x is a variable of type item).

(a) Rewrite(F);

(b) Reset(F);

(c) Get(F);

(d) Put(F);

(e) x := F↑;

(f) F↑ := x;

(g) Eof(F);

POINTERS AND PITFALLS

1. Don't confuse lists with arrays.

2. Choose your data structures as you design your algorithms, and avoid making premature decisions.

3. Practice information hiding: Use procedures and functions to access your data structures.

4. Postpone decisions on the details of implementing your data structures as long as you can.

5. Stacks are the simplest kind of lists; use stacks when possible.

6. Avoid tricky ways of storing your data; tricks usually will not generalize to new situations.

7. Be sure to initialize your data structures.

8. Always be careful about the extreme cases and handle them gracefully. Trace through your algorithm to determine what happens when a data structure is empty or full.

9. Don't optimize your code until it works perfectly, and then only optimize it if improvement in efficiency is definitely required. First try a simple implementation of your data structures. Change to a more sophisticated implementation only if the simple one proves too inefficient.

10. When working with general lists, first decide exactly what operations are needed, then choose the implementation that enables those operations to be done most easily.

REVIEW QUESTIONS

3.1   **1.** What is the difference between an array and a list?

3.2   **2.** What are the operations that can be done on a stack?

3. What are stack frames for subprograms? What do they show?

4. What are the advantages of writing the operations on a data structure as procedures and functions?

3.3   **5.** Define the term *queue*. What operations can be done on a queue?

6. How is a circular array implemented in a linear array?

7. List three different implementations of queues.

3.4   **8.** Define the term *simulation*.

9. Why are random numbers used in computer programs usually not really random?

3.5   **10.** What is a deque?

11. Which of the operations possible for general lists are also possible for queues? for stacks?

12. List three operations possible for general lists that are not allowed for either stacks or queues.

REFERENCES FOR FURTHER STUDY

data abstraction   The separation of properties of data structures and their operations from the implementation of the data structures in memory and procedures is called **data abstraction**. The following book takes this point of view consistently and develops further properties of lists:

JIM WELSH, JOHN ELDER, and DAVID BUSTARD, *Sequential Program Structures*, Prentice-Hall International, London, 1984, 385 pages.

For many topics concerning data structures, the best source for additional information, historical notes, and mathematical analysis is the following series of books, which can be regarded almost like an encyclopaedia for the aspects of computing science that they discuss:

encyclopaedic
reference: KNUTH

DONALD E. KNUTH, *The Art of Computer Programming,* published by Addison-Wesley, Reading, Mass.

Three volumes have appeared to date:

1. *Fundamental Algorithms,* second edition, 1973, 634 pages.

2. *Seminumerical Algorithms,* second edition, 1980, 700 pages.

3. *Sorting and Searching,* 1973, 722 pages.

From now on we shall often give references to this series of books, and for convenience we shall do so by specifying only the name KNUTH together with the volume and page numbers. In particular, stacks, queues, and deques are studied in KNUTH, Volume 1, pp. 234–251, with the inclusion of many interesting extensions and exercises. The algorithms are written both in English and in an assembler language, where KNUTH calculates detailed counts of operations to compare various algorithms.

In Volume 2, pp. 1–177, KNUTH studies the construction and testing of pseudo-random number generators in great depth.

An elementary survey of computer simulations appears in *Byte* 10 (October 1985), pp. 149–251. A simulation of the National Airport in Washington, D.C., appears on pp. 186–190.

C H A P T E R 4

Linked Lists

▶ *This chapter studies the implementation of lists by the use of links. Several examples are developed, and the chapter closes with a discussion of the general principles of abstract data types and data structures.*

4.1 DYNAMIC MEMORY ALLOCATION AND POINTERS

4.1.1 The Problem of Overflow

fixed bounds

In the examples we have studied in the previous chapters we have assumed that all items of data are kept within arrays, arrays that must be declared to have some size that is fixed when the program is written, and that can therefore not be changed while the program is running. When writing a program, we have had to decide on the maximum amount of memory that would be needed for our arrays and set this aside in the declarations. If we run the program on a small sample, then much of this space will never be used. If we decide to run the program on a large set of data, then we may exhaust the space set aside and encounter overflow, even when the computer memory itself is not fully used, simply because our original bounds on the array were too small.

problem of overflow

Even if we are careful to declare our arrays large enough to use up all the available memory, we can still encounter overflow, since one array may reach its limit while a great deal of unused space remains in others. Since different runs of the same program may cause different lists to grow or shrink, it may be impossible to tell before the program actually executes which lists will overflow.

We now exhibit a way to keep lists and other data structures in memory without using arrays, whereby we can avoid these difficulties.

4.1.2 Pointers

The idea we use is that of a pointer. A *pointer,* also called a *link* or a *reference,* is defined to be a variable that gives the location of some other variable, typically of a record containing data that we wish to use. If we use pointers to locate all the records in which we are interested, then we need not be concerned about where the records themselves are actually stored, since by using a pointer, we can let the computer system itself locate the record when required.

Figure 4.1 shows pointers to several records. Pointers are generally depicted as

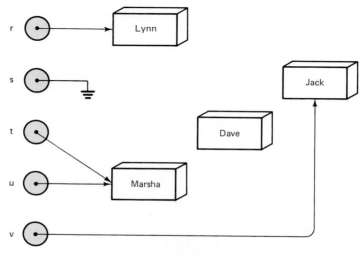

Figure 4.1.   Pointers to records

arrows and records as rectangular boxes. In the diagrams, variables containing pointers are generally shown as colored boxes. Hence in the diagram r is a pointer to the record "Lynn" and v is a pointer to the record "Jack." As you can see, the use of pointers is quite flexible: two pointers can refer to the same record, as t and u do in Figure 4.1, or a pointer can refer to no record at all. We denote this latter situation *pointers referring* within diagrams by the electrical *ground symbol,* as shown for pointer s. Care must *nowhere* be exercised when using pointers, moreover, to be sure that, when they are moved, no record is lost. In the diagram, the record "Dave" is lost, with no pointer referring to it, and therefore there is no way to find it.

linked list   The idea of a **linked list** is, for every record in the list, to put a pointer into the record giving the location of the next record in the list. This idea is illustrated in Figure 4.2.

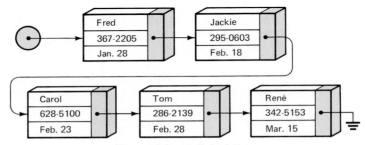

Figure 4.2.   A linked list

As you can see from the illustration, a linked list is simple in concept. It uses the same idea as a children's treasure hunt, where each clue that is found tells where to find the next one. Or consider friends passing a popular cassette around. Fred has it and has promised to give it to Jackie. Carol asks Jackie if she can borrow it and then will next share it with Tom. And so it goes. A linked list may be considered analogous to following instructions where each instruction is given out only upon completion of the previous task. There is then no inherent limit on the number of tasks to be done, since each task may specify a new instruction, and there is no way to tell in advance how many instructions there are. The list implementations studied in Chapter 3, on the other hand, are analogous to a list of instructions written on a single sheet of paper. It is then possible to see all the instructions in advance, but there is a limit to the number of instructions that can be written on the single sheet of paper.

With some practice in their use, you will find that linked lists are as easy to work with as lists implemented within arrays. The methods differ substantially, however, so we must spend some time developing new programming skills. Before we turn to this work, let us consider a few more general observations.

4.1.3 Further Remarks

1. Contiguous and Linked Lists

The word **contiguous** means *in contact, touching, adjoining.* The entries in an array are contiguous, and from now on we shall speak of a list kept in an array as a *contiguous list.* We can then distinguish as desired between contiguous lists and linked lists, and we shall use the unqualified word *list* only to include both.

2. Pointers for Contiguous Lists

A pointer is simply a variable giving the location of some item, and for contiguous lists, we have in fact been using pointers informally throughout the last chapter. The variable *top* is a pointer giving the location of the item on the top of a stack, and the variables *front* and *rear* give the location of the front and rear of a queue. To avoid possible confusion, however, we shall generally reserve the word *pointer* for use with linked lists and continue to use the word *index* (and, later in this chapter, the word *cursor*) to refer to a location within an array.

4.1.4 Dynamic Memory Allocation

As well as preventing unnecessary overflow problems caused by running out of room in arrays, the use of pointers has advantages in a multiprogramming (time-sharing) environment. If we use arrays to reserve in advance the maximum amount of memory that our program might need, then this memory is assigned to us and will be unavailable

time sharing

for other users. If it is necessary to page our job out of memory, then there may be time lost as unused memory is copied to and from a disk. Instead of using arrays to hold all our items, we can begin very small, with space only for the program instructions and simple variables, and whenever we need space for an additional item, we can request the system for the needed memory. Similarly, when an item is no longer needed, its space can be returned to the system, which can then assign it to another user. In this way a program can start small and grow only as necessary, so that when it is small, it can run more efficiently, and when necessary, it can grow to the limits of the computer system.

Even with only one user this dynamic control of memory can prove useful. During one part of a task a large amount of memory may be needed for some purpose, which can later be released and then allocated again for another purpose, perhaps now containing data of a completely different type than before.

4.1.5 Pointers and Dynamic Memory in Pascal

Most newer programming languages, including Pascal, provide powerful facilities for processing pointers and standard procedures for requesting additional memory and for releasing memory during program execution.

1. Static and Dynamic Variables

Variables that can be used during execution of a Pascal program come in two varieties. *Static variables* are those that are declared and named, as usual, while writing the program. Space for them exists as long as the program in which they are declared is running. *Dynamic variables* are created (and perhaps destroyed) during program execution. Since dynamic variables do not exist while the program is compiled, but only when it is run, they cannot be assigned names while it is being written.

The only way to access dynamic variables is by using pointers. Once it is created, however, a dynamic variable does contain data and must have a type like any other variable. Thus we can talk about creating a new dynamic variable of type x and setting a pointer to point to it, or of moving a pointer from one dynamic variable of type x to another, or of returning a dynamic variable of type x to the system.

Static variables, on the other hand, cannot be created or destroyed during execution of the program in which they are declared, and pointer variables cannot be used to point to static variables. Static variables are referenced only by using their names—just as we have always done—and if we wish to refer to positions within arrays, then as before we do so with variables (*indices*) of the same type that indexes the array.

2. Pascal Notation

Pascal uses an upward arrow or caret ($\uparrow$ or $\wedge$) to denote pointers. (These two symbols are usually different representations of the same character.) When this character is not available, the symbol @ is used instead. If node denotes the type of items in which we are interested, then we declare a pointer type that is bound to type node with the declaration

pointer types

type pointer = $\uparrow$node.

The type node to which a pointer refers can be arbitrary, but in most applications, it will be a record. Note that the word pointer is not a reserved word in Pascal; we have declared it like any other identifier denoting a newly defined type. The words link and reference are also frequently used to designate pointer types. As we can with any other type, we can now declare variables that have type pointer, and these variables point to dynamic variables of type node.

When more than one type of dynamic variable is in use, we can name the pointer type to reflect the type of dynamic variables, with declarations such as

type pointitem = $\uparrow$item;
pointnode = $\uparrow$node;

A pointer to dynamic variables or type item is then declared as a variable of type pointitem, and a pointer to a variable of type node is a variable of type pointnode.

3. Type Binding

Pascal sets stringent rules for the use of pointer variables. Each pointer is **bound** to the type of variable to which it points, and the same pointer can never be used to point (at different times) to variables of different types. Variables of two different pointer types cannot be mixed with each other; Pascal will allow assignments between two pointer variables of the same type, but not between pointer variables of different types. If we have declarations

var a, b: pointitem;
x, y: pointnode;

then the assignments x := y and a := b are legal, but the assignment x := a is illegal.

4. Creating and Destroying Dynamic Variables

The creation and destruction of dynamic variables is done with standard procedures in Pascal. If p has been declared as a pointer to type node, then the procedure

new(p)

creates a new dynamic variable of type node and assigns its location to the pointer p. Similarly, the procedure

dispose(p)

returns the space used by the variable of type node to the system. (*Warning:* Some Pascal systems will lose the space and never reuse it.) After the procedure dispose(p) is called, the pointer variable p is undefined, and so cannot be used until it is assigned a new value. These actions are illustrated in Figure 4.3.

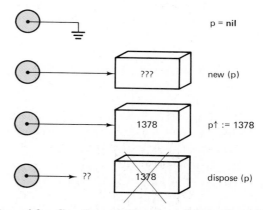

Figure 4.3.   Creating and disposing of dynamic variables

5. Nil Pointers

Sometimes a pointer variable p has no dynamic variable to which it currently refers. This situation can be established by the assignment

p := nil

and subsequently checked by a condition such as

if p <> nil then . . . .

In diagrams we use the electrical ground symbol

nil symbol

for **nil** pointers. The word **nil** is a reserved word in Pascal, not an identifier whose meaning can be changed if desired. It is used in the same way as a constant for pointer types and is generic in that the same value **nil** can be assigned to a variable of any pointer type.

undefined pointers
versus **nil** *pointers*

Note carefully the distinction between a pointer variable whose value is undefined and a pointer variable whose value is **nil**. The assertion p = **nil** means that p currently points to no dynamic variable. If the value of p is undefined, then p might point to any random location in memory. As with all variables, when the program begins execution, the values of pointer variables are undefined. Either a call new(p) or an assignment such as p := q or p := **nil** is required before p can be used. After a call dispose(p), the value of p is undefined, so it is wise to set p := **nil** immediately, to be sure that p is not used with an undefined value.

6. Following the Arrows

Upward arrows (↑) to denote *pointer* appear not only in the declarations of a Pascal program, but also in the action part. But here the arrow appears not to the left of a type, but to the right of a pointer variable. Thus p↑ denotes the variable to which p points. At first, this notation may appear slightly confusing, but its logic will become clear if you remember that ↑ means *points*. Thus the declaration

$$p: \uparrow item$$

dereferencing

is read "p points to an item" and p↑ is read "what p points to." Again the words *link* and *reference* are often used in this connection. The action of taking p↑ is sometimes called "dereferencing the pointer p."

Notice the similarity between this notation and that used in Pascal for a *file window*. If F is a file, then F↑ denotes the one entry of the file that is currently accessible to the program. In other words, F↑ is the position within the file to which the program currently points, just as p↑ is the position within memory to which the pointer p currently points.

7. Restrictions on Pointer Variables

pointer operations

The only use of variables of type ↑item is to find the location of variables of type item. Thus pointer variables can participate in assignment statements, can be checked for equality, and (as parameters) can appear in calls to subprograms, but they can appear nowhere else. The programmer is not allowed to do arithmetic with pointers, since they are addresses, not numbers with intrinsic meaning. Reading or writing the values of pointers is also not allowed, since they are addresses assigned while the program is running, since they may differ from one run of the program to the next, and since their values (as addresses in the computer memory) are implementation features with which the programmer should not be directly concerned. (Some Pascal systems do allow pointer values to be written out, for debugging purposes, so that the programmer can check that appropriate equalities hold, and appropriate pointer assignments have been made.)

Note that these restrictions on using pointers do not apply to the dynamic variables to which the pointers refer. If p is a pointer, then p↑ is not usually a pointer (although it is legal for pointers to point to pointers), but a variable of some other type node, and therefore p↑ can be used in any legitimate way for type node.

assignment

In regard to assignment statements, it is important to remember the difference between p := q and p↑ := q↑, both of which are legal (provided that p and q are bound to the same type), but which have quite different effects. The first statement makes p point to the same object to which q points, but does not change the value of either that object, or of the other object that was formerly p↑. The latter object will be lost unless there is some other pointer variable that still refers to it. The second statement, p↑ := q↑, on the contrary, copies the value of the object q↑ into the object p↑, so that we now have two objects with the same value, with p and q pointing to the two separate copies. Finally, the two assignment statements p := q↑ and p↑ := q have mixed types and are illegal (except in the rare case that both p and q point to pointers of their same type!). Figure 4.4 illustrates these assignments.

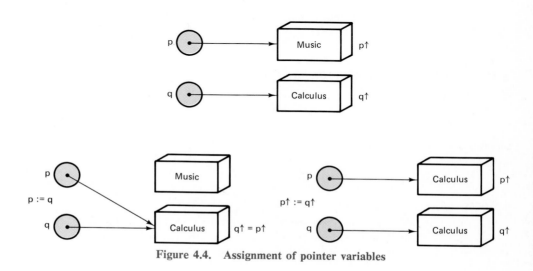

Figure 4.4.   Assignment of pointer variables

Exercises 4.1

These exercises are based on the following declarations, where we assume that the type node has been previously declared in the program.

> **type** pointer = ↑node;
> **var**   p, q, r: pointer;
>   x, y, z: node;

E1. For each of the following statements, either describe its effect or state why it is illegal.

(a) new(p)	**(f)** r := **nil**	**(k)** dispose(r)
(b) new(q↑)	**(g)** z := p↑	**(l)** x := new(p)
(c) new(x)	**(h)** p := ↑x	**(m)** q↑ := **nil**
(d) p := r	**(i)** dispose(y)	**(n)** p↑ := x↑
(e) q := y	**(j)** dispose(p↑)	**(o)** z := **nil**

swap
E2. Write a Pascal procedure to interchange pointers p and q, so that after the procedure is performed, p will point to the node to which q formerly pointed, and vice versa.

E3. Write a Pascal procedure to interchange the values in the dynamic variables to which p and q point, so that after the procedure is performed p↑ will have the value formerly in q↑, and vice versa.

E4. Write a Pascal procedure that makes p point to the same node to which q points and disposes of the node to which p formerly pointed.

E5. Write a Pascal procedure that creates a new variable with p pointing to it, and with contents the same as those of the node to which q points.

4.2 LINKED STACKS AND QUEUES

With these tools of pointers and pointer types we can now begin to consider the implementation of linked lists into Pascal. Since stacks and queues are among the easiest lists to process, we begin with them.

4.2.1 Declarations

1. Nodes and Type Declarations

Recall from Figure 4.2 that each entry of a linked list will be a record containing not only the items of information but also a pointer to the next record in the list. Translating this requirement into Pascal declarations yields

```
type
  pointer = ↑node;
  node    = record
              info: item;          {This part of the record may contain
                                    several fields making up the information in the record.}
              next: pointer        {link to the next node in the list}
            end;
```

use before declaration
Note that we have a problem of circularity in this declaration. A field of type pointer is part of the record of type node, so Pascal requires that type pointer be declared before node, as we have done. On the other hand, type pointer is declared as ↑node and thus uses type node within its declaration. Hence it would appear that type node would have to be declared before pointer. To avoid this problem of circular declarations, in this context Pascal relaxes the rule that every identifier must be declared before being used. Instead, the construction

$$↑\text{sometype}$$

is valid anytime, even if sometype has not yet been declared (although it must be declared at some place before the program ends).

space for pointers

The reason why Pascal can relax its rule in this way and still compile efficiently is that all pointers take the same amount of space in memory, usually the same amount as an integer, no matter to what type they refer. Hence when encountering the declaration of a pointer type, the compiler can set aside the right amount of storage and postpone the problems of checking that all declarations and uses of variables are consistent with the rules.

2. Beginning of the List

In our linked list we shall use the pointer field next to move from any one node in the linked list to the next one, and thereby we can work our way through the list, once we have started. We must now, however, address a small problem that never arises with contiguous lists or other static variables and arrays: How do we find the beginning of the list?

Perhaps an analogy with reading a magazine article will help. If we are in the middle of reading an article, then upon reaching the bottom of a page we often find the instruction "Continued on page . . .," and by following such instructions we can continue reading until we reach the end of the article. But how do we find the beginning? We look in the table of contents, which we expect to find in a fixed location near the beginning of the magazine.

static head

For linked lists also we must refer to some fixed location to find the beginning; that is, we shall use a static variable to locate the first node of the list. One method of doing this is to make the first node in the list a static variable, even though all the remaining nodes are dynamically allocated. In this way the first node will have a unique name to which we can refer. Although we shall sometimes use this method, it has the disadvantage that the first node of the list is treated differently from all the others, a fact that can sometimes complicate the algorithms.

3. Headers

For linked stacks and queues and sometimes for other kinds of linked lists, we shall employ another method that avoids these problems. The *header* for a linked list is a pointer variable that locates the beginning of the list. The header will usually be a static variable, and by using its value, we can arrive at the first (dynamic) node of the list. The header is also sometimes called the *base* or the *anchor* of the list. These terms are quite descriptive of providing a variable that ties down the beginning of the list, but since they are not so widely used, we shall generally employ the term *header*.

initialization

When execution of the program starts we shall wish to initialize the linked list to be empty; with a header pointer, this is now easy. The header is a static variable; so it exists when the program begins, and to set its value to indicate that its list is empty, we need only the assignment

header := **nil;**

4. The End of the List

Finding the end of a linked list is a much easier task than is finding its beginning. Since each node contains a pointer to the next, the pointer field of the last node of the list has nowhere to point, so we give it the special value **nil**. In this way we know that we are at the end of the list if and only if the node we are using has a **nil** pointer to the next. Here we have one small advantage of linked lists over a contiguous implementation: There is no need to keep an explicit counter of the number of nodes in the list.

4.2.2 Linked Stacks

Let us now turn to writing procedures for processing linked stacks. As with the items of contiguous stacks, we shall *push* and *pop* nodes from one end of a linked stack, called its *top*. We now face a small problem of inconsistency with the implementation of stacks in the last chapter: The entries of contiguous stacks were declared to have type item, whereas the entries of linked stacks will have type node, which we have already declared to consist of an item together with a pointer. For some applications of linked stacks we wish to process nodes, but for other applications we wish to be able to process items directly, so that we can substitute a linked implementation of stacks for a contiguous implementation without having to make any changes in the rest of the program.

items and nodes

For this reason we introduce two new procedures, PushNode and PopNode, which will process nodes in a linked stack. We can then use these procedures to write linked versions of the procedures Push and Pop, which, as in the last chapter, will process items directly. If we have an item x that we wish to push onto a linked stack, we must first make a new node and put x into the node, and then push the node onto the stack. Hence we obtain

item *processing*

```
procedure Push(x: item; var S: stack);        {version for linked stack}
var p: pointer;                                {used to make a new node}
begin
   new(p);
   p↑.info := x;
   PushNode(p, S)
end;
```

The connection between the two procedures for popping the stack is just as close.

```
procedure Pop(var x: item; var S: stack);     {version for linked stack}
var p: pointer;                               {used for temporary node}
begin
   PopNode(p, S);
   x := p↑.info;
   dispose(p)
end;
```

node *processing*

Next let us turn to the processing of nodes in a linked stack. The first question to settle is to determine whether the beginning or the end of the linked list will be the top of the stack. At first glance it may appear that (as for contiguous lists) it might be easier to add a node at the end of the list, but this method makes popping the stack difficult: There is no quick way to find the node immediately before a given one in a linked list, since the pointers stored in the list give only one-way directions. Thus, after we remove the last element, to find the new element at the end of the list it might be necessary to trace all the way from the head of the list. To pop our linked stack it is better to make all additions and deletions at the beginning of the list. Each linked list has a header variable that points to its first node; for a linked stack we shall call this header variable top, and it will always point to the top of the stack. Since each node of a linked list points to the next one, the only information needed to keep track of a linked stack is the location of its top. For consistency with other data structures, we shall put this information in a simple record structure, and hence we obtain the following declaration of a linked stack:

type stack = **record** top: pointer **end.**

Let us start with an empty stack, which now means

S.top = **nil,**

and add the first node. We shall assume that this node has already been made somewhere in dynamic memory, and we shall locate this node by using a pointer variable p. The node itself is then referred to as p↑. Pushing p↑ onto the stack consists of the instructions

S.top := p;   p↑.next := **nil.**

As we continue, let us suppose that we already have the stack and that we wish to push a node p↑ onto it. The required adjustments of pointers are shown in Figure 4.5. First, we must set the pointer coming from the new node p↑ to the old

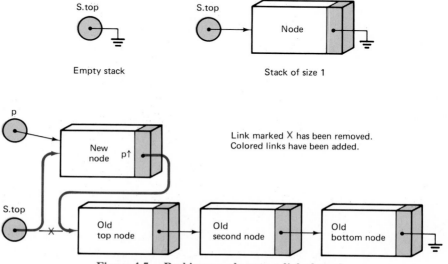

Figure 4.5.   Pushing a node onto a linked stack

top of the stack, and then we must change the top to become the new node. The order of these two assignments is important: If we attempted to do them in the reverse order, the change of top from its previous value would mean that we would lose track of the old part of the list. We thus obtain the following procedure.

push node

```
procedure PushNode(p: pointer; var S: stack);
{Push the node p↑ onto the linked stack S.}
begin
  if p = nil then
    Error                    {Attempt to push a nonexistent node onto the stack.}
  else begin
    p↑.next := S.top;        {The new node points to the former top of the stack.}
    S.top := p                          {Set the top to the new node.}
  end
end;
```

In all our procedures it is important to include error checking and to consider extreme cases. Hence we consider it an error to attempt to push a nonexistent node onto the stack. One extreme case for the procedure is that of an empty stack, which means top = **nil**. Note that in this case the procedure works just as well to add the first node to an empty stack as to add another node to a nonempty stack.

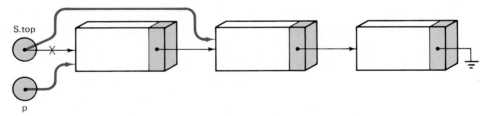

Figure 4.6.   Popping a node from a linked stack

It is equally simple to pop a node from a linked stack. This process is illustrated in Figure 4.6 and is implemented in the following procedure.

pop node

```
procedure PopNode(var p: pointer; var S: stack);
{pops the node p↑ from the linked stack S}
begin
  if S.top = nil then
    Error                              {Attempt to pop an empty stack.}
  else begin
    p := S.top;                              {Pop the top node.}
    S.top := p↑.next              {Move the top down the list.}
  end
end;
```

Note that the principal instructions for popping the linked stack are exactly the reverse of those for pushing a node onto the stack. In popping the stack, it is necessary to check the stack for emptiness, but in pushing it, there is no need to check for overflow, since the procedure itself does not call for any additional memory. The extra memory for the new node is already assigned to p↑.

value and variable parameters

Finally, you should note that both parameters in the procedure that pops the stack are called by reference, but in pushing p↑ onto the stack, only the stack S need be called by reference. The formal reason, of course, is that in procedure PopNode, both the variables S.top and p are changed, while in procedure PushNode, the variable p is not changed. The point of possible confusion, however, is that, even though parameter p is only a local copy of some actual parameter, the local copy p and the actual parameter both point to the same node p↑, and so procedure PushNode is quite capable of making changes in the actual node p↑, whether its parameter p is called by value or by reference.

4.2.3 Application: The Available Space List

In standard Pascal, the way to acquire memory and create a new node is to use the procedure new(p), and the way to return memory to the operating system is to

possible problem with dispose

use the procedure dispose(p). On some systems, however, the procedure dispose(p) either does nothing (in which case the node p↑ becomes lost to the program, and will never be reused), or the procedure runs inefficiently. If our program is one that continually sets up new nodes and disposes of others, then we shall often find it necessary to set up our own procedures to keep track of nodes that are no longer needed, and to reuse the space when new nodes are later required.

Since our nodes come from a linked structure, we can take the nodes that are no longer needed and link them together as a list. The order in which they might be reused makes no difference since they are indistinguishable as empty blocks of

stack of available space

memory, so we might as well put them in a linked stack, since its operations are particularly easy. Thus we need only one variable

var availnode: pointer

which we use to point to the top node on the space-available stack. When we wish to acquire a new node, we should first attempt to pop the stack of nodes that are no longer in use, and only if the stack is empty do we need to go to the computer system by using the procedure new(p). Since at the start of the main program no nodes have been acquired from the system, the program should include at its beginning the statement

initialization

availnode := **nil;**

as initialization, and the following procedure should be used in place of new(p).

new node

```
procedure NewNode(var p: pointer);
begin
  if availnode = nil then           {If nothing is on stack, ask the system.}
    new(p)
  else begin                         {If the stack is not empty, then pop it.}
    p := availnode;
    availnode := p↑.next
  end
end;
```

The procedure replacing dispose(p) never disposes of nodes but instead pushes each unused node p↑ onto the stack.

dispose node

```
procedure DisposeNode(p: pointer);
begin
  if p = nil then
    Error                              {Attempt to dispose of nothing.}
  else begin                           {Push the node onto the stack.}
    p↑.next := availnode;
    availnode := p
  end
end;
```

side effect

packages

In the two procedures just written, availnode is a global variable that is changed by the procedures. In other words, these procedures cause a side effect. This side effect could easily be avoided by listing availnode as a parameter for each of the procedures. It is not certain, however, that doing so would make the program any clearer or more secure. Except for its initialization, the variable availnode should never be used outside the two procedures, and listing it as a parameter might make the programmer think that it should be used elsewhere. What we really want for this application is a feature not available in Pascal, a feature called *information hiding*. Some other languages do provide such features (called *packages* or *modules*) that allow access to variables to be restricted to certain procedures.

4.2.4 Linked Queues

In contiguous storage, queues were significantly harder to manipulate than were stacks, because it was necessary to treat straight-line storage as though it were arranged in a circle, and the extreme cases of full queues and empty queues caused difficulties. It is for queues that linked storage really comes into its own. Linked queues are just as easy to handle as are linked stacks. We need only keep two pointers, front and rear, that will point, respectively, to the beginning and the end of the queue. The operations of insertion and deletion are both illustrated in Figure 4.7.

To show the logical connection between the head and tail pointers of a linked queue, we shall introduce a record type:

type queue

```
type queue = record
               front,
               rear: pointer
             end;
```

A queue should be initialized to be empty with the procedure:

initialize

```
procedure Initialize(var Q: queue);
begin
  Q.front := nil;
  Q.rear  := nil
end;
```

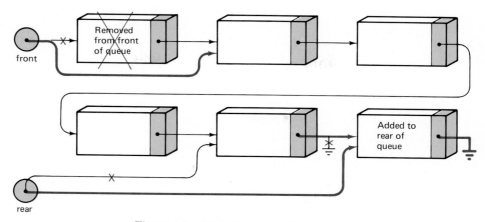

Figure 4.7. Operations on a linked queue

To add a node $p \uparrow$ to the rear of a queue, we then write

insert node

```
procedure AddNode(p: pointer; var Q: queue);
begin                                                    {(procedure AddNode}
  if p = nil then
    Error                              {Attempt to add nonexistent node to the queue.}
  else begin
    with Q do
      if front = nil then              {Q is empty; set both front and rear to p.}
      begin
        front := p;
        rear  := p
      end
      else begin
        rear↑.next := p;               {Place p↑ after the previous rear of queue.}
        rear := p                      {Update the rear to be the new node.}
      end;
      p↑.next := nil                   {Indicate that new node is at the end of list.}
  end
end;                                                     {procedure AddNode}
```

Note that this procedure includes error checking to prevent the insertion of a nonexistent node into the queue. The cases when the queue is empty or not must be treated separately, since the addition of a node to an empty queue requires setting both the front and the rear to the new node, while addition to a nonempty queue requires changing only the rear.

To remove a node from the front of a queue, we use the following procedure:

delete node

```
procedure DeleteNode(var p: pointer; var Q: queue);
begin                                            {procedure DeleteNode}
  with Q do
    if front = nil then
      Error                      {Attempt to delete a node from an empty queue.}
    else begin
      p := front;                    {Pull off the front item as the procedure result.}
      front := front↑.next;    {Advance the front of the queue to the next node.}
      if front = nil then                            {Is the queue now empty?}
        rear := nil
    end
end;                                             {procedure DeleteNode}
```

Again the possibility of an empty queue must be considered separately. It is an error to attempt deletion from an empty queue. It is, however, not an error for the queue to become empty after a deletion, but then the rear and front should both become **nil** to indicate clearly that the queue is empty.

simplicity

If you compare these algorithms for linked queues with those needed for contiguous queues, you will see that the linked versions are both conceptually easier and easier to program.

implementations

The procedures we have developed process nodes; to enable us to change easily between contiguous and linked implementations of queues, we also need versions of procedures AddQueue and DeleteQueue that will process items directly for linked queues. We leave writing these procedures as exercises.

Exercises 4.2

E1. When deleting an item from a linked stack or queue, we checked for emptiness, but when adding an item, we did not check for overflow. Why?

E2. Why is the parameter p in procedure NewNode called by reference, but called by value in procedure DisposeNode?

E3. Write a Pascal procedure to initialize a linked stack to be empty.

E4. For contiguous stacks and queues, we wrote Boolean-valued functions Empty and Full along with the various procedures. Write analogous functions in Pascal for **(a)** linked stacks and **(b)** linked queues.

E5. By making and disposing of new nodes, write procedures **(a)** AddQueue and **(b)** DeleteQueue that will process items directly for linked queues and that can be substituted directly for their contiguous counterparts.

circularly linked list

A *circularly linked list,* illustrated in Figure 4.8, is a linked list in which the node at the tail of the list, instead of having a **nil** pointer, points back to the node at the head of the list. We then need only one pointer tail to access both ends of the list, since we know that tail↑.next points back to the head of the list.

E6. If we implement a queue as a circularly linked list, then we need only one pointer tail (or rear) to locate both the front and the rear. Write Pascal procedures to process a queue stored in this way:

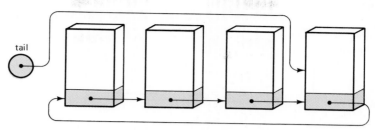

Figure 4.8.   A circularly linked list with tail pointer.

(a) Procedure Initialize.
(b) Procedure AddNode.
(c) Procedure DeleteNode.

deque

E7. Recall (Section 3.5, Exercise 3) that a *deque* is a list in which additions or deletions can be made at either the head or the tail, but not elsewhere in the list. With a deque stored as a circularly linked list, three of the four algorithms to add a node to either end of the deque and to delete a node from either end become easy to write, but the fourth does not.

(a) Which of the four operations is difficult? Why?
(b) Write a Pascal procedure to initialize a circularly linked deque to be empty.
(c) Write Pascal procedures for the three easy operations on a linked deque.
(d) Write a Pascal procedure for the fourth operation.

4.3 FURTHER OPERATIONS ON LINKED LISTS

For stacks and queues all the operations are performed at one of the ends of the list, but for more general linked lists, changes, insertions, or deletions may be made at any point. In fact, all the operations listed in Section 3.5 apply equally well to linked lists as to contiguous lists.

4.3.1 Algorithms for Simply Linked Lists

To illustrate the kind of actions we can perform with linked lists, let us consider for a moment the problem of editing text, and suppose that each node holds one word as well as the link to the next node. The sentence "Stacks are lists" appears as in (a) of Figure 4.9. If we *insert* the word "simple" we obtain the list in (b). Next we decide to *replace* "lists" by "structures" and *insert* the three nodes "but important data" to obtain (c). Afterward, we decide to *delete* "simple but" and so arrive at list (d). Finally, we *traverse* the list to print its contents.

1. List Traversal

As a first example, let us write a procedure to perform *list traversal*, which means to move through the list, visiting each node in turn. What we mean by *visiting* each node depends entirely on the application; it might mean printing out some information, or doing some task that depends on the data in the node. Thus we leave the task unspecified and, as in Section 3.5, use a call to a procedure named Visit(p). To traverse the list, we shall need a local pointer p that will start at the first node on the list

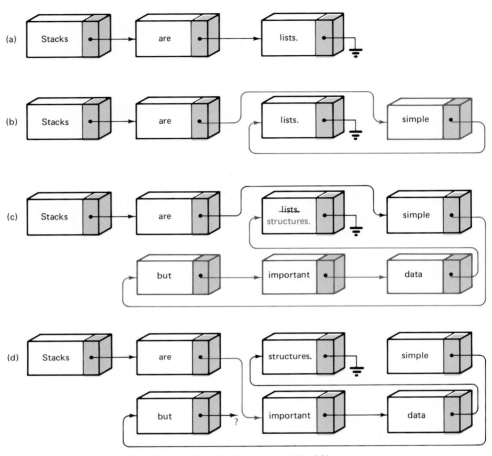

Figure 4.9.   Actions on a linked list

and move from node to node. We need a loop to accomplish this movement, and since we wish to allow the possibility of an empty list (for which the loop will not iterate at all), the correct form will be a **while** loop. Termination occurs when p points off the end of the list, whereupon we have p = **nil**. The procedure then becomes

linked traversal

```
procedure Traverse(head: pointer; procedure Visit(p: pointer));
{Head is the first node of list; Visit(p) does the action at each node.}
var
  p: pointer;                              {local pointer that moves through the list}
begin
  p := head;                              {p starts at the first node.}
  while p <> nil do
  begin
    Visit(p);
    p := p↑.next                         {Move p one node down the list.}
  end
end;
```

Notice the close analogy between traversal of a linked list and traversal of a contiguous list. If head and tail are indices marking the start and finish of a contiguous list inside an array A of items, then traversal of the contiguous list is performed by the following procedure:

contiguous traversal

```
procedure Traverse(head, tail: index; procedure Visit(p: item));
{Head is the first item in list; Visit(p) does the action for each item.}
var
  p: index;                             {local index that moves through the list}
begin
  p := head;                            {p starts at the first item.}
  while p <= tail do
  begin
    Visit(A[p]);
    p := p + 1                          {Move p one item down the list.}
  end
end;
```

Comparing these versions of traversal, we see that the initialization is the same, the general structure is the same, and the instruction p := p↑.next replaces p := p + 1 as the way to advance one node through the list. Figure 4.10 illustrates this process.

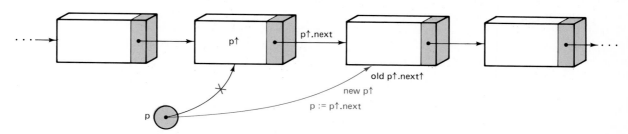

Figure 4.10.   **Advancing one node**

2. Insertion after a Node

Next let us consider the problem of inserting a new node into an arbitrary position in our list. If p is a pointer to some node in the list, and we wish to insert the new node *after* p↑, then the method used for inserting a new node at the rear of a queue works with little change:

```
procedure InsertNodeAfter(p, q: pointer);
{Insert a node q↑ after the node p↑ in a linked list.}
begin
  if (p = nil) or (q = nil) then
    Error             {Both p↑ and q↑ must exist for the insertion to make sense.}
  else begin
    q↑.next := p↑.next;
    p↑.next := q
  end
end;
```

The action of this procedure is illustrated in Figure 4.11.

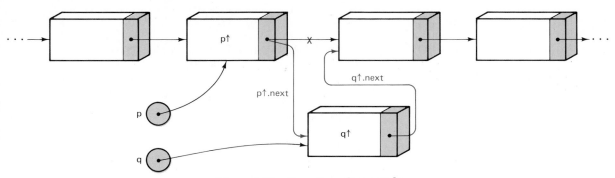

Figure 4.11.   Insertion after a node

3. Insertion before a Node

tracing the list

swap fields

two pointers

Suppose now that p points to some node in the list, and we wish to insert a new node *before* p↑. We now have a difficulty, since the link that must be changed is the one coming into p↑, and there is no way to find this link directly from p and q, since we have no way to move backward through the list.

One way we could use to find the link entering p↑ is to start at the head of the list and traverse it to the desired point, but this is usually not a good method, since its running time is proportional to the length of the list up to p↑, a length that we do not know in advance and that might be prohibitively large.

A second method, the details of which are left as an exercise, is to use a small trick. First, insert the node q↑ after p↑ instead of before p↑. Then, by copying appropriate information fields between the records, swap the information in p↑ and q↑ so that the information in q↑ comes before that in p↑. This method, while it often runs faster than the first one, may become very slow if the information fields are large and will be dangerous if not fatal if there are other variables elsewhere in the program that point to either of the two nodes that were swapped.

Hence we shall consider yet a third method to solve the problem of inserting q↑ before p↑, a method requiring slightly more bookkeeping, but one that moves only pointers, never the information in the nodes, and whose running time does not depend on the length of the list. What we do is to propose keeping a second pointer variable throughout all our processing of the list. This second pointer r will move in lock step with p, with r↑ always kept exactly one node closer to the head of the list than p↑. Inserting the new node q↑ before p↑ is now easy, since it is only inserting q↑ after r↑, and then updating r by setting r := q. Inserting the new node before the first node of the list (in which case the trailing pointer r is undefined) is now a special case, but an easy one, similar to adding a node to a linked stack. This process is illustrated in Figure 4.12, which leads to the following procedure.

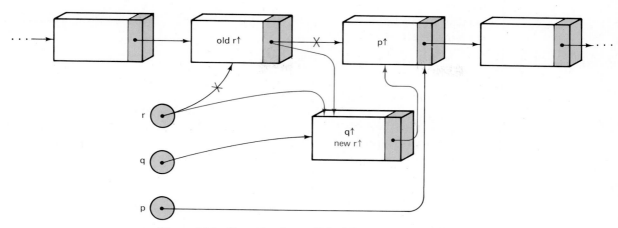

Figure 4.12.   **Insertion into a linked list with two pointers**

insertion between pointers

procedure InsertBetween(q: pointer; **var** head, r, p: pointer);
{Insert q↑ into the list starting at head↑, between the nodes r↑ and p↑, which
   will be maintained with r↑ one node closer to the head of the list.}
begin
  if p = head **then**   {q↑ is to be inserted first in the list.}
  begin
    q↑.next := p;
    r := q;   {r was previously undefined.}
    head := q   {q↑ is now at head of the list.}
  end
  else begin
    q↑.next := p;
    r↑.next := q;
    r := q
  end
end;

4. The Two-Pointer Implementation

new implementation

In writing the procedure just finished we have introduced a subtle change in the structure of our linked list, a change that really amounts to a new implementation of the list, one that requires keeping pointers to two adjacent nodes of the list at all times. In this implementation, some operations (like insertion) become easier, but others may become harder. In list traversal, for example, we must be more careful to get the process started correctly. When p points to the head of the list, then r is necessarily undefined. Thus the first step of traversal must be considered separately. The details are left as an exercise. Similarly, insertion of a new node before the current head of the list is a special case, but an easy one already considered in studying linked stacks.

5. Deletion

Deletion of a node from a linked list is another operation in which the implementation makes a significant difference. From our study of linked stacks and queues, we know that it is never difficult to delete the first node on a linked list. If we wish to delete a node p↑ that is not the first one, however, then to adjust the links, we must locate the link coming into p↑. In a simply linked list with only one pointer, this task is difficult, but with a second pointer r one step behind p, it is easy. After including appropriate error checking, we obtain the following procedure:

two-pointer deletion

```
procedure Delete(var p, r: pointer);
   {deletes node p↑ from a linked list; requires that r be one step behind p}
begin
   if (p = nil) or (r = nil) then
      Error                          {It is an error unless both nodes r↑ and p↑ exist.}
   else if r↑.next <> p then
      Error                          {We must be sure that p is one step ahead of r.}
   else begin
      p := p↑.next;                  {Move p to the first node beyond the one deleted.}
      r↑.next := p                   {Change the link to skip around the deleted node.}
   end
end;
```

This procedure as written keeps no pointer to the node being deleted, but does not dispose of it either. Instead, the procedure assumes that the deleted node is to be used by the calling program and the calling program will keep some pointer other than p with which to find the deleted node.

6. Other Implementations

Many variations are possible in the implementation of linked lists, some of which provide advantages in certain situations. In addition to the one-pointer and two-pointer simply linked lists, we might, for example, consider circularly linked lists in which the last node, rather than containing a **nil** link, has a link to the first node of the list (see Figure 4.8 and Exercise E6 of Section 4.2).

circularly linked list

doubly linked list

Another form of data structure is a ***doubly linked list*** (like the one shown in Figure 4.13) in which each node contains two links, one to the next node in the list and one to the preceding node. It is thus possible to move either direction through the list while keeping only one pointer. With a doubly linked list, traversals in either direction, insertions, and deletions from arbitrary positions in the list can be programmed without difficulty. The cost of a doubly linked list, of course, is the extra space required in each node for a second link.

dummy node

Yet one more variation in implementation is to include a ***dummy node*** at the beginning (or, less commonly, at the end) of a linked list. This dummy node contains no information and is used only to provide a link to the first true node of the list. It is never deleted and, if desired, can even be a static variable (that is, one declared

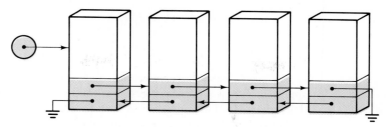

Figure 4.13.   Doubly linked list with header

as the program is written). Use of a dummy node at the head of the list simplifies the form of some procedures. Since the list is never empty, the special case of an empty list need not be considered, and neither does the special case of inserting or deleting at the head of the list.

Some of the exercises at the end of this section request procedures for manipulating doubly linked lists. We shall study linked lists with dummy header nodes in the application in the next section.

4.3.2 Comparison of Implementations

Now that we have seen several algorithms for manipulating linked lists and several variations in their implementation, let us pause to assess some relative advantages of linked and of contiguous implementation of lists.

advantages

The foremost advantage of dynamic storage for linked lists is flexibility. Overflow is no problem until the computer memory is actually exhausted. Especially when the individual records are quite large, it may be difficult to determine the amount of contiguous static storage that might be needed for the required arrays, while keeping

overflow

enough free for other needs. With dynamic allocation, there is no need to attempt to make such decisions in advance.

changes

Changes, especially insertions and deletions, can be made in the middle of a linked list more easily than in the middle of a contiguous list. Even queues are easier to handle in linked storage. If the records are large, then it is much quicker to change the values of a few pointers than to copy the records themselves from one location to another.

disadvantages

The first drawback of linked lists is that the links themselves take space, space that might otherwise be needed for additional data. In most systems, a pointer requires the same amount of storage (one word) as does an integer. Thus a list of integers will require double the space in linked storage that it would require in contiguous storage. On the other hand, in many practical applications, the nodes in the list are quite large, with data fields taking hundreds of words altogether. If each node contains

space use

100 words of data, then using linked storage will increase the memory requirement by only one percent, an insignificant amount. In fact, if extra space is allocated to arrays holding contiguous lists to allow for additional insertions, then linked storage will probably require less space altogether. If each item takes 100 words, then contiguous storage will save space only if all the arrays can be filled to more than 99 percent of capacity.

random access   The major drawback of linked lists is that they are not suited to random access. With contiguous storage, the program can refer to any position within a list as quickly as to any other position. With a linked list, it may be necessary to traverse a long path to reach the desired node.

programming   Finally, access to a node in linked storage may take slightly more computer time, since it is necessary, first, to obtain the pointer and then go to the address. This consideration, however, is usually of no importance. Similarly, you may find at first that writing procedures to manipulate linked lists takes a bit more programming effort, but, with practice, this discrepancy will decrease.

In summary, therefore, we can conclude that contiguous storage is generally preferable when the records are individually very small, when few insertions or deletions need to be made in the middle of a list, and when random access is important. Linked storage proves superior when the records are large and flexibility is needed in inserting, deleting, and rearranging the nodes.

4.3.3 Programming Hints

To close this section we include several suggestions for programming with linked lists, as well as some pitfalls to avoid.

pointers and pitfalls   1. Draw "before" and "after" diagrams of the appropriate part of the linked list, showing the relevant pointers and the way in which they should be changed.

2. To determine in what order values should be placed in the pointer fields to implement the various changes, it is usually better, first, to assign the values to previously undefined pointers, then to those with value **nil**, and finally to the remaining pointers. After one pointer variable has been copied to another, the first is free to be reassigned to its new location.

undefined links   3. Be sure that no links are left undefined at the conclusion of your algorithm, either as links in new nodes that have never been assigned or as links in old nodes that have become dangling, that is, that point to nodes that no longer are used. Such links should either be reassigned to nodes still in use or set to the value **nil**.

extreme cases   4. Always verify that your algorithm works correctly for an empty list and for a list with only one node.

multiple dereferencing   5. Never use constructions such as p↑.next↑.next, even though they are syntactically correct. A single variable should involve only a single pointer reference. Constructions with repeated references usually indicate that the algorithm can be improved by rethinking what pointer variables should be declared in the algorithm, introducing new ones if necessary, so that no variable includes more than one pointer reference (↑).

alias variable   6. It is possible that two (or more) different pointer variables can point to the same node. Since this node can thereby be accessed under two different names, it is called an *alias variable.* The node can be changed using one name and later used with the other name, perhaps without the realization that it has been changed. One pointer can be changed to another node, and the second left dangling. Alias variables are therefore dangerous and should be avoided as much as possible. Be sure you clearly understand whenever you must have two pointers that refer to the same node, and remember that changing one reference requires changing the other.

Exercises 4.3

E1. Write a Pascal function that counts the number of nodes in a linked list.

E2. Draw a before-and-after diagram describing the main action of the Delete procedure presented in the text.

E3. Write a procedure that will concatenate two linked lists. The procedure should have two parameters, pointers to the beginning of the lists, and the procedure should link the end of the first list to the beginning of the second.

E4. Write a procedure that will split a list in two. The procedure will use two pointers as parameters; p will point to the beginning of the list, and q to the node at which it should be split, so that all nodes before q↑ are in the first list and all nodes after q↑ are in the second list. You may decide whether the node q↑ itself will go into the first list or the second. State a reason for your decision.

E5. Write a procedure that will insert a node before the node p↑ of a linked list by the following method. First, insert the new node after p↑, then copy the information fields of p↑ into the new node, and then put the new information fields into p↑. Do you need to make a special case when p↑ is the first node of the list?

E6. Write a procedure to delete the node p↑ from a linked list when you are given only the pointer p without a second pointer in lock step.
  (a) Use the device of copying information fields from one node to another in designing your algorithm.
  (b) Will your procedure work when p↑ is the first or the last node in the list? If not, either describe the changes needed or state why it cannot be done without providing additional information to your procedure.
  (c) Suppose that you are also give a pointer head to the first node of the list. Write a deletion algorithm that does not copy information fields from node to node.

E7. Modify the procedure to traverse a linked list so that it will keep two pointers p and r in lock step, with r↑ always moving one node behind p↑ (that is, r↑ is one node closer to the head of the list). Explain how your procedure gets started and how it handles the special cases of an empty list and a list with only one node.

E8. Write a procedure that will reverse a linked list while traversing it only once. At the conclusion, each node should point to the node that was previously its predecessor; the head should point to the node that was formerly at the end, and the node that was formerly first should have a **nil** link.

E9. Write an algorithm that will split a linked list into two linked lists, so that successive nodes go to different lists. (The first, third, and all odd-numbered nodes go to the first list, and the second, fourth, and all even-numbered nodes go to the second.)

The following exercises concern circularly linked lists. See Figure 4.8 and Exercise 6 of Section 4.2. For each of these exercises, assume that the circularly linked list is specified by a pointer tail to its last node, and ensure that on conclusion your algorithm leaves the appropriate pointer(s) pointing to the tails of the appropriate list(s).

E10. Write a procedure to traverse a circularly linked list, visiting each node. First, do the case where only a single pointer moves through the list, and then describe the changes necessary to traverse the list with two pointers moving in lock step, one immediately behind the other.

E11. Write a procedure to delete a node from a circularly linked list.

E12. Write a procedure that will concatenate two circularly linked lists, producing a circularly linked list.

E13. Write a procedure that will split a circularly linked list into two circularly linked lists.

E14. Devise a procedure that will return all the nodes of a circularly linked list to the stack of available nodes studied in Section 4.2.3, such that the running time of your procedure does not depend on the number of nodes being returned.

E15. Write procedures for manipulating a doubly linked list as follows:
   (a) Add a node after p↑.
   (b) Add a node before p↑.
   (c) Delete node p↑.
   (d) Traverse the list.

E16. A doubly linked list can be made circular by setting the values of links in the first and last nodes appropriately. Discuss the advantages and disadvantages of a circular doubly linked list in doing the various list operations.

E17. Make a chart that will compare the difficulties of doing various operations on different implementations of lists. The rows should correspond to all the operations on lists specified in Section 3.5.3 and the columns to (a) contiguous lists, (b) simply linked lists, and (c) doubly linked lists. Fill in the entries to show the relative difficulty of each operation for each implementation. Take into account both programming difficulty and expected running time.

4.4 APPLICATION: POLYNOMIAL ARITHMETIC

4.4.1 Purpose of the Project

calculator for polynomials

As an application of linked lists, this section outlines a program for manipulating polynomials. Our program will imitate the behavior of a simple calculator that does addition, subtraction, multiplication, division, and perhaps some other operations, but one that performs these operations for polynomials.

There are many kinds of calculators available, and we could model our program after any of them. To provide a further illustration of the use of stacks, however, let us choose to model what is often called a **reverse Polish** calculator. In such a calculator, the operands (numbers usually, polynomials for us) are entered *before* the operation is specified. The operands are pushed onto a stack. When an operation is performed, it pops its operands from the stack and pushes its result back onto the stack. If ? denotes pushing an operand onto the stack, $+$, $-$, $*$, $/$ represent arithmetic operations, and $=$ means printing the top of the stack (but not popping it off), then ? ? $+$ $=$ means reading two operands, then calculating and printing their sum. The instruction ? ? $+$? ? $+$ $*$ $=$ requests four operands. If these are a, b, c, d, then the result printed is (a $+$ b) $*$ (c $+$ d). Similarly, ? ? ? $-$ $=$ $*$? $+$ $=$ pushes a, b, c onto the stack, replaces b, c by b $-$ c and prints its value, calculates a$*$(b $-$ c), pushes d on the stack, and finally calculates and prints (a $*$(b $-$ c)) $+$ d. The advantage of a reverse Polish calculator is that any expression, no matter how complicated, can be specified without the use of parentheses.

This Polish notation is useful for compilers as well as for calculators, and its study forms the major topic of Chapter 12. For the present, however, a few minutes' practice with a reverse Polish calculator will make you quite comfortable with its use.

4.4.2 The Main Program

1. Outline

The task of the calculator program is quite simple in principle. It need only accept new commands and perform them as long as desired. In preliminary outline, the main program takes the form

```
program Calculator(input, output);                        {preliminary outline}
begin
   Initialize(S);                    {Let S be the stack; initialize it to be empty.}
   while there are more commands do
   begin
      GetCommand(com);        {Let com denote the command ready to be done.}
      DoCommand(com, S)
   end
end.
```

2. Performing Commands

To turn this outline into Pascal, we must specify what it means to obtain commands and how this will be done. Before doing so, let us make the decision to represent the commands by the characters ?, $=$, $+$, $-$, $*$, $/$. Given this decision, we can immediately write the procedure DoCommand in Pascal, thereby specifying exactly what each command does:

stack operations

```
procedure DoCommand(com: char; var S: stack);
var
  p, q, r: polynomial;                              {names for the polynomials in use}
begin                                               {procedure DoCommand}
  case com of
```
input
```
    '?': begin                        {Input a polynomial and push it onto the stack.}
           ReadPolynomial(p);
           Push(p, S)
         end;
```
output
```
    '=': WritePolynomial(TopStack(S));
                              {Print the polynomial on the top of the stack.}
          {The function TopStack returns the top of stack, but does not change it.}
```
addition
```
    '+':begin              {Pop the top two polynomials, add them, push answer.}
           Pop(p, S);
           Pop(q, S);
           Add(p, q, r);                                       {sets r := p + q}
           Push(r, S);
           Erase(p);           {Remove the polynomial so its space can be reused.}
           Erase(q)
         end;
```
subtraction
```
    '−':begin         {Pop the top two polynomials, subtract them, push answer.}
           Pop(p, S);
           Pop(q, S);
           Subtract(p, q, r);                                  {sets r := q − p}
           Push(r, S);
           Erase(p);
           Erase(q)
         end;
```
multiplication
```
    '*': begin        {Pop the top two polynomials, multiply them, push answer.}
           Pop(p, S);
           Pop(q, S);
           Multiply(p, q, r);                                  {sets r := p * q}
           Push(r, S);
           Erase(p);
           Erase(q)
         end;
```
division
```
    '/': begin           {Pop the top two polynomials, divide them, push answer.}
           Pop(p, S);
           Pop(q, S);
           Divide(p, q, r);                             {sets r := q divided by p}
           Push(r, S);
           Erase(p);
           Erase(q)
         end
  end
end;                                                   {procedure DoCommand}
```

3. Reading Commands: The Main Program

Now that we have decided that the commands are to be denoted as single characters, we could easily program procedure GetCommand to read one command at a time from the terminal. It is often convenient, however, to read a string of several commands at once, such as ? ? + ? ? + * =, and then perform them all before reading more. To allow for this possibility, let us read a whole line of commands at once and set up an array to hold them. With this decision we can now write the main program in its final form, except for the additional declarations that we shall insert after choosing our data structures. We shall use a procedure ReadCommand to read the string of commands; this procedure will also be responsible for error checking. We shall use the procedure Enquire from Section 1.4.3.

main program

```
program Calculator(input, output);
const
  max = 80;              {maximum number of commands to be done at one time}
type
  index = 0 .. max;
  string = array[1 .. max] of char;
                                {holds the list of commands to be done}
  {Additional type declarations are to be inserted here.}
var
  command:   string;
  i,                             {index of current command}
  n:         index;       {total number of commands in current string}
  S:         stack;
  again:     Boolean;
  {Declarations of procedures and functions are to be inserted later.}
begin                                        {main program Calculator}
  Initialize(S);
  repeat
    Prompt;
    ReadCommand(command, n);
    for i := 1 to n do
      DoCommand(command[i], S);
    Enquire(again)
  until not again
end.                                         {main program Calculator}
```

4. Input Procedures

Before we turn to our principal task (deciding how to represent polynomials and writing procedures to manipulate them), let us complete the preliminaries by giving details for the input procedures. The prompting procedure need only write one line, but note that this line gives the user the opportunity to request further instructions if desired.

prompting user

```
procedure Prompt;
begin
  writeln('Enter a string of commands or ! for instructions.')
end;
```

Procedure ReadCommand must check that the symbols typed in represent legitimate operations and must provide instructions if desired, along with doing its main task. If there is an error or the user requests instructions, then the command string must be reentered from the start.

read commands

```
procedure ReadCommand(var command: string; var n: index);
var
  OK: Boolean;              {Have all characters read so far been acceptable?}
begin                                              {procedure ReadCommand}
  repeat                    {Main loop will repeat until the whole line is OK.}
    n := 0;
    OK := true;
    while OK and (not eoln) do
    begin
      n := n + 1;
      read(command[n]);
      if command[n] in [' ', ','] then
        n := n - 1          {Skip blanks and commas in the command stream.}
      else if command[n] = '!' then               {User requests instructions.}
      begin
        OK := false;
        writeln('Enter a string of instructions in reverse Polish form.');
        writeln('The allowable instructions are:');
        writeln('   ?   Read a polynomial onto stack    =   Print top of stack');
        writeln('   +   Add top two poly''s on stack    −   Subtract top two');
        writeln('   *   Multiply top two on stack       /   Divide top two')
      end
      else
        OK := (command[n] in ['?', '=', '+', '−', '*', '/']) and (n < max)
    end;            {end of while loop considering one character per iteration}
    readln;
    if not OK then                        {Request repetition of the entire line.}
      Prompt
  until OK
end;                                               {procedure ReadCommand}
```

instructions

error checking

5. Stubs and Testing

At this point we have written quite enough of our program that we should pause to compile it, debug it, and test it to make sure that what has been done so far is correct. If we were to wait until all remaining procedures had been written, the program would become so long and complicated that debugging would be much more difficult.

For the task of compiling the program, we must, of course, supply stubs for all the missing procedures. At present, however, we have not even completed the type declarations: The most important one, that of a polynomial, remains unspecified. We could make this type declaration almost arbitrarily and still be able to compile the program, but for testing, it is much better to make the temporary type declaration

temporary type declaration

$$\text{polynomial} = \text{real}$$

and test the program by running it as an ordinary reverse Polish calculator. The following is then typical of the stubs that are needed:

stub

```
procedure Add(p, q: polynomial; var r: polynomial);
begin
   r := p + q
end;
```

stack package

In addition to stubs of the procedures for doing arithmetic and the procedure Erase (which need do nothing), we need a package of procedures to manipulate the stack. If you wish, you may use the package for linked stacks developed in this chapter, but with the items in the stack only real numbers, it is probably easier to use the contiguous stack algorithms developed in Section 3.2. The procedure Initialize and the function TopStack do not appear there, but are trivial to write. With these tools we can fully debug and test the part of the program now written, after which we can turn to the remainder of the project.

4.4.3 Data Structures and Their Implementation

If we carefully consider a polynomial such as

$$3x^5 - 2x^3 + x^2 + 4$$

essence of a polynomial

we see that the important information about the polynomial is contained in the coefficients and exponents of x; the variable x itself is really just a place holder (a dummy variable). Hence, for purposes of calculation, we may think of a polynomial as a sum of terms, each of which consists of a coefficient and an exponent. In a computer we can similarly implement a polynomial as a list of pairs of coefficients and exponents. Each of these pairs will constitute a record, so a polynomial will be represented as a list of records. We must then build into our procedures rules for performing arithmetic on two such lists.

implementation of a polynomial

Should we use contiguous or linked lists? If, in advance, we know a bound on the degree of the polynomials that can occur and if the polynomials that occur have nonzero coefficients in almost all their possible terms, then we should probably do better with contiguous lists. But if we do not know a bound on the degree, or if polynomials with only a few nonzero terms are likely to appear, then we shall find linked storage preferable. To illustrate the use of linked lists, we adopt the latter implementation, as illustrated in Figure 4.14.

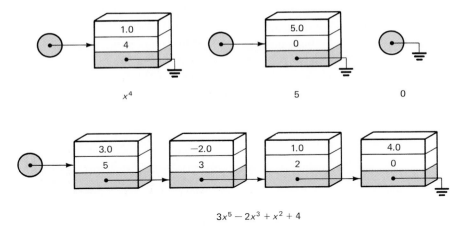

$$3x^5 - 2x^3 + x^2 + 4$$

Figure 4.14.   Polynomials as linked lists

assumptions

We shall consider that each node represents one term of a polynomial, and we shall keep only nonzero terms in the list. The polynomial that is identically 0 will be represented by an empty list. Hence each node will be a record containing a nonzero coefficient, an exponent, and, as usual for linked lists, a pointer to the next term of the polynomial. To refer to polynomials, we shall always use header variables for the lists; hence, it is sensible to make the type polynomial a pointer type and use it for the headers. Moreover, the remaining terms after any given one are again a (smaller) polynomial, so the field next again naturally has type polynomial. As Pascal declarations to insert in the main program, we thus obtain

type polynomial

```
type
  polynomial = ↑term;
  term       = record
                 coef: real;
                 exp:  integer;
                 next: polynomial
               end;
```

We have not yet indicated the order of storing the terms of the polynomial. If we allow them to be stored in any order, then it might be difficult to recognize that

$$x^5 + x^2 - 3 \quad\text{and}\quad -3 + x^5 + x^2 \quad\text{and}\quad x^2 - 3 + x^5$$

restriction

all represent the same polynomial. Hence we adopt the usual convention that the terms of every polynomial are stored in the order of decreasing exponent within the linked list, and we further assume that no two terms have the same exponent and that no term has a zero coefficient.

4.4.4 Reading and Writing Polynomials

With polynomials implemented as linked lists, writing out a polynomial becomes simply a traversal of the list, as follows.

writing

```
procedure WritePolynomial(p: polynomial);
begin                                              {procedure WritePolynomial}
  if p = nil then                  {Make sure something is written for an empty list.}
    writeln('zero polynomial')
  else while p <> nil do
  begin
    write(p↑.coef: 5: 2, 'x↑', p↑.exp: 1);
    p := p↑.next;
    if p <> nil then      {Write a + sign only between terms, not after the last.}
      write(' + ')
  end;
  writeln
end;                                               {procedure WritePolynomial}
```

As we read in a new polynomial, we shall be constructing a new linked list, adding a node to the list for each term (coefficient-exponent pair) that we read. The process of creating a new node, attaching it to the tail of a list, putting in the coefficient and exponent, and updating the tail pointer to point to the new term will reappear in almost every procedure for manipulating polynomials. We therefore write it as a separate utility.

making one term

```
procedure InsertTerm(coef: real; exp: integer; var tail: polynomial);
{Create a new term with the given coefficient and exponent and update tail to
  point to the new term; tail always points to the last term of the polynomial;
  procedure requires that tail <> nil.}
begin                                              {procedure InsertTerm}
  new(tail↑.next);      {Make a new term attached to the end of the polynomial.}
  tail := tail↑.next;                       {Update tail to point to the new term.}
  tail↑.coef := coef;                          {Insert information for the new term.}
  tail↑.exp := exp;
end;                                               {procedure InsertTerm}
```

We can now use this procedure to insert new terms as we read coefficient-exponent pairs. InsertTerm, however, expects to insert the new term *after* the term to which tail currently points, so how do we make the first term of the list? One way is to write a separate section of code. It is easier, however, to use a **dummy header,** as follows. Before starting to read, we make a new node at the head of the list, but we put no information into it. We then insert all the actual terms, each one inserted after the preceding one. When the procedure concludes, the head pointer is advanced one position to the first actual term, and the dummy node is disposed of. This process is illustrated in Figure 4.15 and is implemented in the following procedure:

dummy first node

reading

```
procedure ReadPolynomial(var result: polynomial);
var
    finished:        Boolean;              {Has reading the polynomial been finished?}
    coefficient:     real;
    exponent,
    lastexponent: integer;                 {used to check that exponents descend in size}
    tail:            polynomial;           {used to transverse new polynomial}
begin                                      {procedure ReadPolynomial}
```

instructions

```
    writeln('Enter coefficients and exponents for the polynomial, one per line.');
    writeln('Exponents must be in descending order.');
    writeln('Enter coefficient or exponent of 0 to terminate.');
```

initialize

```
    lastexponent := maxint;
    new(result);                           {Make a temporary dummy head for the polynomial.}
    tail := result;                        {Start traversal at the dummy head.}
```

read one term

```
    repeat
        write('coefficient? ');
        readln(coefficient);
        finished := (coefficient = 0.0);
        if not finished then
        begin
            write('exponent? ');
            readln(exponent);
            if (exponent >= lastexponent) or (exponent < 0) then
```

error checking

```
            begin
                finished := true;
                writeln('Bad exponent. Polynomial is terminated without its last term.')
            end
```

make one term

```
            else begin
                InsertTerm(coefficient, exponent, tail);
                lastexponent := exponent;
                finished := (exponent = 0)
            end
        end
    until finished;
```

conclude

```
    tail↑.next := nil;                     {Terminate the polynomial.}
    tail := result;                        {Prepare to dispose of the dummy head.}
    result := result↑.next;                {Advance result to the first actual term.}
    dispose(tail)
end;                                       {procedure ReadPolynomial}
```

4.4.5 Addition of Polynomials

The requirement that the terms of a polynomial appear with descending exponents
in the list simplifies their addition. To add two polynomials we need only scan through
them once each. If we find terms with the same exponent in the two polynomials,

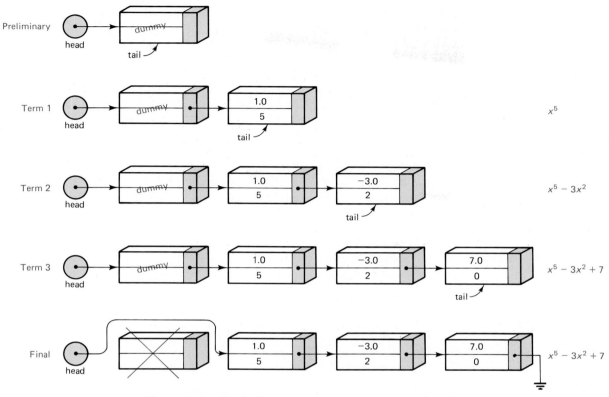

Figure 4.15.   Construction of a linked list with dummy node

then we add the coefficients; otherwise, we copy the term of larger exponent into the sum and go on. When we reach the end of one of the polynomials, then any remaining part of the other is copied to the sum. We must also be careful not to include terms with zero coefficient in the sum.

```
procedure Add(summand1, summand2: polynomial; var result: polynomial);
var
    p,                                       {pointer to traverse first summand}
    q,                                      {pointer to traverse second summand}
    tail: polynomial;                              {pointer to traverse result}
    sum: real;                                 {coefficient of a tentative term}
begin                                                         {procedure Add}
    p := summand1;                      {Start p at the first term of its polynomial.}
    q := summand2;                                                {same for q}
    new(result);                             {Create a new dummy head for the result.}
    tail := result;                    {Tail starts at the dummy head and will be advanced
                                       through the new polynomial by procedure InsertTerm.}
```

initialize

equal-exponent terms
```
                                while (p <> nil) and (q <> nil) do
                                    if p↑.exp = q↑.exp then
                                    begin                                  {Add terms with equal exponents.}
                                        sum := p↑.coef + q↑.coef;
                                        if sum <> 0.0 then
                                                    {A term with 0.0 coefficient is not put into the polynomial.}
                                            InsertTerm(sum, p↑.exp, tail);
                                        p := p↑.next;                              {Advance both pointers.}
                                        q := q↑.next
                                    end
```

unequal exponents
```
                                    else if p↑.exp > q↑.exp then
                                    begin                    {Copy from p, since p has the larger exponent.}
                                        InsertTerm(p↑.coef, p↑.exp, tail);
                                        p := p↑.next
                                    end
                                    else begin               {Copy from q, since q has the larger exponent.}
                                        InsertTerm(q↑.coef, q↑.exp, tail);
                                        q := q↑.next
                                    end;
```

remaining terms
```
                                {At this point the while loop terminates and one of the two summands has
                                been exhausted. At most one of the following copying loops will be executed.}
                                while p <> nil do
                                begin
                                    InsertTerm(p↑.coef, p↑.exp, tail);
                                    p := p↑.next
                                end;
                                while q <> nil do
                                begin
                                    InsertTerm(q↑.coef, q↑.exp, tail);
                                    q := q↑.next
                                end;
```

conclude
```
                                tail↑.next := nil;                    {Finally terminate the result polynomial.}
                                p := result;                 {Remember dummy head of the result polynomial.}
                                result := result↑.next;
                                            {Advance the start from the dummy to the first actual term.}
                                    dispose(p)                                    {Remove the dummy head.}
                            end;                                                      {procedure Add}
```

4.4.6 Completing the Project

1. The Missing Procedures

At this point the remaining procedures for the calculator project are sufficiently similar to those already written that they can be left as exercises. The procedure Erase need only traverse the list (as done in WritePolynomial) disposing of the nodes as it goes. Procedures for the remaining arithmetical operations have the same general form as our procedure for addition. Some of these are easy: Subtraction is almost identical with addition. For multiplication we can first write (a simple) procedure that multiplies a polynomial by a monomial, where *monomial* means a polynomial with only one term. Then we combine use of this procedure with the addition procedure to do a general multiplication. Division is a little more complicated.

2. Group Project

Production of a coherent package of algorithms for manipulating polynomials makes an interesting group project. Different members of the group can write functions or procedures for different operations. Some of these are indicated as projects at the end of this section, but you may wish to include additional features as well. Any additional features should be planned carefully to be sure that they can be implemented in a reasonable time, without disrupting other parts of the program.

specifications

After deciding on the division of work among its members, the most important decisions of the group relate to the exact ways in which the procedures and functions should communicate with each other, and especially with the calling program. If you wish to make any changes in the organization of the program, be certain that the precise details are spelled out clearly and completely for all members of the group.

cooperation

Next, you will find that it is too much to hope that all members of the group will complete their work at the same time, or that all parts of the project can be combined and debugged together. You will therefore need to use program stubs and drivers (see Sections 1.4.1 and 1.4.4) to debug and test the various parts of the project. One member of the group might take special responsibility for these. In any case, you will find it very effective for different members to read, help debug, and test each other's subprograms.

coordination

Finally, there are the responsibilities of making sure that all members of the group complete their work on time, of keeping track of the progress of various aspects of the project, of making sure that no subprograms are integrated into the project before they are thoroughly debugged and tested, and then of combining all the work into the finished product.

Exercises 4.4

E1. Decide whether the stack for the calculator should be contiguous or linked. Justify your decision. Incorporate the necessary procedures to implement the stack in the way you decide.

E2. A function in Pascal can return a pointer as its result. We could therefore write the arithmetic operations as functions, for example,

function Subtract(p, q: polynomial): polynomial;

We could also write Pop(S) as a function that returns the top polynomial on the stack as its result. Then procedure DoCommand could be shortened considerably by writing such statements as

Push(Subtract(Pop(S), Pop(S)), S);

(a) Assuming that this statement works correctly, explain why it would still be bad programming style.

(b) It is possible that two different Pascal compilers, both adhering strictly to standard Pascal, would translate this statement in ways that would give different answers when the program runs. Explain how this could happen.

E3. Find what changes are needed in the procedures and functions of this section so as to use the method of Section 4.2.3 to reuse space for terms on systems where the standard procedure dispose( ) does not work efficiently.

E4. If polynomials are stored as circularly linked lists instead of simply linked lists, then a polynomial can be erased more quickly. What changes are needed to the addition function (and other subprograms) to implement circularly linked lists?

E5. Consider generalizing the project of this section to polynomials in several variables.

Programming Projects 4.4

P1. Write procedure Erase.

P2. Write procedure Subtract.

P3. Write a procedure that will multiply a polynomial by a monomial (that is, by a polynomial consisting of a single term).

P4. Use the procedure of the preceding problem, together with the procedure that adds polynomials, to write the procedure Multiply.

P5. Write procedure Divide.

P6. The procedure ReadCommand, as written, will accept any sequence of commands, but some sequences are illegal. If the stack begins empty, for example, then the sequence + ? ? is illegal, because it is impossible to add two polynomials before reading them in. Modify procedure ReadCommand as follows so that it will accept only legal sequences of commands. The procedure should set up a counter and initialize it to the number of polynomials on the stack. Whenever the command ? appears in the stream, the counter is increased by one (since the read command ? will push an additional polynomial onto the stack), and whenever one of +, −, *, / appears, it is decreased by one (since these commands will pop two polynomials and push one onto the stack). If the counter ever becomes zero or negative then the sequence is illegal.

P7. Many reverse Polish calculators use not only a stack but also provide memory locations where operands can be stored. Extend the project to provide for memory locations for polynomials, and provide additional commands to store the top of the stack into a memory location and to push the polynomial in a memory location onto the stack.

P8. Write a procedure that will discard the top polynomial on the stack, and include this capability as a new command.

P9. Write a procedure that will interchange the top two polynomials on the stack, and include this capability as a new command.

P10. Write a procedure that will add all the polynomials on the stack together, and include this capability as a new command.

P11. Write a procedure that will compute the derivative of a polynomial, and include this capability as a new command.

P12. Write a procedure that, given a polynomial and a real number, evaluates the polynomial at that number, and include this capability as a new command.

P13. [Requires some knowledge of numerical methods]   Write a procedure that will determine all real roots of a polynomial, and include this capability as a new command.

P14. Same as the preceding project, but find all complex roots and multiplicities.

P15. Write a procedure that will print a polynomial as a product of linear factors, arranged attractively, and include this capability as a new command. [Use the procedure of the previous project to find the roots.]

P16. Modify the procedure Divide so that the result of the procedure will be two new polynomials, the quotient and the remainder, where the remainder, if not 0, has degree strictly less than that of the divisor.

4.5 LINKED LISTS IN ARRAYS

old languages

Several of the older but widely used computer languages, such as FORTRAN, COBOL, and BASIC, do not provide facilities for dynamic storage allocation or pointers. Even when implemented in these languages, however, there are many problems where the methods of linked lists are preferable to those of contiguous lists, where, for example, the ease of changing a pointer rather than copying a large record proves advantageous. This section shows how to implement linked lists using only simple integer variables and arrays.

The idea is to begin with a large array (or several arrays to hold different parts of a record) and regard the array as our allocation of unused space. We then set up our own procedures to keep track of which parts of the array are unused and to link entries of the array together in the desired order.

dynamic memory

The one feature of linked lists that we must invariably lose in this implementation method is the dynamic allocation of storage, since we must decide in advance how much space to allocate to each array. All the remaining advantages of linked lists, such as flexibility in rearranging large records or ease in making insertions or deletions anywhere in the list, will still apply, and linked lists still prove a valuable method.

advantages

The implementation of linked lists within arrays even proves valuable in languages like Pascal that do provide pointer types and dynamic memory allocation. The applications where arrays may prove preferable are those where the number of items in a list is known in advance, where the links are frequently rearranged, but relatively few additions or deletions are made, or applications where the same data are sometimes best treated as a linked list and other times as a contiguous list. An example of such an application is illustrated in Figure 4.16, which shows a small part of a student record system. Identification numbers are assigned to students first-come, first-served, so neither the names nor the marks in any particular course are in any special order.

multiple linkages

Given an identification number, a student's records may be found immediately by using the identification number as an index to look in the arrays. Sometimes, however, it is desired to print out the student records alphabetically by name, and this can be done by following the links stored in the array nextname. Similarly, student records can be ordered by marks in any course by following the links in the appropriate array.

cursors

In the implementation of linked lists in arrays, pointers become indices relative to the start of arrays, and the links of a list are stored in an array, each entry of

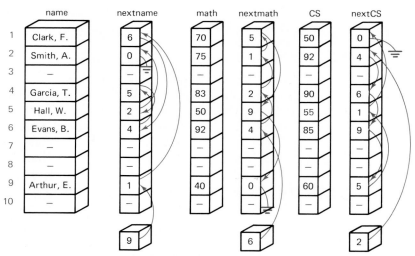

Figure 4.16.   Linked lists in arrays

which gives the index where, within the array, the next entry of the list is stored. To distinguish these indices from the pointers of a linked list in dynamic storage, we shall refer to links within arrays as *cursors* and reserve the word *pointer* for links in dynamic storage.

For the sake of writing programs we shall use two arrays for each linked list, info[ ] to hold the information in the nodes and next[ ] to give the cursor to the next node. These arrays will be indexed from 1 to max, where max is a constant. Since we begin the indices with 1, we can make another arbitrary choice, and use the cursor value 0 to indicate the end of the list, just as the pointer value **nil** is used in dynamic storage. This choice is also illustrated in Figure 4.16.

You should take a moment to trace through Figure 4.16, checking that the cursor values as shown correspond to the arrows shown from each entry to its successor.

To obtain the flavor of implementing linked lists in arrays, let us rewrite several of the algorithms of this chapter with this implementation.

new *and* dispose

Our first task is to set up a list of available space and write procedures to obtain a new node and to return a node to available space. As in Section 4.2.3 we shall set up a stack to keep track of available space, but now this stack will be linked by means of cursors in the array next. To keep track of the stack of available space, we need an integer variable avail that will give the index of its top. If this stack is empty (which will be represented by avail = 0), then we will need to obtain a new node, that is, a position within the array that has not yet been used for any node. Thus we shall keep another integer variable lastnode that will count the total number of positions within our array that have been used to hold list entries. When lastnode exceeds max (the bound we have assumed for array size), then we will have overflow and the program can proceed no further. When the main program starts, both variables avail and lastnode should be initialized to 0, avail to indicate that the stack of space previously used but now available is empty, and lastnode to indicate that no space from the array has yet been assigned. This available-space list is illustrated in Figure

4.17. This figure, by the way, also illustrates how two linked lists can coexist in the same array.

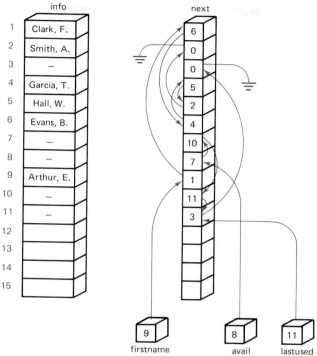

Figure 4.17. The available-space list

The decisions we have made translate into the following declarations:

declarations

```
type
  cursor = 0 .. max;
  table  = array[1 .. max] of cursor;
var
  avail,                              {top of the stack of unused space}
  lastnode,                          {last location in the array used for a node}
  head:    cursor;                    {start of a linked list in the array}
  next:    table;
```

With these declarations we can now rewrite the procedures for keeping track of unused space. At the start of the program, the lists should be initialized by invoking the following:

initialization

```
procedure Initialize(var avail, lastnode: cursor);
begin
  avail := 0;            {The stack of previously used available nodes is empty.}
  lastnode := 0;          {None of the positions in the array has been used yet.}
end;
```

The procedures NewNode and DisposeNode now take the form

new

```
procedure NewNode(var c, avail, lastnode: cursor, var next: table);
{sets c to the index of the first available position}
begin                                                {procedure NewNode}
  if avail <> 0 then
  begin
    c := avail;
    avail := next[avail]
  end
  else if lastnode < max then
  begin
    lastnode := lastnode + 1;
    c := lastnode
  end
  else
    Error                              {Overflow: The array is completely full.}
end;                                                 {procedure NewNode}
```

dispose

```
procedure DisposeNode(c: cursor; var avail: cursor; var next: table);
{returns the node at position c to the stack of available space}
begin                                              {procedure DisposeNode}
  if c = 0 then
    Error                              {attempt to dispose of a nonexistent node}
  else begin
    next[c] := avail;
    avail := c
  end
end;                                               {procedure DisposeNode}
```

The translation of other procedures so as to manipulate linked lists implemented within arrays proceeds in much the same way, and most of these will be left as exercises. To provide further models, however, let us write translations of the procedures to traverse a list and to add a node after a given one in a list.

traverse

```
procedure Traverse(head: cursor; var next: table; procedure Visit(c: cursor));
{Traverse the linked list starting at position head with links in table next; use
    procedure Visit to perform the desired task at each node.}
var
  c: cursor;                               {starts at head and moves through list}
begin                                                {procedure Traverse}
  c := head;
  while c <> 0 do
  begin
    Visit(c);
    c := next[c]
  end
end;                                                 {procedure Traverse}
```

insert after

```
procedure InsertAfter(c, d: cursor; var next: table);
{Insert the node at location c into the linked list after the node at d.}
begin                                              {procedure InsertAfter}
    if (c = 0) or (d = 0) then
        Error                    {Both nodes must exist to perform the insertion.}
    else begin
        next[c] := next[d];            {New node points where old node does.}
        next[d] := c;                     {Old node points to the new one.}
    end
end;                                               {procedure InsertAfter}
```

Exercises 4.5

E1. Draw arrows showing how the list entries are linked together in each of the following next tables. Some tables contain more than one list.

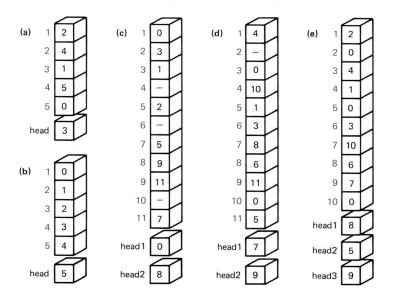

E2. Construct next tables showing how each of the following lists is linked into alphabetical order. Also give the value of the variable head that starts the list.

(a)
1 array
2 stack
3 queue
4 list
5 deque
6 scroll

(b)
1 push
2 pop
3 add
4 delete
5 insert

(c)
1 the
2 of
3 and
4 to
5 a
6 in
7 that
8 is
9 I
10 it
11 for
12 as

(d)
1 London
2 England
3 Rome
4 Italy
5 Madrid
6 Spain
7 Oslo
8 Norway
9 Paris
10 France
11 Warsaw
12 Poland

E3. For the list of cities and countries in part (d) of the previous question construct a next table that produces two linked lists, one containing all the cities in alphabetical order and the other all the countries in alphabetical order. Also give values to the two header variables.

E4. Write a function that counts the number of nodes in a linked list implemented in an array.

E5. Write a procedure that will concatenate two linked lists. The procedure should have two parameters, cursors to the beginning of the lists, and the procedure should link the end of the first list to the beginning of the second.

E6. Write a procedure that will split a list in two. The procedure will use two cursors as parameters; b will point to the beginning of the list and c to the node at which it should be split. It is easier to require that c initially point to the node that will be last in the first list after splitting or to the node that will be first in the second list?

E7. Write a procedure that will reverse a linked list within an array while traversing it only once. At the conclusion, each node should point to the node that was previously its predecessor; the header should point to the node that was formerly at the end, and node that was formerly first should have a 0 cursor.

4.6 ABSTRACT DATA TYPES AND THEIR IMPLEMENTATIONS

4.6.1 Introduction

Suppose that in deciphering a long and poorly documented program you found the following sets of instructions:

$$\text{xxt}\uparrow.\text{xlnk} := \text{w;} \qquad \text{w}\uparrow.\text{xlnk} := \textbf{nil;} \qquad \text{xxt} := \text{w;}$$

reading programs   and

```
if ((xxh = xxt + 1) and (xxt > 0)) or ((xxt = mxx) and (xxh = 1))
   then tryagain
   else begin
      xxt := xxt + 1;
      if xxt > mxx then xxt := 1;
      xx[xxt] := wi
   end;
```

In isolation it may not be clear what either of these sections of code is intended to do, and without further explanation, it would probably take some minutes to realize that in fact they have essentially the same function! Both segments are intended to add an item to the end of a queue, the first queue in a linked implementation and the second queue in contiguous storage.

Researchers working in different subjects frequently have ideas that are fundamentally similar but are developed for different purposes and expressed in different language. Often years will pass before anyone realizes the similarity of the work, but

analogies

when the observation is made, insight from one subject can help with the other. In computer science, even so, the same basic idea often appears in quite different disguises that obscure the similarity. But if we can discover and emphasize the similarities, then we may be able to generalize the ideas and obtain easier ways to meet the requirements of many applications.

similarity

When we first introduced stacks and queues in Chapter 3, we considered them only as they are implemented in contiguous storage, and yet upon introduction of linked stacks and queues in this chapter, we had no difficulty in recognizing the same underlying logical structure. The obscurity of the code at the beginning of this section reflects the programmer's failure to recognize the general concept of a queue and to distinguish between this general concept and the particular implementation needed for each application.

implementation

The way in which an underlying structure is implemented can have substantial effects on program development, and on the capabilities and usefulness of the result. Sometimes these effects can be subtle. The underlying mathematical concept of a real number, for example, is usually (but not always) implemented by computer as a floating-point number with a certain degree of precision, and the inherent limitations in this implementation often produce difficulties with round-off error. Drawing a clear separation between the logical structure of our data and its implementation in computer memory will help us in designing programs. Our first step is to recognize the logical connections among the data and embody these connections in a logical data structure. Later we can consider our data structures and decide what is the best way to implement them for efficiency of programming and execution. By separating these decisions, they both become easier, and we avoid pitfalls that attend premature commitment.

To help us clarify this distinction and achieve greater generality, let us now reconsider some of the data structures we have studied from as general a perspective as we can.

4.6.2 General Definitions

1. Mathematical Concepts

Mathematics is the quintessence of generalization and therefore provides the language we need for our definitions. The place to start is the definition of a type:

DEFINITION
> A *type* is a set, and the elements of the set are called the *values* of the type.

We may therefore speak of the type *integer,* meaning the set of all integers, the type *real,* meaning the set of all real numbers, or the type *character,* meaning the set of symbols that we wish to manipulate in our algorithms.

Notice that we can already draw a distinction between an abstract type and its implementation: The Pascal type integer, for example, is not the set of all integers; it consists only of the set of those integers directly represented in a particular computer, the largest of which is maxint. Similarly, the Pascal type real generally means a certain set of floating-point numbers (separate mantissa and exponent) that is only a small subset of the set of all real numbers. The Pascal type char also varies from computer to computer; sometimes it is the ASCII character set given in Appendix C.3; sometimes it is the EBCDIC character set; sometimes it is some other set of symbols. Even so, all these types, both abstract types and implementations, are sets and hence fit the definition of a type.

2. Atomic and Structured Types

Types such as integer, real, and character are called *atomic* types because we think of their values as single entities only, not something we wish to subdivide. Computer languages like Pascal, however, provide tools such as arrays, files, and pointers with which we can build new types, called *structured* types. A single value of a structured type (that is, a single element of its set) is an array or file or linked list. A value of a structured type has two ingredients: It is made up of *component* elements, and there is a *structure,* a set of rules for putting the components together.

building types   For our general point of view we shall use mathematical tools to provide the rules for building up structured types. Among these tools are sets, sequences, and functions. For the study of lists the one that we need is the *finite sequence,* and for its definition we use mathematical induction. A definition by induction (like a proof by induction) has two parts: First is an intitial case, and second is the definition of the general case in terms of preceding cases.

DEFINITION   A *sequence of length* 0 is empty. A *sequence of length* $n \geq 1$ of elements from a set T is an ordered pair (S_{n-1}, t), where S_{n-1} is a sequence of length $n - 1$ of elements from T, and t is an element of T.

From this definition we can build up longer and longer sequences, starting with the empty sequence and adding on new elements from T, one at a time.

sequential versus   From now on we shall draw a careful distinction between the word *sequential,*
contiguous   meaning that the elements form a sequence, and the word *contiguous,* which we take to mean that the nodes have adjacent addresses in memory. Hence we shall be able to speak of a *sequential* list in either a *linked* or *contiguous* implementation.

3. Abstract Data Types

The definition of a finite sequence immediately makes it possible for us to attempt a definition of a list: A *list* of terms of a type T is simply a finite sequence of elements of the set T. Next we would like to define stacks and queues, but if you consider the definitions, you will realize that there will be nothing regarding the sequence of items to distinguish these structures from a list. The only difference
structure and   among stacks, queues, and more general lists is in the *operations* by which changes
operations   or accesses can be made to the list. Hence, before turning to these other structures, we should complete the definition of a list by specifying what operations can be done with a list. Including a statement of these operations with the structural rules defining a finite sequence, we obtain

DEFINITION   A *list* of elements of type T is a finite sequence of elements of T together with the operations

1. Initialize the list to be empty.
2. Determine whether the list is empty or not.
3. Determine whether the list is full or not.
4. Find the length of the list.
5. Retrieve any node from the list, provided that the list is not empty.
6. Store a new node replacing the node at any position in the list, provided that the list is not empty.
7. Insert a new node into the list at any position, provided that the list is not full.
8. Delete any node from the list, provided that the list is not empty.

It is now easy to see what changes are needed to define stacks and queues.

DEFINITION

*A **stack** of elements of type T is a finite sequence of elements of T together with the operations*

1. Initialize the stack to be empty.
2. Determine if the stack is empty or not.
3. Determine if the stack is full or not.
4. If the stack is not full, then insert a new node at one end of the stack, called its *top.*
5. If the stack is not empty, then retrieve the node at its top.
6. If the stack is not empty, then delete the node at its top.

DEFINITION

*A **queue** of elements of type T is a finite sequence of elements of T together with the operations*

1. Initialize the queue to be empty.
2. Determine if the queue is empty or not.
3. Determine if the queue is full or not.
4. Insert a new node after the last node in the queue, if it is not full.
5. Retrieve the first node in the queue, if it is not empty.
6. Delete the first node in the queue, if it is not empty.

Note that these definitions make no mention of the way in which the abstract data type (list, stack, or queue) is to be implemented. In the past two chapters we have studied different implementations of each of these types, and these new definitions fit any of these implementations equally well. These definitions produce what is called *abstract data types* an ***abstract data type***, often abbreviated as ***ADT***. The important principle is that the definition of any abstract data type involves two parts: First is a description of the way in which the components are related to each other, and second is a statement of the operations that can be performed on elements of the abstract data type.

4.6.3 Refinement of Data Specification

top-down specification

Now that we have obtained such general definitions of abstract data types, it is time to begin specifying more detail, since the objective of all this work is to find general principles that will help with designing programs, and we need more detail to accomplish this objective. There is, in fact, a close analogy between the process of top-down refinement of algorithms and the process of top-down specification of data structures that we have now begun. In algorithm design we begin with a general but precise statement of the problem and slowly specify more detail until we have developed a complete program. In data specification we begin with the selection of the mathematical concepts and abstract data types required for our problem and slowly specify more detail until finally we can describe our data structures in terms of a programming language.

stages of refinement

The number of stages required in this specification process depends on the application. The design of a large software system will require many more decisions than will the design of a single small program, and these decisions should be taken in several stages of refinement. Although different problems will require different numbers of stages of refinement, and the boundaries between these stages sometimes blur, we can pick out four levels of the refinement process.

conceptual

1. On the *abstract* level we decide how the data are related to each other and what operations are needed, but we decide nothing concerning how the data will actually be stored or how the operations will actually be done.

algorithmic

2. On the *data structures* level we specify enough detail so that we can analyze the behavior of the operations and make appropriate choices as dictated by our problem. This is the level, for example, at which we choose between contiguous lists and linked lists. Some operations are easier for contiguous lists and others for linked lists: Finding the length of the list and retrieving the kth element are easier for contiguous lists; inserting and deleting are easier for linked lists. Some applications require many insertions or deletions at arbitrary positions in a list, so we prefer linked lists. For other problems contiguous lists prove better.

programming

3. On the *implementation* level we decide the details of how the data structures will be represented in computer memory. Here, for example, we decide whether a linked list will be implemented with pointers and dynamic memory or with cursors in an array.

4. On the *application* level we settle all details required for our particular application, such as names for variables or special requirements for the operations imposed by the application.

The first two levels are often called *conceptual* because at these levels we are more concerned with problem solving than with programming. The middle two levels can be called *algorithmic* because they concern precise methods for representing data and operating with it. The last two levels are specifically concerned with ***programming***.

Figure 4.18 illustrates these stages of refinement in the case of a queue. We begin with the mathematical concept of a sequence and then the queue considered

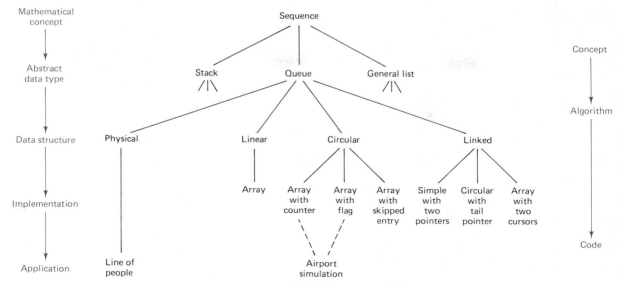

Figure 4.18.   Refinement of a queue

as an abstract data type. At the next level, we choose from the various data structures shown in the diagram, ranging from the physical model (in which all items move forward as each one leaves the head of the queue) to the linear model (in which the queue is emptied all at once) to circular arrays and finally linked lists. Some of these data structures allow further variation in their implementation, as shown on the next level. At the final stage, the queue is coded for a specific application.

Let us conclude this section by restating its most important principles as programming precepts:

> **Programming Precept**
>
> *Let your data structure your program.*
> *Refine your algorithms and data structures at the same time.*

> **Programming Precept**
>
> *Once your data are fully structured,*
> *your algorithms should almost write themselves.*

**Exercises
4.6**

E1. Draw a diagram similar to that of Figure 4.18 showing levels of refinement for **(a)** a stack and **(b)** a list.

E2. Give formal definitions of the terms **(a)** *deque* and **(b)** *scroll,* using the definitions given for stack and queue as models.

E3. In mathematics the ***Cartesian product*** of sets T_1, T_2, . . . , T_n is defined as the set of all n-tuples $(t_1, t_2, . . . , t_n)$, where t_i is a member of T_i for all i, $1 \le i \le n$. Use the Cartesian product to give a precise definition of a ***record*** that has no variant part.

POINTERS AND PITFALLS

1. For general advice on the use of lists, see the Pointers and Pitfalls at the end of Chapter 3.

2. Before choosing implementations, be sure that all the data structures and their associated operations are fully specified on the abstract level.

3. In choosing between linked and contiguous implementations of lists, consider the necessary operations on the lists. Linked lists are more flexible in regard to insertions, deletions, and rearrangement; contiguous lists allow random access.

4. Contiguous lists usually require less computer memory, computer time, and programming effort when the items in the list are small and the algorithms are simple. When the list holds large records, linked lists usually save space, time, and often programming effort.

5. Dynamic memory and pointers allow a program to adapt automatically to a wide range of application sizes and provide flexibility in space allocation among different data structures. Static memory (arrays and cursors) is sometimes more efficient for applications whose size can be completely specified in advance.

6. For advice on programming with linked lists in dynamic memory, see the guidelines at the end of Section 4.3.

REVIEW QUESTIONS

4.1

1. Give two reasons why dynamic memory allocation is a valuable device.

2. Define the terms *pointer, contiguous, static variable,* and *dynamic variable.*

3. What is the difference between "p = **nil**" and "p is undefined"?

4. Is the header for a linked list usually a static variable or a dynamic variable?

4.2

5. In popping a linked stack we first checked that the stack was not empty, but in pushing it we did not first check that it was not full. Why not?

4.3

6. Is it easier to insert a new node before or after a specified node in a linked list? Why?

7. Write a Pascal function that counts the nodes of a linked list.

8. If the items in a list are integers (one word each), compare the amount of space required altogether if (a) the list is kept contiguously in an array 90 percent full, (b) the list is kept contiguously in an array 40 percent full, and (c) the list is kept as a linked list (where the pointers take one word each).

9. Repeat the comparisons of the previous exercise when the items in the list are records taking 200 words each.

10. What is an *alias* variable, and why is it dangerous?

11. What is the major disadvantage of linked lists in comparison with contiguous lists?

4.4

12. Discuss some problems that occur in group programming projects that do not occur in individual programming projects. What advantages does a group project have over individual projects?

4.5

13. What are some reasons for implementing linked lists in arrays with cursors instead of in dynamic memory with pointers?

4.6

14. What two parts must be in the definition of any abstract data type?

15. In an abstract data type, how much is specified about implementation?

16. Name (in order from abstract to concrete) four levels of refinement of data specification.

REFERENCES FOR FURTHER STUDY

The references given at the end of Chapter 3 continue to be appropriate for the current chapter. In particular, linked lists are studied in depth in KNUTH, Volume 1, pp. 251–272, and an algorithm for polynomial addition appears in pp. 272–276. Abstract data types are treated extensively in the book by WELSH, ELDER, and BUSTARD (reference in Chapter 3) and in the book

DANIEL F. STUBBS and NEIL W. WEBRE, *Data Structures with Abstract Data Types and Pascal,* Brooks/Cole Publishing Company, Monterey, Calif., 1985, 459 pages.

For additional details regarding the implementation of pointer types in Pascal, the best reference is the Pascal manual for your system. Several implementations of Pascal either do not use the standard procedures new and dispose or provide alternate methods that may be superior. Since the details of these methods depend on the system, we cannot provide more information here.

Searching

▶ *This chapter studies two important methods for retrieving information from a list: sequential search and binary search. One of our major purposes is to compare various algorithms, to see which are preferable under different conditions. To do this we shall develop sophisticated tools, such as comparison trees, which help to analyze the performance of algorithms. The chapter concludes by showing how algorithm analysis is simplified by using a new mathematical tool, the big Oh notation.*

5.1 SEARCHING: INTRODUCTION AND NOTATION

keys and records

Information retrieval is one of the most important applications of computers. We are given a name and are asked for an associated telephone listing. We are given an account number and are asked for the transactions occurring in that account. We are given an employee name or number and are asked for the personnel records of the employee. In these examples and a host of others, we are given one piece of information, which we shall call a *key,* and we are asked to find a record that contains other information associated with the key. A rule that, for simplicity, we adopt throughout this chapter is that, given a key, there should be at most one record with that key. On the other hand, it is quite possible that, given a key, there is no record at all that has that key.

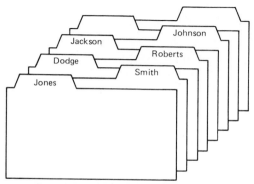

Figure 5.1. Records and their keys

Searching for keys to locate records is often the most time-consuming action in a program, and therefore the way the records are arranged and the choice of method used for searching can make a substantial difference in the program's performance. The searching problem falls naturally into two cases. If there are many records, perhaps each one quite large, then it will be necessary to store the records in files on disk or tape, external to the computer memory. This case is called *external* searching. In the other case the records to be searched are stored entirely within the computer memory. This case is called *internal* searching. In this chapter we consider only internal searching. Although many of the methods we shall develop in this and later chapters are useful for external searching, a comprehensive study of methods for external searching lies beyond the scope of this book.

external and internal searching

Pascal conventions

To write our programs in Pascal, we establish some notation. What we have called records will indeed be Pascal records, and the Pascal type that these records have we shall name as item. One of the fields (or components) of each item will be denoted key and have a type called keytype. We thus assume that the program will have declarations of the form *declarations*

```
type    keytype =       . . .;
        item =      record
                        . . .                              {various components};
                        key:      keytype;
                        . . .                              {more components}
                    end;
```

Typical declarations for the key type are

```
keytype = real;
keytype = integer;
keytype = packed array[1 . . 8] of char.
```

We begin with a *list* of the items to be searched. If we have a linked list (implemented with pointers in dynamic memory), we shall assume the type declarations

```
type
    pointer = ↑node;
    node = record
                info: item;
                next: pointer
            end;
    list = record
                head: pointer
            end;
```

In the case of a contiguous list we use the following declarations, where the constant max is declared elsewhere.

```
type
    list = record
                entry: array[1 . . max] of item;        {entries in the list}
                count: 0 . . max                        {count of items in the list}
            end;
```

target

The key for which we are searching is always called the **target** of the search, and in programs is denoted target. Hence our goal is to find an item in the list whose key is equal to the target.

parameters

Any searching procedure that we write will hence have two input parameters, the target and the list being searched. It will also have two output parameters. The first of these is the Boolean variable found, which indicates whether or not the search was successful in finding an item with the target key. If the search was successful, then the output parameter location will give the place in the list where the target was found. Since we have assumed that each key appears at most once in the list, this location will be uniquely determined. If the search is unsuccessful, then the output parameter location will have an undefined value.

5.2 SEQUENTIAL SEARCH

Beyond doubt the simplest way to do a search is to begin at one end of the list and scan down it until the desired key is found or the other end is reached. This is our first method.

1. Contiguous Version

In the case when the list L is contiguous we obtain the following procedure.

```
procedure SequentialSearch(var L: list; target: keytype;
                           var found: Boolean; var location: integer);
{contiguous version: searches list L for an item with key = target}
begin
  found := false;                                    {Initialize variables.}
  location := 1;
  while (not found) and (location <= L.count) do
    if L.entry[location].key = target then
      found := true
    else
      location := location + 1
end;
```

The **while** loop in this procedure keeps moving through the list as long as the target key target has not been found but terminates as soon as the target is found. If the search is unsuccessful, then found remains false, and at the conclusion location has moved to a position beyond the end of the list (recall that for an unsuccessful search the value of location may be left undefined).

2. Linked Version

A version of sequential search for linked lists is equally easy.

```
procedure SequentialSearch(L: list; target: keytype;
                           var found: Boolean; var location: pointer);
{version for linked lists}
begin
  found := false;                                    {Initialize variables.}
  location := L.head;
  while (not found) and (location <> nil) do
    if location↑.info.key = target then
      found := true
    else
      location := location↑.next
end;
```

3. Comparison of Keys Versus Running Time

importance of comparison count

As you can see, the basic method of sequential search is exactly the same for both the contiguous and linked versions, even though the implementation details differ. In fact, the target is compared to exactly the same keys in the items of the list in either version. Although the running times of the two versions may differ a little because of the different implementations, in both of them all the actions go in lock step with comparison of keys. Hence if we wish to estimate how much computer time sequential search is likely to require, or if we wish to compare it with some other method, then knowing the number of comparisons of keys that it makes will give us the most useful information, information actually more useful than the total running time, which is too much dependent on whether we have the contiguous or linked version, or what particular machine is being used.

4. Analysis of Sequential Search

Short as sequential search is, when we start to count comparisons of keys, we run into difficulties because we do not know how many times the loop will be iterated. We have no way to know in advance whether or not the search will be successful. If it is, we do not know if the target will be the first key on the list, the last, or somewhere between. Thus to obtain useful information, we must do several analyses.

unsuccessful search

successful search

Fortunately, these are all easy. If the search is unsuccessful, then the target will have been compared to all items in the list, for a total of n comparisons of keys, where n is the length of the list. For a successful search, if the target is in position k, then it will have been compared with the first k keys in the list, for a total of exactly k comparisons. Thus the best time for a successful search is 1 comparison, and the worst is n comparisons.

average behavior

We have obtained very detailed information about the timing of sequential search, information that is really too detailed for most uses, in that we generally will not know exactly where in a list a particular key may appear. Instead, it will generally be much more helpful if we can determine the *average* behavior of an algorithm. But what do we mean by average? One reasonable assumption, the one that we shall always make, is to take each possibility once and average the results.

provisos

Note, however, that this assumption may be very far from the actual situation. Not all English words, for example, appear equally often in a typical essay. The telephone operator receives far more requests for the number of a large business than for that of an average family. The Pascal compiler encounters the keywords **if**, **begin**, and **end** far more often than the keywords **label**, **downto**, and **packed**.

There are a great many interesting, but exceedingly difficult, problems associated with analyzing algorithms where the input is chosen according to some statistical distribution. These problems, however, would take us too far afield to be considered here.

Under the assumption of equal likelihood we can find the average number of key comparisons done in a successful sequential search. We simply add the number needed for all the successful searches, and divide by n, the number of items in the list. The result is

$$\frac{1 + 2 + 3 + \cdots + n}{n}.$$

The first formula established in Appendix A is

$$1 + 2 + 3 + \ldots + n = \tfrac{1}{2}n(n + 1).$$

average number of key comparisons

Hence the average number of key comparisons done by sequential search in the successful case is

$$\frac{n(n + 1)}{2n} = \tfrac{1}{2}(n + 1).$$

Exercises 5.2

E1. One good check for any algorithm is to see what it does in extreme cases. Determine what both versions of sequential search do when

(a) There is only one item in the list.

(b) The list is empty.

(c) The list is full (contiguous version only).

E2. Trace the contiguous version of sequential search as it searches for each of the keys present in a list containing three items. Determine how many comparisons are made, and thereby check the formula for the average number of comparisons for a successful search.

E3. If we can assume that the keys in the list have been arranged in order (for example, numerical or alphabetical order), then we can terminate unsuccessful searches more quickly. If the smallest keys come first, then we can terminate the search as soon as a key greater than or equal to the target key has been found. If we assume that it is equally likely that a target key not in the list is in any one of the $n + 1$ intervals (before the first key, between a pair of keys, or after the last key), then what is the average number of comparisons for unsuccessful search in this version?

sentinel

At each iteration, sequential search checks two inequalities, one a comparison of keys to see if the target has been found, and the other a comparison of indices to see if the end of the list has been reached. A good way to speed up the algorithm by eliminating the second comparison is to make sure that eventually key target will be found, by increasing the size of the list and inserting an extra item at the end with key target. Such an item placed in a list to ensure that a process terminates is called a *sentinel*. When the loop terminates, the search will have been successful if target was found before the last item in the list and unsuccessful if the final sentinel item was the one found.

E4. Write a Pascal procedure that embodies the idea of a sentinel in the contiguous version of sequential search.

E5. Find the number of comparisons of keys done by the procedure written in Exercise E4 for

(a) Unsuccessful search.

(b) Best successful search.

(c) Worst successful search.

(d) Average successful search.

E6. In the linked version of sequential search, suppose that (as we have assumed) we are given a pointer only to the start of the list. Explain why adding a sentinel to the list is not a particularly helpful idea. What extra information would make it worthwhile?

Programming Projects 5.2

P1. Write a program to test the contiguous version of sequential search. You should make the appropriate declarations required to set up the list and put keys into it. A good choice for the keys would be the integers from 1 to n. Modify the sequential search procedure so that it keeps a counter of the number of key comparisons that it makes. Find out how many comparisons are done in an unsuccessful search (for some key that you know is not in the list). Also call the procedure to search once for each key that is in the list, and thereby calculate the average number of comparisons made for a successful search. Run your program for representative values of n, such as $n = 10$, $n = 100$, $n = 1000$.

P2. Do Project P1 for a linked list instead of a contiguous list.

P3. Take the driver program written in Project P1 to test the contiguous version of sequential search, and insert the version that uses a sentinel (see Exercises E4–E6). Also insert instructions (system dependent) for obtaining the CPU time used. For various values of n, determine whether the version with or without sentinel is faster. Find the cross-over point between the two versions, if there is one. That is, at what point is the extra time needed to insert a sentinel at the end of the list the same as the time needed for extra comparisons of indices in the version without a sentinel?

5.3 BINARY SEARCH

method

Sequential search is easy to write and efficient for short lists, but a disaster for long ones. Imagine trying to find the name "Thomas Z. Smith" in a large telephone book by reading one name at a time starting at the front of the book! To find any item in a long list, there are far more efficient methods. One of the best is first to compare the item with one in the center of the list and then restrict our attention to only the first or second half of the list, depending on whether the item comes before or after the central one. In this way, at each step we reduce the length of the list to be searched by half. In only twenty comparisons this method will locate any requested name in a list of about a million names.

restrictions

The method we are discussing is called ***binary search.*** This approach requires that the items in the list be of a scalar or other type that can be regarded as having an order and that the list already be completely in order. We shall assume that the keys can be compared under the operations '$<$' and '$>$' (for example, that they are numbers), but the algorithms can easily be extended to care for words or other character strings as keys.

random access

Binary search is not good for linked lists, since it requires jumping back and forth from one end of the list to the middle, an action easy within an array, but slow for a linked list. Hence this section studies only contiguous lists.

dangers

Simple though the idea of binary search is, it is exceedingly easy to program it incorrectly. This method dates back at least to 1946, but the first version free of errors and unnecessary restrictions seems to have appeared only in 1962. One study (reference at the end of the chapter) showed that about 90 percent of professional programmers fail to code binary search correctly, even after working on it for a full hour. Let us therefore take special care to make sure that we make no mistakes. To do this, we must state exactly what our variables designate; we must state precisely what conditions must be true before and after each iteration of the loop contained in the program; and we must make sure that the loop will terminate properly.

Our binary search algorithm will use two indices, top and bottom, to enclose the part of the list in which we are looking for the target key target. At each iteration we shall reduce the size of this part of the list by about half. More formally, we can state the loop invariant that must hold before and after each iteration of the loop in the procedure:

loop invariant

> *The target key, provided it is present, will be found between the indices* bottom *and* top, *inclusive.*

termination

We establish the initial correctness of this statement by setting bottom to 1 and top to L.count, the number of items in the list. Next, we note that the loop should terminate when top $\leq$ bottom, that is, when the remaining part of the list contains at most one item, providing that we have not terminated the loop earlier by finding the target. Finally, we must make progress toward termination by ensuring that the number of items remaining to be searched, top $-$ bottom $+$ 1, strictly decreases at each iteration of the loop.

Several slightly different algorithms for binary search can be written.

5.3.1 The Forgetful Version

Perhaps the simplest variation is to forget the possibility that the target key target might be found quickly and continue, whether target has been found or not, to subdivide the list until what remains has length 1. Our first program proceeds in this way. We shall use three indices in the program: top and bottom will bracket the part of the list that may contain target, and mid will be the midpoint of this reduced list.

```
procedure Binary1(var L: list; target: keytype;
                   var found: Boolean; var location: integer);
{forgetful version of binary search}
var
  top,
  bottom,
  mid:        integer;
begin
  top := L.count;                    {Initialize the bounds to encompass the whole list.}
  bottom := 1;
  while top > bottom do                                          {Check termination.}
  begin
    mid := (top + bottom) div 2;
    if target > L.entry[mid].key then          {Reduce to the top half of the list.}
      bottom := mid + 1
    else                                    {Reduce to the bottom half of the list.}
      top := mid
  end;            {The next if statement guarantees that the invariant still holds.}
  if top = 0 then
    found := false                              {Search of an empty list always fails.}
  else
    found := (target = L.entry[top].key);          {Set the output parameters.}
  location := top
end;
```

loop termination

Note that the **if** statement that divides the list in half is not symmetrical, since the condition tested puts the midpoint into the lower of the two intervals at each iteration. On the other hand, integer division of positive integers always truncates downward. It is only these two facts together that ensure that the loop always terminates. Let us determine what occurs toward the end of the search. The loop will iterate only as long as top > bottom. But this condition implies that when mid is calculated we always have

$$\text{bottom} \le \text{mid} < \text{top}$$

since integer division truncates downward. Next, the **if** statement reduces the size of the interval from top − bottom either to top − (mid + 1) or to mid − bottom, both of which, by the inequality, are strictly less than top − bottom. Thus at each iteration the size of the interval strictly decreases, so the loop will eventually terminate.

After the loop terminates, we must finally check to see if the target key has been found, since all previous comparisons have tested only inequalities.

5.3.2 Recognizing Equality

Although Binary1 is a simple form of binary search, it will often make unnecessary iterations because it fails to recognize that it has found the target before continuing to iterate. Thus we may save computer time with the following variation, which checks at each stage to see if it has found the target.

improved version

```
procedure Binary2(var L: list; target: keytype;
                    var found: Boolean; var location: integer);
{version that recognizes discovery of the target}
var
  top,
  bottom,
  mid:      integer;              {mid will be index of target when it is found in L.}
begin
  top := L.count;                                              {Initialize variables.}
  bottom := 1;
  found := false;
  while (not found) and (top >= bottom) do                      {Check termination.}
  begin
    mid := (top + bottom) div 2;
    if target = L.entry[mid].key then                  {Search terminates successfully.}
      found := true
    else if target < L.entry[mid].key then
      top := mid − 1                             {Reduce to the bottom half of the list.}
    else                                            {Reduce to the top half of the list.}
      bottom := mid + 1
  end;                          {This if statement guarantees that the invariant still holds.}
  location := mid
end;
```

loop termination

Proving that the loop in Binary2 terminates is easier than the proof for Binary1. In Binary2 the form of the **if** statement within the loop guarantees that the length of the interval is reduced by more than half at each iteration. Note that when top = bottom, we allow the loop to iterate one more time. In this way the target can be compared to the final candidate from L without having to write an extra comparison outside the loop.

comparison of methods

Which of these two versions of binary search will do fewer comparisons of keys? Clearly Binary2 will, if we happen to find the target near the beginning of the search. But each iteration of Binary2 requires two comparisons of keys, whereas Binary1 requires only one. Is it possible that if many iterations are needed, then Binary1 may do fewer comparisons? to answer this question we shall develop a new method in the next section.

Exercises 5.3

E1. Suppose that the list L contains the integers 1, 2, . . . , 8. Trace through the steps of Binary1 to determine what comparisons of keys are done in searching for each of the following targets: **(a)** 3, **(b)** 5, **(c)** 1, **(d)** 9, **(e)** 4.5.

E2. Repeat Exercise E1 using Binary2.

E3. Suppose that L_1 and L_2 are lists containing n_1 and n_2 integers, respectively, and both lists are already sorted into numerical order.

(a) Use the idea of binary search to describe how to find the median of the $n_1 + n_2$ integers in the combined lists.

(b) Write a procedure that implements your method.

Programming
Projects
5.3

P1. Adapt the driver program outlined in Project P1 of Section 5.2 so that it can be used to test Binary1. You should check both successful and unsuccessful searches for selected values of n. If your system can provide a measure of elapsed CPU time, you should also obtain timings for average successful and unsuccessful searches for your procedure.

P2. Adapt the program to test Binary2, as in the previous project.

P3. It is redundant to keep three pointers in binary search: bottom, mid, and top, since mid is guaranteed to be halfway between. **(a)** Modify Binary1 so that it keeps only two pointers, mid and the distance from mid to bottom or top. **(b)** Verify the correctness of your algorithm. **(c)** Run both your version and the one in the text to see which is faster.

P4. Do Project P3 for Binary2.

P5. On most computers addition is faster than division. Use the following idea to make a new version of binary search that does no division. First, use addition to construct an auxiliary table of the powers of 2 that are less than the length of the list L.count and then by adding and subtracting appropriate entries from this table reduce the bounds of the interval being searched. Compare the time required by this version to the times required by Binary1 and Binary2.

5.4 COMPARISON TREES

definitions

The *comparison tree* (also called *decision tree* or *search tree*) of an algorithm is obtained by tracing through the action of the algorithm, representing each comparison of keys by a *vertex* of the tree (which we draw as a circle). Inside the circle we put the index of the key against which we are comparing the target key. *Branches* (lines) drawn down from the circle represent the possible outcomes of the comparison and are labeled accordingly. When the algorithm terminates, we put either F (for failure) or the location where the target is found at the end of the appropriate branch, which we call a *leaf*, and draw as a square. Leaves are also sometimes called *end vertices* or *external vertices* of the tree. The remaining vertices are called the *internal vertices* of the tree.

The comparison tree for sequential search is especially simple; it is drawn in Figure 5.2.

definitions

The number of comparisons done by an algorithm in a particular search is the number of internal (circular) vertices traversed in going from the top of the tree (which is called its *root*) down the appropriate path to a leaf. The number of branches traversed to reach a vertex from the root is called the *level* of the vertex. Thus the root itself has level 0, the vertices immediately below it have level 1, and so on. The largest level that occurs is called the *height* of the tree. Hence a tree with only one vertex has height 0. In future chapters we shall sometimes allow trees to be empty, that is, to consist of no vertices at all, and we adopt the convention that an empty tree has height -1.

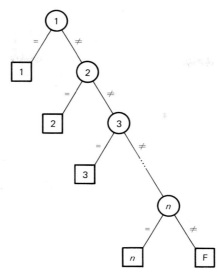

Figure 5.2.   Comparison tree for sequential search

To complete the terminology we use for trees we shall now, as is traditional, mix our metaphors by thinking of family trees as well as botanical trees: We call the vertices immediately below a vertex v the **children** of v and the vertex immediately above v the **parent** of v.

5.4.1 Analysis for $n = 10$

1. Shape of Trees

That sequential search on average does far more comparisons than binary search is obvious from comparing the shape of its tree with that of those of Binary1 and Binary2, which for $n = 10$ are drawn in Figures 5.3 and 5.4, respectively. Sequential search has a long, narrow tree, which means many comparisons, whereas the trees for binary search are much wider and shorter.

2. Three-Way Comparisons and Compact Drawings

two versions

In the tree drawn for Binary2 we have shown the algorithm structure more clearly (and reduced the space needed) by combining two comparisons to obtain one three-way comparison for each pass through the loop. Drawing the tree this way means that every vertex that is not a leaf terminates some successful search and the leaves correspond to unsuccessful searches. Thus the drawing in Figure 5.4 is more compact, but remember that two comparisons are really done for each of the vertices shown, except that only one comparison is done at the vertex at which the search succeeds in finding the target.

It is this compact way of drawing comparison trees that will become our standard method in future chapters.

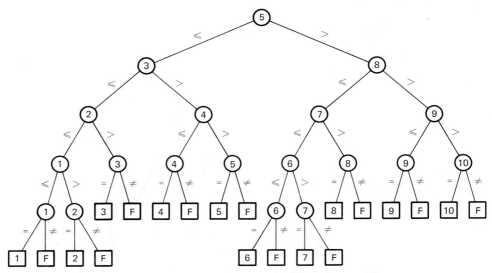

Figure 5.3. Comparison tree for Binary1, $n = 10$

From the trees it is easy to read off how many comparisons will be done when $n = 10$. In the worst case, it is simply one more than the height of the tree; in fact, in every case it is the number of interior vertices lying between the root and the vertex that terminates the search.

3. Binary1 **Comparison Count**

external path length

In Binary1, every search terminates at a leaf; to obtain the average number of comparisons for both successful and unsuccessful searches, we need what is called the ***external path length*** of the tree: the sum of the number of branches traversed in going from

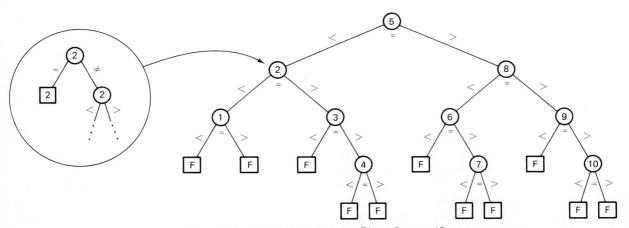

Figure 5.4. Comparison tree for Binary2, $n = 10$

the root once to every leaf in the tree. For the tree in Figure 5.3 the external path length is

$$4 \times 5 + 6 \times 4 + 4 \times 5 + 6 \times 4 = 88.$$

Half the leaves correspond to successful searches, and half to unsuccessful. Hence the average number of comparisons needed for either a successful or unsuccessful search by Binary1 is $44/10 = 4.4$ when $n = 10$.

4. Binary2 **Comparison Count**

internal path length

In the tree as it is drawn for Binary2, all the leaves correspond to unsuccessful searches; hence the external path length leads to the number of comparisons for an unsuccessful search. For successful searches, we need the ***internal path length,*** which is defined to be the sum, over all vertices that are not leaves, of the number of branches from the root to the vertex. For the tree in Figure 5.4 the internal path length is

$$0 + 1 + 2 + 2 + 3 + 1 + 2 + 3 + 2 + 3 = 19.$$

Recall that Binary2 does two comparisons for each non-leaf except for the vertex that finds the target, and note that the number of these internal vertices traversed is one more than the number of branches (for each of the $n = 10$ internal vertices), so we obtain the average number of comparisons for a successful search to be

average successful count

$$2 \times \left(\frac{19}{10} + 1 \right) - 1 = 4.8.$$

The subtraction of 1 corresponds to the fact that one fewer comparison is made when the target is found.

For an unsuccessful search by Binary2, we need the external path length of the tree in Figure 5.4. This is

$$5 \times 3 + 6 \times 4 = 39.$$

We shall assume for unsuccessful searches that the $n + 1$ intervals (less than the first key, between a pair of successive keys, or greater than the largest) are all equally likely; for the diagram we therefore assume that any of the 11 failure leaves are equally likely. Thus the average number of comparisons for an unsuccessful search is

average unsuccessful count

$$\frac{2 \times 39}{11} \approx 7.1.$$

5. Comparison of Algorithms

For $n = 10$, Binary1 does slightly fewer comparisons both for successful and for unsuccessful searches. To be fair, however, we should note that the two comparisons done by Binary2 at each internal vertex are closely related (the same keys are being compared), so that an optimizing compiler may not do as much work as two full comparisons, in which case, in fact, Binary2 may be a slightly better choice than Binary1 for successful searches when $n = 10$.

5.4.2 Generalization

What happens when n is larger than 10? For longer lists, it may be impossible to draw the complete comparison tree, but from the examples with $n = 10$, we can make some observations that will always be true.

1. 2-Trees

Let us define a *2-tree* as a tree in which every vertex except the leaves has exactly two children. Both versions of comparison trees that we have drawn fit this definition, and are 2-trees. We can make several observations about 2-trees that will provide information about the behavior of binary search methods for all values of n.

terminology

Other terms for 2-tree are ***strictly binary tree*** and ***extended binary tree***, but we shall not use these terms, because they are too easily confused with the term *binary tree*, which (when introduced in Chapter 9) has a somewhat different meaning.

number of vertices in a 2-tree

In a 2-tree, the number of vertices on any level can be no more than twice the number on the level above, since each vertex has either 0 or 2 children (depending on whether it is a leaf or not). Since there is one vertex on level 0 (the root), the number of vertices on level t is at most 2^t for all $t \geq 0$. We thus have the facts:

LEMMA 5.1   *The number of vertices on each level of a 2-tree is at most twice the number on the level immediately above.*

LEMMA 5.2   *In a 2-tree, the number of vertices on level t is at most 2^t for $t \geq 0$.*

2. Analysis of Binary1

For Binary1 both successful and unsuccessful searches terminate at leaves; there are thus $2n$ leaves. All these leaves, furthermore, must be on the same level or on two adjacent levels. (This observation can be proved by mathematical induction: It is true for a list of size 1, and when Binary1 divides a larger list in half, the sizes of the two halves differ by at most 1, and the induction hypothesis shows that their leaves are on the same or adjacent levels.) The height (number of levels below root) of the tree is the maximum number of key comparisons that an algorithm does, and for Binary1 is at most one more than the average number, since all leaves are on the same or adjacent levels. By Lemma 5.2 the height is also the smallest integer t such that $2^t \geq 2n$. Take logarithms with base 2. (For a review of properties of logarithms, see Appendix A.2.) We obtain that the number of comparisons of keys done by Binary1 in searching a list of n items is approximately

comparison count, Binary1

$$\lg n + 1.$$

As can be seen from the tree, the number of comparisons is essentially independent of whether the search is successful or not.

3. Notation

The notation for base 2 logarithms just used will be our standard notation. In analyzing algorithms we shall also sometimes need natural logarithms (taken with base $e = 2.71828\ldots$). We shall denote a natural logarithm by ln. We shall rarely need logarithms to any other base. We thus summarize,

logarithms

> ### Convention
> *Unless stated otherwise, all logarithms will be taken with base 2.
> The symbol* lg *denotes a logarithm with base 2,
> and the symbol* ln *denotes a natural logarithm.
> When the base for logarithms is not specified (or is not important),
> then the symbol* log *will be used.*

floor and ceiling

After we take logarithms, we frequently need to move either up or down to the next integer. To specify this action, we define the **floor** of a real number x to be the largest integer less than or equal to x, and the **ceiling** of x to be the smallest integer greater than or equal to x. We denote the floor of x by $\lfloor x \rfloor$ and the ceiling of x by $\lceil x \rceil$.

4. Analysis of Binary2, Unsuccessful Search

To count the comparisons made by Binary2 for a general value of n for an unsuccessful search, we shall examine its comparison tree. For reasons similar to those given for Binary1, this tree is full at the top, with all its leaves on at most two adjacent levels at the bottom. For Binary2, all the leaves correspond to unsuccessful searches, so there are exactly $n + 1$ leaves, corresponding to the $n + 1$ unsuccessful outcomes; less than the smallest key, between a pair of keys, and greater than the largest key. Since these leaves are all at the bottom of the tree, Lemma 5.2 implies that the number of leaves is approximately 2^h, where h is the height of the tree. Taking (base 2) logarithms, we obtain that $h \approx \lg(n + 1)$. This value is the approximate distance from the root to one of the leaves. Since two comparisons of keys are performed for each internal vertex, the number of comparisons done in an unsuccessful search is approximately $2 \lg(n + 1)$.

comparison count for Binary2, unsuccessful case

5. The Path Length Theorem

To calculate the average number of comparisons for a successful search, we first obtain an interesting and important relationship that holds for any 2-tree.

THEOREM 5.3

> *Denote the external path length of a 2-tree by E, the internal path length by I, and let q be the number of vertices that are not leaves. Then*
> $$E = I + 2q.$$

proof

To prove the theorem, we use the method of mathematical induction. If the tree contains only its root, and no other vertices, then $E = I = q = 0$, and the first case of the theorem is trivially correct. Now take a larger tree, and let v be some vertex that is not a leaf, but for which both the children of v are leaves. Let k be the number of branches on the path from the root to v. Now let us delete the two children of v from the 2-tree. Since v is not a leaf but its children are, the number of non-leaves goes down from q to $q - 1$. The internal path length I is reduced by the distance to v, that is, to $I - k$. The distance to each child of v is $k + 1$, so the external path length is reduced from E to $E - 2(k + 1)$, but v is now a leaf, so its distance, k, must be added, giving a new external path length of

$$E - 2(k + 1) + k = E - k - 2.$$

Since the new tree has fewer vertices than the old one, by the induction hypothesis we know that

$$E - k - 2 = (I - k) + 2(q - 1).$$

Rearrangement of this equation gives the desired result.

6. Binary2, Successful Search

In the comparison tree of Binary2, the distance to the leaves is $\lg(n + 1)$, as we have seen. The number of leaves is $n + 1$, so the external path length is about

$$(n + 1) \lg(n + 1).$$

Theorem 5.3 then shows that the internal path length is about

$$(n + 1) \lg(n + 1) - 2n.$$

To obtain the average number of comparisons done in a successful search, we must first divide by n (the number of non-leaves) and then add 1 and double, since two comparisons were done at each internal node. Finally, we subtract 1, since only one comparison is done at the node where the target is found. The result is approximately

$$\frac{2(n + 1)}{n} \lg(n + 1) - 3$$

comparisons of keys.

5.4.3 Comparison of Methods

Note the similarities and differences in the formulae for the two versions of binary search. Recall, first, that we have already made some approximations in our calculations, and hence our formulae are only approximate. For large values of n, the difference between $\lg n$ and $\lg(n + 1)$ is insignificant, and $(n + 1)/n$ is very nearly 1. Hence we can simplify our results as follows:

	Successful Search	*Unsuccessful Search*
Binary1	$\lg n + 1$	$\lg n + 1$
Binary2	$2 \lg n - 3$	$2 \lg n$

In all four cases the times are proportional to $\lg n$, except for small constant terms, and the coefficients of $\lg n$ are, in all cases, the number of comparisons inside the loop. The fact that the loop in Binary2 can terminate early contributes disappointingly little to improving its speed for a successful search; it does not reduce the coefficient of $\lg n$ at all, but only reduces the constant term from $+1$ to -3. A moment's examination of the comparison trees will show why. More than half of the vertices occur at the bottom level, and so their loops cannot terminate early. More than half the remaining ones could terminate only one iteration early. Thus, for large n, the number of vertices relatively high in the tree, say, in the top half of the levels, is negligible in comparison with the number at the bottom level. It is only for this negligible proportion of the vertices that Binary2 can achieve better results than Binary1, but it is at the cost of nearly doubling the number of comparisons for all searches, both successful and unsuccessful ones.

With the smaller coefficient of lg n, Binary1 will do fewer comparisons when n is sufficiently large, but with the smaller constant term, Binary2 may do fewer comparisons when n is small. But for such a small value of n, the overhead in setting up binary search and the extra programming effort probably make it a more expensive

conclusions

method to use than sequential search. Thus we arrive at the conclusion, quite contrary to what we would intuitively conclude, that Binary2 is probably not worth the effort, since for large problems Binary1 is better, and for small problems, SequentialSearch is better. To be fair, however, with some computers and optimizing compilers, the two comparisons needed in Binary2 will not take double the time of the one in Binary1, so in such a situation Binary2 might prove the better choice.

Our object in doing analysis of algorithms is to help us decide which may be better under appropriate circumstances. Disregarding the foregoing provisos, we have now been able to make such a decision, and have available to us information that might otherwise not be obvious.

The numbers of comparisons of keys done in the average successful case by SequentialSearch, Binary1, and Binary2 are graphed in Figure 5.5. The numbers shown in the graphs are from test runs of the procedures; they are not approximations. The first graph in Figure 5.5 compares the three procedures for small values of n, the number of items in the list. In the second graph we compare the numbers over

logarithmic graphs

a much larger range by employing a *log-log graph* in which each unit along an axis represents doubling the corresponding coordinate. In the third graph we wish to compare the two versions of binary search; a *semilog graph* is appropriate here, so that the vertical axis maintains linear units while the horizontal axis is logarithmic.

5.4.4 A General Relationship

Before leaving this section, let us use Theorem 5.3 to obtain a relationship between the average number of key comparisons for successful and for unsuccessful searches, a relationship that holds for any searching method for which the comparison tree

hypotheses

can be drawn as we did for Binary2. That is, we shall assume that the leaves of the comparison tree correspond to unsuccessful searches, that the internal vertices correspond to successful searches, and that two comparisons of keys are made for each internal vertex, except that only one is made at the vertex where the target is found. If I and E are the internal and external path lengths of the tree, respectively, and n is the number of items in the list, so that n is also the number of internal vertices in the tree, then, as in the analysis of Binary2, we know that the average number of comparisons in a successful search is

$$S = 2\left(\frac{I}{n} + 1\right) - 1 = \frac{2I}{n} + 1$$

and the average number for an unsuccessful search is $U = 2E/(n + 1)$. By Theorem 5.3, $E = I + 2n$. Combining these expressions, we can therefore conclude that

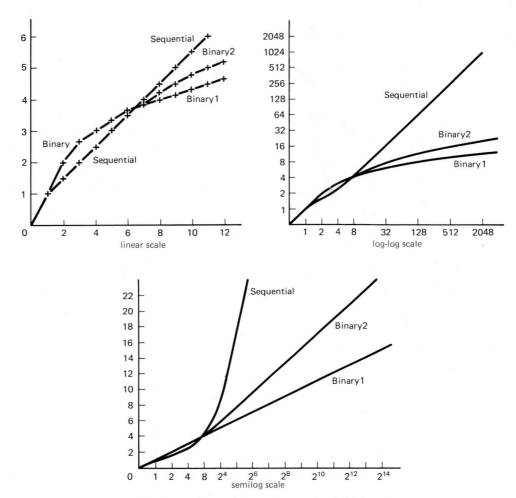

Figure 5.5.   Comparison of average successful searches

<table>
<tr>
<td>THEOREM 5.4

successful and
unsuccessful searches</td>
<td>Under the specified conditions, the average numbers of key comparisons done in successful and unsuccessful searches are related by

$$S = \left(1 + \frac{1}{n}\right) U - 3.$$</td>
</tr>
</table>

In other words, the average number of comparisons for a successful search is almost exactly the same as that for an unsuccessful search. Knowing that an item is in the list is very little help in finding it, if you are searching by means of comparisons of keys.

E1. Draw the comparison trees for Binary1 and Binary2 when

(a) $n = 5$, (b) $n = 7$, (c) $n = 8$, (d) $n = 13$.

Calculate the external and internal path lengths for each of these trees, and verify that the conclusion of Theorem 5.3 holds.

E2. Sequential search has less overhead than binary search, and so may run faster for small n. Find the break-even point where SequentialSearch and Binary1 make the same number of comparisons of keys, in terms of the formulae for the number of comparisons done in the average successful search.

E3. Suppose that you have a list of 10,000 names in alphabetical order in an array and you must frequently look for various names. It turns out that 20 percent of the names account for 80 percent of the retrievals. Instead of doing a binary search over all 10,000 names every time, consider the possibility of splitting the list into two, a high-frequency list of 2000 names and a low-frequency list of the remaining 8000 names. To look up a name, you will first use binary search on the high-frequency list, and 80 percent of the time you will not need to go on to the second stage, where you use binary search on the low-frequency list. Is this scheme worth the effort? Justify your answer by finding the number of comparisons done for the average successful search, both in the new scheme and in a binary search of a single list of 10,000 names.

E4. If you modified binary search so that it divided the list not essentially in half at each pass, but instead into two pieces of sizes about one-third and two-thirds of the remaining list, then what would be the approximate effect on its average count of comparisons?

E5. Write a "ternary" search procedure analogous to Binary2 that examines the key one-third of the way through the list, and if the target key x is greater, then examines the key two-thirds of the way through, and thus in any case at each pass reduces the length of the list by a factor of three. Compare the count of comparisons of your algorithm with binary search.

P1. We have ignored the time needed to initialize the search procedures and to complete index calculations. For this reason, sequential search will be the better method for values of n somewhat larger than your answer to Exercise E2. Modify the test programs written for sequential search and binary search (both versions) in previous sections, so that the programs will record the CPU time used, and determine the break-even point for running time on your computer.

P2. Use the program of Project P1 to compare running times for an average successful search for Binary1 and Binary2. Use values of n about equal to (a) 10, (b) 300, (c) 1000.

P3. Write a program that will do a "hybrid" search, using binary search (your choice of the two algorithms or some variation) for large lists and switching to sequential search when the list is sufficiently reduced. (Because of different overhead, the best switch-over point is not necessarily the same as your answer to Exercise E2 or Project P1.)

5.5 LOWER BOUNDS

We know that for an ordered contiguous list, binary search is much faster than sequential search. It is only natural to ask if we can find another method that is much faster than binary search.

1. Polishing Programs

One approach is to attempt to polish and refine our programs to make them run faster. By being clever we may be able to reduce the work done in each iteration by a bit and thereby speed up the algorithm. One method, called *Fibonacci search,* even manages to replace the division inside the loop by certain subtractions (with no auxiliary table needed), which on some computers will speed up the procedure.

basic algorithms and small variations

Fine tuning of a program may be able to cut its running time in half, or perhaps reduce it even more, but limits will soon be reached if the underlying algorithm remains the same. The reason why binary search is so much faster than sequential search is not that there are fewer steps within its loop (there are actually more) or that the code is optimized, but that the loop is iterated fewer times, about $\lg n$ times instead of n times, and as the number n increases, the value of $\lg n$ grows much more slowly than does the value of n.

In the context of comparing underlying methods, the differences between Binary1 and Binary2 become insignificant. For large lists Binary2 may require nearly double the time of Binary1, but the difference between $2 \lg n$ and $\lg n$ is negligible compared to the difference between n and $2 \lg n$.

2. Arbitrary Searching Algorithms

Let us now ask whether it is possible for any search algorithm to exist that will, in the worst and the average cases, be able to find its target using significantly fewer comparisons of keys than binary search. We shall see that the answer is *no,* providing that we stay within the class of algorithms that rely only on comparisons of keys to determine where to look within an ordered list.

general algorithms and comparison trees

Let us start with an arbitrary algorithm that searches an ordered list by making comparisons of keys, and imagine drawing its comparison tree in the same way as we drew the tree for Binary1. That is, each internal node of the tree will correspond to some comparison of keys and each leaf to one of the possible outcomes. (If the algorithm is formulated as three-way comparisons like those of Binary2, then we expand each internal vertex into two, as shown for one vertex in Figure 5.4.) The possible outcomes to which the leaves correspond include not only the successful discovery of the target but also the different kinds of failure that the algorithm may distinguish. Binary search of a list of length n produces $k = 2n + 1$ outcomes, consisting of n successful outcomes and $n + 1$ different kinds of failure (less than the smallest key, between each pair of keys, or larger than the largest key). On the other hand, our sequential search procedure produced only $k = n + 1$ possible outcomes, since it distinguished only one kind of failure.

height and external path length

As with all search algorithms that compare keys, the height of our tree will equal the number of comparisons that the algorithm does in its worst case, and (since all outcomes correspond to leaves) the external path length of the tree divided by the number of possible outcomes will equal the average number of comparisons done by the algorithm. We therefore wish to obtain lower bounds on the height and the external path length in terms of k, the number of leaves.

3. Observations on 2-Trees

Here is the result on 2-trees that we shall need:

LEMMA 5.5

Let T be a 2-tree with k leaves. Then the height h of T satisfies $h \geq \lceil \lg k \rceil$ and the external path length $E(T)$ satisfies $E(T) \geq k \lg k$. The minimum values for h and $E(T)$ occur when all the leaves of T are on the same level or on two adjacent levels.

proof of last assertion

We begin the proof by establishing the assertion in the last sentence. For suppose that some leaves of T are on level r and some are on level s, where $r > s + 1$. Now take two leaves on level r that are both children of the same vertex v, detach them from v, and attach them as children of some (former) leaf on level s. Then we have changed T into a new 2-tree T' that still has k leaves, the height of T' is certainly no more than that of T, and the external path length of T' satisfies

$$E(T') = E(T) - 2r + (r-1) - s + 2(s+1) = E(T) - r + s + 1 < E(T)$$

since $r > s + 1$. The terms in this expression are obtained as follows. Since two leaves at level r are removed, $E(T)$ is reduced by $2r$. Since vertex v has become a leaf, $E(T)$ is increased by $r - 1$. Since the vertex on level s is no longer a leaf, $E(T)$ is reduced by s. Since the two leaves formerly on level r are now on level $s + 1$, the term $2(s + 1)$ is added to $E(T)$. This process is illustrated in Figure 5.6.

We can continue in this way to move leaves higher up the tree, reducing the external path length and possibly the height each time, until finally all the leaves are on the same or adjacent levels, and then the height and the external path length will be minimal amongst all 2-trees with k leaves.

proof of $h \geq \lceil \lg k \rceil$

To prove the remaining assertions in Lemma 5.5, let us from now on assume that T has minimum height and path length amongst the 2-trees with k leaves, so all leaves of T occur on levels h and (possibly) $h - 1$, where h is the height of T.

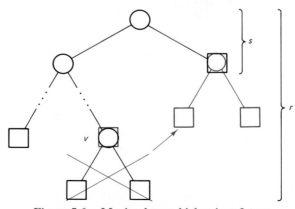

Figure 5.6.   Moving leaves higher in a 2-tree

By Lemma 5.2 the number of vertices on level h (which are necessarily leaves) is at most 2^h. If all the leaves are on level h, then $k \leq 2^h$. If some of the leaves are on level $h - 1$, then each of these (since it has no children) reduces the number of possible vertices on level h by 2, so the bound $k \leq 2^h$ continues to hold. We take logarithms to obtain $h \geq \lg k$, and, since the height is always an integer, we move up to the ceiling $h \geq \lceil \lg k \rceil$.

proof of
$E(T) \geq k \lg k$

For the bound on the external path length, let x denote the number of leaves of T on level $h - 1$, so that $k - x$ leaves are on level h. These vertices are children of exactly $\frac{1}{2}(k - x)$ vertices on level $h - 1$, which, with the x leaves, comprise all vertices on level $h - 1$. Hence, by Lemma 5.2,

$$\tfrac{1}{2}(k - x) + x \leq 2^{h-1},$$

which becomes $x \leq 2^h - k$. We now have

$$
\begin{aligned}
E(T) &= (h - 1)x + h(k - x) \\
&= kh - x \\
&\geq kh - (2^h - k) \\
&= k(h + 1) - 2^h.
\end{aligned}
$$

From the bound on the height, we already know that $2^{h-1} < k \leq 2^h$. If we set $h = \lg k + \epsilon$, then ϵ satisfies $0 \leq \epsilon < 1$, and substituting ϵ into the bound for $E(T)$ we obtain

$$E(T) \geq k(\lg k + 1 + \epsilon - 2^\epsilon).$$

It turns out that, for $0 \leq \epsilon < 1$, the quantity $1 + \epsilon - 2^\epsilon$ is between 0 and 0.0861. Thus the minimum path length is quite close to $k \lg k$ and, in any case, is at least this large, as was to be shown. With this, the proof of Lemma 5.5 is complete.

end of proof

4. Lower Bounds for Searching

Finally, we return to the study of our arbitrary searching algorithm. Its comparison tree may not have all leaves on two adjacent levels, but, even if not, the bounds in Lemma 5.5 will still hold. Hence we may translate these bounds into the language of comparisons, as follows.

THEOREM 5.6

Suppose that an algorithm uses comparisons of keys to search for a target in a list. If there are k possible outcomes, then in its worst case the algorithm must make at least $\lceil \lg k \rceil$ comparisons of keys, and in its average case, it must make at least $\lg k$ comparisons of keys.

Observe that there is very little difference between the worst-case bound and the average-case bound. By Theorem 5.4, moreover, for many algorithms it does not much matter whether the search is successful or not, in determining the bound in the above theorems. When we apply Theorem 5.6 to algorithms like binary search for which, on an ordered list of length n, there are n successful and $n + 1$ unsuccessful outcomes, we obtain a worst-case bound of

$$\lceil \lg(2n + 1) \rceil \geq \lceil \lg(2n) \rceil = \lceil \lg n \rceil + 1$$

and an average-case bound of $\lg n + 1$ comparisons of keys. When we compare these numbers with those obtained in the analysis of Binary1, we obtain

COROLLARY 5.7

> Binary1 *is optimal in the class of all algorithms that search an ordered list by making comparisons of keys. In both the average and worst cases,* Binary1 *achieves the optimal bound.*

5. Other Ways to Search

Just because we have found the bounds in Theorem 5.6, it does not imply that no algorithm can run faster than binary search, only those that rely only on comparisons of keys. To take a simple example, suppose that the keys are the integers from 1 to n themselves. If we know that the target key x is an integer in this range, then we would never perform a search algorithm to locate its item; we would simply store the items in an array indexed from 1 to n and immediately look in index x to find the desired item.

interpolation search

This idea can be extended to obtain another method, called *interpolation search*. We assume that the keys are either numerical or are information, such as words, that can be readily encoded as numbers. The method also assumes that the keys in the list are uniformly distributed, that is, that the probability of a key being in a particular range equals its probability of being in any other range of the same length. To find the target key target, interpolation search then estimates, according to the magnitude of the number target relative to the first and last entries of the list, about where target would be in the list and looks there. It then reduces the size of the list according as target is less than or greater than the key examined. It can be shown that on average, with uniformly distributed keys, interpolation search will take about $\lg \lg n$ comparisons of keys, which, for large n, is somewhat fewer than binary search requires. If, for example, $n = 1{,}000{,}000$, then Binary1 will require about $\lg 10^6 + 1 \approx 21$ comparisons, while interpolation search may need only about $\lg \lg 10^6 \approx 4.32$ comparisons.

Finally, we should repeat that, even for search by comparisons, our assumption that requests for all keys are equally likely may be far from correct. If one or two keys are much more likely than the others, then even sequential search, if it looks for those keys first, may be faster than any other method.

The importance of search, or more generally, information retrieval, is so fundamental that much of data structures is devoted to its methods, and in later chapters we shall return to these problems again and again.

Exercises 5.5

E1. Suppose that a search algorithm makes three-way comparisons like Binary2. Let each internal node of its comparison tree correspond to a successful search and each leaf to an unsuccessful search.

(a) Use Lemma 5.5 to obtain a theorem like Theorem 5.6 giving lower bounds for worst and average case behavior for an unsuccessful search by such an algorithm.

(b) Use Theorem 5.4 to obtain a similar result for successful searches.

(c) Compare the bounds you obtain with the analysis of Binary2.

Programming Project 5.5

P1. Write a program to do interpolation search; verify its correctness (especially termination); and run it on the same sets of data used to test the binary search programs. See the references at the end of the chapter for suggestions and program analysis.

5.6 ASYMPTOTICS

1. Introduction

The time has come to distill important generalizations from our analyses of searching algorithms. As we have progressed we have been able to see more clearly which aspects of algorithm analysis are of great importance and which parts can safely be neglected. It is, for example, certainly true that sections of a program that are performed only once outside loops can contribute but negligibly little to the running time. We have studied two different versions of binary search and found that the most significant difference between them was a single comparison of keys in the innermost loop, which might make one slightly preferable to the other sometimes, but that both versions would run far faster than sequential search for lists of moderate or large size.

designing algorithms for small problems

The design of efficient methods to work on small problems is an important subject to study, since a large program may need to do the same or similar small tasks many times during its execution. As we have discovered, however, for small problems, the large overhead of a sophisticated method may make it inferior to a simpler method. For a list of two or three items, sequential search is certainly superior to binary search. To improve efficiency in the algorithm for a small problem, the programmer must necessarily devote attention to details specific to the computer system and programming language, and there are few general observations that will help with this task.

choice of method for large problems

The design of efficient algorithms for large problems is an entirely different matter. In studying binary search, we have seen that the overhead becomes relatively unimportant; it is the basic idea that will make all the difference between success and a problem too large to be attacked.

asymptotics

The word **asymptotics** that titles this section means the study of functions of a parameter n, as n becomes larger and larger without bound. In comparing searching algorithms, we have seen that a count of the number of comparisons of keys accurately reflects the total running time for large problems, since it has generally been true that all the other operations (such as incrementing and comparing indices) have gone in lock step with comparison of keys.

basic actions

In fact, the frequency of such basic actions is much more important than is a total count of all operations including the housekeeping. The total including housekeeping is too dependent on the choice of programming language and on the programmer's particular style, so dependent that it tends to obscure the general methods. Variations in housekeeping details or programming technique can easily triple the running time of a program, but such a change probably will not make the difference between whether the computation is feasible or not. A change in fundamental method, on the other hand, can make a vital difference. If the number of basic actions is proportional to the size n of the input, then doubling n will about double the running time, no matter how the housekeeping is done. If the number of basic actions is proportional to $\lg n$, then doubling n will hardly change the running time. If the number of basic actions is proportional to n^2, then the time will quadruple, and the computation may still be feasible, but may be uncomfortably long. If the number of basic operations is proportional to 2^n, then doubling n will square this number.

A computation that took 1 second might involve a million (10^6) basic operations, and doubling the input might require 10^{12} basic operations, moving the time from 1 second to 11½ days.

goal

Our desire in formulating general principles that will apply to the analysis of many classes of algorithms, then, is to have a notation that will accurately reflect the way in which the computation time will increase with the size, but that will ignore superfluous details with little effect on the total. We wish to concentrate on one or two basic operations within the algorithm, without too much concern for all the housekeeping operations that will accompany them. If an algorithm does $f(n)$ basic operations when the size of its input is n, then its total running time will be at most $cf(n)$, where c is a constant that depends on the algorithm, on the way it is programmed, and on the computer used, but c does not depend on the size n of the input (at least when n is past a few initial cases).

2. The Big Oh Notation

These ideas are embodied in the following notation:

DEFINITION

> If $f(n)$ and $g(n)$ are functions defined for positive integers, then to write
>
> $$f(n) \text{ is } O(g(n))$$
>
> [read $f(n)$ is *big Oh* of $g(n)$] means that there exists a constant c such that $|f(n)| \leq c|g(n)|$ for all sufficiently large positive integers n.

Under these conditions, we also say that "$f(n)$ has *order* at most $g(n)$" or "$f(n)$ grows no more rapidly than $g(n)$."

common orders

When we apply this notation, $f(n)$ will normally be the operation count or time for some algorithm, and we wish to choose the form of $g(n)$ to be as simple as possible. We thus write $O(1)$ to mean computing time that is bounded by a constant (not dependent on n); $O(n)$ means that the time is directly proportional to n and is called *linear time*. We call $O(n^2)$ *quadratic time*, $O(n^3)$ *cubic*, $O(2^n)$ *exponential*. These five orders, together with *logarithmic time* $O(\log n)$ and $O(n \log n)$, are the ones most commonly used in analyzing algorithms.

Figure 5.7 shows how these seven functions (with constant 1) grow with n. Notice especially how much slower $\lg n$ grows than n; this is essentially the reason why binary search is superior to sequential search for large lists. In the next chapter we shall study algorithms whose time is $O(1)$; notice that both the function 1 and the function $\lg n$ become farther and farther below all the others for large n. Notice also how much more rapidly 2^n grows than any of the other functions. An algorithm for which the time grows exponentially with n will prove usable only for very small values of n.

We can now express the conclusions of our algorithm analyses very simply:

▶   On a list of length n sequential search has time $O(n)$.

▶   On a list of length n binary search has time $O(\log n)$.

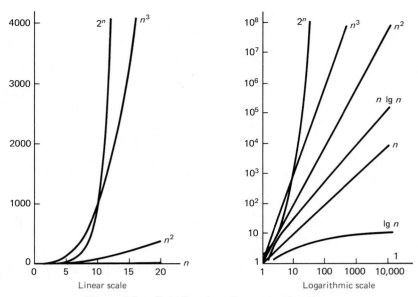

Figure 5.7.   Growth rates of common functions

3. Imprecision of the Big Oh Notation

Note that the constant c in the definition of the big Oh notation depends on which functions $f(n)$ and $g(n)$ are under discussion. Thus we can write that $17n^3 - 5$ is $O(n^3)$ (here $c = 17$ will do, as will any larger c), and also $35n^3 + 100$ is $O(n^3)$ (here $c \geq 35$). Hence, with the big Oh notation, we have lost the distinction in time required by Binary1 and Binary2.

poor uses

Note also that it is equally correct to write that $35n^3$ is $O(n^7)$ as that $35n^3$ is $O(n^3)$. It is correct but uninformative to write that both binary and sequential search have time that is $O(n^5)$. If $h(n)$ is any function that grows faster than $g(n)$, then a function that is $O(g(n))$ must also be $O(h(n))$. Hence the big Oh notation can be used imprecisely, but we shall always refrain from doing so, instead using the smallest possible of the seven functions shown in Figure 5.7.

4. Keeping the Dominant Term

We would often like to have a more precise measure of the amount of work done by an algorithm, and we can obtain one by using the big Oh notation within an expression, as follows. We define

$$f(n) = g(n) + O(h(n))$$

to mean that $f(n) - g(n)$ is $O(h(n))$. Instead of thinking of $O(h(n))$ as the class of all functions growing no faster than $ch(n)$ for some constant c, we think of $O(h(n))$ as a single but arbitrary such function. We then use this function to represent all the terms of our calculation in which we are not interested, generally all the terms except the one that grows the most quickly. The number of comparisons in the average successful search by one of our procedures can now be summarized as:

search comparisons

SequentialSearch	$\frac{1}{2}n + O(1)$
Binary1	$\lg n + O(1)$
Binary2	$2 \lg n + O(1)$

danger

In using the big Oh notation in expressions, it is necessary always to remember that $O(h(n))$ does not stand for a well-defined function but for an arbitrary function from a large class. Hence ordinary algebra cannot be done with $O(h(n))$. For example, we might have two expressions

$$n^2 + 4n - 5 = n^2 + O(n)$$

and

$$n^2 - 9n + 7 = n^2 + O(n)$$

but $O(n)$ represents different functions in the two expressions, so we cannot equate the right sides or conclude that the left sides are equal.

5. Ordering of Common Functions

Although the seven functions graphed in Figure 5.7 are the only ones we shall usually need for algorithm analysis, a few simple rules will enable you to determine the order of many other kinds of functions.

powers

1. The powers of n are ordered according to the exponent: n^a is $O(n^b)$ if and only if $a \leq b$.

logarithms

2. The order of $\log n$ is independent of the base taken for the logarithms; that is, $\log_a n$ is $O(\log_b n)$ for all $a, b > 1$.

3. A logarithm grows more slowly than any positive power of n: $\log n$ is $O(n^a)$ for any $a > 0$, but n^a is never $O(\log n)$ for $a > 0$.

exponentials

4. Any power n^a is $O(b^n)$ for all a and all $b > 1$, but b^n is never $O(n^a)$ for $b > 1$.

5. If $a < b$, then a^n is $O(b^n)$, but b^n is not $O(a^n)$.

products

6. If $f(n)$ is $O(g(n))$ and $h(n)$ is any nonzero function, then $f(n)h(n)$ is $O(g(n)h(n))$.

chain rule

7. The above rules may be applied recursively (a chain rule) by substituting a function of n for n. (Example: $\log \log n$ is $O((\log n)^{1/2})$.)

Exercises 5.6

E1. For each of the following pairs of functions, find the smallest integer value of n for which the first becomes larger than the second.

(a) n^2, $15n + 5$.

(b) 2^n, $8n^4$.

(c) $0.1n$, $10 \lg n$,   when $n > 1$.

(d) $0.1n^2$, $100n \lg n$,   when $n > 1$.

E2. Arrange the following functions into increasing order; that is, $f(n)$ should come before $g(n)$ in your list if and only if $f(n)$ is $O(g(n))$.

1000000	$(\lg n)^3$	2^n
$n \lg n$	$n^3 - 100n^2$	$n + \lg n$
$\lg \lg n$	$n^{0.1}$	n^2

E3. Let x and y be real numbers with $0 < x < y$. Prove that n^x is $O(n^y)$ but that n^y is not $O(n^x)$.

E4. Show that logarithmic time does not depend on the base a chosen for the logarithms. That is, prove that

$$\log_a n \text{ is } O(\log_b n)$$

for any real numbers $a > 1$ and $b > 1$.

Programming Project 5.6

P1. Write a program to test on your computer how long it takes to do $n \lg n$, n^2, 2^n, n^5, and $n!$ additions for $n = 5, 10, 15, 20$.

POINTERS AND PITFALLS

1. In designing algorithms be very careful of the extreme cases, such as empty lists, lists with only one item, or full lists (in the contiguous case).
2. Be sure that all your variables are properly initialized.
3. Double check the termination conditions for your loops, and make sure that progress toward termination always occurs.
4. In case of difficulty, formulate statements that will be correct both before and after each iteration of a loop, and verify that they hold.
5. Avoid sophistication for sophistication's sake. If a simple method is adequate for your application, use it.
6. Don't reinvent the wheel. If a ready-made procedure is adequate for your application, use it.
7. Sequential search is slow but robust. Use it for short lists or if there is any doubt that the keys in the list are properly ordered.
8. Be extremely careful if you must reprogram binary search. Verify that your algorithm is correct and test it on all the extreme cases.
9. Drawing trees is an excellent way both to trace the action of an algorithm and to analyze its behavior.
10. Rely on the big Oh analysis of algorithms for large applications but not for small applications.

REVIEW QUESTIONS

5.3

1. Name three conditions under which sequential search of a list is preferable to binary search.

5.4
2. In searching a list of n items, how many comparisons does sequential search do? binary search, first version?

3. Why was binary search implemented only for contiguous lists, not for simply linked lists?

4. Draw the comparison tree for Binary1 for searching a list of length **(a)** 1, **(b)** 2, **(c)** 3.

5. Draw the comparison tree for Binary2 for searching a list of length **(a)** 1, **(b)** 2, **(c)** 3.

6. If the height of a 2-tree is 3, what are **(a)** the largest and **(b)** the smallest number of vertices that can be in the tree?

7. Define the terms *internal* and *external path length* of a 2-tree. State the path length theorem.

5.5
8. What is the smallest number of comparisons that any method relying on comparisons of keys must make, on average, in searching a list of n items?

9. If Binary2 does 20 comparisons for the average successful search, then about how many will it do for the average unsuccessful search, assuming that the possibilities of the target less than the smallest key, between any pair of keys, or larger than the largest key are all equally likely?

5.6
10. What is the purpose of the big Oh notation?

REFERENCES FOR FURTHER STUDY

The primary reference for this chapter is KNUTH, Volume 3. (See the end of Chapter 3 for the bibliographic details.) Sequential search occupies pp. 389–405; binary search covers pp. 406–414; then comes Fibonacci search, and a section on history. KNUTH studies every method we have touched, and many others besides. He does algorithm analysis in considerably more detail than we have, writing his algorithms in a pseudo-assembly language and counting operations in detail there.

Proving the correctness of the binary search algorithm is the topic of

JON BENTLEY, "Programming pearls: Writing correct programs" (regular column), *Communications of the ACM* 26 (1983), 1040–1045.

In this column BENTLEY shows how to formulate a binary search algorithm from its requirements, points out that about 90 percent of professional programmers whom he has taught were unable to write the program correctly in one hour, and gives a formal verification of correctness.

The following paper studies 26 published versions of binary search, pointing out correct and erroneous reasoning and drawing conclusions applicable to other algorithms:

R. LESUISSE, "Some lessons drawn from the history of the binary search algorithm," *The Computer Journal* 26 (1983), 154–163.

Theorem 5.4 (successful and unsuccessful searches take almost the same time on average) is due to

T. N. HIBBARD, *Journal of the ACM* 9 (1962), 16–17.

Interpolation search is presented in

C. C. GOTLIEB and L. R. GOTLIEB, *Data Types and Structures,* Prentice-Hall, Englewood Cliffs, N.J., 1978, pp. 133–135.

Tables and Information Retrieval

▶ *This chapter continues the study of information retrieval begun in the last chapter, but now concentrating on tables instead of lists. We begin with ordinary rectangular arrays, then other kinds of arrays, and then we generalize to the study of hash tables. One of our major purposes again is to analyze and compare various algorithms, to see which are preferable under different conditions. The chapter concludes by applying the methods of hash tables to the Life game.*

6.1 INTRODUCTION: BREAKING THE lg n BARRIER

In the last chapter we showed that, by use of key comparisons alone, it is impossible to complete a search of n items in fewer than lg n comparisons, on average. But this result speaks only of searching by key comparisons. If we can use some other method, then we may be able to arrange our data so that we can locate a given item even more quickly.

table lookup

In fact, we commonly do so. If we have 500 different records, with an index between 1 and 500 assigned to each, then we would never think of using sequential or binary search to locate a record. We would simply store the records in an array of size 500, and use the index n to locate the record of item n by ordinary table lookup.

functions for information retrieval

Both table lookup and searching share the same essential purpose, that of *information retrieval*. We begin with a key (which may be complicated or simply an index) and wish to find the location of the item (if any) with that key. In other words, both table lookup and our searching algorithms provide *functions* from the set of keys to locations in a list or array. The functions are in fact one-to-one from the set of keys that actually occur to the set of locations that actually occur, since we assume that each item has only one key, and there is only one item with a given key.

tables

In this chapter we study ways to implement and access arrays in contiguous storage, beginning with ordinary rectangular arrays, and then considering tables with restricted location of nonzero entries, such as triangular tables. We turn afterward to more general problems, with the purpose of introducing and motivating the use first of access tables and then hash tables for information retrieval.

We shall see that, depending on the shape of the table, several steps may be needed to retrieve an entry, but, even so, the time required remains $O(1)$—that is, it is bounded by a constant that does not depend on the size of the table—and thus table lookup can be more efficient than any searching method.

6.2 RECTANGULAR ARRAYS

Because of the importance of rectangular arrays, almost all high-level languages provide convenient and efficient means to store and access them, so that generally the programmer need not worry about the implementation details. Nonetheless, computer storage is fundamentally arranged in a contiguous sequence (that is, in a straight line with each entry next to another), so for every access to a rectangular array, the machine must do some work to convert the location within a rectangle to a position along a line. Let us take a slightly closer look at this process.

1. Row- and Column-Major Ordering

Perhaps the most natural way to read a rectangular array is to read the entries of the first row from left to right, then the entries of the second row, and so on until the last row has been read. This is also the order in which most compilers store a rectangular array, and is called *row-major ordering*. For example, if the rows of an array are numbered from 1 to 2 and the columns are numbered from 1 to 3, then the order of indices with which the entries are stored in row-major ordering is

$$[1, 1] \quad [1, 2] \quad [1, 3] \quad [2, 1] \quad [2, 2] \quad [2, 3].$$

FORTRAN

Standard FORTRAN instead uses *column-major ordering,* in which the entries of the first column come first, and so on. This example in column-major ordering is

$$[1, 1] \quad [2, 1] \quad [1, 2] \quad [2, 2] \quad [1, 3] \quad [2, 3].$$

Figure 6.1 further illustrates row- and column-major orderings for an array with three rows and four columns.

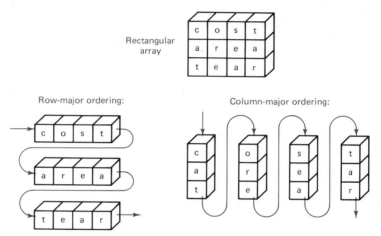

Figure 6.1. **Sequential representation of a rectangular array**

2. Indexing Rectangular Arrays

In the general problem, the compiler must be able to start with an index $[i, j]$ and calculate where the corresponding entry of the array will be stored. We shall derive a formula for this calculation. For simplicity we shall use only row-major ordering and suppose that the rows are numbered from 0 to $m - 1$ and the columns from 0 to $n - 1$. The general case is treated as an exercise. Altogether, the array will have mn entries, as must its sequential implementation. We number the entries in the array from 0 to $mn - 1$. To obtain the formula calculating the position where $[i, j]$ goes, we first consider some special cases. Clearly $[0, 0]$ goes to position 0, and, in fact, the entire first row is easy: $[0, j]$ goes to position j. The first entry of the second row, $[1, 0]$, comes after $[0, n - 1]$, and thus goes into position n. Continuing, we see that $[1, j]$ goes to position $n + j$. Entries of the next row will have two full rows, that is, $2n$ entries, preceding them. Hence entry $[2, j]$ goes to position $2n + j$. In general, the entries of row i are preceded by ni earlier entries, so the desired formula is

index function,
rectangular array

> *Entry* $[i, j]$ *goes to position* $ni + j.$

A formula of this kind, which gives the sequential location of an array entry, is called an *index function.*

3. Variation: An Access Table

The index function for rectangular arrays is certainly not difficult to calculate, and the compilers of most high-level languages will simply write into the machine-language program the necessary steps for its calculation every time a reference is made to a rectangular array. On small machines, however, multiplication can be quite slow, so a slightly different method can be used to eliminate the multiplications.

access table,
rectangular array
This method is to keep an auxiliary array, a part of the multiplication table for n. The array will contain the values

$$0, \quad n, \quad 2n, \quad 3n, \quad \ldots, \quad (m-1)n.$$

Note that this array is much smaller (usually) than the rectangular array, so that it can be kept permanently in memory without losing too much space. Its entries then need be calculated only once (and note that they can be calculated using only addition). For all later references to the rectangular array, the compiler can find the position for $[i, j]$ by taking the entry in position i of the auxiliary table, adding j, and going to the resulting position.

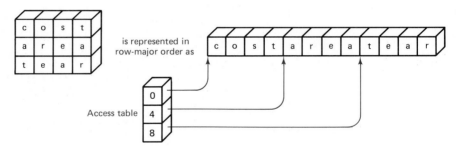

is represented in row-major order as

Access table

Figure 6.2.   **Access table for a rectangular array**

This auxiliary table provides our first example of an *access table* (see Figure 6.2). In general, an access table is an auxiliary array used to find data stored elsewhere. The terms *access vector* and *dope vector* (the latter especially when additional information is included) are also used.

Exercises
6.2
E1. What is the index function for a two-dimensional rectangular array with bounds

$$\textbf{array}[0 \mathinner{\ldotp\ldotp} m-1, \quad 0 \mathinner{\ldotp\ldotp} n-1]$$

under column-major ordering?

E2. Give the index function, with row-major ordering, for a two-dimensional array with arbitrary bounds

$$\textbf{array}[r \mathinner{\ldotp\ldotp} s, \quad t \mathinner{\ldotp\ldotp} u].$$

E3. Find the index function, with the generalization of row-major ordering, for an array with d dimensions and arbitrary bounds for each dimension.

6.3 TABLES OF VARIOUS SHAPES

matrix

Information that is usually stored in a rectangular array may not require every position in the rectangle for its representation. If we define a *matrix* to be an array of numbers, then often some of the positions within the matrix will be required to be 0. Several such examples are shown in Figure 6.3. Even when the entries in a table are not numbers, the positions actually used may not be all of those in a rectangle, and there may be better implementations than using a rectangular array and leaving some positions vacant. In this section, we examine ways to implement tables of various shapes, ways that will not require setting aside unused space in a rectangular array.

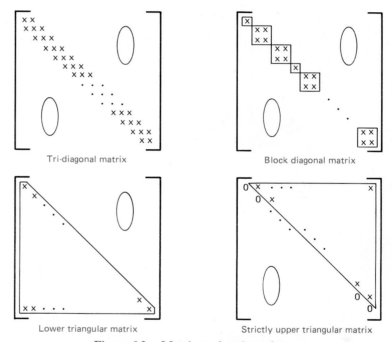

Figure 6.3.   Matrices of various shapes

6.3.1 Triangular Tables

Let us consider the representation of a lower triangular table shown in Figure 6.3. Such a table can be defined formally as a table in which all indices $[i, j]$ are required to satisfy $i \geq j$. We can implement a triangular table in a sequential array by sliding each row out after the one above it, as shown in Figure 6.4.

To construct the index function that describes this mapping, we again make the slight simplification of assuming that the rows and the columns are numbered starting with 0. To find the position where $[i, j]$ goes, we now need to find where row number i starts, and then to locate column j we need only add j to the starting

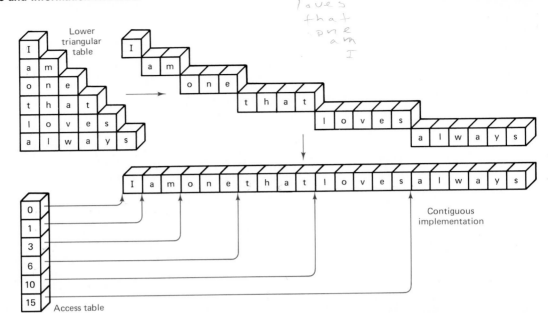

Figure 6.4.   Contiguous implementation of a triangular table

point of row i. If the entries of the contiguous array are also numbered starting with 0, then the index of the starting point will be the same as the number of entries that precede row i. Clearly there are 0 entries before row 0, and only the one entry of row 0 precedes row 1. For row 2 there are $1 + 2 = 3$ preceding entries, and in general we see that preceding row i there are exactly

$$1 + 2 + \cdots + i = \tfrac{1}{2}i(i + 1)$$

entries. Hence the desired function is that entry $[i, j]$ of the triangular table corresponds to entry

index function, triangular table

$$\tfrac{1}{2}i(i + 1) + j$$

of the contiguous array.

As we did for rectangular arrays, we can again avoid all multiplications and divisions by setting up an access table whose entries correspond to the row indices of the triangular table. Position i of the access table will permanently contain the value $\tfrac{1}{2}i(i + 1)$. The access table will be calculated only once at the start of the program, and then used repeatedly at each reference to the triangular table. Note that even the initial calculation of this access table requires no multiplication or division, but only addition to calculate its entries in the order

access table, triangular table

$$0, \quad 1, \quad 1 + 2, \quad (1 + 2) + 3, \quad \cdots .$$

6.3.2 Jagged Tables

In both of the foregoing examples we have considered a rectangular table as made up from its rows. In ordinary rectangular arrays, all the rows have the same length;

in triangular tables, the length of each row can be found from a simple formula. We now consider the case of jagged tables such as the one in Figure 6.5, where there is no predictable relation between the position of a row and its length.

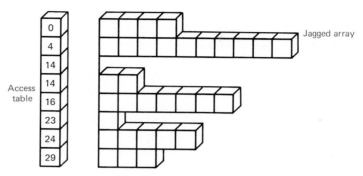

Figure 6.5.   Access table for jagged table

It is clear from the diagram that, even though we are not able to give an *a priori* function to map the jagged table into contiguous storage, the use of an access table remains as easy as in the previous examples, and elements of the jagged table can be referenced just as quickly. To set up the access table, we must construct the jagged table in its natural order, beginning with its first row. Entry 0 of the access table is, as before, the start of the contiguous array. After each row of the jagged table has been constructed, the index of the first unused position of the contiguous storage should then be entered as the next entry in the access table and used to start constructing the next row of the jagged table.

6.3.3 Inverted Tables

Next let us consider an example illustrating multiple access tables, by which we can refer to a single table of records by several different keys at once.

Consider the problem faced by the telephone company in accessing the records of its customers. To publish the telephone book, the records must be sorted alphabetically by the name of the subscriber. But to process long-distance charges, the accounts must be sorted by telephone number. To do routine maintenance, the company also needs to have its subscribers sorted by their address, so that a repairman may be able to work on several lines with one trip. Conceivably the telephone company could keep three (or more) sets of its records, one sorted by name, one by number, and one by address. This way, however, would not only be very wasteful of storage space, but would introduce endless headaches if one set of records were updated but another was not, and erroneous and unpredictable information might be used.

multiple records

By using access tables we can avoid the multiple sets of records, and we can still find the records by any of the three keys almost as quickly as if the records were fully sorted by that key. For the names we set up one access table. The first entry in this table is the position where the records of the subscriber whose name

multiple access tables

is first in alphabetical order are stored, the second entry gives the location of the second (in alphabetical order) subscriber's records, and so on. In a second access table, the first entry is the location of the subscriber's records whose telephone number happens to be smallest in numerical order. In yet a third access table the entries give the locations of the records sorted lexicographically by address. Notice that in this method all the fields that are treated as keys are processed in the same way. There is no particular reason why the records themselves need to be sorted according to one key rather than another, or, in fact, why they need to be sorted at all. The records themselves can be kept in an arbitrary order—say, the order in which they were first entered into the system. It also makes no difference whether the records are in an array, with entries in the access tables being indices of the array, or whether the records are in dynamic storage, with the access tables holding pointers to individual records. In any case, it is the access tables that are used for information retrieval, and, as ordinary contiguous arrays, they may be used for table lookup, or binary search, or any other purpose for which a contiguous implementation is appropriate.

unordered records with ordered access tables

An example of this scheme for a small number of accounts is shown in Figure 6.6.

Index	Name	Address	Phone
1	Hill, Thomas M.	High Towers	2829478
2	Baker, John M.	17 King St.	2884285
3	Roberts, L. B.	53 Ash St.	4372296
4	King, Barbara	High Towers	2863386
5	Hill, Thomas M.	39 King St.	2495723
6	Byers, Carolyn	118 Maple St.	4394231
7	Moody, C. L.	High Towers	2822214

Access Tables		
Name	Address	Phone
2	3	5
6	1	7
1	4	1
5	7	4
4	2	2
7	5	3
3	6	6

Figure 6.6.   Multikey access tables: an inverted array

Exercises 6.3

E1. The *main diagonal* of a square matrix consists of the entries for which the row and column indices are equal. A *diagonal matrix* is a square matrix in which all entries not on the main diagonal are 0. Describe a way to store a diagonal matrix without using space for entries that are necessarily 0, and give the corresponding index function.

E2. A *tri-diagonal matrix* is a square matrix in which all entries are 0 except possibly those on the main diagonal and on the diagonals immediately above and below it. That is, T is a tri-diagonal matrix means that $T[i, j] = 0$ unless $|i - j| \leq 1$.

(a) Devise a space-efficient storage scheme for tri-diagonal matrices, and give the corresponding index function.

(b) The *transpose* of a matrix is the matrix obtained by interchanging its rows with the corresponding columns. That is, matrix B is the transpose of matrix A means that $B[j, i] = A[i, j]$ for all indices i and j corresponding to positions in the matrix. Write a procedure that transposes a tri-diagonal matrix using the storage scheme devised in the previous exercise.

E3. An *upper triangular matrix* is a square array in which all entries below the main diagonal are 0.

(a) Describe the modifications necessary to use the access table method to store an upper triangular matrix.

(b) The transpose of a lower triangular matrix will be an upper triangular matrix. Write a procedure that will transpose a lower triangular matrix, using access tables to refer to both matrices.

E4. Consider a table of the triangular shape shown in Figure 6.7, where the columns are indexed from $-n$ to n and the rows from 0 to n.

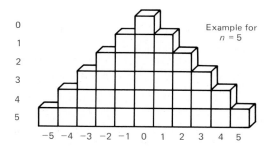

Figure 6.7.   A table symmetrically triangular around 0

(a) Devise an index function that maps a table of this shape into a sequential array.

(b) Write a procedure that will generate an access table for finding the first entry of each row of a table of this shape within the contiguous array.

(c) Write a procedure that will reflect the table from left to right. The entries in column 0 (the central column) remain unchanged, those in columns -1 and 1 are swapped, and so on.

Programming Projects 6.3

Implement the method described in the text that uses an access table to store a lower triangular table, as applied in the following projects.

P1. Write a procedure that will read the entries of a lower triangular table from the terminal.

P2. Write a procedure that will print a lower triangular table at the terminal.

P3. Suppose that a lower triangular table is a table of distances between cities, as often appears on a road map. Write a procedure that will check the triangle rule: The distance from city A to city C is never more than the distance from A to city B, plus the distance from B to C.

6.4 TABLES: A NEW ABSTRACT DATA TYPE

At the beginning of this chapter we studied several *index functions* used to locate entries in tables, and then we turned to *access tables,* which were arrays used for the same purpose as index functions. The analogy between functions and table lookup is indeed very close: With a function, we start with an argument and calculate a corresponding value; with a table, we start with an index and look up a corresponding value. Let us now use this analogy to produce a formal definition of the term *table,* a definition that will, in turn, motivate new ideas that come to fruition in the following section.

1. Functions

domain, codomain, and range

In mathematics a *function* is defined in terms of two sets and a correspondence from elements of the first set to elements of the second. If f is a function from a set A to a set B, then f assigns to each element of A a unique element of B. The set A is called the **domain** of f, and the set B is called the **codomain** of f. The subset of B containing just those elements that occur as values of f is called the **range** of f. This definition is illustrated in Figure 6.8.

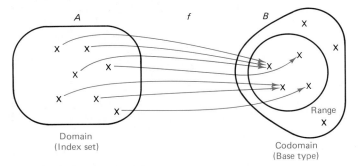

Figure 6.8.   The domain, codomain, and range of a function

index set, value type

Table access begins with an index and uses the table to look up a corresponding value. Hence for a table we call the domain the **index set,** and we call the codomain the **base type** or **value type.** (Recall that in Section 4.6.2 a *type* was defined as a set of values.) If, for example, we have the array declaration

array[m . . n] **of** real

then the index set is the set of integers between m and n, and the base type is the set of all real numbers. As a second example, consider a triangular table with m rows whose entries have type item. The base type is then simply type item, and the index type is the set of ordered pairs of integers

$$\{(i, j) \mid 1 \leq j \leq i \leq m\}.$$

2. An Abstract Data Type

We are now well on the way toward defining *table* as a new abstract data type, but recall from Section 4.6.2 that to complete the definition, we must also specify the operations that can be performed. Before doing so, let us summarize what we know.

DEFINITION

the ADT table

*A **table** with index set I and base type T is a function from I into T together with the following operations.*

1. *Table access:* Evaluate the function at any index in I.

2. *Table assignment:* Modify the function by changing its value at a specified index in I to the new value specified in the assignment.

These two operations are all that are provided by Pascal and some other languages, but that is no reason why we cannot allow the possibility of further operations. If we compare the definition of a list, we find that we allowed insertion and deletion as well as access and assignment. We can do the same with tables.

3. *Insertion:* Adjoin a new element x to the index set I and define a corresponding value of the function at x.

4. *Deletion:* Delete an element x from the index set I and restrict the function to the resulting smaller domain.

Even though these last two operations are not available directly in Pascal, they remain very useful for many applications, and we shall study them further in the next section. In some other languages, such as APL and SNOBOL, tables that change size while the program is running are an important feature. In any case, we should always be careful to program *into* a language and never allow our thinking to be limited by the restrictions of a particular language.

3. Implementation

index functions and access tables

The definition just given is that of an abstract data type and in itself says nothing about implementation, nor does it speak of the index functions or access tables studied earlier. Index functions and access tables are, in fact, implementation methods for more general tables. An index function or access table starts with a general index set of some specified form and produces as its result an index in some subscript range, such as a subrange of the integers. This range can then be used directly as subscripts for arrays provided by the programming language. In this way, the implementation of a table is divided into two smaller problems: finding an access table or index function and programming an array. You should note that both of these are special cases of tables, and hence we have an example of solving a problem by

divide and conquer

dividing it into two smaller problems of the same nature. This process is illustrated in Figure 6.9.

4. Comparisons

lists and tables

Let us compare the abstract data types *list* and *table*. The underlying mathematical construction for a list is the sequence, and for a table, it is the set and the function. Sequences have an implicit order, a first element, a second, and so on, but sets and

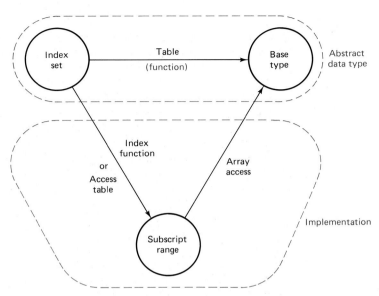

Figure 6.9.   Implementation of a table

retrieval

functions have no such order. (If the index set has some natural order, then sometimes this order is reflected in the table, but this is not a necessary aspect of using tables.) Hence information retrieval from a list naturally involves a search like the ones studied in the previous chapter, but information retrieval from a table requires different methods, access methods that go directly to the desired entry. The time required for searching a list generally depends on the number n of items in the list and is at least $\lg n$, but the time for accessing a table does not usually depend on the number of items in the table; that is, it is usually $O(1)$. For this reason, in many applications table access is significantly faster than list searching.

traversal

On the other hand, traversal is a natural operation for a list but not for a table. It is generally easy to move through a list performing some operation with every item in the list. In general, it may not be nearly so easy to perform an operation on every item in a table, particularly if some special order for the items is specified in advance.

tables and arrays

Finally, we should clarify the distinction between the terms *table* and *array*. *In general, we shall use table* as we have defined it in this section and restrict the term *array* to mean the programming feature available in Pascal and most high-level languages and used for implementing both tables and contiguous lists.

6.5 HASHING

6.5.1 Sparse Tables

1. Index Functions

We can continue to exploit table lookup even in situations where the key is no longer an index that can be used directly as in array indexing. What we can do is to set up a one-to-one correspondence between the keys by which we wish to retrieve information and indices that we can use to access an array. The index function that we produce will be somewhat more complicated than those of previous sections, since it may need to convert the key from, say, alphabetic information to an integer, but in principle it can still be done.

The only difficulty arises when the number of possible keys exceeds the amount of space available for our table. If, for example, our keys are alphabetical words of eight letters, then there are $26^8 \approx 2 \times 10^{11}$ possible keys, a number much greater than the number of positions that will be available in high-speed memory. In practice, however, only a small fraction of these keys will actually occur. That is, the table is *sparse*. Conceptually, we can regard it as indexed by a very large set, but with relatively few positions actually occupied. In Pascal, for example, we might think in terms of conceptual declarations such as

type $\cdots$ = **sparse table** [keytype] **of** item.

Even though it may not be possible to implement a declaration such as this directly, it is often helpful in problem solving to begin with such a picture, and only slowly tie down the details of how it is put into practice.

2. Hash Tables

index function not one-to-one

The idea of a *hash table* (such as the one shown in Figure 6.10) is to allow many of the different possible keys that might occur to be mapped to the same location in an array under the action of the index function. Then there will be a possibility that two records will want to be in the same place, but if the number of records that actually occur is small relative to the size of the array, then this possibility will cause little loss of time. Even when most entries in the array are occupied, hash methods can be an effective means of information retrieval.

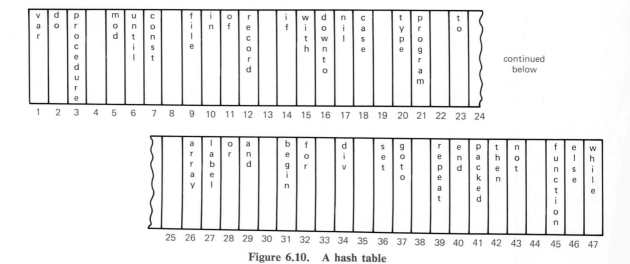

Figure 6.10.   A hash table

hash function

We begin with a *hash function* that takes a key and maps it to some index in the array. This function will generally map several different keys to the same index.

collision

If the desired record is in the location given by the index, then our problem is solved; otherwise, we must use some method to resolve the *collision* that may have occurred between two records wanting to go to the same location. There are thus two questions we must answer to use hashing. First, we must find good hash functions, and, second, we must determine how to resolve collisions.

Before approaching these questions, let us pause to outline informally the steps needed to implement hashing.

3. Algorithm Outlines

keys in table

First, an array must be declared that will hold the hash table. With ordinary arrays, the keys used to locate entries are usually the indices, so there is no need to keep them within the array itself, but for a hash table, several possible keys will correspond to the same index, so one field within each record in the array must be reserved for the key itself.

initialization

Next, all locations in the array must be initialized to show that they are empty. How this is done depends on the application; often it is accomplished by setting the key fields to some value that is guaranteed never to occur as an actual key. With alphanumeric keys, for example, a key consisting of all blanks might represent an empty position.

insertion

To insert a record into the hash table, the hash function for the key is first calculated. If the corresponding location is empty, then the record can be inserted, else if the keys are equal, then insertion of the new record would not be allowed, and in the remaining case (a record with a different key is in the location), it becomes necessary to resolve the collision.

retrieval

To retrieve the record with a given key is entirely similar. First, the hash function for the key is computed. If the desired record is in the corresponding location, then the retrieval has succeeded; otherwise, while the location is nonempty and not all locations have been examined, follow the same steps used for collision resolution. If an empty position is found, or all locations have been considered, then no record with the given key is in the table, and the search is unsuccessful.

6.5.2 Choosing a Hash Function

The two principal criteria in selecting a hash function are that it should be easy and quick to compute and that it should achieve an even distribution of the keys that actually occur across the range of indices. If we know in advance exactly what keys will occur, then it is possible to construct hash functions that will be very efficient, but generally we do not know in advance what keys will occur. Therefore,

method

the usual way is for the hash function to take the key, chop it up, mix the pieces together in various ways, and thereby obtain an index that (like the pseudorandom numbers generated by computer) will be uniformly distributed over the range of indices.

It is from this process that the word *hash* comes, since the process converts the key into something that bears little resemblance. At the same time, it is hoped that any patterns or regularities that may occur in the keys will be destroyed, so that the results will be randomly distributed.

Even though the term *hash* is very descriptive, in some books the more technical terms *scatter-storage* or *key-transformation* are used in its place.

We shall consider three methods that can be put together in various ways to build a hash function.

1. Truncation

Ignore part of the key, and use the remaining part directly as the index (considering non-numeric fields as their numerical codes). If the keys, for example, are eight-digit integers and the hash table has 1000 locations, then the first, second, and fifth digits from the right might make the hash function, so that 62538194 maps to 394. Truncation is a very fast method, but it often fails to distribute the keys evenly through the table.

2. Folding

Partition the key into several parts and combine the parts in a convenient way (often using addition or multiplication) to obtain the index. For example, an eight-digit integer can be divided into groups of three, three, and two digits, the groups added together, and truncated if necessary to be in the proper range of indices. Hence 62538194 maps to $625 + 381 + 94 = 1100$, which is truncated to 100. Since all information in the key can affect the value of the function, folding often achieves a better spread of indices than does truncation by itself.

3. Modular Arithmetic

Convert the key to an integer (using the above devices as desired), divide by the size of the index range, and take the remainder as the result. This amounts to using the Pascal operator **mod.** The spread achieved by taking a remainder depends very much on the modulus (in this case, the size of the hash array). If the modulus is a power of a small integer like 2 or 10, then many keys tend to map to the same

prime modulus

index, while other indices remain unused. The best choice for modulus is a prime number, which usually has the effect of spreading the keys quite uniformly. (We shall see later that a prime modulus also improves an important method for collision resolution.) Hence, rather than choosing a hash table size of 1000, it is better to choose either 997 or 1009; $1024 = 2^{10}$ would usually be a poor choice. Taking the remainder is usually the best way to conclude calculating the hash function, since it can achieve a good spread at the same time that it ensures that the result is in the proper range. About the only reservation is that, on a tiny machine with no hardware division, the calculation can be slow, so other methods should be considered.

4. Pascal Example

As a simple example, let us write a hash function in Pascal for transforming a key consisting of eight alphanumeric characters into an integer in the range

$$0 \, . \, . \; \text{hashsize} - 1.$$

That is, we shall begin with the type

type   keytype = **array**[1 . . 8] **of** char;

We can then write a simple hash function as follows:

```
function Hash(x: keytype): integer;
var
  i:  1 .. 8;
  h: integer;
begin
  h := 0;
  for i := 1 to 8 do
    h := h + ord(x[i]);
  Hash := h mod hashsize
end;
```

We have simply added the integer codes corresponding to each of the eight characters. There is no reason to believe that this method will be better (or worse), however, than any number of others. We could, for example, subtract some of the codes, multiply them in pairs, or ignore every other character. Sometimes an application will suggest that one hash function is better than another; sometimes it requires experimentation to settle on a good one.

6.5.3 Collision Resolution with Open Addressing

1. Linear Probing

The simplest method to resolve a collision is to start with the hash address (the location where the collision occurred) and do a sequential search for the desired key or an empty location. Hence this method searches in a straight line, and it is therefore called *linear probing*. The array should be considered circular, so that when the last location is reached, the search proceeds to the first location of the array.

2. Clustering

The major drawback of linear probing is that, as the table becomes about half full, there is a tendency toward *clustering;* that is, records start to appear in long strings of adjacent positions with gaps between the strings. Thus the sequential searches needed to find an empty position become longer and longer. For consider the example *example of clustering* in Figure 6.11, where the occupied positions are shown in color. Suppose that there are n locations in the array and that the hash function chooses any of them with equal probability $1/n$. Begin with a fairly uniform spread, as shown in the top diagram. If a new insertion hashes to location b, then it will go there, but if it hashes to location a (which is full), then it will also go into b. Thus the probability that b will be filled has doubled to $2/n$. At the next stage, an attempted insertion into any of locations a, b, c, or d will end up in d, so the probability of filling d is $4/n$. After this, e has probability $5/n$ of being filled, and so as additional insertions are made the most likely effect is to make the string of full positions beginning at location a longer and longer, and hence the performance of the hash table starts to degenerate toward that of sequential search.

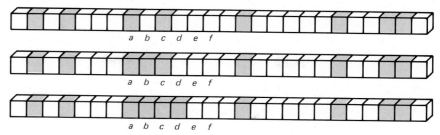

Figure 6.11. Clustering in a hash table

instability

The problem of clustering is essentially one of instability; if a few keys happen randomly to be near each other, then it becomes more and more likely that other keys will join them, and the distribution will become progressively more unbalanced.

3. Increment Functions

rehashing

If we are to avoid the problem of clustering, then we must use some more sophisticated way to select the sequence of locations to check when a collision occurs. There are many ways to do so. One, called **rehashing**, uses a second hash function to obtain the second position to consider. If this position is filled, then some other method is needed to get the third position, and so on. But if we have a fairly good spread from the first hash function, then little is to be gained by an independent second hash function. We will do just as well to find a more sophisticated way of determining the distance to move from the first hash position and apply this method, whatever the first hash location is. Hence we wish to design an increment function that can depend on the key or on the number of probes already made and that will avoid clustering.

4. Quadratic Probing

If there is a collision at hash address h, this method probes the table at locations $h + 1$, $h + 4$, $h + 9$, . . . , that is, at locations $h + i^2$ (mod hashsize) for $i = 1$, $2, ...$ That is, the increment function is i^2.

This method substantially reduces clustering, but it is not obvious that it will probe all locations in the table, and in fact it does not. If hashsize is a power of 2, then relatively few positions are probed. Suppose that hashsize is a prime. If we reach the same location at probe i and at probe j, then

$$h + i^2 \equiv h + j^2 \text{ (mod hashsize)}$$

so that

$$(i - j)(i + j) \equiv 0 \text{ (mod hashsize)}.$$

Since hashsize is a prime, it must divide one factor. It divides $i - j$ only when j differs from i by a multiple of hashsize, so at least hashsize probes have been made. Hashsize divides $i + j$, however, when $j =$ hashsize $- i$, so the total number of distinct positions that will be probed is exactly

number of distinct probes

$$(\text{hashsize} + 1) \textbf{ div } 2.$$

It is customary to take overflow as occurring when this number of positions has been probed, and the results are quite satisfactory.

calculation

Note that quadratic probing can be accomplished without doing multiplications: After the first probe at position x, the increment is set to 1. At each successive probe, the increment is increased by 2 after it has been added to the previous location. Since

$$1 + 3 + 5 + \cdots + (2i - 1) = i^2$$

for all $i \geq 1$ (you can prove this fact by mathematical induction), probe i will look in position

$$x + 1 + 3 + \cdots + (2i - 1) = x + i^2,$$

as desired.

5. Key-Dependent Increments

Rather than having the increment depend on the number of probes already made, we can let it be some simple function of the key itself. For example, we could truncate the key to a single character and use its code as the increment. In Pascal, we might write

increment := ord(k[1]).

A good approach, when the remainder after division is taken as the hash function, is to let the increment depend on the quotient of the same division. An optimizing compiler should specify the division only once, so the calculation will be fast, and the results generally satisfactory.

In this method, the increment, once determined, remains constant. If hashsize is a prime, it follows that the probes will step through all the entries of the array before any repetitions. Hence overflow will not be indicated until the array is completely full.

6. Random Probing

A final method is to use a pseudorandom number generator to obtain the increment. The generator used should be one that always generates the same sequence provided it starts with the same seed. The seed, then, can be specified as some function of the key. This method is excellent in avoiding clustering, but is likely to be slower than the others.

7. Pascal Algorithms

To conclude the discussion of open addressing, we continue to study the Pascal example already introduced, which used alphanumeric keys of the type

type keytype = **array**[1 .. 8] **of** char.

We set up the hash table with the declarations

declarations

```
const
    hashsize = 997;                    {a prime number of appropriate size}
    hashmax = 996;                     {should be 1 less than hashsize}
type
    hashtable = array[0 .. hashmax] of item;
var
    H:          hashtable;
```

initialization

The hash table must be initialized by defining a special key called blankword that consists of eight blanks and setting the key field of each item in H to blankword.

We shall use the hash function already written in Section 6.5.2, part 4, together with quadratic probing for collision resolution. We have shown that the maximum number of probes that can be made this way is (hashsize + 1) **div** 2, and we keep a counter c to check this upper bound.

With these conventions, let us write a procedure to insert a record r, with key r.key, into the hash table H.

insertion

```
procedure Insert(var H: hashtable; r: item);
var
    c,                                 {counter to be sure that table is not full}
    i,                                 {increment used for quadratic probing}
    p: integer;                        {position currently probed in H}
begin                                  {procedure Insert}
    p := Hash(r.key);
    c := 0;
    i := 1;
    while (H[p].key <> blankword)      {Is the location empty?}
        and (H[p].key <> r.key)        {Has the target key been found?}
        and (c <= hashsize div 2) do   {Has overflow occurred?}
    begin
        c := c + 1;
        p := p + i;
        i := i + 2;                    {Prepare increment for the next iteration.}
        if p > hashmax then
            p := p mod hashsize
    end;
    if H[p].key = blankword then
        H[p] := r                      {Insert the new item r.}
    else if H[p].key = r.key then
        Error                          {The same key cannot appear twice.}
    else
        Overflow                       {Counter has reached its limit.}
end;                                   {procedure Insert}
```

quadratic probing

A procedure to retrieve the record (if any) with a given key will have a similar form and is left as an exercise.

8. Deletions

Up to now we have said nothing about deleting items from a hash table. At first glance, it may appear to be an easy task, requiring only marking the deleted location with the special key indicating that it is empty. This method will not work. The reason is that an empty location is used as the signal to stop the search for a target key. Suppose that, before the deletion, there had been a collision or two and that some item whose hash address is the now-deleted position is actually stored elsewhere in the table. If we now try to retrieve that item, then the now-empty position will stop the search, and it is impossible to find the item, even though it is still in the table.

special key

One method to remedy this difficulty is to invent another special key, to be placed in any deleted position. This special key would indicate that this position is free to receive an insertion when desired but that it should not be used to terminate the search for some other item in the table. Using this second special key will, however, make the algorithms somewhat more complicated and a bit slower. With the methods we have so far studied for hash tables, deletions are indeed awkward and should be avoided as much as possible.

6.5.4 Collision Resolution by Chaining

Up to now we have implicitly assumed that we are using only contiguous storage while working with hash tables. Contiguous storage for the hash table itself is, in fact, the natural choice, since we wish to be able to refer quickly to random positions in the table, and linked storage is not suited to random access. There is, however, *linked storage*   no reason why linked storage should not be used for the records themselves. We can take the hash table itself as an array of pointers to the records, that is, as an array of list headers. An example appears in Figure 6.12.

It is traditional to refer to the linked lists from the hash table as *chains* and call this method collision resolution by *chaining*.

1. Advantages of Linked Storage

There are several advantages to this point of view. The first, and the most important *space saving*   when the records themselves are quite large, is that considerable space may be saved. Since the hash table is a contiguous array, enough space must be set aside at compilation time to avoid overflow. If the records themselves are in the hash table, then if there are many empty positions (as is desirable to help avoid the cost of collisions), these will consume considerable space that might be needed elsewhere. If, on the other hand, the hash table contains only pointers to the records, pointers that require only one word each, then the size of the hash table may be reduced by a large factor (essentially by a factor equal to the size of the records), and will become small relative to the space available for the records, or for other uses.

collision resolution

The second major advantage of keeping only pointers in the hash table is that it allows simple and efficient collision handling. We need only add a link field to each record, and organize all the records with a single hash address as a linked list. With a good hash function, few keys will give the same hash address, so the

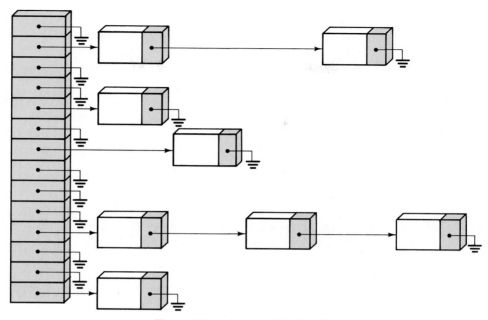

Figure 6.12.   A chained hash table

linked lists will be short and can be searched quickly. Clustering is no problem at all, because keys with distinct hash addresses always go to distinct lists.

overflow

A third advantage is that it is no longer necessary that the size of the hash table exceed the number of records. If there are more records than entries in the table, it means only that some of the linked lists are now sure to contain more than one record. Even if there are several times more records than the size of the table, the average length of the linked lists will remain small, and sequential search on the appropriate list will remain efficient.

deletion

Finally, deletion becomes a quick and easy task in a chained hash table. Deletion proceeds in exactly the same way as deletion from a simple linked list.

2. Disadvantage of Linked Storage

These advantages of chained hash tables are indeed powerful. Lest you believe that chaining is always superior to open addressing, however, let us point out one important disadvantage: All the links require space. If the records are large, then this space is negligible in comparison with that needed for the records themselves; but if the records are small, then it is not.

use of space

small records

Suppose, for example, that the links take one word each and that the items themselves take only one word (which is the key alone). Such applications are quite common, where we use the hash table only to answer some yes-no question about the key. Suppose that we use chaining and make the hash table itself quite small, with the same number n of entries as the number of items. Then we shall use $3n$ words of storage altogether: n for the hash table, n for the keys, and n for the links to find the next node (if any) on each chain. Since the hash table will be nearly full, there will be many collisions, and some of the chains will have several items.

Hence searching will be a bit slow. Suppose, on the other hand, that we use open addressing. The same $3n$ words of storage put entirely into the hash table will mean that it will be only one third full, and therefore there will be relatively few collisions and the search for any given item will be faster.

3. Pascal Algorithms

declarations

A chained hash table in Pascal takes declarations like

```
type
  pointer   = ↑node;
  list      = record head: pointer end;
  hashtable = array [0 . . hashmax] of list;
```

The record type called node consists of an item, called info, and an additional field, called next, that points to the next node on a linked list.

The code needed to initialize the hash table is

initialization

```
for i := 0 to hashmax do H[i].head := nil;
```

We can even use previously written procedures to access the hash table. The hash function itself is no different from that used with open addressing; for data retrieval we can simply use the procedure SequentialSearch (linked version) from Section 5.2, as follows:

retrieval

```
procedure Retrieve(var H: hashtable; target: keytype;
                         var found: Boolean; var location: pointer);
{finds the node with key target in the hash table H, and returns with location
   pointing to that node, provided that found becomes true}
begin
  SequentialSearch(H[Hash(target)], target, found, location)
end;
```

Our procedure for inserting a new entry will assume that the key does not appear already; otherwise, only the most recent insertion with a given key will be retrievable.

insertion

```
procedure Insert(var H: hashtable; p: pointer);
{inserts node p↑ into the chained hash table H, assuming no other node with
   key p↑.info.key is in the table}
var
  i: integer;                              {used for index in hash table}
begin
  i := Hash(p↑.info.key);           {Find the index of the linked list for p↑.}
  p↑.next := H[i].head;                  {Insert p↑ at the head of the list.}
  H[i].head := p                   {Set the head of the list to the new item.}
end;
```

As you can see, both of these procedures are significantly simpler than are the versions for open addressing, since collision resolution is not a problem.

E1. Write a Pascal procedure to insert an item into a hash table with open addressing and linear probing.

E2. Write a Pascal procedure to retrieve an item from a hash table with open addressing and **(a)** linear probing; **(b)** quadratic probing.

E3. Devise a simple, easy-to-calculate hash function for mapping three-letter words to integers between 0 and $n - 1$, inclusive. Find the values of your function on the words

> PAL   LAP   PAM   MAP   PAT   PET   SET   SAT   TAT   BAT

for $n = 11, 13, 17, 19$. Try for as few collisions as possible.

E4. Suppose that a hash table contains hashsize $= 13$ entries indexed from 0 through 12 and that the following keys are to be mapped into the table:

> 10   100   32   45   58   126   3   29   200   400   0.

(a) Determine the hash addresses and find how many collisions occur when these keys are reduced **mod** hashsize.

(b) Determine the hash addresses and find how many collisions occur when these keys are first folded by adding their digits together (in ordinary decimal representation) and then reducing **mod** hashsize.

perfect hash functions

(c) Find a hash function that will produce no collisions for these keys. (A hash function that has no collisions for a fixed set of keys is called *perfect*.)

(d) Repeat the previous parts of this exercise for hashsize $= 11$. (A hash function that produces no collision for a fixed set of keys that completely fill the hash table is called *minimal perfect*.)

E5. Another method for resolving collisions with open addressing is to keep a separate array called the *overflow table*, into which all items that collide with an occupied location are put. They can either be inserted with another hash function or simply inserted in order, with sequential search used for retrieval. Discuss the advantages and disadvantages of this method.

E6. Write an algorithm for deleting a node from a chained hash table.

E7. Write a deletion algorithm for a hash table with open addressing, using a second special key to indicate a deleted item (see part 8 of Section 6.5.3). Change the retrieval and insertion algorithms accordingly.

E8. With linear probing, it is possible to delete an item without using a second special key, as follows. Mark the deleted entry empty. Search until another empty position is found. If the search finds a key whose hash address is at or before the first empty position, then move it back there, make its previous position empty, and continue from the new empty position. Write an algorithm to implement this method. Do the retrieval and insertion algorithms need modification?

Programming Project 6.5

P1. Consider the 35 Pascal reserved words listed in Appendix C.2.1. Consider these words as strings of nine characters, where words less than nine letters long are filled with blanks on the right.

(a) Devise an integer-valued function that will produce different values when applied to all 35 reserved words. [You may find it helpful to write a short program to assist. Your program could read the words from a file, apply the function you devise, and determine what collisions occur.]

(b) Find the smallest integer hashsize such that, when the values of your function are reduced **mod** hashsize, all 35 values remain distinct.

(c) Modify your function as necessary until you can achieve hashsize = 35 in the preceding part. (You will then have discovered a *minimal perfect* hash function for the 35 Pascal reserved words.)

6.6 ANALYSIS OF HASHING

1. The Birthday Surprise

The likelihood of collisions in hashing relates to the well-known mathematical diversion: How many randomly chosen people need to be in a room before it becomes likely that two people will have the same birthday (month and day)? Since (apart from leap years) there are 365 possible birthdays, most people guess that the answer will be in the hundreds, but in fact, the answer is only 24 people.

We can determine the probabilities for this question by answering its opposite: With m randomly chosen people in a room, what is the probability that no two have the same birthday? Start with any person, and check his birthday off on a calendar. The probability that a second person has a different birthday is 364/365. Check it off. The probability that a third person has a different birthday is now 363/365. Continuing this way, we see that if the first $m - 1$ people have different birthdays, then the probability that person m has a different birthday is

$$(365 - m + 1)/365.$$

Since the birthdays of different people are independent, the probabilities multiply, and we obtain that the probability that m people all have different birthdays is

probability

$$\frac{364}{365} \times \frac{363}{365} \times \frac{362}{365} \times \cdots \times \frac{365 - m + 1}{365}.$$

This expression becomes less than 0.5 whenever $m \geq 24$.

collisions likely

In regard to hashing, the birthday surprise tells us that with any problem of reasonable size, we are almost certain to have some collisions. Our approach, therefore, should not be only to try to minimize the number of collisions, but also to handle those that occur as expeditiously as possible.

2. Counting Probes

As with other methods of information retrieval, we would like to know how many comparisons of keys occur on average during both successful and unsuccessful attempts to locate a given target key. We shall use the word *probe* for looking at one item and comparing its key with the target.

The number of probes we need clearly depends on how full the table is. Therefore (as for searching methods), we let n be the number of items in the table, and we let t (which is the same as hashsize) be the number of positions in the array. The *load factor* of the table is $\lambda = n/t$. Thus $\lambda = 0$ signifies an empty table; $\lambda = 0.5$ a table that is half full. For open addressing, λ can never exceed 1, but for chaining, there is no limit on the size of λ. We consider chaining and open addressing separately.

3. Analysis of Chaining

With a chained hash table we go directly to one of the linked lists before doing any probes. Suppose that the chain that will contain the target (if it is present) has k items.

unsuccessful retrieval

If the search is unsuccessful, then the target will be compared with all k of the corresponding keys. Since the items are distributed uniformly over all t lists (equal probability of appearing on any list), the expected number of items on the one being searched is $\lambda = n/t$. Hence the average number of probes for an unsuccessful search is λ.

successful retrieval

Now suppose that the search is successful. From the analysis of sequential search, we know that the average number of comparisons is $\frac{1}{2}(k + 1)$, where k is the length of the chain containing the target. But the expected length of this chain is no longer λ, since we know in advance that it must contain at least one node (the target). The $n - 1$ nodes other than the target are distributed uniformly over all t chains; hence the expected number on the chain with the target is $1 + (n - 1)/t$. Except for tables of trivially small size, we may approximate $(n - 1)/t$ by $n/t = \lambda$. Hence the average number of probes for a successful search is very nearly

$$\tfrac{1}{2}(k + 1) \approx \tfrac{1}{2}(1 + \lambda + 1) = 1 + \tfrac{1}{2}\lambda.$$

4. Analysis of Open Addressing

random probes

For our analysis of the number of probes done in open addressing, let us first ignore the problem of clustering, by assuming that not only are the first probes random, but after a collision, the next probe will be random over all remaining positions of the table. In fact, let us assume that the table is so large that all the probes can be regarded as independent events.

Let us first study an unsuccessful search. The probability that the first probe hits an occupied cell is λ, the load factor. The probability that a probe hits an empty cell is $1 - \lambda$. The probability that the unsuccessful search terminates in exactly two probes is therefore $\lambda(1 - \lambda)$, and, similarly, the probability that exactly k probes are made in an unsuccessful search is $\lambda^{k-1}(1 - \lambda)$. The expected number $U(\lambda)$ of probes in an unsuccessful search is therefore

$$U(\lambda) = \sum_{k=1}^{\infty} k\lambda^{k-1}(1 - \lambda).$$

unsuccessful retrieval

This sum is evaluated in Appendix A.1; we obtain thereby

$$U(\lambda) = \frac{1}{(1 - \lambda)^2}(1 - \lambda) = \frac{1}{1 - \lambda}.$$

To count the probes needed for a successful search, we note that the number needed will be exactly one more than the number of probes in the unsuccessful search made before inserting the item. Now let us consider the table as beginning empty, with each item inserted one at a time. As these items are inserted, the load factor grows slowly from 0 to its final value, λ. It is reasonable for us to approximate this step-by-step growth by continuous growth and replace a sum with an integral. We conclude that the average number of probes in a successful search is approximately

successful retrieval

$$S(\lambda) = \frac{1}{\lambda} \int_0^\lambda U(\mu)\,d\mu = \frac{1}{\lambda} \ln \frac{1}{1-\lambda}.$$

Similar calculations may be done for open addressing with linear probing, where it is no longer reasonable to assume that successive probes are independent. The details, however, are rather more complicated, so we present only the results. For the complete derivation, consult the references at the end of the chapter. For linear probing the average number of probes for an unsuccessful search increases to

linear probing

$$\tfrac{1}{2}\left[1 + \frac{1}{(1-\lambda)^2}\right]$$

and for a successful search the number becomes

$$\tfrac{1}{2}\left[1 + \frac{1}{1-\lambda}\right].$$

5. Theoretical Comparisons

Figure 6.13 gives the values of the foregoing expressions for different values of the load factor.

Load factor	0.10	0.50	0.80	0.90	0.99	2.00
Successful search						
Chaining	1.05	1.25	1.40	1.45	1.50	2.00
Open, Random probes	1.05	1.4	2.0	2.6	4.6	—
Linear probes	1.06	1.5	3.0	5.5	50.5	—
Unsuccessful search						
Chaining	0.10	0.50	0.80	0.90	0.99	2.00
Open, Random probes	1.1	2.0	5.0	10.0	100.	—
Linear probes	1.12	2.5	13.	50.	5000.	—

Figure 6.13.   Theoretical comparison of hashing methods

conclusions

We can draw several conclusions from this table. First, it is clear that chaining consistently requires fewer probes than does open addressing. On the other hand, traversal of the linked lists is usually slower than array access, which can reduce the advantage, especially if key comparisons can be done quickly. Chaining comes into its own when the records are large, and comparison of keys takes significant time. Chaining is also especially advantageous when unsuccessful searches are common, since with chaining, an empty list or very short list may be found, so that often no key comparisons at all need be done to show that a search is unsuccessful.

With open addressing and successful searches, the simpler method of linear probing is not significantly slower than more sophisticated methods, at least until the table is almost completely full. For unsuccessful searches, however, clustering quickly causes linear probing to degenerate into a long sequential search. We might conclude, therefore, that if searches are quite likely to be successful, and the load factor is moderate, then linear probing is quite satisfactory, but in other circumstances another method should be used.

6. Empirical Comparisons

It is important to remember that the computations giving Figure 6.13 are only approximate, and also that in practice nothing is completely random, so that we can always expect some differences between the theoretical results and actual computations. For sake of comparison, therefore, Figure 6.14 gives the results of one empirical study, using 900 keys that are pseudorandom numbers between 0 and 1.

Load factor	0.1	0.5	0.8	0.9	0.99	2.0
Successful search						
Chaining	1.04	1.2	1.4	1.4	1.5	2.0
Open, Quadratic probes	1.04	1.5	2.1	2.7	5.2	—
Linear probes	1.05	1.6	3.4	6.2	21.3	—
Unsuccessful search						
Chaining	0.11	0.53	0.78	0.90	0.99	2.04
Open, Quadratic probes	1.13	2.2	5.2	11.9	126.	—
Linear probes	1.13	2.7	15.4	59.8	430.	—

Figure 6.14. **Empirical comparison of hashing methods**

conclusions　　　In comparison with other methods of information retrieval, the important thing to note about all these numbers is that they depend only on the load factor, not on the absolute number of items in the table. Retrieval from a hash table with 20,000 items in 40,000 possible positions is no slower, on average, than is retrieval from a table with 20 items in 40 possible positions. With sequential search, a list 1000 times the size will take 1000 times as long to search. With binary search, this ratio is reduced to 10 (more precisely, to lg 1000), but still the time needed increases with the size, which it does not with hashing.

Finally, we should emphasize the importance of devising a good hash function, one that executes quickly and maximizes the spread of keys. If the hash function is poor, the performance of hashing can degenerate to that of sequential search.

Exercises
6.6

E1. Suppose that each item (record) in a hash table occupies s words of storage (exclusive of the pointer field needed if chaining is used), and suppose that there are n items in the hash table.

(a) If the load factor is λ and open addressing is used, determine how many words of storage will be required for the hash table.

(b) If chaining is used, then each node will require $s + 1$ words, including the pointer field. How many words will be used altogether for the n nodes?

(c) If the load factor is λ and chaining is used, how many words will be used for the hash table itself? (Recall that with chaining, the hash table itself contains only pointers requiring one word each.)

(d) Add your answers to the two previous parts to find the total storage requirement for load factor λ and chaining.

(e) If s is small, then open addressing requires less total memory for a given λ, but for large s, chaining requires less space altogether. Find the break-even value for s, at which both methods use the same total storage. Your answer will depend on the load factor λ.

E2. Figures 6.13 and 6.14 are somewhat distorted in favor of chaining, because no account is taken of the space needed for links (see part 2 of Section 6.5.4). Produce tables like Figure 6.13, where the load factors are calculated for the case of chaining, and for open addressing the space required by links is added to the hash table, thereby reducing the load factor.

(a) Given n nodes in linked storage connected to a chained hash table, with s words per item (plus 1 more for the link), and with load factor λ, find the total amount of storage that will be used, including links.

(b) If this same amount of storage is used in a hash table with open addressing and n items of s words each, find the resulting load factor. This is the load factor to use for open addressing in computing the revised tables.

(c) Produce a table for the case $s = 1$.

(d) Produce another table for the case $s = 5$.

(e) What will the table look like when each item takes 100 words?

E3. One reason why the answer to the birthday problem is surprising is that it differs from the answers to apparently related questions. For the following, suppose that there are n people in the room, and disregard leap years.

(a) What is the probability that someone in the room will have a birthday on a random date drawn from a hat?

(b) What is the probability that at least two people in the room will have that same random birthday?

(c) If we choose one person and find his birthday, what is the probability that someone else in the room will share the birthday?

E4. In a chained hash table, suppose that it makes sense to speak of an order for the keys, and suppose that the nodes in each chain are kept in order by key. Then a search can be terminated as soon as it passes the place where the key should be, if present. How many fewer probes will be done, on average, in an

ordered hash table

unsuccessful search? In a successful search? How many probes are needed, on average, to insert a new node in the right place? Compare your answers with the corresponding numbers derived in the text for the case of unordered chains.

E5. In our discussion of chaining, the hash table itself contained only pointers, list headers for each of the chains. One variant method is to place the first actual item of each chain in the hash table itself. (An empty position is indicated by an impossible key, as with open addressing.) With a given load factor, calculate the effect on space of this method, as a function of the number of words (except links) in each item. (A link takes one word.)

Programming Project 6.6

P1. Produce a table like Figure 6.14 for your computer, by writing and running test programs to implement the various kinds of hash tables and load factors.

6.7 CONCLUSIONS: COMPARISON OF METHODS

This chapter and the previous one have together explored four quite different methods of information retrieval: sequential search, binary search, table lookup, and hashing. If we are to ask which of these is best, we must first select the criteria by which to answer, and these criteria will include both the requirements imposed by the application and other considerations that affect our choice of data structures, since the first two methods are applicable only to lists and the second two to tables. In many applications, however, we are free to choose either lists or tables for our data structures.

choice of data structures

table lookup

In regard both to speed and convenience, ordinary lookup in contiguous tables is certainly superior, but there are many applications to which it is inapplicable, such as when a list is preferred or the set of keys is sparse. It is also inappropriate whenever insertions or deletions are frequent, since such actions in contiguous storage may require moving large amounts of information.

Which of the other three methods is best depends on other criteria, such as the form of the data.

other methods

Sequential search is certainly the most flexible of our methods. The data may be stored in any order, with either contiguous or linked representation. Binary search is much more demanding. The keys must be in order, and the data must be in random-access representation (contiguous storage). Hashing requires even more, a peculiar ordering of the keys well suited to retrieval from the hash table, but generally useless for any other purpose. If the data are to be available immediately for human inspection, then some kind of order is essential, and a hash table is inappropriate.

near miss

Finally, there is the question of the unsuccessful search. Sequential search and hashing, by themselves, say nothing except that the search was unsuccessful. Binary search can determine which data have keys closest to the target, and perhaps thereby can provide useful information.

6.8 APPLICATION: THE LIFE GAME REVISITED

At the end of Chapter 2 we noted that the bounds we used for the arrays in CONWAY'S game of Life were highly restrictive and artificial. The Life cells are supposed to be on an unbounded grid. In other words, we would really like to have the Pascal declaration

unbounded array

$$\text{\textbf{type} grid} = \text{\textbf{array}[integer, integer] \textbf{of} cell;}$$

which is, of course, illegal. Since only a limited number of these cells will actually be occupied at any one time, we should really regard the grid for the Life game as *sparse table* a sparse table, and therefore a hash table proves an attractive way to represent the grid.

6.8.1 Choice of Algorithm

Before we specify our data structures more precisely, let us consider the basic algorithm that we might use. We already have two versions of the Life simulation, and we should not introduce a third unless we know that it will prove a significant improvement. The first version scanned the entire grid at each generation, an action that is not suitable for a sparse array (where it would be impossibly slow). The second version, on the other hand, was designed essentially to treat the grid as a sparse array. It never explicitly scans through cells that are dead, but uses four lists to locate all cells that need attention. Rather than writing a complete new program *modify* Life2 from scratch, let us therefore see how far we can go to use the overall structure of the second program Life2 in conjunction with a hash table to represent the sparse array.

6.8.2 Specification of Data Structures

We have already decided to represent our sparse array of cells as a hash table, but we have not yet decided between open addressing and chaining. For each cell we must keep the status of the cell (alive or dead), the number of living neighbors, and (since the key itself must be explicitly kept when using a hash table) the row and column of the cell. With these four entries in each record, there are few space *use of space* considerations to advise our decision. With chaining, the size of each record will increase 25 percent to accommodate the necessary pointer, but the hash table itself will be smaller and can take a higher load factor than with open addressing. With open addressing, the records will be smaller, but more room must be left vacant in the hash table to avoid long searches and possible overflow.

flexibility After space considerations, the second question we should ask concerns flexibility. Do we need to make deletions, and, if so, when? We could keep track of all cells until the memory is full, and then delete those that are not needed. But this would require rehashing the full array, which would be slow and painful. With chaining we can easily dispose of cells as soon as they are not needed, and thereby reduce the number of cells in the hash table as much as possible.

access Finally, we should review the requirements for accessing the cells. As we work with a given cell, we need to locate its eight neighbors, and we can use the hash table to do so. Some of these neighbors may be inserted into the four lists live, die, nextlive, and nextdie. When we later retrieve a cell from one of these lists, we could again use the hash table to find it, but doing so would be repeating work. If we use chaining, then we can add a cell to a list either by inserting the cell itself or a pointer to it, rather than by inserting its coordinates as before. In this way we can locate the cell directly with no need for any search. At the same time, linked lists can help to avoid problems with unnecessary overflow.

specification

For reasons both of flexibility and time saving, therefore, let us decide to use dynamic memory allocation, a chained hash table, and linked lists.

list implementation

The most obvious way to implement the four lists is by connecting the cells into one of the lists by means of a pointer field. This would need to be a second pointer field in the record for a cell, since the first pointer field is used for chains from the hash table. A subtle problem arises, however. We have no guarantee that the same cell may not simultaneously be on two of the lists, and with only one available pointer field, the entries of the two lists will become mixed up. The obvious way to cure this problem is to keep a total of five pointer fields for each cell, one for the hash-table chain and four for possible use in the four lists. This solution wastes a great deal of space, since many of the cells will not be on any of the four lists, and very few (if any) will be on more than one.

indirect linked list

A much better way is to put pointers to cells into the four lists, not the cells themselves. The result is illustrated in Figure 6.15. Each node of the list thus contains two pointers, one to a cell and one to the next node of the list.

6.8.3 The Main Program

With these decisions made, we can now tie down the representation and notation for our data structures by writing the main program. Since we are following the method of Life2, the action part is almost identical with that of Life2.

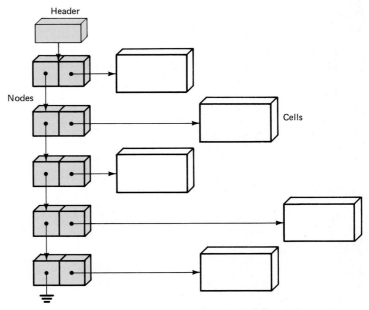

Figure 6.15.   An indirect linked list

```
                    program Life3(input, output);
                    {simulation of Conway's game of Life on an unbounded grid}
                    {version 3}
declarations        const
                      hashsize  = 997;                           {Choose a convenient prime.}
                      hashmax  = 996;                                   {= hashsize − 1}

                    type
                      status     = (alive, dead);
                      count      = 0 . . 8;                       {count of living neighbors}
                      pointcell  = ↑cell;
                      pointnode = ↑node;
cell information      cell       = record                {description of one position in the grid}
                                        state:      status;
                                        numnbrs:    count;
                                        row,
                                        col:        integer;
                                        nextcell:   pointcell
                                   end;
list specification   node       = record              {used to construct indirect linked lists of cells}
                                        entry:      pointcell;
                                        nextnode:   pointnode
                                   end;
                      hashtable = array [0 . . hashmax] of pointcell;

                    var
                      H:           hashtable;           {holds all living cells and dead cells with living
                                                                                          neighbors}
                      live,
                      die,
                      nextlive,
                      nextdie:     pointnode;           {headers for the four indirect linked lists}
                      again:       Boolean              {continue to the next generation?}

                    begin                                              {main program Life3}
                      Initialize(live, die, nextlive, nextdie, H);     {also writes the first map}
main loop             repeat
                        Vivify(live);
                        Kill(die);
                        WriteMap(live, die);
                        AddNeighbors(live, nextlive, nextdie);
                        SubtractNeighbors(die, nextlive, nextdie);
                        Copy(nextlive, live);
                        Copy(nextdie, die);
                        Enquire(again)
                      until not again
                    end.                                             {main program Life3}
```

6.8.4 Procedures

Let us now write several of the procedures, so as to show how processing of the cells and of the lists transpires. The remaining procedures and functions will be left as exercises.

1. Procedure Vivify

The task of the procedure Vivify is to traverse the list live, determine whether each cell on it satisfies the conditions to become alive, and vivify it if so, else delete it from the list. The usual way to facilitate deletion from a linked list is to keep two pointers in lock step, one position apart, while traversing the list. This method appears as an exercise, but here we use another, that gives a simpler program at the expense of a little time and (temporarily) space.

deletion method

Let us take advantage of the indirect linkage of our lists, and when we wish to delete an entry from the list, let us leave the node in place, but set its entry field to **nil**. In this way, the node will be flagged as empty when it is again encountered in the procedure AddNeighbors.

```
procedure Vivify(live: pointnode);
var
   p: pointnode;                          {used to traverse list live}
begin                                     {procedure Vivify}
   p := live;
   while p <> nil do
   with p↑ do begin
      with entry↑ do                      {entry↑ is the cell being examined.}
         if (state = dead) and (numnbrs = 3) then
            state := alive
         else
            entry := nil;                 {Remove the cell from list live.}
      p := nextnode
   end                                    {processing node p↑}
end;                                      {procedure Vivify}
```

2. Procedure AddNeighbors

The task of this procedure is to increase the neighbor count by 1 for each neighbor of all the cells that remain on list live and to add cells to lists nextlive and nextdie when appropriate. The ordering of the cells on these lists is unimportant; hence we shall treat them as stacks, since stacks are the easiest lists to process. We shall use an auxiliary procedure Insert(p: pointnode; q: pointcell) to create a new node pointing to the given cell and push it onto the given list.

insertion and deletion

Finding the neighbors of a given cell will require using the hash table; we shall postpone this task by referring to

hash table retrieval

                         procedure GetCell(row, col: integer; **var** p: pointcell);

which will return a pointer to the cell being sought, creating the cell if it was not previously in the hash table.

```
procedure AddNeighbors(var live, nextlive, nextdie: pointnode);
var
    i, j:       integer;                        {row and column of a neighbor}
    p,                                          {used to traverse list live}
    q:          pointnode;                      {used to delete nodes}
    neighbor: pointcell;                        {points to the cell with coords i, j}
begin                                           {procedure AddNeighbors}
    p := live;
    while p <> nil do
```
get cell from list
```
        with p↑ do
        begin
          if entry <> nil then
            with entry↑ do
```
find a neighbor
```
              for i := row − 1 to row + 1 do
              for j := col − 1 to col + 1 do
                if (i <> row) or (j <> col) then       {exclude row, col itself}
                begin
```
get the neighbor
```
                  GetCell(i, j, neighbor);
                  with neighbor↑ do
                  begin
```
update count and lists
```
                    numnbrs := numnbrs + 1;
                    case numnbrs of
                      0:       writeln('Impossible case in AddNeighbors.');
                      1, 2:;                            {no action needed}
                      3:       if state = dead then Insert(nextlive, neighbor);
                      4:       if state = alive then Insert(nextdie, neighbor);
                      5, 6, 7, 8:;                      {no action needed}
                    end                                 {case statement}
                  end                      {with statement processing one neighbor}
                end;                                    {looping through neighbors}
```
continue traversal
```
        q := p;                  {Prepare to dispose of the node p↑ from list live.}
        p := nextnode;
        dispose(q)
      end;                                              {processing list node}
    live := nil
  end;                                                  {procedure AddNeighbors}
```

3. Processing the Hash Table

If you compare the two foregoing procedures with the corresponding procedures for program Life2 in Chapter 2, you will find that they are almost a direct translation from contiguous storage to linked storage. We now turn to the first basic difference, the procedure that explicitly references the hash table. The task of the procedure

```
GetCell(i, j: integer; var p: pointcell)
```

task

is first to look in the hash table for the cell with the given coordinates. If the search is successful, then the procedure returns a pointer to the cell; otherwise, it must create a new cell, assign it the given coordinates, initialize its other fields to the default values, and put it in the hash table as well as return a pointer to it.

This outline translates into the following Pascal procedure.

```
procedure GetCell(i, j; integer; var p: pointcell);
{gets the cell p with coordinates i, j from the hash table if it is present; otherwise
creates the cell}
var
  location: integer;                      {location returned by the hash function}
  found:    Boolean;                      {Is the cell already in the hash table?}
begin                                                      {procedure GetCell}
  found := false;
  location := Hash(i, j);
  p := H[location];                       {p now points to the start of the chain
                                             containing the cell at i, j.}
  while (not found) and (p <> nil) do    {Search the chain for the desired cell.}
    if (p↑.row = i) and (p↑.col = j) then
      found := true
    else
      p := p↑.nextcell;
    {If the cell was found in table, then we are finished; otherwise, we must
    create a new cell, initialize it, and insert it into the hash table.}
  if not found then
  begin
    new(p);
    with p↑ do begin
      row := i;
      col := j;
      state := dead;
      numnbrs := 0;
      nextcell := H[location];            {Push onto the chain in hash table.}
      H[location] := p
    end                                  {inserting new cell into hash table}
  end                                              {creating new cell}
end;                                              {procedure GetCell}
```

look in hash table

make a new cell

4. The Hash Function

Our hash function will differ slightly from those earlier in the chapter, in that its argument already comes in two parts (row and column), so that some kind of folding can be done easily. Before deciding how, let us for a moment consider the special case of a small array, where the function is one-to-one and is exactly the index function. When there are exactly maxrow entries in each row, the index i, j maps to

$$i + \text{maxrow} * j$$

to place the rectangular array into contiguous storage, one row after the next.

It should prove effective to use a similar mapping for our hash function, where we replace maxrow by some convenient number (like a prime) that will maximize the spread and reduce collisions. Hence we obtain

```
function Hash(i, j: integer): integer;
const
    factor = 101;                          {Choose a convenient prime.}
begin
    Hash := abs(i + factor * j) mod hashsize
end;
```

5. Other Subprograms

The remaining subprograms all bear considerable resemblance either to one of the preceding procedures or to the corresponding procedure in Life2, and these subprograms can therefore safely be left as projects.

Exercise 6.8

E1. Estimate the number of statements executed per generation in Life3, under the same assumptions that were used for Life2 in Section 2.5. Compare the results for the two versions.

Programming Projects 6.8

P1. Write the procedure Kill.

P2. Write the procedure SubtractNeighbors. You will need to remove a cell from the hash table and dispose of it when it reaches the default case: The cell is dead and has a neighbor count of 0.

P3. Write the procedure Insert.

P4. Write the procedure Copy.

P5. Rewrite the procedure Vivify to use two pointers in traversing the list live, and dispose of redundant nodes when they are encountered. Also make the accompanying simplifications in the procedures AddNeighbors and SubtractNeighbors.

P6. The program as we have written it contains a bug, that of dangling pointers. When procedure SubtractNeighbors disposes of a cell, it may still be on one of the lists nextlive or nextdie, since these are allowed to contain redundant entries. Vivify and Kill may then err in the next generation. Correct the bug as follows.

(a) Implement the plan of keeping space-available stacks, as discussed in Section 3.2.3. You will need to keep two stacks, one for available cells and one for available nodes. You will need to write four procedures for obtaining and disposing of cells and nodes.

(b) Suppose that there are some (dangling) pointers to cells that have been placed on the available stack. Show that, when the next generation starts, the procedures Vivify and Kill will safely remove all such dangling pointers, before the available cells are reused.

P7. Run the complete program Life3. Use the same configurations tested on Life2, and compare the time and space requirements.

POINTERS AND PITFALLS

1. Use top-down design for your data structures, just as you do for your algorithms. First determine the logical structure of the data, then slowly specify more detail, and delay implementation decisions as long as possible.

2. Before considering detailed structures, decide what operations on the data will be required, and use this information to decide whether the data belong in a *list* or a *table*. Traversal of the data structure or access to all the data in a prespecified order generally implies choosing a list. Access to any item in time $O(1)$ generally implies choosing a table.

3. For the design and programming of lists, see Chapters 3–5.

4. Use the logical structure of the data to decide what kind of table to use: an ordinary array, a table of some special shape, a system of inverted tables, or a hash table. Choose the simplest structure that allows the required operations and that meets the space requirements of the problem. Don't write complicated procedures to save space that will then remain unused.

5. Let the structure of the data help you decide whether an index function or an access table is better for accessing a table of data. Use the features built into your programming language whenever possible.

6. In using a hash table, let the nature of the data and the required operations help you decide between chaining and open addressing. Chaining is generally preferable if deletions are required, if the records are relatively large, or if overflow might be a problem. Open addressing is usually preferable when the individual records are small and there is no danger of overflowing the hash table.

7. Hash functions must usually be custom-designed for the kind of keys used for accessing the hash table. In designing a hash function, keep the computations as simple and as few as possible while maintaining a relatively even spread of the keys over the hash table. There is no obligation to use every part of the key in the calculation. For important applications, experiment by computer with several variations of your hash function, and look for rapid calculation and even distribution of the keys.

8. Recall from the analysis of hashing that some collisions will almost inevitably occur, so don't worry about the existence of collisions if the keys are spread nearly uniformly through the table.

9. For open addressing, clustering is unlikely to be a problem until the hash table is more than half full. If the table can be made several times larger than the space required for the records, then linear probing should be adequate; otherwise more sophisticated collision resolution may be required. On the other hand, if the table is many times larger than needed, then initialization of all the unused space may require inordinate time.

REVIEW QUESTIONS

6.1   **1.** In terms of the big Oh notation, compare the difference in time required for table lookup and for list searching.

6.2   **2.** What are row- and column-major ordering?

6.3   **3.** Why do jagged tables require access tables instead of index functions?

             4. For what purpose are inverted tables used?

             5. What is the difference in purpose, if any, between an index function and an access table?

6.4   **6.** What operations are available for an abstract table?

             7. What operations are usually easier for a list than for a table?

6.5   **8.** What is the difference in purpose, if any, between an index function and a hash function?

             9. What objectives should be sought in the design of a hash function?

             10. Name three techniques often built into hash functions.

             11. What is *clustering* in a hash table?

             12. Describe two methods for minimizing clustering.

             13. Name four advantages of a chained hash table over open addressing.

             14. Name one advantage of open addressing over chaining.

6.6   **15.** If a hash function assigns 30 keys to random positions in a hash table of size 300, about how likely is it that there will be no collisions?

REFERENCES FOR FURTHER STUDY

The primary reference for this chapter is KNUTH, Volume 3. (See the end of Chapter 3 for bibliographic details.) Hashing is the subject of Volume 3, pp. 506–549. KNUTH studies every method we have touched, and many others besides. He does algorithm analysis in considerably more detail than we have, writing his algorithms in a pseudo-assembly language, and counting operations in detail there.

An alternative treatment that includes careful analysis of algorithms for searching, hashing, as well as other topics, is

LYDIA I. KRONSJO, *Algorithms: Their Complexity and Efficiency,* John Wiley, New York, 1979.

The following book (pp. 156–185) considers arrays of various kinds, index functions, and access tables in considerable detail:

C. C. GOTLIEB and L. R. GOTLIEB, *Data Types and Structures,* Prentice-Hall, Englewood Cliffs, N.J., 1978.

Extensions of the birthday surprise are considered in

M. S. KLAMKIN and D. J. NEWMAN, *Journal of Combinatorial Theory* 3 (1967), 279–282.

Sorting

▶ *This chapter studies several important methods for sorting lists, both contiguous and linked. At the same time, we shall develop further tools that help with the analysis of algorithms.*

7.1 INTRODUCTION AND NOTATION

We live in a world obsessed with keeping information, and to find it, we must keep it in some sensible order. Librarians make sure that no one misplaces a book; income tax authorities trace down every dollar we earn; credit bureaus keep track of almost every detail of our actions. I once saw a cartoon in which a keen filing clerk, anxious to impress the boss, said frenetically, "Let me make sure these files are in alphabetical order before we throw them out." If we are to be the masters of this explosion instead of its victims, we had best learn how to keep track of it all!

practical importance   A few years ago, it was estimated, more than half the time on many commercial computers was spent in sorting. This is perhaps no longer true, since sophisticated methods have been devised for organizing data, methods that do not require that it be kept in any special order. Eventually, nonetheless, the information does go out to people, and then it must be sorted in some way. Because sorting is so important, a great many algorithms have been devised for doing it. In fact, so many good ideas appear in sorting methods that an entire course could easily be built around this one theme. Amongst the differing environments that require different methods, the *external and internal* most important is the distinction between **external** and **internal**, that is, whether *sorting* there are so many records to be sorted that they must be kept in external files on disks, tapes, or the like, or whether they can all be kept internally in high-speed memory. In this chapter we consider only internal sorting.

reference   It is not our intention to present anything close to a comprehensive treatment of internal sorting methods. For such a treatment, see Volume 3 of the monumental work of D. E. KNUTH (reference given at end of Chapter 3). KNUTH expounds about twenty-five sorting methods and claims that they are "only a fraction of the algorithms that have been devised so far." We shall study only five methods in detail, chosen, first, because they are good—each one can be the best choice under some circumstances; second, because they illustrate much of the variety appearing in the full range of methods; and third, because they are easy to write and understand, without too many details to complicate their presentation. Several variations of these methods will also appear as exercises.

notation   Throughout this chapter we use the same notation as in previous chapters, so that L will be a list of items to be sorted. Each item x will have a key x.key by which the items are to be sorted. If we have a contiguous list L, then it will be a record containing an array entry indexed from 1 to count, where the counter count is also a field in L, and the list L will be the parameter for the procedures we write. If we have a linked list, then each node will consist of a field called info of type item and a field called next of type pointer. The list is specified as a record containing the field head that points to the first item in the list.

basic operations   In studying searching algorithms, it soon became clear that the total amount of work done was closely related to the number of comparisons of keys. The same observation is true for sorting algorithms, but sorting algorithms must also either change pointers or move items around within the list, and therefore time spent this way is also important, especially in the case of large items kept in a contiguous list. Our analyses will therefore concentrate on these two basic actions.

analysis

As before, both the worst-case performance and the average performance of a sorting algorithm are of interest. To find the average, we shall consider what would happen if the algorithm were run on all possible orderings of the list (with n items, there are $n!$ such orderings altogether) and take the average of the results.

7.2 INSERTION SORT

example

Every avid player of a card game learns to sort a hand of cards almost automatically. One of the most common approaches is to look at the cards one at a time, and when each new card is seen, to insert it in the proper place in the (partial) hand of cards. This approach leads easily to an algorithm for computer sorting that is so natural that it should be in every programmer's repertoire.

To develop the algorithm, it is better to think of the cards not as held in one's hand, but as being placed face up in a row on a table one at a time as they are being sorted. As each new card is seen, then, it is compared with the row of cards, and some of them are pushed one position to the right to make room to insert the new one. An example is shown in Figure 7.1.

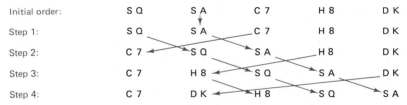

Figure 7.1.   Example of insertion sort

method

The *insertion sort* algorithm thus proceeds on the idea of keeping the first part of the list, when once examined, in the correct order. An initial list with only one item is automatically in order. If we suppose that we have already sorted the first $i - 1$ items, then we take item i and search through this sorted list of length $i - 1$ to see where to insert item i.

7.2.1 Contiguous Version

For a contiguous list, we could use either sequential or binary search to find the place to insert item i. Binary search produces a slightly more complicated algorithm, and this will be pursued in the exercises. To make our algorithm even simpler, however, we shall here choose sequential search instead. A small trick will simplify the algorithm: If we do the search from the last toward the first item in the sorted list, then at the same time as we search, we can move the items to make room to insert L.entry[i] when we find the proper place. Let us now write the algorithm.

contiguous insertion
sort

```
procedure InsertSort(var L: list);
var
   i,                                    {i will be index of first unsorted item.}
   j:        index;                      {j searches sorted part of list.}
   t:        item;                       {t is used to swap entries.}
   found:    Boolean;                    {Has the proper place for L.entry[i] been found?}
begin                                    {procedure InsertSort}
with L do
   for i := 2 to count do
      if entry[i].key < entry[i − 1].key then
                                         {Otherwise, entry[i] is in the proper place.}
      begin
         j := i;
         t := entry[i];                  {Pull entry[i] out of the list.}
         repeat                {Shift all previous entries one place down the list until}
            j := j − 1;                  {the proper place is found.}
            entry[j + 1] := entry[j];    {Position j is now available for insertion.}
            if j = 1 then
               found := true
            else
               found := (entry[j − 1].key <= t.key)
         until found;
         entry[j] := t
      end
end;                                     {procedure InsertSort}
```

The action of the program is nearly self-explanatory. Since a list with only one item is automatically sorted, the loop on i starts with the second item. If it is in the correct place, nothing needs to be done. Otherwise, the new item is pulled out of the list into the variable t, and the **repeat** . . . **until** loop pushes items one position down the list until the correct position is found, and finally t is inserted there before proceeding to the next unsorted item. The case when t belongs in the first position of the list must be treated specially, since in this case there is no item with a smaller key that would terminate the search. We treat this special case by introducing the Boolean variable found and using an **if** statement to set its value.

7.2.2 Linked Version

algorithm

For a linked version of insertion sort, we shall traverse the original list, taking one item at a time and inserting it in the proper place in the sorted list. The pointer variable tail will give the end of the sorted part of the list, and tail↑.next will give the first item that has not yet been inserted into the sorted sublist. We shall let q also point to this item, and use a pointer p to search the sorted part of the list to find where to insert q↑. If q↑ belongs before the current head of the list, then we insert it there. Otherwise, we move p down the list until p↑.info.key >= q↑.info.key and then insert q↑ before p↑. To enable insertion before p↑ (see Section 4.3.1, part 3), we keep a second pointer r in lock step one position closer to the head than p.

stopping a loop

A *sentinel* is an extra item added to one end of a list to ensure that a loop will terminate without having to include a separate check. Since we have tail↑.next = q, the node q↑ is already in place to serve as a sentinel for the search, and the loop moving p is simplified.

Finally, let us note that a list with 0 or 1 item is already sorted, so that we can check these cases separately and thereby avoid trivialities elsewhere. The details appear in the following procedure, and are illustrated in Figure 7.2.

linked insertion sort

```
procedure InsertSort(var L: list);
{linked version of insertion sort}
var
  q,                                      {q↑ is the item being inserted.}
  tail,                                   {tail of sorted sublist}
  p,                                      {used to traverse sorted sublist}
  r:       pointer;                       {always one node closer to head than p}
begin                                     {procedure InsertSort}
  if L.head <> nil then                   {An empty list is already sorted.}
  begin
    tail := L.head;                       {The first node alone makes a sorted sublist.}
    while tail↑.next <> nil do
    begin
      q := tail↑.next;                    {q↑ is the first unsorted node, ready to insert.}
      if q↑.info.key < L.head↑.info.key then
      begin                               {Insert q↑ at the head of the sorted list.}
        tail↑.next := q↑.next;            {Advance the sentinel down the list.}
        q↑.next := L.head;
        L.head := q;
      end
      else begin                          {Search the sorted sublist to insert q↑.}
        r := L.head;
        p := r↑.next;                     {r will stay one step closer to the head than p.}
        while q↑.info.key > p↑.info.key do
        begin
          r := p;
          p := r↑.next
        end;          {At conclusion of the loop, q↑ belongs between r↑ and p↑.}
        if q = p then            {Sentinel was found; q↑ is already in right place.}
          tail := q
        else begin
          tail↑.next := q↑.next;                         {Advance the sentinel.}
          q↑.next := p;                         {Insert q↑ between r↑ and p↑.}
          r↑.next := q
        end                                   {inserting q↑ between r↑ and p↑}
      end                                   {searching list and inserting q↑}
    end                                   {loop through nodes of list}
  end                                   {case where list length is > 0}
end;                                   {procedure InsertSort}
```

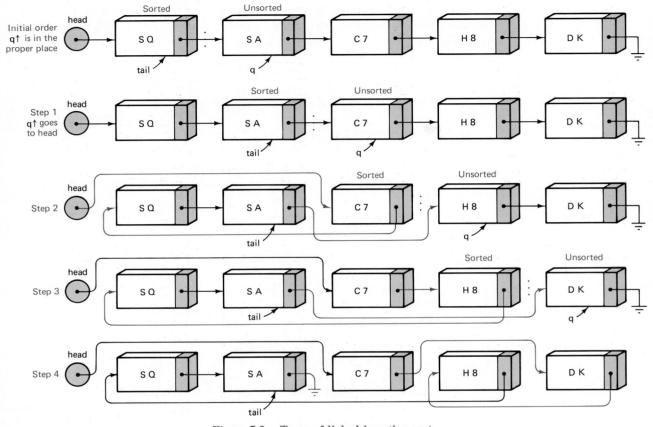

Figure 7.2.   Trace of linked insertion sort

Even though the mechanics of the linked version are quite different from those of the contiguous version, you should be able to see that the basic method is the same. The only real difference is that the contiguous version searches the sorted sublist in reverse order, while the linked version searches it in increasing order of position within the list.

7.2.3 Analysis

Since the basic ideas are the same, let us analyze only the performance of the contiguous version of the program. We also restrict our attention to the case when the list L is initially in random order (meaning that all possible orderings of the keys are equally likely). When we deal with item i, how far back must we go to insert it? There are i possible positions: not moving it at all, moving it one position, up to moving it $i - 1$ positions to the front of the list. Given randomness, these are equally likely. The probability that it need not be moved is thus $1/i$, in which case only one comparison of keys is done, with no moving of items.

inserting one item

The contrary case, when item i must be moved, occurs with probability $(i - 1)/i$. Let us begin by counting the average number of iterations of the **repeat** loop. Since all of the $i - 1$ possible positions are equally likely, the average number of iterations is

$$\frac{1 + 2 + \cdots + (i - 1)}{i - 1} = \frac{(i - 1)i}{2(i - 1)} = \frac{i}{2}.$$

One key comparison and one assignment are done for each of these iterations, with one more key comparison done outside the loop, along with two assignments of items. Hence, in this second case, item i requires, on average, $\frac{1}{2}i + 1$ comparisons and $\frac{1}{2}i + 2$ assignments.

When we combine the two cases with their respective probabilities, we have

$$\frac{1}{i} \times 1 + \frac{i - 1}{i} \times \left(\frac{i}{2} + 1\right) = \frac{i + 1}{2}$$

comparisons and

$$\frac{1}{i} \times 0 + \frac{i - 1}{i} \times \left(\frac{i}{2} + 2\right) = \frac{i + 3}{2} - \frac{2}{i}$$

assignments.

inserting all items

We wish to add these numbers from $i = 2$ to $i = n$, but to avoid complications in the arithmetic, we first use the big Oh notation (see Section 5.6) to approximate each of these expressions by suppressing the terms bounded by a constant. We thereby obtain $\frac{1}{2}i + O(1)$ for both the number of comparisons and the number of assignments of items. In making this approximation, we are really concentrating on the actions within the main loop and suppressing any concern about operations done outside the loop or variations in the algorithm that change the amount of work only by some bounded amount.

To add $\frac{1}{2}i + O(1)$ from $i = 2$ to $i = n$, we apply Theorem A.1 (the sum of the integers from 1 to n), obtaining

$$\sum_{i=2}^{n} \left(\tfrac{1}{2}i + O(1)\right) = \tfrac{1}{2} \sum_{i=2}^{n} i + O(n) = \tfrac{1}{4}n^2 + O(n)$$

for both the number of comparisons of keys and the number of assignments of items.

So far we have nothing with which to compare this number, but we can note that as n becomes larger, the contributions from the term involving n^2 become much larger than the remaining terms collected as $O(n)$. Hence as the size of the list grows, the time needed by insertion sort grows like the square of this size.

best and worst cases

The worst-case analysis of insertion sort will be left as an exercise. We can observe quickly that the best case for insertion sort occurs when the list is already in order, when insertion sort will do nothing except $n - 1$ comparisons of keys. We can now show that no sorting method can possibly do better in its best case.

Theorem 7.1   *Verifying that a list of n items is in the correct order requires at least $n - 1$ comparisons of keys.*

PROOF Consider an arbitrary program that checks whether a list of *n* items is in order or not (and perhaps sorts it if it is not). The program will first do some comparison of keys, and this comparison will involve some two items from the list. Sometime later, at least one of these two items must be compared with a third, or else there would be no way to decide where these two should be in the list relative to the third. Thus this second comparison involves only one new item not previously in a comparison. Continuing in this way, we see that there must be another comparison involving some one of the first three items and one new item. Note that we are not necessarily selecting the comparisons in the order in which the algorithm does them. Thus, except for the first comparison, each one that we select involves only one new item not previously compared. All *n* of the items must enter some comparison, for there is no way to decide whether an item is in the right place unless it is compared to at least one other item. Thus to involve all *n* items requires at least $n - 1$ comparisons, and the proof is complete.

end of proof

With this theorem we find one of the advantages of insertion sort: It verifies that a list is correctly sorted as quickly as can be done. Furthermore, insertion sort remains an excellent method whenever a list is nearly in the correct order and few items are many positions removed from their correct locations.

Exercises
7.2

E1. By hand, trace through the steps insertion sort will use on each of the following lists. In each case, count the number of comparisons that will be made and the number of times an item will be moved.

(a) The following three words to be sorted alphabetically:

triangle   square   pentagon.

(b) The three words in part (a) to be sorted according to the number of sides of the corresponding polygon, in increasing order.

(c) The three words in part (a) to be sorted according to the number of sides of the corresponding polygon, in decreasing order.

(d) The following seven numbers to be sorted into increasing order:

26 33 35 29 19 12 22.

(e) The following list of 14 names to be sorted into alphabetical order:

Tim Dot Eva Roy Tom Kim Guy Amy Jon Ann Jim Kay Ron Jan.

E2. What initial order for a list of keys will produce the worst case for insertion sort in the contiguous version? In the linked version?

E3. How many key comparisons and item assignments does contiguous insertion sort make in its worst case?

E4. Modify the linked version of insertion sort so that a list that is already sorted, or nearly so, will be processed rapidly.

Programming
Projects
7.2

test program for sorting

P1. Write a program that can be used to test and evaluate the performance of insertion sort (and, later, other methods). The following outline may be used.

(a) Write the main program for the case of contiguous lists. The main program should declare the data types (such as item, list, and index) and use procedures to set up the list of items to be sorted, print out the unsorted list if the user wishes, sort the list, and print the sorted list if the user wishes. The program should also determine the amount of CPU time required in the sorting phase, and it should establish counters (which will be updated by inserting code into the sorting procedure) to keep track of the number of comparisons of keys and assignments of items.

(b) Use a random number generator to construct lists of numbers (either integers or reals) to be sorted. Suitable sizes of the lists would be $n = 10, 20, 100,$ and 500. It would be best to keep the lists in permanent files, so that the same lists can be used to evaluate different sorting methods.

(c) Write a procedure to put the random numbers into the keys of items to be sorted. Do at least two cases: First, the records (of type item) should consist of the key alone, and, second, the records should be larger, with about 100 words of storage in each record. The fields other than the key need not be initialized.

(d) Run the program to test the performance of contiguous insertion sort for short lists and long ones, and for small records and large ones.

(e) Rewrite the main program for the case of linked lists instead of contiguous ones.

(f) Rewrite the procedure so that it sets up the records as the nodes of a linked list. Either incorporate the possibility of both small and large records, or explain why there is no need to do so.

(g) Run the program to test the performance of linked insertion sort.

sentinel

P2. Recall that a *sentinel* is an extra item added to one end of a list to ensure that a loop will terminate without having to check separately that the index has reached its limit. Modify the contiguous version of procedure InsertSort to insert a sentinel into the list, so that the phrase "j = 1" can be removed from the termination condition for the loop. Compare the time required for the modified procedure with the original version for the same lists.

P3. Rewrite the contiguous version of procedure InsertSort so that it uses binary search to locate where to insert the next item. Compare the time needed to sort a list with that of the original procedure InsertSort. Is it reasonable to use binary search in the linked version of InsertSort? Why or why not?

scan sort

P4. There is an even easier sorting method, which instead of using two pointers to move through the list, uses only one. We can call it *scan sort,* and it proceeds by starting at one end and moving forward, comparing adjacent pairs of keys, until it finds a pair out of order. It then swaps this pair of items, and starts moving the other way, continuing to swap pairs until it finds a pair in the correct order. At this point it knows that it has moved the one item as far back as necessary, so that the first part of the list is sorted, but, unlike insertion sort, it has forgotten how far forward has been sorted, so it simply reverses direction and sorts forward again, looking for a pair out of order. When it reaches the far end of the list, then it is finished.

(a) Write a Pascal program to implement scan sort for contiguous lists. Your program should use only one index variable (other than L.count), one variable of type item to be used in making swaps, and no other local variables.

(b) Compare the timings for your program with those of InsertSort.

bubble sort   **P5.** A well-known algorithm called **bubble sort** proceeds by scanning the list from left to right, and whenever a pair of adjacent keys is found to be out of order, then those items are swapped. In this first pass, the largest key in the list will have "bubbled" to the end, but the earlier keys may still be out of order. Thus the pass scanning for pairs out of order is put in a loop that first makes the scanning pass go all the way to L.count, and at each iteration stops it one position sooner. **(a)** Write a Pascal procedure for bubble sort. **(b)** Find the number of key comparisons and swaps it makes on average, and compare the results with those for insertion sort.

7.3 SELECTION SORT

Insertion sort has one major disadvantage. Even after most items have been sorted properly into the first part of the list, the insertion of a later item may require that many of them be moved. All the moves made by insertion sort are moves of only one position at a time. Thus to move an item 20 positions up the list requires 20 separate moves. If the items are small, perhaps a key alone, or if the items are in linked storage, then the many moves may not require excessive time. But if the items are very large, records containing hundreds of components like personnel files or student transcripts, and the records must be kept in contiguous storage, then it would be far more efficient if, when it is necessary to move an item, it could be moved immediately to its final position. Our next method accomplishes this goal.

1. The Algorithm

This method is also modeled on sorting a hand of cards, but this time the hand is held by a player who likes to look at all his cards at once. As he looks over his cards, he selects the highest one and puts it where it belongs, selects the second highest and puts it in its place, and continues in this way until the cards are all sorted.

This method (applied to the same hand used to illustrate insertion sort) is demonstrated in Figure 7.3.

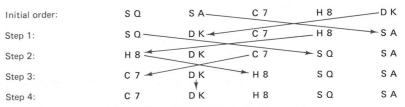

Figure 7.3.   Example of selection sort

This method translates into the following algorithm, called *selection sort*. Since its objective is to minimize data movement, selection sort is primarily useful with contiguous lists, and we therefore give only a contiguous version. The algorithm uses a function called MaxKey, which finds the maximum key on the part of the list L given as the parameters. The procedure Swap simply swaps the two items with the given indices. For convenience in the discussion to follow, we write these two as separate subprograms.

contiguous selection sort

```
procedure SelectSort(var L: list);
var
  i,                                    {index of place being correctly filled}
  m: index;                 {index of largest remaining key (goes to position i)}
  {Declarations of the function MaxKey and the procedure Swap go here.}
begin                                                     {procedure SelectSort}
  for i := L.count downto 2 do
  begin
    m := MaxKey(1, i, L);
    Swap(m, i, L)
  end
end;                                                      {procedure SelectSort}
```

Note that when all items in a list but one are in the correct place, then the remaining one must be also. Thus the **for** loop stops at 2.

largest key in list

```
function MaxKey(low, high: index; var L: list): index;
var
  m,                                          {index of largest key so far}
  j: index;                                   {scans list for largest key}
begin                                                      {function MaxKey}
  with L do
  begin
    m := low;
    for j := low + 1 to high do
      if entry[m].key < entry[j].key then
        m := j;
    MaxKey := m
  end
end;                                                       {function MaxKey}
```

interchange items

```
procedure Swap(x, y: index; var L: list);
var
  t: item;                                              {temporary storage}
begin                                                     {procedure Swap}
  with L do
  begin
    t := entry[x];   entry[x] := entry[y];   entry[y] := t
  end
end;                                                      {procedure Swap}
```

2. Analysis

ordering unimportant

Apropos of algorithm analysis, the most remarkable fact about this algorithm is that both of the loops that appear are of the form **for . . . do . . .** , which means that we can calculate in advance exactly how many times they will iterate. In the number of comparisons it makes, selection sort pays no attention to the original ordering of the list. Hence for a list that is nearly correct to begin with, selection sort is likely to be much slower than insertion sort. On the other hand, selection sort does have the advantage of predictability: Its worst-case time will differ little from its best.

advantage of selection sort

The primary advantage of selection sort regards data movement. If an item is in its correct final position, then it will never be moved. Every time any pair of items is swapped, then at least one of them moves into its final position, and therefore at most $n - 1$ swaps are done altogether in sorting a list of n items. This is the very best that we can expect from any method that relies entirely on swaps to move its items.

We can analyze the performance of procedure SelectSort in the same way that it is programmed. The main procedure does nothing except some bookkeeping and calling the subprograms. Procedure Swap is called $n - 1$ times, and each call does 3 assignments of items, for a total count of $3(n - 1)$. The function MaxKey is called $n - 1$ times, with the length of the sublist ranging from n down to 2. If t is the number of items on the part of the list for which it is called, then MaxKey does exactly $t - 1$ comparisons of keys to determine the maximum. Hence, altogether, there are

comparison count for selection sort

$$(n - 1) + (n - 2) + . . . + 1 = \tfrac{1}{2}n(n - 1)$$

comparisons of keys, which we approximate to $\tfrac{1}{2}n^2 + O(n)$.

3. Comparisons

Let us pause for a moment to compare the counts for selection sort with those for insertion sort. The results are

	Selection	Insertion (average)
Assignments of items	$3.0n + O(1)$	$0.25n^2 + O(n)$
Comparisons of keys	$0.5n^2 + O(n)$	$0.25n^2 + O(n)$

The relative advantages of the two methods appear in these numbers. When n becomes large, $0.25n^2$ becomes much larger than $3n$, and if moving items is a slow process, then insertion sort will take far longer than will selection sort. But the amount of time taken for comparisons is, on average, only about half as much for insertion sort as for selection sort. Under other conditions, then, insertion sort will be better.

Exercises 7.3

E1. By hand, trace through the steps selection sort will use on each of the following lists. In each case, count the number of comparisons that will be made and the number of times an item will be moved.

(a) The following three words to be sorted alphabetically:

triangle   square   pentagon.

(b) The three words in part (a) to be sorted according to the number of sides of the corresponding polygon, in increasing order.

(c) The three words in part (a) to be sorted according to the number of sides of the corresponding polygon, in decreasing order.

(d) The following seven numbers to be sorted into increasing order:

26 33 35 29 19 12 22.

(e) The following list of 14 names to be sorted into alphabetical order:

Tim Dot Eva Roy Tom Kim Guy Amy Jon Ann Jim Kay Ron Jan.

E2. There is a simple algorithm called *count sort* that will construct a new, sorted list from L in a new array, provided we are guaranteed that all the keys in L are different from each other. Count sort goes through L once, and for each key L.entry[i].key scans L to count how many keys are less than L.entry[i].key. If c is this count, then the proper position in the sorted list for this key is $c + 1$. Determine how many comparisons of keys will be done by count sort. Is it a better algorithm than selection sort?

Programming Projects 7.3

P1. Run the test program written as a project in the previous section to compare selection sort with insertion sort (contiguous version). Run at least four cases: with small lists (about 20 entries) and large (about 500), and with small items (key only) and large (about 100 words per item). The keys should be placed in random order.

P2. Write and test a linked version of selection sort.

7.4 SHELL SORT

As we have seen, in some ways insertion sort and selection sort behave in opposite ways. Selection sort moves the items very efficiently but does many redundant comparisons. In its best case, insertion sort does the minimum number of comparisons, but is inefficient in moving items only one place at a time. Our goal now is to derive another method avoiding as much as possible the problems with both of these. Let us start with insertion sort and ask how we can reduce the number of times it moves an item.

diminishing increments

The reason why insertion sort can move items only one position is that it compares only adjacent keys. If we were to modify it so that it first compares keys far apart, then it could sort the items far apart. Afterward, the items closer together would be sorted, and finally the increment between keys being compared would be reduced to 1, to ensure that the list is completely in order. This is the idea implemented in 1959 by D. L. SHELL in the sorting method bearing his name. This method is also sometimes called *diminishing increment sort*. Before describing the algorithm formally, let us work through a simple example of sorting names.

example

Figure 7.4 shows what will happen when we first sort all names that are at distance 5 from each other (so there will be only two or three names on each such list), then re-sort the names using increment 3, and finally perform an ordinary insertion sort (increment 1).

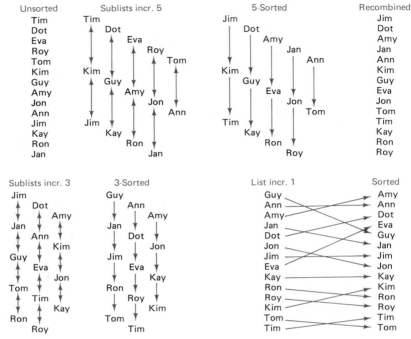

Figure 7.4.   Example of Shell sort

You can see that, even though we make three passes through all the names, the early passes move the names close to their final positions, so that at the final pass (which does an ordinary insertion sort), all the items are very close to their final positions so the sort goes rapidly.

choice of increments   There is no magic about the choice of 5, 3, and 1 as increments. Many other choices might work as well or better. It would, however, probably be wasteful to choose powers of 2, such as 8, 4, 2, and 1, since then the same keys compared on one pass would be compared again at the next, whereas by choosing numbers that are not multiples of each other, there is a better chance of obtaining new information from more of the comparisons. Although several studies have been made of Shell sort, no one has been able to prove that one choice of the increments is greatly superior to all others. Various suggestions have been made. If the increments are chosen close together, as we have done, then it will be necessary to make more passes, but each one will likely be quicker. If the increments decrease rapidly, then fewer but longer passes will occur. The only essential feature is that the final increment be 1, so that at the conclusion of the process, the list will be checked to be completely in order. For simplicity in the following algorithm, we start with increment = L.count and at each pass reduce the increment by

$$\text{increment} := \text{increment } \textbf{div } 3 + 1.$$

We can now outline the algorithm for contiguous lists.

Shell sort

```
procedure ShellSort(var L: list);
  var
    increment,                              {spacing of entries in sublist}
    start:    index;                        {starting point of sublist}
  begin                                     {procedure ShellSort}
    increment := L.count;
    repeat
      increment := increment div 3 + 1;
      for start := 1 to increment do
        Sort(start, increment, L)
    until increment = 1
  end;                                      {procedure ShellSort}
```

The procedure Sort(start, increment, L) is exactly the procedure InsertSort, except that the list starts at the variable start instead of 1 and the increment between successive values is as given instead of 1. The details of modifying InsertSort are left as an exercise.

analysis
The analysis of ShellSort turns out to be exceedingly difficult, and to date, good estimates on the number of comparisons and moves have been obtained only under special conditions. It would be very interesting to know how these numbers depend on the choice of increments, so that the best choice might be made. But even without a complete mathematical analysis, running a few large examples on a computer will convince you that ShellSort is quite good. Very large empirical studies have been made of ShellSort, and it appears that the number of moves, when n is large, is in the range of $n^{1.25}$ to $1.6n^{1.25}$. This constitutes a substantial improvement over insertion sort.

**Exercises
7.4**

E1. By hand, sort the list of 14 names at the beginning of this section using Shell sort with increments of **(a)** 8, 4, 2, 1 and **(b)** 7, 3, 1. Count the number of comparisons and moves that are made in each case.

E2. Explain why Shell sort is ill suited for use with linked lists.

**Programming
Projects
7.4**

P1. Rewrite the procedure InsertSort to serve as the procedure Sort embedded in ShellSort.

P2. Run Shell sort on the same data used to compare sorting algorithms in the previous sections, and check its performance against that of insertion sort and selection sort.

7.5 LOWER BOUNDS

Now that we have seen a method that performs much better than our first attempts, it is appropriate to ask,

How fast is it possible to sort?

To answer, we shall limit our attention (as we did when answering the same question for searching) to sorting methods that rely entirely on comparisons between pairs of keys to do the sorting.

comparison tree

Let us take an arbitrary sorting algorithm of this class and consider how it sorts a list of n items. Imagine drawing its comparison tree. Sample comparison trees for insertion sort and selection sort applied to three numbers a, b, c are shown in Figure 7.5. As each comparison of keys is made, it corresponds to an interior vertex (drawn as a circle). The leaves (square nodes) show the order that the numbers have after sorting.

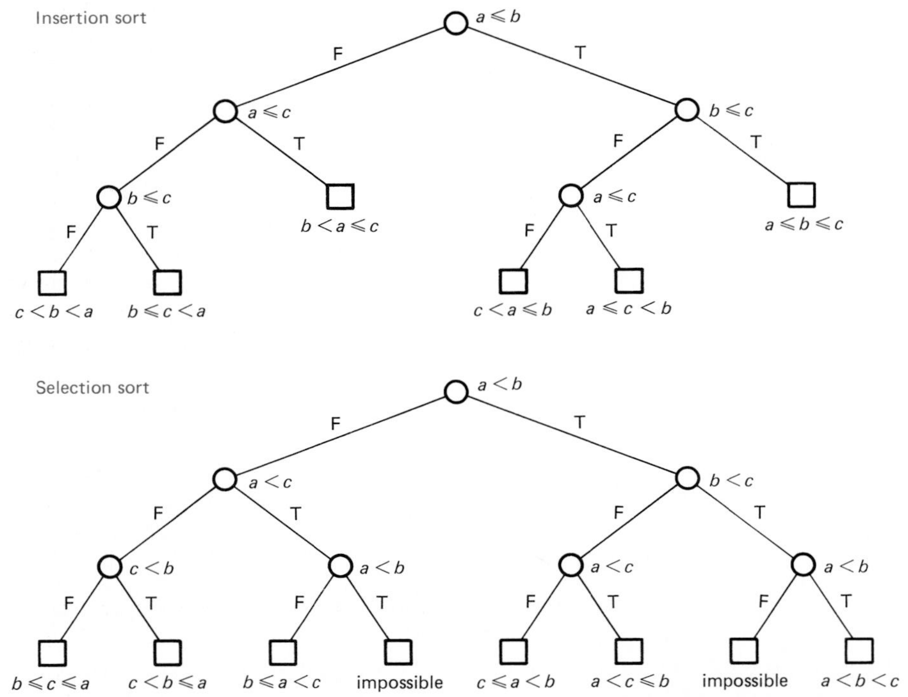

Figure 7.5.   Comparison trees, insertion and selection sort, $n = 3$

Note that the diagrams show clearly that, on average, selection sort makes more comparisons of keys than insertion sort. In fact, selection sort makes redundant comparisons, repeating comparisons that have already been made.

comparison trees:
height and path length

The comparison tree of an arbitrary sorting algorithm displays several features of the algorithm. Its height is the largest number of comparisons that will be made, and hence gives the worst-case behavior of the algorithm. The external path length, after division by the number of leaves, gives the average number of comparisons that the algorithm will do. The comparison tree displays all the possible sequences of comparisons that can be made as all the different paths from the root to the leaves. Since these comparisons control how the items are rearranged during sorting, any two different orderings of the list must result in some different decisions, hence different paths through the tree, which must then end in different leaves. The number of ways that the list containing n items could originally have been ordered is $n!$ (see Appendix A.3.1), and thus the number of leaves in the tree must be at least $n!$. Lemma 5.5 now implies that the height of the tree is at least $\lceil \lg n! \rceil$ and its external path length is at least $n! \lg n!$. Translating these results into the number of comparisons, we obtain

THEOREM 7.2

> *Any algorithm that sorts a list of n items by use of key comparisons must, in its worst case, perform at least $\lceil \lg n! \rceil$ comparisons of keys, and, in the average case, it must perform at least $\lg n!$ comparisons of keys.*

Stirling's formula from Appendix A.3.3 gives an approximation to the factorial of an integer, which, after taking the base 2 logarithm, gives

approximating $\lg n!$

$$\lg n! \approx (n + \tfrac{1}{2})\lg n - (\lg e)n + \lg\sqrt{2\pi} + \frac{\lg e}{12n}.$$

The constants in this expression have the approximate values

$$\lg e \approx 1.442695041$$
$$\lg\sqrt{2\pi} \approx 1.325748069.$$

This approximation to $\lg n!$ is very close indeed, much closer than we shall ever need for analyzing algorithms. For almost all purposes, the following rough approximation will prove quite satisfactory:

$$\lg n! \approx (n + \tfrac{1}{2})(\lg n - 1\tfrac{1}{2}) + 2$$

and often we use only the approximation $\lg n! = n \lg n + O(n)$.

other methods

Before ending this section we should note that there are sometimes methods for sorting that do not use comparisons and can be faster. For example, if you know in advance that you have 100 items and that their keys are exactly the integers between 1 and 100 in some order, with no duplicates, then the best way to sort them is not to do any comparisons, but simply, if a particular item has key i, then place it in location i. With this method we are (at least temporarily) regarding the items to be sorted as being in a table rather than a list, and then we can use the key as an index to find the proper place in the table for each item. Project 1 suggests an extension of this idea to an algorithm.

Exercises 7.5

E1. Draw the comparison trees for **(a)** insertion sort and **(b)** selection sort applied to four objects.

E2. **(a)** Find a sorting method for four keys that is optimal in the sense of doing the smallest possible number of key comparisons in its worst case. **(b)** Find how many comparisons your algorithm does in the average case (applied to four keys). Modify your algorithm to make it come as close as possible to achieving the lower bound of $\lg 4! \approx 4.585$ key comparisons. Why is it impossible to achieve this lower bound?

E3. Suppose that you have a shuffled deck of 52 cards, 13 cards in each of 4 suits, and you wish to sort the deck so that the 4 suits are in order and the 13 cards within each suit are also in order. Which of the following methods is fastest?

(a) Go through the deck and remove all the clubs; then sort them separately. Proceed to do the same for the diamonds, the hearts, and the spades.

(b) Deal the cards into 13 piles according to the rank of the card. Stack these 13 piles back together and deal into 4 piles according to suit. Stack these back together.

(c) Make only one pass through the cards, by placing each card in its proper position relative to the previously sorted cards.

Programming Projects 7.5

interpolation sort

P1. Construct a list of n (pseudo-)random numbers between 0 and 1. Suitable values for n are 10 (for debugging) and 500 (for comparing the program with other methods). Write a program to sort these numbers into a table via the following "interpolation sort." First, clear the table to all -1. For each number from the old list, multiply it by n, take the integer part, and look in that position of the table. If that position is -1, put the number there. If not, move left or right (according to the relative size of the current number and the one in its place) to find the place to insert the new number, moving the entries in the table over if necessary to make room (as in the fashion of insertion sort). Show that your algorithm will really sort the numbers correctly. Compare its running time with that of the other sorting methods applied to the same unsorted list.

linked distribution sort

P2. [Suggested by B. LEE] Write a program to perform a linked distribution sort, as follows. Take the keys to be numbers, as in the previous project; set up an array of linked lists; and distribute the keys into the linked lists according to their magnitude. The linked lists can either be kept sorted as the numbers are inserted or sorted during a second pass, during which the lists are all connected together into one sorted list. Experiment to determine the optimum number of lists to use. (It seems that it works well to have enough lists so that the average length of each list is about 3.)

7.6 DIVIDE AND CONQUER

If you compare the lower bounds derived in the last section with the expected performance of insertion sort and selection sort, then you will see that there is a considerable gap. If $n = 1000$, for example, then insertion sort does about 250,000 comparisons, and selection sort does about 500,000, whereas the lower bound is about 8,500. An optimal method, therefore, should run almost 30 times faster than insertion sort when $n = 1000$. In this section we shall derive more sophisticated sorting algorithms that come close to providing the best performance that the lower bounds will allow.

7.6.1 The Main Ideas

shorter is easier

Making a fresh start is often a good idea, and we shall do so by forgetting (temporarily) almost everything that we know about sorting. Let us try to apply only one important principle that has shown up in every method we have done and that we know from common experience: It is much easier to sort short lists than long ones. If the number of items to be sorted doubles, then the work more than doubles (with insertion or selection sort it quadruples, roughly). Hence if we can find a way to divide the list into two roughly equal-sized lists and sort them separately, then we will save work. If you were working in a library and were given a thousand index cards to put in alphabetical order, then a good way would be to distribute them into piles according to the first letter and sort the piles separately.

divide and conquer

The idea of dividing a problem into smaller but similar subproblems is called *divide and conquer.* First, we note that comparisons by computer are usually two-way branches, so we shall divide the items to sort into two lists at each stage of the process.

What method, you may ask, should we use to sort the reduced lists? Since we have (temporarily) forgotten all the other methods we know, let us simply use the same method, divide and conquer, again, repeatedly subdividing the list. But we won't keep going forever: Sorting a list with only one item doesn't take any work, even if we know no formal sorting methods.

In summary, let us informally outline divide-and-conquer sorting:

divide-and-conquer sorting

```
procedure Sort(list)
   if the list has length greater than 1 then
   begin
      Partition the list into lowlist, highlist;
      Sort(lowlist);
      Sort(highlist);
      Combine(lowlist, highlist)
   end.
```

We still must decide how we are going to partition the list into two sublists and, after they are sorted, how we are going to combine the sublists into a single list. There are two methods, each of which works very well in different circumstances.

1. *Mergesort*

   In the first method we simply chop the list into two sublists of sizes as nearly equal as possible and then sort them separately. Afterward, we carefully merge the two sorted sublists into a single sorted list. Hence this method is called *mergesort.*

2. *Quicksort*

   The second method does more work in the first step of partitioning the list into two sublists, and the final step of combining the sublists then becomes trivial. This method was invented and christened *quicksort* by C. A. R. HOARE. To partition the list, we first choose some key from the list for which, we hope, about half the keys will come before and half after. Call

pivot

this key the *pivot*. Then we partition the items so that all those with keys less than the pivot come in one sublist, and all those with greater keys come in another. Then we sort the two reduced lists separately, put the sublists together, and the whole list will be in order.

7.6.2 An Example

Before we refine our methods into detailed procedures, let us work through an example. We take the following seven numbers to sort:

26 33 35 29 19 12 22.

1. Mergesort Example

The first step of mergesort is to chop the list into two. When (as in this example) the list has odd length, let us establish the convention of making the left sublist one entry larger than the right sublist. Thus we divide the list into

26 33 35 29   and   19 12 22

and first consider the left sublist. It is again chopped in half as

first half

26 33   and   35 29.

For each of these sublists, we again apply the same method, chopping each of them into sublists of one number each. Sublists of length one, of course, require no sorting. Finally, then, we can start to merge the sublists to obtain a sorted list. The sublists 26 and 33 merge to give the sorted list 26 33, and the sublists 35 and 29 merge to give 29 35. At the next step we merge these two sorted sublists of length two to obtain a sorted sublist of length four,

26 29 33 35.

Now that the left half of the original list is sorted, we do the same steps on the right half. First, we chop it into the sublists

second half

19 12   and   22.

The first of these is divided into two sublists of length one, which are merged to give 12 19. The second sublist, 22, has length one so needs no sorting. It is now merged with 12 19 to give the sorted list

12 19 22.

Finally, the sorted sublists of lengths four and three are merged to produce

12 19 22 26 29 33 35.

2. Quicksort Example

choice of pivot

Let us again work through the same example, this time applying quicksort, and keeping careful account of the execution of steps from our outline of the method. To use quicksort, we must first decide, in order to partition the list into two pieces, what key to choose as the pivot. We are free to choose any number we wish, but for consistency, we shall adopt a definite rule. Perhaps the simplest rule is to choose the first number on a list as the pivot, and we shall do so in this example. For practical applications, however, other choices are usually better.

Our first pivot, then, is 26, and the list partitions into sublists

partition

$$19\ 12\ 22 \quad \text{and} \quad 33\ 35\ 29$$

consisting, respectively, of the numbers less than and greater than the pivot. We have left the order of the items in the sublists unchanged from that in the original list, but this decision also is arbitrary. Some versions of quicksort put the pivot into one of the sublists, but we choose to place the pivot into neither sublist.

We now arrive at the next line of the outline, which tells us to sort the first sublist. We thus start the algorithm over again from the top, but this time applied to the shorter list

lower half

$$19\ 12\ 22.$$

The pivot of this list is 19, which partitions its list into two sublists of one number each, 12 in the first and 22 in the second. With only one entry each, these sublists do not need sorting, so we arrive at the last line of the outline, whereupon we combine the two sublists with the pivot between them to obtain the sorted list

$$12\ 19\ 22.$$

Now the call to the sort procedure is finished for this sublist, so it returns whence it was called. It was called from within the sort procedure for the full list of seven numbers, so we now go on to the next line of that procedure.

inner and outer procedure calls

We have now used the procedure twice, with the second instance occurring within the first instance. Note carefully that the two instances of the procedure are working on different lists and are as different from each other as is executing the same code twice within a loop. It may help to think of the two instances as having different colors, so that the instructions in the second (inner) call could be written out in full in place of the call, but in a different color of ink, thereby clearly distinguishing them as a separate instance of the procedure. The steps of this process are illustrated in Figure 7.6.

Returning to our example, we find the next line of the first instance of the procedure to be another call to sort another list, this time the three numbers

upper half

$$33\ 35\ 29.$$

As in the previous (inner) call, the pivot 33 immediately partitions the list, giving sublists of length one that are then combined to produce the sorted list

$$29\ 33\ 35.$$

Sort (26, 33, 35, 29, 19, 12, 22)

Partition into (19, 12, 22) and (33, 35, 29); pivot = 26
Sort (19, 12, 22)

Partition into (12) and (22); pivot = 19
Sort (12)
Sort (22)
Combine into (12, 19, 22)

Sort (33, 35, 29)

Partition into (29) and (35); pivot = 33
Sort (29)
Sort (35)
Combine into (29, 33, 35)

Combine into (12, 19, 22, 26, 29, 33, 35)

Figure 7.6.   Execution trace of quicksort

Finally, this call to sort returns, and we reach the last line of the (outer) instance that sorts the full list. At this point, the two sorted sublists of length three are combined with the original pivot of 26 to obtain the sorted list

recombine

$$12 \ 19 \ 22 \ 26 \ 29 \ 33 \ 35$$

and the process is complete.

7.6.3 Recursion

A procedure like divide and conquer, that calls itself (or calls one procedure that calls another and so on until the first is called again) is termed *recursive*. Recursive procedures are often the easiest and most natural way to solve a problem. At first, some people feel slightly uncomfortable with recursive procedures. Recursion may perhaps appear at first to be an infinite process, but there is no more danger of writing infinite recursion than of writing an infinite iterative loop. In fact, the dangers *termination* are less, since an infinite recursion will soon run out of space and terminate the program, while infinite iteration may continue until manually terminated. In our procedure we have deliberately ensured that when the list has size 1 or less, there is no recursion. When the list is longer, each recursive call is with a list strictly smaller than before. The process will therefore terminate in a finite number of steps.

further study   The importance of recursion makes it the major topic of Chapter 8, where we shall also explain some details of how a recursive procedure works on most computer systems. Appendix B, furthermore, describes methods for converting recursive procedures into equivalent nonrecursive ones. These methods are useful if you must program in one of the older languages (such as FORTRAN, COBOL, or BASIC) that do not provide for recursion.

7.6.4 Tree of Subprogram Calls

With all the recursive calls through which we worked our way, the examples we have studied may lead you to liken recursion to the fable of the Sorcerer's Apprentice, who, when he had enchanted a broom to fetch water for him, did not know how to stop it and so chopped it in two, whereupon it started duplicating itself until there were so many brooms fetching water that disaster would have ensued had the master not returned.

The easy way to keep track of all the calls in our quicksort example is to draw a tree, as in Figure 7.7. The two calls to Sort at each level are shown as the children of the vertex. The sublists of size 1 or 0, which need no sorting, are drawn as the leaves. In the other vertices (to save space) we include only the pivot that is used for the call.

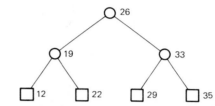

Figure 7.7.   Recursion tree, quicksort of 7 numbers

tree of subprogram calls

Drawing a tree can prove a good way to study the structure of subprogram calls, even when recursion is not involved. The main program is shown as the root of the tree, and all the calls that the main program makes directly are shown as the vertices directly below the root. Each of these subprograms may, of course, call other subprograms, which are shown as further vertices on lower levels. In this way the tree grows into a form like the one in Figure 7.8. We shall call such a tree a *tree of subprogram calls.* We are especially interested in recursion, so that often we draw only the part of the tree showing the recursive calls, and call it a *recursion tree.*

recursion tree

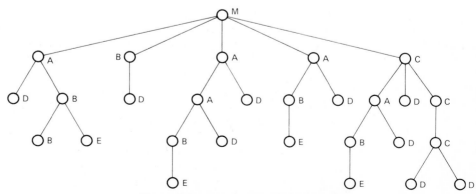

Figure 7.8.   A tree of subprogram calls

From the diagram, you should notice, first, that in drawing the tree recursion is in no way an exception: Different recursive calls appear simply as different vertices that happen to have the same name of a subprogram. Second, note carefully that the tree shows the calls to subprograms, not the nesting of declarations of subprograms. Hence a subprogram called from only one place, but within a loop executed more than once, will appear several times in the tree, once for each execution of the loop. Similarly, if a subprogram is called from a conditional statement that is not executed, then the call will not appear in the tree.

A closely related picture of recursion is that of **stack frames;** refer for a moment to Figure 3.3. The stack frames show the nesting of recursive calls and also illustrate the storage requirements for recursion. If a procedure calls itself recursively several times, then separate copies of the variables declared in the procedure are created for each recursive call. In the usual implementation of recursion, these are kept on

a stack. Note that the amount of space needed for this stack is proportional to the height of the recursion tree, not to the total number of nodes in the tree. That is, the amount of space needed to implement a recursive procedure depends on the *depth* of recursion, not on the *number* of times the procedure is invoked.

If you are still uneasy about the workings of recursion, than you will find it helpful to pause and work through sorting the list of 14 names introduced in previous sections, using both mergesort and quicksort. As a check, Figure 7.9 provides the

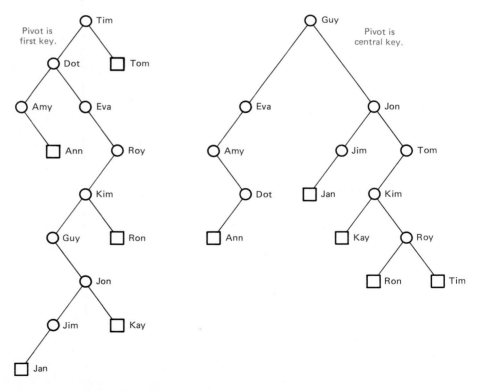

Figure 7.9.   Recursion trees, quicksort of 14 names

tree of calls for quicksort in the same abbreviated form used for the previous example. This tree is given for two versions, one where the pivot is the first key in each sublist, and one where the central key (center left for even-sized lists) is the pivot.

E1. Apply quicksort to the list of seven numbers considered in this section, where the pivot in each sublist is chosen to be **(a)** the last number in the sublist and **(b)** the center (or left-center) number in the sublist. In each case, draw the tree of recursive calls.

E2. Apply mergesort to the list of 14 names considered for previous sorting methods:

   Tim Dot Eva Roy Tom Kim Guy Amy Jon Ann Jim Kay Ron Jan.

E3. Apply quicksort to this list of 14 names, and thereby sort them by hand into alphabetical order. Take the pivot to be **(a)** the first key in each sublist and **(b)** the center (or left-center) key in each sublist. See Figure 7.9.

E4. In both divide-and-conquer methods we have attempted to divide the list into two sublists of approximately equal size, but the basic outline of sorting by divide and conquer remains valid without equal-sized halves. Consider dividing the list so that one sublist has size only 1. This leads to two methods, depending on whether the work is done in splitting one element from the list or in combining the sublists.

(a) Split the list by finding the item with the largest key and making it the sublist of size 1. After sorting the remaining items, the sublists are combined easily by placing the item with largest key last.

(b) Split off the last item from the list. After sorting the remaining items, merge this item into the list.

Show that one of these methods is exactly the same method as insertion sort and the other is the same as selection sort.

7.7 MERGESORT FOR LINKED LISTS

Let us now turn to the writing of formal procedures for each of our sorting methods. In the case of mergesort, we shall write a version for linked lists and leave the case of contiguous lists as an exercise. For quicksort, we shall do the reverse. Both these methods, however, work well for both contiguous and linked lists.

7.7.1 The Procedures

Our outline of the basic method for mergesort translates directly into the following procedure, which should be invoked from the calling program with its calling parameter being a pointer to the head of the list to be sorted. To establish parameter conventions the same as those for the other sorting methods, this calling program should be a procedure with only one parameter, of type list, the head of which is passed to the following procedure.

```
procedure MergeSort(var p: pointer);
   {divides the list starting at p↑ in half, sorts it recursively, and merges the sublists}
   var
      q: pointer;                              {marks the halfway point in the list}
   begin
      If p <> nil then if p↑.next <> nil then
      begin                      {Otherwise, list has 0 or 1 entry, with no need to sort.}
         Divide(p, q);
         MergeSort(p);
         MergeSort(q);
         Merge(p, q, p)
      end
   end;
```

The first subsidiary procedure, Divide(p, q), takes the list to which p points, divides it in half, and returns with q pointing to the start of the second half. The second procedure, Merge(p, q, r), merges the lists to which p and q point, returning a pointer to the merged list as its third parameter r. These subsidiary procedures follow.

```
procedure Divide(var p, q: pointer);
   {takes the list to which p points, divides it in half, and returns with p pointing to
      head of the first half and q to the head of second half; requires that the original
      list contain at least two items, or an error occurs}
   var
      r: pointer;
   begin                                                    {procedure Divide}
      q := p;                              {Start q at position 1 and r at position 3.}
      r := p↑.next;
      r := r↑.next;
      while r <> nil do                    {Move r two positions for each move of q.}
      begin
         r := r↑.next;
         q := q↑.next;
         if r <> nil then
            r := r↑.next
      end;
      {Break the list into halves after q↑.}
      r := q↑.next;
      q↑.next := nil;
      q := r
   end;                                                     {procedure Divide}
```

merge two sorted
linked lists

```
procedure Merge(p, q: pointer; var r: pointer);
{merges two sorted lists into one, that will begin at r: requires that both lists be
   nonempty}
var
   s: pointer;                              {always points to last node of sorted list}
begin                                                            {procedure Merge}
   if (p = nil) or (q = nil) then
      writeln('Merge called with empty lists(s).');
   {First find the head, r, of the merged list.}
   if p↑.info.key <= q↑.info.key then
   begin
      r := p;
      p := p↑.next
   end
   else begin
      r := q;
      q := q↑.next
   end;
   s := r;                        {s always points to the last entry of the merged list.}
   while (p <> nil) and (q <> nil) do
      if p↑.info.key <= q↑.info.key then
      begin
         s↑.next := p;         {Attach the node with the smaller key to the sorted list.}
         s := p;
         p := p↑.next                          {Advance to the next unmerged node.}
      end
      else begin
         s↑.next := q;
         s := q;
         q := q↑.next
      end;
   {After one list is exhausted, attach the remainder of the other one.}
   if p = nil then
      s↑.next := q
   else
      s↑.next := p
end;                                                            {procedure Merge}
```

7.7.2 Analysis of Mergesort

Now that we have a working procedure for mergesort, it is time to pause and determine its behavior, so that we can make reasonable comparisons with other sorting methods. As with other algorithms on linked lists, we need not be concerned with the time needed to move items. We concentrate instead on the number of comparisons of keys that the procedure will do.

1. Counting Comparisons

merge procedure

Comparison of keys is done at only one place in the complete mergesort procedure. This place is within the main loop of the merge (sub-)procedure. After each comparison one of the two nodes is sent to the output list. Hence the number of comparisons certainly cannot exceed the number of nodes being merged. To find the total lengths of these lists, let us again consider the recursion tree of the algorithm, which for simplicity we draw in Figure 7.10 for the case when $n = 2^m$ is a power of 2.

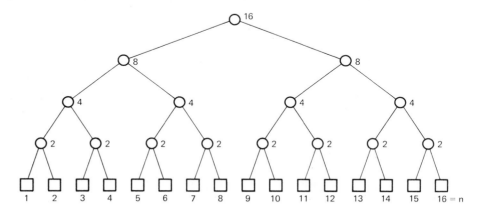

Figure 7.10.   Lengths of sublist merges

It is clear from the tree of Figure 7.10 that the total length of the lists on each level is precisely n, the total number of items. In other words, every item is treated in precisely one merge on each level. Hence the total number of comparisons done on each level cannot exceed n. The number of levels, excluding the leaves (for which no merges are done), is $\lceil \lg n \rceil$. The number of comparisons of keys done by mergesort on a list of n items, therefore, is certainly no more than $n\lceil \lg n \rceil$.

2. Contrast with Insertion Sort

Recall (Section 7.2.3) that insertion sort does more than $\frac{1}{4}n^2$ comparisons of keys, on average, in sorting n items. As soon as n becomes greater than 16, $\lg n$ becomes less than $\frac{1}{4}n$, and when n is of practical size for sorting a list, $\lg n$ is far less than $\frac{1}{4}n$, and therefore the number of comparisons done by mergesort is far less than the number done by insertion sort. When $n = 1024$, for example, then $\lg n = 10$, so that the bound on comparisons for mergesort is 10,240, whereas the average number that insertion sort will do is more than 250,000. A problem requiring a half-hour of computer time using insertion sort will probably require hardly a minute using mergesort.

n lg *n*

The appearance of the expression $n \lg n$ in the preceding calculation is by no means accidental, but relates closely to the lower bounds established in Section 7.5, where it was proved that any sorting method that uses comparisons of keys must do at least

$$\lg n! \approx n \lg n - 1.44n + O(\log n)$$

comparisons of keys. When n is large, the first term of this expression becomes more important than the others. We have now found, in mergesort, an algorithm that comes within reach of this lower bound.

3. Improving the Count

By being somewhat more careful we can, in fact, obtain a more accurate count of comparisons made by mergesort, that will show that its actual performance comes even closer to the best possible number of comparisons of keys allowed by the lower bound.

First, let us observe that merging two lists of total size k never requires k comparisons, but instead at most $k - 1$, since after the second largest key has been put out, there is nothing left to which to compare the largest key, so it goes out without another comparison. Hence we should reduce our total count of comparisons by 1 for each merge that is performed. The total number of merges is essentially

$$\frac{n}{2} + \frac{n}{4} + \frac{n}{8} + \cdots + 1 = n - 1.$$

(This calculation is exact when n is a power of 2 and is a good approximation otherwise.) The total number of key comparisons done by mergesort is therefore less than

$$n \lg n - n + 1.$$

Second, we should note that it is possible for one of the two lists being merged to be finished before the other, and then all items in the second list will go out with no further comparisons, so that the number of comparisons may well be less than we have calculated. Every element of one list, for example, might precede every element of the second list, so that all elements of the second list would come out using no comparisons. The exercises outline a proof that the total count can be reduced, on average, to

improved count
$$n \lg n - 1.1583n + 1$$

and the correct coefficient of n is likely close to -1.25. We thus see that, not only is the leading term as small as the lower bound permits, but the second term is also quite close. By refining the merge procedure even more, the method can be brought within a few percent of the theoretically optimal number of comparisons (see references).

4. Conclusions

advantages of linked mergesort

From these remarks it may appear that mergesort is the ultimate sorting method, and, indeed, for linked lists in random order, it is difficult to surpass. We must remember, however, that considerations other than comparing keys are important. The program we have written spends significant time finding the center of the list, so that it can break it in half. The exercises discuss one method for saving some of this time. The linked version of mergesort uses space efficiently. It needs no large auxiliary arrays or other lists, and since the depth of recursion is only $\lg n$, the amount of space needed to keep track of the recursive calls is very small.

5. Contiguous Mergesort

three-way trade-off for merging

For contiguous lists, unfortunately, mergesort is not such an unqualified success. The difficulty is in merging two contiguous lists without substantial expense in one of (1) space, (2) computer time, or (3) programming effort. The first and most straightforward way to merge two contiguous lists is to use an auxiliary array large enough to hold the combined list and copy the entries into the array as the lists are merged. This method requires extra space proportional to n. For a second method, we could put the sublists to be merged next to each other, forget the amount of order they already have, and use a method like insertion sort to put the combined list into order. This approach uses almost no extra space, but uses computer time proportional to n^2, compared to time proportional to n for a good merging algorithm. Finally (see references), algorithms have been invented that will merge two contiguous lists in time proportional to n while using only a small, fixed amount of extra space. These algorithms, however, are quite complicated.

Exercises 7.7

E1. An article in a 1984 professional journal stated, "This recursive process [mergesort] takes time $O(n \log n)$, and so runs 64 times faster than the previous method [insertion sort] when sorting 256 numbers." Criticize this statement.

E2. The count of key comparisons in merging is usually too high, since it does not account for the fact that one list may be finished before the other. It might happen, for example, that all entries in the first list come before any in the second list, so that the number of comparisons is just the length of the first list. For this exercise, assume that all numbers in the two lists are different and that all possible arrangements of the numbers are equally likely.

(a) Show that the average number of comparisons performed by our algorithm to merge two ordered lists of length 2 is $\frac{8}{3}$. [*Hint:* Start with the ordered list 1, 2, 3, 4. Write down the six ways of putting these numbers into two ordered lists of length 2, and show that four of these ways will use 3 comparisons, and two will use 2 comparisons.]

(b) Show that the average number of comparisons done to merge two ordered lists of length 3 is 4.5.

(c) Show that the average number of comparisons done to merge two ordered lists of length 4 is 6.4.

(d) Use the foregoing results to obtain the improved total count of key comparisons for mergesort.

(e) Show that, as m tends to infinity, the average number of comparisons done to merge two ordered lists of length m approaches $2m - 2$.

fixed-space linear-time merging

E3. [*Challenging*] The straightforward method for merging two contiguous lists by building the merged list in a separate array uses extra space proportional to the number of items in the two lists, but can be written to run efficiently, with time proportional to the number of items. Try to devise a merging method for contiguous lists that will require as little extra space as possible, but that will still run in time (linearly) proportional to the number of items in the lists. [There is a solution using only a small, constant amount of extra space. See references.]

Programming Projects 7.7

P1. Implement mergesort for linked lists on your computer. Use the same conventions and the same test data used for implementing and testing the linked version of insertion sort. Compare the performance of mergesort and insertion sort for short and long lists, as well as for lists nearly in correct order and in random order.

P2. Our mergesort program for linked lists spends significant time locating the center of each sublist, so that it can be broken in half. Implement the following modification that will save most of this time. First set up a record to describe a linked list that will contain not only (a) a pointer to the head of the list, but also (b) a pointer to the center of the list and (c) the length of the list. At the beginning, the original list must be traversed once to determine this information. With this information, it becomes easy to break the list in half and obtain the lengths of the sublists. The center of a sublist can be found by traversing only half the sublist. Rewrite the mergesort procedure to pass the records describing linked lists as calling parameters, and use them to simplify the subdivision of the lists.

P3. Our mergesort procedure pays little attention to whether or not the original *natural mergesort* list was partially in the correct order. In **natural mergesort** the list is broken into sublists at the end of an increasing sequence of keys, instead of arbitrarily at its halfway point. This exercise requests the implementation of two versions of natural mergesort.

one sorted list   In the first version the original list is traversed only once, and only two sublists are used. As long as the order of the keys is correct, the nodes are placed in the first sublist. When a key is found out of order, the first sublist is ended and the second started. When another key is found out of order, the second sublist is ended, and the second sublist merged into the first. Then the second sublist is repeatedly built again and merged into the first. When the end of the original list is reached, the sort is finished. This first version is simple to program, but as it proceeds, the first sublist is likely to become much longer than the second, and the performance of the procedure will degenerate toward that of insertion sort.

several sorted lists   The second version ensures that the lengths of sublists being merged are closer to being equal and, therefore, that the advantages of divide and conquer are fully used. This method keeps a (small) auxiliary array containing (a) the lengths and (b) pointers to the heads of the ordered sublists that are not yet merged. The entries in this array should be kept in order according to the length of sublist. As each (naturally ordered) sublist is split from the original list, it is put into the auxiliary array. If there is another list in the array whose length is between half and twice that of the new list, then the two are merged, and the process repeated. When the original list is exhausted, any remaining sublists in the array are merged (smaller lengths first) and the sort is finished.

There is nothing sacred about the ratio of 2 in the criterion for merging sublists. Its choice merely ensures that the number of entries in the auxiliary array cannot exceed lg n (prove it!). A smaller ratio (required to be greater than 1) will make the auxiliary table larger, and a larger ratio will lessen the advantages of divide and conquer. Experiment with test data to find a good ratio to use.

contiguous mergesort   **P4.** Devise a version of mergesort for contiguous lists. The difficulty is to produce a procedure to merge two sorted lists in contiguous storage. It is necessary to use some additional space other than that needed by the two lists. The easiest solution is to use two arrays, each large enough to hold all the items in the two original lists. The two sorted sublists occupy different parts of the same array. As they are merged, the new list is built in the second array. After the merge is complete, the new list can, if desired, be copied back into the first array. Otherwise, the roles of the two arrays can be reversed for the next stage.

radix sort   **P5.** A formal sorting algorithm predating computers was first devised for use with punched cards, but can be developed into a very efficient sorting method for linked lists. The idea is to consider the key one character at a time and to divide the items, not into two sublists, but into as many sublists as there are possibilities for the given character from the key. If our keys, for example, are words or other alphabetic strings, then we divide the list into 26 sublists at each stage. Punched cards have 12 rows; hence mechanical card sorters work on only one column at a time and divide the cards into 12 piles.

A person sorting words by this method would first distribute the words into 26 lists according to the initial letter, then divide each of these sublists into further sublists according to the second letter, and so on. The following

method   idea eliminates this multiplicity of sublists: Partition the items into sublists first by the least significant position, not the most significant. After this first partition, the sublists are put back together as a single list, in the order given by the character in the least significant position. The list is then partitioned according to the second least significant position and recombined as one list. When, after repetition of these steps, the list has been partitioned by the most significant place and recombined, it will be completely sorted.

program   Implement this method in Pascal for linked lists, where the keys are strings of letters or blanks of fixed length. The sublists should be treated as linked queues, and you will need an array of 27 such queues, indexed by the letters and by the character blank (or some substitute character). Within a loop running from the least to most significant positions, you should traverse the linked list, and add each item to the end of the appropriate queue. After the list has been thus partitioned, recombine the queues into one list by linking the tail of each queue to the head of the next. At the end of the major loop on positions, the list will be completely sorted.

testing   Run radix sort on the same data used to check linked mergesort, and compare the results. Note that the time used by radix sort is proportional to nk, where n is the number of items being sorted and k is the number of characters in a key. The time for mergesort is proportional to n lg n. The relative performance of the methods will therefore relate in some ways to the relative sizes of k and lg n.

7.8 QUICKSORT FOR CONTIGUOUS LISTS

We now turn to the method of quicksort, in which the list is first partitioned into lower and upper sublists for which all keys are, respectively, less than some pivot key or greater than the pivot key. Quicksort can be developed for linked lists with little difficulty, and this project will be pursued in the exercises. The most important applications of quicksort, however, are to contiguous lists, where it can prove to be very fast, and where it has the advantage over contiguous mergesort of not requiring a choice between using substantial extra space for an auxiliary array or investing great programming effort in implementing a complicated and difficult merge algorithm.

7.8.1 The Main Procedure

Our task in developing contiguous quicksort consists essentially in writing an algorithm for partitioning items in an array by use of a pivot key, swapping the items within the array so that all those with keys before the pivot come first, then the item with the pivot key, and then the items with larger keys. We shall let pivotlocation provide the index of the pivot in the partitioned list.

Since the partitioned sublists are kept in the same array, in the proper relative positions, the final step of combining sorted sublists is completely vacuous and thus is omitted from the procedure.

To apply the sorting procedure recursively to sublists, the bounds low and high of the sublists need to be parameters for the procedure. Our other sorting procedures, however, had the list L as the only parameter, so for consistency of notation we do the recursion in a procedure Sort that is invoked by the following procedure:

main procedure, quicksort

```
procedure QuickSort(var L: list);
{main procedure to invoke recursive quicksort}
{Declare procedure Sort here.}
begin
   Sort(L, 1, L.count)
end;
```

The actual quicksort procedure for contiguous lists is then

recursive procedure, quicksort

```
procedure Sort(var L: list; low, high: integer);
{sorts the contiguous list stored in array L.entry, where the list begins at index
   low and ends at index high}
var
   pivotlocation: index;                    {location of the pivot after partitioning}
begin
   if low < high then                       {If not, then no sorting is needed.}
   begin
      Partition(L, low, high, pivotlocation);
      Sort(L, low, pivotlocation − 1);
      Sort(L, pivotlocation + 1, high)
   end
end;
```

7.8.2 Partitioning the List

Now we must construct the procedure Partition. There are several methods that we might use (one of which is suggested as an exercise), methods that sometimes are faster than the algorithm we develop but that are intricate and difficult to get correct. The algorithm we develop is much simpler and easier to understand, and it is certainly not slow; in fact, it does the smallest possible number of key comparisons of any partitioning algorithm.

1. Algorithm Development

Given a pivot value p, we must rearrange the entries of the array and compute the index pivotlocation so that the pivot is at pivotlocation, all entries to its left have keys less than p, and all entries to its right have larger keys. To allow for the possibility that more than one item has key equal to p, we insist that the items to the left of pivotlocation have keys strictly less than p, and the items to its right have keys greater than or equal to p, as shown in the following diagram:

goal (postcondition)

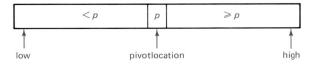

To reorder the items this way, we must compare each key to the pivot. We shall use a **for** loop (running on a variable i) to do this. We shall use a second variable lastsmall such that all items at or before location lastsmall have keys less than p. Suppose that the pivot p starts in the first position, and let us leave it there temporarily. Then in the middle of the loop the array has the following property:

loop invariant

When the procedure inspects entry i, there are two cases. If the entry is greater than or equal to p, then i can be increased and the array still has the required property. If the entry is less than p, then we restore the property by increasing lastsmall and swapping that entry (the first of those at least p) with entry i, as shown in the following diagrams:

restore the invariant

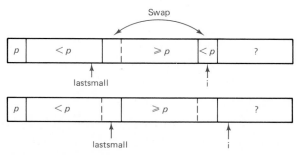

When the loop terminates, we have the situation:

final position

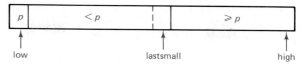

and we then need only swap the pivot from position low to position lastsmall to obtain the desired final arrangement.

2. Choice of Pivot

We are not bound to the choice of the first item in the list as the pivot; we can choose any item we wish and swap it with the first item before beginning the loop that partitions the list. In fact, the first item is often a poor choice for pivot, since if the list is already sorted, then the first key will have no others less than it, and so one of the sublists will be empty. Hence, let us instead choose a pivot near the center of the list, in the hope that our choice will partition the keys so that about half come on each side of the pivot.

pivot from center

3. Coding

With these decisions we obtain the following procedure, in which we use the swap procedure from Section 7.3. For convenience of reference we also include the property that holds during iteration of the loop as an assertion (loop invariant) in the procedure.

```
procedure Partition(var L: list; low, high: index; var pivotlocation: index);
var
  pivot: keytype;                              {will be taken from center of list}
  i,                                           {used to scan through the list}
  lastsmall: index;                            {last key less than pivot}
begin                                          {procedure Partition}
  Swap(low, (low + high) div 2, L);            {Swap the pivot into the first location.}
  pivot := L.entry[low].key;
  lastsmall := low;
  for i := low + 1 to high do
    {Assert: If low < j <= lastsmall then L.entry[j].key < pivot.
             If lastsmall < j < i then L.entry[j].key >= pivot.}
    if L.entry[i].key < pivot then
    begin
      lastsmall := lastsmall + 1;
      Swap(lastsmall, i, L)
                   {Move the large item to the right and the small item i to the left.}
    end;
  Swap(low, lastsmall, L);                     {Put the pivot into its proper position.}
  pivotlocation := lastsmall
end;                                           {procedure Partition}
```

7.8.3 Analysis of Quicksort

It is now time to examine the quicksort algorithm carefully, to determine when it works well and when not, and how much computation it performs.

1. Choice of Pivot

Our choice of a key at the center of the list to be the pivot is arbitrary. This choice may succeed in dividing the list nicely in half, or we may be unlucky and find that one sublist is much larger than the other. Some other methods for choosing the pivot are considered in the exercises. An extreme case for our method occurs for the following list, where every one of the pivots selected turns out to be the largest key in its sublist:

worst case

$$2\ 4\ 6\ 7\ 3\ 1\ 5$$

Check it out, using the Partition procedure in the text. When quicksort is applied to this list, its label will appear to be quite a misnomer, since at the first recursion the nonempty sublist will have length 6, at the second 5, and so on.

If we were to choose the pivot as the first key or the last key in each sublist, then the extreme case would occur when the keys are in their natural order or in their reverse order. These orders, of course, are more likely to happen than some random order, and therefore choosing the first or last key as pivot is likely to cause problems.

2. Count of Comparisons and Swaps

Let us determine the number of comparisons and swaps that contiguous quicksort makes. Let $C(n)$ be the number of comparisons of keys made by quicksort when applied to a list of length n, and let $S(n)$ be the number of swaps of items. We have $C(1) = C(0) = 0$. The partition procedure compares the pivot with every other key in the list exactly once, and thus procedure Partition accounts for exactly $n - 1$ key comparisons. If one of the two sublists it creates has length r, then the other sublist will have length exactly $n - r - 1$. The number of comparisons done in the two recursive calls will then be $C(r)$ and $C(n - r - 1)$. Thus we have

total number of comparisons

$$C(n) = n - 1 + C(r) + C(n - r - 1).$$

To solve this equation we need to know r. In fact, our notation is somewhat deceptive, since the values of $C(\ )$ depend not only on the length of the list but also on the exact ordering of the items in it. Thus we shall obtain different answers in different cases, depending on the ordering.

3. Comparison Count, Worst Case

First, consider the worst case for comparisons. We have already seen that this occurs when the pivot fails to split the list at all, so that one sublist has $n - 1$ entries and the other is empty. In this case, since $C(0) = 0$, we obtain

$$C(n) = n - 1 + C(n - 1).$$

An expression of this form is called a ***recurrence relation*** because it expresses its answer in terms of earlier cases of the same result. We wish to solve the recurrence, which means to find an equation for $C(n)$ that does not involve $C(\ )$ on the other side. Various (sometimes difficult) methods are needed to solve recurrence relations, but in this case we can do it easily by starting at the bottom instead of the top:

$$C(1) = 0.$$
$$C(2) = 1 + C(1) \qquad = 1.$$
$$C(3) = 2 + C(2) \qquad = 2 + 1.$$
$$C(4) = 3 + C(3) \qquad = 3 + 2 + 1.$$

$$\cdots \cdots$$

$$C(n) = n - 1 + C(n - 1) = (n - 1) + (n - 2) + \cdots + 3 + 1$$
$$= \tfrac{1}{2}(n - 1)n$$
$$= (0.5)n^2 - (0.5)n.$$

answer

In this calculation we have applied Theorem A.1 to obtain the sum of the integers from 1 to $n - 1$.

Recall that selection sort makes about

selection sort

$$(0.5)n^2 - (0.5)n$$

key comparisons, and making too many comparisons was the weak point of selection sort (as compared with insertion). Hence in its worst case, quicksort is as bad as the worst case of selection sort.

4. Swap Count, Worst Case

Next let us determine how many times quicksort will swap items, again in its worst case. The partition procedure does one swap inside its loop for each key less than the pivot and two swaps outside its loop. In its worst case, the pivot is the largest key in the list, so the partition procedure will then make $n + 1$ swaps. With $S(n)$ the total number of swaps on a list of length n, we then have the recurrence

$$S(n) = n + 1 + S(n - 1)$$

in the worst case. The partition procedure is called only when $n \geq 2$, and $S(2) = 3$ in the worst case. Hence, as in counting comparisons, we can solve the recurrence by working downward, and we obtain

answer

$$S(n) = (n + 1) + n + \cdots + 3 = \tfrac{1}{2}(n + 1)(n + 2) - 3 = 0.5n^2 + 1.5n - 1$$

swaps in the worst case.

5. Comparisons

In its worst case, contiguous insertion sort must make about twice as many comparisons and assignments of items as it does in its average case, giving a total of $0.5n^2 + O(n)$ for each operation. Each swap in quicksort requires three assignments of items, so quicksort in its worst case does $1.5n^2 + O(n)$ assignments, or, for large n, about three times as many as insertion sort. But moving items was the weak point of insertion sort in comparison to selection sort. Hence, in its worst case, quicksort (so called) is worse than the poor aspect of insertion sort, and, in regard to key comparisons, it is also as bad as the poor aspect of selection sort. Indeed, in the worst-case analysis, quicksort is a disaster, and its name is nothing less than false advertising.

poor worst-case behavior

It must be for some other reason that quicksort was not long ago consigned to the scrap heap of programs that never worked. The reason is the *average* behavior of quicksort when applied to lists in random order, which turns out to be one of

excellent average-case behavior

the best of any sorting methods (using key comparisons and applied to contiguous lists) yet known!

7.8.4 Average-Case Analysis of Quicksort

To do the average-case analysis, we shall assume that all possible orderings of the list are equally likely, and for simplicity, we take the keys to be just the integers from 1 to n.

1. Counting Swaps

When we select the pivot in the procedure Partition, it is equally likely to be any one of the keys. Denote by p whatever key is selected as pivot. Then after the partition, key p is guaranteed to be in index p, since the keys $1, \ldots, p - 1$ are all to its left and $p + 1, \ldots, n$ are to its right.

The number of swaps that will have been made in one call to Partition is $p + 1$, consisting of one swap in the loop for each of the $p - 1$ keys less than p and two swaps outside the loop. Let us denote by $S(n)$ the average number of swaps done by quicksort on a list of length n and by $S(n, p)$ the average number of swaps on a list of length n where the pivot for the first partition is p. We have now shown that, for $n \geq 2$,

$$S(n, p) = (p + 1) + S(p - 1) + S(n - p).$$

We must now take the average of these expressions, since p is random, by adding them from $p = 1$ to $p = n$ and dividing by n. The calculation uses the formula for the sum of the integers (Theorem A.1), and the result is

$$S(n) = \frac{n}{2} + \frac{3}{2} + \frac{2}{n}(S(0) + S(1) + \cdots + S(n - 1)).$$

2. Solving the Recurrence Relation

The first step toward solving this recurrence relation is to note that, if we were sorting a list of length $n - 1$, we would obtain the same expression with n replaced by $n - 1$, provided that $n > 2$:

$$S(n - 1) = \frac{n - 1}{2} + \frac{3}{2} + \frac{2}{n - 1}(S(0) + S(1) + \cdots + S(n - 2)).$$

Multiplying the first expression by n, the second by $n - 1$, and subtracting, we obtain

$$nS(n) - (n - 1)S(n - 1) = n + 1 + 2S(n - 1).$$

or

$$\frac{S(n)}{n + 1} = \frac{S(n - 1)}{n} + \frac{1}{n}.$$

We can solve this recurrence relation as we did a previous one by starting at the bottom. The result is

$$\frac{S(n)}{n+1} = \frac{S(2)}{3} + \frac{1}{3} + \cdots + \frac{1}{n}.$$

The sum of the reciprocals of integers is studied in Appendix A.2.7, where it is shown that

$$1 + \frac{1}{2} + \cdots + \frac{1}{n} = \ln n + O(1).$$

The difference between this sum and the one we want is bounded by a constant, so we obtain $S(n)/(n+1) = \ln n + O(1)$, or, finally,

$$S(n) = n \ln n + O(n).$$

To compare this result with those for other sorting methods, we note that

$$\ln n = (\ln 2)(\lg n)$$

and $\ln 2 \approx 0.69$, so that

$$S(n) \approx 0.69 \, n \lg n + O(n).$$

3. Counting Comparisons

Since a call to the partition procedure for a list of length n makes exactly $n - 1$ comparisons, the recurrence relation for the number of comparisons made in the average case will differ from that for swaps in only one way: Instead of $p + 1$ swaps in the partition procedure, there are $n - 1$ comparisons. Hence the first recurrence for the number $C(n, p)$ of comparisons for a list of length n with pivot p is

$$C(n, p) = n - 1 + C(p - 1) + C(n - p).$$

When we average these expressions for $p = 1$ to $p = n$, we obtain

$$C(n) = n - 1 + \frac{2}{n}(C(0) + C(1) + \cdots + C(n - 1)).$$

Since this recurrence for the number $C(n)$ of key comparisons differs from that for $S(n)$ essentially only by the factor of ½ in the latter, the same steps used to solve for $S(n)$ will yield

$$C(n) = 2n \ln n + O(n) \approx 1.39n \lg n + O(n).$$

7.8.5 Comparison with Mergesort

key comparisons

The calculation just completed shows that, on average, quicksort does about 39 percent more comparisons of keys than required by the lower bound and, therefore, also about 39 percent more than does mergesort. The reason, of course, is that mergesort is carefully designed to divide the list into halves of essentially equal size, whereas the sizes of the sublists for quicksort cannot be predicted in advance. Hence it is possible that quicksort's performance can be seriously degraded, but such an occurrence is unlikely in practice, so that averaging the times of poor performance with those of good performance yields the result just obtained.

data movement

Concerning data movement, we did not derive detailed information for mergesort, since we were primarily interested in the linked version. If, however, we consider the version of contiguous mergesort that builds the merged sublists in a second array, and reverses the use of arrays at each pass, then it is clear that, at each level of the recursion tree, all n items will be copied from one array to the other. The number of levels in the recursion tree is $\lg n$, and it therefore follows that the number of assignments of items in contiguous mergesort is $n \lg n$. For quicksort, on the other hand, we obtained a count of about $0.69n \lg n$ swaps, on average. A good (machine language) implementation should accomplish a swap of items in two assignments.

optimization

Therefore, again, quicksort does about 39 percent more assignments of items than does mergesort. The exercises, however, outline another partition procedure that does, on average, only about one-third as many swaps as the version we developed. With this refinement, therefore, contiguous quicksort may perform fewer than half as many assignments of data items as contiguous mergesort.

Exercises 7.8

E1. How will the quicksort procedure (as presented in the text) function if all the keys in the list are equal?

E2. [Due to KNUTH] Describe an algorithm that will arrange a contiguous list whose keys are real numbers so that all the items with negative keys will come first, then those with nonnegative keys. The final list need not be completely sorted. Make your algorithm do as few movements of items and as few comparisons as possible. Do not use an auxiliary array.

E3. [Due to HOARE] Suppose that, instead of sorting, we wish only to find the mth smallest key in a given list of size n. Show how quicksort can be adapted to this problem, doing much less work than a complete sort.

E4. Given an array of integers, develop a procedure, similar to the partition procedure, that will rearrange the integers so that either all the integers in even-numbered positions will be even or all the integers in odd-numbered positions will be odd. (Your procedure will provide a proof that one or the other of these goals can always be attained, although it may not be possible to establish both at once.)

E5. A different method for choosing the pivot in quicksort is to take the median of the first, last, and central keys of the list. Describe the modifications needed to the procedure QuickSort (contiguous version) to implement this choice. How much extra computation will be done? For $n = 7$, find an ordering of the keys

$$1, 2, \ldots, 7$$

that will force the algorithm into its worst case. How much better is this worst case than that of the original algorithm?

meansort

E6. A different approach to the selection of pivot is to take the mean (average) of all the keys in the list as the pivot. The resulting algorithm is called *meansort.*

(a) Write a procedure to implement meansort. The partition procedure must be modified, since the mean of the keys is not necessarily one of the keys in the list. On the first pass, the pivot can be chosen any way you wish.

As the keys are then partitioned, running sums and counts are kept for the two sublists, and thereby the means (which will be the new pivots) of the sublists can be calculated without making any extra passes through the list.

(b) In meansort the relative *sizes* of the keys determine how nearly equal the sublists will be after partitioning; the initial *order* of the keys is of no importance, except for counting the number of swaps that will take place. How bad can the worst case for meansort be in terms of the relative sizes of the two sublists? Find a set of n integers that will produce the worst case for meansort.

E7. [Requires elementary probability theory]   A good way to choose the pivot is to use a random-number generator to choose the index for the next pivot at each call to Sort. Using the fact that these choices are independent, find the probability that quicksort will happen upon its worst case. **(a)** Do the problem for $n = 7$. **(b)** Do the problem for general n.

E8. At the cost of a few more comparisons of keys, the partition procedure can be rewritten so that the number of swaps is reduced by a factor of about 3, from *optimize* Partition $n/2$ to $n/6$ on average. The idea is to use two indices moving from the ends of the lists toward the center and to perform a swap only when a large key is found by the low index and a small key by the high index. This exercise outlines the development of such a procedure.

(a) Establish two indices i and j, and maintain the invariant property that all keys before position i are less than the pivot and all keys after position j are greater than or equal to the pivot. For simplicity, swap the pivot into the first position, and start the partition with the second element. Write a loop that will increase the index i as long as the invariant holds and another loop that will decrease j as long as the invariant holds. Your loops must also ensure that the indices do not go out of range, perhaps by checking that i ≤ j. When a pair of items, each on the wrong side, is found, then they should be swapped and the loops repeated. What is the termination condition of this outer loop? At the end, the pivot can be swapped into its proper place.

(b) Using the invariant property, verify that your procedure works properly.

(c) Show that each swap performed within the loop puts two items into their final position. From this, show that the procedure does at most $\frac{1}{2}n + O(1)$ swaps in its worst case for a list of length n.

(d) If, after partitioning, the pivot belongs in position p, then the number of swaps that the procedure does is approximately the number of items originally in one of the p positions at or before the pivot, but whose keys are greater than or equal to the pivot. If the keys are randomly distributed, then the probability that a particular key is greater than or equal to the pivot is $(n - p - 1)/n$. Show that the average number of such keys, and hence the average number of swaps, is approximately $p(n - p)/n$. By taking the average of these numbers from $p = 1$ to $p = n$, show that the number of swaps is approximately $n/6 + O(1)$.

(e) The need to check to make sure that the indices i and j in the partition procedure stay in bounds can be eliminated by using the pivot key as a sentinel to stop the loops. Implement this method in your procedure. Be sure to verify that your procedure works correctly in all cases.

(f) [Due to WIRTH]   Consider the following simple and "obvious" way to write the loops using the pivot as a sentinel:

```
repeat
    repeat i := i + 1 until L.entry[i].key >= pivot;
    repeat j := j − 1 until L.entry[j].key <= pivot;
    Swap(i, j, L)
until i >= j;
```

Find a list of keys for which this version fails.

Programming Projects 7.8

P1. Implement quicksort (for contiguous lists) on your computer, and test it with the same data used with previous sorting algorithms. Compare the number of comparisons of keys, assignments of items, and total time required for sorting.

linked quicksort

P2. Write a version of quicksort for linked lists, and run it on your computer for the same test data used for previous methods. The simplest choice for pivot is the first key in the list being sorted. You should find the partition procedure conceptually easier and more straightforward than the contiguous version, since items need not be swapped, but only links changed. You will, however, require a short additional procedure to recombine the sorted sublists into a single linked list.

P3. Because it may involve more overhead, quicksort may be inferior to simpler methods for short lists. Find experimentally a value where, on average, quicksort becomes more efficient than insertion sort. Write a hybrid sorting procedure that starts with quicksort and, when the sublists are sufficiently short, switches to insertion sort. Determine if it is better to do the switch-over within the recursive procedure or to terminate the recursive calls when the sublists are sufficiently short to change methods and then at the very end of the process run through insertion sort once on the whole list.

7.9 REVIEW: COMPARISON OF METHODS

In this chapter we have studied and carefully analyzed quite a variety of sorting methods. Perhaps the best way to summarize this work is to emphasize in turn each of the three important efficiency criteria:

▶   Use of storage space.

▶   Use of computer time.

▶   Programming effort.

1. Use of Space

In regard to space, most of the algorithms we have discussed use little space other than that occupied by the original list, which is rearranged in its original place to be in order. The exceptions are quicksort and mergesort, where the recursion does require a small amount of extra storage to keep track of the sublists that have not yet been sorted. But in a well-written procedure, the amount of extra space used for recursion is $O(\log n)$ and will be trivial in comparison with that needed for other purposes.

Finally, we should recall that a major drawback of mergesort for contiguous lists is that the straightforward version requires extra space equal to that occupied by the original list.

external sorting and merging

In many applications the list to be sorted is much too large to be kept in high-speed memory, and when this is the case, other methods become necessary. A frequent approach is to divide the list into sublists that can be sorted internally within high-speed memory and then merge the sorted sublists externally. Hence much work has been invested in developing merging algorithms, primarily when it is necessary to merge many sublists at once. We shall not discuss this topic further.

2. Computer Time

The second efficiency criterion is use of computer time, which we have already carefully analyzed for each of the methods we have developed.

3. Programming Effort

The third efficiency criterion is often the most important of all: This criterion is the efficient and fruitful use of the programmer's time.

If a list is small, the sophisticated sorting techniques designed to minimize computer time requirements are usually worse or only marginally better in achieving their goal than are the simpler methods. If a program is to be run only once or twice and there is enough machine time, then it would be foolish for a programmer to spend days or weeks investigating many sophisticated algorithms that might, in the end, only save a few seconds of computer time.

When programming in languages like FORTRAN, COBOL, or BASIC that do not support recursion, implementation of mergesort and quicksort becomes more complicated (see Appendix B). Shell sort comes not far behind mergesort and quicksort in performance, does not require recursion, and is easy to program. One should therefore never sell Shell sort short.

simplicity and correctness

The saving of programming time is an excellent reason for choosing a simple algorithm, even if it is inefficient, but two words of caution should always be remembered. First, saving programming time is never an excuse for writing an incorrect program, one that may usually work but can sometimes misbehave. Murphy's law will then inevitably come true. Second, simple programs, designed to be run only a few times and then discarded, often instead find their way into applications not imagined when they were first written. Lack of care in the early stages will then prove exceedingly costly later.

For many applications, insertion sort can prove to be the best choice. It is easy to write and maintain, and it runs efficiently for short lists. Even for long lists, if they are nearly in the correct order, insertion sort will be very efficient. If the list is completely in order, then insertion sort verifies this condition as quickly as can be done.

4. Statistical Analysis

The final choice of algorithm will depend not only on the length of list, the size of records, and their representation in storage, but very strongly on the way in which the records can be expected to be ordered before sorting. The analysis of algorithms from the standpoint of probability and statistics is of great importance. For most algorithms, we have been able to obtain results on the mean (average) performance, but the experience of quicksort shows that the amount by which this performance changes from one possible ordering to another is also an important factor to consider. The *standard deviation* is a statistical measure of this variability. Quicksort has an excellent mean performance, and the standard deviation is small, which signifies that the performance is likely to differ little from the mean. For algorithms like selection sort and mergesort, the best-case and worst-case performances differ little, which means that the standard deviation is almost 0. Other algorithms, like insertion sort, will have a much larger standard deviation in their performance. The particular distribution of the orderings of the incoming lists are therefore an important consideration in choosing a sorting method. To enable intelligent decisions, the professional computer scientist needs to be knowledgeable about important aspects of mathematical statistics as they apply to algorithm analysis.

mean
standard deviation

5. Empirical Testing

Finally, in all these decisions we must be careful to temper the theoretical analysis of algorithms with empirical testing. Different computers and compilers will produce different results. It is most instructive, therefore, to see by experiment how the different algorithms behave in different circumstances.

Exercises 7.9

E1. Classify the sorting methods we have studied into one of the following categories: (a) the method does not require access to the items at one end of the list until the items at the other end have been sorted; (b) the method does not require access to the items that have already been sorted; (c) the method requires access to all items in the list throughout the process.

E2. Some of the sorting methods we have studied are not suited for use with linked lists. Which ones, and why not?

E3. Rank the sorting methods we have studied (both for linked and contiguous lists) according to the amount of extra storage space that they require for indices or pointers, for recursion, and for copies of the items being sorted.

E4. Which of the methods we studied would be a good choice in each of the following applications? Why? If the representation of the list in contiguous or linked storage makes a difference in your choice, state how.

(a) You wish to write a general-purpose sorting program that will be used by many people in a variety of applications.

(b) You wish to sort 1000 numbers once. After you finish, you will not keep the program.

(c) You wish to sort 50 numbers once. After you finish, you will not keep the program.

(d) You need to sort 5 items in the middle of a long program. Your sort will be called hundreds of times by the long program.

(e) You have an array of 1000 keys to sort in high-speed memory, and key comparisons can be made quickly, but each time a key is moved, a corresponding 500 block file on disk must also be moved, and doing so is a slow process.

(f) There is a twelve foot long shelf full of computer science books all catalogued by number. A few of these have been put back in the wrong places by readers, but rarely are they more than one foot from where they belong.

(g) You have a stack of 500 library index cards in random order to sort alphabetically.

(h) You are told that a list of 5000 words is already in order, but you wish to check it to make sure and sort any words found out of order.

E5. Discuss the advantages and disadvantages of designing a general sorting procedure as a hybrid between quicksort and Shell sort. What criteria would you use to switch from one to the other? Which would be the better choice for what kinds of lists?

E6. Summarize the results of the test runs of the sorting methods of this chapter for your computer. Also include any variations of the methods that you have written as exercises. Make charts comparing (a) the number of key comparisons, (b) the number of assignments of items, (c) the total running time, (d) the working storage requirements of the program, (e) the length of the program, and (f) the amount of programming time required to write and debug the program.

E7. Write a one-page guide to help a user of your computer system select one of our sorting algorithms according to his needs.

E8. A sorting procedure is called *stable* if, whenever two items have equal keys, then on completion of the sorting procedure the two items will be in the same order in the list as before sorting. Stability is important if a list has already been sorted by one key and is now being sorted by another key, and it is desired to keep as much of the original ordering as the new one allows. Determine which of the sorting methods of this chapter are stable and which are not. For those that are not, produce a list (as short as possible) containing some items with equal keys whose orders are not preserved. In addition, see if you can discover simple modifications to the algorithm that will make it stable.

POINTERS AND PITFALLS

1. Many computer systems have a general-purpose sorting utility. If you can access this utility and it proves adequate for your application, then use it rather than writing a sorting program from scratch.

2. In choosing a sorting method, take into account the ways in which the keys will usually be arranged before sorting, the size of the application, the amount of time available for programming, the need to save computer time and space, the way in which the data structures are implemented, the cost of moving data, and the cost of comparing keys.

3. For advice on programming and analyzing sorting algorithms, see the Pointers and Pitfalls at the end of Chapter 5.

REVIEW QUESTIONS

7.2   1. How many comparisons of keys are required to verify that a list of n items is in order?

2. Explain in twenty words or less how insertion sort works.

7.3   3. Explain in twenty words or less how selection sort works.

4. On average, about how many more comparisons does selection sort do than insertion sort on a list of 20 items?

5. What is the advantage of selection sort over all the other methods we studied?

7.4   6. What disadvantage of insertion sort does Shell sort overcome?

7.5   7. What is the lower bound on the number of key comparisons that any sorting method must make to put n keys into order, if the method uses key comparisons to make its decisions? Give both the average and worst-case bounds.

8. What is the lower bound if the requirement of using comparisons to make decisions is dropped?

7.6   9. Define the term *divide and conquer.*

10. Explain in twenty words or less how mergesort works.

11. Explain in twenty words or less how quicksort works.

12. What is a recursion tree?

7.7   13. Explain why mergesort is better for linked lists than for contiguous lists.

7.8   14. In quicksort, why did we choose the pivot from the center of the list rather than from one of the ends?

15. On average, about how many more comparisons of keys does quicksort make than the optimum? About how many comparisons does it make in the worst case?

7.9   16. Under what conditions are simple sorting algorithms better than sophisticated ones?

REFERENCES FOR FURTHER STUDY

The primary reference for this chapter is the comprehensive series by D. E. KNUTH (bibliographic details in Chapter 3). Internal sorting occupies Volume 3, pp. 73–180. KNUTH does algorithm analysis in considerably more detail than we have. He writes all algorithms in a pseudo-assembly language and does detailed operation counts there. He studies all the methods we have, several more, and many variations.

The original references to Shell sort and quicksort are, respectively,

D. L. SHELL, "A high-speed sorting procedure," *Communications of the ACM* 2 (1959), 30–32.

C. A. R. HOARE, "Quicksort," *Computer Journal* 5 (1962), 10–15.

The unified derivation of mergesort and quicksort, that can also be used to produce insertion sort and selection sort, is based on the work

JOHN DARLINGTON, "A synthesis of several sorting algorithms," *Acta Informatica* 11 (1978), 1–30.

Mergesort can be refined to bring its performance very close to the optimal lower bound. One example of such an improved algorithm, whose performance is within 6 percent of the best possible, is

R. MICHAEL TANNER, "Minimean merging and sorting: An algorithm," *SIAM Journal on Computing* 7 (1978), 18–38.

A relatively simple contiguous merge algorithm that operates in linear time with a small, constant amount of additional space appears in

HEIKKI MANNILA and ESKO UKKONEN, "A simple linear-time algorithm for *in situ* merging," *Information Processing Letters* 18 (1984), 203–208.

The algorithm for partitioning the list in quicksort was discovered by NICO LOMUTO and was published in

JON L. BENTLEY, "Programming pearls: How to sort," *Communications of the ACM* 27 (1984), 287–291.

"Programming pearls" is a regular column that contains many elegant algorithms and helpful suggestions for programming.

An extensive analysis of the quicksort algorithm is given in

ROBERT SEDGEWICK, "The analysis of quicksort programs," *Acta Informatica* 7 (1976/77), 327–355.

The exercise on meansort (taking the mean of the keys as pivot) comes from

DALIA MOTZKIN, "MEANSORT," *Communications of the ACM* 26 (1983), 250–251; 27 (1984), 719–722.

Expository surveys of various sorting methods are

W. A. MARTIN, "Sorting," *Computing Surveys* 3 (1971), 148–174.

H. LORIN, *Sorting and Sort Systems,* Addison-Wesley, Reading, Mass., 1975, 456 pages.

Programs in Pascal for most of the methods we discuss, along with analysis and empirical results, appear in

N. WIRTH, *Algorithms + Data Structures = Programs,* Prentice-Hall, Englewood Cliffs, N.J., 1976, pp. 56–124.

There is, of course, a vast literature in probability and statistics with potential applications to computers. A classic treatment of elementary probability and statistics is

W. FELLER, *An Introduction to Probability Theory and its Applications,* Vol. 1, second edition, Wiley-Interscience, New York, 1957.

Recursion

▶ *As we have seen from studying sorting methods, recursion is a valuable programming tool. This chapter presents several applications of recursion that further illustrate its usefulness. Some of these applications are simple; others are quite sophisticated. Later in the chapter we analyze how recursion is usually implemented on a computer. In the process, we shall obtain guidelines regarding good and bad uses of recursion, when it is appropriate, and when it should best be avoided.*

The first several sections of this chapter study various applications of recursion, in order to illustrate a range of possible uses. The programs we write are chosen to be especially simple, but to illustrate features that often appear in much more complicated applications.

8.1 DIVIDE AND CONQUER

The uses that we have made of recursion so far are of the form called *divide and conquer,* which can be defined generally as the method of solving a problem by dividing it into two or more subproblems, each of which is similar to the original problem in nature, but smaller in size. Solutions to the subproblems are then obtained separately and are combined to produce the solution of the original problem. Hence we can sort a list by dividing it into two sublists, sort them separately, and combine the results.

An even easier application of divide and conquer is the following recreational problem.

8.1.1 The Towers of Hanoi

In the nineteenth century a game called the *Towers of Hanoi* appeared in Europe, together with promotional material (undoubtedly apocryphal) explaining that the game represented a task underway in the Temple of Brahma. At the creation of the world, the priests were given a brass platform on which were 3 diamond needles. On the first needle were stacked 64 golden disks, each one slightly smaller than the one under it. (The less exotic version, sold in Europe, had 8 cardboard disks and 3 wooden posts.) The priests were assigned the task of moving all the golden disks from the first needle to the third, subject to the conditions that only one disk can be moved at a time, and that no disk is ever allowed to be placed on top of a smaller disk. The priests were told that when they had finished moving the 64 disks, it would signify the end of the world. See Figure 8.1.

the problem

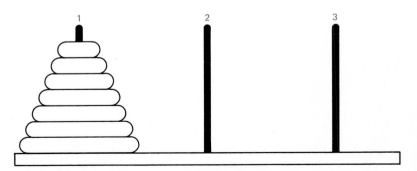

Figure 8.1.   The Towers of Hanoi

Our task, of course, is to write a computer program that will type out a list of instructions for the priests. We can summarize our task by the instruction

Move(64, 1, 3, 2)

which means

Move 64 *disks from needle* 1 *to needle* 3 *using needle* 2 *for intermediate storage.*

8.1.2 The Solution

The idea that gives a solution is to concentrate our attention not on the first step (which must be to move the top disk somewhere), but rather on the hardest step: moving the bottom disk. There is no way to reach the bottom disk until the top 63 disks have been moved, and, furthermore, they must all be on needle 2 so that we can move the bottom disk from needle 1 to needle 3. This is because only one disk can be moved at a time and the bottom (largest) one can never be on top of any other, so that when we move the bottom one, there can be no other disks on needles 1 or 3. Thus we can summarize the steps of our algorithm as

```
Move(63, 1, 2, 3);
Writeln('Move a disk from needle 1 to needle 3.');
Move(63, 2, 3, 1)
```

We now have a small step toward the solution, only a very small one since we must still describe how to move the 63 disks two times, but a significant step nonetheless, since there is no reason why we cannot move the 63 remaining disks in the same way. (In fact, we must do so in the same way since there is again a largest disk that must be moved last.)

This is exactly the idea of recursion. We have described how to do the key step and asserted that the rest of the problem is done in essentially the same way.

8.1.3 Refinement

To write the algorithm formally we shall need to know at each step which needle may be used for temporary storage, and thus we will invoke the procedure in the form

Move(n, a, b, c)

which will mean

Move n *disks from needle* a *to needle* b *using needle* c *as temporary storage.*

Supposedly our task is to be finished in a finite number of steps (even if it does mark the end of the world!), and thus there must be some way that the recursion stops. The obvious stopping rule is that, when there are no disks to be moved, there is nothing to do. We can now write the complete program to embody these rules.

```
program Hanoi(output);
const
   ndisks = 64;
type
   disk   = 0 .. ndisks;
   needle = 1 .. 3;

procedure Move(n: disk; a, b, c: needle);
{moves n disks from a to b using c for temporary storage}
begin
   if n > 0 then begin
      Move(n − 1, a, c, b);
      writeln('Move a disk from', a: 2, ' to', b: 2);
      Move(n − 1, c, b, a)
   end
end;                                           {declaration of Procedure Move}

begin                                                        {main program}
   Move(ndisks, 1, 3, 2)
end.
```

8.1.4 Analysis

Note that this program not only produces a complete solution to the task, but it produces the best possible solution and, in fact, the only solution that can be found except for the possible inclusion of redundant and useless sequences of instructions such as

> *Move a disk from needle* 1 *to needle* 2.
> *Move a disk from needle* 2 *to needle* 3.
> *Move a disk from needle* 3 *to needle* 1.

To show the uniqueness of the irreducible solution, note that, at every stage, the task to be done can be summarized as to move a certain number of disks from one needle to another. There is no way to do this task except to move all the disks except the bottom one first, then perhaps make some redundant moves, then move the bottom one, possibly make more redundant moves, and finally move the upper disks again.

depth of recursion   Next, let us find out how many times the recursion will proceed before starting to return and back out. The first time procedure Move is called, it is with $n = 64$, and each recursive call reduces the value of n by 1. Thus, if we exclude the calls with $n = 0$, which do nothing, we have a total depth of recursion of 64. That is, if we were to draw a tree of recursive calls for the program, it would have 64 levels above its leaves. Except for the leaves, each vertex results in two recursive calls (as well as in writing out one instruction), and so the number of vertices on each level is exactly double that of the level above. The recursion tree for the somewhat smaller task that moves 3 disks instead of 64 appears as Figure 8.2, and the progress of execution follows the path shown in color.

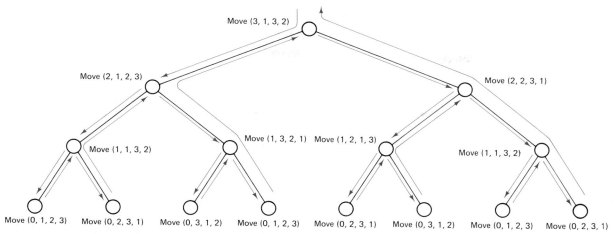

Figure 8.2.   Recursion tree for three disks

From the recursion tree we can easily calculate how many instructions are needed to move 64 disks. One instruction is printed for each vertex in the tree, except for the leaves (which are calls with $n = 0$). The number of non-leaves is

total number of moves
$$1 + 2 + 4 + \cdots + 2^{63} = 2^{64} - 1,$$

and this is the number of moves required altogether.

We can estimate how large this number is by using the approximation

$$10^3 = 1000 < 1024 = 2^{10}.$$

There are about 3.2×10^7 seconds in one year. Suppose that the instructions could be carried out at the rather frenetic rate of one every second (the priests have plenty of practice). Since

$$2^{64} = 2^4 \times 2^{60} > 2^4 \times 10^{18} = 1.6 \times 10^{19},$$

the total task will then take about 5×10^{11} years. If astronomers estimate the age of the universe at about 10 billion (10^{10}) years, then according to this story the world will indeed endure a long time—50 times as long as it already has!

8.2 POSTPONING THE WORK

Divide and conquer, by definition, involves two or more recursive calls within the algorithm being written. In this section we illustrate two applications of recursion each using only one recursive call. In these applications one case or one phase of the problem is solved without using recursion, and the work of the remainder of the problem is postponed to the recursive call.

8.2.1 Generating Permutations

Our first example is the problem of generating the $n!$ permutations of n objects as efficiently as possible. If we think of the number $n!$ as the product

$$n! = 1 \times 2 \times 3 \times \cdots \times n,$$

then the process of multiplication can be pictured as the tree in Figure 8.3 (ignore the labels for the moment).

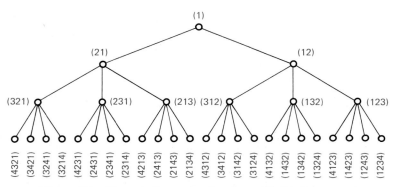

Figure 8.3.   Permutation generation by multiplication, $n = 4$

1. The Idea

We can identify permutations with the nodes as given by the labels in Figure 8.3. At the top is 1 by itself. We can obtain the two permutations of $\{1, 2\}$ by writing 2 first on the left, then on the right of 1. Similarly, the six permutations of $\{1, 2, 3\}$ can be obtained by starting with one of the permutations $(2, 1)$ or $(1, 2)$ and inserting 3 into one of the three possible positions (left, center, or right). The task of generating permutations of $\{1, 2, \ldots, k\}$ can now be summarized as

> *Take a given permutation of $\{1, 2, \ldots, k - 1\}$ and regard it as an ordered list. Insert k, in turn, into each of the k possible positions in this ordered list, thereby obtaining k distinct permutations of $\{1, 2, \ldots, k\}$.*

This algorithm illustrates the use of recursion to complete tasks that have been temporarily postponed. That is, we can write a procedure that will first insert 1 into an empty list and then use a recursive call to insert the remaining numbers from 2 to n into the list. This first recursive call will insert 2 into the list containing only 1, and postpone further insertions to a recursive call. On the nth recursive call, finally, the integer n will be inserted. In this way, having begun with a tree structure as motivation, we have now developed an algorithm for which the given tree becomes the recursion tree.

2. Refinement

Let us restate the algorithm in slightly more formal terms. We shall invoke our procedure as

$$\text{Permute(1, n)}$$

which will mean to insert all integers from 1 to n to build all the $n!$ permutations. When it is time to insert the integer k, the remaining task is

outline

```
procedure Permute(k, n);
begin
    for each possible position in the list L do
    begin
        Insert k into the given position;
        if k = n then ProcessPermutation
                 else Permute(k + 1, n);
        Remove k from the given position
    end
end;
```

The procedure ProcessPermutation will make whatever disposition is desired of a complete permutation of $\{1, 2, \ldots, n\}$. We might wish only to print it out, or we might wish to send it as input to some other task.

3. Data Structures

Let us now make some decisions regarding representation of the data. We use an ordered list to hold the numbers being permuted. This list is global to the recursive invocations of the procedure, that is, there is only the master copy of the list, and each recursive call updates the entries in this master list. Since we must continually insert and delete entries into and from the list, linked storage will be more flexible than will keeping the entries in a contiguous list. But the total number of entries in the list never exceeds n, so we can (probably) improve efficiency by keeping the

linked list in array

linked list within an array, rather than using dynamic memory allocation. Our links are thus integer indices (cursors) relative to the start of the array. With an array, furthermore, the index of each entry, as it is assigned, will happen to be the same as the value of the number being inserted, so the need to keep this numerical value explicitly disappears, so that only the links need to be kept in the array.

artificial mode

Insertions and deletions are further simplified if we put an artificial first node at the beginning of the list, so that insertions and deletions at the beginning of the (actual) list can be treated in the same way as those at other positions, always as insertions or deletions after a node.

This representation of a permutation as a linked list within an array is illustrated in Figure 8.4.

4. Final Program

With these decisions we can write our algorithm as a formal program.

```
program PermutationGenerator(input, output);
const
  maxdegree = 20;                        {maximum number of elements allowed}
type
  cursor = 0 .. maxdegree;               {0 will always denote a nil cursor.}
var
  L: array[cursor] of cursor;
  n: integer;

procedure Permute(k, n: cursor);
var
  p: cursor;                             {cursor to traverse the list in L}
begin                                    {procedure Permute}
  p := 0;
  repeat
    L[k] := L[p]; L[p] := k;             {First insert k after entry p of the list.}
    if k = n then ProcessLinkedPermutation        {defined externally}
             else Permute(k + 1, n);
    L[p] := L[k];                        {Remove k from the list.}
    p := L[p]                            {Advance p one position.}
  until p = 0                            {p = 0 at the end of the list.}
end;                                     {procedure Permute}

begin                                    {main program}
  write('Number of elements to permute?');
  readln(n);
  if (n < 1) or (n > maxdegree) then Error        {defined externally}
  else begin
    L[0] := 0;                           {Set the list to be initially empty.}
    Permute(1, n)
  end
end.                                     {main program PermutationGenerator}
```

Recall that the array L describes a linked list of pointers and does not contain the objects being permuted. If, for example, it is desired to print the integers $\{1, \ldots, n\}$ being permuted, then the auxiliary procedure becomes

```
procedure ProcessLinkedPermutation;
var q: cursor;                           {used to traverse the linked list}
begin
  q := 0;
  while L[q] <> 0 do
  begin
    write(L[q]);
    q := L[q]
  end;
  writeln
end;
```

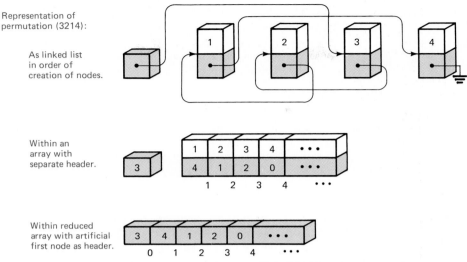

Representation of permutation (3214):

As linked list in order of creation of nodes.

Within an array with separate header.

Within reduced array with artificial first node as header.

Figure 8.4.   Permutation as a linked list in an array

5. Comparisons

It may be interesting to note that the simple algorithm developed here has execution time comparable with the fastest of all published algorithms for permutation generation. R. SEDGEWICK (reference at the end of chapter) gives a survey of such algorithms and singles out the following algorithm, devised by B. R. HEAP, as especially efficient.

```
procedure HeapPermute(n: integer);
var
  c: integer;                         {index to traverse contiguous list in L}
  t: integer;                         {used to swap entries in list}
begin
  c := 1;
  if n > 2 then HeapPermute(n − 1)
          else ProcessContiguousPermutation;
  while c < n do
  begin
    if odd(n) then begin t := L[n];   L[n] := L[1];   L[1] := t   end
              else begin t := L[n];   L[n] := L[c];   L[c] := t   end;
    c := c + 1;
    if n > 2 then HeapPermute(n − 1)
            else ProcessContiguousPermutation
  end
end;
```

timings   On one computer, this algorithm requires 1230 milliseconds to generate the 40,320 permutations of 8 objects, whereas the linked-list algorithm accomplishes the task in 860 milliseconds, an improvement of about 30 percent. With other implementations these numbers will differ, of course, but it is safe to conclude that the linked-list algorithm is at least comparable in efficiency. The correctness of the linked-list method, moreover, is obvious, whereas a proof that this other method actually generates all $n!$ distinct permutations of n objects is much more involved.

8.2.2 Backtracking: Nonattacking Queens

For our second example of an algorithm where recursion allows the postponement of all but one case, let us consider the puzzle of how to place eight queens on a chessboard so that no queen can take another. Recall that a queen can take another piece that lies on the same row, the same column, or the same diagonal (either direction) as the queen. The chessboard has eight rows and columns.

It is by no means obvious how to solve this puzzle, and its complete solution defied even the great C. F. GAUSS, who attempted it in 1850. It is typical of puzzles that do not seem amenable to analytic solutions, but require either luck coupled with trial and error or else much exhaustive (and exhausting) computation. To convince you that solutions to this problem really do exist, two of them are shown in Figure 8.5.

1. Solving the Puzzle

A person attempting to solve the Eight Queens problem will usually soon abandon attempts to find all (or even one) of the solutions by being clever and will start to put queens on the board, perhaps randomly or perhaps in some logical order, but always making sure that no queen placed can take another already on the board. If the person is lucky enough to get eight queens on the board by proceeding in this way, then he has found a solution; if not, then one or more of the queens must be removed and placed elsewhere to continue the search for a solution. To start formulating a program, let us sketch this method in algorithmic form. We denote by n the number of queens on the board; initially, $n = 0$. The key step is described as follows.

outline

```
procedure AddQueen;
    for every unguarded position p on the board do
    begin
        Place a queen in position p;
        n := n + 1;
        if n = 8 then print the configuration else AddQueen;
        Remove the queen from position p;
        n := n − 1
    end.
```

This sketch illustrates the use of recursion to mean "Continue to the next stage and repeat the task." Placing a queen in position p is only tentative; we leave it

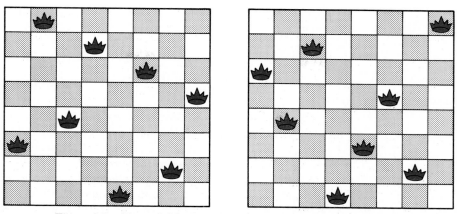

Figure 8.5.   Two configurations showing eight nonattacking queens

there only if we can continue adding queens until we have eight. Whether we reach eight or not, the procedure will return when it finds that it has finished or there are no further possibilities to investigate. After the inner call has returned, then, it is time to remove the queen from position p, because all possibilities with it there have been investigated.

2. Backtracking

This procedure is typical of a broad class called *backtracking algorithms* that attempt to complete a search for a solution to a problem by constructing partial solutions, always ensuring that the partial solutions remain consistent with the requirements of the problem. The algorithm then attempts to extend a partial solution toward completion, but when an inconsistency with the requirements of the problem occurs, the algorithm backs up (*backtracks*) by removing the most recently constructed part of the solution and trying another possibility.

Backtracking proves useful in situations where many possibilities may first appear, but few survive further tests. In scheduling problems, for example, it will likely be easy to assign the first few matches, but as further matches are made, the constraints drastically reduce the number of possibilities. Or consider the problem of designing a compiler. In some languages (but not Pascal) it is impossible to determine the meaning of a statement until almost all of it has been read. Consider, for example, the pair of FORTRAN statements

parsing

$$DO\ 17\ K = 1,6$$
$$DO\ 17\ K = 1.6$$

Both of these are legal: the first initiates a loop, and the second assigns the number 1.6 to the variable DO17K. In such cases where the meaning cannot be deduced immediately, backtracking is a useful method in *parsing* (that is, splitting apart to decipher) the text of a program.

3. Refinement: Choosing the Data Structures

To fill in the details of our algorithm for the Eight Queens problem, we must first decide how we will determine which positions are unguarded at each stage and how we will loop through the unguarded positions. This amounts to reaching some decisions about the presentation of data in the program.

square Boolean array

A person working on the Eight Queens puzzle with an actual chessboard will probably proceed to put queens into the squares one at a time. We can do the same in a computer by introducing an 8×8 array with Boolean entries and by defining an entry to be true if a queen is there and false if not. To determine if a position is guarded, the person would scan the board to see if a queen is guarding the position, and we could do the same, but doing so would involve considerable searching.

A person working the puzzle on paper or on a blackboard often observes that when a queen is put on the board, time will be saved in the next stage if all the squares that the new queen guards are marked off, so that it is only necessary to look for an unmarked square to find an unguarded position for the next queen. Again, we could do the same by defining each entry of our array to be true if it is free and false if it is guarded. A problem now arises, however, when we wish to remove a queen. We should not necessarily change a position that it has guarded from false to true, since it may well be that some other queen still guards that position. We

square integer array

can solve this problem by making the entries of our array integers rather than Boolean, each entry denoting the number of queens guarding the position. Thus, to add a queen we increase the count by 1 for each position on the same row, column, or diagonal as the queen, and to remove a queen we reduce the appropriate counts by 1. A position is unguarded if and only if it has a count of 0.

In spite of its obvious advantages over the previous attempt, this method still involves some searching to find unguarded positions and some calculation to change all the counts at each stage. The algorithm will be adding and removing queens a great many times, so that this calculation and searching may prove expensive. A person working on this puzzle soon makes another observation that saves even more work.

pigeonhole principle

Once a queen has been put in the first row, no person would waste time searching to find a place to put another queen in the same row, since the row is fully guarded by the first queen. There can never be more than one queen in each row. But our goal is to put eight queens on the board, and there are only eight rows. It follows that there must be a queen, exactly one queen, in every one of the rows. (This is called the **pigeonhole principle:** If you have n pigeons and n pigeonholes, and no more than one pigeon ever goes in the same hole, then there must be a pigeon in every hole.)

Thus we can proceed by placing the queens on the board one row at a time, starting with the first row, and we can keep track of where they are with a single array

array of locations

$$\textbf{var col: array}[1 .. 8] \textbf{ of } 1 .. 8$$

where col[i] gives the column containing the queen in row i. To make sure that no two queens are on the same column or the same diagonal, we need not keep and search through an 8×8 array, but we need only keep track of whether each column is free or guarded, and whether each diagonal is likewise. We can do this with three Boolean arrays, colfree, upfree, and downfree, where diagonals from the lower left to the upper right are considered upward and those from the upper left to lower right are considered downward.

guards

How do we identify the positions along a single diagonal? Along the main (downward) diagonal the entries are

$$[1, 1], [2, 2], \ldots , [8, 8],$$

which have the property that the row and column indices are equal; that is, their difference is 0. It turns out that along any downward diagonal the row and column indices will have a constant difference. This difference is 0 for the main diagonal, and ranges from $1 - 8 = -7$ for the downward diagonal of length 1 in the upper right corner, to $8 - 1 = 7$ for the one in the lower left corner. Similarly, along upward diagonals the sum of the row and column indices is constant, ranging from $1 + 1 = 2$ to $8 + 8 = 16$.

After making all these decisions, we can now define all our data structures formally, and, at the same time, we can write the main program.

main program

```
program Queen(output);
var
    col:        array[1 .. 8] of 1 .. 8;          {column with the queen}
    colfree:    array[1 .. 8] of Boolean;         {Is the column free?}
    upfree:     array[2 .. 16] of Boolean;        {Is the upward diagonal free?}
    downfree:   array[-7 .. 7] of Boolean;        {Is the downward diagonal free?}
    row:        0 .. 8;                            {row whose queen is currently placed}
    x:          integer;                          {index to initialize arrays}
{Declaration of Procedure AddQueen to be inserted here}
begin                                             {program Queen}
    row := 0;
    for x := 1 to 8   do colfree[x] := true;
    for x := 2 to 16  do upfree[x] := true;
    for x := -7 to 7  do downfree[x] := true;
    AddQueen
end.                                              {program Queen}
```

Translation of the sketch of the procedure AddQueen into a program is straightforward, given the use of the arrays that have now been defined.

recursive procedure

```
procedure AddQueen;
var
   c: 1 .. 8;                                        {column being tried for the queen}
begin                                                {procedure AddQueen}
   row := row + 1;
   for c := 1 to 8 do
      if colfree[c] and upfree[row + c] and downfree[row − c] then
         begin                                       {Put a queen in position [row, c].}
            col[row] := c;
            colfree[c] := false;
            upfree[row + c] := false;
            downfree[row − c] := false;
            if row = 8 then                          {termination condition}
               WriteBoard
            else
               AddQueen;                             {Proceed recursively.}
            {Now backtrack by removing the queen.}
            colfree[c] := true;
            upfree[row + c] := true;
            downfree[row − c] := true;
         end;                                        {processing queen at column c}
   row := row − 1
end;                                                 {procedure AddQueen}
```

4. Local and Global Variables

Note that in program Queen almost all the variables and arrays are declared in the main program, whereas in program Hanoi the variables were declared in the recursive procedure. If variables are declared within a procedure, then they are local to the procedure and not available outside it. In particular, variables declared in a recursive procedure are local to a single occurrence of the procedure, so if the procedure is called again recursively, the variables are new and different, and the original variables will be remembered after the procedure returns. The copies of variables set up in an outer call are not available to the procedure during an inner recursive call. In program Queen we wish the same information about guarded rows, columns, and diagonals to be available to all the recursive occurrences of the procedure, and to do this, the appropriate arrays are declared not in the procedure, but in the main program. The only reason for the array col[ ] is to communicate the positions of the queens to the procedure WriteBoard. The information in this array is also preserved in the eight local copies of the variable c set up during the recursive calls, but only one of these local copies is available to the program at a given time.

5. Analysis of Backtracking

Finally, let us estimate the amount of work that our program will do. If we had taken the naive approach by writing a program that first placed all eight queens on the board and then rejected the illegal configurations, we would be investigating as many configurations as choosing 8 places out of 64, which is

$$\binom{64}{8} = 4,426,165,368.$$

The observation that there can be only one queen in each row immediately cuts this number to

$$8^8 = 16,777,216.$$

This number is still large, but our program will not investigate nearly this many positions. Instead, it rejects positions whose column or diagonals are guarded. The requirement that there be only one queen in each column reduces the number to

reduced count

$$8! = 40,320$$

which is quite manageable by computer, and the actual number of cases the program considers will be much less than this (see projects), since positions with guarded diagonals in the early rows will be rejected immediately, with no need to make the fruitless attempt to fill the later rows.

effectiveness of backtracking

This behavior summarizes the effectiveness of backtracking: positions that are early discovered to be impossible prevent the later investigation of many fruitless paths.

Another way to express this behavior of backtracking is to consider the tree of recursive calls to procedure AddQueen, part of which is shown in Figure 8.6. It

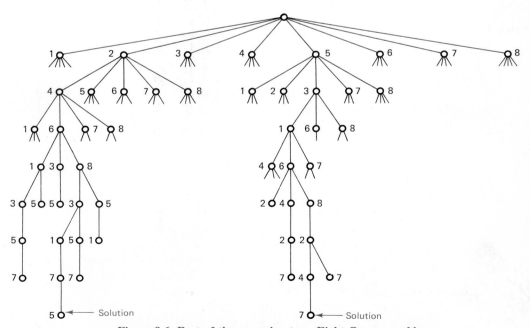

Figure 8.6. Part of the recursion tree, Eight Queens problem

appears formally that each vertex might have up to eight children corresponding to the recursive calls to AddQueen for the eight possible values of c. Even at levels near the root, however, most of these branches are found to be impossible, and the removal of one vertex on an upper level removes a multitude of its descendents. Backtracking is a most effective tool to prune a recursion tree to manageable size.

Exercises
8.2

E1. What is the maximum depth of recursion in program Queen?

E2. Starting with the following partial configuration of five queens on the board, construct the recursion tree of all situations that program Queen will consider in trying to add the remaining three queens. Stop drawing the tree at the point where the program will backtrack and remove one of the original five queens.

E3. Modify the linked-list algorithm for generating permutations so that the position occupied by each number does not change by more than one to the left or to the right from any permutation to the next one generated. [This is a simplified form of one rule for *campanology* (ringing changes on church bells).]

Programming
Projects
8.2

P1. Run program Queen on your computer. You will need to write procedure Write-Board to do the output. In addition, find out exactly how many positions are investigated by including a counter that is incremented every time procedure AddQueen is started. [Note that a method that placed all eight queens before checking for guarded squares would be equivalent to eight calls to AddQueen.]

molecular weight

P2. Write a program that will read a molecular formula such as H_2SO_4 and will write out the molecular weight of the compound that it represents. Your program should be able to handle bracketed radicals such as in $Al_2(SO_4)_3$. [*Hint:* Use recursion to find the molecular weight of a bracketed radical. *Simplifications:* You may find it helpful to enclose the whole formula in parentheses $(\cdots)$. You will need to set up a table of atomic weights of elements, indexed by their abbreviations. For simplicity the table may be restricted to the more common elements. Some elements have one-letter abbreviations, and some two. For uniformity you may add blanks to the one-letter abbreviations.]

maze   **P3.** Describe a rectangular maze by indicating its paths and walls within an array. Write a backtracking program to find a way through the maze.

knight's tour   **P4.** Another chessboard puzzle (this one reputedly solved by GAUSS at the age of four) is to find a sequence of moves by a knight that will visit every square of the board exactly once. Recall that a knight's move is to jump two positions either vertically or horizontally and at the same time one position in the perpendicular direction. Such a move can be accomplished by setting x to either 1 or 2, setting y to $3 - x$, and then changing the first coordinate by $\pm x$ and the second by $\pm y$ (providing the resulting position is still on the board). Write a backtracking program that will input an initial position and search for a knight's tour starting at the given position and going to every square once and no square more than once. If you find that the program runs too slowly, a good method to help the knight find its way is to order the list of squares to which it can move from a given position so that it will first try to go to the squares with the least accessibility, that is, to the squares from which there are the fewest knight's moves to squares not yet visited.

8.3 TREE-STRUCTURED PROGRAMS: LOOK-AHEAD IN GAMES

In games of mental skill the person who can anticipate what will happen several moves in advance has a substantial advantage over a competitor who looks only for immediate gain. In this section we develop a computer algorithm to play games by looking at possible moves several steps in advance. This algorithm can be described most naturally in terms of a tree; afterward we show how recursion can be used to program this tree structure.

8.3.1 Game Trees

We can picture the sequences of possible moves by means of a *game tree*, in which the root denotes the initial situation and the branches from the root denote the legal moves that the first player could make. At the next level down, the branches correspond to the legal moves by the second player in each situation, and so on, with branches from vertices at even levels denoting moves by the first player and branches from vertices at odd levels denoting moves by the second player.

Eight   The complete game tree for the trivial game of *Eight* is shown in Figure 8.7. In this game the first player chooses one of the numbers 1, 2, or 3. At each later turn the appropriate player chooses one of 1, 2, or 3, but the number previously chosen is not allowed. A running sum of the numbers chosen is kept, and if a player brings this sum to exactly 8, then the player wins. If the player takes the sum over 8, then the other player wins. No draws are possible. In the diagram, F denotes a win by the first player, and S a win by the second player.

Even a trivial game like Eight produces a good-sized tree. Games of real interest like Chess or Go have trees so huge that there is no hope of investigating all the branches, and a program that runs in reasonable time can examine only a few levels

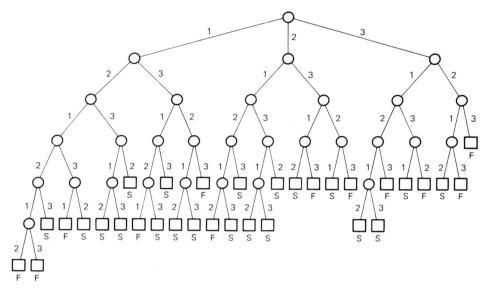

Figure 8.7. Tree for the game of Eight

below the current vertex in the tree. People playing such games are also unable to see every possibility to the end of the game, but they can make intelligent choices, because, with experience, a person comes to recognize that some situations in a game are much better than others, even if they do not guarantee a win. Thus for any interesting game that we propose to play by computer, we shall need some kind of evaluation function that will examine the current situation and return a number assessing its benefits. To be definite, we shall assume that large numbers reflect favorable situations for the first player, and therefore small (or more negative) numbers show an advantage for the second player.

8.3.2 The Minimax Method

Part of the tree for a fictitious game appears in Figure 8.8. Since we are looking ahead, we need the evaluation function only at the leaves of the tree (that is, the positions from which we shall not look further ahead in the game), and from this information we wish to select a move. The move we eventually select is a branch coming from the root, and we take the evaluation function from the perspective of this player, which means that this player selects the maximum value possible. At the next level down, the other player will select the smallest value possible, and so on. By working up from the bottom of the tree, we can assign values to all the vertices. Since we alternately take minima and maxima, this process is called a *minimax* procedure. The result is shown in Figure 8.9 (the dotted lines in color will be explained later, in one of the projects). The value of the current situation is 7, and the current (first) player should choose the leftmost branch.

minimax

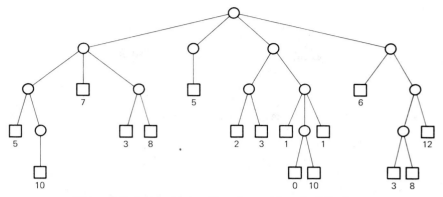

Figure 8.8. A game tree with values assigned at the leaves

8.3.3 Algorithm Development

Next let us see how the minimax method can be embodied in a formal algorithm for looking ahead in a game-playing program. We wish to write a general-purpose algorithm that can be used with any two-player game; we shall therefore leave various types and data structures unspecified, since their choice will depend on the particular game being played. First, we shall need to use a procedure that we call

recommended moves   **procedure** Recommend(P: player; **var** L: list; **var** v: value)

that will return a list L of recommended moves for the player P, as well as a value v that depends on the current situation in the game (but not yet on which of the recommended moves is eventually made). For the player we use the simple type declaration

type player = (first, second)

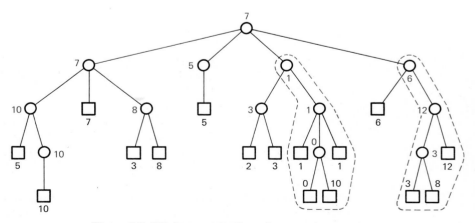

Figure 8.9. Minimax evaluation of a game tree

list implementation

and always take the first player as the one who wishes to maximize the value, while the second player wishes to minimize the value. The value will normally be a number.

How the list of recommended moves is to be implemented depends on the game. In some games the moves can be described concisely, and only a few different kinds of moves are appropriate; for such games a contiguous list may be best. In other games the number of recommended moves can change greatly from one turn to another, and a linked list may prove better. Hence we leave the type list unspecified and use auxiliary procedures FirstEntry(L, m) and NextEntry(L, m) to obtain the first and subsequent moves m from the list, a Boolean function Finished(L) to determine when traversing the list is complete, and an integer function Size(L) to return the number of entries.

termination

Before writing the procedure that looks ahead in the tree, we should decide when the algorithm is to stop looking further. For a game of reasonable complexity, we must establish a number of levels maxdepth beyond which the search will not go. But there are at least two other conditions under which exploring the tree is unnecessary. The first occurs when the procedure Recommend returns a list with only one recommended move, and the other occurs when the outcome of the game is already completely determined (it is a certain win, loss, or tie). We coalesce these two conditions by requiring procedure Recommend to return only one move when the outcome of the game is certain. Thus, even if procedure Recommend finds several winning moves, it must return only one of them.

The basic task of looking ahead in the tree can now be described with the following recursive algorithm.

outline

procedure LookAhead(depth: integer; P: player; **var** m: move; **var** v: value);
{searches as many as depth levels through the game tree; returns the move m
   for player P, and the value v as an assessment of the situation}
begin
   Recommend(P, L, v);
   if the list L contains only one recommended move **then**
      Return the one move and associated value
   else begin
      for each recommended move **do**
         Tentatively make the move and recursively LookAhead for the other play-
            er's best move;
      Select the best value for P among the values returned in the loop above;
      Return the corresponding move and value as the result
   end
end.

8.3.4 Refinement

To specify the details of this algorithm we must, finally, employ two more procedures that depend on the game:

MakeMove(P: player; m: move)   and   UndoMove(P: player; m: move)

that make and undo tentative moves as indicated. In the formal procedure we also rearrange some of the steps from the outline.

```
procedure LookAhead(depth: integer; P: player; var m: move; var v: value);
{searches as many as depth levels through the game tree; returns the move m
  for player P and the value v as an assessment of the situation}
var
  opponent: player;                                        {opponent of P}
  om: move;                                    {recommended move for opponent}
  ov: value;                                  {value returned for opponent's move}
  L: list;                                      {list of recommended moves for P}
  tm: move;                                     {tentative move being tried in tree}
begin                                                    {procedure LookAhead}
  Recommend(P, L, v);
  if Size(L) <= 0 then
    Forfeit                                               {cannot make any move}
  else if (Size(L) = 1) or (depth = 0) then
    FirstEntry(L, m)
                                           {Return the one move as the answer;
                                             the value v has been set by Recommend.}

  else begin
    if P = first then
    begin
      opponent := second;
      v := −infinity                     {Set to a value less than any that occurs.}
    end
    else begin
      opponent := first;
      v := infinity
    end;
    FirstEntry(L, tm);
    repeat
      MakeMove(P, tm);
      LookAhead(depth − 1, opponent, om, ov);
      UndoMove(P, tm);
      if (P = first) and (ov > v) then
        begin  v := ov;   m := tm   end
      else if (P = second) and (ov < v) then
        begin  v:= ov;   m := tm   end;
      NextEntry(L, tm)
    until Finished(L)
  end
end;                                                     {procedure LookAhead}
```

Exercises
8.3

E1. Assign values of +1 for a win by the first player and −1 for a win by the second player in the game of Eight, and apply the minimax procedure to its tree as shown in Figure 8.7.

Nim

E2. A variation of the game of Nim begins with a pile of sticks, from which a player can remove 1, 2, or 3 sticks at each turn. The player must remove at least 1 (but no more than remain on the pile). The player who takes the last stick loses. Draw the complete game tree that begins with **(a)** 5 and **(b)** 6 sticks. Assign appropriate values for the leaves of the tree, and evaluate the other nodes by the minimax method.

tic-tac-toe

E3. Draw the top three levels (showing the first two moves) of the game tree for the game of tic-tac-toe (Noughts and Crosses), and calculate the number of vertices that will appear on the fourth level. You may reduce the size of the tree by taking advantage of symmetries: At the first move, for example, show only three possibilities (the center square, a corner, or a side square) rather than all nine. Further symmetries near the root will reduce the size of the game tree.

E4. Write the auxiliary subprograms FirstEntry(L, m), NextEntry(L, m), Finished(L), and Size(L) for the case when the list is **(a)** contiguous and **(b)** linked.

Programming
Projects
8.3

P1. Write a main program and the other procedures needed to play Eight against a human opponent. Procedure Recommend can return all legal moves at each turn.

P2. Write a look-ahead program for playing tic-tac-toe. In the simplest version, procedure Recommend returns all empty positions as recommended moves. Approximately how many possibilities will then be investigated in a complete search of the game tree? Implement this simple method. Second, modify the procedure Recommend so that it searches for two marks in a row with the third empty, and thereby recommends moves more intelligently. Compare the running times of the two versions.

P3. Consider the following game played on an $n \times n$ board. Each player alternately puts a 1 or a 0 into an empty square (either player can use either number), and the game continues until the board is completely filled. The numbers along each row, column, and the two main diagonals are then added. If there are more odd sums than there are even sums, then the first player wins. If the number of even sums is greater, then the second player wins. Otherwise, the game is a tie. Write a look-ahead program to play this game against a human opponent, who chooses the value of n.

three-dimensional tic-tac-toe

P4. [*Major project*] Write a look-ahead program that plays three-dimensional tic-tac-toe. This game is played on a $4 \times 4 \times 4$ cube, with the usual rules. There are 76 possible winning lines (rows, columns, stacks, and diagonals) with four in a row.

Kalah

P5. [*Major project*] Write a look-ahead program for the game of Kalah (see references at end of chapter for rules and strategy).

alpha-beta pruning

P6. If you have worked your way through the tree in Figure 8.8 in enough detail, you may have noticed that it is not necessary to obtain the values for all the vertices while doing the minimax process, for there are some parts of the tree in which the best strategy certainly cannot appear. Let us suppose that we work our way through the tree starting at the lower left, and filling in the value for a parent vertex as soon as we have the values for all its children. After we have done all the vertices in the two main branches on the left, we find values of 7 and 5, and therefore the maximum value will be at least 7. When we go to the next vertex on level 1 and its left child, we find that the value of this child is 3. At this stage we are taking minima, so the value to be assigned to the parent on level 1 cannot possibly be more than 3 (it is actually 1). Since 3 is less than 7, the first player will take the leftmost branch instead, and we can exclude the other branch. The vertices that, in this way, need never be evaluated, are shown within dotted lines in color in Figure 8.9. The process of eliminating vertices in this way is generally called ***alpha-beta pruning***. The letters α (alpha) and β (beta) are generally used to denote the cutoff points found.

Modify the procedure LookAhead so that it uses alpha-beta pruning to reduce the number of branches investigated. Compare the performance of the two versions in playing several games.

8.4 COMPILATION BY RECURSIVE DESCENT

Consider the problem of designing a compiler that translates a program written in Pascal into machine language. As the compiler reads through the source program written in Pascal, it must understand the syntax and translate each line into the equivalent instructions in machine language.

identifiers

The first part of a Pascal program (or subprogram) contains declarations of labels, constants, types, and variables. The compiler will use this information to allocate space for variables and to determine what kinds of operations can be done with the variables. At the same time, the compiler must remember the identifiers that have been declared as names of types, variables, and the like, so that these identifiers can be interpreted correctly when they appear later in the program. Hence the compiler sets up a ***symbol table*** to keep track of the identifiers. Some compilers use a binary tree to contain the symbol table; others use a hash table; still other compilers use some combination or some other data structure. Although many interesting ideas appear in the design and use of symbol tables, our goal here is only to obtain an overview of how a compiler can use recursion, so we shall not study symbol tables further.

subprograms

The next part of a Pascal program contains declarations of procedures and functions, and the final part consists of the action (statements) of the program. When we come to the declarations of procedures and functions, we can see a good application of recursion. Pascal syntax is designed so that the overall form of a subprogram is the same as that of the main program. Hence there is no need to write another complete section of the compiler to translate the declarations and statements within a subprogram. Instead, the compiler can in essence call itself recursively to compile each subprogram, and after the recursive call returns, it will go on to compile the next subprogram. After all subprograms are compiled, it will translate the statements in the main program. The main program itself, in fact, can be regarded as a subprogram within a mythical outer block in which all the standard identifiers (such as the constant maxint, the types Boolean and text, the procedures writeln and dispose) have already been declared. In this way the main program can be treated almost completely symmetrically with subprograms.

8.4.1 The Main Program

The overall task of the compiler is thus described as follows:

outline

```
program PascalCompiler;
begin
    Set up symbol table and declarations for all standard identifiers;
    Check that first word of the input is 'program';
    DoModule;
    Check that the last symbol is a period '.'
end.
```

The procedure DoModule translates a program, procedure, or function.

tokens

Note that the compiler must continually check what is the next word or symbol in the program. Depending on what this word or symbol is, various actions will be taken. Such a word or symbol is called a *token*, and for our purposes we take a token to be any one of a Pascal reserved word, identifier, literal constant, operator, or punctuation mark. Note, furthermore, that the only way to tell that many constructions in Pascal have terminated is when a token is found that is *not* part of the construction. A statement, for example, terminates when the next token is a semicolon or one of the words **end, else,** or **until**. Hence whenever we start to process part of the program, the variable nexttoken will be the token that initiates that part, and when the processing is complete, then nexttoken will be the first token not in the part just processed. The procedure GetToken will split out the next token.

With this understanding, we can expand the procedure DoModule. The first step it will do is to obtain the next token, so it will effectively skip over the word **program, procedure,** or **function,** and it is almost irrelevant which of these is being processed.

outline

```
procedure DoModule;
begin
    Initialize the symbol table for the symbols in this module.
    GetToken(nexttoken);
    if nexttoken = '(' then DoParameters;          {returns after matching ')'}
    if this module is a function then DoFunctionValue;
    if nexttoken = 'label' then DoLabelSection;
    if nexttoken = 'const' then DoConstantSection;
    if nexttoken = 'type' then DoTypeSection;
    if nexttoken = 'var' then DoVariableSection;
    while (nexttoken = 'function') or (nexttoken = 'procedure') do
        DoModule;
    if nexttoken = 'begin' then DoCompoundStatement else Error
end;
```

8.4.2. Type Declarations

To see a further application of recursion, let us take a slightly more detailed look at the declaration of types. In Pascal, arrays may contain arrays; records may contain records. A well-designed compiler will use a separate procedure to process each of the standard categories of types. Thus there will be a procedure DoType that will, as required, invoke procedures that we call DoArray, DoRecord, DoSet, and DoScalar-Type (amongst others). The way in which these procedures work is closely related to their syntax diagrams. In particular, DoArray will invoke DoScalarType to determine the type by which the array is indexed, and DoType to determine the type of the entries. DoRecord will invoke a procedure called DoVariable for each of the fields within the record. DoVariable will, in turn, invoke DoType to find out the type of the variable. These recursive calls thus eventually work their way down to the simple types, and the meaning of the entire construction is then determined.

top-down parsing

recursive descent

The process of splitting a text or expression into pieces to determine its syntax is called *parsing.* Parsing can proceed either by first examining the atomic (indivisible) building blocks and how they are put together (called *bottom-up parsing*) or by splitting the text or expression into simpler components (called *top-down parsing*). Hence comes the motivation for the term *recursive descent:* the compiler parses large constructions by splitting them into smaller pieces and recursively parses each of the pieces. It thereby descends to simpler and smaller constructions, which are finally split apart into their atomic components, which can be evaluated directly.

As a simple example, consider the following declaration, which results in the tree of procedure calls shown in Figure 8.10. Index is a scalar type previously defined in the program:

example

```
type item = array[index] of
    record
        a: record u: integer; v: index end;
        b: set of index;
        c: array[index] of real;
    end;
```

8.4.3 Parsing Statements

Parsing the action part of a program also proceeds by recursive descent. The action part is a compound statement and is parsed by the procedure DoCompoundStatement. A compound statement is made up of zero or more statements, each of which will be parsed by DoStatement, which, in turn, invokes a different procedure for each possible kind of statement.

As an example, let us see how an **if** statement might be parsed and translated into an assembler language (that is, into a language that corresponds directly with machine-level instructions, but still allows symbolic names and statement labels). From its syntax diagram, we know that an **if** statement consists of the token **if** followed by a Boolean expression, followed by the token **then** and a statement, and finally optionally followed by the token **else** and another statement. See Figure 8.11.

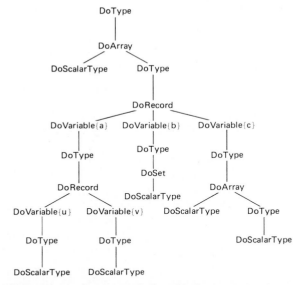

Figure 8.10. Parse tree for a type declaration by recursive descent

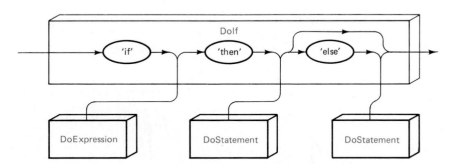

Figure 8.11. Parse tree for an if statement

The assembler-language equivalent of the **if** statement will first evaluate the expression and then use conditional jumps (**goto** statements) to branch around the assembler code corresponding to the statements in the **then** or **else** clauses, as appropriate. The syntax diagram therefore translates into the following procedure.

outline

```
procedure DoIf;
begin
  GetToken(nexttoken);
  DoExpression;
      {This will write the assembler code to evaluate the Boolean expression.}
  if nexttoken <> 'then' then Error
  else begin
    Generate a new assembler-language label x;
    Write assembler code that will cause a conditional jump
            to label x when the Boolean expression is false;
    GetToken(nexttoken);
    DoStatement;
   {This will write the assembler code that corresponds to the statement in the
                                                          then clause.}
  end;
  if nexttoken = 'else' then
  begin
    Generate a new assembler-language label y;
    Write an assembler unconditional jump to label y;
    Write the label x at this point in the assembler code;
    GetToken(nexttoken);
    DoStatement;
        {This will write the assembler code that corresponds to the statement
                                            in the else clause.}
    Write the label y at this point in the assembler code
  end
  else begin                                       {case with no else clause}
    Write the label x at this point in the assembler code
  end
end;
```

Finally, as an exercise you should apply this algorithm to the statement

exercise

if a > 0 **then** b := 1 **else if** a = 0 **then** b := 2 **else** b := 3;

Since this line is made up of two **if** statements, the parsing procedure will call itself recursively and generate a total of four labels. The parse tree for this statement is shown in Figure 8.12.

sample output

In practice, an actual compiler may rearrange some of the jumps and thereby produce an answer superficially different from yours. The output of one such compiler (OMSI Pascal™ for the PDP/11™)* applied to the preceding statement is given in Figure 8.13, where the only changes made from the actual output of the compiler are to replace some numeric displacements calculated by the compiler by their symbolic

---

* OMSI Pascal™ is a trademark of Oregon Software, Inc. PDP™ is a trademark of Digital Equipment Corporation.

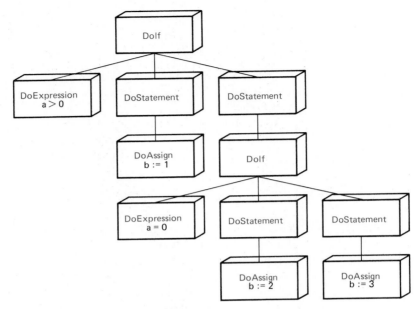

Figure 8.12. Parse tree for nested **if** statement

forms. This particular compiler generates extra statement labels because, for technical reasons, it must follow the wasteful practice of generating branch instructions to do nothing but branch around other jump instructions. In the resulting PDP/11 assembler language, the instruction TST tests the sign of an integer; BEQ branches if the integer is equal to 0, BGT if it is greater than 0. JMP is an unconditional jump. MOV moves the first number given to the second location specified.

```
         TST     A          ; if a > 0 then
         BGT     L0
         JMP     L1
L0:      MOV     #1, B      ; b := 1
         JMP     L2         ; else if a = 0 then
L1:      TST     A
         BEQ     L3
         JMP     L4
L3:      MOV     #2, B      ; b := 2
         JMP     L5         ; else
L4:      MOV     #3, B      ; b := 3
L5:
L2:
```

Figure 8.13. Output from a Pascal compiler

compilers

As you can see from all this, the construction of a compiler is quite a complicated process. A typical Pascal compiler (when written in Pascal) may be five to ten thousand lines of code. The index-writing program we shall study in Chapter 11, by comparison, is only about one thousand lines. The present discussion has attempted only to give a broad overview of the way in which recursion proves useful in writing a compiler. If you take a more detailed view, you will find that we have not only omitted programming steps, but that it is necessary to address many problems that we have not considered at all (for example, error processing). Many interesting ideas arise in the consideration of these problems, so that compiler design and construction constitute a major subject within computer science, one worthy of extensive study in its own right.

Exercises
8.4

E1. For each of the following declarations, draw a tree similar to that in Figure 8.10 showing the subprogram calls that will occur in parsing the declaration.

(a) **type** complex = **record** x: real; y: real **end**;

(b) **type** list = **record** count: index; L: **array**[index] **of** item **end**;

(c) **var** X: list;

(d) **var** A: **array**[index] **of set of** index;

E2. For each of the following statements, draw a tree similar to that in Figure 8.12 showing the subprogram calls that will occur in parsing the statement. You may assume the existence of subprograms such as DoCase, DoWhile, and the like.

(a) **while** x > 0 **do if** x > 10 **then** x := −x **else** x := y − x;

(b) **if** a > b **then if** c > d **then** x := 1 **else if** e > f **then** x := 3;

(c) **begin end**;

E3. Draw parse trees and write outlines of procedures for parsing the following kinds of statements.

(a) **while** expression **do** statement.

(b) Compound statement: **begin** statement(s) **end**.

(c) **case . . . end**.

(d) **for** variable := expression **to** (or **downto**) expression **do** statement.

E4. Write a Pascal procedure GetToken that will read through an input text and return each token (as defined in this section) one at a time as the procedure is invoked.

8.5 PRINCIPLES OF RECURSION

8.5.1 Guidelines for Using Recursion

Recursion is a tool to allow the programmer to concentrate on the key step of an algorithm, without having initially to worry about coupling that step with all the others. As usual with problem solving, the first approach should usually be to consider several simple examples and, as these become better understood, to attempt to formulate a method that will work more generally. In regard to using recursion, you may begin by asking yourself, "How can this problem be divided into parts?" or "How will the key step in the middle be done?" Be sure to keep your answer simple but generally applicable. Do not come up with a multitude of special cases that work only for small problems or at the beginning and end of large ones. Once you have a simple, small step toward the solution, ask whether the remainder of the problem can be done in the same or a similar way, and modify your method if necessary so that it will be sufficiently general.

key step

Once the key step is determined, find a stopping rule that will indicate that the problem or a suitable part of it is done. Build this stopping rule into your key step. You should now be able to write the main program and a recursive procedure that will describe how to carry the step through.

stopping rule

Next, and of great importance, is a verification that the recursion will always terminate. Start with a general situation and check that in a finite number of steps the stopping rule will be satisfied and the recursion terminate. Be sure also that your algorithm correctly handles extreme cases. When called on to do nothing, any algorithm should be able to return gracefully, but it is especially important that recursive algorithms do so, since a call to do nothing is often the stopping rule.

termination

The key tool for the analysis of recursive algorithms is the recursion tree. As we shall see in the next section, the height of the tree is closely related to the amount of memory that the program will require, and the total size of the tree reflects the number of times the key step will be done, and hence the total time the program will use. It is usually highly instructive to draw the recursion tree for one or two simple examples appropriate to your problem.

recursion tree

8.5.2 How Recursion Works

The question of how recursion is actually done in a computer should be carefully separated in our minds from the question of using recursion in designing algorithms. In the design phase, we should use all problem-solving methods that prove to be appropriate, and recursion is one of the most flexible and powerful of these tools. In the implementation phase, we may need to ask which of several methods is the best under the circumstances. There are at least two ways to accomplish recursion in computer systems. At present, the first of these is experimental and only starting to be available in commercial systems, but with changing costs and capabilities of computer equipment, it will probably soon be regarded as quite practical. Our major point in considering two different implementations is that, although restrictions in space and time do need to be considered, they should be considered separately from the process of algorithm design, since different kinds of computer equipment in the future may lead to different capabilities and restrictions.

design versus implementation

1. Multiple Processors: Concurrency

Perhaps the most natural way to think of implementing recursion is to think of each subprogram not as occupying a different part of the same computer, but to think of each subprogram as running on a separate machine. In that way, when one subprogram invokes another, it starts the corresponding machine going, and when the other machine completes its work, then it sends the answer back to the first machine, which can then continue its task. If a procedure makes two recursive calls to itself, then it will simply start two other processors working with the same instructions that it is using. When these processors complete their work, they will send the answers back to the processor that started them going. If they, in turn, make recursive calls, then they will simply start still more processors working.

costs

At one time, the central processor was the most expensive component of a computer system, and any thought of a system including more than one processor would have been considered extravagant. The price of processing power compared to other computing costs has now dropped radically, and in all likelihood we shall, before long, see large computer systems that will include hundreds, if not thousands, of identical microprocessors among their components. When this occurs, implementation of recursion via multiple processors will become commonplace if not inevitable.

With multiple processors, programmers will no longer consider algorithms solely as a linear sequence of actions, but will instead realize that some parts of the algorithm can be done at the same time as other parts. In divide-and-conquer algorithms such as quicksort, for example, the two halves into which the problem is divided often do not depend on each other and can be worked on simultaneously by multiple processors.

concurrency

Processes that take place simultaneously are called *concurrent.* The study of concurrent processes and the methods for communication between them is, at present, an active subject for research in computing science, one in which important developments will undoubtedly improve the ways in which algorithms will be described and implemented in coming years.

2. Single Processor Implementation: Storage Areas

To determine how recursion can be efficiently implemented in a system with only one processor, let us for the moment leave recursion to consider the question of what steps are needed to call a subprogram, on the primitive level of machine-language instructions in a simple computer. The hardware of any computer has a limited range of instructions that includes (amongst other instructions) doing arithmetic on specified words of storage or on registers, moving data to and from the memory, and branching (jumping) to a specified address. When a calling program branches to the beginning of a subprogram, the address of the place whence the call was

return address

made must be stored in memory, or else the subprogram could not remember where to return. The addresses or values of the calling parameters must also be stored where the subprogram can find them, and where the answers can in turn be found by the calling program after the subprogram returns. When the subprogram starts, it will do various calculations on its local variables and storage areas. Once the

local variables

subprogram finishes, however, these local variables are lost, since they are not available outside the subprogram. The subprogram will of course have used the registers within the CPU for its calculations, so normally these would have different values after the subprogram finishes than before it is called. It is traditional, however, to expect that a subprogram will change nothing except its calling parameters or global variables (side effects). Thus it is customary that the subprogram will save all the registers it will use and restore their values before it returns.

storage area   In summary, when a subprogram is called, it must have a storage area (perhaps scattered as several areas); it must save the registers or whatever else it will change, using the storage area also for its return address, calling parameters, and local variables. As it returns, it will restore the registers and the other storage that it was expected to restore. After the return it no longer needs anything in its local storage area.

In this way we implement subprogram calls by changing storage areas, an action that takes the place of changing processors that we considered before. In these considerations it really makes no difference whether the subprogram is called recursively or not, providing that, in the recursive case, we are careful to regard two recursive calls as being different, so that we do not mix the storage areas for one call with those of another, any more than we would mix storage areas for different subprograms, one called from within the other. For a nonrecursive subprogram the storage area can be one fixed area, permanently reserved, since we know that one call to the subprogram will have returned before another one is made, and after the first one returns the information stored is no longer needed. For recursive subprograms, however, the information stored must be preserved until the outer call returns, so an inner call must use a different area for its temporary storage.

Note that the common practice of reserving a permanent storage area for a nonrecursive subprogram can in fact be quite wasteful, since a considerable amount of memory may be consumed in this way, memory that might be useful for other purposes while the subprogram is not active.

3. Re-Entrant Programs

Essentially the same problem of multiple storage areas arises in a quite different context, that of *re-entrant* programs. In a large time-sharing system there may be many users simultaneously using the BASIC interpreter or the text-editing system. These systems programs are quite large, and it would be very wasteful of high-speed memory to keep thirty or forty copies of exactly the same large set of instructions in memory at once, one for each user. What is generally done instead is to write large systems programs like the BASIC interpreter or the text editor with the instructions in one area, but with the addresses of all variables or other data kept in a separate area. Then in the memory of the time-sharing system there will be only one copy of the instructions, but a separate data area for each user.

This situation is somewhat analogous to students writing a test in a room where the questions are written on the blackboard. There is then only one set of questions that all students can read, but each student separately writes answers on different pieces of paper. There is no difficulty for different students to be reading the same or different questions at the same time, and with different pieces of paper their answers will not be mixed with each other. See Figure 8.14.

4. Data Structures: Stacks and Trees

We have yet to specify the data structure that will keep track of all these storage areas for subprograms; to do so, let us look at the tree of subprogram calls. So that an inner subprogram can access variables declared in an outer block, and so that we can return properly to the calling program, we must, at every point in the tree, remember all vertices on the path from the given point back to the root. As we move through the tree, vertices are added to and deleted from one end of this path;

Figure 8.14. Re-entrant processes

stacks

the other end (at the root) remains fixed. Hence the vertices on the path form a stack; the storage areas for subprograms likewise are to be kept as a stack. This process is illustrated in Figure 8.15.

time and space requirements

From Figure 8.15 and our discussion we can immediately conclude that the amount of space needed to implement recursion (which of course is related to the number of storage areas in current use) depends on the height of the recursion tree. Programmers who have not carefully studied recursion sometimes think mistakenly that the space requirement relates to the total number of vertices in the tree. The *time* requirement of the program is related to the number of times subprograms are done, and therefore to the total number of vertices in the tree, but the *space* requirement is only that of the storage areas on the path from a single vertex back to the root. Thus the space requirement is reflected in the height of the tree. A well-balanced, bushy recursion tree hence signifies a recursive process that can do much work with little need for extra space.

Figure 8.15 can, in fact, be interpreted in a broader context than as the process of invoking subprograms. It thereby elucidates an easy but important observation, providing an intimate connection between arbitrary trees and stacks:

THEOREM 8.1

During the traversal of any tree, vertices are added to or deleted from the path back to the root in the fashion of a stack. Given any stack, conversely, a tree can be drawn to portray the life history of the stack, as items are added to or deleted from it.

hardware

In most modern computers efficient means are provided to allow the same instructions to refer to different storage areas as desired. In the IBM 370® series, for example, every instruction that refers to memory calculates the address it uses by adding some value (displacement) to the contents of a specified register called the base register. If the value in the base register is set to the beginning of one storage area then all later instructions will refer to that area. Changing only the one value in the base register will make all the instructions refer to another storage area. A second example

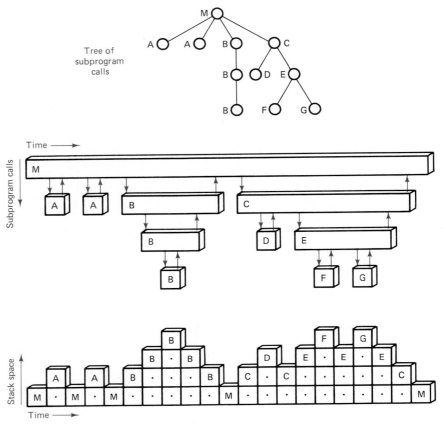

Figure 8.15.   A tree of subprogram calls and the associated stack frames

consists of the machines in the PDP/11 series and most microcomputers. Most of the instructions on these machines can be made to push or pop a stack as automatically as they refer to memory for their operands.

5. Conclusion

The moral of the story is that, when properly implemented, recursion is neither inefficient nor expensive, except perhaps on some machines of quite old design that are rapidly being retired. Some compilers, unfortunately, do make a mess out of recursive procedures, but on a well-designed system there is essentially no additional time overhead for using recursion and no reason to avoid it when it is the natural method.

8.5.3 Tail Recursion

Suppose that the very last action of a procedure is to make a recursive call to itself. In the stack implementation of recursion, as we have seen, the local variables of the procedure will be pushed onto the stack as the recursive call is initiated. When

discarding stack entries

the recursive call terminates, these local variables will be popped from the stack and thereby restored to their former values. But doing so is pointless, because the recursive call was the last action of the procedure, so the procedure now terminates and the just-restored local variables are immediately discarded.

When the very last action of a procedure is a recursive call to itself, it is thus pointless to use the stack, as we have seen, since no local variables need to be preserved. All that is needed is to set the dummy calling parameters to their new values and branch to the beginning of the procedure. We summarize this principle for future reference.

THEOREM 8.2

> *If the last executed statement of a procedure is a recursive call to itself, then this call can be eliminated by changing the values of the calling parameters to those specified in the recursive call, and repeating the whole procedure.*

The process of this transformation is shown in Figure 8.16. Part (a) shows the storage areas used by the calling program M and several copies of the recursive procedure P. The colored arrows show the flow of control. Since each call by P to P is its last action, there is no need to maintain the storage areas after the call, as shown in part (b). Part (c), finally, shows these calls to P as repeated in iterative fashion on the same level.

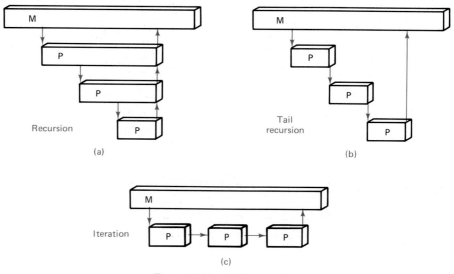

Figure 8.16. Tail recursion

tail recursion

This special case when a recursive call is the last executed statement of the procedure is especially important because it frequently occurs. It is called *tail recursion.* You should carefully note that tail recursion means that the last executed statement is a recursive call, not necessarily that the recursive call is the last statement appearing in the procedure. Tail recursion may appear, for example, within one clause of a **case** statement or an **if** statement where other program lines appear later.

time and space

With most modern compilers there will be little difference in execution *time* whether tail recursion is left in a program or is removed. If *space* considerations are important, however, then the principle of Theorem 8.2 should usually be followed if it is applicable, whether other recursion is being removed or not. By rearranging the termination condition if needed, it is usually possible to repeat the procedure using a **repeat** or a **while** statement.

Consider, for example, a divide-and-conquer algorithm like that devised for the Towers of Hanoi in Section 8.1. By removing tail recursion, procedure Move of the original recursive program can be expressed as

Hanoi without tail recursion

```
procedure Move(n: disk; a, b, c: needle);
{moves n disks from a to b using c for temporary storage}
var
   t: needle;                            {temporary storage to swap needles}
begin
  while n > 0 do begin
    Move(n − 1, a, c, b);
    writeln('Move a disk from ', a: 2, 'to ', b: 2);
    n := n − 1;  t := a;  a := c;  c := t
  end                                    {looping down on n}
end;                                     {declaration of procedure Move}
```

We should have been quite clever had we thought of this version of the procedure when we first looked at the problem, but now that we have discovered it via other considerations, we can give it a natural interpretation. Think of the two needles a and c as in the same class: We wish to use them for intermediate storage as we slowly move all the disks onto b. To move a stack of n disks onto b, then, we must move all except the bottom to the other one of a and c, then move the bottom disk to b, and repeat after interchanging a and c, continuing to shuffle all except the bottom disk between a and c, and at each pass getting a new bottom one onto b.

8.5.4 When Not to Use Recursion

1. Factorials

Many textbooks present the calculation of factorials as the first example of a recursive program:

```
function Factorial(n: integer): integer;            {recursive version}
begin
  if n <= 1 then Factorial := 1
    else Factorial := n * Factorial(n − 1)
end;
```

Although this program is simple and easy, there is an equally simple iterative program:

```
function Factorial(n: integer): integer;
var i, p: integer;
begin
    p := 1;
    for i := 2 to n do p := p * i;
    Factorial := p
end;
```

Which of these programs uses less storage space? At first glance it might appear that the recursive one does, since it has no local variables, and the iterative program has two. But actually (see Figure 8.17) the recursive program will set up a stack and fill it with the $n - 1$ numbers

$$n, n - 1, n - 2, \ldots, 2$$

that are its calling parameters before each recursion and will then, as it works its way out of the recursion, multiply these numbers in the same order as does the second program. The progress of execution for the recursive function is as follows:

trace of recursion
function

$$
\begin{aligned}
\text{Factorial}(6) &= 6 * \text{Factorial}(5) \\
&= 6 * (5 * \text{Factorial}(4)) \\
&= 6 * (5 * (4 * \text{Factorial}(3))) \\
&= 6 * (5 * (4 * (3 * \text{Factorial}(2)))) \\
&= 6 * (5 * (4 * (3 * (2 * \text{Factorial}(1))))) \\
&= 6 * (5 * (4 * (3 * (2 * 1)))) \\
&= 6 * (5 * (4 * (3 * 2))) \\
&= 6 * (5 * (4 * 6)) \\
&= 6 * (5 * 24) \\
&= 6 * 120 \\
&= 720.
\end{aligned}
$$

Thus the recursive program keeps considerably more storage and will take more time as well, since it must store and retrieve all the numbers as well as multiply them.

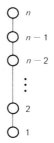

Figure 8.17.   Recursion tree for calculating factorials

2. Fibonacci Numbers

A far more wasteful example than factorials (and one that also appears as an apparently recommended program in some textbooks) is the computation of the *Fibonacci numbers,* which are defined by the recurrence relation

$$F_0 = 0, \quad F_1 = 1, \quad F_n = F_{n-1} + F_{n-2} \quad \text{for } n \geq 2.$$

(If you are interested, consult Appendix A.4 for a discussion of the properties of these numbers.) The recursive program closely follows the definition:

```
function Fib(n: integer): integer;                              {recursive version}
begin
   if n <= 0 then          Fib := 0
   else if n = 1 then      Fib := 1
   else                    Fib := Fib(n − 1) + Fib(n − 2)
end;
```

In fact, this program is quite attractive, since it is of the divide-and-conquer form: The answer is obtained by calculating two simpler cases. As we shall see, however, in this example it is not "divide and conquer" but "divide and complicate."

To assess this algorithm, let us consider, as an example, the calculation of F_7, whose recursion tree is shown in Figure 8.18. The procedure will first have to obtain F_6 and F_5. To get F_6 requires F_5 and F_4, and so on. But after F_5 is calculated on

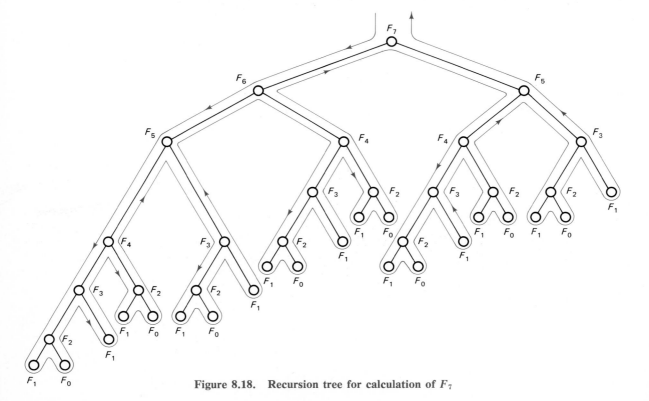

Figure 8.18. Recursion tree for calculation of F_7

the way to F_6, then it will be lost and unavailable when it is later needed to get F_7. Hence, as the recursion tree shows, the recursive program needlessly repeats the same calculations over and over. Further analysis appears as an exercise. It turns out that the amount of time used by the recursive function to calculate F_n grows exponentially with n.

As with factorials, we can produce a simple iterative program by noting that we can start at 0 and keep only three variables, the current Fibonacci number and its two predecessors.

```
function Fib(n: integer): integer;                          {iterative version}
var
  i,                                                    {loop control variable}
  twoback,                                       {second previous number, Fi-2}
  oneback,                                             {previous number, Fi-1}
  current: integer;                                     {current number, Fi}
begin                                                          {function Fib}
  if n <= 0 then
    Fib := 0
  else if n = 1 then
    Fib := 1
  else begin
    twoback := 0;
    oneback := 1;
    for i := 2 to n do
    begin
      current := twoback + oneback;
      twoback := oneback;
      oneback := current
    end;
    Fib := current
  end
end;                                                           {function Fib}
```

The iterative function obviously uses time that is $O(n)$, so that, as we saw in Section 5.6, the time difference between this function and the exponential time of the recursive function will be vast.

If you regard this nonrecursive program as being too tricky, then you can write a straightforward iterative program that sets up a list of length n and calculates F_n simply by starting with F_0 and calculating and storing all the Fibonacci numbers up through F_n. Even this program will use only about n words of storage, which is less than the recursive program will use.

3. Comparisons between Recursion and Iteration

What is fundamentally different between these two examples and the proper uses of recursion that were illustrated in the previous sections of this chapter? To answer this question we shall again turn to the examination of recursion trees. It should already be clear that a study of the recursion tree will provide much useful information to help us decide when recursion should or should not be used.

chain

If a function or a procedure makes only one recursive call to itself, then its recursion tree has a very simple form: It is a chain; that is, each vertex has only one child. This child corresponds to the single recursive call that occurs. Such a simple tree is easy to comprehend. For the factorial function it is simply the list of requests to calculate the factorials from $(n - 1)!$ down to 1!. By reading the recursion tree from bottom to top instead of top to bottom, we immediately obtain the iterative program from the recursive one. When the tree does reduce to a chain, then transformation from recursion to iteration is often easy, and will likely save both space and time.

Note that a procedure's making only one recursive call to itself is not at all the same as having the recursive call made only one place in the procedure, since this place might be inside a loop. It is also possible to have two places that issue a recursive call (such as both the **then** and **else** clauses of an **if** statement) where only one call can actually occur.

duplicate tasks

The recursion tree for calculating Fibonacci numbers is not a chain, but contains a great many vertices signifying duplicate tasks. When a recursive program is run, it sets up a stack to use while traversing the tree, but if the results stored on the stack are discarded rather than kept in some other data structure for future use, then a great deal of duplication of work may occur, as in the recursive calculation of Fibonacci numbers.

change data structures

In such cases it is preferable to substitute another data structure for the stack, one that allows references to locations other than the top. The most obvious choice is that of an ordinary list holding all information calculated so far, and this in fact works nicely for the Fibonacci numbers. The iterative program that we wrote for the Fibonacci numbers, the one that uses only three temporary variables, is in one sense tricky, even though it is easy. The reason is that nothing similar is likely to be found for the numbers defined by the following recurrence relation, one that is similar in form to that for the Fibonacci numbers, and could likely not be separated from it by general programming methods:

$$G_0 = 0, \qquad G_1 = 1, \qquad G_n = G_{n-1} + G_k \quad \text{for } n \geq 2,$$

where $k = \lceil \ln n \rceil$.

After removal of tail recursion, most of the programs written earlier in this chapter each involve only one recursive call, but note carefully that this call is within a loop, and therefore their recursion trees will not reduce to chains. In some cases,

symmetrical tree

nonetheless, it is possible to predict what the parameters of each recursive call will be, and thereby to devise an equivalent nonrecursive program with no stacks. In Appendix B we exploit the complete symmetry of the recursion tree for mergesort, in order to derive an efficient nonrecursive version of this important sorting method.

recursion removal

Finally, by setting up an explicit stack, we can take any recursive program and rearrange it into nonrecursive form. Appendix B describes methods for doing so. The resulting program, however, is often more complicated and harder to understand than is the recursive version, and for many applications the saving of space and time is insignificant. On machines with hardware stack instructions, in fact, the nonrecursive form may actually require more running time than the equivalent recursive program. Appendix B develops a nonrecursive version of quicksort as an example.

8.5.5 Guidelines and Conclusions

In making a decision, then, about whether to write a particular algorithm in recursive or nonrecursive form, a good starting point is to consider the recursion tree. If it has a simple form, the iterative version may be better. If it involves duplicate tasks, then data structures other than stacks will be appropriate, and the need for recursion may disappear. If the recursion tree appears quite bushy, with little duplication of tasks, then recursion is likely the natural method.

top-down design

The stack used to resolve recursion can be regarded as a list of postponed obligations for the program. If this list can be easily constructed in advance, then iteration is probably better; if not, recursion may be. Recursion is something of a top-down approach to problem solving; it divides the problem into pieces or selects out one key step, postponing the rest. Iteration is more of a bottom-up approach; it begins with what is known and from this constructs the solution step by step.

stacks or recursion

It is always true that recursion can be replaced by iteration and stacks. It is also true, conversely (see references for the proof), that any (iterative) program that manipulates a stack can be replaced by a recursive program with no stack. Thus the careful programmer should not only ask whether recursion should be removed, but should also ask, when a program involves stacks, whether the introduction of recursion might produce a more natural and understandable program that could lead to improvements in the approach and in the results.

Exercises 8.5

E1. Determine which procedures written in earlier sections of this chapter have tail recursion, and rewrite them to remove the tail recursion.

E2. In the recursive calculation of F_n, determine exactly how many times each smaller Fibonacci number will be calculated. From this, determine the order-of-magnitude time and space requirements of the recursive function. [You may find out either by setting up and solving a recurrence relation (top-down approach), or by finding the answer in simple cases and proving it more generally by mathematical induction (bottom-up approach). Consult Appendix A.4.]

E3. The *greatest common divisor* (GCD) of two positive integers is the largest integer that divides both of them. Thus the GCD of 8 and 12 is 4, the GCD of 9 and 18 is 9, and the GCD of 16 and 25 is 1. Write a recursive function

GCD(x, y: integer)

that implements the *division algorithm:* If y = 0, then the GCD of x and y is x; otherwise, the GCD of x and y is the same as the GCD of y and x **mod** y. Rewrite the function in iterative form.

E4. The binomial coefficients may be defined by the following recurrence relation, which is the idea of *Pascal's triangle,* the top of which is shown in Figure 8.19.

$$C(n, 0) = 1 \quad \text{and} \quad C(n, n) = 1 \qquad \text{for } n \geq 0.$$
$$C(n, k) = C(n-1, k) + C(n-1, k-1) \quad \text{for } n > k > 0.$$

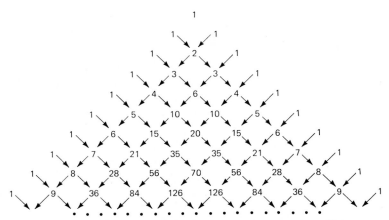

Figure 8.19.   The top of Pascal's triangle of binomial coefficients

(a) Write a recursive function to generate $C(n, k)$ by the above formula.

(b) Draw the recursion tree for calculating $C(6, 4)$.

(c) Use a square array and write a nonrecursive program to generate Pascal's triangle in the lower left half of the array.

(d) Write a nonrecursive program with neither array nor stack to calculate $C(n, k)$ for arbitrary $n \geq k \geq 0$.

(e) Determine the asymptotic space and time requirements for each of the algorithms devised in parts (a), (c), and (d).

E5. *Ackermann's function,* defined as follows, is a standard device to determine how well recursion is implemented on a computer.

$$A(0, n) = n + 1 \qquad\qquad \text{for } n \geq 0.$$
$$A(m, 0) = A(m - 1, 1) \qquad \text{for } m > 0.$$
$$A(m, n) = A(m - 1, A(m, n - 1)) \quad \text{for } m > 0 \text{ and } n > 0.$$

(a) Write a recursive function to calculate Ackermann's function.

(b) Calculate the following values:

$$A(0, 0) \quad A(0, 9) \quad A(1, 8) \quad A(2, 2) \quad A(2, 0)$$
$$A(2, 3) \quad A(3, 2) \quad A(4, 2) \quad A(4, 3) \quad A(4, 0)$$

(c) Write a nonrecursive function to calculate Ackermann's function.

POINTERS AND PITFALLS

1. Recursion should be used freely in the initial design of algorithms. It is especially appropriate where the main step toward solution consists of reducing a problem to one or more smaller cases.

2. Be very careful that your algorithm always terminates and handles trivial cases correctly.

3. Tail recursion should be removed if space considerations are important (Theorem 8.2).

4. The recursion tree should be studied to see whether the recursion is needlessly repeating work, or if the tree represents an efficient division of the work into pieces.

5. A tree that reduces a chain implies that recursion can be replaced by iteration.

6. If the recursion tree shows complete regularity that can be determined in advance, then sometimes this regularity can be built into the algorithm in a way that will improve efficiency and perhaps remove the recursion.

7. Recursive procedures and iterative procedures using stacks can accomplish exactly the same tasks. Consider carefully whether recursion or iteration will lead to a clearer program and give more insight into the problem.

8. Recursion can always be translated into iteration, but the general rules (Appendix B) will often produce a result that greatly obscures the structure of the program. Such obfuscation should be tolerated only when the programming language makes it unavoidable, and even then it should be well documented.

REVIEW QUESTIONS

8.1   **1.** Define the term *divide and conquer.*

8.2   **2.** Describe *backtracking* as a problem-solving method.

        3. State the *pigeonhole principle.*

8.3   **4.** Determine the value of the following game tree by the *minimax* method.

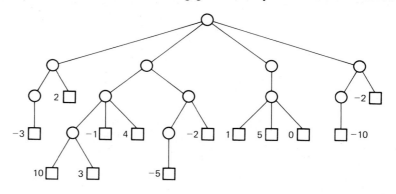

8.4   **5.** Draw a parse tree for the type declaration

        list = **record**   e: **array**[1 .. max] **of** item;   n: 0 .. max   **end;**

        6. Draw a parse tree for the statement

        for i := 1 **to** 10 **do if** odd(i) **then** Process(i) **else** Redo(i);

8.5   **7.** Name two different ways to implement recursion.

8. What is a *re-entrant* program?

9. How does the time requirement for a recursive procedure relate to its recursion tree?

10. How does the space requirement for a recursive procedure relate to its recursion tree?

11. What is *tail* recursion?

12. Rewrite the quicksort procedure Sort of Section 7.8.1 to remove tail recursion.

13. Describe the relationship between the shape of the recursion tree and the efficiency of the corresponding recursive algorithm.

REFERENCES FOR FURTHER STUDY

The examples and applications studied in this chapter come from a variety of sources. The Towers of Hanoi is quite well known and appears in several textbooks. A survey of related papers is

> D. WOOD, "The Towers of Brahma and Hanoi revisited," *Journal of Recreational Mathematics* 14 (1981–82), 17–24.

Our treatment of the Eight Queens problem especially follows that given in

> N. WIRTH, *Algorithms + Data Structures = Programs,* Prentice-Hall, Englewood Cliffs, N.J., 1976, pp. 143–147.

This book by WIRTH also contains a solution of the Knight's Tour (pp. 137–142) problem, as well as a chapter (pp. 280–349) on compiling and parsing.

The algorithm that generates permutations by insertion into a linked list was published in the ACM *SIGCSE Bulletin* 14 (February 1982), 92–96. Useful surveys of many methods of generating permutations are

> R. SEDGEWICK, "Permutation generation methods," *Computing Surveys* 9 (1977), 137–164; addenda, ibid., 314–317.

> R. W. TOPOR, "Functional programs for generating permutations," *Computer Journal* 25 (1982), 257–263.

The original reference for the efficient algorithm by HEAP is

> B. R. HEAP, "Permutations by interchanges," *Computer Journal* 6 (1963), 293–294.

The applications of permutations to campanology (change ringing of bells) produce interesting problems amenable to computer study. An excellent source for further information is

> F. J. BUDDEN, *The Fascination of Groups,* Cambridge University Press, Cambridge, England, 1972, pp. 451–479.

Compilation by recursive descent is a standard topic in compiler design, a topic treated in detail in most newer textbooks in compiler theory. Consult, for example,

ALFRED V. AHO and JEFFREY D. ULLMAN, *Principles of Compiler Design,* Addison-Wesley, Reading, Mass., 1977.

Many other applications of recursion appear in books such as

E. HOROWITZ and S. SAHNI, *Fundamentals of Computer Algorithms,* Computer Science Press, Rockville, Md., 1978, 626 pages.

This book (pp. 290–302) contains more extensive discussion and analysis of game trees and look-ahead programs. An outline of a programming project for the game of Kalah appears in

CHARLES WETHERELL, *Etudes for Programmers,* Prentice-Hall, Englewood Cliffs, N.J., 1978.

The general theory of recursion forms a topic of current research. A readable presentation from a theoretical approach is

R. S. BIRD, *Programs and Machines,* John Wiley, New York, 1976.

See also

R. S. BIRD, "Notes on recursion elimination," *Communications of the ACM* 20 (1977), 434–439.

R. S. BIRD, "Improving programs by the introduction of recursion," *Communications of the ACM* 20 (1977), 856–863.

A computer system made up from 64 small computers is described in

CHARLES L. SEITZ, "The cosmic cube," *Communications of the ACM* 28 (1985), 22–33.

The proof that stacks may be eliminated by the introduction of recursion appears in

S. BROWN, D. GRIES, and T. SZYMANSKI, "Program schemes with pushdown stores," *SIAM Journal on Computing* 1 (1972), 242–268.

Binary Trees

▶ *Linked lists have great advantages of flexibility over the contiguous representation of data structures, but they have one weak feature. They are sequential lists; that is, they are arranged so that it is necessary to move through them only one position at a time. In this chapter we overcome these disadvantages by studying trees as data structures, using the methods of pointers and linked lists for their implementation. Data structures organized as trees will prove valuable for a range of applications, especially for problems of information retrieval.*

Consider the problem of searching an ordinary linked list for some target key. There is no way to move through the list other than one node at a time, and hence searching through the list must always reduce to a sequential search. As you know, sequential search is usually very slow in comparison with binary search. The pivotal question for this chapter is,

> *Can we find a method for rearranging the nodes of a linked list so that we can search in time $O(\log n)$ instead of $O(n)$?*

If we consider applying binary search to the list of names in Figure 9.1, then the order in which comparisons will be made is shown in the accompanying comparison tree.

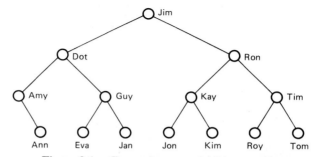

Figure 9.1.   Comparison tree for binary search

From the diagram it may already be clear that the way in which we can keep the advantages of linked storage and obtain the speed of binary search is to store the nodes in the structure of the comparison tree itself, with links used to describe the relations of the tree.

9.1 DEFINITIONS

In binary search, when we make a comparison with a key we then move either left or right depending on the outcome of the comparison. It is thus important to keep the relation of left and right in the structure we build. It is also possible that the part of the tree on one side or both below a given node is empty. In the example of Figure 9.1, the name Amy has an empty left subtree. For all the leaves, both subtrees are empty.

We can now give the formal definition of a new data structure.

DEFINITION
> A *binary tree* is either empty, or it consists of a node called the *root* together with two binary trees called the *left subtree* and the *right subtree* of the root.

ADT

Note that this definition is that of a mathematical structure. To specify binary trees as an abstract data type, we must state what operations can be performed on binary trees. Rather than doing so at once, we shall develop the operations while the chapter progresses.

Note also that this definition makes no reference to the way in which binary trees will be implemented in memory. As we shall presently see, a linked representation is natural and easy to use, but other methods are possible as well. Note finally that this definition makes no reference to keys or the way in which they are ordered. Binary trees are used for many purposes other than searching; hence we have kept the definition general. Information retrieval is, nonetheless, one of the most important uses for binary trees, and therefore we use a special term for binary trees in which there are keys with a special order:

DEFINITION

> A binary *search tree* is a binary tree that is either empty or in which each node contains a key that satisfies the conditions:
>
> 1. All keys (if any) in the left subtree of the root precede the key in the root.
> 2. The key in the root precedes all keys (if any) in its right subtree.
> 3. The left and right subtrees of the root are again search trees.

Before we consider search trees further, let us return to the general definition of binary trees and see how the recursive nature of the definition works out in the construction of small binary trees.

The first case, which involves no recursion, is that of an empty binary tree. For ordinary trees we would never think of allowing an empty tree, but for binary trees it is convenient, not only in the definition, but in algorithms, since the empty binary tree will be naturally represented by a **nil** pointer.

The only way to construct a binary tree with one node is to make that node its root, and to make both the left and right subtrees empty. Thus a single node with no branches is a binary tree.

small binary trees

With two nodes in the tree, one of them will be the root and the other will be in a subtree. Thus one of the left or right subtrees must be empty, and the other will contain one node. Hence there are two different binary trees with two nodes.

At this point you should note that the concept of a binary tree differs from that of an ordinary tree, in that left and right are important. The two binary trees with two nodes can be drawn as

left and right

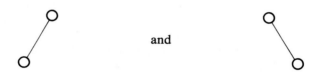

and

which are different from each other, but neither can be distinguished from

as ordinary trees.

2-trees

Binary trees, moreover, are not the same class as the 2-trees studied in the analysis of algorithms. Each node in a 2-tree has either 0 or 2 children, never 1 as can happen with a binary tree. Left and right are not important for 2-trees, but they are crucial in working with binary trees.

For the case of a binary tree with three nodes, one of these will be the root, and the others will be partitioned between the left and right subtrees in one of the ways

$$2 + 0 \qquad 1 + 1 \qquad 0 + 2.$$

Since there are two binary trees with two nodes and only one empty tree, the first case gives two binary trees. The third case does similarly. In the second case, the left and right subtrees both have one node, and there is only one binary tree with one node, so there is one binary tree in the second case. Altogether, then, there are five binary trees with three nodes.

These binary trees are all drawn in Figure 9.2. Before proceeding, you should pause to construct all fourteen binary trees with four nodes. This exercise will further help you establish the ideas behind the definition of binary trees.

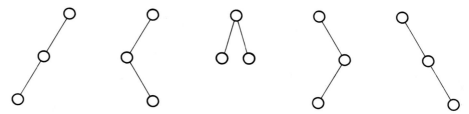

Figure 9.2.   The binary trees with three nodes

linked implementation

A binary tree has a natural implementation in linked storage. As usual, we shall wish all the nodes to be acquired as dynamic storage, so we shall need a separate pointer variable to enable us to find the tree. Our usual name for this pointer variable will be **root**, since it will point to the root of the tree. With this pointer variable, it is easy to recognize an empty binary tree as precisely the condition

root = **nil.**

Each node of a binary tree (as the root of some subtree) has both a left and a right subtree, which we can reach with pointers by declaring

type pointer = ↑node;
    node = **record**
        {information fields within the node go here}
        left,
        right**:** pointer
    end

These declarations turn the comparison tree for the 14 names from Figure 9.1 into the linked binary tree of Figure 9.3. As you can see, the only difference between the comparison tree and the linked binary tree is that we have explicitly shown the **nil** links in the latter, whereas it is customary in drawing trees to omit all empty subtrees and the branches going to them. The tree of Figure 9.3, furthermore, is automatically a binary search tree, since the decision to move left or right at each node is based on the same comparisons of keys used in the definition of a search tree.

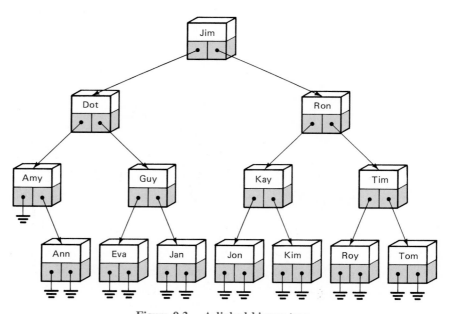

Figure 9.3.   A linked binary tree

9.2 TREESEARCH

At this point we should tie down some of the major ideas by writing a short procedure to search through a linked binary tree for the item with a particular key. First, let us write some declarations that would appear in the main program, in a form similar to those introduced for searching in Chapter 5. Recall that we used item as the name for the records in the list, each of which contained a key field. We leave keytype undefined, assuming that it is some type, such as a number or a string, for which any two keys can be compared to determine which should be first.

> *In this chapter, we always assume that no two items have the same key.*

The items are placed in nodes that embody the tree structure, as follows.

Pascal declaration of binary search tree

```
type pointer = ↑node;
     node   = record
       info: item;
       left,
       right: pointer
     end;

var  root,                        {pointer to the root of the binary tree}
     p:      pointer;             {temporary pointer that moves through tree}
     target: keytype;                    {key for which we search}
```

To search for the target we first compare it with the key at the root of the tree. If it is not the same, we go to the left subtree or right subtree as appropriate and repeat the search in that subtree. What event will be the termination condition? Clearly if we find the key, the procedure succeeds. If not, then we continue searching until we hit an empty subtree. By using a pointer p to move through the tree, we can use p also to send the results of the search back to the calling program. Thus,

precondition and postcondition

> *Procedure* TreeSearch *uses a pointer* p *as its calling parameter. Before invoking the procedure, the pointer should be set to the root of the tree:*
>
> p := root.
>
> *When the procedure returns,* p *will point to the node containing the target if the search was successful, and* p *will be* **nil** *if it was unsuccessful.*

Perhaps the simplest way to write the procedure is to use recursion:

recursive search

```
procedure TreeSearch(var p: pointer; target: keytype);
begin
  if p <> nil then
    if target <> p↑.info.key then
      if target < p↑.info.key then
        begin p := p↑.left; TreeSearch(p, target) end
      else
        begin p := p↑.right; TreeSearch(p, target) end
end;
```

The recursion in this procedure can easily be removed, since it is tail recursion, essentially by writing a loop in place of the nested **if** statements. The body of the procedure then consists essentially of the statement

```
while (p <> nil) and (target <> p↑.info.key) do
  if target < p↑.info.key then p := p↑.left else p := p↑.right
```

With standard Pascal, however, this statement must be rewritten to avoid a run-time error when the search is unsuccessful, since it may attempt to look up p↑

even though p = **nil.** Perhaps the simplest way is to introduce a Boolean variable, as implemented in the following procedure.

nonrecursive search

```
procedure TreeSearch(var p: pointer; target: keytype);
var finished: Boolean;
begin
  repeat
    if p = nil then finished := true
    else if p↑.info.key = target then finished := true
    else begin
      finished := false;
      if target < p↑.info.key then p := p↑.left else p := p↑.right
    end
  until finished
end;
```

9.3 TRAVERSAL OF BINARY TREES

In many applications it is necessary, not only to find a node within a binary tree, but to be able to move through all the nodes of the binary tree, visiting each one in turn. If there are n nodes in the binary tree, then there are $n!$ different orders in which they could be visited, but most of these have little regularity or pattern. When we write an algorithm to traverse a binary tree we shall almost always wish to proceed so that the same rules are applied at each node. At a given node, then, there are three tasks we shall wish to do in some order: We shall visit the node itself; we shall traverse its left subtree; and we shall traverse its right subtree. If we name these three tasks V, L, and R, respectively, then there are six ways to arrange them:

$$V\,L\,R \qquad L\,V\,R \qquad L\,R\,V \qquad V\,R\,L \qquad R\,V\,L \qquad R\,L\,V.$$

By standard convention these six are reduced to three by considering only the ways in which the left subtree is traversed before the right. The other three are clearly similar. These three remaining ways are given names:

preorder, inorder, and postorder

$V\,L\,R$	$L\,V\,R$	$L\,R\,V$
Preorder	**Inorder**	**Postorder**

These three names are chosen according to the step at which the given node is visited. With *preorder traversal* the node is visited before the subtrees, with *inorder traversal* it is visited between them, and with *postorder traversal* the root is visited after both of the subtrees.

Inorder traversal is also sometimes called *symmetric order,* and postorder traversal may be called *endorder.*

The translation from the definitions to formal procedures to traverse a linked binary tree in these ways is especially easy. As usual, we take root to be a pointer to the root of the tree, and we assume the existence of another procedure Visit( ) that does the desired task for each node.

```
procedure Preorder(root: pointer);        procedure Inorder(root: pointer);
begin                                      begin
   if root <> nil then                        if root <> nil then
   begin                                      begin
      Visit(root);                               Inorder(root↑.left);
      Preorder(root↑.left);                      Visit(root);
      Preorder(root↑.right)                      Inorder(root↑.right)
   end                                        end
end;                                       end;

                 procedure Postorder(root: pointer);
                 begin
                    if root <> nil then
                    begin
                       Postorder(root↑.left);
                       Postorder(root↑.right);
                       Visit(root)
                    end
                 end;
```

expression tree

    The choice of the names *preorder*, *inorder,* and *postorder* is not accidental, but relates closely to a motivating example of considerable interest, that of expression trees. An *expression tree* is built up from the simple operands and operators of an (arithmetical or logical) expression by placing the simple operands as the leaves of a binary tree, and the operators as the interior nodes. For each binary operator, the left subtree contains all the simple operands and operators in the left operand of the given operator, and the right subtree contains everything in the right operand. For a unary operator, one subtree will be empty.

operators

    We traditionally write some unary operators to the left of their operands, such as '—' (unary negation) or the standard functions like log( ) and cos( ). Others are written on the right, such as the factorial function ( )!, or the function that takes the square of a number, ( )². Sometimes either side is permissible, such as the derivative operator, which can be written as d/dx on the left, or as ( )′ on the right, or the incrementing operator $++$ in the language "C" (where the actions on the left and right are different). If the operator is written on the left, then in the expression tree we take its left subtree as empty. If it appears on the right, then its right subtree will be empty.

    The expression trees of a few simple expressions are shown in Figure 9.4, together with the slightly more complicated example of the quadratic formula in Figure 9.5, where we denote exponentiation by ↑.

Polish notation

    If you apply the traversal algorithms to these trees, you will immediately see how their names are related to the well-known *Polish forms* of expressions: Traversal of an expression tree in preorder yields the *prefix form* of the expression, in which every operator is written before its operand(s); inorder traversal gives the *infix form* (the customary way to write the expression); and postorder traversal gives the *postfix form,* in which all operators appear after their operand(s). A moment's consideration will convince you of the reason: The left and right subtrees of each node are its

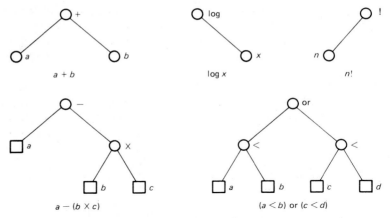

Figure 9.4.   Expression trees

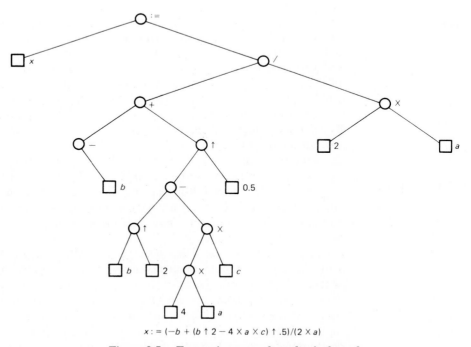

$x := (-b + (b \uparrow 2 - 4 \times a \times c) \uparrow .5)/(2 \times a)$

Figure 9.5.   Expression tree of quadratic formula

operands, and the relative position of an operator to its operands in the three Polish forms is the same as the relative order of visiting the components in each of the three traversal methods. The Polish notation is the major topic of Chapter 12.

9.4 TREESORT

As a further example, let us take the binary tree of 14 names from Figure 9.1 or Figure 9.3, and write them in the order given by each traversal method:

example of search tree traversal

preorder:

Jim Dot Amy Ann Guy Eva Jan Ron Kay Jon Kim Tim Roy Tom

inorder:

Amy Ann Dot Eva Guy Jan Jim Jon Kay Kim Ron Roy Tim Tom

postorder:

Ann Amy Eva Jan Guy Dot Jon Kim Kay Roy Tom Tim Ron Jim

It is no accident that inorder traversal produces the names in alphabetical order. A search tree is set up so that all the nodes in the left subtree of a given node come before it in the ordering, and all the nodes in its right subtree come after it. Hence inorder traversal produces all the nodes before a given node first, then the given node, and then all the later nodes.

treesort

We now have the idea for an interesting sorting method, called *treesort*. We simply take the items to be sorted, build them into a binary search tree, and use inorder traversal to put them out in order. This method has the great advantage, as we shall see, that it is easy to make changes in the list of items considered. Adding and deleting items in a sorted contiguous list is oppressively slow and painful; searching for an item in a sequential linked list is equally inefficient.

Treesort has the considerable advantages that it is almost as easy to make changes as in a linked list, the sort is as fast as quicksort, and searches can be made with the efficiency of binary search.

9.4.1 Insertion into a Search Tree

The first part of treesort is to build a sequence of nodes into a binary search tree. We can do so by starting with an empty binary tree and inserting one node at a time into the tree, always making sure that the properties of a search tree are preserved. The first case, inserting a node into an empty tree, is easy. We need only make root point to the new node. If the tree is not empty, then we must compare the key with the one in the root. If it is less, then the new node must be inserted into the left subtree; if it is more, then it must be inserted into the right subtree. If the keys are equal, then our assumption that no two nodes have the same key is violated.

From this outline we can now write our procedure, using the same declarations employed for the procedure TreeSearch.

recursive insertion

```
procedure Insert(var root: pointer; newnode: pointer);
begin                                            {procedure Insert}
  if root = nil then
  begin
    root := newnode;
    root↑.left := nil;
    root↑.right := nil
  end
  else with root↑ do
    if newnode↑.info.key < info.key then
      Insert(left, newnode)
    else if newnode↑.info.key > info.key then
      Insert(right, newnode)
    else Error
end;                                             {duplicate key}
                                                 {procedure Insert}
```

The use of recursion in this procedure is not essential, since it is tail recursion. To replace recursion with iteration we must introduce a local pointer variable p that will move to the left or right subtree. We use the condition p = **nil** to terminate the loop.

nonrecursive insertion

```
procedure Insert(var root: pointer; newnode: pointer);
var p: pointer;                                  {used to move through tree}
begin                                            {procedure Insert}
  p := root;
  while p <> nil do with p↑ do
    if newnode↑.info.key < info.key then
      if left <> nil then
        p := left
      else
        begin left := newnode; p := nil end
    else if newnode↑.info.key > info.key then
      if right <> nil then
        p := right
      else
        begin right := newnode; p := nil end
    else Error;                                  {duplicate key}
  newnode↑.left := nil;
  newnode↑.right := nil;
  if root = nil then root := newnode             {care for empty tree}
end;                                             {procedure Insert}
```

9.4.2 The Treesort Algorithm

Now that we can insert new nodes into the search tree, we can build it up and thus devise the new sorting method. In the resulting procedure, we assume the existence of a procedure GetNode( ) that will provide a pointer to the next node to be sorted.

GetNode(p) returns the value p = **nil** when there are no more nodes to be inserted. The procedure will return as its result the pointer root to the search tree it builds.

sorting

```
procedure TreeSort(var root: pointer);
var p: pointer;
begin                                              {procedure TreeSort}
  root := nil;
  GetNode(p);
  while p <> nil do
  begin
    Insert(root, p);
    GetNode(p)
  end;
  Inorder(root)                                    {Traverse the final tree.}
end;                                               {procedure TreeSort}
```

Note carefully that, if the same set of nodes is presented to TreeSort in a different order, then the search tree that is built may have a different shape. When it is traversed in inorder, the keys will still be properly sorted, but the particular location of nodes within the tree depends on the way in which they were initially presented to Treesort. If the 14 names of Figure 9.1, for example, are presented in the order

Tim Dot Eva Roy Tom Kim Guy Amy Jon Ann Jim Kay Ron Jan

then the resulting search tree will be the one in Figure 9.6. If the names are presented sorted in their alphabetical order, then the search tree will degenerate into a chain.

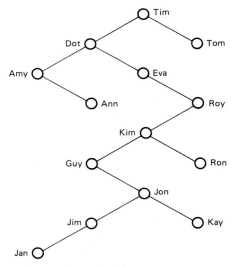

Figure 9.6.   Search tree of 14 names

key comparisons

Let us briefly study what comparisons of keys are done by treesort. The first node goes directly into the root of the search tree, with no key comparisons. As each succeeding node comes in, its key is first compared to the key in the root and then it goes either into the left subtree or the right subtree. Notice the similarity with quicksort, where at the first stage every key is compared with the first pivot key, and then put into the left or the right sublist. In treesort, however, as each node comes in it goes into its final position in the linked structure. The second node becomes the root of either the left or right subtree (depending on the comparison of its key with the root key). From then on all keys going into the same subtree are compared to this second key. Similarly, in quicksort all keys in one sublist are compared to the second pivot, the pivot for that sublist. Continuing in this way, we can make the following observation.

THEOREM 9.1

Treesort makes exactly the same comparisons of keys as does quicksort when the pivot for each sublist is chosen to be the first key in the sublist.

advantages

As we know, quicksort is usually an excellent method. On average, only mergesort among the methods we have studied makes fewer key comparisons. Hence, on average, we can expect treesort also to be an excellent sorting method in terms of key comparisons. Quicksort, however, needs to have access to all the items to be sorted throughout the process. With treesort, the nodes need not all be available at the start of the process, but are built into the tree one by one as they become available. Hence treesort is preferable for applications where the nodes are received one at a time. The major advantage of treesort is that its search tree remains available for later insertions and deletions, and that the tree can subsequently be searched in logarithmic time, whereas all our previous sorting methods either required contiguous lists, for which insertions and deletions are difficult, or produced simply linked lists for which only sequential search is available.

drawbacks

The major drawback of treesort is already implicit in Theorem 9.1. Quicksort has a very poor performance in its worst case, and, although a careful choice of pivots makes this case extremely unlikely, the choice of pivot to be the first key in each sublist makes the worst case appear whenever the keys are already sorted. If the keys are presented to treesort already sorted, then treesort too will be a disaster—the search tree it builds will reduce to a chain. Treesort should never be used if the keys are already sorted, or are nearly so. There are few other reservations about treesort that are not equally applicable to all linked structures. For small problems with small items, contiguous storage is usually the better choice, but for large problems and bulky records, linked storage comes into its own.

9.4.3 Deletion from a Search Tree

method

At the beginning of the discussion of treesort, the ability to make changes in the search tree was mentioned as an advantage. We have already obtained an algorithm that adds a new node to the search tree, and it can be used to update the tree as easily as to build it from scratch. But we have not yet considered how to delete a node from the tree. If the node to be deleted is a leaf, then the process is easy: We need only replace the link to the deleted node by **nil.** The process remains easy if the deleted node has only one subtree: We adjust the link from the parent of the deleted node to point to its subtree.

When the node to be deleted has both left and right subtrees nonempty, however, the problem is more complicated. To which of the subtrees should the parent of the deleted node now point? What is to be done with the other subtree? This problem is illustrated in Figure 9.7, together with one possible solution. (An exercise outlines another, sometimes better solution.) What we do is to attach the right subtree in place of the deleted node, and then hang the left subtree onto an appropriate node of the right subtree.

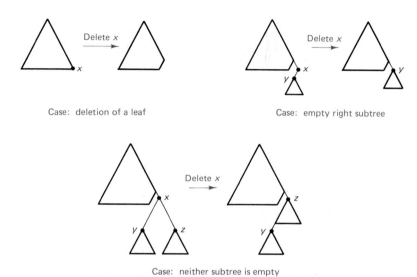

Figure 9.7.   Deletion of a node from a search tree

To which node of the right subtree should the former left subtree be attached? Since every key in the left subtree precedes every key of the right subtree, it must be as far to the left as possible, and this point can be found by taking left branches until an empty left subtree is found.

We can now write a procedure to implement this plan. As a calling parameter it will use a pointer p to the node to be deleted. Since the object is to update the search tree, we must assume that the corresponding actual parameter is one of the links of the tree, and not just a copy, or else the tree structure itself will not be changed as it should. In other words, if the node at the left of $x\uparrow$ is to be deleted, the call should be

requirement

$$Delete(x\uparrow.left)$$

and if the root is to be deleted, the call should be

$$Delete(root).$$

On the other hand, the following call will not work properly:

$$y := x\uparrow.left; \; Delete(y).$$

deletion

```
procedure Delete(var p: pointer);
var
   q:  pointer;                      {used to look for the place to hang the left subtree}
begin                                                           {procedure Delete}
   if p = nil then
      Error                                         {attempt to delete a nonexistent node}
   else if p↑.right = nil then
      begin                                   {Reattach the left subtree in place of p↑.}
      q := p;
      p := p↑.left;
      Dispose(q)
   end
   else if p↑.left := nil then
      begin                                   {Reattach the right subtree in place of p↑.}
      q := p;
      p := p↑.right;
      Dispose(q)
   end
   else                                                {Neither subtree is empty.}
      begin
      q := p↑.right;                        {Move right, then as far left as possible.}
      while q↑.left <> nil do q := q↑.left;
      q↑.left := p↑.left;
      q := p;
      p := p↑.right;
      Dispose(q)
   end
end;                                                            {procedure Delete}
```

You should trace through this procedure to check that all pointers are updated properly, especially in the case when neither subtree is empty. Note the steps needed to make the loop stop at a node with empty left subtree, but not to end at the empty subtree itself.

This procedure is far from optimal, in that it can greatly increase the height of the tree. Two examples are shown in Figure 9.8. When the roots are deleted from these two trees, the one on the top reduces its height, but the one below increases its height. Thus the time required for a later search can substantially increase, even though the total size of the tree has decreased. There is, moreover, often some tendency for insertions and deletions to be made in sorted order, that will further elongate the search tree. Hence, to optimize the use of search trees, we need methods to make the left and right subtrees more nearly balanced. We shall consider this important topic later in this chapter.

balancing

Exercises 9.4

E1. Construct the 14 binary trees with four nodes.

E2. Write a function that will count all the nodes of a linked binary tree.

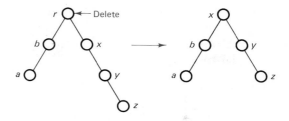

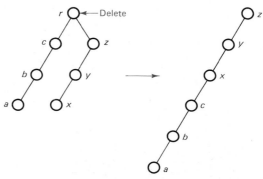

Figure 9.8.   Deletions from two search trees

E3. Determine the order in which the vertices of the following binary trees will be visited under **(1)** preorder, **(2)** inorder, and **(3)** postorder traversal.

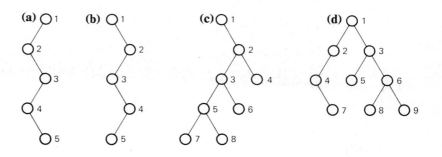

E4. Draw the expression tree for each of the following expressions, and give the order of visiting the nodes in **(1)** preorder, **(2)** inorder, and **(3)** postorder.

(a) $\log n!$ **(c)** $a - (b - c)$

(b) $(a - b) - c$ **(d)** $(a < b)$ and $(b < c)$ and $(c < d)$

E5. Write a function that will count the leaves (i.e., the nodes with both subtrees empty) of a linked binary tree.

E6. Write a function that will find the height of a linked binary tree.

double-order traversal **E7.** Write a procedure to perform a ***double-order traversal*** of a binary tree, meaning that at each node of the tree, the procedure first visits the node, then traverses its left subtree (in double order), then visits the node again, then traverses its right subtree (in double order).

E8. For each of the binary trees in Exercise E3, determine the order in which the nodes will be visited in the mixed order given by invoking procedure A:

```
procedure A(p: pointer);            procedure B(p: pointer);
begin                               begin
    if p <> nil then begin              if p <> nil then begin
        Visit(p);                           A(p↑.left);
        B(p↑.left);                         Visit(p);
        B(p↑.right);                        A(p↑.right)
    end                                 end
end;                                end;
```

E9. Write a procedure that will make a copy of a linked binary tree. The procedure should obtain the necessary new nodes from the system and copy the information fields from the nodes of the old tree to the new one.

printing a binary tree **E10.** Write a procedure that will print the keys from a binary tree in the ***bracketed form***

(key : LT, RT)

where key is the key in the root, LT denotes the left subtree of the root printed in bracketed form, and RT denotes the right subtree in bracketed form. *Optional part:* Modify the procedure so that it prints nothing instead of **(:,)** for an empty tree, and x instead of **(x:,)** for a tree consisting of only one node with key x.

E11. Write a procedure that will interchange all left and right subtrees in a linked binary tree. (See the example in Figure 9.9.)

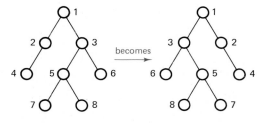

Figure 9.9. **Reversal of a binary tree**

E12. Draw the search trees that procedure TreeSort will construct for the list of 14 names presented in each of the following orders.

(a) Jan Guy Jon Ann Jim Eva Amy Tim Ron Kim Tom Roy Kay Dot

(b) Amy Tom Tim Ann Roy Dot Eva Ron Kim Kay Guy Jon Jan Jim

(c) Jan Jon Tim Ron Guy Ann Jim Tom Amy Eva Roy Kim Dot Kay

(d) Jon Roy Tom Eva Tim Kim Ann Ron Jan Amy Dot Guy Jim Kay

deletion   **E13.** Write a procedure that will delete a node from a linked binary tree, using the following method in the case when the node to be deleted has both subtrees nonempty. First, find the immediate predecessor of the node under inorder traversal (the immediate successor would work just as well), by moving to its left child and then as far right as possible. This immediate predecessor is guaranteed to have at most one child (why?), so it can be deleted from its current position without difficulty. It can then be placed into the tree in the position formerly occupied by the node that was supposed to be deleted, and the properties of a search tree will still be satisfied (why?).

level-by-level traversal   **E14.** Write a procedure that will traverse a binary tree level by level. That is, the root is visited first, then the immediate children of the root, then the grandchildren of the root, and so on. [*Hint:* Use a queue.]

                    E15. Write a function that will return the width of a linked binary tree, that is, the maximum number of nodes on the same level.

doubly linked list   **E16.** Write a procedure that converts a binary tree into a doubly linked list, in which the nodes have the order of inorder traversal of the tree. At the conclusion of the procedure, the pointer root should point to the leftmost node of the doubly linked list, and the links right and left should be used to move through the list, and be **nil** at the two ends of the list.

traversal sequences   For the following exercises, it is assumed that the keys stored in the nodes of the binary trees are all distinct, but it is not assumed that the trees are search trees. That is, there is no necessary connection between the ordering of the keys and their location in the trees. If a tree is traversed in a particular order, and each key printed when its node is visited, the resulting sequence is called the sequence corresponding to that traversal.

                    E17. Suppose that you are given two sequences that supposedly correspond to the preorder and inorder traversals of a binary tree. Prove that it is possible to reconstruct the binary tree uniquely.

                    E18. Either prove or disprove (by finding a counterexample) the analogous result for inorder and postorder traversal.

                    E19. Either prove or disprove the analogous result for preorder and postorder traversal.

                    E20. Find a pair of (short) sequences of the same keys that could not possibly correspond to the preorder and inorder traversals of the same binary tree.

Programming Project 9.4   **P1.** Write a procedure for searching, using a binary search tree with sentinel as follows. Introduce a new sentinel node, and keep a pointer to it. See Figure 9.10. Replace all the **nil** links within the search tree with links to the sentinel. Then, for each search, first store the target into the sentinel. Run both this procedure and the original procedure TreeSearch to compare the time needed both for successful and unsuccessful search.

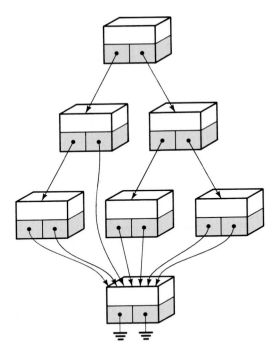

Figure 9.10.   Binary search tree with sentinel

9.5 BUILDING A BINARY SEARCH TREE

Suppose that we have a list of nodes that is already in order, perhaps a file of records, with keys already sorted alphabetically. If we wish to use these nodes to look up information, add additional nodes, or make other changes, then we would like to take the list or file of nodes and make it into a binary search tree.

We could, of course, start out with an empty binary tree and simply use the tree insertion algorithm to insert each node into it. But the nodes were given already in order, so the resulting search tree will become one long chain, and using it will be too slow—with the speed of sequential search rather than binary search. We wish instead, therefore, to take the nodes and build them into a tree that will be as bushy as possible, so as to reduce both the time to build the tree and all subsequent search time. When the number of nodes, n, is 31, for example, we wish to build the tree of Figure 9.11.

goal

In Figure 9.11 the nodes are numbered in their natural order, that is, in inorder sequence, which is the order in which they will be received and built into the tree. If you examine the diagram for a moment, you may notice an important property of the labels. The labels of the leaves are all odd numbers; that is, they are not divisible by 2. The labels of the nodes one level above the leaves are 2, 6, 10, 14, 18, 22, 26, and 30. These numbers are all double an odd number; that is, they are

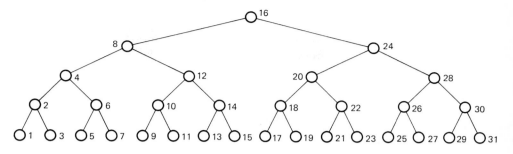

Figure 9.11.   Complete binary tree with 31 nodes

all even, but are not divisible by 4. On the next level up, the labels are 4, 12, 20, and 28, numbers that are divisible by 4, but not by 8. Finally, the nodes just below the root are labeled 8 and 24, and the root itself is 16. The key observation is

key property

> *If the nodes of a complete binary tree are labeled in inorder sequence, then each node is exactly as many levels above the leaves as the highest power of 2 that divides its label.*

Let us now put one more constraint on our problem: Let us suppose that we do not know in advance how many nodes will be built into the tree. If the nodes are coming from a file or a linked list, then this assumption is quite reasonable, since we may not have any convenient way to count the nodes before receiving them.

This assumption also has the advantage that it will stop us from worrying about the fact that, when the number of nodes is not exactly one less than a power of 2, then the resulting tree will not be complete and cannot be as symmetric as the one in Figure 9.11. Instead, we shall design our algorithm as though it were completely symmetric, and after receiving all nodes we shall determine how to tidy up the tree.

9.5.1. Getting Started

There is no doubt what to do with node number 1 when it arrives. It will be a leaf, and therefore its left and right pointers should both be set to **nil**. Node number 2 goes above node 1, as shown in Figure 9.12. Since node 2 links to node 1, we obviously must keep some way to remember where node 1 is. Node 3 is again a leaf, but it is in the right subtree of node 2, so we must remember a pointer to node 2.

Does this mean that we must keep a list of pointers to all nodes previously processed, to determine how to link in the next one? The answer is no, since when node 3 is received, all connections for node 1 are complete. Node 2 must be remembered until node 4 is received to establish the left link from node 4, but then a pointer to node 2 is no longer needed. Similarly, node 4 must be remembered until node 8 has been processed. In Figure 9.12 colored arrows point to each node that must be remembered as the tree grows.

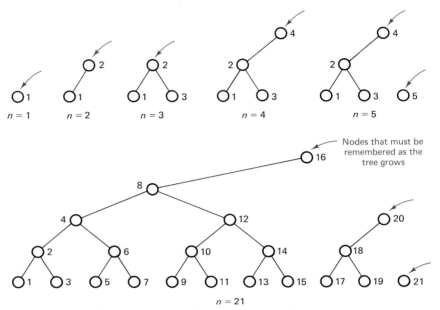

Figure 9.12.   Building the first nodes into a tree

It should now be clear that to establish future links, we need only remember pointers to one node on each level, the last node processed on that level. We keep these pointers in an array called lastnode that will be quite small. For example, a tree with 20 levels can accommodate

$$2^{20} - 1 > 1,000,000$$

nodes.

As each new node arrives, it is clearly the last one received in the order, so we can set its right pointer to **nil** (at least temporarily). The left pointer of the new node is **nil** if it is a leaf, and otherwise is the entry in lastnode one level lower than the new node. So that we can treat the leaves in the same way as other nodes, we consider the leaves to be on level 0, index the array lastnode from -1 to the maximum height allowed, and ensure that lastnode[-1] = **nil**.

9.5.2 Declarations and the Main Procedure

We can now write down declarations of the variables needed for our task, and, while we are at it, we can outline the main procedure. The first step will be to receive all the nodes and insert them into the tree. To obtain each new node, we assume the existence of an auxiliary procedure

GetNode(p)

that returns with p pointing to the new node, or p = **nil** when all nodes have been delivered. After all the nodes have been inserted, we must find the root of the tree and then connect any right subtrees that may be dangling (see Figure 9.12 in the case of 5 or 21 nodes).

    The main procedure thus becomes

main procedure

```
procedure BuildTree(var root: pointer);
{uses an auxiliary procedure GetNode(p) to obtain a list of items in proper order
     of keys, and builds them into a binary search tree}
const maxheight = 20;
type
  level = −1 .. maxheight;                         {number of steps above leaves}
var
  lastnode: array[level] of pointer;                      {contains a pointer to
                                                the last node processed on each level}
  counter: integer;                                {number of nodes read in so far}
  p: pointer;                                      {p↑ is the present input node.}
  lev: level;                                      {level of p↑}
begin                                              {procedure BuildTree}
  for lev := −1 to maxheight do lastnode[lev] := nil;
  counter := 0;
  GetNode(p);
  while p <> nil do
  begin
    counter := counter + 1;
    Insert(p);
    GetNode(p)
  end;                                             {receiving and processing input}
  FindRoot;
  ConnectSubtrees
end;                                               {procedure BuildTree}
```

9.5.3 Inserting a Node

The discussion in the previous section shows how to set up the left links of each node correctly, but for some of the nodes, the right link should not permanently have the value **nil**. When a new node arrives, it cannot yet have a proper right subtree, since it is the latest node (under the ordering) so far received. The node, however, may be the right child of some previous node. On the other hand, it may instead be a left child, in which case its parent node has not yet arrived. We can tell which case occurs by looking in the array lastnode. If lev denotes the level of the new node, then its parent has level lev + 1. We look at lastnode[lev + 1]↑. If its right link is still **nil**, then its right child must be the new node; if not, then its right child has already arrived, and the new node must be the left child of some future node.

    We can now formally describe how to insert a new node into the tree.

insertion

```
procedure Insert(p: pointer);
{inserts p↑ as rightmost node of a partial binary search tree}
var
  lev : level;                                          {level of p↑}
begin                                              {procedure Insert}
  lev := Power2(counter);
  p↑.right := nil;
  p↑.left := lastnode[lev − 1];
  lastnode[lev] := p;
  if lastnode[lev + 1] <> nil then
    with lastnode[lev + 1]↑ do
      if right = nil then right := p
end;                                               {procedure Insert}
```

This procedure uses a short function to find the level of p↑:

finding the level

```
function Power2(c: integer): level;
{finds the highest power of 2 that divides c; requires c ≠ 0}
var
  lev : level;
begin                                                {function Power2}
  lev := 0;
  while not odd(c) do
    begin c := c div 2; lev := lev + 1 end;
  Power2 := lev
end;                                                 {function Power2}
```

9.5.4 Finishing the Task

Finding the root of the tree is easy: the root is the highest node in the tree; hence its pointer is the highest entry not equal to **nil** in the array lastnode. We therefore have

finding the root

```
procedure FindRoot;
var
  lev: level;
begin                                              {procedure FindRoot}
  if counter = 0 then
    root := nil                                         {Tree is empty.}
  else begin                                            {nonempty tree}
    lev := maxheight;      {Find the highest occupied level; it gives the root.}
    while lastnode[lev] = nil do lev := lev − 1;
    root := lastnode[lev]
  end
end;                                               {procedure FindRoot}
```

Finally, we must determine how to tie in any subtrees that may not yet be connected properly after all the nodes have been received. The difficulty is that some nodes in the upper part of the tree may still have their right links set to **nil**, even though further nodes have come in that belong in their right subtrees.

Any node for which the right child is still **nil** will be one of the nodes in lastnode. Its right child should be set to the highest node in lastnode that is not already in its left subtree. We thus arrive at the following algorithm.

tying subtrees together

```
procedure ConnectSubtrees;
var
  p:    pointer
  lev:  level;
  s:    level;
begin                                          {procedure ConnectSubtrees}
  lev := maxheight;
  while (lastnode[lev] = nil) and (lev > 1) do
    lev := lev − 1;                            {Find the highest node: root.}
  while lev > 1 do                   {Nodes on levels 1 and 0 are already OK.}
    with lastnode[lev]↑ do
    if right <> nil then
      lev := lev − 1                {Search down for the highest dangling node.}
    else begin                            {case: Right subtree is undefined.}
      p := left;                         {Find the highest entry in lastnode that}
      s := lev − 1;                                {is not in the left subtree.}
      repeat
        p := p↑.right;
        s := s − 1
      until (p = nil) or (p <> lastnode[s]);
      right := lastnode[s];
      lev := s                {Nodes on levels between lev and s are on the left.}
    end                                       {connecting dangling subtrees}
end;                                           {procedure ConnectSubtrees}
```

9.5.5 Evaluation

The algorithm of this section produces a binary search tree that is not always completely balanced. If 32 nodes come in, for example, then node 32 will become the root of the tree, and all 31 remaining nodes will be in its left subtree. Thus the leaves are five steps removed from the root. If the root were chosen optimally, then most of the leaves would be four steps from it, and only one would be five steps. Hence one comparison more than necessary will usually be done.

One extra comparison in a binary search is not really a very high price, and it is easy to see that a tree produced by our method is never more than one level away from optimality. There are sophisticated methods for building a binary search tree that is as balanced as possible, but much remains to recommend a simpler method, one that does not need to know in advance how many nodes are in the tree.

The exercises outline ways in which our algorithm can be used to take an arbitrary binary search tree and rearrange the nodes to bring it into better balance, so as to improve search times. Again, there are more sophisticated methods (which, however will likely be slower) for rebalancing a tree. In Section 9.6 we shall study AVL trees, in which we perform insertions and deletions in such a way as always to maintain the tree in a state of near balance. For many practical purposes, however, the simpler algorithm described in this section should prove sufficient.

9.5.6 Random Search Trees and Optimality

To conclude this section, let us ask whether it is worthwhile on average to keep a binary search tree balanced or to rebalance it. If we assume that the keys have arrived in random order, then, on average, how many more comparisons are needed in a search of the resulting tree than would be needed in a completely balanced tree?

extended binary tree
In answering the question we first convert the binary search tree into a 2-tree, as follows. Think of all the vertices of the binary tree as drawn as circles, and add on new, square vertices replacing all the empty subtrees (**nil** links). This process is shown in Figure 9.13. All the vertices of the original binary tree become internal vertices of the 2-tree, and the new vertices are all external (leaves). A successful search terminates at an interior vertex of the 2-tree, and an unsuccessful search at a leaf. Hence the internal path length gives us the number of comparisons for a successful search, and the external path length gives the number for an unsuccessful search.

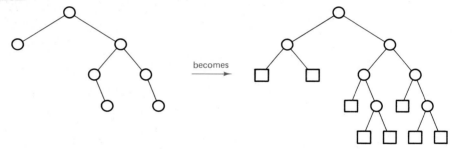
becomes

Figure 9.13.   Extension of a binary tree into a 2-tree

We shall assume that the $n!$ possible orderings of keys are equally likely in building the tree. When there are n nodes in the tree, we denote by $S(n)$ the number of comparisons done in the average successful search and by $U(n)$ the number in the average unsuccessful search.

counting comparisons
The number of comparisons needed to find any key in the tree is exactly one more than the number of comparisons that were needed to insert it in the first place, and inserting it required the same comparisons as the unsuccessful search showing that it was not yet in the tree. We therefore have the relationship

$$S(n) = 1 + \frac{U(0) + U(1) + \cdots + U(n-1)}{n}.$$

The relation between internal and external path length, as presented in Theorem 5.4, states that

$$S(n) = (1 + 1/n)U(n) - 1.$$

The last two equations together give

recurrence relation
$$(n + 1)U(n) = 2n + U(0) + U(1) + \cdots + U(n - 1).$$

We solve this recurrence by writing the equation for $n - 1$ instead of n,

$$nU(n - 1) = 2(n - 1) + U(0) + U(1) + \cdots + U(n - 2),$$

and subtracting, to obtain

$$U(n) = U(n - 1) + \frac{2}{n + 1}.$$

The sum

$$H_n = 1 + \frac{1}{2} + \frac{1}{3} + \cdots + \frac{1}{n}$$

harmonic number
is called the nth **harmonic number,** and it is shown in Appendix A.2.7 that this number is approximately the natural logarithm $\ln n$. Since $U(0) = 0$, we can now evaluate $U(n)$ by starting at the bottom and adding:

$$U(n) = 2 \left[\frac{1}{2} + \frac{1}{3} + \cdots + \frac{1}{n + 1} \right] = 2H_{n + 1} - 2 \approx 2 \ln n.$$

By Theorem 5.4 the number of comparisons for a successful search is also approximately $2 \ln n$. By Theorem 5.6, the optimal number of comparisons in a search of n items is the base 2 logarithm, $\lg n$. But (see Appendix A.2.5)

$$\ln n = (\ln 2)(\lg n).$$

Finally, therefore, we have

THEOREM 9.2
The average number of comparisons needed in the average binary search tree with n nodes is approximately $2 \ln n = (2 \ln 2)(\lg n)$.

COROLLARY 9.3
The average binary search tree requires approximately $2 \ln 2 \approx 1.39$ *times as many comparisons as a completely balanced tree.*

cost of not balancing
In other words, the average cost of not balancing a binary search tree is approximately 39 percent more comparisons. In applications where optimality is important, this cost must be weighed against the extra cost of balancing the tree, or of maintaining it in balance. Note especially that these latter tasks involve not only the cost of computer time, but the cost of the extra programming effort that will be required.

**Exercises
9.5**

E1. Draw the sequence of partial search trees (like Figure 9.12) that the method in this section will construct for $n = 6$ through $n = 8$.

E2. Write a procedure GetNode(p) that will traverse a linked list and get each node from the list in turn. Assume that the list is simply linked with the links in the right field of each node.

E3. Combine the algorithm for converting a binary tree to a doubly-linked list (requested in Exercise E16 of Section 9.4) with Exercise E2 and the algorithm of this section to obtain a self-contained procedure to put a binary search tree into better balance.

E4. Write a version of procedure GetNode(p) that traverses a binary tree in inorder without first converting it into a linked sequential list. Make sure that the algorithm of this section will not change any links in the tree until your traversal algorithm no longer needs them. Thereby obtain a self-contained procedure for putting a binary search tree into better balance with only one pass through its nodes.

E5. Write a procedure GetNode(p) that will read a record from a file, check that the key is in the proper order, and return a new node containing the record. Thereby obtain a self-contained procedure for reading a balanced binary search tree from an ordered sequential file.

E6. Suppose that the number of nodes in the tree is known in advance. Modify the algorithm of this section to take advantage of this knowledge, and produce a tree in which any imbalance is of at most one level, and occurs at the leaves rather than near the root.

E7. There are $6 = 3!$ possible orderings of three keys, but only 5 distinct binary trees with three nodes. Therefore these binary trees are not equally likely to occur as search trees. Find which search tree corresponds to each possible order, and thereby find the probability for building each of the binary search trees from randomly ordered input.

E8. Repeat Exercise E7, with the $4! = 24$ orderings of four keys and the 14 binary trees with four nodes.

9.6 HEIGHT BALANCE: AVL TREES

The algorithm of Section 9.5 can be used to build a nearly balanced binary search tree, or to restore balance when it is feasible to restructure the tree completely. In many applications, however, insertions and deletions occur continually, with no predictable order. In some of these applications, it is important to optimize search times by keeping the tree very nearly balanced at all times. The method of this section for achieving this goal was described in 1962 by two Russian mathematicians, G. M. ADEL'SON-VEL'SKIĬ and E. M. LANDIS, and the resulting binary search trees are called *AVL trees* in their honor.

AVL trees achieve the goal that searches, insertions, and deletions in a tree with n nodes can all be achieved in time that is $O(\log n)$, even in the worst case. The height of an AVL tree with n nodes, as we shall establish, can never exceed $1.44 \lg n$, and thus even in the worst case, the behavior of an AVL tree could not be much below that of a random binary search tree. In almost all cases, however, the actual length of a search is very nearly $\lg n$, and thus the behavior of AVL trees closely approximates that of the ideal, completely balanced binary search tree.

9.6.1 Definition

In a completely balanced tree, the left and right subtrees of any node would have the same height. Although we cannot always achieve this goal, by building a search tree carefully we can always ensure that the heights of every left and right subtree never differ by more than 1. We accordingly make the following:

DEFINITION

An *AVL tree* is a binary search tree in which the heights of the left and right subtrees of the root differ by at most 1 and in which the left and right subtrees are again AVL trees.

AVL tree

With each node of an AVL tree is associated a *balance factor* that is *left high, equal,* or *right high* according, respectively, as the left subtree has height greater than, equal to, or less than that of the right subtree.

In drawing diagrams, we shall show a left-high node by '/', a node whose balance factor is equal by '—', and a right-high node by '\'. Figure 9.14 shows several small AVL trees, as well as some binary trees that fail to satisfy the definition.

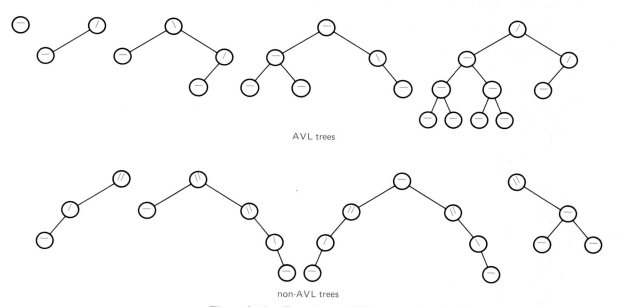

AVL trees

non-AVL trees

Figure 9.14. **Examples of AVL trees and other binary trees**

Note that the definition does not require that all leaves be on the same or adjacent levels. Figure 9.15 shows several AVL trees that are quite skewed, with right subtrees having greater height than left subtrees.

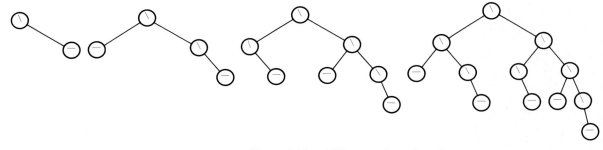

Figure 9.15. **AVL trees skewed to the right**

9.6.2 Insertion of a Node

1. Introduction

problem

We can insert a new node into an AVL tree by first using the usual binary tree insertion algorithm, comparing the key of the new node with that in the root, and inserting the new node into the left or right subtree as appropriate. It often turns out that the new node can be inserted without changing the height of the subtree, in which case neither the height nor the balance of the root will be changed. Even when the height of a subtree does increase, it may be the shorter subtree that has grown, so that only the balance factor of the root will change. The only case that can cause difficulty occurs when the new node is added to a subtree of the root that is strictly taller than the other subtree, and the height is increased. This would cause one subtree to have height 2 more than the other, whereas the AVL condition is that the height difference is never more than 1. Before we consider this situation more carefully, let us illustrate in Figure 9.16 the growth of an AVL tree through several insertions, and then we shall tie down the ideas by outlining our algorithm in Pascal.

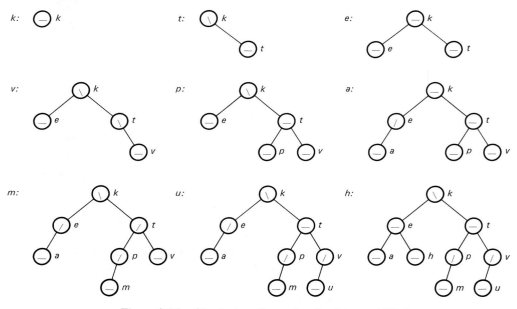

Figure 9.16.   Simple insertions of nodes into an AVL tree

2. Pascal Conventions

The basic structure of our algorithm will be the same as the ordinary binary tree insertion algorithm of Section 9.4.1, but with certain additions to accommodate the structure of AVL trees. First, each record corresponding to a node will have an additional field (along with its information field and left and right pointers), defined as

bf: balancefactor;

where we employ the enumerated type

$$\textbf{type } \text{balancefactor} = (\text{LH, EH, RH});$$

which symbols denote *left high, equal height,* and *right high,* respectively. Second, we must keep track of whether an insertion has increased the height or not, so that the balance factors can be changed appropriately. This we do by including an additional calling parameter taller of type Boolean. The task of restoring balance when required will be done in the subsidiary procedures LeftBalance and RightBalance.

AVL tree insertion

```
procedure Insert(var root: pointer; newnode: pointer; var taller: Boolean);
var
   tallersubtree: Boolean;                    {Has the height of a subtree increased?}
begin                                                        {procedure Insert}
  if root = nil then
  begin
    root := newnode;
    root↑.left := nil;
    root↑.right := nil;
    root↑.bf := EH;
    taller := true
  end
  else with root↑ do
    if newnode↑.info.key = info.key then
      Error                              {Duplicate key is not allowed in search tree.}
    else if newnode↑.info.key < info.key then
    begin                                             {Insert in the left subtree.}
      Insert(left, newnode, tallersubtree);
      if tallersubtree then                          {Change the balance factors.}
        case bf of
          LH: LeftBalance;
          EH: begin bf := LH; taller := true end;
          RH: begin bf := EH; taller := false end
        end
      else taller := false
    end
    else begin                                        {Insert in the right subtree.}
      Insert(right, newnode, tallersubtree);
      if tallersubtree then
        case bf of
          LH: begin bf := EH; taller := false end;
          EH: begin bf := RH; taller := true end;
          RH: RightBalance
        end
      else taller := false
    end
end;                                                          {procedure Insert}
```

3. Rotations

Let us now consider the case when a new node has been inserted into the taller subtree of the root and its height has increased, so that now one subtree has height 2 more than the other, and the tree no longer satisfies the AVL requirements. We must now rebuild part of the tree to restore its balance. To be definite, let us assume that we have inserted the new node into the right subtree, its height has increased, and the original tree was right high. That is, we wish to consider the case covered by the procedure RightBalance. Let r be the root of the tree and x the root of its right subtree.

There are three cases to consider, depending on the balance factor of x.

4. Case 1: Right High

left rotation

The first case, when x is right high, is illustrated in Figure 9.17. The action needed in this case is called a *left rotation;* we have rotated the node x upward to the root, dropping r down into the left subtree of x; the subtree T_2 of nodes with keys between those of r and x now becomes the right subtree of r rather than the left subtree of x. A left rotation is succinctly described in the following Pascal procedure. Note especially that, when done in the appropriate order, the steps constitute a rotation of the values in three pointer variables. Note also that, after the rotation, the height of the rotated tree has decreased by 1; it had previously increased because of the insertion; hence the height finishes where it began.

```
procedure RotateLeft(var p: pointer);
                                    {p is the root of the subtree being rotated.}
var
  temp: pointer;
begin                                                      {procedure RotateLeft}
  if p = nil then
    Error                                    {It is impossible to rotate an empty tree.}
  else if p↑.right = nil then
    Error                        {It is impossible to make an empty subtree the root.}
  else begin
    temp := p↑.right;
    p↑.right := temp↑.left;              {Move the subtree of intermediate nodes.}
    temp↑.left := p;                            {Drop the root into the left subtree.}
    p := temp                        {Change the root to the former right subtree.}
  end
end;                                                        {procedure RotateLeft}
```

5. Case 2: Left High

double rotation

The second case, when the balance factor of x is left high, is slightly more complicated. It is necessary to move two levels, to the node w that roots the left subtree of x, to find the new root. This process is shown in Figure 9.18 and is called a *double rotation*, because the transformation can be obtained in two steps by first rotating the subtree with root x to the right (so that w becomes its root), and then rotating the tree with root r to the left (moving w up to become the new root).

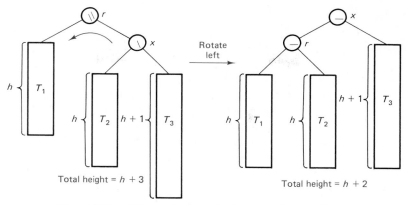

Figure 9.17.   First case: Restoring balance by a left rotation

In this second case, the new balance factors for r and x depend on the previous balance factor for w. The diagram shows the subtrees of w as having equal heights, but it is possible that w may be either left or right high. The resulting balance factors are

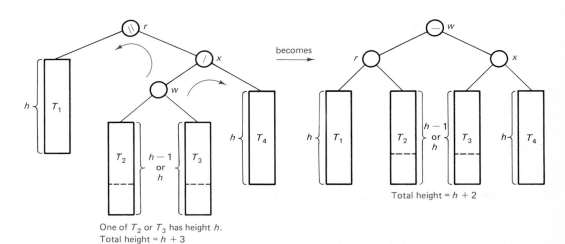

Figure 9.18.   Second case: Restoring balance by double rotation

6. Case 3: Equal Height

impossible case

It would appear, finally, that we must consider a third case, when the two subtrees of x have equal heights, but this case, in fact, can never happen. To see why, let us recall that we have just inserted a new node into the subtree rooted at x, and this subtree now has height 2 more than the left subtree of the root. The new node went either into the left or right subtree of x. Hence its insertion increased the height of only one subtree of x. If these subtrees had equal heights after the insertion, then the height of the full subtree rooted at x was not changed by the insertion, contrary to what we already know.

7. Pascal Procedure for Balancing

It is now straightforward to incorporate these transformations into a Pascal procedure. The forms of procedures RotateRight and LeftBalance are clearly similar to those of RotateLeft and RightBalance, respectively, and are left as exercises.

restoring balance

```
procedure RightBalance;                        {to be written into procedure Insert}
var
  x,                                           {pointer to right subtree of root}
  w: pointer;                                  {left subtree of x↑}
                            {also uses variables root and taller from procedure Insert}
begin                                          {procedure RightBalance}
  x := root↑.right;
  case x↑.bf of
    RH: begin                                  {single rotation left}
          root↑.bf := EH;
          x↑.bf := EH;
          RotateLeft(root);
          taller := false
        end;
    EH: Error;                                 {impossible case}
    LH: begin                                  {double rotation left}
          w := x↑.left;
          case w↑.bf of
            EH: begin root↑.bf := EH; x↑.bf := EH end;
            LH: begin root↑.bf := EH; x↑.bf := RH end;
            RH: begin root↑.bf := LH; x↑.bf := EH end
          end;
          w↑.bf := EH;
          RotateRight(x);
          root↑.right := x;
          RotateLeft(root);
          taller := false
        end
  end
end;                                           {procedure RightBalance}
```

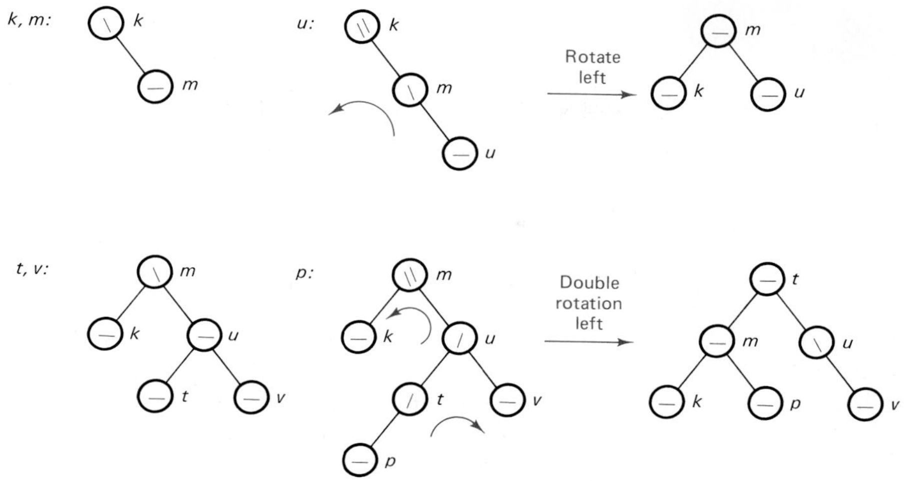

Figure 9.19.   AVL insertions requiring rotations

Examples of insertions requiring single and double rotations are shown in Figure 9.19.

8. Behavior of the Algorithm

counting rotations

The number of times that procedure Insert calls itself recursively to insert a new node can be as large as the height of the tree. At first glance it may appear that each one of these calls might induce either a single or double rotation of the appropriate subtree, but, in fact, at most only one (single or double) rotation will ever be done. To see this, let us recall that rotations are done only in procedures RightBalance and LeftBalance and that these procedures are called only when the height of a subtree has increased. When these procedures return, however, the rotations have removed the increase in height, so, for the remaining (outer) recursive calls, the height has not increased, and no further rotations or changes of balance factors are done.

Most of the insertions into an AVL tree will induce no rotations. Even when rotations are needed, they will usually occur near the leaf that has just been inserted. Even though the algorithm to insert into an AVL tree is complicated, it is reasonable to expect that its running time will differ little from insertion into an ordinary search tree of the same height. Later we shall see that we can expect the height of AVL trees to be much less than that of random search trees, and therefore both insertion and retrieval will be significantly more efficient in AVL trees than in random binary search trees.

9.6.3 Deletion of a Node

Deletion of a node x from an AVL tree requires the same basic ideas, including single and double rotations, that are used for insertion. We shall give only the steps of an informal outline of the method, leaving the writing of complete algorithms as a programming project.

method

1. Reduce the problem to the case when the node x to be deleted has at most one child. For suppose that x has two children. Find the immediate predecessor y of x under inorder traversal (the immediate successor would be just as good), by first taking the left child of x, and then moving right as far as possible to obtain y. The node y is guaranteed to have no right child, because of the way it was found. Place y (or a copy of y) into the position in the tree occupied by x (with the same parent, left and right children, and balance factor that x had). Now delete y from its former position, by proceeding as follows, using y in place of x in each of the following steps.

2. Delete the node x from the tree. Since we know (by step 1) that x has at most one child, we delete x simply by linking the parent of x to the single child of x (or to **nil**, if no child). The height of the subtree formerly rooted at x has been reduced by 1, and we must now trace the effects of this change on height through all the nodes on the path from x back to the root of the tree. We use a Boolean variable shorter to show if the height of a subtree has been shortened. The action to be taken at each node depends on the value of shorter, on the balance factor of the node, and sometimes on the balance factor of a child of the node.

3. The Boolean variable shorter is initially true. The following steps are to be done for each node p on the path from the parent of x to the root of the tree, provided shorter remains true. When shorter becomes false, then no further changes are needed, and the algorithm terminates.

4. *Case* 1: The current node p has balance factor equal. The balance factor of p is changed according as its left or right subtree has been shortened, and shorter becomes false.

5. *Case* 2: The balance factor of p is not equal, and the taller subtree was shortened. Change the balance factor of p to equal, and leave shorter as true.

6. *Case* 3: The balance factor of p is not equal, and the shorter subtree was shortened. The height requirement for an AVL tree is now violated at p, so we apply a rotation as follows to restore balance. Let q be the root of the taller subtree of p (the one not shortened). We have three cases according to the balance factor of q.

7. *Case* 3*a*: The balance factor of q is equal. A single rotation (with changes to the balance factors of p and q) restores balance, and shorter becomes false.

8. *Case* 3*b*: The balance factor of q is the same as that of p. Apply a single rotation, set the balance factors of p and q to equal, and leave shorter as true.

9. *Case* 3*c*: The balance factors of p and q are opposite. Apply a double rotation (first around q, then around p), set the balance factor of the new root to equal and the other balance factors as appropriate, and leave shorter as true.

In cases 3a, b, and c, the direction of the rotations depends on whether a left or right subtree was shortened. Some of the possibilities are illustrated in Figure 9.20, and an example of the deletion of a node appears in Figure 9.21.

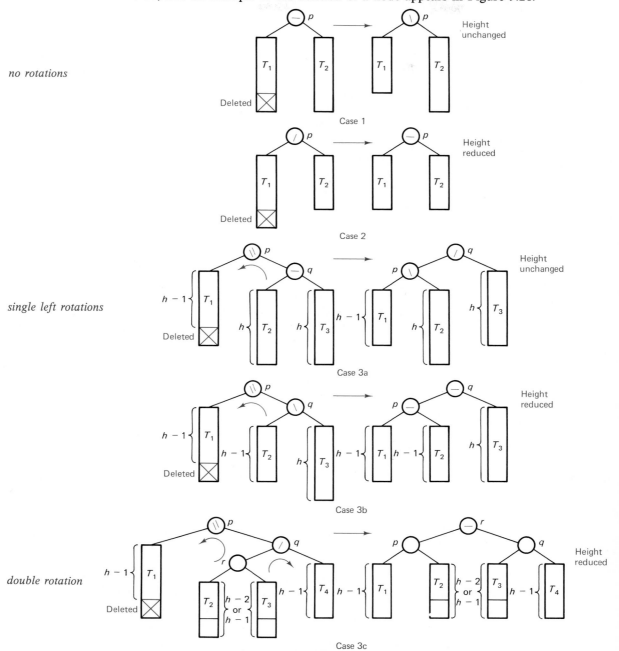

Figure 9.20.   Sample cases, deletion from an AVL tree

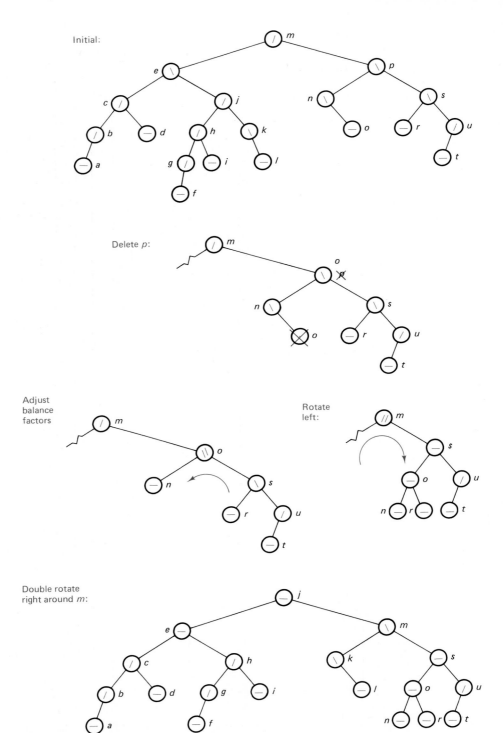

Figure 9.21.   Example of deletion from an AVL tree

9.6.4 The Height of an AVL Tree

It turns out to be very difficult to find the height of the average AVL tree, and thereby to determine how many steps are done, on average, by the algorithms of this section. It is much easier, however, to find what happens in the worst case, and these results show that the worst-case behavior of AVL trees is essentially no worse than the average behavior of random trees. Empirical evidence suggests that the average behavior of AVL trees is much better than that of random trees, almost as good as that which could be obtained from a perfectly balanced tree.

worst-case analysis

To determine the maximum height that an AVL tree with n nodes can have, we can instead ask what is the minimum number of nodes that an AVL tree of height h can have. If F_h is such a tree, and the left and right subtrees of its root are F_l and F_r, then one of F_l and F_r must have height $h - 1$, say, F_l, and the other has height either $h - 1$ or $h - 2$. Since F_h has the minimum number of nodes among AVL trees of height h, it follows that F_l must have the minimum number of nodes among AVL trees of height $h - 1$ (that is, F_l is of the form F_{h-1}), and F_r must have height $h - 2$ with minimum number of nodes (so that F_r is of the form F_{h-2}).

Fibonacci trees

The trees built by this rule, which are therefore as sparse as possible for AVL trees, are called **Fibonacci trees**. The first few are shown in Figure 9.22.

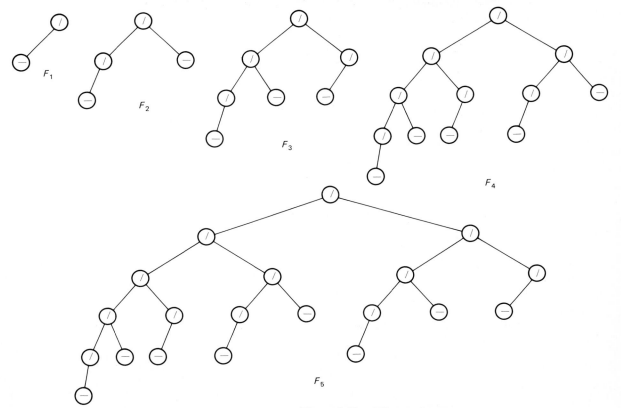

Figure 9.22.   **Fibonacci trees**

*counting nodes of a
Fibonacci tree*

If we write $|T|$ for the number of nodes in a tree T, we then have (counting the root as well as the subtrees) the recurrence relation

$$|F_h| = |F_{h-1}| + |F_{h-2}| + 1,$$

where $|F_0| = 1$ and $|F_1| = 2$. By adding 1 to both sides, we see that the numbers $|F_h| + 1$ satisfy the definition of the Fibonacci numbers (see Appendix A.4), with the subscripts changed by 3. By the evaluation of Fibonacci numbers in Appendix A.4, we therefore see that

$$|F_h| + 1 \approx \frac{1}{\sqrt{5}}\left[\frac{1+\sqrt{5}}{2}\right]^{h+3}.$$

Next, we solve this relation for h by taking the logarithms of both sides, discarding all except the largest terms. The approximate result is that

*height of Fibonacci
tree*

$$h \approx 1.44 \lg|F_h|.$$

worst-case bound

This means that the sparsest possible AVL tree with n nodes has height approximately $1.44 \lg n$. A perfectly balanced binary tree with n nodes has height about $\lg n$, and a degenerate tree has height as large as n. Hence the algorithms for manipulating AVL trees are guaranteed to take no more than about 44 percent more time than the optimum. In practice, AVL trees do much better than this. It can be shown that, even for Fibonacci trees, which are the worst case for AVL trees, the average search time is only 4 percent more than the optimum. Most AVL trees are not nearly as sparse as Fibonacci trees, and therefore it is reasonable to expect that average search times for average AVL trees are very close indeed to the optimum. Empirical studies, in fact, show that the average number of comparisons seems to be about

*average-case
observation*

$$\lg n + 0.25$$

when n is large.

**Exercises
9.6**

E1. Determine which of the following binary search trees are AVL trees. For those that are not, find all nodes at which the requirements are violated.

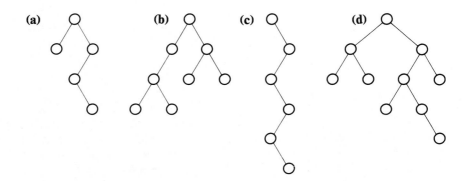

E2. In each of the following, insert the keys, in the order shown, to build them into an AVL tree.

(a) A, Z, B, Y, C, X.   (d) A, Z, B, Y, C, X, D, W, E, V, F.

(b) A, B, C, D, E, F.   (e) A, B, C, D, E, F, G, H, I, J, K, L.

(c) M, T, E, A, Z, G, P.   (f) A, V, L, T, R, E, I, S, O, K.

E3. Delete each of the keys inserted in Exercise 2 from the AVL tree, in LIFO order (last key inserted is first deleted).

E4. Delete each of the keys inserted in Exercise 2 from the AVL tree, in FIFO order (first key inserted is first deleted).

E5. Prove that the number of (single or double) rotations done in deleting a key from an AVL tree cannot exceed half the height of the tree.

Programming Projects 9.6

P1. Write a Pascal program that will accept keys from the user one at a time, build them into an AVL tree, and write out the tree at each stage. You will need a procedure to print a tree, perhaps in the bracketed form defined in Exercise E10 of Section 9.4.

P2. Write Pascal procedures to delete a node from an AVL tree, following the steps in the text.

P3. [*Major project*]   Conduct empirical studies to estimate, on average, how many rotations are needed to insert an item and to delete an item from an AVL tree.

9.7 CONTIGUOUS REPRESENTATION OF BINARY TREES: HEAPS

There are several ways other than the usual linked structures to implement binary trees, and some of these ways lead to interesting applications. This section presents one such example: a contiguous implementation of binary trees that is employed in a sorting algorithm for contiguous lists called *heapsort*. This algorithm sorts a contiguous list of length n with $O(n \log n)$ comparisons and movements of items, even in the worst case. Hence it achieves worst-case bounds better than those of quicksort, and for contiguous lists is better than mergesort, since it needs only a small and constant amount of space apart from the array being sorted.

9.7.1 Binary Trees in Contiguous Storage

Let us begin with a complete binary tree such as the one shown in Figure 9.23, and number the vertices, beginning with the root, from left to right on each level.

We can now put the binary tree into a contiguous array by storing each node in the position shown by its label. We conclude that

finding the children

> *The left and right children of the node with index k are in positions $2k$ and $2k + 1$, respectively. If these positions are beyond the bounds of the array, then these children do not exist.*

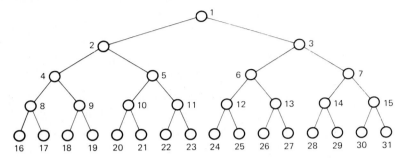

Figure 9.23.   Complete binary tree with 31 vertices

This contiguous implementation can, in fact, be extended to arbitrary binary trees, provided that we can flag locations in the array to show that the corresponding nodes do not exist. The results for several binary trees are shown in Figure 9.24.

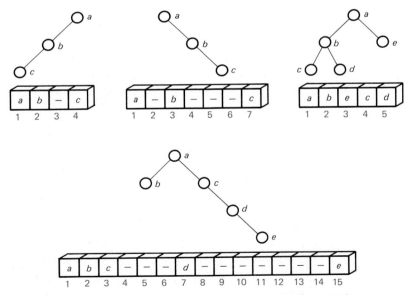

Figure 9.24.   Binary trees in contiguous implementation

It is clear from the diagram that, if a binary tree is far from a complete tree, then the contiguous representation wastes a great deal of space. Under other conditions, however, no space at all is wasted. It is this case that we shall now apply.

9.7.2 Heaps and Heapsort

1. Definition

DEFINITION

> A *heap* is defined to be a binary tree with a key in each node, such that
>
> 1. All the leaves of the tree are on two adjacent levels.
> 2. All leaves on the lowest level occur to the left and all levels, except possibly the lowest, are filled.
> 3. The key in the root is at least as large as the keys in its children (if any), and the left and right subtrees (if they exist) are again heaps.

not search trees

The first two conditions ensure that the contiguous representation of the tree will be space efficient. The third condition determines the ordering. Note that a heap is definitely *not* a search tree. The root, in fact, must have the largest key in the heap. Figure 9.25 shows four trees, the first of which is a heap, with the others violating one of the three properties.

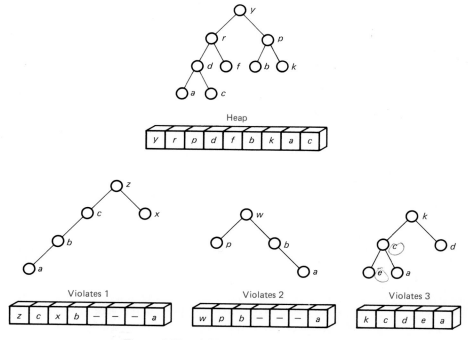

Figure 9.25. A heap and three other trees

REMARK   Some implementations of Pascal refer to the area used for dynamic memory as the "heap"; this use of the word "heap" has nothing to do with the present definition.

2. Outline of Heapsort

two-phase procedure

Heapsort proceeds in two phases. The entries in the array being sorted are interpreted as a binary tree in contiguous implementation. The first two properties of a heap are automatically satisfied, but the keys will not generally satisfy the third property. Hence the first phase of heapsort is to convert the tree into a heap.

For the second phase, we recall that the root (which is the first entry of the array as well as the top of the heap) has the largest key. This key belongs at the end of the list. We therefore move the first entry to the last position, replacing an entry x. We then decrease a counter k that keeps track of the size of the list, thereby excluding the largest entry from further sorting. The entry x that has been moved from the last position, however, may not belong on the top of the heap, and therefore we must insert x into the proper position to restore the heap property before continuing to loop in the same way.

Let us summarize this outline by rewriting it in Pascal. We use the same notation and conventions used for all the contiguous sorting algorithms of Chapter 7.

main procedure

```
procedure HeapSort(var L: list);
var
   x: item;                              {temporary storage for moving items}
   k: index;                            {Entries beyond k have been sorted.}
begin                                                {procedure HeapSort}
   BuildHeap;                                                 {first phase}
   for k := L.count downto 2 do
   begin
      x := L.entry[k];                  {Extract the last element from the list.}
      L.entry[k] := L.entry[1];         {Move top of the heap to end of the list.}
      InsertHeap(x, 1, k − 1) {Restore the heap properties for the shortened list.}
   end
end;                                                  {procedure HeapSort}
```

3. An Example

Before we begin work on the two procedures BuildHeap and InsertHeap, let us see what happens in the first few stages of sorting the heap shown as the first diagram in Figure 9.25. These stages are shown in Figure 9.26. In the first step, the largest key, y, is moved from the first to the last entry of the list. The first diagram shows the resulting tree, with y removed from further consideration, and the last entry, c, put aside as the temporary variable x. To find how to rearrange the heap and insert c, we look at the two children of the root. Each of these is guaranteed to have a larger key than any other entry in its subtree, and hence the largest of these two entries or the new entry $x = c$ belongs in the root. We therefore promote r to the top of the heap, and repeat the process on the subtree whose root has just been removed. Hence the largest of d, f and c is now inserted where r was formerly. At the next step, we would compare c with the two children of f, but these do not exist, so the promotion of entries through the tree ceases, and c is inserted in the empty position formerly occupied by f.

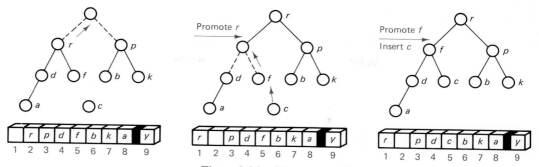

Figure 9.26.   First stage of heapsort

At this point we are ready to repeat the algorithm, again moving the top of the heap to the end of the list and restoring the heap property. The sequence of actions that occurs in the complete sort of the list is shown in Figure 9.27.

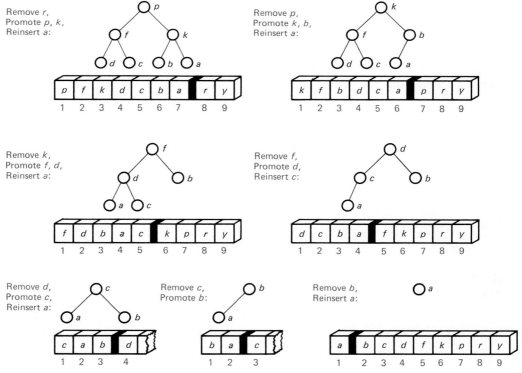

Figure 9.27.   Trace of heapsort

4. The Procedure InsertHeap

It is only a short step from this example to a formal procedure for inserting the entry x into the heap.

heap insertion

```
procedure InsertHeap(x: item; a, b: index);
{Insert item x into the partial heap with empty root in index a. The heap occupies
    locations a through b of the array L.entry.}
var
  m: integer;                        {index of the child of L.entry[a] with the larger key}
begin                                                         {procedure InsertHeap}
  m := 2 * a;                                                 {m is now the left child of a.}
  while m <= b do
  begin
    if m < b then if L.entry[m].key < L.entry[m + 1].key then
      m := m + 1;                           {m is now the child of a with the larger key.}
    if x.key >= L.entry[m].key then                    {If so, x belongs in position a.}
      m := b + 1                          {Set m as a flag to terminate the loop.}
    else begin                         {Promote L.entry[m] and move down the tree.}
      L.entry[a] := L.entry[m];
      a := m;
      m := 2 * a
    end
  end;
  L.entry[a] := x
end;                                                          {procedure InsertHeap}
```

5. Building the Initial Heap

initialization

The remaining task that we must specify is to build the initial heap from a list in
arbitrary order. To do so, we first note that a binary tree with only one node automatically satisfies the properties of a heap, and therefore we need not worry about any
of the leaves of the tree, that is, about any of the entries in the second half of the
list. If we begin at the midpoint of the list and work our way back toward the
start, we can use the procedure InsertHeap to insert each entry into the partial heap
consisting of all later entries, and thereby build the complete heap. The desired procedure is therefore simply

```
procedure BuildHeap;
begin
  for k := (L.count div 2) downto 1 do
  begin
    x := L.entry[k];
    InsertHeap(x, k, L.count)
  end
end;
```

9.7.3 Analysis of Heapsort

From the example we have worked it is not at all clear that heapsort is efficient,
and in fact heapsort is not a good choice for short lists. It seems quite strange that
we can sort by moving large keys slowly toward the beginning of the list before
finally putting them away at the end. When n becomes large, however, such small

quirks become unimportant, and heapsort proves its worth as one of very few sorting algorithms for contiguous lists that is guaranteed to finish in time $O(n \log n)$ with minimal space requirements.

worst-case insertion   First, let us determine how much work InsertHeap does in its worst case. At each pass through the loop, the index a is doubled; hence the number of passes cannot exceed lg(b **div** a); this is also the height of the subtree rooted at L.entry[a]. Each pass through the loop does two comparisons of keys (usually) and one assignment of items. Therefore, the number of comparisons done in InsertHeap is at most 2 lg(b **div** a) and the number of assignments lg(b **div** a).

Let $m = \lfloor \frac{1}{2}n \rfloor$. In BuildHeap we make m calls to InsertHeap, for values of $k = $ a ranging from m down to 1. Hence the total number of comparisons is about

first phase

$$2 \sum_{k=1}^{m} \lg(n/k) = 2(m \lg n - \lg m!) \approx 5m \approx 2.5n,$$

since, by Stirling's approximation (Corollary A.6) and $\lg m = \lg n - 1$, we have

$$\lg m! \approx m \lg m - 1.5m \approx m \lg n - 2.5m.$$

Similarly, in the sorting and insertion phase, we have about

second phase

$$2 \sum_{k=2}^{n} \lg k = 2 \lg n! \approx 2n \lg n - 3n$$

comparisons. This term dominates that of the initial phase, and hence we conclude *total worst-case counts* that the number of comparisons is $2n \lg n + O(n)$.

One assignment of items is done in InsertHeap for each two comparisons (approximately). Therefore the total number of assignments is $n \lg n + O(n)$.

From Section 7.8.4 we can see that the corresponding numbers for quicksort in the average case are $1.39n \lg n + O(n)$ comparisons and $0.69 \, n \lg n + O(n)$ swaps, *comparison with* which can be reduced to $0.23 \, n \lg n + O(n)$ swaps. Hence the worst case for heapsort *quicksort* is somewhat poorer than is the average case for quicksort. Quicksort's worst case, however, is $O(n^2)$, which is far worse than the worst case of heapsort for large n. An average-case analysis of heapsort appears to be very complicated, but empirical studies show that (as for selection sort) there is relatively little difference between the average and worst cases, and heapsort usually takes about twice as long as quicksort. Heapsort, therefore, should be regarded as something of an insurance policy: On average, heapsort costs about twice as much as quicksort, but heapsort avoids the slight possibility of a catastrophic degradation of performance.

9.7.4 Priority Queues

To conclude this section, we briefly mention another application of heaps. A *priority queue* is a data structure with only two operations:

1. Insert an item.

2. Remove the item having the largest (or smallest) key.

If items have equal keys, then the usual rule is that the first item inserted should be removed first.

applications

In a time-sharing computer system, for example, a large number of tasks may be waiting for the CPU. Some of these tasks have higher priority than others. Hence the set of tasks waiting for the CPU forms a priority queue. Other applications of priority queues include simulations of time-dependent events (like the airport simulation in Chapter 3) and solution of sparse systems of linear equations by row reduction.

implementations

We could represent a priority queue as a sorted contiguous list, in which case removal of an item is immediate, but insertion would take time proportional to n, the number of items in the queue. Or we could represent it as an unsorted list, in which case insertion is rapid but removal is slow. If we used an ordinary binary search tree (sorted by the size of the key) then, on average, insertion and removal could both be done in time $O(\log n)$, but the tree could degenerate and require time $O(n)$. Extra time and space may be needed, as well, to accommodate the linked representation of the binary search tree.

Now consider the properties of a heap. The item with largest key is on the top and can be removed immediately. It will, however, take time $O(\log n)$ to restore the heap property for the remaining keys. If, however, another item is to be inserted immediately, then some of this time may be combined with the $O(\log n)$ time needed to insert the new item. Thus the representation of a priority queue as a heap proves advantageous for large n, since it is represented efficiently in contiguous storage and is guaranteed to require only logarithmic time for both insertions and deletions.

Exercises
9.7

E1. Determine the contiguous representation of each of the following binary trees. Which of these trees are heaps? For those that are not, state which rule(s) is (are) violated at which node(s).

(a)

(b)

(c)

(d)

(e)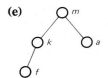

(f)

(g)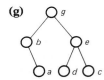

(h)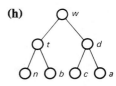

E2. By hand, trace the action of HeapSort on each of the following lists. Draw the initial tree to which the list corresponds, show how it is converted into a heap, and show the resulting heap as each item is removed from the top and the new item inserted.

(a) The list of five playing cards used in Chapter 7:
$$\text{S Q} \quad \text{S A} \quad \text{C 7} \quad \text{H 8} \quad \text{D K.}$$

(b) The list of seven numbers:

$$26 \quad 33 \quad 35 \quad 29 \quad 19 \quad 12 \quad 22.$$

(c) The list of 14 names:

Tim Dot Eva Roy Tom Kim Guy Amy Jon Ann Jim Kay Ron Jan.

E3. (a) Design a procedure that will insert a new item into a heap, obtaining a new heap. (The procedure InsertHeap in the text requires that the root be unoccupied, whereas for this exercise the root will already contain the item with largest key, which must remain in the heap. Your procedure will increase the count of items in the list.) (b) Analyze the time and space requirements of your procedure.

E4. (a) Design a procedure that will delete the item with largest key (the root) from the top of the heap and restore the heap properties of the resulting, smaller list. (b) Analyze the time and space requirements of your procedure.

E5. (a) Design a procedure that will delete the item with index i from a heap, and restore the heap properties of the resulting, smaller list. (b) Analyze the time and space requirements of your procedure.

E6. Consider a heap of n keys, with x_k being the key in position k (in the contiguous representation) for $1 \le k \le n$. Prove that the height of the subtree rooted at x_k is $\lfloor \lg(n/k) \rfloor$, for $1 \le k \le n$. [*Hint:* Use "backward" induction on k, starting with the leaves and working back toward the root, which is x_1.]

E7. Define the notion of a *ternary heap,* analogous to an ordinary heap except that each node of the tree except the leaves has three children. Devise a sorting method based on ternary heaps, and analyze the properties of the sorting method.

Programming Project 9.7

P1. Conduct empirical studies to compare the performance of HeapSort with Quick-Sort.

POINTERS AND PITFALLS

1. Consider binary search trees as an alternative to lists (indeed, as a way of implementing the abstract data type *list*). At the cost of an extra pointer field in each node, binary search trees allow random access (with $O(\log n)$ key comparisons) to all nodes while maintaining the flexibility of linked lists for insertions, deletions, and rearrangement.

2. Consider binary search trees as an alternative to tables (indeed, as a way of implementing the abstract data type *table*). At the cost of access time that is $O(\log n)$ instead of $O(1)$, binary search trees allow traversal of the data structure in the order specified by the keys while maintaining the advantage of random access provided by tables.

3. In choosing your data structures, always consider carefully what operations will be required. Binary trees are especially appropriate when random access, traversal in a predetermined order, and flexibility in making insertions and deletions are all required.

4. While choosing data structures and algorithms, remain alert to the possibility of highly unbalanced binary trees. If the incoming data are likely to be in random order, then an ordinary binary search tree should prove entirely adequate. If the data come in a sorted or nearly sorted order, then the algorithms should take appropriate action. If there is only a slight possibility of serious imbalance, it might be ignored. If, in a large project, there is greater likelihood of serious imbalance, then there may still be appropriate places in the software where the trees can be checked for balance and rebuilt if necessary. For applications in which it is essential to maintain logarithmic access time at all times, AVL trees provide nearly perfect balance at a slight cost in computer time and space but with considerable programming cost.

5. Binary trees are defined recursively; algorithms for manipulating binary trees are usually best written recursively. In programming with binary trees, be aware of the problems generally associated with recursive algorithms. Be sure that your algorithm terminates under any condition and that it correctly treats the trivial case of an empty tree.

6. Although binary trees are usually implemented as linked structures, remain aware of the possibility of other implementations. In programming with linked binary trees, keep in mind the pitfalls attendant on all programming with linked lists.

7. Priority queues are important for many applications, and heaps provide an excellent implementation of priority queues.

8. Heapsort is like an insurance policy: It is usually slower than quicksort, but it guarantees that sorting will be completed in $O(n \log n)$ comparisons of keys, as quicksort cannot always do.

REVIEW QUESTIONS

9.1

1. Define the term *binary tree*.

2. Define the term *binary search tree*.

3. What is the difference between a binary tree and an ordinary tree in which each vertex has at most two branches?

9.2

4. If a binary search tree with *n* nodes is well balanced, what is the approximate number of comparisons of keys needed to find a target? What is the number if the tree degenerates to a chain?

9.3

5. Give the order of visiting the vertices of each of the following binary trees under **(1)** preorder, **(2)** inorder, and **(3)** postorder traversal.

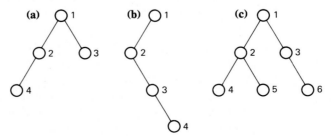

6. Draw the expression trees for each of the following expressions, and show the result of traversing the tree in (1) preorder, (2) inorder, and (3) postorder.
   (a) $a - b$.
   (b) $n!/m!$.
   (c) $\log m!$.
   (d) $(\log x) + (\log y)$.
   (e) $x \times y \leq x + y$.
   (f) $a > b$ or $b \geq a$.

9.4

7. In twenty words or less explain how treesort works.

8. What is the relationship between treesort and quicksort?

9. What causes deletion from a search tree to be more difficult than insertion into a search tree?

9.5

10. When is the algorithm for building a binary search tree developed in Section 9.5 useful, and why is it preferable to simply using the procedure for inserting an item into a search tree for each item in the input?

11. How much slower, on average, is searching a random binary search tree than is searching a completely balanced binary search tree?

9.6

12. What is the purpose for AVL trees?

13. What condition defines an AVL tree among all binary search trees?

14. Draw a picture explaining how balance is restored when an insertion into an AVL tree puts a node out of balance.

15. How does the worst-case performance of an AVL tree compare with the worst-case performance of a random binary search tree? With its average-case performance? How does the average-case performance of an AVL tree compare with that of a random binary search tree?

9.7

16. What is a heap?

17. How does heapsort work?

18. Compare the worst-case performance of heapsort with the worst-case performance of quicksort, and compare it also with the average-case performance of quicksort.

19. What is a priority queue?

20. Give three possible implementations of priority queues, and give the approximate number of key comparisons needed, on average, for insertion and deletion in each implementation.

REFERENCES FOR FURTHER STUDY

The most comprehensive source of information on binary trees is the series of books by KNUTH. The properties of binary trees, other classes of trees, traversal, path length, and history, altogether occupy pp. 305–405 of Volume 1. Volume 3, pp. 442–480, discusses binary search trees, AVL trees, and related topics. Heapsort is discussed in pp. 145–149 of Volume 3. The proof of Theorem 9.2 is from Volume 3, p. 427.

An alternative study of binary trees, with Pascal programs presented in detail, is

N. WIRTH, *Algorithms + Data Structures = Programs,* Prentice-Hall, Englewood Cliffs, N.J., 1976.

This book also contains (pp. 189–264) an exposition, with Pascal algorithms, of binary trees, balancing methods, and generalizations, including (pp. 215–226) algorithms for insertion and deletion in AVL trees.

A mathematical analysis of the behavior of AVL trees appears in

E. M. REINGOLD, J. NIEVERGELT, and N. DEO, *Combinatorial Algorithms: Theory and Practice,* Prentice-Hall, Englewood Cliffs, N.J., 1977.

The original reference for AVL trees is

G. M. ADEL'SON-VEL'SKIĬ and E. M. LANDIS, *Dokl. Akad. Nauk SSSR* 146 (1962), 263–266; English translation: *Soviet Math. (Dokl.)* 3 (1962), 1259–1263.

Heapsort was discovered and so named by

J. W. J. WILLIAMS, *Communications of the ACM* 7 (1964), 347–348.

Several algorithms for constructing a balanced binary search tree are discussed in

HSI CHANG and S. S. IYENGAR, "Efficient algorithms to globally balance a binary search tree," *Communications of the ACM* 27 (1984), 695–702.

A simple but complete development of algorithms for heaps and priority queues appears in one of the regular columns:

JON BENTLEY, "Programming pearls: Thanks, heaps," *Communications of the ACM* 28 (1985), 245–250.

Trees and Graphs

▶ *This chapter continues the study of trees as data structures, now concentrating on trees with more than two branches at each node. We then turn to algorithms for graphs, which are more general structures that include trees as a special case. Each of the major sections of this chapter is independent of the others and can be studied separately.*

10.1 ORCHARDS, TREES, AND BINARY TREES

Binary trees, as we have seen, are a powerful and elegant form of data structures. Even so, the restriction to no more than two children at each node is severe, and there are many possible applications for trees as data structures where the number of children of a node can be arbitrary. This section elucidates a pleasant and helpful surprise: Binary trees provide a convenient way to represent what first appears to be a far broader class of trees.

10.1.1 On the Classification of Species

free tree

Since we have already sighted several kinds of trees in the applications we have studied, we should, before exploring further, put our gear in order by settling the definitions. In mathematics, the term *tree* has a quite broad meaning: It is any set of points (called vertices) and any set of pairs of distinct vertices (called edges or branches) such that (1) there is a sequence of edges (a path) from any vertex to any other, and (2) there are no circuits, that is, no paths starting from a vertex and returning to the same vertex.

In computer applications we usually do not need to study trees in such generality, and when we do, for emphasis we call them *free trees*. Our trees are almost always tied down by having one particular vertex singled out as the *root,* and for emphasis we call such a tree a *rooted tree.*

rooted tree

A rooted tree can be drawn in our usual way by picking it up by its root and shaking it so that all the branches and other vertices hang downward, with the leaves at the bottom. Even so, rooted trees still do not have all the structure that we usually use. In a rooted tree there is still no way to tell left from right, or, when one vertex has several children, to tell which is first, second, and so on. If for no other reason, the restraint of sequential execution of instructions (not to mention sequential organization of storage) usually imposes an order on the children of each vertex. Hence we

ordered tree

define an *ordered tree* to be a rooted tree in which the children of each vertex are assigned an order.

Note that ordered trees for which no vertex has more than two children are still not the same class as binary trees. If a vertex in a binary tree has only one child, then it could be either on the left side or on the right side, and the two resulting binary trees are different, but both would be the same as ordered trees.

2-tree

As a final remark related to the definitions, let us note that the 2-trees that we studied as part of algorithm analysis are rooted trees (but not necessarily ordered trees) with the property that every vertex has either 0 or 2 children. Thus 2-trees do not coincide with any of the other classes we have introduced.

Figure 10.1 shows what happens for the various kinds of trees with a small number of vertices. Note that each class of trees after the first can be obtained by taking the trees from the previous class and distinguishing those that differ under the new criterion. Compare the list of five ordered trees with four vertices with the list of fourteen binary trees with four vertices constructed as an exercise in Section 9.4. You will find that, again, the binary trees can be obtained from the appropriate ordered trees by distinguishing a left branch from a right branch.

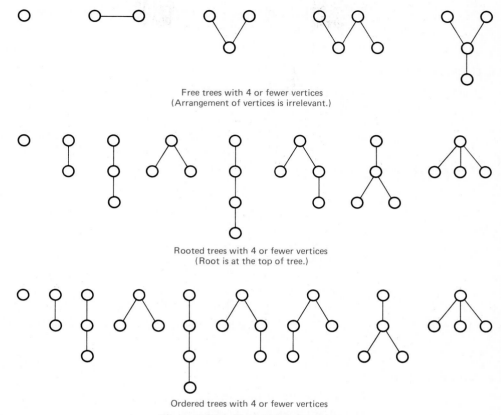

Free trees with 4 or fewer vertices
(Arrangement of vertices is irrelevant.)

Rooted trees with 4 or fewer vertices
(Root is at the top of tree.)

Ordered trees with 4 or fewer vertices

Figure 10.1.   Various kinds of trees

10.1.2 Ordered Trees

1. Computer Implementation

If we wish to use an ordered tree as a data structure, the obvious way to implement it in computer memory would be to extend the standard way to implement a binary tree, keeping as many fields in each node as there may be subtrees, in place of the two links needed for binary trees. Thus in a tree where some nodes have as many as ten subtrees, we would keep ten link fields in each node. But this will result in a great many of the link fields being **nil**. In fact, we can easily determine exactly how many. If the tree has n nodes and each node has k link fields, then there are $n \times k$ links altogether. There is exactly one link that points to each of the $n - 1$ nodes other than the root, so the proportion of **nil** links must be

multiple links

$$\frac{(n \times k) - (n - 1)}{n \times k} > 1 - \frac{1}{k}.$$

Hence if a vertex might have ten subtrees, then more than ninety percent of the links will be **nil**. Clearly, this method of representing ordered trees is very wasteful of space. The reason is that, for each node, we are maintaining a contiguous list of links to all its children, and these contiguous lists reserve much unused space. We now investigate a way that replaces these contiguous lists with linked lists and leads to an elegant connection with binary trees.

2. Linked Implementation

To keep the children of each node in a linked list, we shall need two kinds of links. First comes the header for each such list; this will be a link from each node to its leftmost child, which we may call firstchild. Second, each node except the root will appear in one of these lists, and hence requires a link to the next node on the list, that is, to the next child of the parent. We may call this second link nextchild. This implementation is illustrated in Figure 10.2.

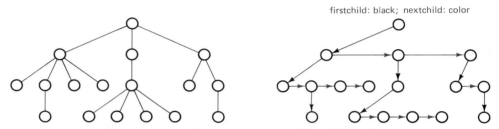

Figure 10.2.   Linked implementation of an ordered tree

3. The Natural Correspondence

For each node of the ordered tree we have defined two links (that will be **nil** if not otherwise defined), firstchild and nextchild. By using these two links we now have the structure of a binary tree; that is, the linked implementation of an ordered tree is a linked binary tree. If we wish, we can even form a better picture of a binary tree by taking the linked implementation of the ordered tree and rotating it a few degrees clockwise, so that downward (firstchild) links point leftward and the horizontal (nextchild) links point downward and to the right.

4. Inverse Correspondence

Suppose that we reverse the steps of the preceding process, by beginning with a binary tree and trying to recover an ordered tree. The first observation that we must make is that not every binary tree is obtained from a rooted tree by the above process: Since the nextchild link of the root is always **nil**, the root of the corresponding binary tree will always have an empty right subtree. To study the inverse correspondence more carefully, we must consider another class of structures.

10.1.3 Forests and Orchards

In our work so far with binary trees we have profited from using recursion, and for other classes of trees we shall continue to do so. Employing recursion means reducing a problem to a smaller one. Hence we should see what happens if we take a rooted tree or an ordered tree and strip off the root. What is then left is (if not empty) a set of rooted trees or an ordered set of ordered trees, respectively.

forest

The standard term for an arbitrary set of trees is *forest,* but when we use this term, we generally assume that the trees are rooted. The phrase *ordered forest* is sometimes used for an ordered set of ordered trees, but we shall adopt the equally descriptive (and more colorful) term *orchard* for this class. (Although this term is not yet in common use, perhaps it will soon become standard.)

orchard

Note that not only can we obtain a forest or an orchard by removing the root from a rooted tree or an ordered tree, respectively, but we can build a rooted or an ordered tree by starting with a forest or an orchard, attaching a new vertex at the top, and adding branches from the new vertex (which will be the root) to the roots of all trees in the forest or the orchard.

recursive definitions

We shall use this observation to give a new, recursive definition of ordered trees and orchards, one that yields a formal proof of the connection with binary trees. First, let us consider how to start. Recall that it is possible that a binary tree be empty; that is, it may have no vertices. It is also possible that a forest or an orchard be empty; that is, that it contain no trees. It is however, not possible that a rooted or an ordered tree be empty, since it is guaranteed to contain a root, at least. If we wish to start building trees and forests, we can note that the tree with only one vertex is obtained by attaching a new root to an empty forest. Once we have this tree, we can make a forest consisting of as many one-vertex trees as we wish and attach a new root to build all rooted trees of height 1. In this way we can continue to construct all the rooted trees in turn in accordance with the following mutually recursive definitions.

DEFINITION

> A *rooted tree* consists of a single vertex v, called the *root* of the tree, together with a forest F, whose trees are called the *subtrees* of the root.
>
> A *forest* F is a (possibly empty) set of rooted trees.

A similar construction works for ordered trees and orchards.

DEFINITION

> An *ordered tree* T consists of a single vertex v, called the *root* of the tree, together with an orchard O, whose trees are called the *subtrees* of the root v. We may denote the ordered tree with the ordered pair
>
> $$T = \{v, O\}.$$
>
> An *orchard* O is either the empty set $\varnothing$, or consists of an ordered tree T, called the *first tree* of the orchard, together with another orchard O' (which contains the remaining trees of the orchard). We may denote the orchard with the ordered pair
>
> $$O = (T, O').$$

Notice how the ordering of trees is implicit in the definition of orchard. A non-empty orchard contains a first tree, and the remaining trees form another orchard, which again has a first tree, which is the second tree of the original orchard. Continuing to examine the remaining orchard yields the third tree, and so on, until the remaining orchard is the empty one.

10.1.4 The Formal Correspondence

We can now obtain the principal result of this section.

THEOREM 10.1

> *Let S be any finite set of vertices. There is a one-to-one correspondence f from the set of orchards whose set of vertices is S to the set of binary trees whose set of vertices is S.*

PROOF

Let us use the notation introduced in the definitions to prove the theorem. First, we need a similar notation for binary trees: A binary tree B is either the empty set $\emptyset$ or consists of a root vertex v with two binary trees B_1 and B_2. We may thus denote a binary tree with the ordered triple

$$B = [v, B_1, B_2].$$

We shall prove the theorem by mathematical induction on the number of vertices in S. The first case to consider is the empty orchard $\emptyset$, which will correspond to the empty binary tree:

$$f(\emptyset) = \emptyset.$$

If the orchard O is not empty, then it is denoted by the ordered pair

$$O = (T, O_2)$$

where T is an ordered tree and O_2 another orchard. The ordered tree T is denoted as the pair

$$T = \{v, O_1\}$$

where v is a vertex and O_1 is another orchard. We substitute this expression for T in the first expression, obtaining

$$O = (\{v, O_1\}, O_2).$$

By the induction hypothesis f provides a one-to-one correspondence from orchards with fewer vertices than in S to binary trees, and O_1 and O_2 are smaller than O, so the binary trees $f(O_1)$ and $f(O_2)$ are determined by induction hypothesis. We define the correspondence f from the orchard O to a binary tree by

$$f(\{v, O_1\}, O_2) = [v, f(O_1), f(O_2)].$$

It is now obvious that the function f is a one-to-one correspondence between orchards and binary trees with the same vertices. For any way to fill in the sumbols v, O_1, and O_2 on the left side, there is exactly one way to fill in the same symbols on the right, and vice versa.

end of proof

10.1.5 Rotations

We can also use this notational form of the correspondence to help us form the picture of the transformation from orchard to binary tree. In the binary tree $[v, f(O_1), f(O_2)]$ the left link from v goes to the root of the binary tree $f(O_1)$, which in fact was the first child of v in the ordered tree $\{v, O_1\}$. The right link from v goes to the vertex that was formerly the root of the next ordered tree to the right. That is, "left link" in the binary tree corresponds to "first child" in an ordered tree, and "right link" corresponds to "next sibling." In geometrical terms the transformation reduces to the rules:

1. Draw the orchard so that the first child of each vertex is immediately below the vertex, rather than centering the children below the vertex.
2. Draw a vertical link from each vertex to its first child, and draw a horizontal link from each vertex to its next sibling.
3. Remove the remaining original links.
4. Rotate the diagram 45 degrees clockwise, so that the vertical links appear as left links and the horizontal links as right links.

This process is illustrated in Figure 10.3.

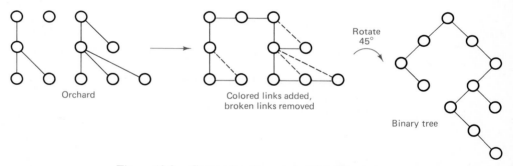

Orchard   Colored links added,   Rotate 45°   Binary tree
broken links removed

Figure 10.3.   Conversion from orchard to binary tree

10.1.6 Summary

We have seen three ways to describe the correspondence between orchards and binary trees:

▶   firstchild and nextchild links,

▶   rotations of diagrams,

▶   formal notational equivalence.

Most people find the second way, rotation of diagrams, the easiest to remember and to picture. It is the first way, setting up links to give the correspondence, that is usually needed in actually writing computer programs. The third way, the formal correspondence, finally, is the one that proves most useful in constructing proofs of various properties of binary trees and orchards.

Exercises
10.1

E1. Convert each of the following orchards into a binary tree.

(a)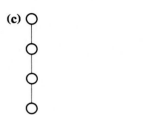

(b)

(c)

(d)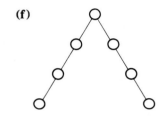

(e)

(f)

(g)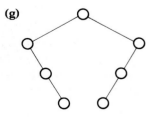

(h)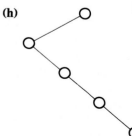

E2. Convert each of the following binary trees into an orchard.

(a) ○

(b)

(c)

(d)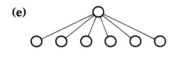

(e)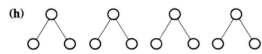

(f)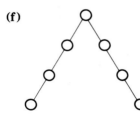

(g)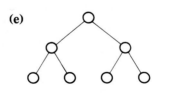

(h)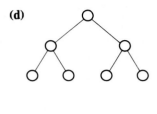

E3. Draw all the **(a)** free trees, **(b)** rooted trees, and **(c)** ordered trees with five vertices.

E4. We can define the *preorder traversal* of an orchard as follows. If the orchard is empty, do nothing. Otherwise, first visit the root of the first tree, then traverse the orchard of subtrees of the first tree in preorder, and then traverse the orchard of remaining trees in preorder. Prove that preorder traversal of an orchard and preorder traversal of the corresponding binary tree will visit the vertices in the same order.

E5. We can define the *inorder traversal* of an orchard as follows. If the orchard is empty, do nothing. Otherwise, first traverse the orchard of subtrees of the first tree's root in inorder, then visit the root of the first tree, and then traverse the orchard of remaining subtrees in inorder. Prove that inorder traversal of an orchard and inorder traversal of the corresponding binary tree will visit the vertices in the same order.

E6. Describe a way of traversing an orchard that will visit the vertices in the same order as postorder traversal of the corresponding binary tree. Prove that your traversal method visits the vertices in the correct order.

10.2 LEXICOGRAPHIC SEARCH TREES: TRIES

multiway branching

Several times in previous chapters we have contrasted searching a list with looking up an entry in a table. We can apply the idea of table lookup to information retrieval from a tree by using a key or part of a key to make a multiway branch.

Instead of searching by comparisons of entire keys, we can consider a key as a sequence of characters (letters or digits, for example), and use these characters to determine a multiway branch at each step. If our keys are alphabetic names, then we make a 26-way branch according to the first letter of the name, followed by another branch according to the second letter, and so on. This multiway branching is the idea of a thumb index in a dictionary. A thumb index, however, is generally used only to find the words with a given initial letter; some other search method is then used to continue. In a computer we can proceed two or three levels by multiway branching, but then the tree will become too large, and we shall need to resort to some other device to continue.

10.2.1 Tries

One method is to prune from the tree all the branches that do not lead to any key. In English, for example, there are no words that begin with the letters 'bb', 'bc', 'bf', 'bg', . . . , but there are words beginning 'ba', 'bd', or 'be'. Hence all the corresponding branches and nodes can be removed from the tree. The resulting tree is called a *trie*. (This term originated as letters extracted from the word *retrieval,* but is usually pronounced like the word "try.")

A trie of order m can be defined formally as being either empty or consisting of an ordered sequence of exactly m tries of order m.

10.2.2 Searching for a Key

A trie describing the words (as listed in the *Oxford English Dictionary*) made up only from the letters *a*, *b*, and *c* is shown in Figure 10.4. Along with the branches to the next level of the trie, each node contains a pointer to a record of information about the key, if any, that has been found when the node is reached. The search for a particular key begins at the root. The first letter of the key is used as an index to determine which branch to take. An empty branch means that the key being sought is not in the tree. Otherwise, we use the second letter of the key to determine the branch at the next level, and so continue. When we reach the end of the word, the information pointer directs us to the desired information. A **nil** information pointer shows that the string is not a word in the trie. Note, therefore, that

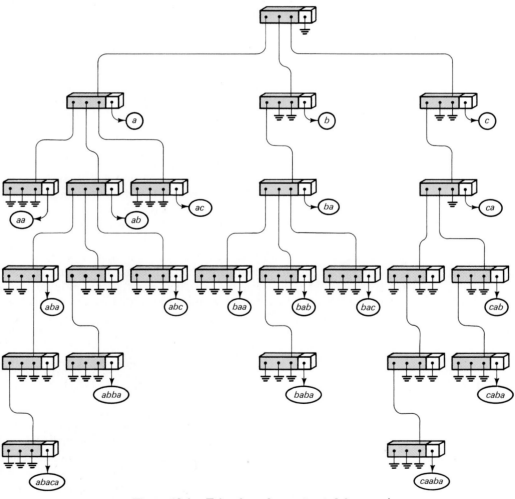

Figure 10.4. Trie of words constructed from *a*, *b*, *c*

the word *a* is a prefix of the word *aba*, which is a prefix of the word *abaca*. On the other hand, the string *abac* is not an English word, and therefore has a **nil** information pointer.

10.2.3 Pascal Algorithm

The search process just described translates easily into a procedure. First, we need some declarations.

trie declaration

```
type
  letter  = 'a' .. 'z';
  key     = array[1 .. maxlength] of char;          {contains only ' ' and 'a' .. 'z'}
  pointer = ↑node;
  node    = record
              branch: array[letter] of pointer;
              info: keyinfo
            end;
```

The constant maxlength giving the maximum length of a key and the pointer type keyinfo bound to some type that contains the desired information for each key are assumed to be declared elsewhere. We shall assume that all keys contain only lowercase letters and blanks and that a key is terminated by the first blank it contains. The searching method then becomes the following procedure.

trie retrieval

```
procedure TrieSearch(root: pointer; target: key; var p: pointer);
{Root points to the root of a trie; at the conclusion, p will point to the trie record
    that points to the information record for the target if the search is successful;
    p will be nil if the search is unsuccessful.}
var
  i: integer;
begin                                               {procedure TrieSearch}
  p := root;
  i := 1;
  while (i <= maxlength) and (p <> nil) do
    if target[i] = ' ' then
      i := maxlength + 1                {terminates search for a blank in target}
                              {p is left pointing to the node with information for target.}
    else begin
      p := p↑.branch[target[i]]; {Move down the appropriate branch of the trie.}
      i := i + 1                          {Move to the next character of the target.}
    end;
  if p <> nil then if p↑.info = nil then p := nil
end;                                                {procedure TrieSearch}
```

The termination condition for the loop is made more complicated to avoid an index error after an iteration with i = maxlength. At the conclusion, p (if not **nil**) points to the node in the trie corresponding to the target. The information field can then be obtained from p↑.info.

10.2.4 Insertion into a Trie

Adding a new key to a trie is quite similar to searching for the key: We must trace our way down the trie to the appropriate point and set the info pointer to the information record for the new key. If, on the way, we hit a **nil** branch in the trie, we must now not terminate the search, but instead we must add new nodes to the trie so as to complete the path corresponding to the new key. We thereby obtain the following procedure.

trie insertion

```
procedure InsertTrie(var root: pointer; k: key; info: keyinfo);
var
    i: integer;
    p: pointer;
    ch: letter;
begin                                                    {procedure InsertTrie}
    if root = nil then                       {Create a new trie with all empty subtries.}
    begin
        new(root);
        for ch := 'a' to 'z' do
            root↑.branch[ch] := nil;
        root↑.info := nil
    end;
    p := root;                                       {Start a search down the trie.}
    i := 1;
    while i <= maxlength do
        if k[i] = ' ' then              {Terminate the search for a blank in the target.}
            i := maxlength + 1
        else begin
            if p↑.branch[k[i]] <> nil then        {Move down the appropriate branch.}
                p := p↑.branch[k[i]]
            else begin                    {Make a new node on the route for key k.}
                new(p↑.branch[k[i]]);
                p := p↑.branch[k[i]];
                for ch := 'a' to 'z' do
                    p↑.branch[ch] := nil;
                p↑.info := nil
            end;
            i := i + 1                           {Continue to the next character in k.}
        end;
                    {At this point, we have tested for all nonblank characters of k.}
    if p↑.info <> nil then
        Error                                    {k duplicates a key already in the trie.}
    else
        p↑.info := info
end;                                                     {procedure InsertTrie}
```

10.2.5 Deletion from a Trie

The same general plan used for searching and insertion also works for deletion from a trie. We trace down the path corresponding to the key being deleted, and when we reach the appropriate node, we set the corresponding info field to **nil**. If now, however, this node has all its fields **nil** (all branches and the info field), then we should dispose of this node. To do so, we can set up a stack of pointers to the nodes on the path from the root to the last node reached. Alternatively, we can use recursion in the deletion algorithm and avoid the need for an explicit stack. In either case, we shall leave the programming as an exercise.

10.2.6 Assessment of Tries

The number of steps required to search a trie (or insert into it) is proportional to the number of characters making up a key, not to a logarithm of the number of keys, as in other tree-based searches. If this number of characters is small relative to the (base 2) logarithm of the number of keys, then a trie may prove superior to a binary tree. If, for example, the keys consist of all possible sequences of five letters, then the trie can locate any of $n = 26^5 = 11,881,376$ keys in 5 iterations, whereas the best that binary search can do is $\lg n \approx 23.5$ key comparisons.

comparison with binary search

In many applications, however, the number of characters in a key is larger, and the set of keys that actually occur is sparse in the set of all possible keys. In these applications the number of iterations required to search a trie may very well exceed the number of key comparisons needed for a binary search.

The best solution, finally, may be to combine the methods. A trie can be used for the first few characters of the key, and then another method can be employed for the remainder of the key. If we return to the example of the thumb index in a dictionary, we see that, in fact, we use a multiway tree to locate the first letter of the word, but we then use some other search method to locate the desired word among those with the same first letter.

Exercises 10.2

E1. Draw the tries constructed from each of the following sets of keys.

    (a) All three-digit integers containing only 1, 2, 3 in decimal representation.

    (b) All three-letter sequences built from a, b, c, d where the first letter is a.

    (c) All four-digit binary integers (built from 0 and 1).

    (d) The words

        pal   lap   a   papa   al   papal   all   ball   lab

    built from the letters a, b, l, p.

E2. Write a procedure that will traverse a trie and print out all its words in alphabetical order.

E3. Write a procedure that will traverse a trie and print out all its words, with the order determined first by the length of the word, with shorter words first, and, second, by alphabetical order for words of the same length.

E4. Write a procedure that will delete a word from a trie.

P1. Run the insertion, search, and deletion procedures for appropriate test data, and compare the results with similar experiments for binary search trees.

10.3 EXTERNAL SEARCHING: B-TREES

In our work throughout this book we have assumed that all our data structures are kept in high-speed memory; that is, we have considered only *internal* information retrieval. For many applications, this assumption is reasonable, but for many other important applications, it is not. Let us now turn briefly to the problem of *external* information retrieval, where we wish to locate and retrieve records stored in a disk file.

10.3.1 Access Time

The time required to access and retrieve a word from high-speed memory is a few microseconds at most. The time required to locate a particular record on a disk is measured in milliseconds, and for floppy disks can exceed a second. Hence the time required for a single access is thousands of times greater for external retrieval than for internal retrieval. On the other hand, when a record is located on a disk, the normal practice is not to read only one word, but to read in a large *page* or *block* of information at once. Typical sizes for blocks range from 256 to 1024 characters or words.

Our goal in external searching must be to minimize the number of disk accesses, since each access takes so long compared to internal computation. With each access, however, we obtain a block that may have room for several records. Using these records, we may be able to make a multiway decision concerning which block to access next. Hence multiway trees are especially appropriate for external searching.

10.3.2 Multiway Search Trees

Binary search trees generalize directly to multiway search trees in which, for some integer m called the *order* of the tree, each node has at most m children. If $k \leq m$ is the number of children, then the node contains exactly $k - 1$ keys, which partition all the keys into k subsets. If some of these subsets are empty, then the corresponding children in the tree are empty. Figure 10.5 shows a 5-way search tree in which some of the children of some nodes are empty.

10.3.3 Balanced Multiway Trees

Our goal is to devise a multiway search tree that will minimize file accesses; hence we wish to make the height of the tree as small as possible. We can accomplish this by insisting, first, that no empty subtrees appear above the leaves (so that the division of keys into subsets is as efficient as possible); second, that all leaves be on

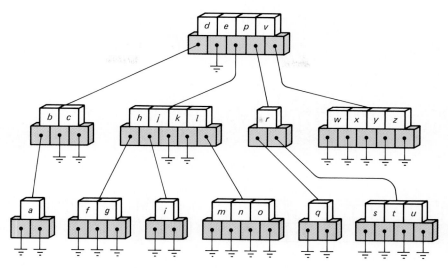

Figure 10.5.   A 5-way search tree

the same level (so that searches will all be guaranteed to terminate with about the same number of accesses); and, third, that every node (except the leaves) have at least some minimal number of children. We shall require that each node (except the leaves) have at least half as many children as the maximum possible. These conditions lead to the following formal definition.

DEFINITION

A **B-tree of order** m is an m-way tree in which

1. All leaves are on the same level.
2. All internal nodes except the root have at most m (nonempty) children, and at least $\lceil m/2 \rceil$ (nonempty) children.
3. The number of keys in each internal node is one less than the number of its children, and these keys partition the keys in the children in the fashion of a search tree.
4. The root has at most m children, but may have as few as 2 if it is not a leaf, or none if the tree consists of the root alone.

The tree in Figure 10.5 is not a B-tree, since some nodes have empty children, and the leaves are not all on the same level. Figure 10.6 shows a B-tree of order 5 whose keys are the 26 letters of the alphabet.

10.3.4 Insertion into a B-Tree

The condition that all leaves be on the same level forces a characteristic behavior of B-trees: In constrast to binary search trees, B-trees are not allowed to grow at their leaves; instead, they are forced to grow at the root. The general method of

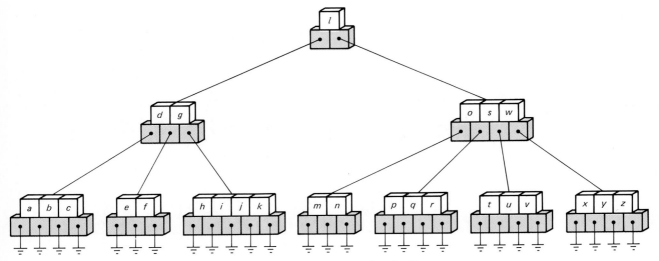

Figure 10.6.   A B-tree of order 5

method

insertion is as follows. First, a search is made to see if the new key is in the tree. This search (if the key is truly new) will terminate in failure at a leaf. The new key is then added to the leaf node. If the node was not previously full, then the insertion is finished. When a key is added to a full node, then the node splits into two nodes on the same level, except that the median key is not put into either of the two new nodes, but is instead sent up the tree to be inserted into the parent node. When a search is later made through the tree, therefore, a comparison with the median key will serve to direct the search into the proper subtree. When a key is added to a full root, then the root splits in two and the median key sent upward becomes a new root.

This process is greatly elucidated by studying an example such as the growth of the B-tree of order 5 shown in Figure 10.7. We shall insert the keys

$$a\ g\ f\ b\ k\ d\ h\ m\ j\ e\ s\ i\ r\ x\ c\ l\ n\ t\ u\ p$$

into an initially empty tree, in the order given.

node splitting

The first four keys will be inserted into one node, as shown in the first diagram of Figure 10.7. They are sorted into the proper order as they are inserted. There is no room, however, for the fifth key, k, so its insertion causes the node to split into two, and the median key, $f,$ moves up to enter a new node, which is a new root. Since the split nodes are now only half full, the next three keys can be inserted without difficulty. Note, however, that these simple insertions can require rearrangement of the keys within a node. The next insertion, j, again splits a node, and this time it is j itself that is the median key, and therefore moves up to join f in the root.

upward propagation

The next several insertions proceed similarly. The final insertion, that of p, is more interesting. This insertion first splits the node originally containing $k\ l\ m\ n$, sending the median key m upward into the node containing $c\ f\ j\ r$, which is, however, already full. Hence this node in turn splits, and a new root containing j is created.

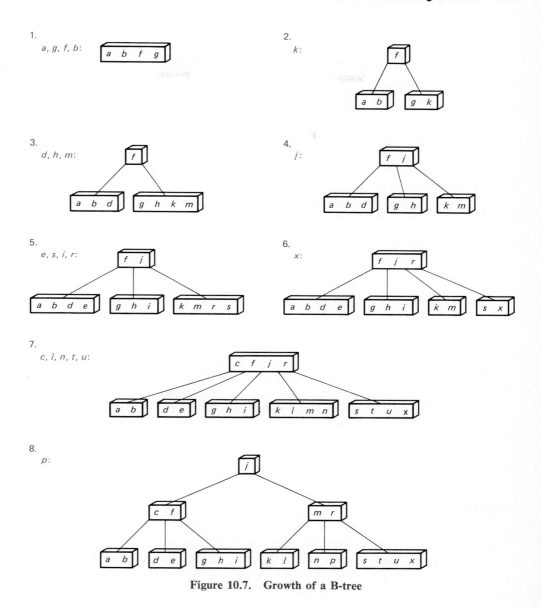

Figure 10.7.   Growth of a B-tree

improving balance

Two comments regarding the growth of B-trees are in order. First, when a node splits, it produces two nodes that are now only half full. Later insertions, therefore, can more likely be made without need to split nodes again. Hence one splitting prepares the way for several simple insertions. Second, it is always a median key that is sent upward, not necessarily the key being inserted. Hence repeated insertions tend to improve the balance of the tree, no matter in what order the keys happen to arrive.

10.3.5 Pascal Algorithms: Searching and Insertion

To develop Pascal algorithms for searching and insertion in a B-tree, let us begin with the declarations needed to set up a B-tree. For simplicity we shall construct our B-tree entirely in high-speed memory, using Pascal pointers to describe its structure. In most applications, these pointers would be replaced by the addresses of various blocks or pages on a disk, and taking a pointer reference would become making a disk access. We shall also construct our tree from keys alone; in any practical application each key would be associated with other information.

1. Declarations

We assume that keytype is defined already. Within one node there will be a list of keys and a list of pointers to the children of the node. Since these lists are short, we shall, for simplicity, use contiguous arrays and a separate variable count for their representation.

B-tree implementation

```
const
  max = 4;                  {maximum number of keys in a node; max = m − 1}
  min = 2;                  {minimum number of keys in a node; min = ⌈ ½m ⌉ − 1}
type
  pointer = ↑node;
  position = 0 .. max;
  node = record
    count: position;              {Except for the root, the lower limit is min.}
    key: array[1 .. max] of keytype;
    branch: array[position] of pointer
  end;
```

The way in which the indices are arranged implies that in some of our algorithms we shall need to investigate branch[0] separately, and then consider each key in association with the branch on its right.

2. Searching

As a simple first example we write a procedure to search through a B-tree for a target key. The input parameters for the procedure are the target key and a pointer to the root of the B-tree. The first output parameter is a Boolean variable found that indicates if the target was found in the tree. If the target is found, then the second output parameter points to the node where the target was found, and the third parameter is the position of the target within that node. The general method of searching by working our way down through the tree is similar to a search through a binary search tree. In a multiway tree, however, we must examine each node more extensively to find which branch to take at the next step. This examination is done by the auxiliary procedure SearchNode that returns output parameters found and targetpos, which is the position of the target if found, and otherwise is the number of the branch on which to continue the search.

B-tree retrieval

```
procedure Search(target: keytype; root: pointer;
    var found: Boolean; var targetnode: pointer; var targetpos: position);
begin                                              {procedure Search}
  if root = nil then
    found:= false
  else begin
    SearchNode(target, root, found, targetpos);
    if found then
      targetnode := root
    else
      Search(target, root↑.branch[targetpos], found, targetnode, targetpos)
  end
end;                                               {procedure Search}
```

This procedure has been written recursively to exhibit the similarity of its structure to that of the insertion procedure to be developed shortly. The recursion is tail recursion, however, and can easily be replaced by iteration if desired.

3. Searching a Node

This procedure determines if the target is in the current node, and, if not, finds which of the count + 1 branches will contain the target key. For convenience, the possibility of taking branch 0 is considered separately, and then a sequential search is made through the remaining possibilities.

sequential search

```
procedure SearchNode(target: keytype; p: pointer; var found: Boolean;
                                              var k: position);
{searches keys in node p↑ for target; returns location k of target, or branch on
    which to continue search}
begin                                              {procedure SearchNode}
  with p↑ do
    if target < key[1] then
    begin                                          {Take the leftmost branch.}
      found := false;
      k := 0
    end
    else begin                    {Start a sequential search through the keys.}
      k := count;
      while (target < key[k]) and (k > 1) do
        k := k − 1;
      found := (target = key[k])
    end
end;                                               {procedure SearchNode}
```

For B-trees of large order, this procedure should be modified to use binary search.

4. Insertion: The Main Procedure

Insertion can be most naturally formulated as a recursive procedure, since after insertion in a subtree has been completed, a (median) key may remain that must be reinserted higher in the tree. Recursion allows us to keep track of the position within the tree and work our way back up the tree without need for an explicit auxiliary stack.

parameters

We shall assume that the key being inserted is not already in the tree. The insertion procedure then needs only two parameters: newkey, the key being inserted, and root, the root of the B-tree. For the recursion, we need three additional output parameters. The first of these is the Boolean variable pushup, which indicates whether the root of the subtree has split into two, also producing a (median) key to be reinserted higher in the tree. When this happens, we shall adopt the convention that the old root node contains the left half of the keys and a new node contains the right half of the keys. When a split occurs, the second output parameter x is the median key, and the third parameter xr is a pointer to the new node, the right half of the former root p↑ of the subtree.

To keep all these parameters straight, we shall do the recursion in a procedure called PushDown. This situation is illustrated in Figure 10.8.

The recursion is started by the main procedure Insert. If the outermost call to procedure PushDown should return with pushup true, then there is a key to be placed in a new root, and the height of the entire tree will increase. The main procedure appears as follows.

B-tree insertion: main procedure

```
procedure Insert(newkey: keytype; var root: pointer);
   {inserts newkey into the B-tree with the given root; requires that newkey is not
       already present in the tree}

   var
      pushup:        Boolean;          {Has the height of the tree increased?}
      x:             keytype;          {node to be reinserted as new root}
      xr,                              {subtree on right of x}
      p:             pointer;          {pointer for temporary use}
   begin                              {procedure Insert}
      PushDown(newkey, root, pushup, x, xr);
      if pushup then                   {Tree grows in height.}
      begin                            {Make a new root.}
         new(p);
         with p↑ do
         begin
            count := 1;
            key[1] := x;
            branch[0] := root;
            branch[1] := xr;
            root := p
         end                           {with statement}
      end                              {making new root}
   end;                               {procedure Insert}
```

new root

5. Recursive Insertion into a Subtree

Next we turn to the recursive procedure PushDown. In a B-tree, a new key is first inserted into a leaf. We shall thus use the conditon p = **nil** to terminate the recursion; that is, we shall continue to move down the tree searching for newkey until we hit an empty subtree. Since the B-tree does not grow by adding new leaves, we do not then immediately insert target, but instead set pushup true and send the key back up (now called x) for insertion.

When a recursive call returns and pushup is true, then we attempt to insert the key x in the current node. If there is room, then we are finished. Otherwise, the current node p↑ splits into p↑ and xr↑ and a (possibly different) median key x is sent up the tree. The procedure uses three auxiliary procedures: SearchNode (same as before); PushIn puts the key x into node p↑ provided that there is room; and Split chops a full node p↑ into two.

found the leaf where key goes

return from recursion

insert into node

split node

```
procedure PushDown(newkey: keytype; p: pointer; var pushup: Boolean;
                                          var x: keytype; var xr: pointer);
var
    k:      position;                {branch on which to continue the search}
    found:  Boolean;                 {Is newkey already in the tree (error)?}
begin                                                     {procedure PushDown}
  if p = nil then
  begin                 {cannot insert into empty tree; recursion terminates}
    pushup := true;
    x := newkey;
    xr := nil
  end
  else begin                                          {Search the current node.}
    SearchNode(newkey, p, found, k);
    if found then
      writeln('Error: inserting duplicate key');
    PushDown(newkey, p↑.branch[k], pushup, x, xr);
    if pushup then                                 {Reinsert the median key x.}
    with p↑ do
      if count < max then
      begin
        pushup := false;
        PushIn(x, xr, p, k)
      end
      else begin
        pushup := true;
        Split(x, xr, p, k, x, xr)
      end
  end
end;                                                      {procedure PushDown}
```

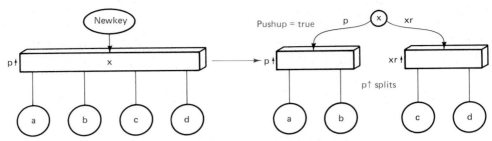

Figure 10.8.   Action of PushDown **procedure**

6. Insert a Key into a Node

The next procedure inserts the key x and its right-hand pointer xr into the node p↑. The procedure is called only when there is room for the insertion.

```
procedure PushIn(x: keytype; xr, p: pointer; k: position);
{inserts key x and pointer xr into node p↑ at position k; requires that the node
    was not previously full}
var
   i: position;                              {index to move keys to make room for x}
begin                                                        {procedure PushIn}
   with p↑ do begin
     for i := count downto k + 1 do
     begin                                 {Shift all the keys and branches to the right.}
       key[i + 1] := key[i];
       branch[i + 1] := branch[i]
     end;
     key[k + 1] := x;
     branch[k + 1] := xr;
     count := count + 1
   end
end;                                                        {procedure PushIn}
```

7. Splitting a Full Node

The next procedure inserts the key x with subtree pointer xr into the full node p↑; splits the right half off as new node yr↑; and sends the median key y upward for reinsertion later. It is, of course, not possible to insert key x directly into the full node: We must instead first determine whether x will go into the left or right half, divide the node (at position median) accordingly, and then insert x into the appropriate half. While this work proceeds, we shall leave the median key y in the left half.

procedure Split(x: keytype; xr, p: pointer; k: position; **var** y: keytype;
$\qquad\qquad\qquad\qquad\qquad\qquad\qquad\qquad\qquad$**var** yr: pointer);
{splits node p↑ with key x and pointer xr at position k into nodes p↑ and yr↑
with median key y}
var
  i,$\qquad\qquad\qquad\qquad\qquad\qquad\qquad\qquad${used for copying from p↑ to new node}
  median: position;
begin$\qquad\qquad\qquad\qquad\qquad\qquad\qquad\qquad\qquad${procedure Split}

find splitting point	**if** k <= min **then** {Determine if the new key x goes to the left or right half.}
	  median := min
	else
	  median := min + 1;
	new(yr);$\qquad\qquad\qquad\qquad\quad${Get a new node and put it on the right.}
	with p↑ **do begin**

move keys to right node	**for** i := median + 1 **to** max **do**$\qquad\qquad\qquad${Move half the keys.}
	  begin
	    yr↑.key[i − median] := key[i];
	    yr↑.branch[i − median] := branch[i]
	  end;
	  yr↑.count := max − median;
	  count := median;

insert new key	**if** k <= min **then**$\qquad\qquad\qquad\qquad\qquad${Push in the new key.}
	    PushIn(x, xr, p, k)
	  else
	    PushIn(x, xr, yr, k − median);
	  y := key[count];
	  yr↑.branch[0] := branch[count];
	  count := count − 1
	end
	end;$\qquad\qquad\qquad\qquad\qquad\qquad\qquad\qquad${procedure Split}

10.3.6 Deletion from a B-Tree

1. Method

During insertion, the new key always goes first into a leaf. For deletion we shall also wish to remove a key from a leaf. If the key that is to be deleted is not in a leaf, then its immediate predecessor (or successor) under the natural order of keys is guaranteed to be in a leaf (prove it!). Hence we can promote the immediate predecessor (or successor) into the position occupied by the deleted key, and delete the key from the leaf.

If the leaf contains more than the minimum number of keys, then one can be deleted with no further action. If the leaf contains the minimum number, then we first look at the two leaves (or, in the case of a node on the outside, one leaf) that are immediately adjacent and children of the same node. If one of these has more than the minimum number of keys, then one of them can be moved into the parent node, and the key from the parent moved into the leaf where the deletion is occurring.

If, finally, the adjacent leaf has only the minimum number of keys, then the two leaves and the median key from the parent can all be combined as one new leaf, that will contain no more than the maximum number of keys allowed. If this step leaves the parent node with too few keys, then the process propagates upward. In the limiting case, the last key is removed from the root, and then the height of the tree decreases.

2. Example

The process of deletion in our previous B-tree of order 5 is shown in Figure 10.9. The first deletion, h, is from a leaf with more than the minimum number of keys, and hence causes no problem. The second deletion, r, is not from a leaf, and therefore the immediate successor of r, which is s, is promoted into the position of r, and then s is deleted from its leaf. The third deletion, p, leaves its node with too few keys. The key s from the parent node is therefore brought down and replaced by the key t.

Deletion of d has more extensive consequences. This deletion leaves the node with too few keys, and neither of its sibling nodes can spare a key. The node is therefore combined with one of the siblings and with the median key from the parent node, as shown by the dotted line in the first diagram and the combined node $a\,b\,c\,e$ in the second diagram. This process, however, leaves the parent node with only the one key f. The top three nodes of the tree must therefore be combined, yielding the tree shown in the final diagram of Figure 10.9.

3. Pascal Procedures

We can write a deletion algorithm with overall structure similar to that used for insertion. Again we shall use recursion, with a separate main procedure to start the recursion. Rather than attempting to pull a key down from a parent node during an inner recursive call, we shall allow the recursive procedure to return even though there are too few keys in its root node. The outer procedure will then detect this occurrence and move keys as required.

The main procedure is as follows.

B-tree deletion

```
procedure Delete(target: keytype; var root: pointer);
{deletes the key target from the B-tree with the given root}

var
  found: Boolean;                     {Has the target been found in a subtree?}
  p: pointer;                         {used to dispose of an empty root}
begin                                 {procedure Delete}
  RecDelete(target, root, found);
  if not found then
    Error                             {Target was not in the B-tree.}
  else if root↑.count = 0 then        {Root is now empty.}
  begin
```

dispose of empty root

```
    p := root;
    root := root↑.branch[0];
    dispose(p)
  end
end;                                  {procedure Delete}
```

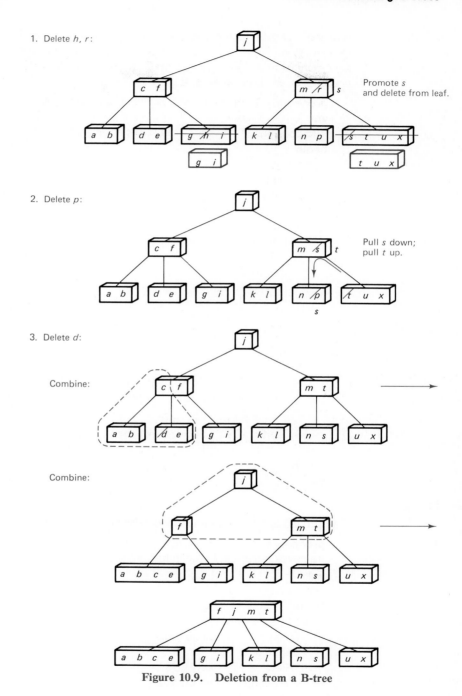

Figure 10.9. Deletion from a B-tree

4. Recursive Deletion

Most of the work is done in the recursive procedure. It first searches the current node for the target. If it is found, and the node is not a leaf, then the immediate successor of the key is found and is placed in the current node, and the successor is deleted. Deletion from a leaf is straightforward, and otherwise the process continues by recursion. When a recursive call returns, the procedure checks to see if enough keys remain in the appropriate node, and, if not, moves keys as required. Auxiliary procedures are used in several of these steps.

```
procedure RecDelete(target: keytype; p: pointer; var found: Boolean);
var
   k: position;                          {location of target or of branch on which to search}
begin                                                               {procedure RecDelete}
   if p = nil then
      found := false                                   {Hitting an empty tree is an error.}
   else with p↑ do begin
      SearchNode(target, p, found, k);
```
found node with target
```
      if found then
         if branch[k − 1] = nil then                              {case: p↑ is a leaf}
            Remove(p, k)                          {removes key from position k of p↑}
         else begin
            Successor(p, k);                       {replaces key[k] by its successor}
            RecDelete(key[k], branch[k], found);
            if not found then
               Error                      {We know that the new key[k] is in the leaf.}
         end
      else                             {Target was not found in the current node.}
```
search a subtree
```
         RecDelete(target, branch[k], found);
                        {At this point, the procedure has returned from a recursive call.}

      if branch[k] <> nil then
         if branch[k]↑.count < min then
            Restore(p, k)
   end
end;                                                               {procedure RecDelete}
```

5. Auxiliary Procedures

The procedures Remove and Successor are straightforward.

remove key from a leaf
```
procedure Remove(p: pointer; k: position);
{removes key[k] and branch[k] from p↑}
var
   i: position;                                        {index to move entries}
begin                                                            {procedure Remove}
   with p↑ do begin
      for i := k + 1 to count do
      begin
         key[i − 1] := key[i];
         branch[i − 1] := branch[i]
      end;
      count := count − 1
   end
end;                                                            {procedure Remove}
```

copy successor of key

```
procedure Successor(p: pointer; k: position);
{replaces p↑.key[k] by its immediate successor under natural order}
var
  q: pointer;                              {used to move down the tree to a leaf}
begin                                                      {procedure Successor}
  q := p↑.branch[k];
  while q↑.branch[0] <> nil do
    q := q↑.branch[0];
  p↑.key[k] := q↑.key[1]
end;                                                       {procedure Successor}
```

Finally, we must show how to restore p↑.branch[k] to the minimum number of keys if a recursive call has reduced its count below the minimum. The procedure we write is somewhat biased to the left; that is, it looks first to the sibling on the left, and uses the right sibling only when necessary. The steps that are needed are illustrated in Figure 10.10.

```
procedure Restore(p: pointer; k: position);
{finds a key and inserts it into p↑.branch[k]↑ so as to restore minimum}
begin                                                      {procedure Restore}
  if k = 0 then                                           {case: leftmost key}
    if p↑.branch[1]↑.count > min then
      MoveLeft(p, 1)
    else
      Combine(p, 1)
  else if k = p↑.count then                              {case: rightmost key}
    if p↑.branch[k − 1]↑.count > min then
      MoveRight(p, k)
    else
      Combine(p, k)
```

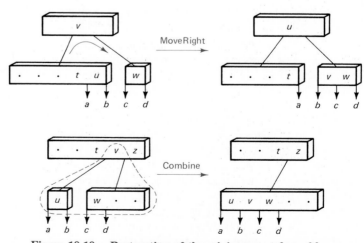

Figure 10.10. Restoration of the minimum number of keys

```
                else                                        {remaining cases}
                  if p↑.branch[k − 1]↑.count > min then
                      MoveRight(p, k)
                  else if p↑.branch[k + 1]↑.count > min then
                      MoveLeft(p, k + 1)
                  else
                      Combine(p, k)
            end;                                            {procedure Restore}
```

The actions of the remaining three procedures MoveRight, MoveLeft, and Combine are clear from Figure 10.10, but for completeness, they are written in full below.

```
              procedure MoveRight(p: pointer; k: position);
              var
                  c: position;
              begin                                         {procedure MoveRight}
                with p↑.branch[k]↑ do begin
```
move a key to the right
```
                  for c := count downto 1 do
                  begin                                     {Shift all keys in right node one position.}
                      key[c + 1] := key[c];
                      branch[c + 1] := branch[c]
                  end;
                  branch[1] := branch[0];                   {Move key from parent into right node.}
                  count := count + 1;
                  key[1] := p↑.key[k]
                end;
                with p↑.branch[k − 1]↑ do begin             {Move last key of left node into parent.}
                  p↑.key[k] := key[count];
                  p↑.branch[k]↑.branch[0] := branch[count];
                  count := count − 1
                end
              end;                                          {procedure MoveRight}
```

move a key to the left
```
              procedure MoveLeft(p: pointer; k: position);
              var
                  c: position;
              begin                                         {procedure MoveLeft}
                with p↑.branch[k − 1]↑ do begin             {Move key from parent into left node.}
                  count := count + 1;
                  key[count] := p↑.key[k];
                  branch[count] := p↑.branch[k]↑.branch[0]
                end;
```

```
        with p↑.branch[k]↑ do begin
          p↑.key[k] := key[1];                    {Move key from right node into parent.}
          branch[0] := branch[1];
          count := count − 1;
          for c := 1 to count do
          begin                        {Shift all keys in right node one position leftward.}
            key[c] := key[c + 1];
            branch[c] := branch[c + 1]
          end
        end
      end;                                                            {procedure MoveLeft}
```

combine adjacent
nodes

```
      procedure Combine(p: pointer; k: position);
      var
        c: position;
        q: pointer;          {points to the right node, which will be emptied and deleted}
      begin                                                           {procedure Combine}
        q := p↑.branch[k];
        with p↑.branch[k − 1]↑ do begin                               {Work with left node.}
          count := count + 1;                                       {Insert key from parent.}
          key[count] := p↑.key[k];
          branch[count] := q↑.branch[0];
          for c := 1 to q↑.count do                          {Insert all keys from right node.}
          begin
            count := count + 1;
            key[count] := q↑.key[c];
            branch[count] := q↑.branch[c]
          end
        end;
        with p↑ do begin
          for c := k to count − 1 do                           {Delete key from parent node.}
          begin
            key[c] := key[c + 1];
            branch[c] := branch[c + 1]
          end;
          count := count − 1
        end;
        dispose(q)                                      {Dispose of the empty right node.}
      end;                                                            {procedure Combine}
```

Exercises 10.3

E1. Insert the six remaining letters of the alphabet in the order

$$z, v, o, q, w, y$$

into the final B-tree of Figure 10.7.

E2. Insert the keys below, in the order stated, into an initially empty B-tree of order
(a) 3, **(b)** 4, **(c)** 7.

$$a \; g \; f \; b \; k \; d \; h \; m \; j \; e \; s \; i \; r \; x \; c \; l \; n \; t \; u \; p.$$

E3. What is the smallest number of keys that, when inserted in an appropriate order, will force a B-tree of order 5 to have height 2 (that is, 3 levels)?

E4. If a key in a B-tree is not in a leaf, prove that both its immediate predecessor and immediate successor (under the natural order) are in leaves.

E5. Remove the tail recursion from the procedure Search.

E6. Rewrite the procedure SearchNode to use binary search.

E7. A *B*-tree* is a B-tree in which every node, except possibly the root, is at least two-thirds full, rather than half full. Insertion into a B*-tree moves keys between sibling nodes (as done during deletion) as needed, thereby delaying splitting a node until two sibling nodes are completely full. These two nodes can be split into three, each of which will be at least two-thirds full.

(a) Specify the changes needed to the insertion algorithm so that it will maintain the properties of a B*-tree.

(b) Specify the changes needed to the deletion algorithm so that it will maintain the properties of a B*-tree.

(c) Discuss the relative advantages and disadvantages of B*-trees compared to ordinary B-trees.

Programming Project 10.3

P1. Combine all the procedures of this section into a complete program for manipulating B-trees. You will need to add procedures to input keys to be inserted or deleted, to traverse a B-tree, and to print its keys.

10.4 GRAPHS

This section introduces an important mathematical structure that has applications in subjects as diverse as sociology, chemistry, geography, and electrical engineering.

10.4.1 Mathematical Background

1. Definitions and Examples

graphs and directed graphs

A *graph G* consists of a set *V*, whose members are called the *vertices* of *G*, together with a set *E* of pairs of distinct vertices from *V*. These pairs are called the *edges* of *G*. If *e* = (*v*, *w*) is an edge with vertices *v* and *w*, then *v* and *w* are said to *lie on e*, and *e* is said to be *incident* with *v* and *w*. If the pairs are unordered, then *G* is called an *undirected graph;* if the pairs are ordered, then *G* is called a *directed graph.* The term *directed graph* is often shortened to *digraph,* and the unqualified term *graph* usually means *undirected graph.*

drawings

The natural way to picture a graph is to represent vertices as points or circles and edges as line segments or arcs connecting the vertices. If the graph is directed, then the line segments or arcs have arrowheads indicating the direction. Figure 10.11 shows several examples of graphs.

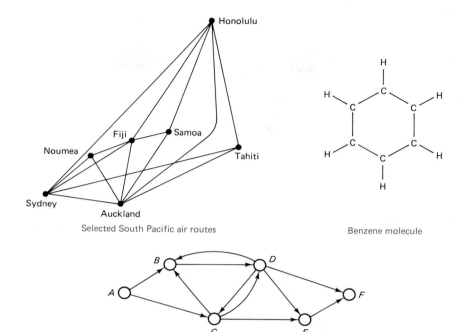

Selected South Pacific air routes

Benzene molecule

Message transmission in a network

Figure 10.11.   Examples of graphs

applications

Graphs find their importance as models for many kinds of processes or structures. Cities and the highways connecting them form a graph, as do the components on a circuit board with the connections among them. An organic chemical compound can be considered a graph with the atoms as the vertices and the bonds between them as edges. The people living in a city can be regarded as the vertices of a graph with the relationship *is acquainted with* describing the edges. People working in a corporation form a directed graph with the relation "supervises" describing the edges.

2. Undirected Graphs

paths, cycles, connected

Several kinds of undirected graphs are shown in Figure 10.12. Two vertices in an undirected graph are called *adjacent* if there is an edge from the first to the second. Hence, in the undirected graph of panel (a), vertices 1 and 2 are adjacent, as are 3 and 4, but 1 and 4 are not adjacent. A *path* is a sequence of distinct vertices, each adjacent to the next. Panel (b) shows a path. A *cycle* is a path containing at least three vertices such that the last vertex on the path is adjacent to the first. Panel (c) shows a cycle. A graph is called *connected* if there is a path from any vertex to any other vertex; panels (a), (b), and (c) show connected graphs, and panel (d) shows a disconnected graph.

free tree

Panel (e) of Figure 10.12 shows a connected graph with no cycles. You will notice that this graph is, in fact, a tree, and we take this property as the definition: A *free tree* is defined as a connected undirected graph with no cycles.

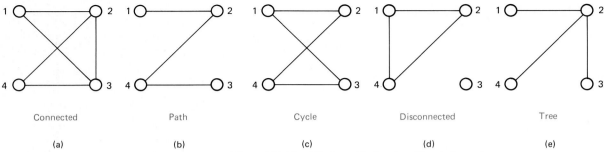

Figure 10.12.   **Various kinds of undirected graphs**

3. Directed Graphs

directed paths and cycles

For directed graphs we can make similar definitions. We require all edges in a path or a cycle to have the same direction, so that following a path or a cycle means always moving in the direction indicated by the arrows. Such a path (cycle) is called a ***directed*** path (cycle). A directed graph is called ***strongly connected*** if there is a directed path from any vertex to any other vertex. If we suppress the direction of the edges and the resulting undirected graph is connected, we call the directed graph ***weakly connected.*** Figure 10.13 illustrates directed cycles, strongly connected directed graphs, and weakly connected directed graphs.

multiple edges

self-loops

The directed graphs in panels (b) and (c) of Figure 10.13 show pairs of vertices with directed edges going both ways between them. Since directed edges are ordered pairs and the ordered pairs (v, w) and (w, v) are distinct if $v \neq w$, such pairs of edges are permissible in directed graphs. Since the corresponding unordered pairs are not distinct, however, in an undirected graph there can be at most one edge connecting a pair of vertices. Similarly, since the vertices on an edge are required to be distinct, there can be no edge from a vertex to itself. We should remark, however, that (although we shall not do so) sometimes these requirements are relaxed to allow multiple edges connecting a pair of vertices and self-loops connecting a vertex to itself.

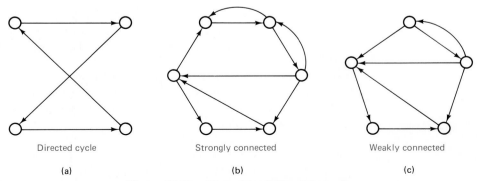

Figure 10.13.   **Examples of directed graphs**

10.4.2 Computer Representation

If we are to write programs for solving problems concerning graphs, then we must first find ways to represent the mathematical structure of a graph as some kind of data structure. There are two methods in common use, which differ fundamentally in the choice of abstract data type used, and there are several variations depending on the implementation of the abstract data type.

1. The Set Representation

Graphs are defined in terms of sets, and it is natural to look first to sets to determine their representation as data. First, we have a set of vertices, and, second, we have the edges as a set of pairs of vertices. Rather than attempting to represent this set of pairs directly, we divide it into pieces by considering the set of edges attached to each vertex separately. In other words, we can keep track of all the edges in the graph by keeping, for all vertices v in the graph, the set E_v of edges containing v, or, equivalently, the set A_v of all vertices adjacent to v. In fact, we can use this idea to produce a new, equivalent definition of a graph:

DEFINITION

A *graph* G consists of a set V, called the *vertices* of G, and, for all $v \in V$, a subset A_v of V, called the set of vertices *adjacent* to v.

From the subsets A_v we can reconstruct the edges as ordered pairs by the rule: The pair (v, w) is an edge if and only if $w \in A_v$. It is easier, however, to work with sets of vertices than with pairs. This new definition, moreover, works for both directed and undirected graphs; the graph is undirected means that it satisfies the following symmetry property: $w \in A_v$ implies $v \in A_w$ for all $v, w \in V$.

2. Implementation of Sets

sets as bit strings

There are two general ways for us to implement sets of vertices in data structures and algorithms. One way is to represent the set as a *list* of its elements; this method we shall study presently. The other implementation, often called a *bit string*, keeps a Boolean value (hence a single bit) for each possible member of the set to indicate whether or not it is in the set. This latter method is used in the Pascal type constructor **set**, which we consider first. To employ Pascal sets, we must begin with an ordinal type whose values correspond to the possible vertices. For simplicity, we shall consider that these vertices are indexed with the integers from 1 to n, where n denotes the number of vertices. Since we shall wish n to be variable, we shall also introduce a constant max bounding the number of vertices, with which we can fully specify the first representation of a graph:

first implementation: sets

```
type
    vertex = 1 .. max;                    {Identify vertices with their indices.}
    adjacencyset = set of vertex;
    graph = record
        n: 0 .. max;                      {number of vertices in the graph}
        A: array[vertex] of adjacencyset
    end;
```

In this implementation the array entry A[v] is the set of all vertices adjacent to the vertex v.

3. Adjacency Tables

restrictions

There is one practical problem with the foregoing implementation: The type constructor **set** is not available in all programming languages, and, when it is, there are often impractically small limits on the maximum size of a set. We can overcome this difficulty, however, and at the same time obtain a better representation of graphs.

sets as arrays

We have already seen that the Pascal type **set of** vertex is essentially implemented as **array**[vertex] **of** Boolean, where each array entry indicates whether or not the corresponding vertex is a member of the set. If we substitute this array for the adjacency set, we find that the array A in the declaration of type graph can be changed to an array of arrays, that is, to a two-dimensional array, as follows:

second implementation: adjacency table

```
type
    vertex = 1 .. max;                          {Identify vertices with their indices.}
    adjacencytable = array[vertex, vertex] of Boolean;
    graph = record
              n: 0 .. max;                       {number of vertices in the graph}
              A: adjacencytable
            end;
```

meaning

The adjacency table A has a natural interpretation: A[v, w] is true if and only if vertex v is adjacent to vertex w. If the graph is directed, we interpret A[v, w] as indicating whether or not the edge from v to w is in the graph. If the graph is undirected, then the adjacency table is symmetric; that is, A[v, w] = A[w, v] for all v and w. The representation of a graph by adjacency sets and by an adjacency table is illustrated in Figure 10.14.

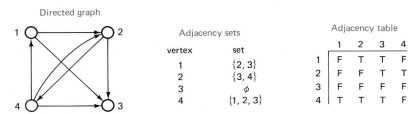

Figure 10.14.   Adjacency set and an adjacency table

4. Adjacency Lists

Another way to represent a set is as a *list* of its elements. For representing a graph we shall then have both a list of vertices and, for each vertex, a list of adjacent vertices. We shall consider implementation of graphs by using both contiguous lists and simply linked lists. For more advanced applications, however, it is often useful to employ more sophisticated implementations of lists as binary or multiway search trees or as heaps.

Note that by identifying vertices with their indices in the previous representations we have *ipso facto* implemented the vertex set as a contiguous list, but now we should make a deliberate choice concerning the use of contiguous or linked lists.

5. Linked Implementation

Greatest flexibility is obtained by using linked lists for both the vertices and the adjacency lists. This implementation is illustrated in panel (a) of Figure 10.15 and results in a declaration such as the following:

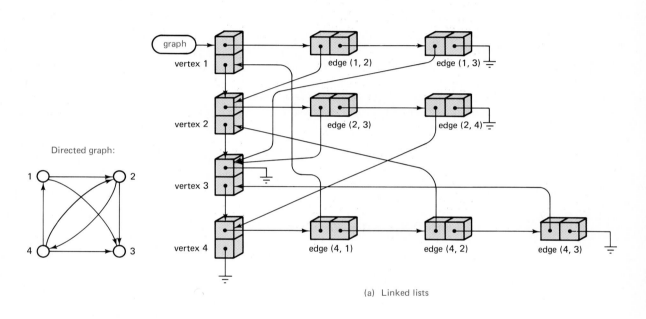

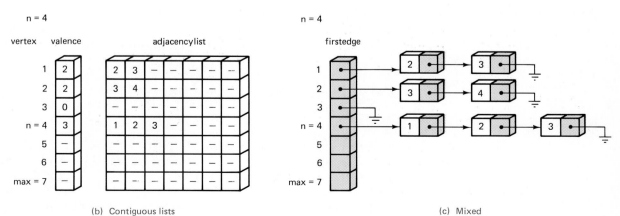

Figure 10.15.   Implementations of a graph with lists

<table>
<tr><td>third implementation:
linked lists</td><td>

type
  pointvertex = ↑vertex;
  pointedge = ↑edge;
  vertex = **record**
       firstedge: pointedge;
       nextvertex: pointvertex
     end;
  edge = **record**
       endpoint: pointvertex;
       nextedge: pointedge;
     end;
  graph = pointvertex;

</td><td>

{start of the adjacency list}
{next vertex on the linked list}

{vertex to which the edge points}
{next edge on the adjacency list}

{header for the list of vertices}

</td></tr>
</table>

6. Contiguous Implementation

Although this linked implementation is very flexible, it is sometimes awkward to navigate through the linked lists, and many algorithms require random access to vertices. Therefore the following contiguous implementation is often better. For a contiguous adjacency list we must keep a counter, and for this we use standard notation from graph theory: the *valence* of a vertex is the number of edges on which it lies, hence also the number of vertices adjacent to it. This contiguous implementation is illustrated in panel (b) of Figure 10.15.

<table>
<tr><td>fourth
implementation:
contiguous lists</td><td>

type
  vertex = 1 .. max;
  counter = 0 .. max;
  adjacencylist = **array**[vertex] **of** vertex;
  graph = **record**
       n: counter;
       valence: **array**[vertex] **of** counter:
       A: **array**[vertex] **of** adjacencylist
     end;

</td><td>

{number of vertices in the graph}

</td></tr>
</table>

7. Mixed Implementation

The final implementation uses a contiguous list for the vertices and linked storage for the adjacency lists. This mixed implementation is illustrated in panel (c) of Figure 10.15.

<table>
<tr><td>fifth implementation:
mixed lists</td><td>

type
  vertex = 1 .. max;
  pointedge = ↑edge;
  edge = **record**
       endpoint: vertex;
       next: pointedge
     end;
  graph = **record**
       n: 0 .. max;
       firstedge: **array**[vertex] **of** pointedge
     end;

</td><td>

{number of vertices in graph}

</td></tr>
</table>

8. Information Fields

Many applications of graphs require not only the adjacency information specified in the various representations but also further information specific to each vertex or each edge. In the linked representations, this information can be included as additional fields within appropriate records, and in the contiguous representations it can be included by making array entries into records.

networks, weights

An especially important case is that of a **network**, which is defined as a graph in which a numerical **weight** is attached to each edge. For many algorithms on networks, the best representation is an adjacency table where the entries are the weights rather than Boolean values.

10.4.3 Graph Traversal

1. Methods

In many problems we wish to investigate all the vertices in a graph in some systematic order, just as with binary trees we developed several systematic traversal methods. In tree traversal, we had a root vertex with which we generally started; in graphs we often do not have any one vertex singled out as special, and therefore the traversal may start at an arbitrary vertex. Although there are many possible orders for visiting the vertices of the graph, two methods are of particular importance.

depth-first

Depth-first traversal of a graph is roughly analogous to preorder traversal of an ordered tree. Suppose that the traversal has just visited a vertex v, and let $w_1, w_2, \ldots, w_k$ be the vertices adjacent to v. Then we shall next visit w_1 and keep $w_2, \ldots, w_k$ waiting. After visiting w_1 we traverse all the vertices to which it is adjacent before returning to traverse $w_2, \ldots, w_k$.

breadth-first

Breadth-first traversal of a graph is roughly analogous to level-by-level traversal of an ordered tree. If the traversal has just visited a vertex v, then it next visits *all* the vertices adjacent to v, putting the vertices adjacent to these in a waiting list to be traversed after all vertices adjacent to v have been visited. Figure 10.16 shows the order of visiting the vertices of one graph under both depth-first and breadth-first traversal.

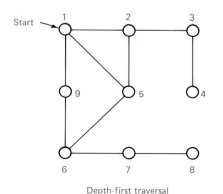 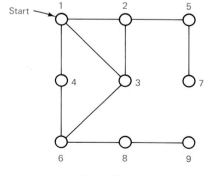

Depth-first traversal   Breadth-first traversal

Note: The vertices adjacent to a given one are considered as arranged in clockwise order.

Figure 10.16. Graph traversal

2. Depth-First Algorithm

Depth-first traversal is naturally formulated as a recursive algorithm. Its action, when it reaches a vertex v, is

outline

```
Visit(v);
for all vertices w adjacent to v do
    Traverse(w);
```

complications

In graph traversal, however, two difficulties arise that cannot appear for tree traversal. First, the graph may contain cycles, so our traversal algorithm may reach the same vertex a second time. To prevent infinite recursion, we therefore introduce a Boolean-valued array visited, set visited[v] to true before starting the recursion, and check the value of visited[w] before processing w. Second, the graph may not be connected, so the traversal algorithm may fail to reach all vertices from a single starting point. Hence we enclose the action in a loop that runs through all vertices.

With these refinements we obtain the following outline of depth-first traversal. Further details depend on the choice of implementation of graphs, and we postpone them to application programs.

*main
procedure*

```
procedure DepthFirst(var G: graph; procedure Visit(var v: vertex));
var
    visited: array[vertex] of Boolean;
    v: vertex;
begin                                        {procedure DepthFirst}
    for all v in G do
        visited[v] := false;
    for all v in G do
        if not visited[v] then
            Traverse(v)
end;                                         {procedure DepthFirst}
```

The recursion is performed in the following procedure, to be declared within the previous one.

*recursive
traversal*

```
procedure Traverse(v: vertex);
var
    w: vertex;
begin                                        {recursive depth-first traversal}
    visited[v] := true;
    Visit(v);
    for all w adjacent to v do
        if not visited[w] then
            Traverse(w)
end;                                         {recursive depth-first traversal}
```

3. Breadth-First Algorithm

stacks and queues

Since using recursion and programming with stacks are essentially equivalent, we could formulate depth-first traversal with a stack, pushing all unvisited vertices adjacent to the one being visited onto the stack and popping the stack to find the next vertex to visit. The algorithm for breadth-first traversal is quite similar to the resulting algorithm for depth-first traversal, except that a queue is needed instead of a stack. Its outline follows.

breadth-first traversal

```
procedure BreadthFirst(var G: graph; procedure Visit(var v: vertex));
var
    Q:        vertexqueue;
    visited:  array[vertex] of Boolean;
    v, w:     vertex;
begin                                          {procedure BreadthFirst}
  for all v in G do
    visited[v] := false;
  Initialize(Q);                               {Set the queue to be empty.}
  for all v in G do
    if not visited[v] then
    begin
      AddQueue(v, Q);
      repeat
        DeleteQueue(v, Q);
        visited[v] := true;
        Visit(v);
        for all w adjacent to v do
        if not visited[w] then
          AddQueue(w)
      until Empty(q)
    end
end;                                            {procedure BreadthFirst}
```

10.4.4 Topological Sorting

1. The Problem

topological order

If G is a directed graph with no directed cycles, then a *topological order* for G is a sequential listing of all the vertices in G such that, for all vertices v, $w \in G$, if there is an edge from v to w, then v precedes w in the sequential listing. Throughout this section we shall consider only directed graphs that have no directed cycles.

applications

As a first application of topological order, consider the courses available at a university as the vertices of a directed graph, where there is an edge from one course to another if the first is a prerequisite for the second. A topological order is then a listing of all the courses such that all prerequisites for a course appear before it does. A second example is a glossary of technical terms that is ordered so that no term is used in a definition before it is itself defined. Similarly, the author of a textbook

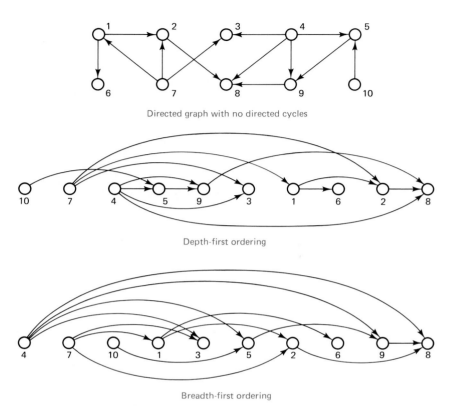

Figure 10.17.   Topological orderings of a directed graph

uses a topological order for the topics in the book. An example of two different topological orders of a directed graph is shown in Figure 10.17.

As an example of algorithms for graph traversal, we shall develop procedures that produce a topological ordering of the vertices of a directed graph that has no cycles. We shall develop two procedures, first for depth-first traversal and then for breadth-first traversal. Both the procedures will operate on a graph G given in the *graph representation* mixed implementation (with a contiguous list of vertices and linked adjacency lists), and both procedures will produce an array of type

$$\text{toporder} = \textbf{array}[\text{vertex}] \textbf{ of } \text{vertex};$$

that will specify the order in which the vertices should be listed to obtain a topological order.

2. Depth-First Algorithm

In a topological order each vertex must appear before all the vertices ·that are its successors in the directed graph. For a depth-first topological ordering, we therefore *method* start by finding a vertex that has no successors and place it last in the order. After we have, by recursion, placed all the successors of a vertex into the topological order, then we can place the vertex itself in a position before any of its successors. The variable place indicates the position in the topological order where the next vertex to be ordered will be placed. Since we first order the last vertices, we begin with place equal to the number of vertices in the graph. The main procedure is a direct implementation of the general algorithm developed in the last section.

depth-first topological sorting

```
procedure TopSort(var G: graph; var T: toporder);
{G is a directed graph with no cycles implemented with a contiguous list of vertices
    and linked adjacency lists; the procedure makes a depth-first traversal of G
    and generates the resulting topological order in the array T.}
var
    visited: array[vertex] of Boolean;          {checks that G contains no cycles}
    v:       vertex;                   {next vertex whose successors are to be ordered}
    place: 0 .. max;                   {next position in the topological order to be filled}
begin                                                       {procedure TopSort}
    for v := 1 to G.n do
        visited[v] := false;
    place:= G.n;
    for v := 1 to G.n do
        if not visited[v] then
            Sort(v, place);
end;                                                        {procedure TopSort}
```

The procedure Sort that performs the recursion, based on the outline for the general procedure Traverse, first places all the successors of v into their positions in the topological order and then places v into the order.

recursive traversal

```
procedure Sort(v: vertex; var place: integer);
{puts all the successors of v and finally v itself into the topological order, beginning
    at position place and working down}
var
    w: vertex;                          {one of the vertices that immediately succeed v}
    p: pointedge;                  {traverses the adjacency list of vertices succeeding v}
begin                                                  {recursive topological sort}
    visited[v] := true;
    p := G.firstedge[v];                              {Find the first vertex succeeding v.}
    while p <> nil do
    begin
        w := p↑.endpoint;                             {w is an immediate successor of v.}
        if not visited[w] then
            Sort(w, place);                       {Order all the successors of w and w itself.}
        p := p↑.next                         {Go on to the next immediate successor of v.}
    end;
    T[place] := v;                                   {Put v itself into the topological order.}
    place := place − 1
end;                                                   {recursive topological sort}
```

performance

Since this algorithm visits each node of the graph exactly once and follows each edge once, doing no searching, its running time is $O(n + e)$, where n is the number of nodes and e is the number of edges in the graph.

3. Breadth-First Algorithm

method

In a breadth-first topological ordering of a directed graph with no cycles, we start by finding the vertices that should be first in the topological order and then apply the fact that every vertex must come before its successors in the topological order. The vertices that come first are those that are not successors of any other vertex. To find these we set up an array predecessorcount such that predecessorcount[v] will be the number of immediate predecessors of each vertex v. The vertices that are not successors are those with no predecessors. We therefore initialize the breadth-first traversal by placing these vertices into the queue of vertices to be visited. As each vertex is visited, it is removed from the queue, assigned the next available position in the topological order (starting at the beginning of the order), and then removed from further consideration by reducing the predecessor count for each of its immediate successors by one. When one of these counts reaches zero, all predecessors of the corresponding vertex have been visited, and the vertex itself is then ready to be processed, so it is added to the queue. We therefore obtain the following procedure.

*breadth-first
topological order*

```
procedure TopSort(var G: graph; var T: toporder);
  {G is a directed graph with no cycles implemented with a contiguous list of vertices
    and linked adjacency lists; the procedure makes a breadth-first traversal of
    G and generates the resulting topological order in T.}
var
  predecessorcount: array[vertex] of integer;
                            {number of immediate predecessors of each vertex}
  Q:     queue;                        {vertices ready to be placed into the order}
  v,                                        {vertex currently being visited}
  w:     vertex;                      {one of the immediate successors of v}
  p:     pointedge;                   {traverses the adjacency list of v}
  place: integer;                     {next position in topological order}
begin                                        {procedure TopSort}
  {Initialize all the predecessor counts to 0.}
  for v := 1 to G.n do
    predecessorcount[v] := 0;
  {Increase the predecessor count for each vertex that is a successor.}
  for v := 1 to G.n do
```

set predecessor counts

```
  begin
    p := G.firstedge[v];
    while p <> nil do
    begin
      predecessorcount[p↑.endpoint] := predecessorcount[p↑.endpoint] + 1;
      p := p↑.next
    end
  end;
```

find vertices going first

process a vertex

performance

```
Initialize(Q);
{Place all vertices with no predecessors into the queue.}
for v := 1 to G.n do
   if predecessorcount[v] = 0 then
      AddQueue(v, Q);
{Start the breadth-first traversal.}
place := 0;
while not Empty(Q) do
begin
   DeleteQueue(v, Q);              {Visit v by placing it into the topological order.}
   place := place + 1;
   T[place] := v;
   p := G.firstedge[v];           {Traverse the list of immediate successors of v.}
   while p <> nil do
   begin        {Reduce the predecessor count for each immediate successor.}
      w := p↑.endpoint;
      predecessorcount[w] := predecessorcount[w] − 1;
      if predecessorcount[w] = 0 then
         {w has no further predecessors, so it is ready to process.}
         AddQueue(w, Q);
      p := p↑.next
   end
end
end;                                                        {procedure TopSort}
```

This algorithm requires auxiliary procedures for processing the queue. The entries in the queue are to be vertices, and the queue can be implemented in any of the ways described in Chapters 3 and 4; the details are left as an exercise.

As with depth-first traversal, the time required by the breadth-first procedure is $O(n + e)$, where n is the number of vertices and e is the number of edges in the directed graph.

10.4.5 A Greedy Algorithm: Shortest Paths

1. The Problem

shortest path

As a final application of graphs, one requiring somewhat more sophisticated reasoning, we consider the following problem. We are given a directed graph G in which every edge has a nonnegative *weight* attached, and our problem is to find a path from one vertex v to another w such that the sum of the weights on the path is as small as possible. We call such a path a **shortest path**, even though the weights may represent costs, time, or some quantity other than distance. We can think of G as a map of airline routes, for example, with each vertex representing a city and the weight on each edge the cost of flying from one city to the second. Our problem is then to find a routing from city v to city w such that the total cost is a minimum. Consider the directed graph shown in Figure 10.18. The shortest path from vertex 1 to vertex

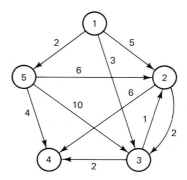

Figure 10.18. A directed graph with weights

2 goes via vertex 3 and has a total cost of 4, compared to the cost of 5 for the edge directly from 1 to 2 and the cost of 8 for the path via vertex 5.

It turns out that it is just as easy to solve the more general problem of starting at one vertex, called the *source,* and finding the shortest path to *every* other vertex, instead of to just one destination vertex. For simplicity, we take the source to the vertex 1, and our problem then consists of finding the shortest path from vertex 1 to every vertex in the graph. We require that the weights are all nonnegative.

source

2. Method

The algorithm operates by keeping a set S of those vertices whose shortest distance from 1 is known. Initially, 1 is the only vertex in S. At each step we add to S a remaining vertex for which the shortest path from 1 has been determined. The problem is to determine which vertex to add to S at each step. Let us think of the vertices already in S as having been labeled with some color, and think of the edges making up the shortest paths from the source 1 to these vertices as also colored.

distance table

We shall maintain a table D that gives, for each vertex v, the distance from 1 to v along a path all of whose edges are colored, except possibly the last one. That is, if v is in S, then $D[v]$ gives the shortest distance to v and all edges along the corresponding path are colored. If v is not in S, then $D[v]$ gives the length of the path from 1 to some vertex w in S plus the weight of the edge from w to v, and all the edges of this path except the last one are colored. The table D is initialized by setting $D[v]$ to the weight of the edge from 1 to v if it exists and to ∞ if not.

greedy algorithm

To determine what vertex to add to S at each step, we apply the *greedy* criterion of choosing the vertex v with the smallest distance recorded in the table D, such that v is not already in S.

verification

We must prove that for this vertex v the distance recorded in D really is the length of the shortest path from 1 to v. For suppose that there were a shorter path from 1 to v, such as shown in Figure 10.19. This path first leaves S to go to some vertex x, then goes on to v (possibly even reentering S along the way). But if this path is shorter than the colored path to v, then its initial segment from 1 to x is

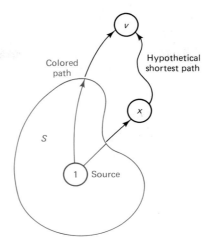

Figure 10.19.   Finding a shortest path

end of proof

also shorter, so that the greedy criterion would have chosen x rather than v as the next vertex to add to S, since we would have had $D[x] < D[v]$.

When we add v to S we think of v as now colored and also color the shortest path from 1 to v (every edge of which except the last was actually already colored). *maintain the invariant* Next, we must update the entries of D by checking, for each vertex w not in S, whether a path through v and then directly to w is shorter than the previously recorded distance to w. That is, we replace $D[w]$ by $D[v]$ plus the weight of the edge from v to w if the latter quantity is smaller.

3. Example

Before writing a formal procedure incorporating this method, let us work through the example shown in Figure 10.20. For the directed graph shown in panel (a), the initial situation is shown in panel (b): The set S (colored vertices) consists of 1 alone, and the entries of the distance table D are shown as numbers in color beside the other vertices. The distance to vertex 5 is shortest, so 5 is added to S in panel (c), and the distance $D[4]$ is updated to the value 6. Since the distances to vertices 2 and 3 via vertex 5 are greater than those already recorded in T, their entries remain unchanged. The next closest vertex to 1 is vertex 3, and it is added in panel (d), which also shows the effect of updating the distances to vertices 2 and 4, whose paths via vertex 3 are shorter than those previously recorded. The final two steps, shown in panels (e) and (f), add vertices 2 and 4 to S and yield the paths and distances shown in the final diagram.

4. Implementation

For the sake of writing a procedure to embody this algorithm for finding shortest distances, we must choose an implementation of the directed graph. Use of the adjacency-table implementation facilitates random access to all the vertices of the graph,

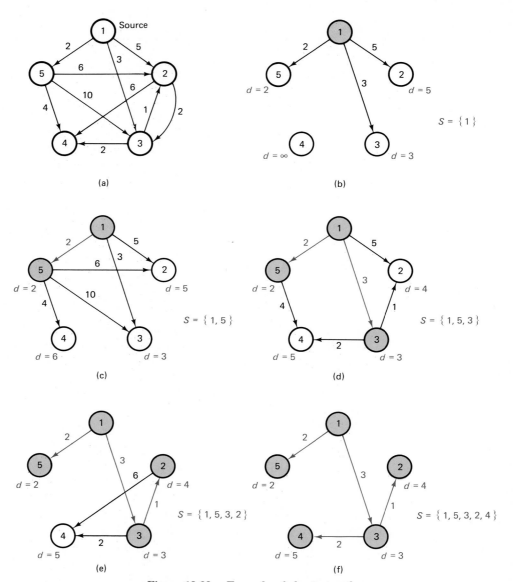

Figure 10.20.   Example of shortest paths

as we need for this problem. Moreover, by storing the weights in the table we can use the table to give weights as well as adjacencies. We shall place a special large value ∞ in any position of the table for which the corresponding edge does not exist. These decisions are incorporated in the following Pascal declarations to be included in the calling program.

graph representation

```
const
  max = {to be provided; maximum number of vertices in the graph};
  infinity = maxint;
type
  weight = integer;
  count  = 0 .. max;
  vertex = 1 .. max;
  adjacencytable = array[vertex, vertex] of weight;
  distancetable = array[vertex] of weight;
var
  n:    count;                          {number of vertices in the graph}
  cost: adjacencytable;                        {describes the graph}
  D:    distancetable;             {shortest distances from vertex 1}
```

The procedure that we write will accept the adjacency table and the count of vertices in the graph as its input parameters and will produce the table of closest distances as its output parameter.

shortest-distance procedure

```
procedure Distance(n: count; var cost: adjacencytable; var D: distancetable);
{calculates cost of the shortest path from vertex 1 to each vertex of the graph}
var
  final: array[vertex] of Boolean;
                              {Has the final distance from 1 to v been found?}
                              {final[v] is true if and only if v is in the set S.}
  i,                                      {repetition count for the main loop}
                           {One distance is finalized on each pass through the loop.}
  w,                                     {a vertex not yet added to the set S}
  v:    vertex;                  {vertex with minimum tentative distance in D[ ]}
  min: weight;                               {distance of v, equals D[v]}
begin                                             {procedure Distance}
  final[1] := true;                   {Initialize with vertex 1 alone in the set S.}
  D[1] := 0;
  for v := 2 to n do
  begin
    final[v] := false;
    D[v] := cost[1, v]
  end;
  for i := 2 to n do {Start the main loop; add one vertex v to S on each pass.}
  begin
    min := infinity;                          {Find the closest vertex v to vertex 1.}
    for w := 2 to n do
      if not final[w] then
        if D[w] < min then
        begin
          v := w;
          min := D[w]
        end;
```

```
                    final[v] := true;                          {Add v to the set S.}
                    for w := 2 to n do              {Update the remaining distances in D.}
                        if not final[w] then
                            if min + cost[v, w] < D[w] then
                                D[w] := min + cost[v, w]
                end
            end;                                           {procedure Distance}
```

performance   To estimate the running time of this procedure, we note that the main loop is executed $n - 1$ times, and within it are two other loops, each executed $n - 1$ times, so these loops contribute a multiple of $(n - 1)^2$ operations. Statements done outside the loops contribute only $O(n)$, so the running time of the algorithm is $O(n^2)$.

10.4.6 Graphs as Data Structures

In this section we have studied a few applications of graphs, but we have hardly begun to scratch the surface of the broad and deep subject of graph algorithms. In many of these algorithms, graphs appear, as they have in this section, as mathematical structures capturing the essential description of a problem rather than as computational tools for its solution.

mathematical structures and data structures   Note that in this section we have spoken of graphs as mathematical structures, and not as data structures, for we have used graphs to formulate mathematical problems, and to write algorithms we have then implemented the graphs within data structures like tables and lists. Graphs, however, can certainly be regarded as data structures themselves, data structures that embody relationships among the data more complicated than those describing a list or a tree.

flexibility and power   Because of their generality and flexibility, graphs are powerful data structures that prove valuable in more advanced applications such as the design of data base management systems. Such powerful tools are meant to be used, of course, whenever necessary, but they must always be used with care so that their power is not turned to confusion. Perhaps the best safeguard in the use of powerful tools is to insist on regularity, that is, to use the powerful tools only in carefully defined and well-understood ways. Because of the generality of graphs, it is not always easy to impose this discipline on their use.

irregularity   In this world, nonetheless, irregularities will always creep in, no matter how hard we try to avoid them. It is the bane of the systems analyst and programmer to accommodate these irregularities while trying to maintain the integrity of the underlying system design. Irregularity even occurs in the very systems that we use as models for the data structures we devise, models such as the family trees whose terminology we have always used. An excellent illustration of what can happen is the following classic story, quoted by N. WIRTH from a Zurich newspaper of July 1922.

I married a widow who had a grown-up daughter. My father, who visited us quite often, fell in love with my step-daughter and married her. Hence, my father became my son-in-law, and my step-daughter became my mother. Some months later, my wife gave birth to a son, who became the brother-in-law of my father as well as my uncle. The wife of my father, that is my step-daughter, also had a son. Thereby, I got a brother and at the same time a grandson. My wife is my grandmother, since she is my mother's mother. Hence, I am my wife's husband and at the same time her step-grandson; in other words, I am my own grandfather.

Exercises
10.4

E1. (a) Find all the cycles in each of the following graphs. **(b)** Which of these graphs are connected? **(c)** Which of these graphs are free trees?

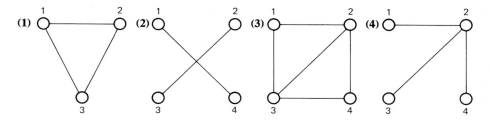

E2. For each of the graphs shown in Exercise E1, give the implementation of the graph as **(a)** an adjacency table, **(b)** a linked vertex list with linked adjacency lists, **(c)** a contiguous vertex list of contiguous adjacency lists.

E3. A graph is *regular* if every vertex has the same valence (that is, if it is adjacent to the same number of other vertices). For a regular graph, a good implementation is to keep the vertices in a linked list and the adjacency lists contiguous. The length of all the adjacency lists is called the *degree* of the graph. Write Pascal declarations for this implementation of regular graphs.

E4. The topological sorting procedures as presented in the text are deficient in error checking. Modify the **(a)** depth-first and **(b)** breadth-first procedures so that they will detect any (directed) cycles in the graph and indicate what vertices cannot be placed in any topological order because they lie on a cycle.

Programming
Projects
10.4

P1. Write Pascal procedures called ReadGraph that will read from the terminal the number of vertices in an undirected graph and lists of adjacent vertices. Be sure to include error checking. The graph is to be implemented as **(a)** an adjacency table, **(b)** a linked vertex list with linked adjacency lists, **(c)** a contiguous vertex list of linked adjacency lists.

P2. Write Pascal procedures called WriteGraph that will write pertinent information specifying a graph to the terminal. The graph is to be implemented as **(a)** an adjacency table, **(b)** a linked vertex list with linked adjacency lists, **(c)** a contiguous vertex list of linked adjacency lists.

P3. [Requires graphics capability] Rewrite the procedures WriteGraph to use a graphics-capable terminal and draw the graph.

P4. Use the procedures ReadGraph and WriteGraph to implement and test the topological sorting procedures developed in this section for **(a)** depth-first order and **(b)** breadth-first order. In part **(b)** you will also need to use procedures for processing the queue.

P5. Implement and test the procedure for determining shortest distances in directed graphs with weights.

POINTERS AND PITFALLS

1. Trees are flexible and powerful structures both for modeling problems and for organizing data. In using trees in problem solving and in algorithm design, first decide on the kind of tree needed (ordered, rooted, free, or binary) before considering implementation details.

2. Most trees can be described easily by using recursion; their associated algorithms are often best formulated recursively.

3. For problems of information retrieval, consider the size, number, and location of the records along with the type and structure of the keys while choosing the data structures to be used. For small records or small numbers of keys, high-speed internal memory will be used, and binary search trees will likely prove adequate. For information retrieval from disk files, methods employing multiway branching, such as tries, B-trees, and hash tables, will usually be superior. Tries are particularly suited to applications where the keys are structured as a sequence of symbols and where the set of keys is relatively dense in the set of all possible keys. For other applications, methods that treat the key as a single unit will often prove superior. B-trees, together with various generalizations and extensions, can be usefully applied to many problems concerned with external information retrieval.

4. Graphs provide an excellent way to describe the essential features of many applications, thereby facilitating specification of the underlying problems and formulation of algorithms for their solution. Graphs sometimes appear as data structures but more often as mathematical abstractions useful for problem solving.

5. Graphs may be implemented in many ways by the use of different kinds of data structures. Postpone implementation decisions until the applications of graphs in the problem-solving and algorithm-development phases are well understood.

6. Many applications require graph traversal. Let the application determine the traversal method: depth first, breadth first, or some other order. Depth-first traversal is naturally recursive (or can use a stack). Breadth-first traversal normally uses a queue.

7. Greedy algorithms represent only a sample of the many paradigms useful in developing graph algorithms. For further methods and examples, consult the references.

REVIEW QUESTIONS

10.1

1. Define the terms (a) *free tree,* (b) *rooted tree, and* (c) *ordered tree.*

2. Draw all the different (a) free trees, (b) rooted trees, and (c) ordered trees with three vertices.

3. Name three ways describing the correspondence between orchards and binary trees, and indicate the primary purpose for each of these ways.

10.2   4. What is a trie?

5. How may a trie with six levels and a five-way branch in each node differ from the rooted tree with six levels and five children for every node except the leaves? Will the trie or the tree likely have fewer nodes, and why?

6. Discuss the relative advantages in speed of retrieval of a trie and a binary search tree.

10.3   7. How does a multiway search tree differ from a trie?

8. What is a B-tree?

9. What happens when an attempt is made to insert a new key into a full node of a B-tree?

10. Does a B-tree grow at its leaves or at its root? Why?

11. In deleting a key from a B-tree, when is it necessary to combine nodes?

12. For what purposes are B-trees especially appropriate?

10.4   13. In the sense of this chapter, what is a graph?

14. What does it mean for a directed graph to be strongly connected? weakly connected?

15. Describe three ways to implement graphs in computer memory.

16. Explain the difference between *depth-first* and *breadth-first* traversal of a graph.

17. What data structures are needed to keep the waiting vertices during **(a)** depth-first and **(b)** breadth-first traversal?

18. For what kind of graphs is *topological sorting* defined?

19. What is a topological order for such a graph?

20. Why is the algorithm for finding shortest distances called *greedy*?

REFERENCES FOR FURTHER STUDY

One of the most thorough available studies of trees is in the series of books by KNUTH. The correspondence from ordered trees to binary trees appears in Volume 1, pp. 332–347. Volume 3, pp. 471–505, discusses multiway trees, B-trees, and tries. Mathematical results concerning trees and graphs are in Volume 1, pp. 362–385. Topological sorting (with the breadth-first algorithm) appears in Volume 1, pp. 258–268.

Tries were first studied in

EDWARD FREDKIN, "Trie memory," *Communications of the ACM* 3 (1960), 490–499.

The original reference for B-trees is

R. BAYER and E. MCCREIGHT, "Organization and maintenance of large ordered indexes," *Acta Informatica* 1 (1972), 173–189.

An interesting survey of applications and variations of B-trees is

D. COMER, "The ubiquitous B-tree," *Computing Surveys* 11 (1979), 121–137.

The quotation at the end of the chapter is taken from

N. WIRTH, *Algorithms + Data Structures = Programs,* Prentice-Hall, Englewood Cliffs, N.J., 1976, p. 170.

This book also contains (pp. 242–264) an exposition of B-trees with Pascal algorithms for insertion and deletion.

The study of graphs and algorithms for their processing is a large subject and one that involves both mathematics and computing science. Three books, each of which contains many interesting algorithms, are

R. E. TARJAN, *Data Structures and Network Algorithms,* Society for Industrial and Applied Mathematics, Philadelphia, 1983, 131 pages.

SHIMON EVEN, *Graph Algorithms,* Computer Science Press, Rockville, Md., 1979, 249 pages.

E. M. REINGOLD, J. NIEVERGELT, N. DEO, *Combinatorial Algorithms: Theory and Practice,* Prentice-Hall, Englewood Cliffs, N.J., 1977, 433 pages.

The original reference for the greedy algorithm determining the shortest paths in a graph is

E. W. DIJKSTRA, "A note on two problems in connexion with graphs," *Numerische Mathematik* 1 (1959), 269–271.

Case Study: An Index Writer

▶ *This chapter develops a program that makes a list of all the distinct words appearing in a text. This case study illustrates both principles of program design and of data structuring, exhibiting applications and interactions of arrays, files, hash tables, linked lists, and binary search trees.*

11.1 SPECIFYING THE PROBLEM

concordance

restrictions

specifications

There are several good reasons for making a list, in alphabetical order, of all the distinct words that appear in a document. First, a list of the important words is helpful in preparing an index for the document, especially if page numbers are included along with the words. Second, we may wish, for a broader class of words, to be able to locate all the occurrences of each word, so that we can quickly find the context of a short section that we remember. Such a list of words with all their occurrences is called a **concordance.** Third, we might like to have a list of all the words with a count of how many times each word is used. Different authors use different styles; and often substantial differences occur in the relative frequencies of using common words. Word counts provide important clues to scholars attempting to determine doubtful authorships. Fourth (but not least important), a word list is of great help in recognizing inconsistencies in spelling words. The word list cannot, by itself, serve as a spelling corrector, but it can certainly recognize many misprints that might otherwise not be detected. It is often reasonable to expect that an author is inconsistent in spelling a word if he is not sure of its correct spelling, and these inconsistencies can be spotted quickly in the list and used to flag words whose spelling should be checked.

You may already have guessed that the first major application of the program we develop in this chapter is the very text of this book itself. The first and fourth reasons are clearly important for this application, with the second and third capabilities being interesting by-products. A document of about 150,000 words is usually too large to keep in the high-speed memory of a computer at one time, and sorting 150,000 items is a very big task. Hence our first restriction on our project: We must spurn the simple solution of reading the whole document into memory, splitting it into a long list of words, and sorting the list. Instead, we shall assume that we are using a small computer and have memory enough for two or three thousand words, but no more.

Our second restriction is that the program should run efficiently, so that, if possible, it will run on a microcomputer in reasonable time, or, if that is not possible, it will at least run successfully on a quite small computer system. The program will probably also need to request some information from the user. It should therefore run quickly enough to be used interactively on a time-sharing system, without frustrating the user with long delays.

With these restrictions in mind, let us describe the task of our project more precisely. We wish to have a list of the distinct words in the text, arranged in alphabetical order. For some words (as specified by the user), we wish a list of all the pages on which the word appears. For some words (as specified by the user), we wish a count of the number of appearances of the word. There may remain other words for which we desire no special information. Hence we may regard the words as going into one of three categories, which we shall call *index, count,* and *forget.*

At the first appearance of each word, the program must ask the user which of these three dispositions to make. The program should never ask the user twice about the same word.

remaining requirements

At this point it may appear that we have spelled out the requirements for the program completely, but we have not. For example, we have not specified exactly what constitutes a word; this task we postpone to a later section. Nor have we specified the form of input and output. For documents of any significant size, we shall clearly wish to read the document from a file, rather than type it in as input from a terminal. We could type the word list out at the terminal, but this would be prohibitively long for a large document and is not as useful as making the word list into another file that can later be examined and appropriate information extracted. Finally, in the future we shall presumably wish to run the program on other documents. If so, we may not wish to specify the disposition of each word all over again. Hence the program should set up a master word list, update it with the new words from the current document, and keep the updated list as another file. For backup purposes, the previous master word list should not be destroyed or altered.

postpone decisions

Note carefully that, at this point, although we have a good idea of what the program should do and the way in which it will communicate with its environment (via files and the interactive user), we have said nothing about the way the data will be kept while the program is running, nor of the method that will be used to process the data (other than to eschew one obvious possible method). By the time we have settled these questions, we shall have devised the essence of the program, and in a project this large, it is essential that we avoid jumping to premature decisions.

11.2 STRUCTURING THE DATA: THE MAIN PROGRAM

11.2.1 Requirements on Data Organization

Our problem includes several conflicting requirements that greatly limit the ways of representing our data. The master word list, first of all, will be too large to be kept in memory all at once. Second, our program is supposed to run efficiently, and accesses to files (on disk or otherwise outside high-speed memory) are very slow compared to operations within memory. It is therefore impractical to consider looking up each word separately in the master word list. With a large document, it will, in any case, take significant time for the program to read all the way through the document, so we should, if possible, avoid reading the same information more than once from a file. Finally, as we have previously noted, the input text will be too large to fit into memory. Hence we would like to be able to read the input text only once, read the master word list only once, and in this single pass produce the word list for the input document in alphabetical order with page references or frequency counts as desired.

read once

1. Two-Phase Program

This goal is unattainable. It might happen that the first word of the input text belongs at the very end of the word list. Since we cannot keep all the words in memory at once, it will be necessary to use some kind of auxiliary files to remember the words from the input text until they can be compared to the master word list and processed accordingly. Thus the first phase of our program will read the input text, split it into individual words, and put them away for further processing.

2. Common Words

It now appears as though we must read the entire input at least twice, once as a document and again after it has been split into a long list of words. One simple observation, fortunately, will spare most of the words from going into the auxiliary files and having to be processed further in a second phase. This observation is that, in English (or any other human language), some words occur far more frequently than others. A dictionary of reasonable size contains perhaps 50,000 entries; an unabridged dictionary more than 100,000, but only a few common words make up the bulk of the words in almost any text. In the present book, for example, a vocabulary of fewer than 1000 words will cover more than 80 percent of all words in the text. In ordinary English discourse, it usually takes only 134 distinct words to account for half of all the words in a text.

reduce problem

During the input phase, therefore, let us keep the most common words in memory and look up each word as soon as it is read in. If it is present, then we can process it at once; if not, then it must be put into an auxiliary file for later processing.

choice of data structure

In what kind of data structure should we keep these common words? Our use is that of table lookup: For each incoming word we wish to determine as quickly as possible whether it is present or not. The keys are the words themselves, and there are too many possible words to use simple array indexing; the study in Chapter 6 shows this task to be an appropriate application for a hash table. Our table of common words will not (after it is constructed) be subject to insertions or deletions; with a good hash function open addressing will probably prove better than chaining. Let us therefore reach the decision to keep the common words in memory during the first phase in a hash table with open addressing.

hash table

For simplicity we shall (arbitrarily) decide that the common words in the hash table coincide with the common words for which no information is to be kept. Hence, when a word is found in the hash table, no further processing is needed, and we sometimes write the category *hash* in place of *forget.*

3. Auxiliary Files

Our next task is to decide how to store the words that do require further processing in the second phase. The simplest way is to set up an auxiliary file and write the words into it one at a time. The file is then reset and read in the second phase. If there is enough room to read all these words into memory at once, then the second phase can proceed efficiently: The words can first be sorted alphabetically and then compared with the master word list as it is read. If we are sure that the program will never be used for documents of more than about 10,000 words, and the first phase disposes of about 80 percent of them, then there may be enough room to proceed in this way, and it is then a good choice of method.

For generality, however, we would like to be able to process larger documents. The time required for sorting, moreover, grows faster than the number of words, and therefore, if we can find a way to divide the problem into a series of smaller problems, then the total time required for sorting will be shortened, and the available memory can accommodate a larger document.

distribution: divide and conquer

The idea that we shall use to subdivide the problem is the same idea used in a distribution sort: Instead of putting the words into one auxiliary file, we divide them into twenty-six auxiliary files, according to the first letter of the word. As we shall see, this requires essentially no extra time in the first phase, and it divides the second phase into twenty-six similar but smaller problems that will, together, run faster than one large sorting problem.

4. The Third Phase

merging

Recall that the words from the current document were to be used to update the master word list (keeping a backup copy). This task could be done while the second phase is in progress, but for simplicity and clarity, we shall instead use a third phase, that will merge the word list for the current document with the master word list, and will also update the list of common words kept as the hash table.

5. Filters

Our program design as it has developed is typical of many applications where the work to be done splits naturally into a series of tasks or phases that can be considered separately. A good way to think of the work is as starting with raw input and passing it through a series of *filters,* each of which converts the data into a form closer to the desired result. This approach is the basis of the popular UNIX* operating system, which is made up of a large number of filters, each of which does only one task, usually quite a simple task. The power of the operating system comes from the flexibility and generality of the ways in which filters can be combined.

smaller independent modules

In our program, too, we should consider each of the three phases as independently from the others as we can. Not only will this approach help to keep the design simple, but we may find that one or another part of the program will prove to be useful for some unanticipated application. Within a UNIX or UNIX-like system it would probably be best to write each of the three phases as a separate program. With other systems, however, it is not so convenient to direct the output of one program to become the input of another, and therefore we shall consider the more difficult case of writing the three phases within one program. Even so, we can improve the modularity of the project by keeping the interface between phases as simple as we can, and by insisting, for example, that all temporary files remain in human-readable form.

---

* UNIX™ is a trademark of Bell Laboratories.

11.2.2 The Main Program

At this point, let us reinforce our decisions concerning data representation by establishing the notation that will be used both for communication with the outside environment and for sending information from the first phase to the second phase. These notations constitute the declarations placed in the main program.

declarations

The **const** declaration section includes all constants used in the program, even those used in only one phase or subprogram. By collecting all the constants in one place, it becomes easier to see what changes must be made to adapt the program to a particular computer system.

A program that manipulates words or other character strings will necessarily have some dependence on the way in which characters are represented in computer memory. For definiteness, this chapter has been written for the ASCII representation. A comment is inserted at every point where this assumption makes a difference, noting what changes may be needed for other representations.

ASCII

main program

```
program IndexText(InText, InIndex, NewIndex, OutIndex, HashFile,
                  NewHashFile, Input, Output);
{Produces word counts and list of references for the document file InText. Uses
  the master word list in file InIndex, if provided. Output word list for the new
  text goes to file NewIndex. The merger of these two files becomes OutIndex.
  HashFile contains the common words to be ignored. If not specified, it is created
  on output, containing the words so flagged by the user.}
const
```

limits

```
  maxwd        = 20;              {More letters in a word will be ignored.}
  minwd        = 3;                  {Shorter words will be ignored.}
  hashsize     = 2003;           {should be a prime; size of hash table}
  linesperpage = 66;             {assumes standard spacing and paper}
  maxheight    = 20;             {for building binary tree in phase 2}
```

characters

```
  A            = 'A';
  Z            = 'Z';
  hyphen       = '–';
  blank        = ' ';
  apostrophe   = '''';           {requires two "s to represent one}
  underscore   = '_';
  ordbackspace = 8;              {ASCII control character for backspace}
  ordformfeed  = 12;             {ASCII control character for new page}
  changecase   = 32;             {ASCII difference between upper- and lowercase}
```

types

```
type
  word      = packed array[1 .. maxwd] of char;
  reference = record
                wd: word;
                pg: integer                           {page number}
              end;
  fileref   = file of reference;                      {used for local files}
  letter    = A .. Z;
  hashentry = 1 .. hashsize;
```

files

```
        var
          InText,                                    {document being processed}
          InIndex,                                   {master word list}
          NewIndex,                                  {word list of current document}
          OutIndex:     text;                        {updated master word list}
          HashFile,
          NewHashFile: file of word;        {local file, used to update HashFile}
          RefFile:     array[letter] of fileref;  {local files used for auxiliary storage of
                       words from phase 1 to phase 2: separate file for each initial letter}
          blankword:   word;                         {will contain all blanks}
```

division into phases

```
        begin                                        {main program}
          SplitWords;                                {phase 1}
          ClassifyWords;                             {phase 2}
          UpdateHashFile;                            {phase 3, first part}
          MergeIndices;                              {phase 3, second part}
        end.
```

11.2.3 Word Processing

1. Storage of a Word

strings

Our program needs to keep a considerable number of different words in storage and must be able to compare, move, and change these words efficiently. The length of a word varies considerably: One reasonable approach would be to keep words stored as a linked list of characters. This method, however, would use considerable space for links, and would make comparison of two words a fairly slow process. For simplicity, therefore, we shall represent a word as a (packed) array of characters of fixed length maxwd. All positions in the array after the end of the word will be filled with blanks.

We shall frequently need to perform various standard tasks with words. Standard Pascal allows two arrays to be checked for equality, but does not necessarily provide the other facilities we need, which we therefore write as auxiliary subprograms. Many Pascal compilers, however, do provide these other capabilities, which should then probably be used in place of the subprograms given here.

2. Comparing Words

precedence of words

```
        function Lt(u, v: word): Boolean;
        {Determine if word u precedes word v lexicographically.}
        var
          i: 1 .. maxwd;                             {loop variable}
        begin                                        {function Lt}
          i := 1;
          while (i < maxwd) and (u[i] = v[i]) do i := i + 1;
          Lt := (u[i] < v[i])
                    {Above is the version that works with ASCII code. For codes where
                      blank comes after letters, modifications are necessary.}
        end;                                         {function Lt}
```

3. Reading and Writing a Word

For convenience in processing, we shall treat all the words put in the files generated by our program in the same way as words in memory, that is, as having the fixed length of maxwd characters, with blanks added to make up this length. The procedures below are applied only to files whose words are of this fixed length (not, for example, to the terminal input, where the user could not be expected to type in extra blanks to complete a word).

file input

```
procedure ReadWord(var F: text; var w: word);
{reads word w from text file F; assumes not at end of file}
var
  c: 1 .. maxwd;
begin                                        {procedure ReadWord}
  for c := 1 to maxwd do
    read(F, w[c])
end;                                         {procedure ReadWord}
```

file output

```
procedure WriteWord(var F: text; w: word);
{writes word w to text file F}
var
  c: 1 .. maxwd;
begin                                        {procedure WriteWord}
  for c := 1 to maxwd do
    write(F, w[c])
end;                                         {procedure WriteWord}
```

11.3 PHASE 1: SPLITTING THE TEXT INTO WORDS

task

The task of this phase is, briefly, to read the input text, split it into individual words, look up each word in the hash table, and, if it is not there, put it in the appropriate auxiliary file for later processing.

11.3.1 The Main Procedure

This action translates into the outline coded as the following procedure, which in turn invokes three other procedures. Initialize sets up the hash table and the necessary variables; GetWord splits off a single word from the input text; and Conclude tidies up after the input text has been completely read.

As we did in the main program, we declare in this main procedure several variables that are used only in the subprocedures. These include various counters and other information needed to identify words and determine the page number corresponding to each word.

first phase

```
procedure SplitWords;
{sets up hash table, reads text, and divides into 26 word lists}
```

declarations

```
var
   hash:          array[hashentry] of word;              {hash table}
   pagecount,                           {keeps the current page number}
   addpage,                     {amount to increase pagecount after word}
   linecount:     integer;                 {line number on the current page}
   outcount:      array[letter] of integer;         {counters for word files}
   wordcount:     integer;                   {count of all words in the text}
   w:             word;                  {word currently being processed}
   x:             hashentry;              {location of w, if in hash table}
   endinput:      Boolean;           {true if and only if input has all been read}
   firstletter:   char;                   {Into which file does word w go?}
```

"constants" for GetWord

```
{The following variables are kept for use in procedure GetWord, and for efficiency
   are set up only once in procedure Initialize.}

   backspace,
   formfeed:      char;                          {ASCII control characters}
   contchar,                         {characters OK in the middle of a word}
   alphabet:      set of char;              {letters only—to start a word}
{Implementation dependent: A good Pascal compiler should allow "set of char";
   otherwise, a restricted range is required.}

begin                                                 {procedure SplitWords}
   Initialize;                          {sets up files, hash table, constants}
   GetWord(w);                          {obtains a single word from InText}
   while not endinput do
   begin
     x := HashAddress(w);
     if w <> hash[x] then
     begin                                 {Not in hash table; put into RefFile.}
       firstletter := w[1];
       outcount[firstletter] := outcount[firstletter] + 1;
       with RefFile[firstletter]↑ do
       begin
         wd := w;
         pg := pagecount
       end;
       Put(RefFile[firstletter])
     end;
     GetWord(w)
   end;
   Conclude                                  {writes word counts to Output}
end;                                                 {procedure SplitWords}
```

11.3.2 Designing the Hash Function and Table

The first auxiliary subprogram needed in phase 1 concerns the processing of the hash table. We have already decided to use open addressing in the hash table of common words used in the above procedure. An unoccupied position in the table will contain the special word blankword consisting of all blanks. Since the table will run a load factor of perhaps 0.5, linear probing may prove unsatisfactory; let us instead use quadratic probing. Finally comes the question of error processing: What if we attempt to insert a word into a completely full table? We could either check for this condition in the function determining the hash address, or in phase 3 when inserting additional words into the file. If we do the check in the function, then it will be needlessly invoked for every access to the hash table; hence, instead, we postpone the check to phase 3.

hash table retrieval

```
function HashAddress(w: word): hashentry;
{calculates the location in hash table of word w, or, if none, returns pointing to
    the blank word where w should go}
var
  x,                                                {calculated location}
  inc: integer;                          {increment for open addressing}
begin                                          {function HashAddress}
  x := (ord(w[1]) * ord(w[3]) * ord(w[4]) + ord(w[6])) mod hashsize + 1;
  {Hash function assumes long word length. For short word machines, we must
      ensure that the result is nonnegative, and worry about overflow.}
  if (hash[x] <> w) and (hash[x] <> blankword) then
  begin
    inc := 1;
    repeat
      x := x + inc;
      if x > hashsize then x := x - hashsize;
      inc := inc + 2
    until (w = hash[x]) or (blankword = hash[x])
  end;
  HashAddress := x
end;                                          {function HashAddress}
```

11.3.3 Initialization

The procedure initializing all the variables involves no really new ideas. Nevertheless, you should especially note the error checking included at several points.

initialization

```
procedure Initialize;
{sets up constant-valued sets for use in GetWord; opens the text file and initializes
    various counters; opens file holding hash table (if any), and reads or otherwise
    initializes the table}
var
  ch: char;                                        {used as an index}
  i: integer;                           {general-purpose loop control}
```

```
                          begin                                          {procedure Initialize}
set up "constants"          backspace := chr(ordbackspace);
                            formfeed := chr(ordformfeed);               {Initialize ASCII control characters.}
                            alphabet := ['A' .. 'Z', 'a' .. 'z'];              {letters only, to start a word}
                            contchar := alphabet + [hyphen, apostrophe, backspace, underscore];
                                                                {characters that will not terminate the word}

                          for i := 1 to maxwd do
                            blankword[i] := blank;

input                     reset(InText);
                          endinput := eof(InText);
                          repeat
                            write( 'What is the page number on which the text begins?');
                            readln(pagecount);
                            if pagecount < 0 then
                              writeln('Must be a non-negative integer.')
                          until pagecount >= 0;
                          linecount := 0;
                          addpage := 0;
                          wordcount := 0;

output                    for ch := A to Z do
                          begin
                            rewrite( RefFile[ch] );
                            outcount[ch] := 0
                          end;

hash table                reset(HashFile);
                          if eof(HashFile) then
                          begin              {There is no previous table; initialize the table to all blanks.}
                            writeln('Cannot open file for hash table. Creating a new table.');
                            for i := 1 to hashsize do
                              hash[i] := blankword
                          end
                          else begin                                {Retrieve the previous hash table.}
                            i := 0;
                            repeat
                              i := i + 1;
                              hash[i] := HashFile↑;
                              get(HashFile)
                            until eof(HashFile) or (i >= hashsize);
                            if (not eof(HashFile)) or (i <> hashsize) then
                              writeln('Error in reading hash table. Incorrect number of entries.')
                          end
                          end;                                                   {procedure Initialize}
```

11.3.4 Finding One Word

Before we can begin to write the procedure that obtains one word from the input text, we must finally address the question,

specifications

> *What is a word?*

The naive answer is, "any sequence of letters," but a few moments' consideration will show that our problems are considerably more complicated.

1. Numerals

Should numerals be allowed in words? Numbers like "1000" or "1728" are frequently written with numerals (as done here), but treated like words. In computer programs, names like A1 and A2 are considered distinct. For the sake of completeness, it might be a good idea to allow numerals within words and treat them in the same way as letters. For simplicity, however, we shall follow the practice of dictionaries and shall exclude numerals. Hence digits appearing between words will be ignored, and the appearance of a digit will terminate a word.

2. Upper- and Lowercase

Perhaps the simplest way to treat upper- and lowercase letters is to regard them as identical. This way, however, loses information. The acronym "SAM" (Sequential Access Method) is not the same as the man's name "Sam." The name "IBM" would be misspelled in lowercase letters. On the other hand, a word should not be considered different because it happens to appear at the beginning of a sentence, and is therefore capitalized. Let us therefore adopt the same convention used in dictionaries: The first letter of every word will be converted to uppercase, but the remaining letters will be left in the same case in which they appear. In comparisons upper- and lowercase will be considered different.

3. Separators

A word ends when a blank is encountered, the line ends, or any character other than a letter or numeral appears (such as punctuation), except for a few special characters that we shall consider separately. All characters in the input should then be ignored until the next word starts, and this will be with the next letter that appears.

4. Hyphens

Hyphens are used for two purposes. At the end of a line, a hyphen means that a word continues on the next line. In this case, we shall delete both the hyphen and the end of line, combining the two parts into a single word. When not at the end of a line, a hyphen connects two words (or radicals) to form a single word. It is quite reasonable to regard each constituent as a separate word, but we shall instead elect to treat a hyphenated word as a single unit. In a word like "pre-empt" neither half is an independent word, and a term like "Come-by-chance" (a town in Newfoundland) has meaning quite distinct from any of its constituent words. Note that our conventions will have the effect of stripping the hyphen from a hyphenated word that happens to be divided after its hyphen between two lines. This situation should arise infrequently. Finally, hyphens are occasionally attached to the end of words, as in the phrase "in-, post-, or preorder traversal." We shall delete such hyphens.

Note that hyphens are not the same as dashes—such as the one in this sentence. In typewritten or computer-input text, however, a dash is frequently represented as two consecutive hyphens. Hence we shall treat two consecutive hyphens as the termination of a word.

5. Apostrophes

Apostrophes have three common uses. They frequently appear as quotation marks, in which case they should terminate words like other punctuation. Second, they appear within contractions, where they should be treated like letters and allow the word to continue. Third, they denote the possessive form of a noun. There is little reason to regard the word "cat's" as different from "cat"; hence we remove a final apostrophe followed by "s." The possessive form "s' " causes no difficulty, of course, since its apostrophe will terminate the word like other punctuation. Finally, within the inner part of a hyphenated term, we shall leave the possessive form intact: An early version of this chapter's program produced a strange result by stripping the possessive from *bird's-eye,* a term appearing both in Chapter 11 and in Chapter 2.

The only time when the rules formulated here will go wrong is that they regard the possessive form "its" as distinct from its variant "it" and fail to recognize the contraction "it's," instead converting it to the word "it."

6. Underlining

Some texts contain the underscore character '_' together with associated backspace characters to produce underlined words. We shall ignore all such characters, removing them from the words before further processing.

11.3.5 Getting a Word from InText

We can now build all these decisions into the key procedure of phase 1, which reads through the file InText and returns the next word. We use a subsidiary procedure GetChar to obtain a single character from InText, and at the same time keep track of ends of lines and the end of file, via the variables endln and endinput, respectively. Since the end of file is discovered in the subsidiary procedure, a statement label

goto statement

and **goto** are used to exit from the outer procedure when the file ends. The end of a page is also detected by GetChar, but the page number associated with a word should be that where the word begins, which might not be the same as where it ends. Hence the variable keeping track of page numbers is updated in GetWord rather than in GetChar.

A second subsidiary procedure, AddChar, appends a character to the word cur-

long and short words

rently being read, and ensures that the word does not exceed maxwd characters. (The constant maxwd is declared in the main program.) Longer words are truncated. The program also ignores all words less than minwd characters, in order to speed the processing.

Since the end of a word is determined by finding the first character not in the word, and since the treatment of several of the special characters depends on what

buffering

comes after the character, the character buffer ch will often contain the character *after* the one being currently processed.

procedure GetWord(**var** w: word);
{Gets words from input file InText, and returns only words at least minwd characters long. Parameter endinput becomes true if and only if the end of InText is reached with no word to return. This parameter is set by the subsidiary procedure GetChar. The procedure also updates global variables wordcount and linecount, updates the global variable pagecount after each linesperpage cr's, or after each formfeed, whichever comes first, and uses the sets alphabet and contchar and various character constants.}

goto and **label**

```
label 1;                          {used by GetChar to exit procedure on eof(InText)}
var   c:          0 .. maxwd;                     {count of characters in word}
      ch:         char;                           {character currently processed}
      endln:      Boolean;                        {At the end of a line?}
begin                                             {procedure GetWord}
  repeat                          {until current word is at least minwd chars long}
    c := 0;
```

find start of word

```
    repeat
      GetChar(ch)                      {Find a letter that will start the word.}
    until ch in alphabet;
```

update page

```
    pagecount := pagecount + addpage;
    addpage := 0;
    if ch in ['a' .. 'z'] then              {Translate the first letter to uppercase.}
      ch := chr(ord(ch) − changecase);                      {system dependent}
    AddChar(ch);                                  {Put first letter into the word.}
    GetChar(ch);
```

continue with word

```
    while ch in contchar do
      if ch in alphabet then                      {Add letters directly to word.}
      begin                                       {processing letter}
        AddChar(ch);
        GetChar(ch)
      end                                         {processing letter}
      else if ch = hyphen then
```

hyphens

```
      begin                                       {processing hyphen}
        GetChar(ch);                              {Find what comes after hyphen.}
        if endln then
          GetChar(ch)              {Delete both the hyphen and the end of line.}
        else if ch = hyphen then               {Two hyphens represent a dash.}
          ch := blank                       {Use a blank to terminate the word.}
        else if ch in alphabet then
          AddChar(hyphen)                    {Include hyphens between letters.}
        else {nothing}                              {Delete all other hyphens.}
      end                                         {processing hyphen}
```

apostrophe

```
               else if ch= apostrophe then
                 begin                              {processing apostrophe}
                   GetChar(ch);
                   if ch = 's' then                 {Delete ''s' at end of word only.}
                   begin
                     GetChar(ch);
                     if ch in contchar then
                     begin
                       AddChar(apostrophe);
                       AddChar('s')
                     end
                   end
                 else if ch in alphabet then
                   AddChar(apostrophe)              {Allow contractions.}
                 end                                {processing apostrophe}
               else              {Remaining possibilities are backspace and underscore.}
```

other

```
                 GetChar(ch);                      {Delete these characters.}
               {while loop on continuing characters ends here.}
               wordcount := wordcount + 1
             until c >= minwd;                      {Skip over short words.}
             while c < maxwd do                     {Fill with blanks.}
```

blank fill

```
             begin
               c := c + 1;
               w[c] := blank
             end;
             1:         {When end of file occurs, program will exit to here from GetChar.}
           end;                                     {procedure GetWord}
```

1. Getting One Character

```
             procedure GetChar(var ch: char);
             {gets a character from input text into ch; checks for eof; updates page count
               and line count}
               begin                                {procedure GetChar}
                 if eof(InText) then
                 if c >= minwd then
                   ch := '.'                         {special character to end the current word}
                 else begin                          {no word to return; set endinput}
                   endinput := true;
```

*use **goto** at end of file*

```
                   goto 1                            {Exit from GetWord.}
                 end
```

```
                    else begin                    {not at end of file: process next character}
                       ch := InText↑;
                       endln := eoln(InText);
                       get(InText);
                       if endln then
```
end of line
```
                       begin
                          linecount := linecount + 1;
                          if linecount >= linesperpage then
                             begin
                                addpage := addpage + 1;
                                linecount := 0
                             end
                       end;
                       if ch = formfeed then
```
end of page
```
                       begin
                          addpage := addpage + 1;
                          linecount := 0;
                          endln := true;                   {Treat formfeed like end of line.}
                          ch := blank
                       end
                    end
                 end;                                      {procedure GetChar}
```

2. Adding a Character to the Word

```
                 procedure AddChar(ch: char);
                 {adds given character to word, if possible}
                 begin                                     {procedure AddChar}
                    if c < maxwd then
                    begin
                       c := c + 1;
                       w[c] := ch
                    end
                 end;                                       {procedure AddChar}
```

11.3.6 Tidying Up

To complete the first phase of the program, we need only close or reset all the files so that the second phase can read them.

procedure Conclude;

{Writes out counts of various word lists. For some systems, it is necessary to close files, which should be done in this procedure.}
var
  ch: char;   {loop index}
begin   {procedure Conclude}

information for user

  writeln('The total number of words read in is', wordcount:7);
  writeln;
  writeln('The number of words to process further in the next stage,');
  writeln('beginning with each letter, is below.');
  writeln;
  for ch := 'A' **to** 'M' **do** write('   ', ch: 1, '   ');
  writeln;
  for ch := 'A' **to** 'M' **do** write(outcount[ch]: 4, ' ');
  writeln;
  writeln;
  for ch := 'N' **to** 'Z' **do** write('   ', ch: 1, '   ');
  writeln;
  for ch := 'N' **to** 'Z' **do** write(outcount[ch]: 4, ' ');
  writeln;
  writeln
end;   {procedure Conclude}

{procedure Conclude}

**Exercises
11.3**

E1. As written, the program ignores all words with fewer than three letters. What single change will make the program keep track of shorter words?

E2. What would be the easiest way to modify the program to translate all letters to uppercase and, hence, ignore the distinction between upper- and lowercase?

E3. Describe the modifications needed in the program so that it would treat digits in the same way as letters.

E4. Describe the changes needed so that the program will regard the parts of a hyphenated term as separate words (except when a hyphen is at the end of a line).

E5. Some dialects of Pascal (such as those usually used for microcomputers), unfortunately, do not allow an array of files. First, describe how to simplify the program so that all words requiring further processing go into a single auxiliary file. Second, devise a scheme by which some of the advantages of sorting with multiple files can be kept, but using fewer than 26 files, and not in an array.

E6. Some operating systems limit the number of files that can be simultaneously open to fewer than 26. Describe how to modify the program to use an array of fewer than 26 files, where now words with several different initial letters go to the same file. If, for example, the array has 8 files, then dividing the letters as follows will achieve a fairly uniform spread of (English) words among the files:

A—B C—D E—G H—L M—O P—R S T—Z.

11.4 PHASE 2: CLASSIFYING THE WORDS

Our task in phase 2 is to process the words that were put in the temporary files in phase 1. More specifically, for each initial letter from A to Z, we wish to read the references from the appropriate temporary file, read the entries from the master word list InIndex with the same initial letter, produce a word count or list of page numbers for words in the master word list, and, on the first occurrence of a word not in InIndex, request the user to assign it to the appropriate category.

11.4.1 Choosing Data Structures

There are several ways to store the data in memory, each of which brings both advantages and disadvantages. Let us first recall the requirements for the data in this second phase. One requirement is that the finished word lists are to be in alphabetical order, available for human inspection. Hence the words must be sorted at some stage in the process. Second, the process is to run efficiently. Sorting tends to be a slow process, so we must exercise care how and when to do it. Third, memory is limited, so we must attempt to avoid storing duplicate information and otherwise try to avoid overflow.

1. Sort, Then Merge

If there is enough room in memory for all the references from one of the temporary files, then perhaps the easiest way to solve the problem is, first, to read in all these references, second, sort them alphabetically, and, finally, read through the master word list, comparing entries as we go. This comparison stage is akin to merging two files. If the same word appears in both lists, then the word list can be updated. If a word is in the new list but not the old, then its disposition can be learned by asking the user, and the proper action can then be taken.

2. Collect, Then Sort and Merge

The major difficulty with the preceding method is that there may not be enough room for all the references from the temporary file. Any writer, working on one document, tends to use a somewhat restricted vocabulary, but to use the same words many times. (This observation is especially true of technical writing.) Hence the total number of references may be too large for memory, but the total number of distinct words will probably not be. As we read the temporary file, therefore, we should amalgamate the references belonging to the same word.

new hash table   One commendable method (left as an exercise) to do this is to set up a new hash table and insert each reference as it is received, amalgamating those that are found to belong together. After the file is exhausted, the hash table is sorted and is compared to the master word list.

3. Collect, Sort and Compare Simultaneously

binary tree   In yet another method (the one that we shall develop), the references are amalgamated and sorted and compared with the master word list as they are received. Instead of concentrating on the file of references, we read in the appropriate part of the master word list and build it into a binary tree. The master word list is already in alphabetical order, so this task will go very quickly—its time is linear in the number of words. As each reference is read in, we search for it in the binary tree with the speed of binary search. If it is present, then the corresponding node is updated; if not, then it is inserted into the tree at the appropriate place. A final inorder traversal of the tree yields the new word list in alphabetical order.

11.4.2 The Main Procedure

We can now establish our notation by writing the main procedure for phase 2. We shall, of course, use linked storage for the binary tree, and the type node is a record with variants according to the disposition of the associated word. The list of page numbers for each word is kept as a simply linked list, with nodes of type reflist. The two associated pointer types are called pointer and pointref, respectively.

procedure ClassifyWords;
{For each letter of the alphabet, the procedure reads in a list of words from InIndex, builds them into a binary tree, supplements it with entries from RefFile, and writes the result to NewIndex and NewHashFile.}

declarations   **type**
    wordtype = (hash, count, index);   {three ways to process a word}
    pointref = ↑reflist;
    reflist = **record**   {list of references}
        pg: integer;
        next: pointref
      end;
    pointer = ↑node;
    node = **record**   {vertex of the binary tree}
        wd: word;
        left,
        right: pointer;
      case kind: wordtype **of**
      hash:
        ( ); {empty}
      count:
        (ct: integer);
      index:
        (ref: pointref)
    end;

```
                          var
                             root: pointer;                              {root of the binary tree}
                             ch: char;                                   {Loop on the first letter of word.}
                          begin                                          {procedure ClassifyWords}
instructions                 writeln('At the appearance of each word, give its disposition:');
                             writeln(' F — Forget all occurrences of this word.');
                             writeln(' C — Count how many times this word appears.');
                             writeln(' I — Index this word: list the pages on which it appears.');
                             reset(InIndex);
                             rewrite(NewIndex);
                             rewrite (NewHashFile);
main loop                    for ch := A to Z do            {Start main loop on first letter of word.}
                             begin
build tree from file            BuildTree(root, ch);   {Get the part of master wordlist starting with ch from
                                                             the file InIndex, and build it into a binary tree.}
                                reset(RefFile[ch]);
                                while not eof(RefFile[ch]) do
                                begin
update tree                        Process(RefFile[ch]↑);
                                                      {Use new words from RefFile[ch] to update the tree.}
                                   get(RefFile[ch])
                                end;
output                          OutputTree(root)
                                    {Write the contents of the tree into files NewIndex and NewHashFile.}
                             end                                {main loop on letters of alphabet}
                          end;                                          {procedure ClassifyWords}
```

11.4.3 Setting Up the Search Tree

The entries in the master word list InIndex are already sorted alphabetically; hence they can be built into the search tree by the method developed in Section 9.5. The procedure BuildTree needed here is precisely the procedure BuildTree developed in Section 9.5. The only difference is that the character ch should be passed through as a second calling parameter. The letter ch is not used in BuildTree itself, but should be passed to the subsidiary procedure GetNode(p, ch). Here it determines which entries should be read from InIndex, and when the reading should stop.

Since the procedures are almost identical to those developed there, we refer to Section 9.5 for the procedure BuildTree and its subsidiary subprograms Insert, Power2, FindRoot, and ConnectSubtrees. For the present application we need only write the procedure GetNode.

1. File Structure

Note that, up to this late time in writing the program, we have not needed to decide the format of the master word file InIndex. Now, however, we shall write the procedure to read this file and must therefore specify its structure. First, this file is to be accessible for human inspection or for use by other programs; hence the file should be of type *text file* text rather than of some privately defined type not available to other programs or systems. Hence, although we shall regard the entries of the file as a kind of record, they will not be treated as such by Pascal. We shall, instead, place all of the information for a single word as one *line* of the file in Pascal.

The first piece of information in each entry is, of course, the word itself. This will occupy maxwd characters. Next we must indicate whether the word is to be indexed, or its occurrences counted. We do so by placing either the letter "i" or "c" after the word. Finally comes a list of page numbers for "i" words, or a single integer count for "c" words.

2. Setting Up a Node

read word from file

```
procedure GetNode(var p: pointer; ch: char);
{reads a word from file InIndex and sets node correspondingly;
returns p = nil at eof or when next word starts later than ch}
var
  wordcode: char;                               {letter indicating type of word}
begin                                                    {procedure GetNode}
  while (not eof(InIndex)) and (InIndex↑ = blank) do
    Get(InIndex);                                    {Skip all the leading blanks.}
  if eof(InIndex) then
    p := nil
  else if InIndex↑ > ch then
    p := nil
  else begin
    new(p);
    with p↑ do begin
      ReadWord(InIndex, wd);
      Read(InIndex, wordcode);
      if wordcode = 'i'
        then begin kind := index; ref := nil end
      else if wordcode = 'c'
        then begin kind := count; ct := 0 end
      else
        writeln('Erroneous word code in file InIndex.')
    end;                                {with statement setting up the node}
    readln(InIndex)                     {Advance to the start of the next entry.}
  end
end;                                                    {procedure GetNode}
```

Note that this procedure sets either the reference list to be empty or the count to be 0 (depending on the word type) for each word. The values to be put into the tree concern the new input document only; these values will be combined with the former values in InIndex during the third phase of the program.

11.4.4 Processing a Reference

Now that the binary tree has been built, the next task to be done in phase 2 is to process the references from the temporary file. The references are read in by the main procedure; we now can write the subsidiary procedure that processes a single reference, updating the binary tree appropriately. This procedure, of course, invokes several others. Its basic task is to search the binary tree for a node corresponding to the reference given as its calling parameter. If it finds such a node, then it invokes UpdateNode; if not, then it invokes NewWord to create a new node for the word and InsertTree to put it into the binary tree.

The basic structure of these procedures is similar to that of corresponding procedures developed in Chapter 9, but the differences required by the specific application are enough that they are rewritten here in full.

1. The Tree Search

```
procedure Process(r: reference);
{takes the word and page reference r and updates the binary tree}
var
   p:   pointer;                                   {Trace through the tree.}
   found:   Boolean;                              {Is the word in the tree?}
begin                                               {procedure Process}
   if root = nil then                             {The tree might be empty.}
      NewWord(root, r)
   else begin                                      {case of nonempty tree}
      p := root;                                   {Begin a tree search.}
      found := false;
      repeat
         if r.wd = p↑.wd then
            found := true
         else if Lt(r.wd, p↑.wd) then
            p := p↑.left
         else
            p := p↑.right
      until found or (p = nil);

      if found then UpdateNode(p, r)
      else begin                           {p↑ was not found: add it to the tree.}
         NewWord(p, r);
         InsertTree(root, p)
      end
   end
end;                                                {procedure Process}
```

2. Updating a Node

```
procedure UpdateNode(p: pointer; r: reference);
{uses reference r to update information in node p↑}
var
    q: pointref;                            {used to add reference to list}

begin                                       {procedure UpdateNode}
    with p↑ do
      case kind of
        hash:;                              {no action needed}
        count: ct := ct + 1;
        index: if ref = nil then
                 begin
                   new(ref);
                   ref↑.pg := r.pg;
                   ref↑.next: = nil
                 end
               else if ref↑.pg <> r.pg then
                 begin                      {Add the new reference to the list.}
                   new(q);
                   q↑.pg: = r.pg;
                   q↑.next := ref;
                   ref: = q
                 end
      end                                   {case statement to update tree}
end;                                        {procedure UpdateNode}
```

3. Creating a New Node

```
procedure NewWord(var p: pointer; r: reference);
{Creates a node for the first occurrence of a new reference r. A pointer to the
  new node is returned in p.}
var
    response: char;                         {answer received from user}
begin                                       {procedure NewWord}
    new(p);
    with p↑ do
    begin
      wd := r.wd;
      left := nil;
      right := nil;
```
ask user about word
```
      repeat                                {Ask user what kind of word.}
        WriteWord(output, wd);
        write('is (F, C, I)?');
        readln(response)
      until response in ['F', 'C', 'I', 'f', 'c', 'i'];
```

```
                        case response of
                          'F', 'f': kind := hash;
                          'C', 'c': begin
                                       kind := count;
                                       ct := 1
                                    end;
                          'I', 'i':  begin
                                       kind := index;
                                       new(ref);
                                       ref↑.pg := r.pg;
                                       ref↑.next := nil;
                                     end
                        end                                            {case statement}
                      end                                              {with statement}
                    end;                                               {procedure NewWord}
```

4. Inserting a New Node into the Tree

```
                    procedure InsertTree(r, p: pointer);
```
{adds a node p↑ to the tree with root r↑; requires that r ≠ **nil** and p↑ not be in
   the tree; proceeds by recursion}
```
                    begin                                             {procedure InsertTree}
                      if Lt(p↑.wd, r↑.wd) then
                        if r↑.left = nil then r↑.left := p
                        else InsertTree(r↑.left, p)
                      else
                        if r↑.right = nil then r↑.right := p
                        else InsertTree(r↑.right, p)
                    end;                                               {procedure InsertTree}
```

11.4.5 Output the Tree

The only remaining task in phase 2 is to write the information from the binary tree
into the output files. The overall structure of this task is a simple inorder traversal
of the binary tree, as follows.

1. Binary Tree Traversal

```
                    procedure OutputTree(p: pointer);
```
{traverses the tree for which p↑ is the root in inorder}
```
                    begin                                             {procedure OutputTree}
                      if p <> nil then
                      with p↑ do
                      begin
                        OutputTree(left);                             {Traverse the left subtree.}
                        PutNode(p);
                        OutputTree(right);                            {Traverse the right subtree.}
                        Dispose(p)
                      end
                    end;                                               {procedure OutputTree}
```

2. Output One Node

The information in a node of the binary tree will be written out in the same format as it was read from the text file InIndex. For nodes of types index or count, the information is written to file NewIndex, which in phase 3 will be merged with InIndex. For the nodes of type forget (hash), the words should not go into the word lists, but into a temporary file NewHashFile, which in phase 3 will be used to update the permanent HashFile.

```
procedure PutNode(p: pointer);
var
   q: pointref;                               {used to traverse list of references}
begin                                                       {procedure PutNode}
   with p↑ do
     case kind of
        hash:   begin
                  NewHashFile↑ := wd;
                  put(NewHashFile)
                end;
        count:  if ct <> 0 then       {Otherwise, word is not in the document.}
                begin
                  WriteWord(NewIndex, wd);
                  write(NewIndex, 'c');
                  writeln(NewIndex, ct: 5)
                end;
        index:  if ref <> nil then
                begin
                  WriteWord(NewIndex, wd);
                  write(NewIndex, 'i');
                  q := ref;
                  repeat
                    write(NewIndex, q↑.pg: 5);
                    q := q↑.next
                  until q = nil;
                  writeln(NewIndex)
                end
     end                                                      {case statement}
end;                                                       {procedure PutNode}
```

Exercises 11.4

E1. Some Pascal systems provide facilities for returning blocks of storage to the system that are more efficient than the dispose procedure. If your system has such a facility, show how it can be used in this chapter's program.

E2. Describe the changes needed to keep lists of unused space and reuse this space instead of relying on the standard procedures new and dispose.

E3. Suppose that the temporary files of references are small enough that each of them will fit in memory. Implement the first plan for phase 2, wherein the list of references is first sorted and then compared with the master word list InIndex.

E4. Implement the second plan for phase 2, in which each reference is first inserted into a hash table and multiple entries are amalgamated. Afterward, the contents of the hash table are sorted and compared with the master word list InIndex.

E5. The master word list can become a large file (for this book it is more than 150,000 characters). A great deal (perhaps half) of this space is taken by blanks, since we represent each word as a blank-filled sequence of exactly maxwd characters. Describe the changes needed so that each word in the file will be terminated by its first blank and extra blanks will not be stored in the file.

11.5 PHASE 3: UPDATING THE PERMANENT FILES

11.5.1 The Hash File

The new entries for the hash table are in the file NewHashFile. We need only use the same function HashAddress written in phase 1 to insert these entries into the table and write the resulting table out to HashFile.

We now face a small organizational problem. If the same function HashAddress is needed both in phase 1 and in phase 3, should it not be declared at the level immediately within the main program, so that it will be available in both phases? It would certainly be reasonable to do so, but if we do, then we must also save space for the hash table at the same time, since the function refers to the table, and we would otherwise have undeclared variables. But in phase 2 we do not use the hash table and cannot afford to lose the space that it would occupy. We are therefore unable to declare the table and its function at the outer level and must instead write the same declarations out twice, once in phase 1 and once in phase 3.

scope rules   The preceding problem points out a major deficiency of Pascal. Declarations have a strictly hierarchical range of validity in Pascal, which does not always meet the requirements of a program. In the current project, we would really like to use a *package* that would combine the hash table with its associated function, declare the package only once, and instruct the compiler that it should be included in phase 1 and phase 3, but not in phase 2. A good name for packages such as this is *information*

information hiding   *hiding module,* since we have no need to access the hash table except through the function in the one specific way.

With the conventions of standard Pascal, however, we have no choice except to write the function HashAddress a second time. While we are doing so, we can make a slight change in the function to include error checking. It is conceivable that the hash table becomes full, in which case the function will search interminably for an empty position. This search should be prevented by inserting a condition such as

if inc $>$ (hashsize **div** 2) **then** $\cdots$

after inc is incremented by 2. The conditional statement should take appropriate action for overflow.

```
                    procedure UpdateHashFile;
                    {reads in old hash table, inserts file of new entries; writes out to HashFile}
                    var
                        hash: array[hashentry] of word;
                        x: hashentry;
                        w: word;
                    begin                                        {procedure UpdateHashFile}
read old file           reset(HashFile);
                        if eof(HashFile) then                {HashFile is empty; create new table.}
                            for x := 1 to hashsize do
                                hash[x] := blankword
                        else
                            for x := 1 to hashsize do
                                read(HashFile, hash[x]);
                    {Some versions of Pascal do not allow procedures read and write for files other
                        than text. For such systems, expand to use get and put.}

read new file       reset (NewHashFile);
                    while not eof(NewHashFile) do
                    begin
                        read(NewHashFile, w);
                        hash[HashAddress(w)] := w
                        {If the table is full, new entries will replace old ones.}
                    end;
output              rewrite(HashFile);
                    for x := 1 to hashsize do
                        write(HashFile, hash[x])
                    end;                                         {procedure UpdateHashFile}
```

11.5.2 Merging the Word Lists

The procedure for merging the new word list into the master word list involves no really new ideas, but the procedure is somewhat complicated by the need to combine two records into one when the same word appears in both lists. This task is assisted by the subsidiary procedure CopyLine. This procedure uses two Boolean parameters to determine whether it is beginning a new line (so that it should write out the word being processed) and whether it should end the current line. The procedure also reads in the word from the next record, in order to continue the usual buffering of one record.

```
procedure MergeIndices;
{merges files NewIndex and InIndex into file OutIndex}
var
   u, v: word;                              {from new and old indices; respectively}
   m, n: integer;                                        {counts for above entries}
   ukind,
   vkind: char;                                            {Is the word of kind i or c?}
begin                                                        {procedure MergeIndices}
   reset(NewIndex);
   reset(InIndex);
   if eof(NewIndex) or eof(InIndex) then
      writeln('One of the indices is empty. No merge will be done.')
   else begin
      rewrite(OutIndex);
      ReadWord(NewIndex, u);
      ReadWord(InIndex, v);
      repeat
```
different words
```
         if Lt(u,v) then
            CopyLine(u, NewIndex, true, true)
               {Boolean parameters mean, respectively: start new line; end the line.}
         else if Lt(v,u) then
            CopyLine(v, InIndex, true, true)
```
same word
```
         else begin                  {Words are equal. Determine the kind of word.}
            read(NewIndex, ukind);
            read(InIndex, vkind);
            if ukind <> vkind then
               writeln('Inconsistent word types found in merge.');
            WriteWord(OutIndex, u);
            write(OutIndex, ukind);
            if ukind = 'c' then
            begin
               readln(NewIndex, m);
               readln(InIndex, n);
               m := m + n;
               writeln(OutIndex, m: 5);
               if not eof(NewIndex) then ReadWord(NewIndex, u);
               if not eof(InIndex) then ReadWord(InIndex, v)
            end
            else begin                           {Copy both lists of page numbers.}
               CopyLine(u, NewIndex, false, false);
               CopyLine(v, InIndex, false, true)
            end
         end
      until eof(NewIndex) or eof(InIndex);
```

copy remainder of file

```
                              while not eof(NewIndex) do
                                 CopyLine(u, NewIndex, true, true);
                              while not eof(InIndex) do
                                 CopyLine(v, InIndex, true, true)
                              {At most one of the two loops above will iterate.}
                           end
                        end;                                    {procedure MergeIndices}
```

1. Copying a Line

```
                        procedure CopyLine(var w: word; var F: text; newline, endline: Boolean);
                        {Copies the remainder of a line from the file F to OutIndex. If newline is true,
                           then the word w is also written, and kind is copied. If endline is true, then
                           the line written to OutIndex is ended. The procedure also reads a new word
                           w from the next line in F.}

                        var
                           n: integer;                          {number copied from file to file}
                           kind: char;                          {word code copied from file to file}

                        begin                                   {procedure CopyLine}
                           if newline then
                           begin
                              WriteWord(OutIndex, w);
                              read(F, kind);
                              write(OutIndex, kind)
                           end
                           else
                              while (not eof(F)) and (not eoln(F)) and (F↑ = blank) do
                                 get(F);
                           while (not eof(F)) and (not eoln(F)) do
                           begin
                              read(F, n);
                              write(OutIndex, n: 5);
                              while(not eoln(F)) and (F↑ = blank) do
                                 get(F);                        {Skip blanks.}
                           end;
                           readln(F);
                           if not eof(F) then
                              ReadWord(F, w);
                           If endline then writeln(OutIndex)
                        end;                                    {procedure CopyLine}
```

1.	**program** IndexText(InText, InIndex, NewIndex, OutIndex, HashFile, Input, Output);	{main program}
2.	**function** Lt(u, v: word): Boolean;	
3.	**procedure** ReadWord(**var** F: text; **var** w: word);	
4.	**procedure** WriteWord(**var** F: text; w: word);	

phase 1

5.	**procedure** SplitWords;	{phase 1}
6.	**function** HashAddress(w: word): hashentry;	
7.	**procedure** Initialize;	
8.	**procedure** GetWord;	
9.	**procedure** GetChar(**var** ch: char);	
10.	**procedure** AddChar(ch: char);	
11.	**procedure** Conclude;	

phase 2

12.	**procedure** ClassifyWords;	{phase 2}
13.	**procedure** BuildTree(**var** root: pointer; ch: char);	
14.	**procedure** Insert(p: pointer);	
15.	**function** Power2(c: integer): level;	
16.	**procedure** FindRoot;	
17.	**procedure** ConnectSubtrees;	
18.	**procedure** GetNode(**var** p: pointer; ch: char);	
19.	**procedure** Process(r: reference);	
20.	**procedure** UpdateNode(p: pointer; r: reference);	
21.	**procedure** NewWord(**var** p: pointer; r: reference);	
22.	**procedure** InsertTree(r, p: pointer);	
23.	**procedure** OutputTree(p: pointer);	
24.	**procedure** PutNode(p: pointer);	

phase 3

25.	**procedure** UpdateHashFile;	{phase 3}
26.	**function** HashAddress(w: word); hashentry;	
27.	**procedure** MergeIndices;	
28.	**procedure** CopyLine	

Table 11.1.   Nesting of subprogram declarations

11.5.3 Summary

too big to remember

With this procedure, the program has been completely written. It is, as you can see, by far the longest program that has appeared in this book. It illustrates an inescapable feature of large programs: It is impossible to keep all the details in mind at once. By concentrating first on the overall outline, and then on one section at a time, it is possible to write and debug the entire program. In the end, even so, the program must be put together to function as a single unit. At this stage the skills of a librarian become important, simply to keep track of all the subprograms and to put them in their proper places. In summary, then, the organizational structure of our program is shown in Table 11.1. All the necessary subprograms are listed, and the indenting shows the appropriate nesting of declarations.

11.6 REVIEW, ANALYSIS, AND MAINTENANCE

not final

Experience can either reinforce or change priorities, desires, and goals. Experience in working with a program can show which features are strong and which are not, which capabilities are valuable and which should be modified. The index writing program of this chapter is by no means in final form. In fact, it is not presented here in the form in which it is actually used. The program is, instead, presented in a form as close as possible to that in which it was first designed and written (with bugs removed). The reason for this presentation is to illustrate that computer programming, like engineering or art, is an experimental subject where a first effort will usually need further refinement and polishing before it achieves complete satisfaction.

This section discusses some proposed changes for the program, some possible extensions of its capabilities, and some improvements that can be made in its structure. This section should be regarded as an extended set of exercises, an outline of various projects, some of which can be pursued almost indefinitely.

11.6.1 Convenience of Use

friendliness

In its current form, our program is not as friendly as it might be. With a good-sized file the first phase will take significant time, during which the user is left in total silence. The program should keep the user informed of its progress during execution. At a minimum, one line might be printed for each page processed, indicating how the work is going. On the other hand, it is certainly possible to make the program too verbose. Printing the entire text as it is read would probably be excessive.

error handling

interrupts

Failures can occur in the execution of any program, but every effort should be made to make them unlikely, and to minimize their effects. The input and output of our program should be refined (according to the features and requirements of a particular system) so that file-handling errors are completely processed and will not cause catastrophic failure. A large program like ours is always in danger of being manually interrupted by the user or the system (for example, time limits). At the moment, such interruption may destroy all the work already complete. All the files opened for output, for example, may be lost. If your system provides facilities for programmed processing of interrupts, or allows the program to complete an orderly shutdown, then by all means these facilities should be included in the program. If it is possible to salvage the incomplete files, then auxiliary programs should be written to do so and, if possible, to allow the program to continue from where it was interrupted.

11.6.2 Flexibility and Generality

incorrect words

As written, our program tacitly assumes that the document is in its final form, with no errors and ready to be completely indexed. The major application of the program, however, will be to documents that are not in final form. The program is especially useful in checking spelling and consistency of word choice in different parts of a document. The output files should therefore not necessarily become part of a permanent record. The third phase of the program, which merges these output files into the permanent hash table and master word list, should probably be a separate program that could be run if the document is in final form, and otherwise need not be.

misspellings

The program treats misspelled words in exactly the same way as correctly spelled words. There should be a special category for misspelled words or others that are questionable. After the program finishes, the words in this category should be collected for the user in some form to facilitate their investigation and correction. In fact, I find it convenient to split the "index" category of the program into three categories: category "i" contains the important terms that will be placed in an index; category "p" contains words that occur only a few times, and for which page references (a concordance) will be given. Category "?" includes the misspelled words and others that will probably be changed. Words in this last category are never merged into the permanent records.

frequency counts

Just because a word occurs frequently, it is not necessarily uninteresting. Frequency counts could certainly be kept for the words in the hash table, and would be of interest for some purposes. When first running the program to set up the initial word lists, it may not be evident to the user into which category to place some words. Words placed in the hash table may turn out to be not so common as other words. An interesting extension of phase 3 of the program would be another program to reallocate words among the various categories. The relative frequencies of words in the hash table, in category "c" and category "p" (give page references) would be determined, and appropriate criteria used to move words from one category to another.

revision of hash table

A related project is to rehash the hash table, according to frequency. The order in which words are inserted in the hash table is that in which they first appear. If the table is nearly full, then searches of several entries may be needed to find a particular word. Depending on the order of first appearance, common words can require longer searches than less common ones. Future runs of the program can therefore be speeded up by sorting all the words in the hash table according to frequency and then inserting them all over again into an empty table according to this order.

filters

Finally, it would probably be better to write the program as a series of several independent programs (*filters*), as proposed in part 5 of Section 11.2.1. In this way, different parts of the program could be used separately if needed in a particular application.

11.6.3 Use of Space

Our decision to represent words as fixed-length arrays of exactly maxwd = 20 characters wastes a great deal of space. Space in the files can easily be saved by eliminating trailing blanks from the words (as proposed in an exercise). Saving space in high-speed memory is more difficult, given the constraints of standard Pascal. It might be practical to use linked storage, with blocks of several letters in each node, but the programming would then become more complicated.

trailing blanks

A more sophisticated method is to recognize that the usual way of representing individual letters in computer storage takes up a great deal of space, much more

encoding

than is actually needed. Eight binary digits are usually used for each character. Within our words we allow upper- and lowercase letters, hyphens, and apostrophes, for a total of only 54 characters. In six binary digits we can represent 64 distinct characters. Hence by using six instead of eight bits, we can immediately reduce our space requirements by 25 percent. With a little more work we can save a great deal more. Not all characters are equally likely. The letter 'e' occurs much more frequently than does 'z' or 'j'. A *Huffman encoding* is a system that produces a representation in which the common characters have very short codes, and the uncommon characters much longer codes, and thereby reduces the average space needed for a word.

If we look at sequences of letters we can do even better. In English the pair of letters 'th' occurs very frequently, while 'jj' or 'qb' almost never occur. In one large experiment (see the paper of MCMAHON, CHERRY, and MORRIS in the references) considering triples of letters and blanks, of the 21952 possible combinations, only 4923, or 22.4 percent, actually occur in a large text of about a half-million words. By using this and further methods, it is possible to devise representations of English text that will reduce the space needed, on average, to little more than 1.5 bits per character.

Such packing of characters requires execution time, of course. On the other hand, the speed of reading and writing files is slow compared to calculation. It is necessary, therefore, to reach a balance between a system that requires a great deal of calculation, but can minimize file accesses by keeping more information in high-speed memory, and a system that calculates very quickly but requires more file processing.

11.6.4 Spelling Correction

A highly desirable extension of the program is that it should not only detect words that are probably misspelled, but that it should be able to suggest or make corrections in the spelling. Such a goal cannot be completely within our reach until we can devise programs that understand the meaning rather than just the form of a text. Nonetheless, misprints tend to occur in predictable ways, and it is possible to use some of these patterns to suggest corrections. This topic is open ended and the subject of considerable current work. See the references for summaries of some of this activity.

REFERENCES FOR FURTHER STUDY

A good starting point for learning some of the various approaches for designing programs like that of this chapter is the following survey paper.

JAMES L. PETERSON, "Computer programs for detecting and correcting spelling errors," *Communications of the ACM* 23 (1980), 676–687; related correspondence and comments: *Ibid.* 24 (1981), 322, 331–332, 608–609, 618–619.

As you see from this list of pages, this survey paper has elicited considerable correspondence regarding alternative methods. This correspondence reflects substantial current interest in the development of spelling-correcting programs.

This paper includes an annotated bibliography of 44 items, constituting excellent source material for further study of the topics raised in this chapter. Let us single out a few of these sources, with some further references.

First is a book in which the author describes a much more elaborate spelling checking and correcting program (made up of 105 procedures).

JAMES L. PETERSON, *Design of a spelling program: An experiment in program design,* Lecture Notes in Computer Science, Volume 96, Springer-Verlag, Berlin, Heidelberg, New York, 1980.

A simple spelling corrector is described in

PETER ROBINSON and DAVE SINGER, "Another spelling correction program," *Communications of the ACM* 24 (1981), 296–297.

An interesting idea for a spelling checker, using multiple hashing functions to determine with high probability if a word is misspelled while using only 20 percent of the space needed for a dictionary, is

ROBERT NIX, "Experience with a space efficient way to store a dictionary," *Communications of the ACM* 24 (1981), 297–298.

The observations in this chapter about word frequencies are taken from the following paper, which provides a good tutorial on a statistical approach to spelling checking and text compression:

L. E. MCMAHON, L. L. CHERRY, AND R. MORRIS, "Statistical text processing," *Bell System Technical Journal* 57 (1978), 2137–2154.

Word frequencies and other statistical information for a text of more than a million words are given in

H. KUCERA and W. FRANCIS, *Computational Analysis of Present-Day American English,* Brown University Press, Providence, R.I., 1967.

A very elementary exposition of techniques for text compression by (variable-length) Huffman codes is

JONATHAN AMSTERDAM, "Data compression with Huffman coding," *Byte* 11, no. 5 (May 1986), 99–108.

Since the ability to locate a passage containing a given term is important for scholars, concordances have been used for many years, and, before the advent of computers, a great deal of labor was invested in developing such concordances. One of the best examples is the following book, which lists the chapter and verse of every word appearing in the King James translation of the Bible, and except for the 47 most common words, lists every occurrence of each word with its surrounding context.

JAMES STRONG, *Exhaustive Concordance of the Bible,* Methodist Book, 1894 (available in many reprint editions).

Case Study: The Polish Notation

▶ *This chapter studies the Polish notation for arithmetic or logical expressions, first in terms of problem solving, and then as applied to a program that interactively accepts an expression, compiles it, and evaluates it. This chapter illustrates uses of recursion, stacks, and trees, as well as their interplay in problem solving and algorithm design.*

12.1 THE PROBLEM

One of the most important accomplishments of the early designers of computer languages was allowing a programmer to write arithmetic expressions in something close to their usual mathematical form. It was a real triumph to design a compiler that understood expressions such as

$$(x + y) * exp(x - z) - 4.0$$
$$a * b + c / d - c * (x + y)$$
$$\textbf{not } (p \textbf{ and } q) \textbf{ or } (x < = 7.0)$$

and produced machine-language output. In fact, the name FORTRAN stands for

etymology: FORTRAN

FORmula TRANslator

in recognition of this very accomplishment. It often takes only one simple idea that, when fully understood, will provide the key to an elegant solution of a difficult problem, in this case the translation of expressions into sequences of machine-language instructions.

The triumph of the method to be developed in this chapter is that, in contrast to the first approach a person might take, it is not necessary to make repeated scans through the expression to decipher it, and, after a preliminary translation, neither parentheses nor priorities of operators need to be taken into account, so that evaluation of the expression can be achieved with great efficiency.

12.1.1 The Quadratic Formula

Before we discuss this idea, let us briefly imagine the problems an early compiler designer might have faced when confronted with a fairly complicated expression. Even the quadratic formula produces problems:

$$x := (-b + (b \uparrow 2 - (4 \times a) \times c) \uparrow \frac{1}{2})/(2 \times a).$$

(Here, and throughout this chapter, we denote exponentiation by '$\uparrow$'. We limit our attention to one of the two roots.) Which operations must be done before others? What are the effects of parentheses? When can they be omitted? As you answer these questions for this example, you will probably look back and forth through the expression several times.

In considering how to translate such expressions, the compiler designers soon settled on the conventions that are familiar now: Operations are ordinarily done left to right, subject to the priorities assigned to operators, with exponentiation highest, then multiplication and division, then addition and subtraction. This order can be altered by parentheses. For the quadratic formula, the order of operations is

$$x := (- b + (b \uparrow 2 - (4 \times a) \times c) \uparrow \frac{1}{2})/(2 \times a)$$

$$\begin{array}{cccccccccc} \uparrow & \uparrow & \uparrow & \uparrow & \uparrow & \uparrow & \uparrow & \uparrow & \uparrow & \uparrow \\ 10 & 1 & 7 & 2 & 5 & 3 & 4 & 6 & 9 & 8 \end{array}$$

Note that assignment ':=' really is an operator that takes the value of its right operand and assigns it to the left operand. The priority of ':=' will be the lowest of any operator, since it cannot be done until the expression is fully evaluated.

12.1.2 Unary Operators and Priorities

With one exception, all the operators in the quadratic equation are *binary;* that is, they have two operands. The one exception is the leading minus sign in $-b$. This is a *unary* operator, and unary operators provide a slight complication in determining priorities. Normally we interpret -2^2 as -4, which means that negation is done after exponentiation, but we interpret 2^{-2} as ¼ and not as -4, so that here negation is done first. It is reasonable to assign unary operators the same priority as exponentiation and, in order to preserve the usual algebraic conventions, to evaluate operators of this priority from right to left. Doing this, moreover, also gives the ordinary interpretation of $2 \uparrow 3 \uparrow 2$ as

$$2^{(3^2)} = 512 \qquad \text{and not as} \qquad (2^3)^2 = 64.$$

There are unary operators other than negation. These include such operations as taking the factorial of x, denoted $x!$, the derivative of a function f, denoted f', as well as all functions of a single variable, such as the trigonometric, exponential, and logarithmic functions. There is also the Boolean operator **not**, which negates a Boolean variable.

Several binary operators also have Boolean results: the operators **and** and **or** as well as the comparison operators '=', '≠', '<', '>', '≤', and '≥'. These comparisons are normally done after the arithmetic operators, but before **and, not** and assignment.

We thus obtain the following list of priorities to reflect our usual customs in evaluating operators:

priority list

Operators	Priority
↑, all unary arithmetic operators	6
× / **div** **mod**	5
+ − (binary)	4
= ≠ < > ≤ ≥	3
not	2
and or	1
:=	0

Note that these priorities are not those used in Pascal, where **and** has priority 5 and **or** has priority 4. As long as we are designing our own system, however, we are free to set our own conventions, provided that they are consistent, reasonable, and appropriate.

12.2 THE IDEA

12.2.1 Expression Trees

Drawing a picture is often an excellent way to gain insight into a problem. For our current problem, the appropriate picture is the *expression tree,* as first introduced in Section 9.3. Recall that an expression tree is a binary tree in which the leaves are the simple operands and the interior vertices are the operators. If an operator is binary, then it has two nonempty subtrees that are its left and right operands (either simple operands or subexpressions). If an operator is unary, then only one of its subtrees is nonempty, the one on the left or right according as the operator is written on the right or left of its operand. You should review Figure 9.4 for several simple expression trees, as well as Figure 9.5 for the expression tree of the quadratic formula.

Let us determine how to evaluate an expression tree such as, for example, the one shown in panel (a) of Figure 12.1. It is clear that we must begin with one of the leaves, since it is only the simple operands for which we know the values when starting. To be consistent, let us start with the leftmost leaf, whose value is 2.9. Since, in our example, the operator immediately above this leaf is unary negation,

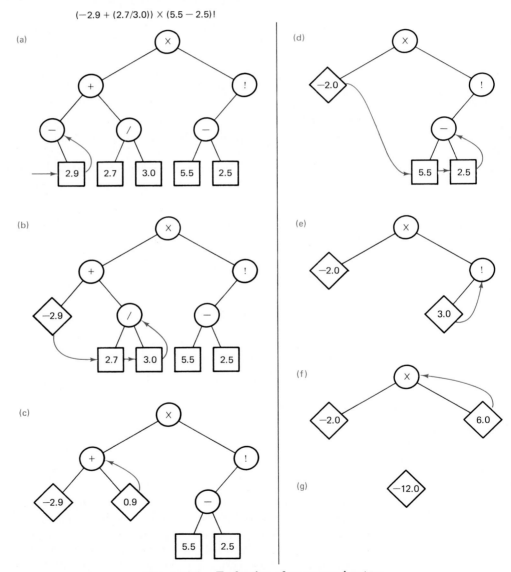

Figure 12.1. Evaluation of an expression tree

we can apply it immediately and replace both the operator and its operand by the result, −2.9. This step results in the diamond-shaped node in panel (b) of the diagram.

The parent of the diamond-shaped node in panel (b) is a binary operator, and its second operand has not yet been evaluated. We cannot, therefore, apply this operator yet, but must instead consider the next two leaves, as shown by the colored path. After moving past these two leaves, the path moves to the parent operator, which can now be evaluated, and the result placed in the second diamond-shaped node, as shown in panel (c).

At this stage, both operands of the addition are available, so we can perform it, obtaining the simplified tree in panel (d). And so we continue, until the tree has been reduced to a single node, which is the final result. In summary, we have processed the nodes of the tree in the order

$$2.9 \quad - \quad 2.7 \quad 3.0 \quad / \quad + \quad 5.5 \quad 2.5 \quad - \quad ! \quad \times.$$

postorder traversal

The general observation is that we should process the subtree rooted at any given operator in the order: "Evaluate its left subtree; Evaluate its right subtree; Perform the operator." (If the operator is unary, then one of these steps is vacuous.) This order is precisely a postorder traversal of the expression tree. We have already observed in Section 9.3 that the postorder traversal of an expression tree yields the postfix form of the expression, in which each operator is written after its operands, instead of between them.

This simple idea is the key to efficient calculation of expressions by computer.

As a matter of fact, our customary way to write arithmetic or logical expressions with the operator between its operands is slightly illogical. The instruction

Take the number 12 *and multiply by* · · ·.

is incomplete until the second factor is given. In the meantime it is necessary to remember both a number and an operation. From the viewpoint of establishing uniform rules it makes more sense either to write

Take the numbers 12 *and* 3; *then multiply.*

or to write

Do a multiplication. The numbers are 12 *and* 3.

12.2.2 Polish Notation

This method of writing all operators either before their operands, or after them, is called *Polish notation,* in honor of its discoverer, the Polish mathematician JAN ŁUKASIEWICZ. When the operators are written before their operands, it is called the *prefix form.* When the operators come after their operands, it is called the *postfix form* or, sometimes, *reverse Polish form* or *suffix form.* Finally, in this context, it is customary to use the coined phrase *infix form* to denote the usual custom of writing binary operators between their operands.

The expression $a \times b$ becomes $\times\, a\, b$ in prefix form and $a\, b\, \times$ in postfix form. In the expression $a + b \times c$, the multiplication is done first, so we convert it first, obtaining first $a + (b\, c\, \times)$ and then $a\, b\, c\, \times\, +$ in postfix form. The prefix form of this expression is $+\, a \times b\, c$. Note that prefix and postfix forms are not related by taking mirror images or other such simple transformation. Note also that all parentheses have been omitted in the Polish forms. We shall justify this omission later.

As a more complicated example we can write down the prefix and postfix forms of the quadratic formula, starting from its expression tree, as shown in Figure 9.5.

preorder traversal

First, let us traverse the tree in preorder. The operator in the root is the assignment ':=', after which we move to the left subtree, which consists only of the operand x. The right subtree begins with the division '/ ', and then moves leftward to '+' and to the unary negation '−'.

We now have an ambiguity that will haunt us later if we do not correct it. The first '−' (minus) in the expression is unary negation, and the second is binary subtraction. In Polish form it is not obvious which is which. When we go to evaluate the prefix string we will not know whether to take one operand for '−' or two, and the results will be quite different. To avoid this ambiguity we shall reserve '−' to denote binary subtraction and use the special symbol '$\div$' for unary negation. (This terminology is certainly not standard. There are other ways to resolve the problem.)

The preorder traversal up to this point has yielded

$$:=\quad x\quad /\quad +\quad \div\quad b,$$

and the next step is to traverse the right subtree of the operator '+'. The result is the sequence

$$\uparrow\quad -\quad \uparrow\quad b\quad 2\quad \times\quad \times\quad 4\quad a\quad c\quad \text{½}.$$

Finally, we traverse the right subtree of the division '/ ', obtaining

$$\times\quad 2\quad a.$$

Hence the complete prefix form for the quadratic formula is

$$:=\, x\, /\, +\, \div\, b\, \uparrow\, -\, \uparrow\, b\, 2 \times \times 4\, a\, c\, \text{½} \times 2\, a.$$

You should verify yourself that the postfix form is

$$x\, b\, \div\, b\, 2 \uparrow 4\, a \times c \times -\, \text{½} \uparrow +\, 2\, a \times /\, :=.$$

12.2.3 Pascal Method

Before concluding this section, we should remark that most Pascal compilers do not use Polish forms in translating expressions into machine language (although many other languages do). Most Pascal compilers, instead, use the method of recursive descent as introduced in Section 8.4. In this method, each priority of operator requires a separate procedure for its compilation (and a separate syntax diagram for its definition). This requirement may partially explain why Pascal uses a truncated list of priorities in comparison with those employed throughout this chapter.

parsing

Translation of an expression by recursive descent is called ***top-down parsing***, whereas this chapter's method of translating an expression by looking at each of its components in turn is an example of ***bottom-up parsing***.

Exercises
12.2

(a) Draw the expression tree for each of the following expressions. Using the tree, convert the expression into **(b)** prefix and **(c)** postfix form. Use the table of priorities developed in this section, not those in Pascal.

E1. $a + b < c$.

E2. $a < b + c$.

E3. $a - b < c - d$ **or** $e < f$.

E4. $n!$ **div** $(k! \times (n - k)!)$
(formula for binomial coefficients).

E5. $s := (n \ / \ 2) \times (2 \times a + (n - 1) \times d)$.
(This is the sum of the first n terms of an arithmetic progression.)

E6. $g := a \times (1 - r \uparrow n)/(1 - r)$.
(This is the sum of the first n terms of a geometric progression.)

E7. $a = 1$ **or** $b \times c = 2$ **or** $(a > 1$ **and not** $b < 3)$.

12.3 EVALUATION OF POLISH EXPRESSIONS

We first introduced the postfix form as a natural order of traversing an expression tree in order to evaluate the corresponding expression. Later in this section we shall formulate an algorithm for evaluating an expression directly from the postfix form, but first (since it is even simpler) we consider the prefix form.

12.3.1 Evaluation of an Expression in Prefix Form

Preorder traversal of a binary tree works from the top down. The root is visited first, and the remainder of the traversal then divided into two parts. The natural way to organize the process is as a recursive, divide-and-conquer algorithm. The same situation holds for an expression in prefix form. The first symbol (if there is more than one) is an operator (the one that will actually be done last), and the remainder of the expression comprises the operand(s) of this operator (one for a unary operator, two for a binary operator). Our procedure for evaluating the prefix form should hence begin with this first symbol. If it is a unary operator, then the procedure should invoke itself recursively to determine the value of the operand. If the first symbol is a binary operator, then it should make two recursive calls for its two operands. The recursion terminates in the remaining case: When the first symbol is a simple operand, it is its own prefix form and the procedure should only return its value.

The following outline thus summarizes the evaluation of an expression in prefix form:

outline

```
procedure Evaluate (expression, result);
  Let t be the first symbol in expression, and move one position through the
  expression;
  if t is a unary operator then
  begin
    Evaluate(expression, x);
    Set the result to the value of operator t applied to x
  end
  else if t is a binary operator then
  begin
    Evaluate(expression, x);
    Evaluate(expression, y);
    Set the result to the value of operator t applied to x and y
  end
  else                                              {t is a simple operand.}
    Set the result to the value of t
end;
```

12.3.2 Pascal Conventions

To tie down the details in this outline, let us establish some conventions and rewrite the algorithm in Pascal. The operators and operands in our expression may well have names that are more than one character long; hence we do not scan the expression one character at a time. Instead we define a *token* to be a single operator or operand from the expression. To emphasize that the procedure scans through the expression only once, we shall employ an auxiliary procedure

token

GetToken(**var** t: token)

that will move through the expression and return one token at a time. We need to know whether the token is an operand, a unary operator, or a binary operator, so we assume the existence of a function Kind( ) that will return one of the three words

operand,   unaryop,   binaryop.

(In Pascal these identifiers together constitute an *enumerated type.*)

For simplicity we shall assume that all the operands and the results of evaluating the operators are of the same type, which we leave unspecified and call value. In many applications, this type would be one of integer, real, complex, or Boolean.

Finally, we must assume the existence of three auxiliary functions that return a result of type value.

DoUnary(t: token, x: value): value
DoBinary(t: token, x, y: value): value

actually perform the given operation on their operand(s). They need to recognize the symbols used for the operation t and the operands x and y and invoke the necessary machine-language instructions. Similarly,

$$GetValue(t: token): value$$

returns the actual value of a simple operand t, and might need, for example, to convert a constant from decimal to binary form, or look up the value of a variable. The actual form of these functions will depend very much on the application. We cannot settle all these questions here, but want only to concentrate on designing one important part of a compiler or expression evaluator.

12.3.3 Pascal Procedure for Prefix Evaluation

With these preliminaries we can now translate our outline into a Pascal program to evaluate prefix expressions.

```
procedure EvaluatePrefix(var result: value);
var
    t:     token;
    x, y: value;
begin                                          {procedure EvaluatePrefix}
  GetToken(t);
  case Kind(t) of
    unaryop: begin
                EvaluatePrefix(x);
                result := DoUnary(t, x)
             end;
    binaryop: begin
                EvaluatePrefix(x);
                EvaluatePrefix(y);
                result := DoBinary(t,x,y)
             end;
    operand: result := GetValue(t)
  end
end;                                           {procedure EvaluatePrefix}
```

12.3.4 Evaluation of Postfix Expressions

It is almost inevitable that the prefix form so naturally calls for a recursive function for its evaluation, since the prefix form is really a "top-down" formulation of the algebraic expression: The outer, overall actions are specified first, then later in the expression the component parts are spelled out. On the other hand, in the postfix form the operands appear first, and the whole expression is slowly built up from its simple operands and the inner operators, in a "bottom-up" fashion. Therefore iterative programs using stacks appear more natural for the postfix form. (It is of course possible to write either recursive or nonrecursive programs for either form. We are here discussing only the motivation, or what first appears more natural.)

stacks

To evaluate an expression in postfix form, it is necessary to remember the operands until their operator is eventually found some time later. The natural way to remember them is to put them on a stack. Then when the first operator to be done is encountered, it will find its operands on the top of the stack. If it puts its result back on the stack, then its result will be in the right place to be an operand for a later operator. When the evaluation is complete, the final result will be the only value on the stack. In this way, we obtain a procedure to evaluate a postfix expression.

At this time we should note a significant difference between postfix and prefix expressions. There was no need, in the prefix procedure, to check explicitly that the end of the expression had been reached, since the entire expression automatically constituted the operand(s) for the first operator. Reading a postfix expression from left to right, however, we can encounter subexpressions that are, by themselves, legitimate postfix expressions. For example, if we stop reading

$$b \quad 2 \quad \uparrow \quad 4 \quad a \quad \times \quad c \quad \times \quad -$$

after the '$\uparrow$', we find that it is a legal postfix expression. To remedy this problem we shall suppose that the expression ends with a special sentinel, and for this sentinel token the function Kind( ) returns the special value

endexpression.

The remaining defined types in Pascal, as well as the other auxiliary procedures and functions are the same as for the prefix evaluation. In addition, we shall represent the stack as an array declared in our procedure, with subsidiary procedures as follows.

```
procedure Push(v: value);              procedure Pop(var v: value);
begin                                  begin
  if nstack >= maxstack then Error       if nstack <= 0 then Error
  else begin                             else begin
    nstack := nstack + 1;                  v := stack[nstack];
    stack[nstack] := v                     nstack := nstack - 1
  end                                    end
end;                                   end;
```

```
procedure EvaluatePostfix(var result: value);
const
  maxstack = 100;                        {maximum size of the stack}
var
  stack:    array[1 .. maxstack] of value;
  nstack:   0 .. maxstack;               {number of values in the stack}
  t:        token;                       {current operator or operand}
  x, y:     value;                       {operands of current operator}
```

```
begin                                          {procedure EvaluatePostfix}
   nstack := 0;                                {Initialize the stack to be empty.}
   repeat
      GetToken(t);
      case Kind(t) of
         operand:
                 Push(GetValue(t));
         unaryop:
                    begin
                       Pop(x);
                       Push(DoUnary(t, x))
                    end;
         binaryop:
                    begin
                       Pop(y);                  {second operand}
                       Pop(x);                  {first operand}
                       Push(DoBinary(t, x, y))
                    end;
         endexpression:
                    if nstack = 1 then
                       Pop(result)
                    else
                       Error               {There must be exactly one entry at the end.}
      end                                       {case statement}
   until Kind(t) = endexpression;
end;                                            {procedure EvaluatePostfix}
```

In this program we have included error checking in the Push and Pop procedures, to catch the possibility that the appearance of an operator might call for popping the stack without enough operands on the stack. Similarly at the end there is an error if there is more than one result or no result on the stack.

12.3.5 Proof of the Program: Counting Stack Entries

So far we have given only an informal motivation for the preceding program, and it may not be clear that it will produce the correct result in every case. Fortunately it is not difficult to give a formal justification of the program and, at the same time, to discover a useful criterion as to whether an expression is properly written in postfix form or not.

The method we shall use is to keep track of the number of entries in the stack. When each operand is obtained, it is immediately pushed onto the stack. A unary operator first pops, then pushes the stack, and thus makes no change in the number of entries. A binary operator pops the stack twice and pushes it once, giving a net decrease of one entry in the stack. More formally, we have *running-sum condition*

> For a sequence *E* of operands, unary operators, and binary operators, form a running sum by starting at the left end of *E* and counting $+1$ for each operand, 0 for each unary operator, and -1 for each binary operator. *E* satisfies the **running-sum condition** provided that this running sum never falls below 1, and is exactly 1 at the right-hand end of *E*.

The sequence of running sums for an evaluation of the postfix form of the quadratic formula is illustrated in Figure 12.2. We shall prove the following two theorems at the same time.

THEOREM 12.1

> *If E is a properly formed expression in postfix form, then E must satisfy the running-sum condition.*

THEOREM 12.2

> *A properly formed expression in postfix form will be correctly evaluated by procedure* EvaluatePostfix.

PROOF   We shall prove the theorems together by using mathematical induction on the length of the expression *E* being evaluated.

induction proof   The starting point for the induction is the case that *E* is a single operand alone, with length 1. This operand contributes $+1$, and the running-sum condition is satisfied. The procedure, when applied to a simple operand alone, gets its value, pushes it on the stack (which was previously empty) and at the end pops it as the final value of the procedure, thereby evaluating it correctly.

For the induction hypothesis we now assume that *E* is a proper postfix expression of length more than 1, that the program correctly evaluates all postfix expressions of length less than that of *E*, and that all such shorter expressions satisfy the running-sum condition. Since the length of *E* is more than 1, *E* is constructed at its last step either as *F op*, where *op* is a unary operator and *F* a postfix expression, or as *F G op*, where *op* is a binary operator and *F* and *G* are postfix expressions. In either case the lengths of *F* and *G* are less than that of *E*, so by induction hypothesis both of them satisfy the running-sum condition, and the procedure would evaluate either of them separately and would obtain the correct result.

unary operator   First, take the case when *op* is a unary operator. Since *F* satisfies the running-sum condition, the sum at its end is exactly $+1$. As a unary operator, *op* contributes

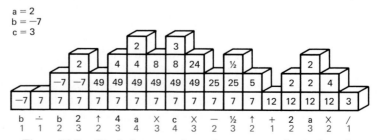

Figure 12.2.   Stack frames and running sums, quadratic formula

0 to the sum, so the full expression E satisfies the running-sum condition. When the procedure reaches the end of F, similarly, it will, by induction hypothesis, have evaluated F correctly and left its value as the unique stack entry. The unary operator *op* is then finally applied to this value, which is popped as the final result.

binary operator

Finally, take the case when *op* is binary. When the procedure reaches the last token of F, the value of F will be the unique entry on the stack. Similarly, the running sum will be 1. At the next token the program starts to evaluate G. By the induction hypothesis the evaluation of G will also be correct, and its running sum alone never falls below 1, and ends at exactly 1. Since the running sum at the end of F is 1, the combined running sum never falls below 2 and ends at exactly 2 at the end of G. Thus the evaluation of G will proceed and never disturb the single entry on the bottom of the stack, which is the result of F. When the evaluation reaches the final binary operator *op*, the running sum is correctly reduced from 2 to 1, and the operator finds precisely its two operands on the stack, where after evaluation it leaves its unique result. This completes the proof of Theorems 12.1 and 12.2.

end of proof

This error checking by keeping a running count of the number of entries on the stack provides a handy way to verify that a sequence of tokens is in fact a properly formed postfix expression and is especially useful because its converse is also true:

THEOREM 12.3

If E is any sequence of operands and operators that satisfies the condition on running sums, then E is a properly formed expression in postfix form.

PROOF

We shall again use mathematical induction to prove Theorem 12.3. The starting point is an expression containing only one token. Since the running sum (same as final sum) for a sequence of length 1 will be 1, this one token must be a simple operand. One simple operand alone is indeed a syntactically correct expression.

induction proof

Now, for the inductive step, suppose that the theorem has been verified for all expressions strictly shorter than E, and E has length greater than 1. If the last token of E were an operand, then it would contribute $+1$ to the sum, and since the final sum is 1, the running sum would have been 0 one step before the end, contrary to the assumption that the running-sum condition is satisfied. Thus the final token of E must be an operator.

If the operator is unary, then it can be omitted and the remaining sequence still satisfies the condition on running sums, so by induction hypothesis is a syntactically correct expression, and all of E then also is.

Finally, suppose that the last token is a binary operator *op*. To show that E is syntactically correct, we must find where in the sequence the first operand of *op* ends and the second one starts, by using the running sum. Since the operator *op* contributes -1 to the sum, it was 2 one step before the end. This 2 means that there were two items on the stack, the first and second operands of *op*. As we step backward through the sequence E, eventually we will reach a place where there is only one entry on the stack (running sum 1), and this one entry will be the first operand of *op*. Thus the place to break the sequence is at the last position before the end where the running sum is exactly 1. Such a position must exist, since at the far left end of E (if not before) we will find a running sum of 1. When we break E at its last 1, then it takes the form $F\ G\ op$. The subsequence F satisfies the condition on running sums, and ends with a sum of 1, so by induction hypothesis it is a correctly formed postfix expression. Since the running sums during G of $F\ G$ op never again fall to 1, and end at 2 just before op, we may subtract 1 from each of them and conclude that the running sums for G alone satisfy the condition. Thus by induction hypothesis G is also a correctly formed postfix expression. Thus both F and G are correct expressions and can be combined by the binary operator op into a correct expression E. Thus, the proof of the theorem is complete.

end of proof

We can take the proof one more step, to show that the last position where a sum of 1 occurs is the *only* place where the sequence E can be split into syntactically correct subsequences F and G. For suppose it was split elsewhere. If at the end of F the running sum is not 1, then F is not a syntactically correct expression. If the running sum is 1 at the end of F, but reaches 1 again during the G part of $F\ G$ op, then the sums for G alone would reach 0 at that point, so G is not correct. We have now shown that there is only one way to recover the two operands of a binary operator. Clearly there is only one way to recover the single operand for a unary operator. Hence we can recover the infix form of an expression from its postfix form, together with the order in which the operations are done, which we can denote by bracketing the result of every operation in the infix form with another pair of parentheses.

We have therefore proved

THEOREM 12.4

An expression in postfix form that satifies the running-sum condition corresponds to exactly one fully bracketed expression in infix form. Hence no parentheses are needed to achieve the unique representation of an expression in postfix form.

Similar theorems hold for the prefix form; their proofs are left as exercises. The theorems of this section provide both a theoretical justification of the use of Polish notation and a convenient way to check an expression for correct syntax.

12.3.6 Recursive Evaluation of Postfix Expressions

Most people find that the recursive procedure for evaluating prefix expressions is easier to understand than the stack-based (nonrecursive) procedure for evaluating postfix expressions. In this (optional) section we show how the stack can be eliminated in favor of recursion for postfix evaluation.

First, however, let us see why the natural approach leads to a recursive procedure for prefix evaluation but not for postfix. We can describe both prefix and postfix expressions by the syntax diagrams of Figure 12.3. In both cases there are three possibilities: The expression consists of only a single operand, or the outermost operator is unary or is binary.

prefix evaluation

In tracing through the diagram for prefix form, the first token we encounter in the expression determines which of the three branches we take, and there are then no further choices to make (except within recursive calls, which need not be considered

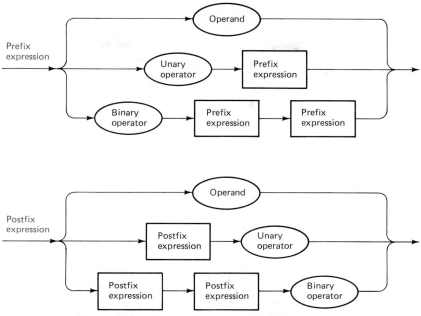

Figure 12.3. Syntax diagrams of Polish expressions

just now). Hence the structure of the recursive procedure for prefix evaluation closely resembles the syntax diagram.

postfix evaluation

With the postfix diagram, however, there is no way to tell from the first token (which will always be an operand) which of the three branches to take. It is only when the last token is encountered that the branch is determined. This fact does, however, lead to one easy recursive solution: Read the expression from right to left, reverse all the arrows on the syntax diagram, and use the same procedure as for prefix evaluation!

If we wish, however, to read the expression in the usual way from left to right, then we must work harder. Let us consider separately each of the three kinds of tokens in a postfix form. We have already observed that the first token in the expression must be an operand; this follows directly from the fact that the running sum after the first token is (at least) 1. Since unary operators do not change the running sum, unary operators can be inserted anywhere after the initial operand. It is the third case, binary operators, whose study leads to the solution.

running sum

Consider the sequence of running sums, and the place(s) in the sequence where the sum drops from 2 to 1. Since binary operators contribute -1 to the sum, such places must exist if the postfix expression contains any binary operators, and must correspond to the places in the expression where the two operands of the binary operator constitute the whole expression to the left. Such situations are illustrated in the stack frames of Figure 12.2. The entry on the bottom of the stack is the first operand; a sequence of positions where the height is at least 2, starting and ending at exactly two, make up the calculation of the second operand, and, taken in isolation, this sequence is itself a properly formed postfix expression. A drop in height from 2 to 1 marks one of the binary operators in which we are interested.

After the binary operator more unary operators may appear, and then the process may repeat itself (if the running sums again increase) with more sequences that are self-contained postfix expressions followed by binary and unary operators. In summary, we have shown that postfix expressions are described by the syntax diagram of Figure 12.4, which translates easily into the recursive procedure that follows. The Pascal conventions are the same as in the previous procedures.

left recursion

The situation appearing in the postfix diagram of Figure 12.3 is called *left recursion,* and the steps we have taken in the transition to the diagram in Figure 12.4 are typical of those needed to remove left recursion.

```
procedure EvaluatePostfix(var result: value);              {recursive version}
var
   t:   token;
begin                                              {procedure EvaluatePostfix}
   GetToken(t);
   if Kind(t) <> operand then
     Error
   else
     P(result);
   if Kind(t) <> endexpression then
     Error
end;                                               {procedure EvaluatePostfix}

procedure P(var result: value);
{Recursively evaluates postfix expression beginning at token t, which is guaran-
   teed to be an operand when P is invoked. At the conclusion, t is the first
   token beyond the expression evaluated, and will be either a binary operator
   or endexpression.}
var
   x: value;
begin                                              {recursive postfix evaluation}
   result := GetValue(t);
   GetToken(t);
   while (Kind(t) = unaryop) or (Kind(t) = operand) do
   begin
     if Kind(t) = unaryop then
       result := DoUnary(t, result)
     else                                          {t must be an operand.}
     begin
       P(x);
       if Kind(t) = binaryop then
         result := DoBinary(t, result, x)
       else
         Error
     end;
     GetToken(t)
   end
end;                                               {recursive postfix evaluation}
```

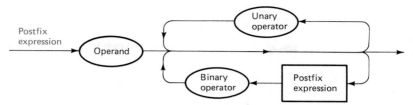

Figure 12.4.   Alternative syntax diagram, postfix expression

Exercises 12.3

E1. Trace the action on each of the following expressions by the procedure Evaluate-Postfix in **(1)** nonrecursive and **(2)** recursive versions. For the recursive procedure, draw the tree of recursive calls, indicating at each node which tokens are being processed. For the nonrecursive procedure, draw a sequence of stack frames showing which tokens are processed at each stage.

(a) a b $+$ c $\times$.
(b) a b c $+$ $\times$.
(c) a $!$ b $!$ $/$ c d $-$ a $!$ $-$ $\times$.
(d) a b $<$ **not** c d $\times$ $<$ e **or**.

E2. Trace the action of the procedure EvaluatePrefix on each of the following expressions, by drawing a tree of recursive calls showing which tokens are processed at each stage.

(a) $/$ $+$ x y $!$ n.
(b) $/$ $+$ $!$ x y n.
(c) **and** $<$ x y **or**   **not** $=$ $+$ x y z $>$ x 0.

E3. Which of the following are syntactically correct postfix expressions? Show the error in each incorrect expression. Translate each correct expression into infix form, using parentheses as necessary to avoid ambiguities.

(a) a b c $+$ $\times$ a $/$ c b $+$ d $/$ $-$.
(b) a b $+$ c a $\times$ b c $/$ d $-$.
(c) a b $+$ c a $\times$ $-$ c $\times$ $+$ b c $-$.
(d) a $\div$ b $\times$.
(e) a $\times$ b $\div$.
(f) a b $\times$ $\div$.
(g) a b $\div$ $\times$.

E4. Translate each of the following expressions from prefix form into postfix form.
(a) $/$ $+$ x y $!$ n.
(b) $/$ $+$ $!$ x y n.
(c) **and** $<$ x y **or**   **not** $=$ $+$ x y z $>$ x 0.

E5. Write a Pascal algorithm to translate an expression from prefix form into postfix form. Use the Pascal conventions of this chapter.

E6. Translate each of the following expressions from postfix form into prefix form.
(a) a b $+$ c $\times$.
(b) a b c $+$ $\times$.
(c) a $!$ b $!$ $/$ c d $-$ a $!$ $-$ $\times$.
(d) a b $<$ **not** c d $\times$ $<$ e **or**.

E7. Write a Pascal algorithm to translate an expression from postfix form into prefix form. Use the Pascal conventions of this chapter.

E8. A *fully bracketed* expression is one of the following forms:
(1) a simple operand;
(2) (*op E*) where *op* is a unary operator and *E* is a fully bracketed expression,
(3) (*E op F*) where *op* is a binary operator and *E* and *F* are fully bracketed expressions.

Hence, in a fully bracketed expression, the results of every operation are enclosed in parentheses. Examples of fully bracketed expressions are $((a + b) - c)$, $(-a)$, $(a + b)$, $(a + (b + c))$. Write Pascal algorithms that will translate expressions from **(a)** prefix and **(b)** postfix form into fully bracketed form.

E9. Formulate and prove theorems analogous to Theorems **(a)** 12.1, **(b)** 12.3, and **(c)** 12.4 for the prefix form of expressions.

12.4 TRANSLATION FROM INFIX FORM TO POLISH FORM

Very few (if any) programmers habitually write algebraic or logical expressions in Polish form, or even in fully bracketed form. To make convenient use of the algorithms we have developed, we must have an efficient method to translate arbitrary expressions from infix form into Polish notation. As a first simplification, we shall consider only the postfix form. Secondly, we shall exclude unary operators that are placed to the right of their operands. Such operators cause no conceptual difficulty, but would make the algorithms more complicated.

One method that we could use would be to build the expression tree from the infix form, and traverse the tree to obtain the postfix form, but, as it turns out, constructing the tree is actually more complicated than constructing the postfix form directly. Since, in postfix form, all operators come after their operands, the task of translation from infix to postfix form is simply

delaying operators

> *Delay each operator until its right-hand operand has been translated. Pass each simple operand through without delay.*

This action is illustrated in Figure 12.5.

The major problem we must resolve is to find what token will terminate the right-hand operand of a given operator. We must take both parentheses and priorities of operators into account. The first problem is easy. If a left parenthesis is in the operand, then everything through the matching right parenthesis must also be. For the second problem, that of priorities of operators, we consider binary operators separately from those of priority 6, namely, unary operators and exponentiation.

finding the end of the right operand

Most binary operators are evaluated from left to right. Let op_1 be such a binary operator, and let op_2 be the first nonbracketed operator to the right of op_1. If the priority of op_2 is less than or equal to that of op_1, then op_2 will not be part of the

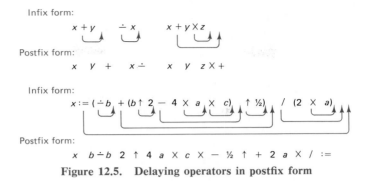

Figure 12.5. Delaying operators in postfix form

right operand of op_1, and its appearance will terminate the right operand of op_1. If the priority of op_2 is greater than that of op_1, then op_2 is part of the right operand of op_1, and we can continue through the expression until we find an operator of priority less than or equal to that of op_1; this operator will then terminate the right operand of op_1.

right-to-left evaluation

Next suppose that op_1 has priority 6 (it is unary or exponentiation), and recall that operators of this priority are to be evaluated from right to left. If the first operand op_2 to the right of op_1 has equal priority, it therefore will be part of the right operand of op_1, and the right operand is terminated only by an operator of strictly smaller priority.

There are two more ways in which the right operand can terminate: The expression can end, or the given operator may itself be within a bracketed subexpression, in which case its right operand will end when an unmatched right parenthesis ')' is encountered. In summary, we have the rules

> *If op is an operator in an infix expression, then its right-hand operand contains all tokens on its right until one of the following is encountered:*
>
> *(a) The end of the expression.*
> *(b) An unmatched right parenthesis ')'.*
> *(c) An operator of priority less than or equal to that of op, and not within a bracketed subexpression, if op has priority less than 6.*
> *(d) An operator of priority strictly less than that of op, and not within a bracketed subexpression, if op has priority 6.*

stack of operators

From these rules we can see that the appropriate way to remember the operators being delayed is to keep them on a stack. If operator op_2 comes on the right of operator op_1 but has higher priority, then op_2 will be output before op_1 is. Thus the operators are output in the order first in, last out.

The key to writing an algorithm for the translation is to make a slight change in our point of view by asking, as each token appears in the input, which of the operators previously delayed (that is, on the stack) now have their right operands terminated because of the new token, so that it is time to move them into the output. The preceding conditions then become

> (a) *At the end of the expression, all operators are output.*
> (b) *A right parenthesis causes all operators found since the corresponding left parenthesis to be output.*
> (c) *An operator of priority not* 6 *causes all other operators of greater or equal priority to be output.*
> (d) *An operator of priority* 6 *causes all other operators of strictly greater priority to be output, if such operators exist.*

To implement rule (b), we shall put each left parenthesis on the stack when it is encountered. Then when the matching right parenthesis appears, and the operators have been popped from the stack, the pair can both be discarded.

We can now incorporate these rules into a procedure. To do so, we shall use the same auxiliary types and procedures as in the last section, except that now the function Kind(··) can return two additional values

leftparen   rightparen

that denote, respectively, left and right parentheses. The procedures Push and Pop will now process tokens (operators) rather than values. In addition to the procedure GetToken( ) that obtains the next token from the input (infix expression), we use an auxiliary procedure

PutToken(t: token)

that puts the given token into the postfix expression. Thus these two procedures might read and write with files or might only refer to arrays already set up, depending on the desired application. Finally, we shall use a function Priority(op) that will return the priority of an operator op.

With these conventions we can write the procedure.

```
procedure Translate;
const
  maxstack = 100;                              {maximum allowable size of stack};
var
    stack:    array[1 .. maxstack] of token;
    nstack:   0 .. maxstack;                    {number of operators on the stack}
    t,                                          {token currently being processed}
    x:        token;                            {operator popped from stack}
    endright: Boolean;                          {end of right operand reached?}
```

```
begin                                                    {procedure Translate}
  nstack := 0;                                           {Initialize stack to be empty.}
  repeat
    GetToken(t);
    case Kind(t) of
        operand:        PutToken(t);
        leftparen:      Push(t);
        rightparen:     begin
                          Pop(t);
                          while Kind(t) <> leftparen do
                          begin
                            PutToken(t);
                            Pop(t)           {Discard the left parenthesis.}
                          end
                        end;
        unaryop,        {treat both kinds of operators together}
        binaryop:       begin
                          repeat
                            if nstack = 0 then
                              endright := true
                            else if Kind( stack[nstack] ) = leftparen then
                              endright := true
                            else if Priority(stack[nstack]) < Priority(t) then
                              endright := true
                            else if  (Priority(stack[nstack]) = Priority(t))
                                     and (Priority(t) = 6) then
                              endright := true
                            else begin
                              endright := false;
                              Pop(x);
                              PutToken(x)
                            end
                          until endright;
                          Push(t)
                        end;                               {processing operator}
        endexpression:
                        while nstack > 0 do                {empty the stack}
                        begin
                          Pop(x);
                          PutToken(x)
                        end
      end                                                  {case statement}
  until Kind(t) = endexpression;
  PutToken(t);                                             {Put endexpression into postfix.}
end;                                                       {procedure Translate}
```

Input Token	Contents of Stack (rightmost token is on top)					Output Token(s)	
x						x	
:=	:=						
(	:=	(					
÷	:=	(	÷				
b	:=	(	÷			b	
+	:=	(	+			÷	
(	:=	(	+	(			
b	:=	(	+	(		b	
↑	:=	(	+	(	↑		
2	:=	(	+	(	↑	2	
−	:=	(	+	(	−	↑	
4	:=	(	+	(	−	4	
×	:=	(	+	(	−×		
a	:=	(	+	(	−×	a	
×	:=	(	+	(	−×	×	
c	:=	(	+	(	−×	c	
)	:=	(	+			×	−
↑	:=	(	+	↑			
½	:=	(	+	↑		½	
)	:=					↑	+
/	:=	/					
(	:=	/	(				
2	:=	/	(			2	
×	:=	/	(	×			
a	:=	/	(	×		a	
)	:=	/				×	
endexpression						/	:=

Figure 12.6. Translation of quadratic formula into postfix form

Figure 12.6 shows the steps performed to translate the quadratic formula

$$x := (\dot{-}b + (b \uparrow 2 - 4 \times a \times c) \uparrow \frac{1}{2})/(2 \times a)$$

into postfix form, as an illustration of this algorithm. (Recall that we are using '$\dot{-}$' to denote unary negation.)

This completes the discussion of translation into postfix form. There will clearly be similarities in describing the translation into prefix form, but some difficulties arise because of the seemingly irrelevant fact that, in European languages, we read from left to right. If we were to translate an expression into prefix form working from left to right, then not only would the operators need to be rearranged but operands would need to be delayed until after their operators were output. But the relative order of operands is not changed in the translation, so the appropriate data structure to keep the operands would not be a stack (it would in fact be a queue). Since stacks would not do the job, neither would recursive programs with no explicit arrays, since these two kinds of programs can do equivalent tasks. Thus a left-to-right translation into prefix form would need a different approach. The trick is to translate into prefix form by working from right to left through the expression, using methods quite similar to the left-to-right postfix translation that we have developed. The details are left as an exercise.

E1. Note that in procedure Translate the action taken at the end of the input is much the same as when a right parenthesis is encountered. Suppose that the entire expression is enclosed in a pair of parentheses to serve as sentinels for the beginning and end. Write a simplified version of procedure Translate that no longer needs to check explicitly for the end of input.

E2. Procedure Translate is sadly deficient in error checking. Unmatched parentheses, for example, may send it off into a nonexistent part of the expression. Add error checking to the procedure so that it will detect syntax errors in its input (infix) expression.

E3. Modify procedure Translate so that it will accommodate unary operators that are written to the right of their operands. You should assume that the function Kind(···) returns the answer rightunary when such an operator appears.

E4. Rewrite procedure Translate as a recursive procedure that uses no stack or other array.

12.5 AN INTERACTIVE EXPRESSION EVALUATOR

There are many applications for a program that can evaluate a function that is typed in interactively while the program is running. One such application is a program that will draw the graph of a mathematical function (either on a plotter or on a graphics video terminal). Suppose that you are writing such a program to be used to help first-year calculus students graph functions. Most of these students will not know how to write or compile programs, so you wish to include in your program some way that the user can put in an expression for a function such as

$$x * \log(x) - x \uparrow 1.25$$

while the program is running. The program can then graph the function for appropriate values of x.

goal

The goal of this section is to describe such a program, and especially to complete the writing of two subprograms to help with this problem. The first subprogram will take as input an expression involving constants, variable(s), arithmetic operators, and standard functions, with bracketing allowed, as typed in from the terminal. It will then translate the expression into postfix form and keep it in an appropriate array. The second subprogram will evaluate the expression for values of the variable(s) given as its calling parameter(s) and return the answer.

purpose

We undertake this project for several reasons. It shows how to take the ideas already developed for working with Polish notation and build these ideas into a complete, concrete, and functioning program. In this way, the project illustrates a problem-solving approach to program design, in which we begin with solutions to the key questions and complete the structure with auxiliary procedures as needed. Finally, since this project is intended for use by people with little computer experience, it provides opportunity to test *robustness,* that is, the ability of the program to withstand unexpected or incorrect input without catastrophic failure.

12.5.1 The Main Program

The main program outlines how the work is divided into procedures; hence we look at it first.

```
program GraphFunction(input, output);
    {reads an expression from the terminal; converts it into postfix form; evaluates
        the postfix expression and graphs it over a specified range}
    {Declarations of constants, types, variables, procedures and functions will be
        inserted here.}
begin                                                        {main program}
    writeln('Welcome to the function-graphing program.');
    write('Do you wish instructions');
    if Yes then Instruct;
    DefineTokens;
    repeat                                        {Start using a new expression.}
        StartExpression;
        repeat                                    {Start making a new graph.}
            ReadGraphLimits;
            ReadParameters;
            x := xlow;
            repeat
                Lexicon[firstoperand].val := x;
                    {By convention, x is always the first entry in the list of operands.}
                EvaluatePostfix(y);
                Graph(x, y);
                x := x + increment
            until x > xhigh;
            write('Repeat for new graphing limits')
        until not Yes;
        write('Repeat for a new expression')
    until not Yes;
    writeln('Graphing program has finished.')
end.                                                         {main program}
```

1. Instructions

As with most programs written for casual users, the first step is to determine if instructions should be given. To save space, however, we shall not include a text for procedure Instruct here. The response to questions to the user is obtained through the following function Yes.

```
function Yes: Boolean;
var
  ch: char;
begin                                            {function Yes}
  repeat
    write(' (y,n)?');
    readln(ch)
  until ch in ['N', 'n', 'Y', 'y'];
  Yes := ch in ['Y', 'y']
end;                                             {function Yes}
```

2. Error Processing

In several procedures we shall use a procedure

procedure Error(s: message)

that will print a message and terminate the program. That is, for simplicity, we shall make all errors that the program detects be fatal to its execution. The type message will be a string of alphanumeric characters. Many versions of Pascal permit variable-length strings as parameters, but standard Pascal requires such strings to have a fixed length, and therefore we must include blanks to fill each error message to the same length.

3. Further Procedures

The second task of the main program is to establish the definitions of the predefined tokens (such as the operators $+$, $-$, $*$ amongst others, the operand x that will be used in the graphing, and perhaps some constants). We shall write procedure Define-Tokens after we have decided on the data structures.

Procedure StartExpression reads in an expression, splits it into tokens, and translates it into postfix form. Here arise several design problems, and the greatest need to check the input for possible errors that the user might make.

graphing

Procedure ReadGraphLimits sets up any initialization required to draw the graph, obtains the bounds and scale for drawing, and determines the range of value for x and the increment to be used. These requirements, unfortunately, differ greatly from one system to another, so we cannot hope to write a procedure that is widely applicable. For testing the program, therefore, we must be content with a small stub that only obtains the bounds and increment for x. Similarly, procedure Graph(x, y) that actually graphs the point (x, y) is also system dependent, and so is not included here. For testing our program, a stub that writes out the values of x and y will suffice.

expression parameters

It may be that the expression as typed in contains variables other than x, the one used for graphing. If so, our program will treat these other variables as parameters that will keep the same value while one graph is drawn, but whose values can be changed from one graph to the next, without other change in the expression. Procedure ReadParameters obtains values for these variables.

The innermost loop of the main program moves through the range of values for x, sets them into the place where they can be found by procedure EvaluatePostfix, and graphs the results.

12.5.2 Representation of the Data

Our data-structure decisions concern how to store and retrieve the tokens used in Polish expressions and their evaluation. For each different token we must remember (1) its name (as a string of characters), so that we can recognize it in the input expression; (2) its kind (unaryop, binaryop, operand, leftparen, rightparen, or endexpression); (3) for operators, its priority; for operands, its value. It is reasonable to think of representing each token as a record containing this information. One small difficulty arises: The same token may appear several times in an expression. If it is an operand, then we must be certain that it is given the same value each time. If we put the records themselves into the expressions, then when a value is assigned to an operand we must be sure that it is updated in all the records corresponding to that operand. We can avoid having to keep chains of references to a given variable by associating an integer code with each token, and placing this code in the expression, rather *lexicon* than the full record. We shall then set up a ***lexicon*** for the tokens, which will be an array indexed by the integer codes, and which will hold the full records for the tokens. In this way, if k is the code for a variable, then every appearance of k in the expression will cause us to look in position k of the lexicon for the corresponding value, and we are automatically assured of getting the same value each time.

Placing integer codes rather than records in the expressions also has the advantage of saving some space, but space for tokens is unlikely to be a critical restraint for this project. The time required to evaluate the postfix expression at many different values of the argument x is more likely to prove expensive.

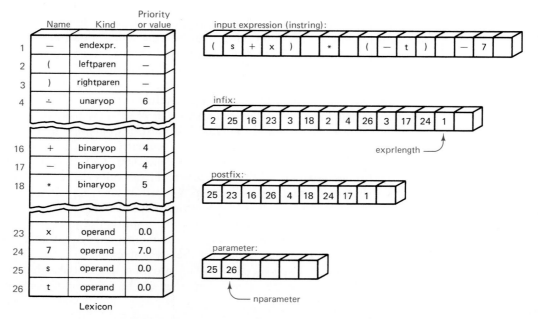

Figure 12.7.   Data structures for program GraphFunction

As the input expression is decoded, the program may find constants and new variables (parameters), which it will then add to the lexicon. These will all be classed as operands, but recall that, in the case of parameters, the user will be asked to give values before the expression is evaluated. Hence it is necessary to keep one more list, a list of the codes that correspond to parameters.

All these data structures are illustrated in Figure 12.7, along with some of the data structures used in the principal procedures.

Let us summarize the data representation by giving the declarations to be inserted into the main program.

declarations in main program

const

maxstring	= 100;	{maximum number of tokens in an expression}
maxstack	= 100;	{bound on stack size}
maxtoken	= 100;	{maximum number of distinct kinds of tokens}
maxpriority	= 6;	{largest priority of any operator}
maxparameter	= 50;	{largest number of variables allowed}
namelength	= 7;	{number of characters in an identifier}
firstunary	= 4;	{Where among the tokens is first unary operator?}
lastunary	= 15;	{last code of a unary operator}
firstbinary	= 16;	{What is the code of the first binary operator?}
lastbinary	= 22;	{What is the code of the last binary operator?}
firstoperand	= 23;	{Where do the operands start?}
		{By convention, firstoperand is the code for the variable x.}
lastoperand	= 25;	{Last predefined operand; other operands may be introduced by the user within the expression.}

type

value	= real;	
		{For simplicity, keep all the variables having the same type.}
priorrange	= 1 .. maxpriority;	
token	= 0 .. maxtoken;	{codes; 0 denotes undefined}
tokenkind	= (operand, unaryop, binaryop, endexpression, leftparen, rightparen);	
string	= **packed array**[1 .. maxstring] **of** char;	
message	= **packed array**[1 .. 45] **of** char;	
name	= **packed array**[1 .. namelength] **of** char;	
deftoken	= **record**	

    nm: name;
    case k: tokenkind **of**
     operand: (val: value);
     unaryop,
     binaryop: (pri: priorrange);
     endexpression,
     leftparen,
     rightparen: ( )   {empty}
    end;

expression	= **array**[1 .. maxstring] **of** token;	
exprindex	= 0 .. maxstring;	
paramindex	= 0 .. maxparameter;	

var
    postfix: expression;
    Lexicon: **array**[token] **of** deftoken;   {information on all tokens}
    nparameter: paramindex;   {count of number of parameters}
    parameter: **array**[paramindex] **of** token; {list of operands whose values
                                                  must be read in before graphing}
    x, y,   {y is expression evaluated at x.}
    xlow, xhigh,   {bounds on x for plotting}
    ylow, yhigh,   {bounds on y for plotting}
    increment: value;   {increment for plotting}

12.5.3 Predefined Tokens

The only task to be done by procedure DefineTokens is to place the names, kinds, priorities (for operators), and values (for operands) of all the predefined tokens into the lexicon. Hence the procedure consists only of a long series of assignment statements, which we omit to save space.

The complete list of predefined tokens used in this implementation is shown in Figure 12.8. Note that we can add operators that are not a standard part of a computer

Token	Name	Kind	Priority/Value	
1		endexpression		
2	(	leftparen		
3	)	rightparen		
4	−	unaryop	6	{negation}
5	abs	unaryop	6	
6	sqr	unaryop	6	
7	sqrt	unaryop	6	
8	exp	unaryop	6	
9	ln	unaryop	6	
10	lg	unaryop	6	{base 2 log}
11	sin	unaryop	6	
12	cos	unaryop	6	
13	arctan	unaryop	6	
14	round	unaryop	6	
15	trunc	unaryop	6	
16	+	binaryop	4	
17	−	binaryop	4	
18	*	binaryop	5	
19	/	binaryop	5	
20	div	binaryop	5	
21	mod	binaryop	5	
22	↑	binaryop	6	
23	x	operand	0.00000	
24	pi	operand	3.14159	
25	e	operand	2.71828	

Figure 12.8. **Predefined tokens for GraphFunction program**

language (such as the base 2 logarithm lg) and constants such as e and π. The expressions in which we are interested in this section begin and end with real numbers. Hence we do not include any Boolean or set-valued operations. Several integer-valued operations are included, since integers can sensibly be regarded as real numbers.

12.5.4 Translation of the Expression

In this section of the program, we must read an expression in ordinary (infix) form, check that it is syntactically correct, split it apart into tokens, and find their codes. As a sequence of tokens, the expression can then be converted to postfix form by the procedure written in Section 12.4.

1. Finding the Definitions of Tokens

As each token is split from the input string, we must find its code. This is an information retrieval problem: The name of the token is the key, and the integer code must be retrieved. In the expression there will usually be no more than a few dozen tokens, and it is quite arguable that the best way to retrieve the code is by sequential search through the lexicon. Sequential search would be easy to program, would require no further data structures, and the cost in time over more sophisticated methods would be negligible. One object of this project, however, is to illustrate larger applications, where the expense of sequential search may no longer be negligible. In a compiler, for example, there may be many hundreds of distinct symbols that must be recognized, and more sophisticated symbol tables must be used. A good choice is to use a hash table together with the lexicon. In the hash table we shall store only codes, and use these to look in the lexicon to locate the token with a given name.

In this way, we obtain the following procedures.

2. The Main Procedure

```
procedure StartExpression;
const
    hashsize    = 101;
type
    address    = 0 .. hashsize;
    indexname  = 0 .. namelength;        {used to loop through a name}
    indexstring = 0 .. maxstring;        {used to traverse input string}
var
    infix:       expression;    {output from ReadExpression; input to Translate}
    H:           array[address] of token;              {hash table}
    tokencount: token;            {count of number of distinct tokens}
begin                                          {procedure StartExpression}
    MakeHashTable;
    ReadExpression;
    Translate
end;                                           {procedure StartExpression}
```

3. Processing the Hash Table

```
function Hash(x: name): address;
var
  a: integer;
  ch: char;
  found: Boolean;
begin                                              {function Hash}
  ch := x[1];
  a  := abs(ord(ch)) mod hashsize;
  repeat
    if H[a] = 0 then
      found := true
    else if Lexicon[H[a]].nm = x then
      found := true
    else begin
      ch := x[2];
      a := a + abs(ord(ch));
      if a > hashsize then a := a mod hashsize;
      found := false
    end
  until found;
  Hash := a
end;                                               {function Hash}
```

Since many of the tokens have names only one character long, we have written the hash function to give special emphasis to this possibility. The spread achieved by this function appears fairly good, although other functions may do better.

It is also necessary to initialize the hash table with entries corresponding to the predefined tokens. The first such token, however, is endexpression, which is determined by reaching the end of the input, and not by looking in the hash table. Hence token 1 is not placed in H.

```
procedure MakeHashTable;
var
  a:        address;
  t:        token;
begin                                              {procedure MakeHashTable}
  for a := 0 to hashsize do
    H[a] := 0;
  for t := 2 to lastoperand do
    H[Hash(Lexicon[t].nm)] := t
end;                                               {procedure MakeHashTable}
```

4. Decoding the Expression

Figure 12.8 includes both some tokens whose names are single special characters and some tokens whose names are words beginning with a letter. These latter may be any of unary or binary operators or operands. It is also possible to have tokens that are numbers, that is, which are made up of digits (and possibly a decimal point). Hence in splitting the input expression into tokens, we shall consider three cases, using three procedures in the main loop,

FindWord   FindNumber   FindSymbol,

that will determine the name of the token and put its code into the output expression (still in infix at this stage).

input format

We must now establish conventions regarding the input format. Let us assume that the input expression is typed as one line, so that when we reach the end of the line, we have also reached the end of the input string. Let us use the conventions of Pascal concerning spaces: Blanks are ignored between tokens, but the occurrence of a blank terminates a token. If a token is a word, then it begins with a letter, which can be followed by letters or digits. Let us translate all lowercase letters to uppercase and use only uppercase in comparisons (be sure that the predefined tokens are hashed as uppercase only). Let us truncate names to namelength characters, where the constant namelength is defined in the main program.

error checking

It is in reading the input string that the greatest amount of error checking is needed to make sure that the syntax of the input expression is correct, and to make our program as robust as possible. Most of this error checking will be done in the subsidiary procedures, but in the main procedure, we keep a counter to make sure that parentheses are nested correctly, that is, that more right than left parentheses never appear and at the end the parentheses are balanced.

With these provisions, we obtain the following procedure:

```
procedure ReadExpression;
var
    lengthinstring: indexstring;          {length of input expression}
    instring:       string;               {expression as typed in}
    exprlength:     exprindex;            {length of postfix expression}
    position:       indexstring;          {moves through input string}
    parencount:     integer;              {checks for balanced parentheses}
    digit,
    alphabet,
    lower:          set of char;
begin                                     {procedure ReadExpression}
    tokencount := lastoperand;
    writeln('Type in the expression to graph on the following line:');
    position := 1;
    while (position < maxstring − 1) and (not eoln) do
    begin
      read (instring[position]);
      position := position + 1
    end;
```

```
                    instring[position] := ' ';                    {The blank is a sentinel for searches.}
                    lengthinstring := position;
                    exprlength := 0;
                    nparameter := 0;
                    parencount := 0;
                    position := 1;
                    lower := ['a' .. 'z'];                        {Assumes the letters are contiguous, as in}
                    alphabet := lower + ['A' .. 'Z'];                 {ASCII; wrong for EBCDIC}
                    digit := ['0' .. '9'];
                    while position <= lengthinstring do
                      if instring[position] = ' ' then             {Skip all blanks between tokens.}
                        position := position + 1
                      else if instring[position] in alphabet then
                        FindWord
                      else if instring[position] in (digit + ['.']) then
                        FindNumber
                      else
                        FindSymbol;
                    {At this point, position has moved to the end of the input string.}
                  if parencount <> 0 then
                    Error('Number of left and right parentheses not same            ');
                  if Leading then
                    Error('Input expression is incomplete.                          ');
                  PutToken(1)                              {Put endexpression into the infix expression.}
                end;                                                  {procedure ReadExpression}
```

5. Error Checking for Correct Syntax

The most important aspect of error checking that makes its first appearance in this procedure is the Boolean-valued function Leading. To motivate the inclusion of this function, let us first consider a special case. Suppose that an expression is made up only from simple operands and binary operators, with no parentheses or unary operators. Then the only syntactically correct expressions are of the form

operand binaryop operand binaryop · · · *operand*

where the first and last tokens are operands, and the two kinds of tokens alternate. It is illegal for two operands to be adjacent, or for two binary operators to be adjacent. In the leading position there must be an operand, as there must be after each operator, so we can consider these positions also as "leading," since the preceding operator must lead to an operand.

leading positions

Now suppose that unary operators are to be inserted into this expression. Any number of unary operators can be placed before any operand (recall that we are allowing only unary operators that go to the left of their operands), but it is illegal to place a unary operator immediately before a binary operator. That is, unary operators can appear exactly where operands are allowed, in leading positions but only there. On the other hand, the appearance of a unary operator leaves the position still as a "leading" position, since an operand must still appear before a binary operator becomes legal.

Let us now, finally, also allow parentheses in the expression. A bracketed subexpression is treated as an operand and, therefore, can appear exactly where operands are legal. Hence left parentheses can appear exactly in leading positions, and leave the position as leading, and right parentheses can appear only in nonleading positions, and leave the position as nonleading.

All the possibilities are summarized in Figure 12.9.

	Previous Token *Any One of*	*Legal Tokens* *Any One of*
Leading position:		
	start of expression	operand
	binary operator	unary operator
	unary operator	left parenthesis
	left parenthesis	
Nonleading position:		
	operand	binary operator
	right parenthesis	right parenthesis
		end of expression

Figure 12.9.   **Tokens legal in leading and nonleading positions**

These requirements are built into the following function that will be used in the subsidiary procedures to check the syntax of the input.

```
function Leading: Boolean;
var k: tokenkind;
begin                                          {function Leading}
   if exprlength = 0 then                       {This is start of expression.}
      Leading := true
   else begin
      k := Kind(infix[exprlength]);             {Look at the preceding token.}
      Leading := (k = leftparen) or (k = unaryop) or (k = binaryop)
   end
end;                                            {function Leading}
```

6. Auxiliary Subprograms

Amongst the other auxiliary subprograms needed are the procedure

PutToken(t: token);

that adds a token to the list in the array infix, and the function

Kind(t: token): tokenkind;

that returns the kind of a token. PutToken is straightforward, and we leave it as an exercise. Kind could just as easily be written in line each time it is used, since we employ a record structure for tokens, but to remain consistent with earlier sections of this chapter (where Kind was used but not yet programmed), we instead use a separate function whose body consists of the single statement

Kind := Lexicon[t].k

7. Case: Token Is a Word

We now turn to the three subsidiary procedures for processing words, numbers, and special symbols. The first of these must implement the decisions about the structure of words that we made in part 4 of this section. From Figure 12.8 we see that a word token can be any one of an operand, unary operator, or binary operator. The error checking must be adjusted accordingly. Or it may be that the word token does not yet appear in the lexicon, in which case it represents the first appearance of a new parameter, which must be entered accordingly into the lexicon and into the list of parameters. These requirements translate into the following procedures, the first of which extracts a word from the input string, and the second processes the word.

```
procedure ExtractWord (   var s: string; var position: indexstring;
                          var word: name);
{Extracts a name called word (letters and digits) from string s starting at position;
    at conclusion position has moved to the first character beyond the name.}
var
    i:          integer;
    start,
    stop:       indexstring;
    ch:         char;
begin                                                       {procedure ExtractWord}
    start := position;
    while instring[position] in (alphabet + digit) do
        position := position + 1;
        {Position now points to the first character beyond the end of the word.}
    stop := position − 1;
    if stop >= start + namelength then
    begin
        write('Warning: The name ');
        for i := start to stop do
            write(instring[i]);
        writeln(' has been truncated to', namelength:2, ' characters.');
        stop := start + namelength − 1
    end;
    for i := 1 to namelength do
        if start + i − 1 <= stop then
        begin
            word[i] := instring[start + i − 1];
            if word[i] in lower then
                begin  ch := word[i];   word[i] := chr(ord(ch) − 32)  end
                {Above statement changes to capital letters, assuming ASCII ordering.}
        end
        else
            word[i] := ' '
end;                                                        {procedure ExtractWord}
```

```
    procedure FindWord;
    var
        word:       name;
        t:          token;
    begin                                           {procedure FindWord}
      ExtractWord(instring, position, word);
      t := H[Hash(word)];
      if t <> 0 then                                {Token is one already defined.}
        if Leading then
          if Kind(t) = binaryop then
            Error('Binary operator in illegal position                ')
          else PutToken(t)                {Other kinds are legal in leading position.}
        else                                    {Case: not in leading position}
          if Kind(t) <> binaryop then
            Error('Binary operator expected                           ')
          else
            PutToken(t)
      else                      {New name for a token; must set up its definition.}
        if tokencount >= maxtoken then
          Error('Too many distinct variables and constants            ')
        else if not Leading then
          Error('Operand follows ) or another operand.                ')
        else begin
          tokencount := tokencount + 1;
          H[ Hash(word) ] := tokencount;
          lexicon[tokencount].nm := word;
          lexicon[tokencount].k := operand;
          if nparameter >= maxparameter then
            Error('Expression contains too many parameters.            ')
          else begin
            nparameter := nparameter + 1;
            parameter[nparameter] := tokencount;
            PutToken(tokencount)
          end
        end
    end;                                            {procedure FindWord}
```

8. Case: Token Is a Number

The treatment of numbers is generally similar to that of variables, but with two differences. One is that we must convert the number to binary so that we can use its value directly from the lexicon, rather than reading its value into a list of parameters. The other difference is that there is not necessarily a unique name for a number. If namelength is large enough so that a string can hold as many digits as the precision of the machine, then unique names can be assigned, but if not, two different numbers might get the same name. To guard against this possibility, we shall regard every occurrence of a number as a newly defined token, and act accordingly. We do assign the number a name, but only for debugging purposes, and we do not even enter the name into the hash table.

In converting the number into binary, for simplicity we exclude the scientific notation and consider the integer and fractional parts separately. We use an auxiliary function to convert a string of digits into an integer (stored as a real). This function, which appears after the procedure, accepts an empty string and returns 0. Therefore our program will correctly interpret real numbers such as 7. or .5 that are not legal syntax in Pascal.

```
procedure FindNumber;
var
      x:              string;
      xlength,
      decpoint,                               {position of decimal point, if any}
      newposition: indexstring;
      fraction,
      r:              value;                   {value of number, converted to binary}
      i:              integer;
begin                                          {procedure FindNumber}
   if not Leading then
      Error('Constant in illegal position                        ')
   else if tokencount > = maxtoken then
      Error('Too many constants and variables                   ')
   else begin                                  {Legal case: make a new token.}
      newposition := position;
      while instring[newposition] in digit do
         newposition := newposition + 1;
      r := ConvertReal(instring, position, newposition − 1);
      if instring[newposition] = '.' then
      begin                                    {fractional part}
         decpoint := newposition;
         repeat
            newposition := newposition + 1
         until not (instring[newposition] in digit);
         fraction := ConvertReal(instring, decpoint + 1, newposition − 1);
         for i := 1 to newposition − decpoint − 1 do
            fraction := fraction/10.0;
         r := r + fraction
      end;                                     {fractional part}
```

```
        if instring[newposition] in ['E', 'e'] then
          Error('Sorry, scientific notation is not allowed.                   ')
        else begin
          tokencount := tokencount + 1;
          Lexicon[tokencount].nm := 'number';
          Lexicon[tokencount].k := operand;
          Lexicon[tokencount].val := r;
          PutToken(tokencount);
          position := newposition
        end
      end                                                    {legal case}
    end;                                                 {procedure FindNumber}

  function ConvertReal(x: string; start, stop: indexstring): value;
  {converts the digits between positions start and stop in string x into an integer,
    which is stored as a real to avoid overflow problems}
  var
    ch: char;
    i: indexstring;
    sum: value;
  begin                                                  {function ConvertReal}
    sum := 0.0;
    for i := start to stop do
    begin
      ch := x[i];
      if not (ch in digit) then
        Error ('Nondigit encountered in a number.                    ');
      sum := (10.0 * sum) + (ord(ch) − ord('0'))
              {Assumes that the ten digits have contiguous codes, as in ASCII}
    end;
    ConvertReal := sum
  end;                                                   {function ConvertReal}
```

9. Case: Token Is a Special Symbol

The third subsidiary procedure treats the special symbols. Most of its work is simpler than the previous cases; it need create no new tokens: If it fails to recognize a symbol then an error occurs. The special symbols are all one character long, so counting positions in instring is easier.

The only complication concerns the two symbols '+' and '−', which can be either unary or binary operators. Fortunately, the function Leading will tell us which case occurs, since only a unary operator is legal in a leading position. We shall take no action for a unary '+', since it has no effect, and we replace a unary '−' by our private notation '∸'. Note, however, that this change is local to our program. The user is not required—or even allowed—to use the symbol '∸' for unary negation.

```
procedure FindSymbol;
var
  i: integer;
  x: name;
  t: token;
begin                                    {procedure FindSymbol}
  x[1] := instring[position];
  for i := 2 to namelength do
    x[i] := ' ';
  t := H[Hash(x)];
  if t = 0 then
    Error('Unrecognized symbol in expression                    ')
  else if Leading then
    if Kind(t) = rightparen then
      Error(badexpr, 'Illegal place for closing parenthesis              ')
    else if Kind(t) = binaryop then
              {A binary operator is illegal here; it must be a unary operator.}
      if x = '+        ' then                 {Do nothing; forget a unary +.}
      else if x = '-        ' then
      begin
        x := '-        ';
        t := H[Hash(x)];
        PutToken(t)
      end
      else Error('Binary operator in illegal position             ')
    else PutToken(t)            {Other kinds are legal in leading position.}
  else                                     {Case: not in leading position}
    if (Kind(t) = rightparen) or (Kind(t) = binaryop) then
      PutToken(t)
    else
      Error('Binary operator or ) expected                    ');
  if Kind(t) = leftparen then
    parencount := parencount + 1
  else if Kind(t) = rightparen then
  begin
    parencount := parencount - 1;
    if parencount < 0 then
      Error('More right than left parentheses             ')
  end;
  position := position + 1
end;                                     {procedure FindSymbol}
```

10. Translation into Postfix Form

At the conclusion of procedure ReadExpression, the input expression has been converted into an infix sequence of tokens, in exactly the form needed by procedure Translate as derived in Section 12.4. In fact, we now arrive at the key step of our algorithm and can apply the previous work without essential change; the only modifications needed in procedure Translate are the addition of two variables used to index the input and output expressions, and even this indexing is done only in the straightforward subsidiary procedures GetToken and PutToken, which we leave as exercises.

We also omit the auxiliary subprograms Push, Pop, and Priority, since they involve no new problems or ideas.

When procedure Translate has finished, the expression is a sequence of tokens in postfix form, and can be evaluated efficiently in the next stage. This efficiency, in fact, is important so that a graph can be drawn without undue delay, even though it requires evaluation of the expression for a great many different values.

12.5.5 Evaluating the Expression

1. Reading the Parameters

The first step in evaluating the expression is to establish values for the parameters, if any. This is done only once for each graph, in the straightforward procedure:

```
procedure ReadParameters;
var
  i: paramindex;
begin                                    {procedure ReadParameters}
  if nparameter > 0 then
  begin
    writeln('Type in values for each of the following parameters.');
    for i := 1 to nparameter do
      with Lexicon[parameter[i]] do
      begin
        write (' ', nm,'?');
        readln(val)
      end
  end
end;                                     {procedure ReadParameters}
```

2. Postfix Evaluation

To evaluate the postfix expression, we again use a procedure developed in the first part of this chapter. Either the recursive or the nonrecursive version of procedure EvaluatePostfix can be used, again with no significant change (the nonrecursive version requires Push and Pop procedures for values). There will likely be no significant difference in running time between the two versions, so it is a matter of taste which to use. Both versions, however, require subsidiary functions GetValue, DoUnary, and DoBinary, to which we now turn.

3. Evaluation of Operands

The first function need only look in the lexicon:

```
function GetValue(t: token): value;
begin
  if Kind(t) <> operand then
    Error('Attempt to get value for nonoperand                    ')
  else
    GetValue := Lexicon[t].val
end;
```

4. Operators

Since we have integer codes for all the tokens, the application of operators can be done within a simple but long **case** statement. We leave the one for unary operators as an exercise. For binary operators, we have the following function.

```
function DoBinary(t: token; x, y: value): value;
begin                                                    {function DoBinary}
  if (t < firstbinary) or (t > lastbinary) then
    Error('Binary operator code out of range
  else case t of
    16: DoBinary := x + y;
    17: DoBinary := x − y;
    18: DoBinary := x * y;
    19: if y <> 0.0 then
          DoBinary := x/y
        else
          Error('Division by 0.0                                   ');
    20: if round(y) <> 0 then
          DoBinary := round(x) div round(y)
        else
          Error ('Integer division by 0                            ');
    21: if round(y) <> 0 then
          DoBinary := round(x) mod round(y)
        else
          Error('Attempt to use a 0 modulus                        ');
    22: DoBinary := Exponent(x, y)
  end
end;                                                      {function DoBinary}
```

Note that we can easily use the structure of this function to improve the error checking usually provided to the user by the operating system. The messages given for division by 0 will likely prove more helpful than something like

Floating point error,

which may be all that the system normally provides.

Since Pascal does not provide an exponentiation operator, we can also take this opportunity to write an exponentiation function. We use two different methods as appropriate: If the power is an integer (or very close to one), then we use a loop and multiplication or division to evaluate the exponent; otherwise, we use logarithms.

```
function Exponent(x, y: value): value;
const
    epsilon = 0.000001;              {tolerance to regard a number as an integer}
var
  i: integer;
  p: value;
begin                                                      {function Exponent}
  if abs(y − round(y)) < epsilon then
  begin                                                   {Treat y like an integer.}
    p := 1.0;
    if y >= 0.0 then
      for i := 1 to round(y) do
        p := p * x
    else if x = 0.0 then
      Error('Negative power of 0.0                              ')
    else
      for i := −1 downto round(y) do
        p := p/x;
    Exponent := p
  end
  else if x > 0.0 then                  {Use logarithms and exponents.}
    Exponent := exp(y * ln(x))
  else if abs(x) < epsilon then
    Exponent := 0.0
  else
    Error('Attempt to take negative number to noninteger power      ')
end;                                                       {function Exponent}
```

12.5.6 Summary

At this point, we have surveyed the entire project. Figure 12.10 lists all the subprograms required for this project, arranged in their proper hierarchy of declaration. Most of these appear in the text, but several have been left as exercises for the programmer to supply. These are marked with an asterisk (*) in the right margin.

```
program GraphFunction;
function Kind(t: token): tokenkind;
function Yes: Boolean;
procedure Error(message: string);                                    *
procedure Instruct;                                                  *
procedure DefineTokens;                                             *

procedure StartExpression;
    function Hash(x: name): address;
    procedure MakeHashTable;

    procedure ReadExpression;
        procedure  PutToken(t : token);          {into infix expression} *
        function    Leading: Boolean;
        procedure  ExtractWord
        procedure  FindWord;
        procedure  FindNumber;
        function    ConvertReal(x: string): value;
        procedure  FindSymbol;

    procedure Translate;
        procedure Push(t: token);                            {token} *
        procedure Pop(var t: token);                         {token} *
        procedure GetToken(var t: token);         {from infix expression} *
        procedure PutToken(t: token);            {into postfix expression} *
        function Priority(t: token): integer;                          *

procedure ReadParameters;

procedure ReadGraphLimits;                                           *

procedure Graph(x, y: value);                                       *

procedure EvaluatePostfix (var result: value);            {recursive or not}
    procedure Push(v: value);          {value, for nonrecursive only}
    procedure Pop(var v: value);       {value, for nonrecursive only}
    procedure P(var result: value);        {for recursive version only}
    procedure  GetToken(var t: token);      {from postfix expression} *
    function GetValue(t: token): value;
    function DoUnary(t: token; x: value): value;                    *
    function DoBinary(t: token; x, y: value): value;
        function Exponent(x, y: value): value;
```

Figure 12.10.   Summary of subprograms for GraphFunction

E1. State precisely what changes in the program are needed to add the base 10 logarithm function log( ) as an additional unary operator.

E2. Naive users of this program might (if graphing a function involving money) write a dollar sign '$' within the expression. What will the present program do if this happens? What changes are needed so that the program will ignore a '\$'?

E3. Pascal or PL/1 programmers might accidentally type a semicolon ';' at the end of the expression. What changes are needed so that a semicolon will be ignored at the end of the expression, but will be an error elsewhere?

E4. Explain what changes are needed to allow the program to accept either square brackets [···] or curly brackets {···} as well as round brackets (···). The nesting must be done with the same kind of brackets; that is, an expression of the form (··[··)··] is illegal, but forms like [··(··)··{··}··] are permissible.

Programming Projects 12.5

P1. Provide the missing subprograms (marked with asterisks in Figure 12.10) and implement program GraphFunction on your computer. Most of the subprograms are straightforward, although several involve graphics and will be system dependent.

P2. Modify the program so that it will accept unary operators that are written on the right of the operand. Two examples of such operators that might be included are the factorial operator '!' and the percentage operator '%' that divides its operand by 100.0.

P3. Modify the error checking so that several severities of errors are detected and appropriate actions are taken for each. Error severities might include

(a) Warning: Continue execution.

(b) Bad value: Repeat with new bounds.

(c) Bad expression: Ask user to re-enter the expression.

(d) Fatal: The program is internally inconsistent.

REFERENCES FOR FURTHER STUDY

The Polish notation is so natural and useful that one might expect its discovery to be hundreds of years ago. It may be surprising to note that it is a discovery of this century:

JAN ŁUKASIEWICZ, *Elementy Logiki Matematyczny,* Warsaw, 1929; English translation: *Elements of Mathematical Logic,* Pergamon Press, Oxford, 1963.

The development of iterative algorithms to form and evaluate Polish expressions (usually postfix form) can be found in several data structures books, as well as more advanced books on compiler theory. The iterative algorithm for translating an expression from infix to postfix form appears to be due independently to E. W. DIJKSTRA and to C. L. HAMBLIN, and appears in

E. W. DIJKSTRA, "Making a Translator for ALGOL 60," *Automatic Programming Information,* no. 7 (May 1961); reprinted in *Annual Review of Automatic Programming* 3 (1963), 347–356.

C. L. HAMBLIN, "Translation to and from Polish notation," *Computer Journal 5* (1962), 210–213.

The recursive algorithm (Section 12.3.6) for evaluation of postfix expressions is derived, albeit from a rather different point of view, and for binary operators only, in

EDWARD M. REINGOLD, "A comment on the evaluation of Polish postfix expressions," *Computer Journal* 24 (1981), 288.

Mathematical Methods

▶ *The first part of this appendix supplies several mathematical results used in algorithm analysis. The final two sections (Fibonacci and Catalan numbers) are optional topics for the mathematically inclined reader.*

A.1 SUMS OF POWERS OF INTEGERS

The following two formulas are useful in counting the steps executed by an algorithm.

THEOREM A.1

$$1 + 2 + \cdots + n = \frac{n(n+1)}{2}.$$

$$1^2 + 2^2 + \cdots + n^2 = \frac{n(n+1)(2n+1)}{6}.$$

PROOF   The first identity has a simple and elegant proof. We let S equal the sum on the left side, write it down twice (once in each direction), and add vertically:

algebraic proof

$$
\begin{array}{ccccccccccccc}
1 & + & 2 & + & 3 & + & \cdots & + & n-1 & + & n & = & S \\
n & + & n-1 & + & n-2 & + & \cdots & + & 2 & + & 1 & = & S \\
\hline
n+1 & + & n+1 & + & n+1 & + & \cdots & + & n+1 & + & n+1 & = & 2S
\end{array}
$$

There are n columns on the left; hence $n(n+1) = 2S$ and the identity follows.

The first identity also has the proof without words shown in Figure A.1.

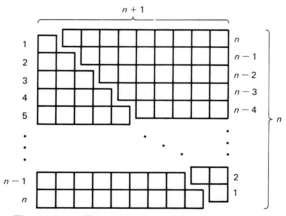

Figure A.1.   Geometrical proof for sum of integers

proof by induction   We shall use the method of **mathematical induction** to prove the second identity. This method requires that we start by establishing an initial case, called the **induction base,** which for our formula is the case $n = 1$. In this case the formula becomes

$$1^2 = \frac{1(1+1)(2+1)}{6},$$

which is true, so the induction base is established. Next, using the formula for the case $n - 1$, we must establish it for case n. For case $n - 1$ we thus shall assume

$$1^2 + 2^2 + \cdots + (n-1)^2 = \frac{(n-1)n(2(n-1)+1)}{6}.$$

It follows that

$$1^2 + 2^2 + \cdots + (n-1)^2 + n^2 = \frac{(n-1)n(2(n-1)+1)}{6} + n^2$$

$$= \frac{2n^3 - 3n^2 + n + 6n^2}{6}$$

$$= \frac{n(n+1)(2n+1)}{6},$$

end of proof

which is the desired result, and the proof by induction is complete.

A convenient shorthand for a sum of the sort appearing in these identities is to use the capital Greek letter sigma

summation notation

$$\Sigma$$

in front of the typical summand, with the initial value of the index controlling the summation written below the sign, and the final value above. Thus the preceding identities can be written

$$\sum_{k=1}^{n} k = \frac{n(n+1)}{2}$$

and

$$\sum_{k=1}^{n} k^2 = \frac{n(n+1)(2n+1)}{6}.$$

Two other formulas are also useful, particularly in working with trees.

THEOREM A.2

$$1 + 2 + 4 + \cdots + 2^{m-1} = 2^m - 1.$$
$$1 \times 1 + 2 \times 2 + 3 \times 4 + \cdots + m \times 2^{m-1} = (m-1) \times 2^m + 1.$$

In summation notation these equations are

$$\sum_{k=0}^{m-1} 2^k = 2^m - 1.$$

sums, powers of 2

$$\sum_{k=1}^{m} k \times 2^{k-1} = (m-1) \times 2^m + 1.$$

PROOF

The first formula will be proved in a more general form. We start with the following identity, which, for any value of $x \neq 1$, can be verified simply by multiplying both sides by $x - 1$:

$$\frac{x^m - 1}{x - 1} = 1 + x + x^2 + \cdots + x^{m-1}$$

for any $x \neq 1$. With $x = 2$ this expression becomes the first formula.

To establish the second formula we take the same expression in the case of $m + 1$ instead of m:

$$\frac{x^{m+1} - 1}{x - 1} = 1 + x + x^2 + \cdots + x^m$$

for any $x \neq 1$, and differentiate with respect to x:

$$\frac{(x - 1)(m + 1)x^m - (x^{m+1} - 1)}{(x - 1)^2} = 1 + 2x + 3x^2 + \cdots + mx^{m-1}$$

end of proof

for any $x \neq 1$. Setting $x = 2$ now gives the second formula.

Suppose that $|x| < 1$ in the preceding formulas. As m becomes large, it follows that x^m becomes small, that is,

$$\lim_{m \to \infty} x^m = 0.$$

Taking the limit as $m \to \infty$ in the preceding equations gives

THEOREM A.3

infinite series

If $|x| < 1$ then

$$\sum_{k=0}^{\infty} x^k = \frac{1}{1 - x}.$$

$$\sum_{k=1}^{\infty} kx^{k-1} = \frac{1}{(1 - x)^2}.$$

A.2 LOGARITHMS

The primary reason for using logarithms is to turn multiplication and division into addition and subtraction, and exponentiation into multiplication. Before the advent of pocket calculators, logarithms were an indispensable tool for hand calculation: Witness the large tables of logarithms and the once ubiquitous slide rule. Even though we now have other methods for numerical calculation, the fundamental properties of logarithms give them importance that extends far beyond their use as computational tools.

The behavior of many phenomena, first of all, reflects an intrinsically logarithmic structure; that is, by using logarithms we find important relationships that are not otherwise obvious. Measuring the loudness of sound, for example, is logarithmic: If one sound is 10 db (decibels) louder than another, then the actual acoustic energy is 10 times as much. If the sound level in one room is 40 db and it is 60 db in another, then the human perception may be that the second room is half again as noisy as the first, but there is actually 100 times more sound energy in the second room. This phenomenon is why a single violin soloist can be heard above a full orchestra (when playing a different line), and yet the orchestra requires so many violins to maintain a proper balance of sound.

physical measurements

large numbers

Logarithms, secondly, provide a convenient way to handle very large numbers. The scientific notation, where a number is written as a small real number (often in the range from 1 to 10) times a power of 10, is really based on logarithms, since the power of 10 is essentially the logarithm of the number. Scientists who need to use very large numbers (like astronomers, nuclear physicists, and geologists) frequently speak of orders of magnitude, and thereby concentrate on the logarithm of the number.

A logarithmic graph, thirdly, is a very useful device for displaying the properties of a function over a much broader range than a linear graph. With a logarithmic graph, we can arrange to display detailed information on the function for small values of the argument and at the same time give an overall view for much larger values. Logarithmic graphs are especially appropriate when we wish to show percentage changes in a function.

A.2.1 Definition of Logarithms

base

Logarithms are defined in terms of a real number $a > 1$, which is called the **base** of the logarithms. (It is also possible to define logarithms with base a in the range $0 < a < 1$, but doing so would introduce needless complications into our discussion.) For any number $x > 0$, we define $\log_a x = y$ where y is the real number such that $a^y = x$. The logarithm of a negative number, and the logarithm of 0, are not defined.

A.2.2 Simple Properties

From the definition and from the properties of exponents we obtain

$$\log_a 1 = 0,$$
$$\log_a a = 1,$$
$$\log_a x < 0$$

for all x such that $0 < x < 1$.

$$0 < \log_a x < 1$$

for all x such that $1 < x < a$.

$$\log_a x > 1$$

for all x such that $a < x$.

The logarithm function has a graph like the one in Figure A.2. We also obtain the identities

$$\log_a (xy) = (\log_a x) + (\log_a y)$$
$$\log_a (x/y) = (\log_a x) - (\log_a y)$$
$$\log_a x^z = z \log_a x$$
$$\log_a a^z = z$$
$$a^{\log_a x} = x$$

that hold for any positive real numbers x and y, and for any real number z.

From the graph in Figure A.2 you will observe that the logarithm grows more and more slowly as x increases. The graphs of positive powers of x less than 1, such as the square root of x or the cube root of x, also grow progressively more slowly, but never become as flat as the graph of the logarithm. In fact,

As x grows large, $\log x$ grows more slowly than x^c, for any $c > 0$.

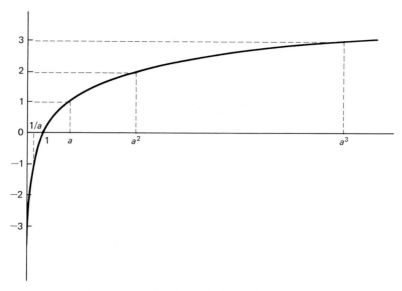

Figure A.2.   Graph of the logarithm function

A.2.3 Choice of Base

common logarithm

Any real number $a > 1$ can be chosen as the base of logarithms, but certain special choices appear much more frequently than others. For computation and for graphing, the base $a = 10$ is often used, and logarithms with base 10 are called ***common*** logarithms. In studying computer algorithms, however, base 10 appears infrequently, and we do not often use common logarithms. Instead, logarithms with base 2 appear the most frequently, and we therefore reserve the special symbol

$$\lg x$$

to denote a logarithm with base 2.

A.2.4 Natural Logarithms

In studying mathematical properties of logarithms, and in many problems where logarithms appear as part of the answer, the number that appears as the base is

$$e = 2.718281828459\cdots.$$

Logarithms with base e are called ***natural*** logarithms. In this book we always denote the natural logarithm of x by

$$\ln x.$$

In many mathematics books, however, other bases than e are rarely used, in which case the unqualified symbol $\log x$ usually denotes a natural logarithm. Figure A.3 shows the graph of logarithms with respect to the three bases 2, e, and 10.

The properties of logarithms that make e the natural choice for the base are thoroughly developed as part of the calculus, but we can mention a few of these

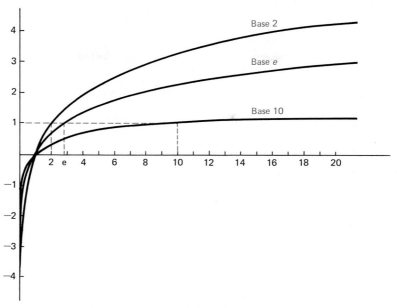

Figure A.3.   Logarithms with three bases

properties without proof. First, the graph of ln x has the property that its slope at each point x is $1/x$; that is, the derivative of ln x is $1/x$ for all real numbers $x > 0$. Second, the natural logarithm satisfies the infinite series

$$\ln(x + 1) = x - \frac{x^2}{2} + \frac{x^3}{3} - \frac{x^4}{4} + \cdots$$

for $-1 < x < 1$, but this series requires a great many terms to give a good approximation and, therefore, is not useful directly for computation. It is much better to consider *exponential function* instead the exponential function that "undoes" the logarithm, and that satisfies the series

$$e^x = 1 + x + \frac{x^2}{2!} + \frac{x^3}{3!} + \cdots$$

for all real numbers x. This exponential function e^x also has the important property that it is its own derivative.

A.2.5 Change of Base

Logarithms with respect to one base are closely related to logarithms with respect to any other base. To find this relation, we start with the following relation that is essentially the definition

$$x = a^{\log_a x}$$

for any $x > 0$. Then

$$\log_b x = \log_b a^{\log_a x} = (\log_a x)(\log_b a).$$

The factor $\log_b a$ does not depend on x, but only on the two bases. Therefore,

> *Logarithms can be converted from one base to another simply by multiplying by a constant factor, the logarithm of the first base with respect to the second.*

The most useful numbers for us in this connection are

conversion factors
$$\begin{aligned} \lg e &\approx 1.442695041, \\ \ln 2 &\approx 0.693147181, \\ \ln 10 &\approx 2.302585093. \end{aligned}$$

A.2.6 Logarithmic Graphs

In a logarithmic scale the numbers are arranged as on a slide rule, with larger numbers closer together than smaller numbers. In this way, equal distances along the scale represent equal *ratios* rather than the equal *differences* represented on an ordinary linear scale. A logarithmic scale should be used when percentage change is important to measure, or when perception is logarithmic. Human perception of time, for example, would seem to be nearly linear in the short term—what happened two days ago is twice as distant as what happened yesterday—but is more nearly logarithmic in the long term: We draw less distinction between one million years ago and two million years ago than we do between ten years ago and one hundred years ago.

log-log graphs
Graphs in which both the vertical and horizontal scales are logarithmic are called **log-log graphs.** In addition to phenomena where the perception is naturally logarithmic in both scales, log-log graphs are useful to display the behavior of a function over a very wide range. For small values the graph records a detailed view of the function, and for large values a broad view of the function appears on the same graph. For searching and sorting algorithms, we wish to compare methods both for small problems and large problems; hence log-log graphs are appropriate. See Figure A.4.

One observation is worth noting: Any power of x graphs as a straight line with a log-log scale. To prove this, we start with an arbitrary power function $y = x^n$ and take logarithms on both sides, obtaining

$$\log y = n \log x.$$

A log-log graph in x and y becomes a linear graph in $u = \log x$ and $v = \log y$, and the equation becomes $v = nu$ in terms of u and v, which indeed graphs as a straight line.

A.2.7 Harmonic Numbers

As a final application of logarithms, we obtain an approximation to a sum that appears frequently in the analysis of algorithms, especially that of sorting methods. The nth **harmonic number** is defined to be the sum

$$H_n = 1 + \frac{1}{2} + \frac{1}{3} + \cdots + \frac{1}{n}$$

of the reciprocals of the integers from 1 to n.

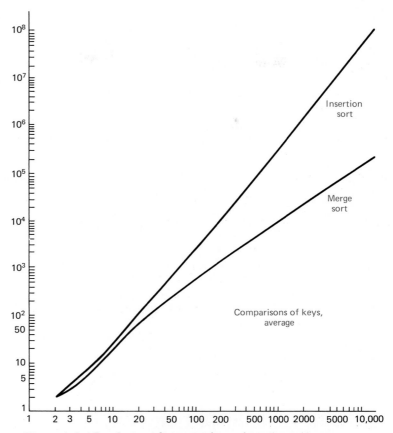

Figure A.4.   Log-log graph, comparisons, insertion and merge sorts

To evaluate H_n we consider the function $1/x$, and the relationship shown in Figure A.5. The area under the step function is clearly H_n, since the width of each step is 1, and the height of step k is $1/k$, for each integer k from 1 to n. This area is approximated by the area under the curve $1/x$ from ½ to $n + $ ½. The area under the curve is

$$\int_{1/2}^{n+1/2} \frac{1}{x}\,dx \;=\; \ln(n + \text{½}) - \ln \text{½} \;\approx\; \ln(n) + 0.7.$$

When n is large, the fractional term 0.7 is insignificant, and we obtain $\ln n$ as a good approximation to H_n.

By refining this method of approximation by an integral, it is possible to obtain a very much closer approximation to H_n, if such is desired. Specifically,

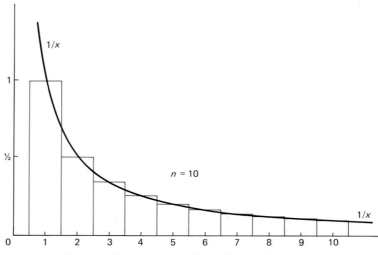

Figure A.5.   Approximation of harmonic numbers

THEOREM A.4

The harmonic number H_n, $n \geq 1$, satisfies

$$H_n = \ln n + \gamma + \frac{1}{2n} - \frac{1}{12n^2} + \frac{1}{120n^4} - \epsilon,$$

*where $0 < \epsilon < 1/(252n^6)$ and $\gamma \approx 0.577215665$ is known as **Euler's constant**.*

A.3   PERMUTATIONS, COMBINATIONS, FACTORIALS

A.3.1   Permutations

A *permutation* of objects is an ordering or arrangement of the objects in a row. If we begin with n different objects, then we can choose any of the n objects to be the first one in the arrangement. There are then $n - 1$ choices for the second object, and since these choices can be combined in all possible ways, the number of choices multiplies. Hence the first two objects may be chosen in $n(n - 1)$ ways. There remain $n - 2$ objects, any one of which may be chosen as the third in the arrangement. Continuing in this way, we see that the number of permutations of n distinct objects is

count of permutations

$$n! = n \times (n - 1) \times (n - 2) \times \cdots \times 2 \times 1.$$

Objects to permute: a b c d					
choose a first:	a b c d	a b d c	a c b d	a c d b	a d b c	a d c b
choose b first:	b a c d	b a d c	b c a d	b c d a	b d a c	b d c a
choose c first:	c a b d	c a d b	c b a d	c b d a	c d a b	c d b a
choose d first:	d a b c	d a c b	d b a c	d b c a	d c a b	d c b a

Figure A.6.   Constructing permutations

Note that we have assumed that the objects are all distinct, that is, that we can tell each object from every other one. It is often easier to count configurations of distinct objects than when some are indistinguishable. The latter problem can sometimes be solved by temporarily labeling the objects so they are all distinct, then counting the configurations, and finally dividing by the number of ways in which the labeling could have been done. The special case in the next section is especially important.

A.3.2 Combinations

A *combination* of n objects taken k at a time is a choice of k objects out of the n, without regard for the order of selection. The number of such combinations is denoted either by

$$C(n, k) \quad \text{or by} \quad \binom{n}{k}.$$

We can calculate $C(n, k)$ by starting with the $n!$ permutations of n objects and form a combination simply by selecting the first k objects in the permutation. The order, however, in which these k objects appear is ignored in determining a combination, so we must divide by the number $k!$ of ways to order the k objects chosen. The order of the $n - k$ objects not chosen is also ignored, so we must also divide by $(n - k)!$. Hence,

count of combinations

$$C(n, k) = \frac{n!}{k!(n - k)!}.$$

Objects from which to choose: a b c d e f				
a b c	a c d	a d f	b c f	c d e
a b d	a c e	a e f	b d e	c d f
a b e	a c f	b c d	b d f	c e f
a b f	a d e	b c e	b e f	d e f

Figure A.7.   **Combinations of 6 objects, taken 3 at a time**

binomial coefficients   The number of combinations $C(n, k)$ is called a *binomial coefficient,* since it appears as the coefficient of $x^k y^{n-k}$ in the expansion of $(x + y)^n$. There are hundreds of different relationships and identities about various sums and products of binomial coefficients. The most important of these can be found in textbooks on elementary algebra and on combinatorics.

A.3.3 Factorials

We frequently use permutations and combinations in analyzing algorithms, and for these applications we must estimate the size of $n!$ for various values of n. An excellent approximation to $n!$ was obtained by JAMES STIRLING in the eighteenth century:

THEOREM A.5

$$n! \approx \sqrt{2\pi n}\left(\frac{n}{e}\right)^n\left[1 + \frac{1}{12n} + O\left(\frac{1}{n^2}\right)\right].$$

We usually use this approximation in logarithmic form instead:

COROLLARY A.6

$$\ln n! \approx (n + \tfrac{1}{2}) \ln n - n + \tfrac{1}{2} \ln(2\pi) + \frac{1}{12n} + O\left(\frac{1}{n^2}\right).$$

Note that, as n increases, the approximation to the logarithm becomes more and more accurate; that is, the difference approaches 0. The difference between the direct approximation to the factorial and $n!$ itself will not necessarily become small (that is, the difference need not go to 0), but the percentage error becomes arbitrarily small (the ratio goes to 1). KNUTH (Volume 1, page 111) gives refinements of Stirling's approximation that are even closer.

The complete proof of Stirling's approximation requires techniques from advanced calculus that would take us too far afield here. We can, however, use a bit of elementary calculus to illustrate the first step of the approximation. First, we take the natural logarithm of a factorial, noting that the logarithm of a product is the sum of the logarithms:

$$\ln n! = \sum_{x=1}^{n} \ln x.$$

Next, we approximate the sum by an integral, as shown in Figure A.8. It is clear from the diagram that the area under the step function, which is exactly $\ln n!$, is approximately the same as the area under the curve, which is

$$\int_{1/2}^{n+1/2} \ln x \, dx = (x \ln x - x) \Big|_{1/2}^{n+1/2}$$
$$= (n + \tfrac{1}{2})\ln(n + \tfrac{1}{2}) - n + \tfrac{1}{2} \ln 2.$$

For large values of n, the difference between $\ln n$ and $\ln(n + \tfrac{1}{2})$ is insignificant, and hence this approximation differs from Stirling's only by the constant difference between $\tfrac{1}{2} \ln 2$ (about 0.35) and $\tfrac{1}{2} \ln(2\pi)$ (about 0.919).

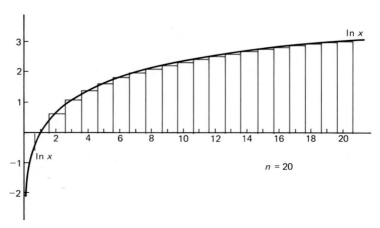

Figure A.8.   Approximation of $\ln n!$ by an integral

A.4 FIBONACCI NUMBERS

rabbits

The Fibonacci numbers originated as an exercise in arithmetic proposed by LEONARDO FIBONACCI in 1202:

> *How many pairs of rabbits can be produced from a single pair in a year? We start with a single newly born pair; it takes one month for a pair to mature, after which they produce a new pair each month, and the rabbits never die.*

In month 1, we have only one pair. In month 2, we still have only one pair, but they are now mature. In month 3, they have reproduced, so we now have two pairs. And so it goes. The number F_n of pairs of rabbits that we have in month n satisfies

definition: recurrence relation

$$F_0 = 0, \quad F_1 = 1, \quad \text{and} \quad F_n = F_{n-1} + F_{n-2} \text{ for } n \geq 2.$$

This same sequence of numbers, called the **Fibonacci sequence**, appears in many other problems. In Section 9.6.4, for example, F_n appears as the minimum number of nodes in an AVL tree of height n. Our object in this section is to find a formula for F_n.

generating function

We shall use the method of **generating functions**, which is important for many other applications. The generating function is a formal infinite series in a symbol x, with the Fibonacci numbers as coefficients:

$$F(x) = F_0 + F_1 x + F_2 x^2 + \cdots + F_n x^n + \cdots.$$

We do not worry about whether this series converges, or what the value of x might be, since we are not going to set x to any particular value. Instead, we shall only perform formal algebraic manipulations on the generating function.

Next, we multiply by powers of x,

$$\begin{aligned}
F(x) &= F_0 + F_1 x + F_2 x^2 + \cdots + F_n x^n + \cdots \\
x F(x) &= \qquad\quad F_0 x + F_1 x^2 + \cdots + F_{n-1} x^n + \cdots \\
x^2 F(x) &= \qquad\qquad\qquad F_0 x^2 + \cdots + F_{n-2} x^n + \cdots
\end{aligned}$$

and subtract the second two equations from the first,

$$(1 - x - x^2) F(x) = F_0 + (F_1 - F_0) x = x,$$

since $F_0 = 0$, $F_1 = 1$, and $F_n = F_{n-1} + F_{n-2}$ for all $n \geq 2$. We therefore obtain

closed form

$$F(x) = \frac{x}{1 - x - x^2}.$$

The roots of $1 - x - x^2$ are $\frac{1}{2}(-1 \pm \sqrt{5})$. By the method of partial fractions we can thus rearrange the formula for $F(x)$ as

$$F(x) = \frac{1}{\sqrt{5}} \left(\frac{1}{1 - \phi x} - \frac{1}{1 - \psi x} \right)$$

where

$$\phi = \tfrac{1}{2}(1 + \sqrt{5}) \quad \text{and} \quad \psi = 1 - \phi = \tfrac{1}{2}(1 - \sqrt{5}).$$

(Check this equation for $F(x)$ by putting the two fractions on the right over a common denominator.) The next step is to expand the fractions on the right side by dividing their denominators into 1:

$$F(x) = \frac{1}{\sqrt{5}}(1 + \phi x + \phi^2 x^2 + \cdots - 1 - \psi x - \psi^2 x^2 - \cdots).$$

The final step is to recall that the coefficients of $F(x)$ are the Fibonacci numbers and, therefore, to equate the coefficients of each power of x on both sides of this equation. We thus obtain

solution

$$F_n = \frac{1}{\sqrt{5}}(\phi^n - \psi^n).$$

Approximate values for ϕ and ψ are

$$\phi \approx 1.618034 \quad \text{and} \quad \psi \approx -0.618034.$$

This surprisingly simple answer to the values of the Fibonacci numbers is interesting in several ways. It is, first, not even immediately obvious why the right side should always be an integer. Second, ψ is a negative number of sufficiently small absolute value that we always have $F_n = \phi^n/\sqrt{5}$ rounded to the nearest integer.

golden mean

Third, the number ϕ is itself interesting. It has been studied since the times of the ancient Greeks—it is often called the *golden mean*—and the ratio of ϕ to 1 is said to give the most pleasing shape of a rectangle.

A.5. CATALAN NUMBERS

The purpose of this section is to count the binary trees with n vertices. We shall accomplish this result via a slightly circuitous route, discovering along the way several other problems that have the same answer. The resulting numbers, called the *Catalan numbers*, are of considerable interest in that they appear in the answers to many apparently unrelated problems.

A.5.1 The Main Result

DEFINITION

For $n \geq 0$, the nth *Catalan number* is defined to be

$$\text{Cat}(n) = \frac{C(2n, n)}{n + 1} = \frac{(2n)!}{(n + 1)! \, n!}$$

THEOREM A.7

The number of distinct binary trees with n vertices, $n \geq 0$, is the nth Catalan number $\text{Cat}(n)$.

A.5.2 The Proof by One-to-One Correspondences

1. Orchards

Let us first recall the one-to-one correspondence (Theorem 10.1) between the binary trees with n vertices and the orchards with n vertices. Hence to count binary trees, we may just as well count orchards.

2. Well-Formed Sequences of Parentheses

Second, let us consider the set of all well-formed sequences of n left parentheses '('
and n right parentheses ')'. Such a sequence is ***well formed*** means that, when scanned
from left to right, the number of right parentheses encountered never exceeds the
number of left parentheses. Thus '((()))' and '()()()' are well-formed, but '())(()' is
not, nor is '(()', since the total numbers of left and right parentheses in the expression
must be equal.

LEMMA A.8

*There is a one-to-one correspondence between the orchards with n vertices
and the well-formed sequences of n left parentheses and n right parentheses,
$n \geq 0$.*

To define this correspondence, we first recall that an orchard is either empty
or is an ordered sequence of ordered trees. We define the ***bracketed form*** of an
orchard to be the sequence of bracketed forms of its trees, written one after the
next in the same order as the tree in the orchard. The bracketed form of the empty
orchard is empty. We recall also that an ordered tree is defined to consist of its
root vertex, together with an orchard of subtrees. We thus define the ***bracketed form***
of an ordered tree to consist of a left parenthesis '(' followed by the (name of the)
root, followed by the bracketed form of the orchard of subtrees, and finally a right
parenthesis ')'.

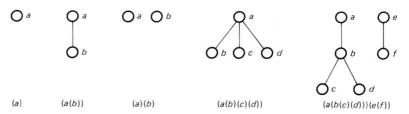

Figure A.9.   Bracketed form of orchards

The bracketed forms of several ordered trees and orchards appear in Figure
A.9. It should be clear that the mutually recursive definitions above produce a unique
bracketed form for any orchard and that the resulting sequence of parentheses is
well formed. If, on the other hand, we begin with a well-formed sequence of parentheses, then the outermost pair(s) of parentheses correspond to the tree(s) of an
orchard, and within such a pair of parentheses is the description of the corresponding
tree in terms of its root and its orchard of subtrees. In this way, we have now
obtained a one-to-one correspondence between the orchards with n vertices and the
well-formed sequences of n left and n right parentheses.

In counting orchards we are not concerned with the labels attached to the vertices,
and hence we shall omit the labels and, with the correspondence just outlined, shall
now count well-formed sequences of n left and n right parentheses, with nothing
else inside the parentheses.

3. Stack Permutations

Let us note that, by replacing each left parenthesis by $+1$ and each right parenthesis by -1, the well-formed sequences of parentheses correspond to sequences of $+1$ and -1 such that the partial sums from the left are always nonnegative, and the total sum is 0. If we think of each $+1$ as pushing an item onto a stack, and -1 as popping the stack, then the partial sums count the items on the stack at a given time. From this it can be shown that the number of stack permutations of n objects (see exercises in Section 4.2) is yet another problem for which the Catalan numbers provide the answer. Even more, if we start with an orchard and perform a complete traversal (walking around each branch and vertex in the orchard as though it were a decorative wall), counting $+1$ each time we go down a branch and -1 each time we go up a branch (with $+1$ -1 for each leaf), then we thereby essentially obtain the correspondence with well-formed sequences over again.

4. Arbitrary Sequences of Parentheses

Our final step is to count well-formed sequences of parentheses, but to do this we shall instead count the sequences that are *not* well formed, and subtract from the number of all possible sequences. We need a final one-to-one correspondence:

LEMMA A.9

The sequences of n left and n right parentheses that are not well formed correspond exactly to all sequences of n − 1 left parentheses and n + 1 right parentheses (in all possible orders).

To prove this correspondence, let us start with a sequence of n left and n right parentheses that is not well formed. Let k be the first position in which the sequence goes wrong, so the entry at position k is a right parenthesis, and there is one more right parenthesis than left up through this position. Hence strictly to the right of position k there is one fewer right parenthesis than left. Strictly to the right of position k, then, let us replace all left parentheses by right and all right parentheses by left. The resulting sequence will have $n − 1$ left parentheses and $n + 1$ right parentheses altogether.

Conversely, let us start with a sequence of $n − 1$ left parentheses and $n + 1$ right parentheses, and let k be the first position where the number of right parentheses exceeds the number of left (such a position must exist, since there are more right than left parentheses altogether). Again let us exchange left for right and right for left parentheses in the remainder of the sequence (positions after k). We thereby obtain a sequence of n left and n right parentheses that is not well formed and have constructed the one-to-one correspondence as desired.

5. End of the Proof

With all these preliminary correspondences, our counting problem reduces to simple combinations. The number of sequences of $n − 1$ left and $n + 1$ right parentheses is the number of ways to choose the $n − 1$ positions occupied by left parentheses from the $2n$ positions in the sequence, that is, the number is $C(2n, n − 1)$. By Lemma A.9, this number is also the number of sequences of n left and n right parentheses that are not well formed. The number of all sequences of n left and n right parentheses is similarly $C(2n, n)$, so the number of well-formed sequences is

$$C(2n, n) - C(2n, n - 1)$$

which is precisely the nth Catalan number.

Because of all the one-to-one correspondences, we also have

COROLLARY A.10

The number of well-formed sequences of n left and n right parentheses, the number of permutations of n objects obtainable by a stack, the number of orchards with n vertices, and the number of binary trees with n vertices are all equal to the nth Catalan number Cat(n).

A.5.3 History

It is, surprisingly, for none of the above questions that Catalan numbers were first discovered, but rather for questions in geometry. Specifically, Cat(n) provides the number of ways to divide a convex polygon with $n + 2$ sides into triangles by drawing $n - 1$ nonintersecting diagonals. See Figure A.10. This problem seems to have been proposed by L. EULER and solved by J. A. V. SEGNER in 1759. It was then solved again by E. CATALAN in 1838. Sometimes, therefore, the resulting numbers are called the *Segner numbers,* but more often they are called *Catalan numbers.*

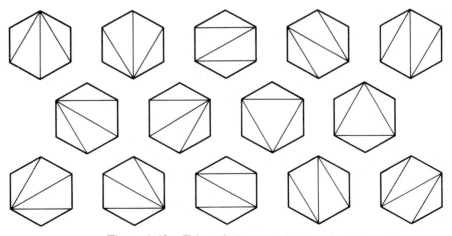

Figure A.10.   Triangulations of a hexagon by diagonals

A.5.4 Numerical Results

We conclude this section with some indications of the sizes of Catalan numbers. The first 20 values are given in Figure A.11.

n	Cat(n)	n	Cat(n)
0	1	10	16,796
1	1	11	58,786
2	2	12	208,012
3	5	13	742,900
4	14	14	2,674,440
5	42	15	9,694,845
6	132	16	35,357,670
7	429	17	129,644,790
8	1,430	18	477,638,700
9	4,862	19	1,767,263,190

Figure A.11.   The first 20 Catalan numbers

For larger values of n, we can obtain an estimate on the size of the Catalan numbers by using Stirling's approximation. When it is applied to each of the three factorials, and the result is simplified, we obtain

$$\text{Cat}(n) \approx \frac{4^n}{(n+1)\sqrt{\pi n}} \cdot$$

When compared with the exact values in Figure A.11, this estimate gives a good idea of the accuracy of Stirling's approximation. When $n = 10$, for example, the estimated value for the Catalan number is 17,007, compared to the exact value of 16,796.

REFERENCES FOR FURTHER STUDY

More extensive discussions of proof by induction, the summation notation, sums of powers of integers, and logarithms appear in many algebra textbooks. These books will also provide examples and exercises on these topics. An excellent discussion of the importance of logarithms and of the subtle art of approximate calculation is

logarithms

N. DAVID MERMIN, "Logarithms!", *American Mathematical Monthly* 87 (1980), 1–7.

Several interesting examples of estimating large numbers and thinking of them logarithmically are discussed in

DOUGLAS R. HOFSTADTER, "Metamagical themas" (regular column), *Scientific American* 246, no. 5 (May 1982), 20–34.

Several surprising and amusing applications of harmonic numbers are given in the nontechnical article

harmonic numbers

RALPH BOAS, "Snowfalls and elephants, pop bottles and π", *Two-Year College Mathematics Journal* 11 (1980), 82–89.

The detailed estimates for both harmonic numbers and factorials (Stirling's approximation) are quoted from KNUTH, Volume 1, pp. 108–111, where detailed proofs may be found. KNUTH, Volume 1, is also an excellent source for further information

factorials

regarding permutations, combinations, and related topics. The original reference for Stirling's approximation is

> JAMES STIRLING, *Methodus Differentialis* (1730), p. 137.

The branch of mathematics concerned with the enumeration of various sets or classes of objects is called **combinatorics.** This science of counting can be introduced on a very simple level, or studied with great sophistication. Two elementary textbooks containing many further developments of the ideas introduced here are

combinatorics

> GERALD BERMAN and K. D. FRYER, *Introduction to Combinatorics,* Academic Press, New York, 1972.

> ALAN TUCKER, *Applied Combinatorics,* John Wiley, New York, 1980.

The derivation of the Fibonacci numbers will appear in almost any book on combinatorics, as well as in KNUTH, Volume 1, pp. 78–86, who includes some interesting history as well as many related exercises. The appearance of Fibonacci numbers in nature is illustrated in

Fibonacci numbers

> PETER STEVENS, *Patterns in Nature,* Little, Brown, Boston, 1974.

Many hundreds of other properties of Fibonacci numbers have been and continue to be found; these are often published in the research journal *Fibonacci Quarterly.*

Catalan numbers

A derivation of the Catalan numbers (applied to triangulations of convex polygons) appears in the first of the above books on combinatorics (pp. 230–232). KNUTH, Volume 1, pp. 385–406, enumerates several classes of trees, including the Catalan numbers applied to binary trees. A list of 46 references providing both history and applications of the Catalan numbers appears in

> W. G. BROWN, "Historical note on a recurrent combinatorial problem," *American Mathematical Monthly* 72 (1965), 973–977.

The following article expounds many other applications of Catalan numbers:

> MARTIN GARDNER, "Mathematical games" (regular column), *Scientific American* 234, no. 6 (June 1976), 120–125.

The original references for the derivation of the Catalan numbers are

> J. A. V. SEGNER, "Enumeratio modorum, quibus figuræ planæ rectilinæ per diagonales dividuntur in triangula," *Novi Commentarii Academiæ Scientiarum Imperialis Petropolitanæ* 7 (1758–1759), 203–209.

> E. CATALAN, "Solution nouvelle de cette question: un polygone étant donné, de combien de manieres peut-on le partager en triangles au moyen de diagonales?" *Journal de Mathématiques Pures et Appliquées* 4 (1839), 91–94.

Removal
of Recursion

▶ *In some contexts (like FORTRAN and COBOL) it is not possible to use recursion. This appendix discusses methods for reformulating algorithms to remove recursion. First comes a general method that can always be used, but is quite complicated and yields a program whose structure may be obscure. Next is a simpler transformation that, although not universally applicable, covers many important applications. This transformation yields, as an example, an efficient nonrecursive version of quicksort. A nonrecursive version of mergesort is also developed to illustrate other techniques for recursion removal. Finally this appendix studies threaded binary trees, which provide all the capabilities of ordinary binary trees without reference to recursion or stacks.*

Although the methods developed in this appendix can be used with any higher-level algorithmic language, they are most appropriate in contexts that do not allow recursion. When recursion is available, the techniques described here are unlikely to save enough computer time or space to prove worthwhile or to compensate for the additional programming effort that they demand. Although, for the sake of clarity, the sample programs are written in Pascal, they are designed to facilitate translation into languages not allowing recursion.

prerequisite

Section 8.5 (Principles of Recursion) should be studied before consulting this appendix.

B.1 GENERAL METHODS FOR REMOVING RECURSION

Recall from Section 8.5.2 that each call to a subprogram (recursive or not) requires that the subprogram have a storage area where it can keep its local variables, its calling parameters, and its return address (that is, the location of the statement following the one that made the call). In a recursive implementation, the storage areas for subprograms are kept in a stack. Without recursion, one permanent storage area is often reserved for each subprogram, so that an attempt to make a recursive call would change the values in the storage area, thereby destroying the ability of the outer call to complete its work and return properly.

To simulate recursion we must therefore eschew use of the local storage area reserved for the subprogram, and instead set up a stack, in which we shall keep all the local variables, calling parameters, and the return address for the procedure.

B.1.1 Preliminary Assumptions

It is frequently true that stating a set of rules in the most general possible form requires so many complicated special cases that it obscures the principal ideas. Such is indeed true for recursion removal, so we shall instead develop the methods only for a special case and separately explain how the methods can be applied to all other categories of subprograms.

direct and indirect recursion

Recursion is said to be **direct** if a subprogram calls itself; it is **indirect** if there is a sequence of more than one subprogram call that eventually calls the first subprogram, such as when procedure A calls procedure B, which in turn calls A. We shall first assume that the recursion is direct; that is, we deal only with a single subprogram that calls itself.

For simplicity we shall, second, assume that we are dealing with a procedure rather than a function. This is no real restriction, since any function can be turned into a procedure by including one extra calling parameter that will be used to hold the output value. This output parameter is then used instead of the function name in the calling program.

parameters
We have used two kinds of parameters for procedures: those called by value and those called by address (reference). Parameters called by value are copied into local variables within the procedure that are discarded when the procedure returns; parameters called by address exist in the calling program, so that the procedure refers to them there. The same observations are true of all other variables used by the procedure: They are either declared locally within the procedure or exist outside, globally to the procedure. Parameters and variables in the first category are created anew every time the procedure is started; hence, before recursion they must be pushed onto a stack so that they can be restored after the procedure returns. Parameters and variables of the second category must not be stacked, since every time the procedure changes them it is assumed that the global variables have been changed, and if they were restored to previous values the work of the procedure would be undone.

If the procedure has parameters called by address (those in Pascal declared with **var** in the procedure heading), then we shall assume that the actual parameters are exactly the same in every call to the procedure. This is again no real restriction, since we can introduce an additional global variable, say, t, and instead of writing P(x) and P(y) for two different calls to the procedure, we can write

$$\textbf{begin}\quad t := x; \quad P(t); \quad x := t \quad \textbf{end}$$

for one and

$$\textbf{begin}\quad t := y; \quad P(t); \quad y := t \quad \textbf{end}$$

for the other.

B.1.2 General Rules

We now take P to satisfy these assumptions; that is, P is a directly recursive procedure for which the actual parameters called by address in P are the same in every call to P. We can translate P into a nonrecursive procedure by including instructions in P to accomplish the following tasks. These steps involve insertion of statement labels and **goto** statements as well as other constructions that will make the result appear messy. At the moment, however, we are proceeding mechanically, essentially playing compiler, and doing these steps is the easiest way to go, given that the original procedure works properly. Afterward, we can clean and polish the procedure, making it into a form that will be easier to follow and be more efficient.

initialization
1. Declare a stack (or stacks) that will hold all local variables, parameters called by value, and flags to specify whence P was called (if it calls itself from several places). As the first executed statement of P, initialize the stack(s) to be empty by setting the counter to 0. The stack(s) and the counter are to be treated as global variables, even though they are declared in P.

2. To enable each recursive call to start at the beginning of the original procedure P, the first executable statement of the original P should have a label (statement number) attached to it.

The following steps should be done at each place inside P where P calls itself.

recursive call

3. Make a new statement label L_i (if this is the ith place where P is called recursively) and attach the label to the first statement after the call to P (so that a return can be made to this label).

4. Push the integer i onto the stack. (This will convey on return that P was called from the ith place.)

5. Push all local variables and parameters called by value onto the stack.

6. Set the dummy parameters called by value to the values given in the new call to P.

7. Replace the call to P with a **goto** to the statement label at the start of P.

At the end of P (or wherever P returns to its calling program), the following steps should be done.

return

8. If the stack is empty then the recursion has finished; make a normal return.

9. Otherwise, pop the stack to restore the values of all local variables and parameters called by value.

10. Pop an integer i from the stack and use this to go to the statement labeled L_i. In FORTRAN this can be done with a *computed go to* statement, in BASIC with an on $\cdots$ go to, and in Pascal with a **case** statement.

By mechanically following the preceding steps we can remove direct recursion from any procedure.

B.1.3 Indirect Recursion

The case of indirect recursion requires slightly more work, but follows the same idea. Perhaps the conceptually simplest way (which avoids **goto**'s from one procedure to another) is first to rename variables as needed to ensure that there are no conflicts of names of local variables or parameters between any of the mutually recursive procedures, and then write them one after another, not as separate procedures, but as sections of a longer one. The foregoing steps can then be carried through for each of the former procedures, and the **goto**'s used according as which procedure is calling which. Separate stacks can be used for different procedures, or all the data can be kept on one stack, whichever is more convenient.

B.1.4 Towers of Hanoi

As an illustration of this method, let us write out a nonrecursive version of the program for the Towers of Hanoi, as it was developed in Section 8.1, to which you should compare the following program. This program is obtained as a straightforward application of the rules just formulated. You should compare the result with the original version.

```
procedure Move(n: disk; a, b, c: needle);
{moves n disks from a to b using c for temporary storage}
{nonrecursive version}
label
   0,                                {marks start of original procedure}
   1,                                {return from first recursive call}
   2;                                {return from second recursive call}

type
   place = 0 .. 2;                   {place to return from a recursive call}
   stackentry = record              {information needed for recursive calls}
                   n: disk;
                   a, b, c: needle;
                   address: place
                end;
   stack = record
              count: 0 .. ndisks;
              entry: array[1 .. ndisks] of stackentry
           end;

var
   S: stack;
   returnaddress: place;            {selects place to return after recursion}

begin                                              {procedure Move}
   S.count := 0;                                   {Initialize stack.}
0:                  {marks the start of the original recursive procedure}
   if n > 0 then
   begin
      Push(n, a, b, c, 1, S);
      n := n − 1;
      Swap(b, c);
      goto 0;                                 {Make the first recursive call.}
1:                              {marks the return from the first recursive call}
      writeln('Move a disk from', a:2, ' to', b:2);
      Push(n, a, b, c, 2, S);
      n := n − 1;
      Swap(a, c);
      goto 0;
2:;                         {marks the return from the second recursive call}
   end;                     {now at the end of the original recursive procedure}
                                   {Prepare to return from a recursive call.}
```

local storage simulating recursion

first recursive call

second recursive call

```
    if S.count > 0 then
    begin
      Pop(n, a, b, c, returnaddress, S);
      case returnaddress of
        0:;                                        {error: impossible case}
        1: goto 1;
        2: goto 2
      end                                          {case statement}
    end                                            {Return from recursive call.}
  end;                                             {procedure Move}
```

This version of procedure Move uses several auxiliary procedures, as follows:

```
procedure Push(n: disk; a, b, c: needle; address: place; var S: stack);
begin                                              {procedure Push}
  S.count := S.count + 1;
  S.entry[S.count].n := n;
  S.entry[S.count].a := a;
  S.entry[S.count].b := b;
  S.entry[S.count].c := c;
  S.entry[S.count].address := address
end;                                               {procedure Push}


procedure Pop(var n: disk; var a,b,c: needle; var address: place; var S: stack);
begin                                              {procedure Pop}
  n := S.entry[S.count].n;
  a := S.entry[S.count].a;
  b := S.entry[S.count].b;
  c := S.entry[S.count].c;
  address := S.entry[S.count].address;
  S.count := S.count - 1
end;                                               {procedure Pop}


procedure Swap(var x, y: needle);
var
  t: needle;
begin
  t := x;   x := y;   y := t
end;
```

As you can see, a short and easy recursive procedure has turned into a complicated mess. The procedure even contains branches that jump from outside into the middle of the block controlled by an **if** statement, an occurrence that should always be regarded as very poor style, if not an actual error. Fortunately, much of the complication results only from the mechanical way in which the translation was done. We can now make several simplifications.

Note what happens when the procedure recursively returns from a call at the second place (returnaddress = 2). After the stack is popped it branches to statement 2, which does nothing except run down to pop the stack again. Thus what was popped off the stack the first time is lost, so that there was no need to push it on in the first place. In the original recursive procedure, the second recursive call to Move occurs at the end of the procedure. At the end of any procedure its local variables are discarded; thus there was no need to preserve all the local variables before the second recursive call to Move since they will be discarded when it returns in any case.

tail recursion   This situation is ***tail recursion,*** and from this example we see graphically the unnecessary work that tail recursion can induce. Before translating any program to nonrecursive form, we should be careful to apply Theorem 8.2 and remove the tail recursion.

B.1.5 Further Simplifications

While we are considering simplifications, we can make a more general observation about local variables and parameters called by value. In a procedure being transformed to nonrecursive form, these will need to be pushed onto the stack before a recursive call only when they have both been set up before the call, and will be used again after the call, with the assumption that they have unchanged values. Some variables may have been used only in sections of the procedure not involving recursive calls, so there is no need to preserve their values across a recursive call. For example, the index variable of a **for** loop might be used to control loops either before or after a recursive call or even both before and after, but if the index variable is initialized when a loop starts after the call, there is no need to preserve it on the stack. On the other hand, if the recursive call is in the middle of a **for** loop, then the index variable must be stacked. By applying these principles we can simplify the resulting program and conserve stack space, and thereby perform optimizations of the program that a recursive compiler would likely not do, since it would probably preserve all local variables on the stack.

B.2 RECURSION REMOVAL BY FOLDING

B.2.1 Program Schemata

We can now further simplify our method for removing recursion: A procedure that includes a recursive call from only one place will not need to include flags to show where to return, since there is only one possibility. In many cases, we can also rearrange parts of the program to clarify it by removing **goto**'s.

After removal of the tail recursion, the second recursive version of the procedure Move for the Towers of Hanoi, as given in Section 8.5.3, is a program of the general schema:

recursive schema

```
procedure P( {parameters} );                                    {recursive version}
  {local declarations to be inserted here}
begin
  while not termination do begin
    Block A;                        {first part of program; empty for our example}
    P;                              {only recursive call to procedure itself}
    Block B;                                        {next part of program}
  end;
  Block C;                          {final part of program; empty for our example}
end;                                                              {procedure}
```

Our general rules presented in the last section will translate this schema into the nonrecursive form:

first nonrecursive
schema

```
procedure P( {parameters} );                    {preliminary nonrecursive version}
label 100, 101;                                 {used to simulate recursive returns}
  {local declarations to be inserted here}
  {declaration of stack goes here}
begin
  Set stack to be empty;
100:
  while not termination do
  begin
    Block A;                                           {first part of program}
    Push data onto stack and change parameters;
    goto 100;
101:
    Block B;                                           {next part of program}
  end;
  Block C;                                             {final part of program}
  if stack not empty then
  begin
    Pop data from stack;
    goto 101
  end
end;                                                              {procedure}
```

If we terminate the **while** loop after the line changing the parameters, then we can eliminate the **label** 100 and the **goto** 100. Doing this will require that, when Block B is complete, we go back to the **while** statement. By moving the part of the schema that pops the stack to the front of Block B, we no longer need the other **goto**. On the first time through, the stack will be empty, so the popping section will be skipped. These steps can all be accomplished by enclosing the procedure in a statement

repeat ... until stack is empty.

We thus obtain

procedure P({parameters});   {nonrecursive version}
{local declarations to be inserted here}
{declaration of stack goes here}
begin
   Set stack to be empty;
   repeat
     if stack is not empty **then begin**
       Pop data from stack;
       Block B;   {next part of program}
     end;
     while not termination **do begin**
       Block A;   {first part of program}
       Push data onto stack and change parameters;
     end;
     Block C;   {final part of program}
   until stack is empty
end;

This rearrangement is essentially *folding* the loop around the recursive call. Thus the part coming after the recursive call now appears at the top of the program instead of the bottom.

B.2.2 Proof of the Transformation

Since deriving this rearrangement has required several steps, let us now pause to provide a formal verification that the changes we have made are correct.

THEOREM B.1

The recursive procedure P of the form given previously and the folded, nonrecursive version of P both accomplish exactly the same steps.

To prove the theorem, we shall trace through the recursive and the folded nonrecursive versions of P and show that they perform exactly the same sequence of blocks A, B, and C. The remaining parts of both versions do only bookkeeping, so that if the same sequence of the blocks is done, then the same task will be accomplished. In tracing through the programs, it will help to note that there are two ways to call a recursive procedure: either from outside, or from within itself. We refer to

these as *external* and *internal* calls, respectively. These two forms of call are indistinguishable for the recursive version, but are quite different for the nonrecursive form. An external call starts at the beginning of the procedure and finishes at the end. An internal call starts after the data are pushed onto the stack and the parameters are changed and finishes when the line is reached that pops the stack.

We shall prove the theorem by using mathematical induction on the height of the recursion tree corresponding to a given call to P. The starting point is the case when P is called with the termination condition already true, so that no recursion takes place (the height of the tree is 0). In this case the recursive version performs Block C once, and nothing else is done. For the nonrecursive version we consider the two kinds of calls separately. If the call is external, then the stack is empty, so that the **if** statement does nothing, and the **while** statement also does nothing since the termination condition is assumed to be true. Thus only Block C is done, and since the stack is empty, the procedure terminates. Now suppose that the call to P is internal. Then P has arrived at the line that pushes the stack (so it is not empty). Since the termination condition is true, the **while** loop now terminates, and Block C is done. Since the stack is not empty, the **repeat** loop next proceeds to the line that pops the stack, and this line corresponds to returning from the internal call. Thus in every case when the recursion tree has height 0, only Block C is done once.

induction step

For the induction step we consider a call to P where the recursion tree has height $k > 0$, and by induction we assume that all calls whose trees have height less than k will translate correctly into nonrecursive form. Let r be the number of times that the **while** loop iterates in the call to P under consideration.

This situation is illustrated in the sample recursion tree shown in Figure B.1. Each node in this tree should be considered as expanded to show the sequence of blocks being performed at each stage. The tree also, of course, shows when the stack will be pushed and popped. Consider traversing the tree by walking around it in a counterclockwise direction following each edge both down and up and going around

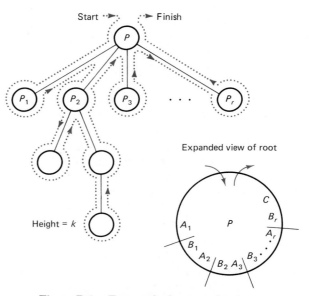

Figure B.1. Traversal of a recursion tree

each node. It is precisely as a branch is traversed going downward that the stack is pushed, and as we return up a branch the stack is popped.

The recursive version thus performs a sequence of blocks and calls:

$$A_1 \quad P_1 \quad B_1 \quad A_2 \quad P_2 \quad B_2 \quad \ldots \quad A_r \quad P_r \quad B_r \quad C$$

where the subscripts specify only the iteration at which the block or call is done. The calls to P denoted $P_1, P_2, \ldots, P_r$ all have recursion trees of heights strictly less than k (at least one has height exactly $k - 1$), so by induction hypothesis the sequence of blocks embedded in these calls will be the same for the recursive and nonrecursive versions (provided that we can show that the sequence of outer blocks is the same, so that the calling parameters will be the same). In tracing through the nonrecursive procedure, we again consider the two kinds of calls separately.

external call　　If the call is external, then the stack is initially empty, so the **while** loop begins iterating. First Block A is done, and then an internal call to P is started by pushing the stack. The corresponding return occurs when the stack is eventually popped and becomes empty again. The sequence of blocks and calls occurring in the meantime all correspond to the recursive call P_1, and by induction hypothesis correspond correctly to the recursive version. When the stack is popped and empty, then Block B is done and we reach the **while** statement to begin the second iteration. The program thus continues, with each iteration starting with Block A, then an internal call, then Block B. After r iterations the total sequence of blocks will have been the same as in the recursive version, and therefore the termination condition will become true for the first time, and so the **while** loop will be skipped. Block C is then done, and since the stack is empty, the procedure terminates. Hence the total sequence of blocks is the same as in the recursive version.

internal call　　Finally, consider that the call (with tree of height k) is internal. The call then begins where the stack is pushed, so it then has $s > 0$ sets of data. Next Block A is done, and another internal call instituted, that includes all steps until the stack is popped and again has exactly s sets of data. Next Block B is done, and the iterations continue as in the previous case, except that now the returns from internal calls that interest us are those leaving s sets of data on the stack. After r iterations the termination condition becomes true, so the **while** loop terminates, and Block C is done. The stack has $s > 0$ entries, so the procedure now moves to the line that pops the stack, which constitutes the return from the internal call that we have been tracing. Thus in every case the sequence of blocks done is the same, and the *end of proof*　　proof of the theorem is complete.

B.2.3 Towers of Hanoi: The Final Version

With the method of folding that we have now developed, we can now write our final nonrecursive version of the program for the Towers of Hanoi, a version that is much clearer than the first nonrecursive one, although still not as natural as the recursive program.

```
procedure Move(n: disk; a, b, c: needle);
{moves n disks from a to b using c for temporary storage}
{folded nonrecursive version}
type
  stackentry = record                         {information needed for recursive calls}
                 n: disk;
                 a, b, c: needle
               end;
  stack = record
            count: 0 .. ndisks;
            entry: array[1 .. ndisks] of stackentry
          end;
var
  S: stack;
begin                                          {procedure Move}
  S.count := 0;                                {Initialize stack.}
  repeat
    if S.count <> 0 then
    begin
      Pop(n, a, b, c, S);                      {Pop is modified from previous version.}
      writeln('Move a disk from', a:2, ' to', b:2);
      n := n − 1;
      Swap(a, c)
    end;
    while n > 0 do
    begin
      Push(n, a, b, c, S);                     {Push is modified from previous version.}
      n := n − 1;
      Swap(b, c)
    end
  until S.count = 0
end;                                           {procedure Move}
```

Exercises B.2

E1. Remove the tail recursion from the algorithm for preorder traversal of a linked binary tree (Section 9.3). Show that the resulting program fits the schema of Theorem B.1, and thereby devise a nonrecursive algorithm, using a stack, that will traverse a binary tree in preorder.

E2. Repeat Exercise E1 for inorder traversal.

E3. Devise a nonrecursive algorithm, using one or more stacks, that will traverse a linked binary tree in postorder. Why is this project more complicated than the preceding two exercises?

E4. Consider a pair of mutually recursive procedures P and Q that have the following schemata.

```
procedure P;                        procedure Q;
{local declarations for P}          {local declarations for Q}
begin                               begin
  while not termP do                  while not termQ do
  begin                               begin
    Block A;                            Block X;
    Q;                                  P;
    Block B;                            Block Y;
  end;                                end;
  Block C;                            Block Z;
end;                                end;
```

Assume that there are no conflicts of names between local variables or dummy parameters in P and in Q.

(a) Write a nonrecursive procedure made up from the blocks in P and Q that will perform the same action as a call to P.

(b) Prove that your translation is correct in a way similar to the proof of Theorem B.1.

Programming Project B.2

P1. Show that the program Queen from Section 8.2.2 has the schema needed for Theorem B.1, and apply folding to remove the recursion. Run both the recursive and nonrecursive versions to see which is faster.

B.3 NONRECURSIVE QUICKSORT

Because of its importance as an efficient sorting algorithm for contiguous lists, we shall devise a nonrecursive version of quicksort, as an application of the methods of the last section. Before proceeding, you should briefly review Section 7.8, from which we take all the notation.

The first observation to make about the original recursive procedure Sort written for quicksort is that its second call is tail recursion, which can easily be removed. We thus obtain the following intermediate form.

tail recursion removed

```
procedure Sort(var L: list; low, high: integer);
var
  pivotlocation: index;
begin
  while low < high do
  begin
    Partition(L, low, high, pivotlocation);
    Sort(L, low, pivotlocation −1);
    low := pivotlocation + 1
  end
end;
```

This procedure is in precisely the form covered by Theorem B.1, so it can be folded to remove the recursive call. The only variables needed after the recursive call are low and pivotlocation, so only these two variables need to be stacked.

Before we proceed with the program transformation, let us note that, in doing the sorting, it really makes no difference which half of the list is sorted first. The calling parameters to be stacked mark the bounds of sublists yet to be sorted. It turns out that it is better to put the longer sublist on the stack and immediately sort the shorter one. The longer sublist along with the pivot will account for at least half of the items. Hence at each level of recursion, the number of items remaining to be sorted is reduced by half or more, and therefore the number of items on the stack is guaranteed to be no more than $\lg n$. In this way, even though quicksort has a worst-case running time that is $O(n^2)$, the extra space needed for its stack can be guaranteed not to exceed $O(\log n)$.

stack space

This decision to stack the larger sublist at each stage does not affect the application of folding, but only introduces an **if** statement at the appropriate point. We thus arrive at the following nonrecursive version of quicksort:

```
procedure NRQuickSort(var L: list);
const
  maxstack      = 20;                    {allows sorting up to 1,000,000 items}
var
  low, high,                             {bounds of list being sorted}
  pivotlocation: index;
  lowstack,                             {Declare two arrays for the stack.}
  highstack:     array[1 .. maxstack] of index;
  nstack:        0 .. maxstack;
begin                                    {procedure NRQuickSort}
  nstack := 0;
  low := 1;
  high := L.count;
  repeat
    if nstack > 0 then
    begin                                {Pop the stack.}
      low := lowstack[nstack];
      high := highstack[nstack];
      nstack := nstack − 1
    end;
    while low < high do
    begin
      Partition(L, low, high, pivotlocation);
      {Push larger sublist onto stack, and do smaller.}
      if pivotlocation − low < high − pivotlocation then
      begin                              {Stack right sublist and do left.}
        if nstack >= maxstack then Overflow;    {separate procedure}
        nstack := nstack + 1;
        lowstack[nstack] := pivotlocation + 1
        highstack[nstack] := high;
        high := pivotlocation − 1
      end                                {continued on next page}
```

```
        else begin                              {Stack left sublist and do right.}
            if nstack >= maxstack then Overflow;     {separate procedure}
            nstack := nstack + 1;
            lowstack[nstack] := low;
            highstack[nstack] := pivotlocation − 1;
            low := pivotlocation + 1
        end
    end
until nstack = 0
end;                                             {procedure NRQuickSort}
```

B.4 STACKLESS RECURSION REMOVAL: MERGESORT

This section discusses point 5 of the guidelines for using recursion in Section 8.5.5; that is, the translation of a program into nonrecursive form by exploiting the regularity of its recursion tree, thereby avoiding the need to use a stack. The program we develop in this section is not likely to prove a great improvement over the recursive version, since the stack space saved is only $O(\lg n)$. It is primarily a matter of taste which version to use.

Mergesort is one of the most efficient sorting methods we have studied; it and heapsort are the only ones we considered for which the number of comparisons in the worst case, as well as in the average case, is $O(n \log n)$. Mergesort is therefore a good choice for large sorting problems when time constraints are critical. The recursion used in mergesort, however, may entail some overhead costs that can be avoided by rewriting mergesort in nonrecursive form.

Let us begin by considering the tree of recursive calls that mergesort will make in sorting a list; this tree for $n = 16$ is drawn in Figure B.2. In the recursive formulation of mergesort, we begin at the root of the tree and divide the list in half. We then look at the left list (move to the left subtree) and repeat the division. Afterward, we look at the right sublist and move to the right subtree. In other words,

Recursion in mergesort performs a preorder traversal of the tree.

Now let us determine the order in which the merges are actually done. No sublists are actually merged until the list has been divided all the way down to sublists of one element each. The first two one-element sublists, represented as the leftmost two leaves in the tree, are then merged. Then the next two one-element sublists are merged, and afterward the resulting two-element sublists are merged into a four-element sublist. In this way the process continues building small sublists into larger ones. In fact,

The order in which the merges are actually done
constitutes a postorder traversal of the tree.

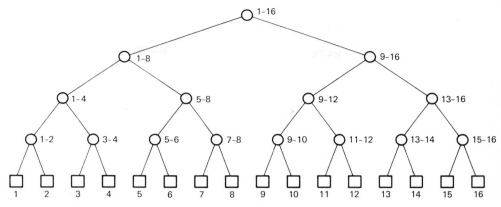

Figure B.2   Recursion tree for mergesort, $n = 16$

traversal orders

Translating mergesort into nonrecursive form amounts to rewriting the algorithm to perform a postorder traversal of the tree instead of a preorder traversal. We could, of course, use a stack to assist with the postorder traversal, but instead we shall take advantage of the fact that, when n is a power of 2, the tree has a completely symmetric structure. Using this structure we can obtain a nonrecursive traversal algorithm with no need for a stack. The idea that we shall employ is the same as that used in Section 9.5, where we developed an algorithm for building elements from an ordered list into a balanced binary search tree. In fact, the algorithm we now need differs from that of Section 9.5 only in that we now wish to make a postorder traversal of the tree, whereas in Section 9.5 we did an inorder traversal.

We shall also find that, when n is not a power of 2 (as in Section 9.5), few further difficulties arise. The present algorithm will also have the advantage over the recursive form, that it is not necessary to know or calculate in advance how many items are in the list being sorted. (Recall that our original recursive version of mergesort spent significant time finding the center of a linked list.)

To design our algorithm, let us imagine receiving the elements of the unsorted list one at a time, and as each element arrives, let us continue the postorder traversal of the tree by doing as many merges as possible with the elements that we have available. When only the first element has arrived, no merge can be done; when the second element comes, the first two sublists of size 1 will be merged. Element 3 does not induce any merges, but element 4 is first compared with element 3, and the resulting two-element sublist is then merged with the first two-element sublist. Continuing in this way, we see that element 5 does not induce any merge, element 6 induces only 1, element 7 none, and element 8 induces 3 merges. Further study of the tree will convince you that:

> *When mergesort processes the item in position c of its input, then the number of times that sublists are merged before proceeding to the next element is exactly the highest power of 2 that divides c.*

In writing our algorithm we shall, as in Section 7.7, consider only a version sorting linked lists. In this way, we can use the same function presented in Section 7.7 to merge two sorted sublists, and we need not consider the auxiliary space or complicated algorithms needed to accomplish merging in contiguous lists.

As we progress through the tree, we shall find that at various stages several sublists will have been constructed that have not yet been merged with each other. We shall keep track of these sublists by using an auxiliary array of pointers. At any point in the process, there can be at most one such sublist corresponding to each level in the tree; hence the size of this array grows only logarithmically with the length of the list being sorted, and the amount of additional memory that it requires is inconsequential.

The main part of our algorithm can now be described completely: We shall traverse the linked list of input and use the function Power2(c) (taken from Section 9.5) to determine the number mergecount of times that sublists will be merged. We do these merges using the sublists whose headers are in the auxiliary array. After the appropriate merges are made, a pointer to the resulting sorted sublist is placed in location mergecount of the auxiliary array.

It now remains only for us to describe what must be done to complete the sort after the end of the input list is reached. If n is an exact power of 2, then the list will be completely sorted at this point. Otherwise, it turns out that

> *At the end of receiving input, the sorted sublists that must still be merged occupy precisely the same relative positions in the auxiliary array as those occupied by the nonzero digits in the representation of the counter* c *as a binary integer.*

proof by induction

We can prove this observation by mathematical induction. When $n = 1$ it is certainly true. In fact, when n is any exact power of 2, $n = 2^k$, the first part of the algorithm will have merged all the items as received into a single sorted sublist, and the integer n when written in binary has a single 1 in the digit position k corresponding to the power of 2, and 0's elsewhere. Now consider the algorithm for an arbitrary value of n, and let 2^k be the largest power of 2 such that $2^k \le n$. The binary representation of n contains a 1 in position k (the count of digits starts at 0), which is its largest nonzero digit. The remaining digits form the binary representation of $m = n - 2^k$. When the first 2^k items have been received, the algorithm will have merged them into a single sublist, a pointer to which is in position k of the auxiliary array, corresponding properly to the digit 1 in position k of the binary representation of n. As the remaining m items are processed, they will, by induction hypothesis, produce sublists with pointers in positions corresponding to 1's in the binary representation of m, which, as we have observed, is the same as the remaining

end of proof

positions in the binary representation of n. Hence the proof is complete.

With this background, we can now produce a formal description of the algorithm. The notational conventions are those of Section 7.7.

procedure NRMergeSort(**var** head: pointer);

{Nonrecursive version of mergesort. Uses a counter c to determine the number of sublists to merge at each stage.}

```
const
  maxlog = 20;                                     {allows over 1,000,000 entries in list}
var
  sublist: array[0. .maxlog] of pointer;
  p,                                               {first unsorted item from list}
  q:        pointer;                               {head of a (partial) merged list}
  i,                                               {used to control for loop}
  c,                                               {counter (index) of current item}
  mergecount,                                      {largest power of 2 dividing c}
  d:        integer;                               {a digit in binary representation of c}
begin                                              {procedure NRMergeSort}
  p := head;
  c := 0;
  while p <> nil do                                {Traverse the unsorted list.}
  begin
    c := c + 1;
    mergecount := Power2(c);
    q := p;
    p := p↑.next;
    q↑.next := nil;                                {Split off q↑ as a sublist of size 1.}
    for i := 0 to mergecount − 1 do
      Merge(q, sublist[i], q);
    sublist[mergecount] := q
  end;
```

{At this point, the list has been traversed. The unmerged sublists correspond to the 1's in the binary representation of the counter c. Note that p = **nil** at this point.}

```
  mergecount := −1;
  while c <> 0 do
  begin
    d := c mod 2;                                  {d is a binary digit in c.}
    c := c div 2;
    mergecount := mergecount + 1;
    if d <> 0 then
      if p = nil then
        p := sublist[mergecount]       {This case occurs only for first nonzero d.}
      else
        Merge(p, sublist[mergecount], p)
                                                   {This case occurs always thereafter.}
  end;
  head := p
end;                                               {procedure NRMergeSort}
```

Exercise
B.4

E1. The algorithm for the Towers of Hanoi has a completely symmetric recursion tree. Design a nonrecursive program for this problem that uses no stacks, lists, or arrays.

Programming
Project
B.4

P1. Run the nonrecursive mergesort of this section, and compare timings with those of the recursive version of Section 7.7.

B.5 THREADED BINARY TREES

Because of the importance of linked binary trees, it is worthwhile to develop nonrecursive algorithms to manipulate them, and to study the time and space requirements of these algorithms. We shall find that, by changing the **nil** links in a binary tree to special links called *threads,* it is possible to perform traversals, insertions, and deletions without using either a stack or recursion.

B.5.1 Introduction

First, let us note that the second recursive call in the ordinary recursive versions of both preorder and inorder traversal of a linked binary tree is tail recursion, and so can be removed easily, with no need to set up a stack. From now on we shall assume that this has been done, so that preorder and inorder traversal each involve only one recursive call.

The situation with postorder traversal is more complicated, so we shall postpone its study to the end of the section.

use of stack

Removal of the remaining recursive call in preorder or inorder traversal does at first appear to require a stack. Let us see how many entries can possibly be on the stack. Since the procedures use no local variables, the only value to be stacked is the calling parameter, which is a (simple, one-word) pointer variable, a pointer to the current position in the tree. After the pointer has been stacked, the algorithm moves to the left subtree as it calls itself. (Note that when the algorithm later moves to the right subtree it need only change the pointer, not push it onto the stack, since the tail recursion has been removed.) The pointers stop being stacked and the recursion terminates when a leaf is reached. Thus the total number of pointers that may appear on the stack is the number of left branches taken in a path from the root to a leaf of the tree, plus one more since a pointer to the leaf itself is stacked. The algorithms could easily be rewritten to avoid stacking this last pointer.

Since most binary trees are fairly bushy, the number of pointers on the stack is likely to be $O(\log n)$ if the tree has n nodes. Since lg n is generally small in comparison to n, the space taken by the stack is usually small in comparison to the space needed for the nodes themselves. Thus, if it is reasonable to assume that the tree is quite bushy, then it is probably not worth the effort to pursue sophisticated methods to save space, and either the recursive algorithms or their straightforward translation to nonrecursive form with a stack will likely be satisfactory.

stack space

It is, on the other hand, certainly possible that a binary tree will have few right branches and many left branches. In fact, the tree that is a chain moving to the left will put pointers to every one of its nodes onto the stack before working out of the recursion. Hence, if we wish to ensure that the traversal algorithms will never fail for want of space, we must be careful to reserve stack space for $n + 1$ pointers if there are n nodes in the binary tree. (Keeping the recursion for the system to handle will, of course, not help at all, since the system must still find space for the stack, and will likely also use space for stacking return addresses, etc., and so will need more than $n + 1$ words of memory.) If we are working with a large binary tree that takes almost all the memory, then finding extra stack space can be a problem.

Whenever you run out of some resource, a good question to ask yourself is whether some of that same resource is being left unused elsewhere. In the current problem, the answer is *yes*. For all the leaves of any binary tree, both the left and right pointers are **nil**, and often for some of the other nodes one of the pointers is **nil**. In fact, the following easy observation shows that there are exactly enough **nil** pointers in the tree to take care of the stack.

LEMMA B.2

*A linked binary tree with n nodes, n ≥ 0, has exactly n + 1 **nil** links.*

PROOF

We first note that each node of the tree contains two pointers, so there are $2n$ pointers altogether in a tree with n nodes, plus one more in the header. There is exactly one pointer to each of the n nodes of the tree (coming from the parent of each node except the root, and from the header to the root). Thus the number of **nil** pointers is exactly

end of proof

$$(2n + 1) - n = n + 1.$$

With this result, we could devise an algorithm to use the space occupied by **nil** pointers and traverse the tree with no need for auxiliary space for a stack.

We shall not solve the problem this way, however, because of one danger in such a method. If the program should happen to crash in the middle of traversing the binary tree, having changed various pointers within the tree to reflect a (now-forgotten) current situation, it may later be difficult or impossible to recover the structure of the original tree. We might thereby lose all our data, with far more serious consequences than the original crash.

goal

What we want, then, is a way to set up the pointers within the binary tree permanently so that the **nil** pointers will be replaced with information that will make it easy to traverse the tree (in either preorder or inorder) without setting up a stack or using recursion.

Let us see how far ordinary inorder traversal can go before it must pop the stack. It begins by moving left as many times as it can, while the left subtree is not empty. Then it visits the node and moves to the right subtree (if nonempty) and repeats the process, moving to the left again. Only when it has just visited a node and finds that its right subtree is empty must it pop the stack to see where to go next. In Pascal we could write

```
p := root;                                    {pointer that moves through the tree}
while p <> nil do
begin
  while p↑.left <> nil do p := p↑.left;
  Visit(p);
  p := p↑.right
end;
```

When this sequence of instructions is complete, we have p = **nil**, and we must find some way to locate the next node under inorder traversal.

B.5.2 Threads

In a *right-threaded binary tree* each **nil** right link is replaced by a special link to the successor of that node under inorder traversal, called a *right thread.* Using right threads we shall find it easy to do an inorder traversal of the tree, since we need only follow either an ordinary link or a thread to find the next node to visit. For later applications, we shall also find it useful to put *left threads* into the tree, which means to replace each **nil** left link by a special link to the predecessor of the node under inorder traversal. The result is called a *fully threaded binary tree.* The word *fully* is omitted if there is no danger of confusion. Figure B.3 shows a threaded binary tree, where the threads are shown as colored lines.

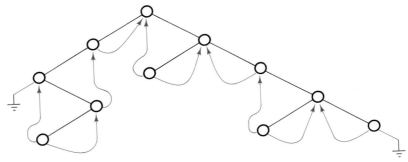

Figure B.3.   A fully threaded binary tree

Note that two threads have been left as **nil** in the diagram, the left thread from the first node under inorder traversal, and the right thread from the last node. We shall leave these two pointers as **nil**. Another convention that is sometimes useful is to let these two nodes have threads pointing back to the root of the tree. This convention sometimes makes termination conditions slightly more complicated, but sometimes allows easier repetition of the full traversal of the tree, if that is desired.

implementation   In implementing threads in a programming language, we must have some way to determine whether each link is a true pointer to a nonempty subtree, or a thread to some node higher in the tree. With Pascal pointer types, the usual way to do this would be to attach to each pointer a Boolean variable (that need only take one bit) that specifies if the pointer is a link or a thread.

In some environments, however, we can represent threads even more compactly. Nonrecursive traversal is most commonly used in nonrecursive languages, and in this case the nodes are usually represented as entries of arrays, and the pointers are indices (cursors) within the arrays. Thus true links are represented as positive integers, and the **nil** link is usually represented as 0. We can then easily represent threads as negative integers, so that if a pointer variable p is less than 0, then it is a thread to the node at $-p$.

For the remainder of this section we shall adopt this positive-negative convention and use the implementation of linked lists with cursors in a workspace array that was developed in Section 4.5. This decision is implemented in the following declarations, for which the constant max gives the size (in nodes) of the workspace **ws**.

```
type
    cursor = 0 .. max;
    extcursor = −max .. max;                    {either a cursor or a thread}
    node = record
              key: keytype;
              {Other information fields go here.}
              left,
              right: extcursor
           end;
var
    ws:   array [1 .. max] of node;             {workspace for linked trees}
    root: cursor;                               {root of threaded binary search tree}
```

B.5.3 Inorder and Preorder Traversal

First, let us see how easy it now is to traverse a threaded binary tree in inorder.

```
procedure Inorder(root: cursor);
var
    p: extcursor;
begin                                           {procedure Inorder}
    p := root;                  {Find the first (leftmost) node for inorder traversal.}
    if p > 0 then
      while ws[p].left > 0 do
        p := ws[p].left;
    while p <> 0 do             {Now visit node, and go to its successor.}
    begin
      Visit(p);
      p := ws[p].right;
      if p < 0 then             {If this is a thread link, then it gives the successor.}
        p := −p
      else if p > 0 then        {Otherwise, move as far left as possible.}
        while ws[p].left > 0 do
          p := ws[p].left
    end             {If neither section is done, then p = 0 and the traversal is done.}
end;                                            {procedure Inorder}
```

As you can see, this algorithm is somewhat longer than the original algorithm for inorder traversal. A direct translation of the original algorithm into nonrecursive form would be of comparable length and would require additional space for a stack that is not needed when we use threaded trees.

It is a surprising fact that preorder traversal of an inorder threaded tree is just as easy to write:

```
procedure Preorder(root: cursor);
{preorder traversal of binary tree with (inorder) threads}
var
  p: extcursor;
begin                                                      {procedure Preorder}
  p := root;             {In preorder, we first visit node, then move left, then right.}
  while p > 0 do
  begin
    Visit(p);
    if ws[p].left > 0 then
      p := ws[p].left
    else if ws[p].right > 0 then
      p := ws[p].right
{Otherwise, p is a leaf. We must take its right thread, which will return to a
    node already visited, and then move to the right again.}
    else begin
      while ws[p].right < 0 do
        p := —ws[p].right;
      p := ws[p].right
    end
  end
end;                                                       {procedure Preorder}
```

B.5.4 Insertion in a Threaded Tree

To use threaded trees, we must be able to set them up. Thus we need an algorithm to add a node to the tree. We first consider the case where a node is added to the left of a node that previously had an empty left subtree. The other side is similar. Since the node we are considering has empty left subtree, its left link is a thread to its predecessor under inorder traversal, which will now become the predecessor of the new node being added. The successor of the new code will be the node to which it is attached on the left. This situation is illustrated in Figure B.4 and implemented in the following procedure.

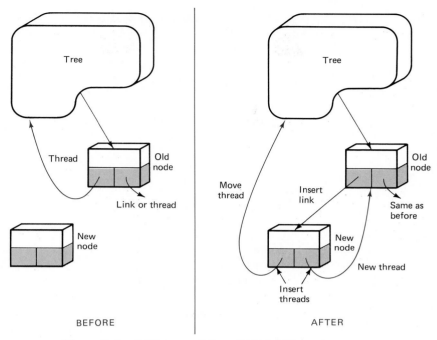

BEFORE   AFTER

Figure B.4.   Adding a node to a threaded binary tree

This process translates directly into the following algorithm.

```
procedure LeftInsert(q, p: cursor);
{inserts the node at cursor q as the left subtree of the node at p}
begin
   if ws[p].left > 0 then
      Error
   else begin
      ws[q].left  := ws[p].left;
      ws[q].right := −p;
      ws[p].left  := q;
   end
end;
```

The general insertion algorithm for a threaded binary search tree can now be formulated like the nonrecursive insertion procedure developed in Section 9.4.1.

```
procedure Insert(q: cursor; var root: cursor);
{inserts the node at cursor q into the threaded search tree with the given root}
var
   k:        cursor;
   finished: Boolean;
begin                                                  {procedure Insert}
   if root = 0 then
   begin                                               {Insert into an empty tree.}
      root := q;
      ws[q].left := 0;
      ws[q].right := 0
   end
   else begin        {Search for the place for the new key, starting at the root.}
      k := root;
      finished := false;
      repeat
         if ws[q].key < ws[k].key then
            if ws[k].left <= 0 then
            begin        {We have an empty left subtree and can insert the node.}
               LeftInsert(q, k);
               finished := true
            end
            else                      {Move to left subtree and continue search.}
               k := ws[k].left
         else if ws[q].key > ws[k].key then
            if ws[k].right <= 0 then
            begin        {We have an empty right subtree and can insert the node.}
               RightInsert(q,k);
               finished := true
            end
            else                     {Move to right subtree and continue search.}
               k := ws[k].right
         else begin                      {We have found a duplicate of the new key.}
            writeln('Error: duplicate key: ', ws[q].key,' at positions ', q, k);
            finished := true
         end
      until finished
   end
end;                                                   {procedure Insert}
```

As you can see, this algorithm is only a little more complicated than that required to add a node to an unthreaded tree. Similarly, an algorithm to delete a node (which is left as an exercise) is not much more difficult than before. It is only in the traversal algorithms where the additional cases lengthen the programs. Whether the saving of stack space is worth the programming time needed to use threads depends, as usual, on the circumstances. The differences in running time will usually be insignificant; it is only the saving in stack space that need be considered. Even this is lessened if the device of using negative indices to represent threads is not available (as it is not, for example, with Pascal pointer types).

Finally, we should mention the possibility of shared subtrees. In some applications a subtree of a binary tree is sometimes processed separately from other actions taken on the entire tree. With ordinary binary trees this can be done easily by setting the root of the subtree to the appropriate node of the larger tree. With threads, however, traversal of the smaller tree will fail to terminate properly, since after all nodes of the subtree have been traversed, there may still be a thread pointing to some successor node in the larger tree. Hence threads are often better avoided when processing complicated data structures with shared substructures.

B.5.5 Postorder Traversal

Traversal of a threaded binary tree in postorder, using neither recursion nor stacks, is somewhat more complicated than the other traversal orders. The reason is that postorder traversal investigates each node several times. When a node is first reached, its left subtree is traversed. The traversal then returns to the node in order to traverse its right subtree. Only when it returns to the node the third time does it actually visit the node. Finally, it must find the parent of the node to continue the traversal.

We can obtain an initial outline of an algorithm by following these steps. We shall use the following enumerated type to indicate the stage of processing the node.

$$\textbf{type } action = (goleft, goright, visitnode);$$

outline

```
procedure PostOrder;
while not all nodes have been visited do
   case nextaction of
      goleft:    begin
                    Traverse the left subtree;
                    Return to the node;
                    nextaction := goright
                 end;
      goright:   begin
                    Traverse the right subtree;
                    Return to the node;
                    nextaction := visitnode
                 end;
      visitnode: begin
                    Visit the node;
                    Find the parent of the node;
                    Set nextaction appropriately for the parent
                 end
   end;
```

Note that this algorithm is written so that it performs three iterations for each node. In this way, at every point we need only know the value of nextaction to determine at what stage of the traversal we are. Had we written the three stages sequentially within a single iteration of the loop, then we would need to use recursion or a stack to determine our status upon completion of traversal of a subtree.

Closer consideration, however, will show that even this outline does not yet succeed in avoiding the need for a stack. As we traverse a subtree, we shall continually change nextaction as we process each node of the subtree. Hence we must use some method to determine the previous value as we return to the original node. We shall first postpone this problem, however, by assuming the existence of an auxiliary procedure Parent, which will determine the parent of a node and the new value of nextaction.

With these assumptions, we arrive at the following procedure.

```
procedure PostOrder(root: cursor);
{performs a postorder traversal of a binary tree with (inorder) threads}
var
  p: extcursor;
  nextaction: action;
begin                                              {procedure PostOrder}
  p := root;
  nextaction := goleft;
  while p <> 0 do
    case nextaction of
      goleft:                        {Traverse the left subtree if it is nonempty.}
        if ws[p].left > 0 then
          p := ws[p].left
        else
          nextaction := goright;
      goright:                       {Traverse the right subtree if it is nonempty.}
        if ws[p].right > 0 then
        begin
          p := ws[p].right;
          nextaction := goleft
        end
        else
          nextaction := visitnode;
      visitnode:                     {Visit the node and find its parent.}
        begin
          Visit(p);
          Parent(p, p, nextaction)
        end
    end
end;                                               {procedure PostOrder}
```

finding the parent

Finally, we must solve the problem of locating the parent of a node and determining the proper value of the code, without resorting to stacks or recursion. The solution to this problem, fortunately, already appears in the outline obtained earlier. If we have just finished traversing a left subtree, then we should now set nextaction to goright; if we have traversed a right subtree, then nextaction becomes visitnode. We can determine which of these cases has occurred by using the threads, and at the same time we can find the node that is the parent node of the last one visited. If we are in a left subtree, then we find the parent by moving right as far as possible in the subtree, and then take a right thread. If the left child of this node is the original node, we know that we have found the parent and are in a left subtree. Otherwise, we must do the similar steps through left branches to find the parent. This process is illustrated in Figure B.5.

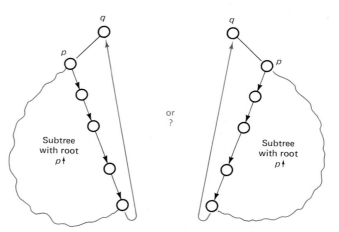

Figure B.5.   Finding the parent of a node in a threaded tree

The translation of this method into a formal procedure is straightforward.

procedure Parent(p: cursor; **var** q: extcursor; **var** nextaction: action);
{Finds the parent of node p, and sets q to the parent. Returns nextaction = goright if p is the left child of q, and nextaction = visitnode if p is the right child of q. If p is the root, returns q = 0.}

```
begin                                              {procedure Parent}
  q := p;                            {Locate the inorder successor of p; set it to q.}
  while q > 0 do
    q := ws[q].right;
  if q = 0 then                          {No successor: p cannot be a left child.}
    nextaction := visitnode
  else                                               {must have q < 0}
    if ws[−q].left = p then
    begin                                      {Case: p is the left child of −q.}
      nextaction := goright;
      q := −q
    end
    else
      nextaction := visitnode;
```
{If nextaction = goright, then we are finished. If nextaction = visitnode, find the parent as the inorder predecessor of subtree of p.}

```
        if nextaction = visitnode then
        begin
          q := p;
          while q > 0 do
            q := ws[q].left;
          q := -q;
          if (q > 0) and (ws[q].right <> p) then
            Error
        end
      end;
```
{procedure Parent}

Exercises
B.5

E1. Write the threaded-tree algorithms in Pascal for **(a)** insertion of a new node on the left, **(b)** inorder traversal, and **(c)** preorder traversal, using dynamic memory and Boolean flags to determine whether links are threads or real branches.

E2. What changes must be made in the algorithm of Section 9.2 in order to search for a key in a threaded binary search tree?

E3. Write a procedure to insert a new node on the right of a node in a threaded binary tree.

E4. Write a procedure to delete a node from a threaded binary tree.

E5. Write a procedure that will insert threads into an unthreaded binary tree by traversing it once in inorder, using a stack.

E6. Modify the procedure of Exercise E5, so that it uses no extra space for a stack, but the unused link space and threads already constructed instead.

E7. Write a procedure to insert a new node between two others in a threaded binary tree. That is, if p is a link to a node in the threaded tree, and p has nonempty left subtree, insert the new node (with q the pointer to it) as the left subtree of the one at p, with the left subtree of q being the former left subtree of p, and the right subtree of q being empty. Be sure to adjust all threads properly.

REFERENCES FOR FURTHER STUDY

Techniques and procedures for the removal of recursion are a topic of current research. Some good ideas appear in

D. E. KNUTH, "Structured programming with goto statements," *Computing Surveys* 6 (1974), 261–302.

R. S. BIRD, "Notes on recursion elimination," *Communications of the ACM* 20 (1977), 434–439.

R. S. BIRD, "Improving programs by the introduction of recursion," *Communications of the ACM* 20 (1977), 856–863.

KNUTH (*op. cit.,* page 281) writes

> There has been a good deal published about recursion elimination . . .; but I'm amazed that very little of this is about "down to earth" problems. I have always felt that the transformation from recursion to iteration is one of the most fundamental concepts of computer science, and that a student should learn it at about the same time he is studying data structures.

A nonrecursive program using no stack is developed for the Towers of Hanoi in the paper

> HELMUT PARTSCH and PETER PEPPER, "A family of rules for recursion removal," *Information Processing Letters* 5 (1976), 174–177.

Further papers on the Towers of Hanoi appear sporadically in the *SIGPLAN Notices* published by the ACM.

Presentation of nonrecursive versions of quicksort is a common topic, but so many slight variations are possible that few of the resulting programs are exactly the same. More extensive analysis is given in

> ROBERT SEDGEWICK, "The analysis of quicksort programs," *Acta Informatica* 7 (1976/77), 327–355.

Threaded binary trees constitute a standard topic in data structures, and some discussion will appear in most textbooks on data structures. Many of these books, however, leave the more complicated algorithms (such as postorder traversal) as exercises. The original reference for right-threaded binary trees is

> A. J. PERLIS and C. THORNTON, "Symbol manipulation by threaded lists," *Communications of the ACM* 3 (1960), 195–204.

Fully threaded trees were independently discovered by

> A. W. HOLT, "A mathematical and applied investigation of tree structures for syntactic analysis," Ph.D. dissertation (mathematics), University of Pennsylvania, Philadelphia, 1963.

Pascal
Notes

▶ *This appendix supplies several tables and lists of guidelines and rules, to serve as a reference for the writing of Pascal programs.*

C.1 SYNTAX DIAGRAMS

explanation

The syntax of Pascal is determined by tracing through the diagrams in the direction shown by arrows. Symbols or words within circles or ovals must be included exactly as given. These Pascal keywords are shown in all capital letters. Rectangular boxes refer to other syntax diagrams. The syntax of all classes such as {function} identifier, {variable} identifier, or {type} identifier all have the same syntax as identifier: The qualifying words in braces are intended only to clarify the meanings of the diagrams.

These diagrams are based on the ISO draft international standard DIS 7185 for Pascal and include some features, such as conformant array schemata, that may not be available on all compilers. These features are marked with asterisks (*) in the diagrams.

program

program

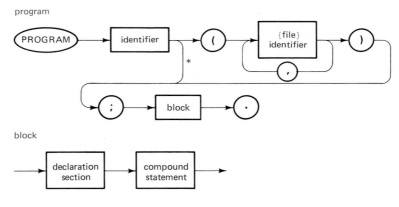

block

declarations

declaration section

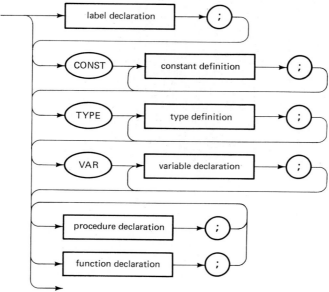

label declaration

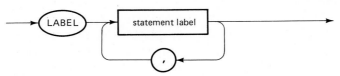

constant definition

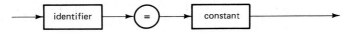

type definition

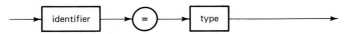

variable declaration

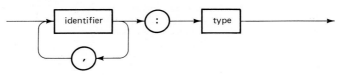

subprograms

procedure declaration

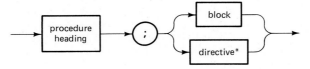

function declaration

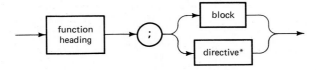

procedure heading

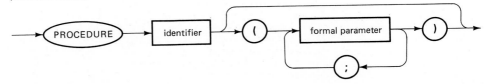

function heading

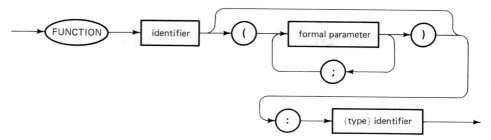

formal parameter

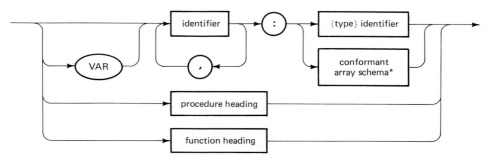

*(not always
implemented)*

conformant array schema*

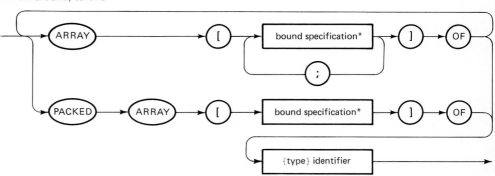

bound specification*

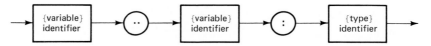

statement label

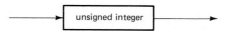

string

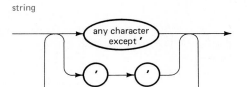

identifier,
directive*

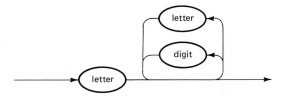

numbers

constant

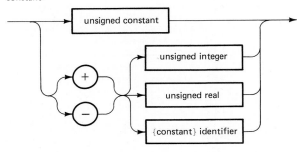

unsigned constant

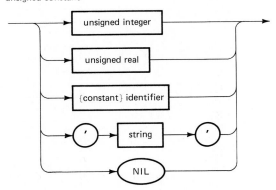

unsigned integer

unsigned real

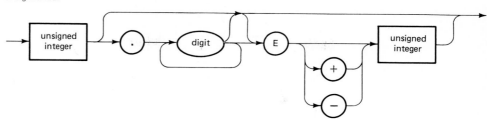

types

type

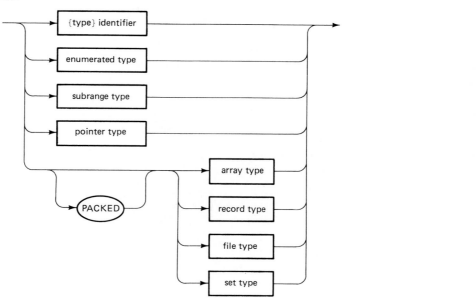

enumerated type

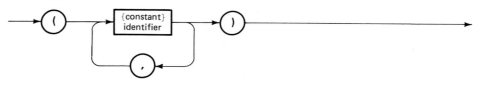

subrange type

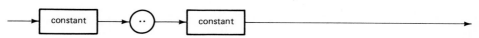

pointer type

array type

record type

field list

variant

file type

set type

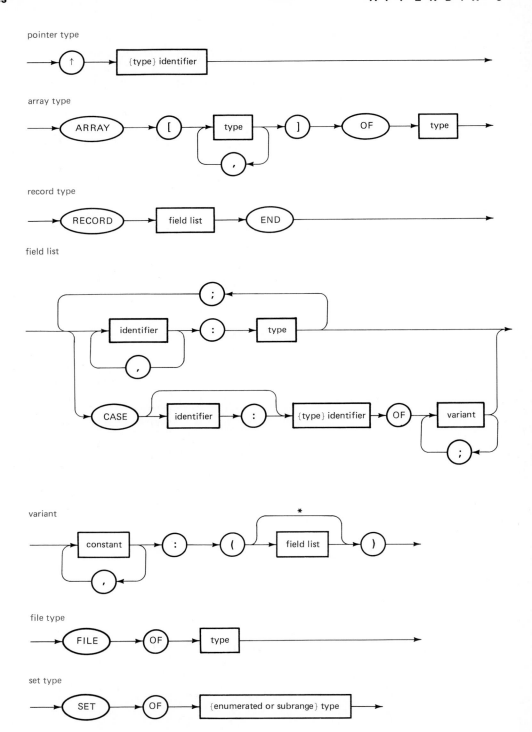

statements

compound statement

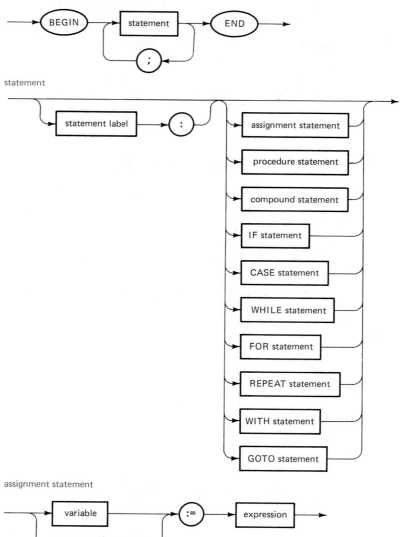

statement

assignment statement

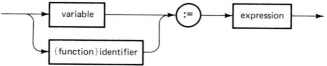

procedure statement

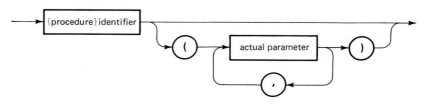

selection statements

IF statement

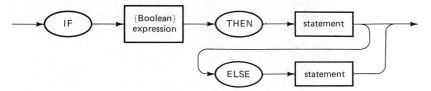

CASE statement

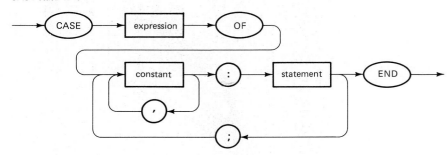

iteration statements

WHILE statement

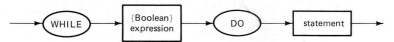

FOR statement

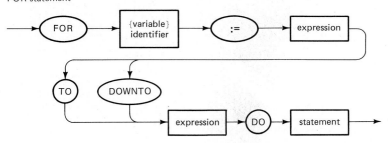

REPEAT statement

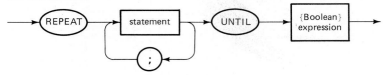

WITH statement

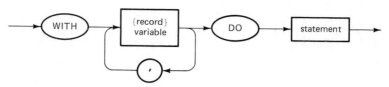

GOTO statement

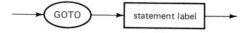

actual parameter

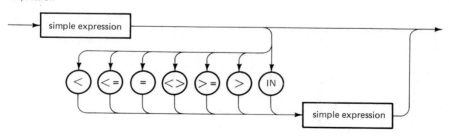

expressions

expression

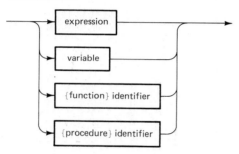

simple expression

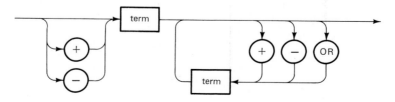

term

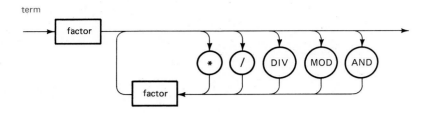

factor

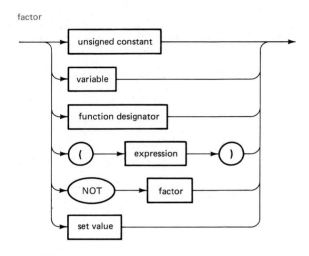

function designator

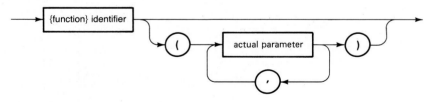

set value

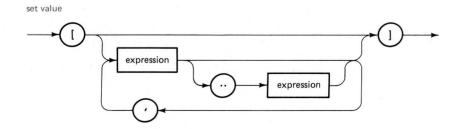

variable

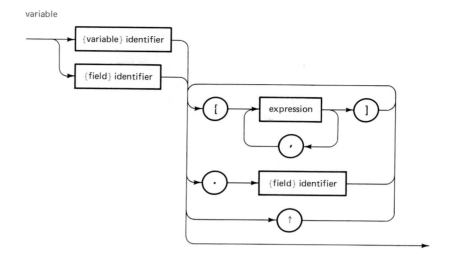

C.2 GENERAL RULES

C.2.1 Identifiers

An identifier can be as long as desired, subject to the following rules.

1. No blanks (spaces) can be inside an identifier.
2. An identifier cannot be divided between two lines (thus its maximum length is the length of a line, usually 80 characters).
3. Standard Pascal requires that, to be regarded as different, identifiers must differ somewhere in the first eight characters. (Many Pascal compilers relax this rule to recognize differences in any position.)
4. Small letters and capital letters can be used as desired (if both are available). Most, but not all, compilers treat small and capital letters as the same.
5. The following *reserved words* may not be used as identifiers, or for any purpose other than the uses specified for them in appropriate syntax diagrams:

reserved words

and	downto	if	or	then
array	else	in	packed	to
begin	end	label	procedure	type
case	file	mod	program	until
const	for	nil	record	var
div	function	not	repeat	while
do	goto	of	set	with

underscore   6. Although it is not standard Pascal, some compilers allow the underscore character '_' within identifiers. How this symbol is treated depends on the compiler: It may be ignored, treated like a letter, or treated like a numeral.

7. The following *standard identifiers* are predefined as part of the Pascal language. It is legal for the programmer to use these identifiers for purposes other than the usual ones, but it is generally unwise to do so, since by declaring a different use, the original use is lost. You can, for example, declare the word write to be a variable if you so desire, but if you do so, you will be unable to use the standard procedure that writes to a file or the terminal. The complete list of standard identifiers follows.

standard identifiers

abs	eoln	new	read	sqrt
arctan	exp	odd	readln	succ
Boolean	false	ord	real	text
char	get	output	reset	true
chr	input	pack	rewrite	trunc
cos	integer	page	round	unpack
dispose	ln	pred	sin	write
eof	maxint	put	sqr	writeln

8. See Section 1.3.1 for guidelines on choosing identifiers.

C.2.2 Rules for Spaces

1. Spaces are never allowed inside identifiers, reserved words, numbers or the special symbols made up of more than one character (e.g., $<=$, $<>$, $>=$, $:=$).

2. At least one space must be included when needed to prevent one identifier, reserved word, or number from running into another (For example,

    ForX:=AtoBdo

    would be a syntactically correct assignment statement in Pascal if the variables were declared, not the beginning of a **for** loop).

3. Inside of apostrophes '...' (i.e., in a string constant) spaces are treated like any other character.

4. Except in the preceding cases, all spaces are ignored and may be inserted where desired.

5. The end of a line is treated in exactly the same way as a space, and therefore a statement can be continued from one line to the next at any place where a space is allowed.

6. A comment is treated in exactly the same way as a space, can be inserted wherever a space is allowed, and can be continued from one line to the next.

C.2.3 Guidelines Used in Book for Program Format

The following guidelines for indenting are used in most, but not all, programs in this book.

1. The words **const, type, var**, and **record** appear alone on a line, unless the complete declaration easily fits on one line.

2. Only one item is declared per line, except when several logically related items share exactly the same declaration.

3. The lines containing items being declared are each indented slightly.

4. The word **begin** appears on a line by itself, except in the phrase **else begin**, which usually appears on one line.

5. The word **end** appears on a line by itself, and is lined up with the corresponding word or phrase **begin, else begin, case**, or **record**.

6. Statements or declarations between one of these words or phrases and its corresponding **end** are indented slightly.

7. A single statement immediately following one of the words **then, do, repeat**, or **else** is indented slightly, but the word **begin** is not indented after any of these words.

8. Normally only one assignment statement appears per line.

9. Each alternative of a **case** statement appears on a new line, indented slightly beyond the word **case**.

10. Blank lines are inserted in longer programs wherever needed to separate logical sections of the program.

11. In the text, the declarations of functions and procedures are generally separated from that of the main program. When the declarations are inserted in their proper place, however, they are surrounded by enough blank space to show clearly where one subprogram stops and the next starts.

C.2.4 Punctuation

The syntax diagrams provide precise rules for the punctuation of a Pascal program, and when difficulties arise, you should check the syntax diagrams to locate the errors. Even so, there remain several errors common for programmers new to Pascal, for which some guidelines and hints may help.

commas and semicolons

1. Items that Pascal is to treat in the same way are generally separated by commas, and items that may be treated differently by semicolons. Thus variables with exactly the same declaration are separated by commas, as are the indices in a (multidimensional) array, the actual parameters for a subprogram, and the alternatives sharing the same action in a **case** statement. On the other hand, semicolons separate declarations of variables of (possibly)

different types, separate different statements, separate formal parameters (which may be declared differently) of subprograms, and different alternatives in a **case** statement.

2. Semicolons are used to *separate* items or statements, not to *terminate* statements.

3. The illegal inclusion or omission of a semicolon will usually not produce an error diagnostic for the line on which the error occurs, but will usually produce a strange and irrelevant diagnostic for the line *after* the error.

4. A semicolon is always illegal immediately before (or at the end of the line immediately preceding) one of the words

and	downto	mod	or	set
array	else	nil	packed	then
div	file	not	program	to
do	in	of	record	

Of all these reserved words, the only one likely to cause trouble is **else**.

5. A semicolon is almost never needed immediately after **begin** or immediately before **end** or **until**, but its redundant inclusion is not an error.

C.2.5 Alternative Symbols

On systems where certain standard symbols are not available, the following substitutions are made:

For ↑ or ∧ substitute @.
For { and } substitute (* and *).
For [and] substitute (. and .).

C.3 STANDARD DECLARATIONS

C.3.1 Constants

The predefined constants are false, true, and maxint.

1. Common Values for maxint

Most 8 and 16 bit machines: maxint = 32,767
Most 32 bit machines: maxint = 2,147,483,647
Most 60 bit machines: maxint = 281,474,976,710,655

2. ASCII Codes for Characters, with Ordinals

0 NUL	16 DLE	32 SP	48 0	64 @	80 P	96 `	112 p
1 SOH	17 DC1	33 !	49 1	65 A	81 Q	97 a	113 q
2 STX	18 DC2	34 "	50 2	66 B	82 R	98 b	114 r
3 ETX	19 DC3	35 #	51 3	67 C	83 S	99 c	115 s
4 EOT	20 DC4	36 $	52 4	68 D	84 T	100 d	116 t
5 ENQ	21 NAK	37 %	53 5	69 E	85 U	101 e	117 u
6 ACK	22 SYN	38 &	54 6	70 F	86 V	102 f	118 v
7 BEL	23 ETB	39 '	55 7	71 G	87 W	103 g	119 w
8 BS	24 CAN	40 (	56 8	72 H	88 X	104 h	120 x
9 HT	25 EM	41)	57 9	73 I	89 Y	105 i	121 y
10 LF	26 SUB	42 *	58 :	74 J	90 Z	106 j	122 z
11 VT	27 ESC	43 +	59 ;	75 K	91 [	107 k	123 {
12 FF	28 FS	44 ,	60 <	76 L	92 \	108 l	124 |
13 CR	29 GS	45 −	61 =	77 M	93]	109 m	125 }
14 SO	30 RS	46 .	62 >	78 N	94 ↑	110 n	126 ~
15 SI	31 US	47 /	63 ?	79 O	95 _	111 o	127 DEL

Alternative symbols are

Code 94 may print as $\wedge$.
Code 126 may print as $\neg$.

3. EBCDIC Codes for Characters, with Ordinals

0 NUL	21 NL	43 CU2	79 |	124 @	150 o	195 C	227 T
1 SOH	22 BS	45 ENQ	80 &	125 '	151 p	196 D	228 U
2 STX	23 IL	46 ACK	90 !	126 =	152 q	197 E	229 V
3 ETX	24 CAN	47 BEL	91 $	127 "	153 r	198 F	230 W
4 PF	25 EM	50 SYN	92 *	129 a	155 }	199 G	231 X
5 HT	26 CC	52 PN	93)	130 b	161 ~	200 H	232 Y
6 LC	27 CU1	53 RS	94 ;	131 c	162 s	201 I	233 Z
7 DEL	28 IFS	54 UC	95 ¬	132 d	163 t	208 }	240 0
10 SMM	29 IGS	55 EOT	96 −	133 e	164 u	209 J	241 1
11 VT	30 IRS	59 CU3	97 /	134 f	165 v	210 K	242 2
12 FF	31 IUS	60 DC4	106 ‖	135 g	166 w	211 L	243 3
13 CR	32 DS	61 NAK	107 ,	136 h	167 x	212 M	244 4
14 SO	33 SOS	63 SUB	108 %	137 i	168 y	213 N	245 5
15 SI	34 FS	64 SP	109 _	139 {	169 z	214 O	246 6
16 DLE	36 BYP	74 ¢	110 >	145 j	173 [	215 P	247 7
17 DC1	37 LF	75 .	111 ?	146 k	189]	216 Q	248 8
18 DC2	38 ETB	76 <	121 `	147 l	192 {	217 R	249 9
19 DC3	39 ESC	77 (	122 :	148 m	193 A	224 \	250 |
20 RES	42 SM	78 +	123 #	149 n	194 B	226 S	

4. Meanings of Common Control Codes

The *control codes* are the characters with ASCII ordinals of 32 or less, together with 127, or the EBCDIC characters with ordinals of 64 or less. These characters do not produce a visible printed output, but may produce special effects. The meanings of some of the common control codes are below.

NUL null (ignored)	HT horizontal tab	CR carriage return
ETX end of text	LF line feed	ESC escape
BEL rings a bell	VT vertical tab	SP space (blank)
BS back space	FF form feed	DEL delete

C.3.2 Types

The predeclared types are

```
integer
real
Boolean = (false, true)
char
text = packed file of char
```

The terms used to display various categories of types are shown in Figure C.1.

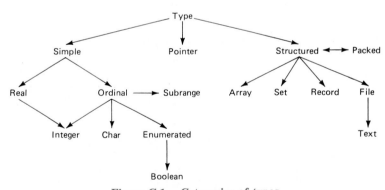

Figure C.1.   Categories of types

C.3.3 Variables

The only predeclared variables are the files, with type text,

Input   Output.

C.3.4 Procedures

The predeclared procedures are

For input and output:

Reset, Rewrite, Get, Put, Read, Write, Readln, Writeln, Page.

For pointer types:

New, Dispose.

For packed data:

Pack, Unpack.

C.3.5 Functions

Name	Argument	Result	Action
Arithmetic functions:			
Abs	integer, real	*same as argument*	*Absolute value*
Sqr	integer, real	*same as argument*	*Square of argument*
Sqrt	integer, real	real	*Square root of argument*
Exp	integer, real	real	*Exponential*
Ln	integer, real	real	*Natural logarithm*
Sin	integer, real	real	*Sine*
Cos	integer, real	real	*Cosine*
Arctan	integer, real	real	*Angle with given tangent*
Type conversion:			
Chr	integer	char	*Character with given code*
Ord	*ordinal type*	integer	*Ordinal code of argument*
Round	real	integer	*Rounds to closest integer*
Trunc	real	integer	*Truncates to integer part*
File processing:			
Eof	*file type*	Boolean	*Checks end of file*
Eoln	text	Boolean	*Checks end of line*
Miscellaneous:			
Odd	integer	Boolean	*Is integer odd?*
Succ	*ordinal type*	*same type*	*Next value in order*
Pred	*ordinal type*	*same type*	*Preceding value in order*

C.4 OPERATORS

Operator	Operand type(s)	Result type	Action
Assignment:			
:=	*any type but file*	*same type*	*copies right operand to left*
Arithmetic:			
+	integer, real	*same type*	*addition or unary positive*
−	integer, real	*same type*	*subtraction or unary negative*
*	integer, real	*same type*	*multiplication*
div	integer	integer	*division with truncation*
mod	integer	integer	*remainder after* **div**
/	integer, real	real	*division*
Comparison:			
=	*any type but file*	Boolean	*equality*
<>	*any type but file*	Boolean	*not equals*
<	*any simple type*	Boolean	*less than, precedes*
>	*any simple type*	Boolean	*greater than, follows*
<=	*any simple type*	Boolean	*less than or equal to*
>=	*any simple type*	Boolean	*greater than or equal to*
Logical:			
not	Boolean	Boolean	*logical negation*
and	Boolean	Boolean	*conjunction*
or	Boolean	Boolean	*disjunction*
Set operations:			
+	*any set type*	*same type*	*set union*
*	*any set type*	*same type*	*set intersection*
−	*any set type*	*same type*	*set difference*
<=	*any set type*	Boolean	*set inclusion*
>=	*any set type*	Boolean	*set containment*
in	*left: ordinal type*	Boolean	*set membership*
	right: set of type of left operand		
[]	*ordinal type*	**set of** *type*	*constructs set of operand(s)*

Priorities of operators:

	1.	* / **div mod and**
Highest:	2.	+ − **or**
	3.	= < <= > >= <> **in**
Lowest:	4.	:=

INDEX